Secretarial Office Procedures
Eighth Edition

James R. Meehan
*Professor of Business Education and
Dean of Administration
Hunter College
of the City University of New York*

Mary Ellen Oliverio
*Professor of Education
Teachers College
Columbia University*

William R. Pasewark
*Chairman, Business Education Department
Texas Tech University*

Published by
SOUTH-WESTERN PUBLISHING CO.

K32

Cincinnati Chicago Dallas Pelham Manor, N.Y. Palo Alto, Calif. Brighton, England

Copyright © 1972

Philippine Copyright 1972

by

South-Western Publishing Co.
Cincinnati, Ohio 45227

All Rights Reserved

The text of this publication, or any part thereof, may not be reproduced or transmitted in any form or by any means, electronic or mechanical, including photocopying, recording, storage in an information retrieval system, or otherwise, without the prior written permission of the publisher.

ISBN: 0-538-11320-0
Library of Congress Catalog Card Number 70-153449

5 6 7 K 8 7 6 5 4

Printed in the United States of America

PREFACE

Modern society needs competent, dedicated office workers. Such people not only make a valuable contribution to the business world, but they also derive great personal satisfaction from their participation. In this eighth edition of *Secretarial Office Procedures*, the prospective secretary is introduced to the capabilities and techniques that are critical in becoming fully prepared to meet the demands of the business world.

The material in this textbook is based on careful study and analysis of the most up-to-date procedures. These procedures are presented realistically so that the student will be able to cope with the demands of her first job and will be prepared for the promotional opportunities that await the well-qualified office worker.

The modern office reflects the application of the most advanced technology in the world — automation, electronic computers, instant communications around the world via satellites. Changes will continue, but the student will be ready to meet them when she has mastered the material to which she is introduced in *Secretarial Office Procedures*.

Secretarial Office Procedures is organized to assist the student in meeting the following objectives:

1. Aid in mastering office tasks that are not ordinarily included in other business courses, such as handling incoming and outgoing mail; filing rules, applications, and systems; and the actual duties of the office receptionist.
2. Provide refresher instruction and application in previously acquired skills that are partially lost if not used constantly, such as production typing and the use of numbers.
3. Integrate previous and newly acquired skills through a series of simulated office assignments based on actual job situations.
4. Develop desirable personal and professional qualities to enable the beginning employee to work harmoniously with her immediate supervisor and her co-workers and to avoid personality conflicts.
5. Develop an understanding and appreciation of the importance of the office function in the modern business world.

Embodying all these aims, *Secretarial Office Procedures* also develops a business background that qualifies the new employee for promotion to more responsible positions in the secretarial field.

In preparing this edition of *Secretarial Office Procedures*, the authors have

1. Reorganized the text into short, teachable assignments, arranged in logical sequence. These units are designed, however, so that they are interchangeable, enabling the teacher to start at any point in the book.
2. Introduced new topics and updated information that includes
    (a) Data processing
    (b) Modern recording and transcribing equipment
    (c) Changes in the field of reproduction and copying equipment
    (d) Recent changes in telephone equipment and techniques
    (e) Recent changes in postal service and regulations
    (f) Detailed information on specialized secretarial positions, such as the legal secretary, the medical secretary, the educational secretary, and the administrative assistant
    (g) Federal, state, and municipal civil service announcements and requirements
    (h) Flow charting of operations
3. Maintained the emphasis on the *you* approach. The text material is personalized and well within the understanding of the students.
4. Reviewed carefully the vocabulary to keep the text at an appropriate reading level for high school students.
5. Included a Vocabulary Builder at the beginning of each unit that gives the part of speech, definition, and an example of each of the difficult words as they are used in sentences in the text.
6. Introduced each part of each unit with an anecdote relating to a secretary in a typical office situation.
7. Rewritten the end-of-part material which includes
    (a) **Questions** — a series of questions that should be easily answered by the student who has carefully studied the text material
    (b) **Judgment** — thought-provoking business problems that should lead to stimulating discussions
    (c) **Personal Qualities** — case problems designed to improve human relations, ethical behavior, and work habits
    (d) **Language Usage** — exercises that provide a much needed review of the language arts
    (e) **Secretarial Work** — exercises that present the student with simulated office situations and applications. Although not necessary for the completion of these work assignments, stationery and business forms that provide for realistic practice are available in a correlated workbook, which also has been carefully updated.

The authors wish to acknowledge the invaluable assistance of countless business teachers, certified professional secretaries, and office supervisors who offered many suggestions that have been incorporated in the eighth edition of *Secretarial Office Procedures*. The authors also are indebted to the many business firms and government agencies which supplied instructional materials, business forms, photographs, and other illustrations.

James R. Meehan
Mary Ellen Oliverio
William R. Pasewark

CONTENTS

UNIT 1 THE SECRETARY
    PART 1 You and Your Job 3
    PART 2 Personal and Professional Qualities 17

UNIT 2 DICTATION AND TRANSCRIPTION
    PART 1 Dictation 33
    PART 2 Transcription 44
    PART 3 Dictating and Transcribing Machines 55

UNIT 3 THE MAILABLE LETTER
    PART 1 Letter Placement and Styles 65
    PART 2 Parts of the Letter 73
    PART 3 Stationery 88

UNIT 4 SECRETARIAL LETTER WRITING
    PART 1 Key Skills 97
    PART 2 Letters Composed by Secretaries 107

UNIT 5 SECRETARIAL TYPEWRITING
    PART 1 Preparing Business Reports 123
    PART 2 Parts of Business Reports 132
    PART 3 Financial Statements and Reports 147
    PART 4 Legal Papers, Minutes, and Resolutions 161

UNIT 6 PROCESSING DATA
    PART 1 How Data Is Processed 181
    PART 2 Computing and Recording Machines 193
    PART 3 Business Forms 206

UNIT 7 MAILING AND SHIPPING SERVICES
    PART 1 Incoming Mail 221
    PART 2 Outgoing Mail 232
    PART 3 Air and Surface Shipping 250

UNIT 8 THE SECRETARY AND THE PUBLIC
    PART 1 Greeting Callers 261
    PART 2 Good Language Usage 275

UNIT 9 TELEPHONE AND TELEGRAPH SERVICES

PART 1	Receiving Calls	287
PART 2	Placing Calls	299
PART 3	Special Telephone Equipment	309
PART 4	Special Communications Services	318
PART 5	Domestic and International Telegraph Services	325

UNIT 10 COPYING AND DUPLICATING

PART 1	Copying and Reproducing Machines	341
PART 2	Duplicating Machines	349

UNIT 11 BUSINESS FILING

PART 1	Records Control	367
PART 2	Alphabetic Filing Rules for Names of Individuals	375
PART 3	Alphabetic Filing Rules for Business Firms and Other Organizations	384
PART 4	Filing Equipment and Supplies for Correspondence	405

UNIT 12 RECORDS MANAGEMENT

PART 1	Basic Filing Procedures	419
PART 2	Charge-Out, Follow-Up, Transfer, and Retention	433
PART 3	Numeric, Subject, and Geographic Filing	441
PART 4	Special Files and Information Systems	460

UNIT 13 TRAVEL

PART 1	Travel Services and Arrangements	475
PART 2	Itineraries and Travel Expense Reports	488

UNIT 14 SECRETARIAL ACCOUNTING

PART 1	Petty Cash — Handwritten	505
PART 2	The Checkbook and the Bank	513
PART 3	Making Cash Payments	528
PART 4	Income Tax Procedures	535

UNIT 15 YOU AS A SECRETARY

PART 1	Job Opportunities	545
PART 2	The Personal Data Sheet and the Application Form	553
PART 3	The Interview	565
PART 4	Specialized Secretarial Positions	573
PART 5	Up the Secretarial Ladder and Beyond	591

APPENDIX

A	Grammar	599
B	Punctuation	613
C	Word Choice and Spelling	623
D	Abbreviations	631
E	Titles, Capitalization, and Numbers	636
F	Special Forms of Address, Salutations, and Complimentary Closings	642
G	Reference Books	648

INDEX 657

Unit 1 THE SECRETARY

Part 1. You and Your Job
     2. Personal and Professional Qualities

The secretary is an important person in every office. She must be intelligent, highly skilled, and willing to accept responsibility. No executive can hope to work at top efficiency without the assistance of a competent secretary.

VOCABULARY BUILDER

Mend your speech a little, lest it mar your fortune.
Shakespeare

secretaries ....
noun: those employed to handle correspondence and manage ... work for a superior

initiative ....
noun: an introductory step; energy or aptitude displayed in starting action

accurately ....
adverb: free from mistake or error; conforming exactly to truth or to a standard

replenish ....
verb: to fill or build up again; to replace

attitude ....
noun: a mental position with regard to a fact or state

appropriate ....
adjective: especially suitable; fitting

environment ....
noun: surroundings; the total of social and cultural conditions that influence the life of an individual or a community

chaos ....
noun: a state of utter confusion; a confused mass

nullify ....
verb: annul; to make of no value or consequence

integrity ....
noun: honesty; soundness; quality or state of being complete or undivided; adherence to a code of moral, artistic, or other values

p. 5   In general, you will find that **secretaries** are assistants to people who hold executive positions.

p. 5   The National Secretaries Association defines the secretary as an executive assistant ... who exercises **initiative** and judgment ....

p. 8   Executives value the skill of secretaries who can take their messages quickly and **accurately** ....

p. 12   Lillie needs to learn how to use her calendar to note supplies that are low and schedule a regular time to **replenish** them ....

p. 12   Develop the **attitude** of a professional secretary.

p. 19   ... each has achieved a skillful combination of clothing **appropriate** for work ....

p. 23   You will want to think about the type of **environment** in which you will be able to become fully involved in your work.

p. 24   **Chaos** develops quickly if a secretary just shoves papers in the desk drawers or lets them pile up on file cabinets.

p. 24   The fact that the trade magazine contained an article that was of interest to her employer ... did not **nullify** the consequences ....

p. 30   **Integrity** is a quality that an employer evaluates when interviewing candidates for positions ....

PART 1 YOU AND YOUR JOB—
YOUR BASIC SKILLS, YOUR TRAINING, YOUR REWARDS

Kathy Cunningham is secretary to Mr. Carlos Perez who is sales manager for Latin America with a large manufacturing company that has headquarters in Philadelphia. Mr. Perez spends much of his time traveling in the countries in which he supervises sales representatives. Kathy stays in the office during her employer's trips and carries on his work so that there is no delay in the matters that come to his desk. While Mr. Perez is away, he talks with Kathy on the telephone on a regular schedule. Kathy keeps a record of all the questions for which she needs answers, so that when Mr. Perez calls no time is lost in trying to remember what the questions are. Mr. Perez has said to his fellow executives when he is in the home office, "Kathy carries on my work as though I were at my desk. I could not do what I must do away from the office if it were not for Kathy. She is a topflight secretary."

Kathy understands her employer's work. She has a large map of Latin America on the wall behind her desk which helps her keep track of Mr. Perez's travels. She can talk with so much understanding of the activities in these countries that it is difficult to remember that Kathy has not visited these places!

What are Kathy's key tasks? They are writing business letters for her employer after she has gathered all the information needed, keeping a record of all the matters that must be discussed with Mr. Perez when he telephones, planning transportation and hotel arrangements for Mr. Perez and his assistants when they are leaving for a trip, sending memorandums to other executives in the company that keep them informed of Mr. Perez's activities while he is traveling.

....

Carolyn Rom is secretary to Mr. Walter Stevens who is the director of public relations for a large radio and television company. Mr. Stevens' title gives a clue to what he does: *public relations* is the art of promoting understanding and goodwill between the company and the public. Mr. Stevens' office answers a great deal of mail from people inquiring about the nature of the business and requesting informational bulletins. Such mail comes from all parts of the world. Also, Mr. Stevens spends some of his time in learning how the public is reacting to the programs provided by his company and in sensing what future interests might be among listeners. Carolyn serves as a valuable assistant in seeing that all the tasks are carried through smoothly and graciously.

What are Carolyn's major responsibilities? They include serving as receptionist to many callers, keeping an accurate calendar of Mr. Stevens' activity-filled days, maintaining a file of people who have taken part in meetings and conferences sponsored by the company, arranging for meetings that are held both in company quarters and in local hotels, and in handling much of the correspondence on her own.

Kathy and Carolyn are just two of over four million women workers who are included among the United States Bureau of the Census category of "clerical and kindred workers." There are also about a hundred thousand men so classified in the United States. The secretaries in this general category do many different tasks. While one secretary's major jobs may differ from those of another secretary, surveys of how secretaries spend their workdays show that they do have common tasks.

Illus. 1-1
Secretaries are assistants to people who hold executive positions.

Ohio National Life Insurance Company

In general, you will find that secretaries are assistants to people who hold executive positions. Executives direct the work of their organizations. Secretarial tasks are related to executive responsibilities. In dictation secretaries take the correspondence and reports that relay policies and decisions to others; they maintain files of the products made or the services rendered; they gather information needed by the executive; they give messages by telephone and in person to other executives and customers.

The National Secretaries Association defines the secretary as "an executive assistant who possesses a mastery of office skills, who demonstrates the ability to assume responsibility without direct supervision, who exercises initiative and judgment, and who makes decisions within the scope of assigned authority."[1]

THE SECRETARY AMONG OFFICE WORKERS

In business organizations there are typists, file clerks, clerk-typists, stenographers, secretaries, and administrative assistants. You may wonder what the differences are among all these titles. What makes a secretary a secretary and not a stenographer or a typist?

This question can be answered only *in general*, because titles are used differently from company to company. The table on page 6 shows the differences in several common office positions.

As you can see, the typist has a limited range of tasks. This means that she is spending most of her working day at the typewriter. However, the typing that she does may vary considerably each day. For example, on one day a group of typists in a large office in Chicago typed form letters, rough drafts of manuscripts, stencils, statistical tables, and forms. The stenographer's tasks are more varied than those of a typist but not as varied as those of a secretary. Stenographers generally work for a number of executives and spend much of their day taking dictation and transcribing it. Along with these principal duties they may handle telephone calls and maintain records.

Beginning Office Workers

Beginning office workers are generally assigned to positions where the tasks are not highly varied, so that you will find beginners holding

---

[1] We will refer to the secretary as *she* throughout this book since the majority of secretaries at this time are women. This does not mean, however, that there are not excellent opportunities for male secretaries in all types of organizations. In fact, male secretaries have unusually fine opportunities for employment, particularly in engineering, mining, construction, and railroading, to name only a few fields.

OFFICE POSITIONS

Position	Range of Tasks	Primary Tasks	Primary Requirements
Typist	Limited	Typing letters, filling in forms	Typewriting
File Clerk	Slightly varied	Filing materials, finding materials, typing	Knowledge of filing, typewriting
Clerk-Typist	Slightly varied	Typing, maintaining records, computing	Typewriting, knowledge of filing, skill in use of calculating machines
Stenographer	Slightly varied	Taking dictation, transcribing	Stenography, typewriting
Secretary	Varied	Handling correspondence, including taking dictation and transcribing; managing paper work; handling telephone and callers	Stenography, typewriting, knowledge of work of office and company, human relations skills
Administrative Assistant	Highly varied	Organizing work of the office and carrying through with little direction, supervising other office workers, establishing priorities	Thorough knowledge of work of office and company, high level office skills, knowledge of office management, human relations skills

Illus. 1-2

positions as typists, file clerks, clerk-typists, and stenographers. All these positions require that the worker have skills. Beginners are not expected to understand the functions of the company in which they find employment. Their first positions provide a means for them to gain understanding of the work of the company and thus become qualified for higher level positions. In any job where you handle some part of the paper work of the organization, you can learn much about the company that will aid you in developing the understanding necessary to assume more responsibility.

The Secretary

The secretary is not a beginner in the office. She has had some experience in the company that has prepared her for the broader responsibilities she is to assume. From time to time, however, a secretary with experience in another organization is employed and is given an on-the-job introduction to her work. Since she has had job experience in another company, she will learn about the new company in very little time. A secretary does, at one time or another, all the tasks that typists, file clerks, clerk-typists, and stenographers do; but she also has many other responsibilities. A secretary works for one executive and sometimes for two. An executive expects his secretary to take messages by telephone and to place calls for him, to compose some letters, to do research for and prepare materials for his reports, and to act as his representative in dealing with the public and the staff in the company. Secretaries make appointments, prepare travel schedules, keep office files, and inform their employers of forthcoming conferences and appointments.

Promotions

Many companies follow the policy of promoting from within the company when they are filling secretarial positions. When a personnel manager was asked about his company's reason for this practice, he said:

> Secretaries are very important persons in our company. To be effective in their jobs, they must not only know the office in which they work, but they must also understand the purpose of our total organization. We find that some of those who have stayed with our company have become familiar with our business. We want to take advantage of what they have learned, so that when we need to fill a vacancy in a secretarial position, we look to our office staff to discover who has good office skills and has developed an understanding of our company's business. One of these will be appointed to the secretarial job.

Through your study of secretarial office procedures you will become familiar with the wide range of tasks that secretaries face as they work each day. You will also see the usefulness of the office skills you have already learned and will continue to use.

BASIC SKILLS OF THE SECRETARY

A study of secretarial workers includes the finding that there are almost nine hundred different duties carried out by secretaries! It would be a long discussion if we were to include all of these. Some, as you already know, are more central to the main secretarial tasks than others. Among the basic skills are these:

Taking Dictation and Transcribing

The twin skills of taking dictation and transcribing are at the center of the secretary's responsibilities. Executives value the skill of secretaries who can take their messages quickly and accurately and prepare transcripts that need only signatures. Competent secretaries are able to answer immediately a call to "take a letter" and can follow through when there are corrections to be made, facts to be checked, and changes to be made in language.

Typewriting

While a secretary will not sit at her typewriter all day as a typist does, she still makes use of her typewriting skill frequently. What kinds of jobs do secretaries type? Let's list some of the tasks of a group of secretaries on just one day: A secretary to the public relations director of a chemical company typed a news release concerning a new product; a secretary to the editor of a monthly magazine typed a rough draft of an editorial which her employer had typed on his own typewriter; a secretary to a university professor of history typed stencils of a new reading list for one of the professor's courses; a secretary to a lawyer typed a contract for a client; a secretary to a doctor typed a case history on a patient.

The secretary does use the typewriter as an important tool in preparing various kinds of materials that are sent to many different places.

Handling Communications

Many businessmen think of their offices as the center of a network of communications, and the secretary plays a key role in maintaining this network effectively. Secretaries answer the telephone, talk with visitors, and write memorandums and letters on their own. All these tasks require skill in the use of both oral and written English. Secretaries who score high in handling communications have these important skills:

1. Ability to spell, including the checking of words in a dictionary when in doubt
2. Ability to speak pleasantly and smoothly with good usage of language
3. Ability to write briefly and to the point
4. Ability to understand the meaning of messages

An executive, talking about his secretary, said:

> I am always getting compliments about the manner in which Amy handles telephone calls. Our customers remark about her gracious manner, her excellent use of language, and the quickness with which she grasps the message and follows through with an answer that is directly to the point. After struggling with a young woman who never understood messages and who left them on my desk in meaningless form, you can understand my enthusiasm for Amy. She keeps communications flowing smoothly and pleasantly.

Operating Calculating Machines

There are many machines in the modern office that make tasks easier. For example, there is a calculating machine that simplifies computational tasks. Betty, a secretary to an architect, finds the printing calculator an aid when she is determining the total cost of a new project from notes which her employer provides her. Lynn finds an adding machine a great aid in checking the figures on invoices in a central buying office of a chain of department stores. Using calculating machines properly and fully can cut off minutes from many tasks.

Illus. 1-3

Some secretaries use calculators for checking figures and simplifying their work.

Eastman Kodak Company

Copying and Duplicating

Secretaries are often given tasks that require making multiple copies. They need to know the advantages of each of the methods available to them and the cost of each method. Modern businesses often have equipment for making copies directly as well as for reproducing copies from various kinds of masters and stencils. When a secretary is handed a complicated drawing by her architect employer and is asked for three copies, she realizes that a photocopying machine should be used. On the other hand, when he gives her a memorandum that is to be sent to three hundred persons in the company, she will prepare a stencil that will be sent to the duplicating office for reproduction.

Maintaining Records

Well-organized records and an orderly procedure for using them indicate an efficient secretary. Frequently a secretary is called on for information that is needed immediately. Claire, a secretary to a physician who is frequently invited to address meetings in all parts of the world, comments,

> I have to be able to find needed materials immediately, for it is not uncommon for Dr. Hughes to be on the telephone talking with a doctor in Stockholm when he will call me and say, "What is the title of the talk I am giving in London in late May?" And, as you would guess, I have to be able to put my hand on the file with the details of the London visit in seconds!

Secretaries are expected to maintain their records and keep track of those that are removed temporarily. Unfiled stacks of material are a sign of poor attention to this important office task.

Handling Travel Arrangements

Most executives spend much time traveling, and their secretaries must become skillful travel agents if trips are to be well planned. Secretaries need to know the preferences of their employers when traveling and the travel possibilities. Making arrangements also requires a thorough understanding of the executive's schedule. Gail, a secretary in Fresno, California, for example, arranged an air trip for her employer who had to give an address on the East Coast at six in the evening. She made a reservation for a morning flight at ten. Fortunately, Mr. Gage looked at his ticket when it was placed on his desk about a week before the departure and noted that he would not be in New York in time for the dinner meeting. Gail had *forgotten* about the time difference between the two coasts! An executive who finds himself in an airport terminal at three in the morning with no connecting flight to his destination, where he must appear at nine the next morning, does not think kindly of his secretary and her skill in planning travel arrangements.

When all the details for a trip have been worked out, the secretary is expected to prepare an itinerary. An *itinerary* is an outline of the trip which includes the date and the exact time of departure and arrival for each part of the trip, the means of transportation to be used, the accommodations for which reservations have been made, appointments to be kept, and any other details that provide a full account of the trip. The itinerary should be placed on the executive's desk prior to the day of departure so that if any changes are necessary there will be time to make them.

Illus. 1-4

When all the details of a trip have been worked out, the secretary prepares an itinerary.

AT&T

Part 1 / You and Your Job

Planning the Day's Work

Secretaries work without direct supervision and, therefore, assume responsibility for deciding the order in which they will do the tasks before them. The *establishing of priorities*, which means putting the tasks in one, two, three order, cannot be done unless the secretary has a complete understanding of the work of her office. Often she and her employer will discuss the jobs to be done and together establish an order for them. However, unexpected events can change the plans and at such times the secretary must know how to revise her own work schedule to take account of the changing situation.

The secretary's desk calendar, her employer's calendar, and her *tickler*, or follow-up, file — all serve to keep her on her schedule. She knows how to use these scheduling devices so that they are faithful aids to her memory. One distressed secretary, Lillie, said,

> Do you know that I had to go to the supply room three times today? First, I didn't realize that I didn't have enough stencils for the job I had to do this morning. Then later I found that I had run out of postal cards. This afternoon I needed a dozen oversized envelopes. I must begin to plan my work better so that I will be better organized for doing the jobs that come up.

Lillie needs to learn how to use her calendar to note supplies that are low and schedule a regular time to replenish them so that she can complete her work without unnecessary delays.

TRAINING FOR SECRETARIAL POSITIONS

Now that you have an overview of some of the key responsibilities of secretaries, you may be asking yourself: How do I prepare to enter such a professional position? There are three steps in the process of becoming a fully prepared secretary:

1. Acquire the basic skills and develop them so that you can use them in a wide variety of situations.
2. Develop an understanding of the nature of business offices and organizations and of the knowledge needed to work properly in such surroundings.
3. Develop the attitude of a professional secretary. A *professional* secretary is one who has deep interest in doing excellent work on every task she undertakes, has thorough concern with the total operation of the organization in which she is employed, and has developed her own means of evaluating how well she is doing.

REWARDS OF SECRETARIAL POSITIONS

When secretaries are asked about the rewards of their positions, their comments reflect varying sources of satisfaction.

Fulfillment in Serving Society

June is secretary to the director of a major government agency. She says,

> My employer is making decisions and guiding activities that affect the economic lives of millions and millions of American workers and their employers. I like to be a part of such an important function.

Phyllis, a secretary to a professor of biology, states,

> Some of the most important research in the basic behavior of cells is under way in our laboratories. I like being a part of activities that may unlock some of the key mysteries of human life.

Rae works for the director of international sales for a chemical company. She comments,

> Our company sells materials to countries around the world that aid farmers in increasing the productivity of their land. I like to think that I am helping in some small way to reduce hunger in the world.

Working Conditions

Most offices are attractive places with modern furniture and tastefully designed decorations. Secretaries like the places in which they work. In fact, in one study of secretaries' attitudes toward their work, over 94 percent said that they found their present offices pleasant places in which to work.[2] Offices are often air-conditioned and scientifically lighted so that fatigue is minimized.

Secretaries tend to work approximately 35 hours a week, five days a week. Almost all firms pay secretaries for any overtime that they must work, and paid vacations are a standard fringe benefit for most workers who have been on their jobs for a minimum of six months.

Opportunities for Employment

Secretaries are needed everywhere — in small companies, in small towns, in giant corporations, in the largest cities of the world. The need

---

[2] *Nation's Business* (March, 1968) (Study made by National Office Products Association).

for secretaries seems to be endless. Projections to 1975 indicate an increase of 27 percent in the employment of secretaries and stenographers between 1965 and 1975. This figure is projected in a period when the rate of increase in the use of computers and other types of automatic office equipment continues upward.

Salaries

Salaries vary in different parts of the country and at different times, depending on business conditions, the cost of living, and the available supply of office workers. Beginners can expect to earn from $80 to $115 a week, with fringe benefits adding up to another $10 to $20 a week. Secretaries with several years of experience may command salaries from $160 up. Though rare, there are executive secretaries who are earning salaries of $15,000 or more.

QUESTIONS

1. Describe a secretary as defined by the National Secretaries Association.
2. Sally tells you that she spends all day taking dictation from a staff of five men and transcribing her dictation. Would you classify Sally as a secretary? Explain.
3. What are the advantages to a company in promoting company personnel to secretarial positions?
4. What are some jobs that secretaries do at their typewriters?
5. Why is good language usage considered an important skill of a secretary?
6. Aside from taking dictation, transcribing, and typing, name at least three other skills needed by a good secretary.
7. What information is generally included on an itinerary?
8. Explain what a secretary must do when she *establishes priorities*.
9. What are some aids the secretary can use in planning her work effectively?
10. What are some rewards of a secretarial position?

JUDGMENT

1. What experience in an organization do you believe would aid an office worker who assumes a secretarial position?
2. A friend of yours makes this comment to you, "I don't understand why you would be interested in secretarial work. You will just sit at a typewriter and type letters all day and answer the telephone and take simple messages such as 'Bill called' or 'Why wasn't our order shipped?' " What would you say to your friend?

PERSONAL QUALITIES

Ann Clifford has just been employed as a stenographer, but she realizes that she can become a secretary if her work proves to be satisfactory over a reasonable length of time.

During her first morning in the office, however, she is asked to assemble and staple a 12-page duplicated report and to copy a typed report. She is not given any dictation, despite the fact that she had to pass a stenographic test before she was hired. At lunch time Ann expresses dismay at not having been asked to take dictation. She appears very upset and unhappy.

Assume that you and Ann are co-workers. What would be your comment?

LANGUAGE USAGE

A noun is a name of a person	Examples: Sally, Donald, Leo, friend, child, author
name of a place	Examples: Cape Cod, Caspian Sea, White House
name of a thing	Examples: table, notebook, typewriter
name of a condition or relation	Examples: happiness, initiative, democracy

Copy the sentences below and underline all nouns.
Example: The <u>tables</u> will be transported to <u>Cleveland</u> by <u>railroad</u>.

1. The company is celebrating its fifty-year anniversary.
2. Does California have a larger population than Illinois?
3. We cannot expect the committee to make a decision before the end of next week.
4. A secretarial job is one that requires a wide variety of skills.
5. What are the reference books that secretaries should have on their desks?
6. J. E. Cannon is the president of the branch bank in this town.
7. Can an agenda be drawn up before the meeting gets under way this afternoon?
8. Is judgment a quality that one can observe in office workers?
9. A future office worker can learn much through studying secretarial procedures.
10. Information is constantly sought by employers as they carry through their tasks.

SECRETARIAL WORK

1. You have studied eight key tasks that secretaries have in common in this part. During this course you will have many experiences to help you become skilled in handling these tasks. Prepare an outline with the major headings of these key tasks and under each heading indicate the specific skills and abilities that you would expect to develop during this course.

   Example: WHAT I EXPECT TO LEARN THIS YEAR

   A. Taking dictation and transcribing
      (a) Improve my ability to take dictation at a rapid rate
      (b) Improve my ability to write outlines for words that are unfamiliar to me

2. Below are four questions relating to the secretarial profession. Choose two of these and write one short paragraph on each.

   Is a secretary saving time when she leaves the proofreading of her transcription to her employer?

   In what ways may a position as stenographer aid a beginner in becoming qualified for a promotion to a secretarial position?

   How is the dictation that a secretary takes in a job *likely* to differ from that which stenographic students get in their classes?

   What could a future secretary do to improve her spelling and English grammar skills?

PART 2 PERSONAL AND PROFESSIONAL QUALITIES

Helen Mathis is highly respected by Mr. Dickinson, president of the major department store in a town of 57,000 people. Helen has worked for Mr. Dickinson for two years. Before working for Mr. Dickinson, she was a stenographer in the buying office. Helen was promoted to the top secretarial position because of her skills, her understanding of the company, and her exceptionally attractive personality. Her fellow workers would elect her "the worker with whom I would most prefer to work" if there were such an election; for Helen is cooperative, generous in taking on a job to be done, honest in all her relationships with others, and loyal to those with whom she works. As one of the vice-presidents said, "Helen is a gem of a young woman. She keeps the president's office operating smoothly, but beyond that she keeps it one of the happiest places in this whole store. She is fair and gracious no matter what the complications are. In the hectic world of a retail store, we certainly do appreciate Helen."

If you were to enter a roomful of secretaries and talk with them, you would soon realize that not all secretaries are alike! You would find that some are friendly; others are reserved. You would see some who are very gracious, others less so. You would notice that most are poised and self-confident; others are shy and seemingly lack self-confidence. You would find that you could not describe the typical "secretarial personality." Secretaries are not alike if you try to compare them in a social group. Of course, we would come to the same conclusion if we were with a group of scientists, baseball players, or television stars! We must, therefore, not simplify secretarial traits by talking about the "secretarial personality." However, studies have been made that have tried to identify secretarial traits that are prized by employers and fellow workers. Secretaries who seek to improve their professional behavior and future secretaries try to develop these traits. They are always alert to their shortcomings and make a continuous effort to improve their personalities and make themselves more pleasing to those with whom they associate. Some of the key qualities of a secretary will be discussed here.

PERSONAL QUALITIES

Business executives like their activities to be orderly and systematic. With a goal of efficiency, organizations choose office workers who reflect orderliness. The personal appearance of secretaries is, therefore, of concern to a company. Neatness is a valuable trait, and secretaries who dress and behave in good taste project a favorable image of their organizations.

Illus. 1-5

Secretaries who dress and behave in good taste project a favorable image of their organizations.

Personal Care

An attractive appearance begins with perfect personal care, and the secretary has to learn that attention to basic grooming needs can never be neglected. Some rules that should never be broken are:

1. Take a bath or shower at least once each day.
2. Use an antiperspirant or deodorant daily.
3. Brush your teeth at least twice each day.
4. Clean and wash your face thoroughly twice each day.
5. Manicure your nails regularly, and be kind to your hands by using a lotion regularly, particularly if you are in a cold climate during the winter months.
6. Wash your hair regularly and brush it often.

Dress

Proper selection and care of clothes are reflected in the way a secretary looks when she appears at her office each morning. Well-dressed secretaries do not dress alike, but each has achieved a skillful combination of clothing appropriate for work and becoming to the individual's figure. We live in a society that allows considerable freedom in selection of clothing. Most companies respect this freedom, but assume that secretaries will choose clothing that indicates an understanding of what is acceptable for office wear. Clothes that are comfortable but not casual are generally acceptable. With the range of styles and types of clothing available for the many activities modern young women engage in, there are times when without thinking a young woman will choose an unsuitable costume for a workday! Such a selection shows poor taste and causes embarrassment in the office. As one supervisor said,

> Miriam is such a lovely girl, but her long peasant-style gathered skirt and bandanna did look out of place in our glass and chrome offices. I told her gently about how inappropriate her attire was. Her response was, "I'm sorry. I just wasn't thinking, and this is just the most comfortable outfit I own." I don't believe she will make such an error again!

Clothes that are simple and fit well and are of a length that is accepted in the community are usually fully satisfactory for the office.

The secretary chooses shoes that are appropriate for her clothing and are comfortable so that she can walk gracefully and easily. Accessories such as purses, scarves, gloves, and jewelry should be selected with care. Purses should be of sufficient size to hold personal belongings but should not bulge. Scarves, gloves, and jewelry should be chosen with an eye toward enhancing total appearance.

Modern developments in fabrics and in clothing construction have reduced the time required to maintain your clothing and accessories in good condition. You should read labels carefully to be sure that you handle each item properly. You should plan a regular schedule for washing, cleaning, and repairing all your wearing apparel. From time to time the orderly secretary takes stock of her personal wardrobe giving special attention to the condition of her shoes, purses, coats, and dresses. She plans for purchases that she will have to make in the near future.

Hair Styles

Hair styles, in much the same way as clothing, vary considerably. Again, appropriateness and good taste should be given major consideration when making your decision about "How shall I wear my hair?" A hair style that is attention-getting is out of place in an office and shows poor taste. Simple, easy-to-care-for styles are best for daytime wear and require little attention.

Makeup

Women have always been interested in fashion and in making themselves attractive. Makeup should complement the clothes you wear. If it is too obvious it can detract from a quiet, well-groomed appearance. Makeup should be used to enhance the good features of your face. It should not call attention to an awkwardly applied collection of concoctions! You should carefully study the art of making up your face so that you add to its beauty in a *natural* manner. The observer should think, My, what a pretty face!, not, My, she has a great deal of makeup on her face! General advice for office makeup is to wear little; keep the full range of application for evening wear.

Health

Respect for oneself begins with attention to basic health needs. Sufficient sleep, proper foods, and a reasonable amount of exercise are *absolutely* necessary if you are to be healthy. An authority on feminine beauty in commenting on good health said,

> A woman who wants to look her *very* best will never cheat herself of sleep. Women of forty who look no older than thirty are women who have respected the rule of getting a good night's sleep *every* night.

Proper food provides the nutrients needed to maintain a healthy body with all the energy that you demand for the many activities in which you participate. While nutrition experts tell us about the importance of a good breakfast, many people fail to heed the advice. Do you begin the day with a good breakfast which you eat in an unhurried fashion? Properly selected foods for lunch and dinner deserve attention, too.

To function well the body requires exercise. Plan your leisure hours to include activities that provide relaxation and a chance to use muscles that get little use in your regular work. Walking, bicycling, and sports, such as tennis, bowling, and swimming, will help you keep your body in fine form.

> Christine is an attractive young woman who enjoys good health. She seems always to be functioning at her best and never complains of fatigue. However, when you learn about her life style it is easy to understand her good health. She follows a relatively regular schedule on week days so that she has

sufficient time for three meals, approximately eight hours of sleep, and some hours for recreation. She lives in a large metropolitan area; so she must plan for her recreation. She bicycles several times each week in a beautiful park that is not far from her apartment. She also plays tennis and takes long walks weekly.

Kelly Services

Illus. 1-6

Shiny hair, sparkling eyes, radiant health, and abundant energy are the rewards for the secretary who eats properly and gets sufficient rest and relaxation.

Posture and Poise

One of the outstanding features of a successful actress or fashion model is her posture and her poise — the gracefulness of her movements and the sense of well-being that she reflects. You, too, can develop such gracefulness and ease of movement by paying attention to your behavior. Are you aware of how you walk? of how you sit? of how you move across a room? Practice movements that exhibit gracefulness and graciousness. Take time to be conscious of your movements and of your responses to people.

While posture is a significant part of conveying a sense of poise, there is more to the concept of *poise*. Poise is difficult to define. One definition is that it is the ability to remain gracious under all circumstances. The dictionary gives several definitions for this term. The one that is most appropriate for our discussion is "balance, equilibrium, stability." When we say that a woman is poised we **usually have observed** that she seems to

Part 2 / Personal and Professional Qualities

know how to behave appropriately in a situation. She maintains her equilibrium, her sense of balance. Now we mean "her equilibrium, her sense of balance" in a more than physical sense. It is true that a woman who drops and breaks a cup and saucer when she extends her hand for a handshake would appear unusually awkward and not poised. But beyond the physical awkwardness there likely may be communicated a sense of emotional awkwardness — the young woman was not quite able to cope with the prospect of being introduced to someone. Try movements and responses that will reveal your personality favorably. An employer discussed a young woman who failed to win a promotion by saying,

> Janice is a wonderful young woman. Her skills are excellent; she is one of the best workers in the stenographic pool. However, I could not use her in this office. She walks around the office as though she is afraid of everyone. She doesn't look up when someone talks to her. You never see her eyes. She responds without looking up, also. She is lacking in self-confidence. I have to have someone in this office who is poised and can meet and talk with people in a warm, comfortable fashion. The supervisor in the stenographic pool is going to talk with Janice to see if she can help her to see how much talent she has that is unused because of her behavior and the image that she presents to others.

Voice and Language Usage

The quality of your voice and the skill with which you use the language are important in a secretarial position. A pleasant, clear voice is attractive. A loud, demanding voice is unattractive; a very low, retiring voice makes communication difficult.

Secretaries should use a vocabulary that demonstrates wise and precise use of the language. The slang expressions of teenage talk sessions are out of place in the modern business office. "Isn't this groovy?" is just not the most appropriate reaction to a personnel bulletin announcing a new fringe benefit for all office workers! A secretary who responds "Search me!" when she is asked a question she cannot answer doesn't convey a mature attitude toward her work.

PROFESSIONAL QUALITIES

> Wilma was an exceptionally hard-working secretary, but she just couldn't be a member of our team. There were times when she needed to take care of callers. We found that if she was busy at her typewriter, she would refuse to look up to greet someone who had come to her desk. We just didn't like our visitors to be treated in such an unfriendly manner. Also,

> Wilma felt that if I couldn't find something on my desk, it was my fault; I had obviously misplaced it and she would never come to my assistance. She was not willing to change her manner, so we had to dismiss her.

Wilma will undoubtedly be happier working in a position where she has no need to share tasks with others!

Cooperation

A secretary works with others. In some instances she works closely with one executive; in other instances she may work with several executives as well as with a number of other office workers. To be an effective co-worker, a secretary must be aware of the needs of others and be willing to provide information and assistance when they are needed. Good secretaries enjoy helping others and maintain an awareness of where help is needed throughout the day.

Involvement

Have you ever heard the comment, "He couldn't do a good job because his heart wasn't in it"? Do you know what this statement means? Good secretaries know what it means. They know that much of their success depends on their being fully involved in the work of the company. Their interest in what is going on is genuine and lasts through easy days as well as demanding days. The secretary to a dedicated legislator in the federal government commented:

> My job is so challenging that I don't know what time it is. I consider it a full-time job; and on many days, when important legislation is being debated, we are at work long after the traditional closing hour of five. When you care about what you are doing, you don't turn off your interest at a particular time. I would not be happy having just a job — something I did merely to earn a living. My work is an important part of my life, and I must believe in it and commit myself to it fully.

This secretary has captured the significance of behaving professionally and has gained much joy and satisfaction from her work.

You will want to think about the type of environment in which you will be able to become fully involved in your work. Do you like a busy, active place where you must give attention to several matters at the same time and must be able to meet deadlines that arise regularly? Or would you prefer to be in a carefully organized, smoothly functioning office where all that must be done is known long ahead of time and can be scheduled so that there are no last minute rushes? Do you prefer to work with others in cooperative activity? Or would you rather have a set of tasks that are only slightly related to the work of others so that you can work alone? There are many variations in offices; you will want to get to know yourself so that you can make a wise choice.

Orderliness

It is not clear if people are born orderly or if they acquire the ability in school. We do observe differences in the way in which people keep their notebooks, their desks, and their personal possessions. Regardless of the origin of an orderly nature, to be successful, secretaries *must be* orderly. Chaos develops quickly if a secretary just shoves papers in the desk drawers or lets them pile up on file cabinets. A work station must be well organized to avoid wasting time in finding room to work and in locating the supplies needed.

A secretary has to determine the best arrangement for her materials and then see that she follows through with putting materials back in place. A place for everything and everything in its place is a good motto for a secretary. Work stations must be organized so that others can locate items needed if the secretary is away from her desk.

One executive was distressed because he needed a draft of a speech that he had given his secretary to type. She had gone to lunch and when he went to her desk, he was completely confused; there was no way for him to figure out the system that his secretary was following. She had no "Work in Progress" folder or basket. She should have had such a guide for her employer! When she returned, a somewhat unhappy executive asked, "Belle, where is the draft of my speech?" Her reply — "Oh, I stuck it in that copy of your trade magazine that came in this morning's mail!" There was no need to ask, "Why did you do that?" This young woman had not realized how necessary it was to have a system for maintaining everything at her desk. The fact that the trade magazine contained an article that was of interest to her employer in connection with his speech did not nullify the consequences of her unexplained act.

Trustworthiness

Executives frequently comment on their appreciation of a secretary whom they can trust. When one executive was asked to describe the behavior of a secretary who is trustworthy, he said,

> My present secretary is a perfect model. I can depend on her to continue to work when I am out of town or at a conference. She is careful about being on time regardless of my schedule. In other words, she doesn't need to be "checked in"

> each morning or at lunch time in order to be on time. I handle a wide range of jobs and I have no time to check up to see if something has been done. When I ask my secretary to get a copy of a report and mail it with a note of explanation to someone, I need not worry again about that task. The request is taken care of. We have tasks that are not immediately required. I know that my secretary has not filed them away; she has them listed in her "jobs to be done" folder and will use relatively quiet periods to make some progress on such jobs. I never need to remind her of such pending jobs.

A secretary that an executive can *trust* adds many hours to the time he can devote to other jobs. If an employer has to check on his secretary, he isn't getting real work from her. If he subtracts his checking-up time from the time she spends on the job, her contribution to the work load may be very small.

Secretaries are in positions of confidence. They perform tasks that bring them in contact with highly confidential information about what is going on in an organization. They know about new developments before they become public announcements. To reveal such developments can seriously change the position of a company in relation to the public or in relation to competitive firms. You will need to cultivate the attitude that the business of your employer is not to be communicated to *anyone*.

Initiative

Anticipating what needs to be done is a valuable trait. Being able to take action on one's own increases the helpfulness of a secretary. Initiative, which is the ability to identify accurately what needs to be done and then follow through with the correct action, is a key characteristic of good secretaries. Most executives are grateful to secretaries who show initiative in their jobs. The secretary to the dean of a college had exceptional skill in taking the initiative, and her employer thoroughly appreciated her skill.

> Diane has a sixth sense in understanding what is coming next. I received a letter asking me to speak at a college in Artesia, New Mexico, and when the letter arrived on my desk there was a note attached indicating the kind of transportation service available into this small town. She read the letter and realized that this was a small town obviously not on a direct airline route, and she knew that I would question transportation services.
>
> I will unthinkingly call a meeting of a group of twenty with no plans for a meeting room. Diane knows my office is too small for such a group; she immediately checks to find out if

there is a room available at the suggested time before she types the meeting notice. You can imagine what my life would be like if twenty people showed up at my office and only then did I realize that I hadn't made provisions for a conference room!

There are dozens of times each day that Diane is doing the kind of forward thinking that makes life pleasant.

Loyalty

To be *loyal* means that you are faithful and true to your employer. Secretaries are helpful and concerned about the work of their employers. To be loyal implies that the secretary is *genuinely* helpful and concerned — she has not merely learned how to *act* in the presence of her employer. Rather, she can continue to be faithful and true when her employer is away or when she is talking with others. The loyal secretary has no wish to engage in office gossip. She is satisfied with her business associates and has no need to talk critically about them to others. A secretary who talks freely about her employer's personality weaknesses, for example, has an extremely poor attitude toward her responsibilities and her listener will soon lose respect for her.

THE ENVIRONMENT IN WHICH YOU WORK

A secretary's conduct is influenced by the behavior she meets in her work surroundings. Human beings are responsive to their environments and often encounter difficulty in living up to the standards that they have set for themselves. The qualities that have been described in this part are those that we wish to find in workers. Actually many workers, including executives, secretaries, and other office personnel, do not measure up to the highest score on each of the desired traits or characteristics. Nonetheless, many people strive to improve the quality of their behavior. You must respect the efforts of those around you to improve their behavior in much the same fashion that you want others to respect your efforts.

You, as a future secretary, want to develop your own ideas of the kind of person you wish to become. Become aware of your own conduct and judge it against your own standards. Environments differ: in some, it will be easy to measure up; while in others you will have to think through carefully what you should do. Each environment will offer some challenge to you to grow into a more mature personality. Sandra described a situation in this fashion:

When I first met Mr. Cooper, I wondered if I could work for him for more than a day. He seemed in such a hurry, and he gave me instructions for five different jobs at the same moment.

There was no preliminary discussion of the general routine of the office. My reaction was: Here is a truly thoughtless man! That day was about six months ago! I must confess that the first two days were hectic — and I made a few mistakes. However, I soon realized that Mr. Cooper was seriously interested in the company and in doing his job well. He gives his full attention to his work. He assumes that a secretary is *just* as interested as he is. I began to feel more confident. Then I realized that I liked his attitude toward a secretary, and I have grown to have respect for Mr. Cooper. I find it very easy to be loyal to him and to do my work in a fully professional manner.

Whether or not you become a good secretary depends a good deal upon yourself. Your goals are largely dependent upon the value you place upon yourself and your own desire to succeed. As you are introduced to the responsibilities of secretarial work, you will want to assess not only your technical skills in handling such work, but you will also want to think about the personal qualities that are closely related to doing the work in a fully professional manner.

Illus. 1-7

Your personality is the total of your characteristics — personal and professional — and is an important factor in your success.

Pitney Bowes

QUESTIONS

1. Do you agree with the statement: All successful secretaries must have outgoing, aggressive personalities. Discuss your answer.
2. On what basis does a secretary choose clothing for her working days?
3. How much makeup is appropriate for office use?
4. What are important rules for good personal care?
5. Describe a situation where a secretary can show how poised she is.
6. Why should a secretary be interested in developing her vocabulary?
7. Why is cooperation important among the workers in an office?
8. How would you explain *commitment to one's work* in relation to secretarial work?
9. Why is it important for a secretary to be trustworthy?
10. In what ways does a loyal secretary differ from a disloyal secretary?

JUDGMENT

1. A young secretary likes to talk about her failure to eat regular meals and to get sufficient hours of sleep. In fact, she has commented, "I never bother with meals; I'm too busy to eat and I think sleeping is a waste of time. I often get only four hours' sleep a night."

   Do you agree with this secretary? Explain.
2. Mr. Nickerman stated, "Skills are important in this job; however, if the secretary is not a responsible person, she will be of little value to me." What do you believe Mr. Nickerman is suggesting as important qualities?
3. Describe the work habits of a secretary who scores high on "ability to organize her work."
4. Mr. Trent asked his secretary, Florence, to be sure a report gets in the day's outgoing special delivery mail. Mr. Trent is called out to a meeting at three and tells Florence that inasmuch as his meeting will last until seven, he will not return to the office. Florence then decides that she doesn't have to rush the report. She will do it the next day. What qualities are revealed in this decision?

PERSONAL QUALITIES

1. You and a friend, Vicki, are discussing the requirements of business dress which an older mutual friend, Helene, has to follow. Helene works in an old, established bank in the heart of the financial district of the city. Helene has told you:

   "When I was interviewed for my position, the personnel manager told me that the company was considered a stable, serious enterprise and that all employees had to reflect this image. I learned that I would have to dress in conservative, quiet fashions and wear very little makeup. As I talked with the interviewer, I found myself thinking about wearing such attire to work. Then I realized that she was describing the way in which I like to dress when I go to work, and I knew that I could fit into such an environment easily."

Your friend, Vicki, interrupts at this point and says,

"I do not believe that a company should dictate to an employee. I would *never* accept such restrictions on what I wear. I don't believe I would even consider a position in such a firm."

You and Vicki are close friends and you speak freely with each other. What would you say in response to Vicki's comment and what is *your* reaction to Helene's attitude?

2. A young office worker makes this comment to you:

"I work for one reason only: to make as much money as I can. I give just so much of my effort to my job. I don't like to get too involved because then I use a great deal of my energy at work and need to rest at night. I consider my life as beginning when I leave the office. I would *never* work overtime. I cannot imagine what is so important as to keep me tied to my desk after the regular hours are over."

Is this young worker *likely* to be promoted? Explain.

LANGUAGE USAGE

Pronouns are words that serve as substitutes for nouns. They must agree with their antecedents (nouns for which they stand) in person, number, and gender.

Illustration: Sally is using the gloves *that* Terri gave *her* for Christmas. *Sally* (third person, singular number, feminine gender) is the antecedent of *her*, which is in the same person, number, and gender. The word *gloves* (third person, plural number, neuter gender) is the antecedent of *that*, which is in the same person, number, and gender.

Write the following sentences, indicating correct pronouns.

1. Neither Jane nor Betsy feels that (her, their) project is ready for discussion at this time.
2. This is a very important concern of both William and (I, me).
3. They were not sure (who, whom) they should approach with the suggestion.
4. Every office worker should have a dictionary available to (him, them).
5. (They, them), along with a group from another organization, will be attending the convention in late October.

6. The secretary, as well as the typists in her office, was not sure what (her, their) responsibility was in such an emergency.
7. The committee has promised to have (its, their) recommendations ready for review by the end of next week.
8. Integrity is a quality that an employer evaluates when interviewing candidates for positions in (his, their) company.
9. A secretary (who, whom) is cooperative is appreciated by (her, their) employer.
10. The three people (who, which) are sitting in the reception area are waiting to talk with Mr. Erwin.

SECRETARIAL WORK

1. Your teacher will probably want to have information about you just as an employer would want information about a new employee.

   Write a short report about your background, including part-time and full-time employment, if any, and the schools you have attended, including a list of the business courses you have taken in this and other schools.

2. You have just studied the personal and professional qualities that are necessary to become a good secretary. Write a short report on qualities which you consider important to develop. In the report, tell why these qualities are important for secretaries.

Unit 2 DICTATION AND TRANSCRIPTION

Part 1. Dictation
    2. Transcription
    3. Dictating and Transcribing Machines

The secretary spends a great deal of time taking dictation and transcribing letters. Her shorthand and typewriting skills must be superior if she is to help her organization keep the cost of correspondence as low as possible.

VOCABULARY BUILDER

He who does not know the force of words cannot know men.
　　　　　　　　　　　　　　　Confucius

encounter..............................
　　verb: to come upon face to face; to meet; to come upon unexpectedly

indistinctly..............................
　　adverb: not sharply outlined; blurred; faint; not clearly understandable

flexible..............................
　　adjective: yielding to influence; capable of responding or conforming to changing or new situations

competent..............................
　　adjective: qualified; capable; fit; able

illegible..............................
　　adjective: the quality or state of not being readable

strive..............................
　　verb: to devote serious effort or energy; to try hard; to take pains; to struggle

consecutive..............................
　　adjective: following one right after the other without gaps; continuous

varied..............................
　　adjective: having numerous types or forms

supplement..............................
　　noun: something that completes or makes an addition; a continuation of a book or periodical containing corrections or additions

accompanying..............................
　　verb: to go with or attend as an associate or companion

p. 35　While the basic vocabulary with which you will deal will be fully understood, you will ... **encounter** new words.

p. 35　Some employers dictate slowly and clearly; others dictate rapidly and, at times, almost **indistinctly**.

p. 41　There may be times when you may make ... suggestions, but you must be **flexible** enough in your attitude to pleasantly accept his procedures.

p. 44　As a **competent** secretary you will probably have a time schedule for the day.

p. 47　To make a large number of carbon copies, use lightweight carbon paper ... otherwise the last ... copies may be blurred, smudgy, and **illegible**.

p. 48　Strikeovers ... should never appear in the finished work of a secretary who **strives** to do her best.

p. 51　Avoid dividing words at the end of two or more **consecutive** lines.

p. 55　To accommodate these **varied** uses, equipment is available in ....

p. 57　In a company where a network system has been installed, executives tend to use the service as a **supplement** to that provided by their secretaries.

p. 58　When either the dictation is finished or the record is filled, the tape or disc and its **accompanying** indicator slip are then ....

PART 1 DICTATION

Ann Winston is secretary to Mr. William Thurmond, regional manager for a major motion picture corporation. One of the most important tasks that Ann performs each day is taking dictation from her employer and preparing copies of the materials dictated for theater managers. To record the dictation smoothly and accurately, Ann has developed considerable knowledge and understanding of her employer's responsibilities which help her to respond to a variety of questions which Mr. Thurmond asks while he dictates, such as, "Did we send a copy of the Monday night preview report to Dick Sayles?" or "Have we received reports on attendance figures from our managers in Alexandria, Newport News, Richmond, and Roanoke?"

BASIC SKILLS FOR TAKING DICTATION

As a future secretary, you already possess the basic skills for taking dictation. These must be adapted to the situation in which you will work as a secretary; but you will find that these skills, if properly developed, will give you the foundation upon which to build high-level competency in performing your stenographic tasks.

The first skill you must have is the ability to write shorthand at a rate that is somewhat faster than that which normally will be required of you in the business office. You will want to have some reserve skill. You might well ask, Why is it necessary to have reserve skill? Let us say, for example, that an employer dictates at an average rate of 100 words a minute. Would a secretary who takes dictation at 100 words a minute be able to record whatever her employer says? No, not necessarily. His actual speaking rate will vary, and there may be short spurts of dictation at the rate of 150 words or more a minute. The secretary, therefore, must have some skill beyond the average speed to be able to handle such spurts. Also, a secretary taking dictation on an unfamiliar topic will be unable to write at even her normal rate. In fact, if you can normally take dictation at 100 words a minute you may be able to write only 80 words a minute when the subject of the dictation is unfamiliar to you. You must have reserve skill in these situations.

Illus. 2-1

A secretary must be alert. A slight change in voice indicates an instruction that is not part of the dictation.

AT&T

Another basic skill that you must have is the ability to be fully alert to what is being said. This is necessary so that you can quickly grasp the slight change in tone which announces that what follows is an instruction to you and not a part of the dictated message. It is necessary, furthermore, that if there is an interruption and the dictator asks that a portion of the material dictated be read back, you will be able to read quickly and with understanding. As a matter of fact, your employer should not have to ask you to read back dictation after an interruption. As soon as he puts down the phone or terminates a conversation with anyone who has come into his office you should immediately reread at least the last three or five words of the last phrase that he has dictated. This will refresh his memory and enable him to proceed smoothly. If the interruption has been lengthy, he may request you to reread a sentence or more.

You must also have the skill of writing unfamiliar outlines. While the basic vocabulary with which you will deal will be fully understood, you will from time to time undoubtedly encounter new words. The competent secretary is able to write these from sound and, later, with the aid of a dictionary, determine what has been dictated.

LEARNING YOUR EMPLOYER'S WORK

From your study of stenography, you have realized that if you are familiar with the subject of the material dictated to you, you find it much easier to take dictation at the rate given. On the other hand, when the material dictated is foreign to you, it is much more difficult to take all the dictation. Familiarity with the subject is an important aid in your work as a secretary. There are a number of ways in which you can develop an understanding of your employer's work.

First, you will be acquainted with the correspondence that he handles. As you open the mail, sort it, and attach related files to the correspondence that your employer must answer, you will become familiar with what you are reading. You should read with interest and attention so that when you take dictation replying to incoming letters, you will do so with understanding and awareness.

Second, many of the activities you will perform in the office will be related. If you note this connection, you will understand the dictation. The professional and trade publications which your employer receives, the reports of your company, the file copies of letters that come to your employer — all are sources that will help you become fully acquainted with your employer's work.

TAKING DICTATION

There is no "typical" manner in which employers handle their dictation, for there are many differences in dictation habits. Some employers set aside a certain time each day for dictation; others dictate from time to time during the day. Some employers make notes as they read their correspondence which aid them in dictating smoothly and quickly; others seemingly think through their responses while in the process of dictating. Some employers dictate slowly and clearly; others dictate rapidly and, at times, almost indistinctly. Some employers expect the secretary to sit by quietly with no reaction whatsoever during dictation; others like their secretaries to interrupt if there is something that is not clear or doesn't seem to make sense.

It is the dictator's responsibility to dictate his messages and reports to his secretary in as efficient and effective a manner as he can. However, the secretary, at least in her early experiences with a particular employer, can do little to make suggestions which she believes will improve the way in which the employer handles his dictation. The role of the secretary requires that she be fully cooperative in assisting her employer.

The secretary must learn either directly from her employer or from watching how he works the manner in which she is to handle the dictation.

Suppose a secretary notices that during dictation the employer must ask her for related correspondence or other materials that are necessary before he can complete a letter. This may be a clue that she is not reading the incoming mail with enough attention to determine all the materials that should have been on her employer's desk with his mail.

Dictation Readiness

Whether the employer dictates only once each day or at different times throughout the day, it is the responsibility of the secretary to be prepared to answer immediately a request for taking dictation. You may be summoned to your employer's desk by direct oral call if your desk is nearby, by a buzzer, or by some other interoffice communication device.

Illus. 2-2

A secretary must always be prepared to take dictation. Circumstances require dictation readiness at a moment's notice.

AT&T

You should have on your desk, within easy reach, a notebook and pen and pencils. As soon as you acknowledge the executive's call you should take your notebook and writing tools for dictation and go into his office. Sometimes the call will not be for dictation, but for other instructions. You will find it helpful to make notes of any instructions or directions that your employer may wish to give you.

There are times when the executive's call interrupts an important task. Your first responsibility is to answer the call. If you are in the process of doing a task that must be completed shortly, you can tactfully mention this to your employer and let him decide whether his need to dictate is more important than what you are doing.

When you leave your desk, you must remember to take care of any confidential information that may be on your desk. It will take only a few seconds to turn over such material or insert it in a folder. If there is something in your typewriter that should not be read by others, you should quickly roll the platen back so that the copy cannot be seen by anyone passing your desk.

If you must be away from your desk while your employer is in his office, you should ask someone to respond to any call from your employer while you are away. If your employer should call during such a time, your fellow worker will be able to tell him where you are, when you will be back, or how he can reach you.

Dictation Position

When you take dictation for a long period of time you should arrange your materials, your chair, and your location at your employer's desk or near it in a manner that will be the least tiring and the most comfortable. You will probably find it easier to hear the dictator when facing him — experienced secretaries usually do. You may, therefore, arrange to sit directly across from the dictator, resting your notebook on his desk. Another position many secretaries find convenient is to the left or right of the dictator, resting their notebooks on the sliding desk shelf. If it is not possible to use your employer's desk and you must take dictation with your notebook on your knee, get a clipboard on which to rest your notebook. You may also use the clipboard to keep materials your employer may give you during the dictation period. A clipboard helps avoid the possibility of dropping them.

Dictation Tools

A good secretary is careful in handling the tools with which she works. Your notebook and pen or pencils should be readily available. You will want to place a paper clip or a rubber band around the used portion of your notebook so that you can open it easily to a clean sheet where you can begin to take your notes. Also, it is important to date your notebooks so that if you must refer to your notes at a later date, you will find the task of locating the desired message much easier. Many secretaries follow the practice of writing the date in the bottom right-hand corner of the first page of the dictation. This corner reference makes it easy to flip through a notebook when searching for a particular day's dictation.

Dictation Procedures

You will want to be sure to mark clearly the beginning of each letter or report that is dictated. If there are special instructions that will be important and helpful to you when you begin transcribing, these should be written (in shorthand) in sufficient detail to be understandable when you get back to your desk. Many secretaries use only the left column of the shorthand pad for taking dictation so that the right column is free for recording instructions as well as corrections that the executive may make as he dictates.

Many executives hand the letter or report to which they have dictated a reply to the secretary as they complete the response. The material which the secretary has been given may be numbered with the same number as the response in her notebook. If it is turned face down, the letters in her notebook will be in the same order as the correspondence that is related to those letters.

When the dictator pauses to collect his thoughts, or is interrupted by the telephone or someone stopping in his office, the secretary should

Illus. 2-3

When the dictator is interrupted a secretary rereads her notes, makes necessary corrections, and codes spelling or definition problems.

Unit 2 / Dictation and Transcription

make use of such free moments. At such times she can read notes, insert necessary punctuation marks, correct poor outlines, make longhand notes where necessary, or insert symbols to show words which must be checked for meaning or spelling.

When changes are to be made in the notes you have taken, you will want to be sure that you make them carefully so that there will be no confusion when you begin to transcribe. If the dictator decides that what has just been dictated is to be taken out of the letter, you should merely draw a single line through the notes and begin the correction immediately after the part that was removed. If additions are made after the letter has been dictated, you should place a circled *A* at the point in your notes where the addition is to be typed when a transcript is prepared. Another circled *A* should appear at the beginning of the addition, wherever it appears, and double diagonal lines at the end of the addition. For a second addition *B* can be used, and so on as illustrated on page 40.

If questions arise in your mind as you are taking dictation, it is a good idea to make a note of the questions so that you can ask them when the dictation is completed. Some secretaries keep separate notebooks for use in jotting down such questions. Others have a small pad on which they quickly note questions; still others use small cards for such a purpose. You will want to be sure that you have all the information needed to complete the transcription of the material dictated as quickly and efficiently as possible. For example, you may need to know how many copies are to be prepared, whether or not certain letters are to be completed first, and further details about some references in a particular letter.

KINDS OF DICTATION

While much of the dictation that a secretary handles consists of letters, there may be interoffice memorandums, telegrams, reports, and instructions. Each type of dictation requires careful attention to details.

When a letter is dictated, the dictator will often begin with the salutation and expect the secretary to locate the address of the person or business to whom the letter is written. Generally the dictator will pass on to the secretary the letter he is answering, and on it the secretary will find the information for the address. It is very important that the name of the addressee be spelled correctly and that the proper title be used. If the dictator is not answering a letter, he may dictate the name and address. In such instances, the secretary may want to write the proper names in longhand to be sure that the name is spelled correctly. Many names that sound the same have different spellings, such as Brown and Browne or Burns and Byrnes. The secretary must be certain of the correct spelling.

Illus. 2-4

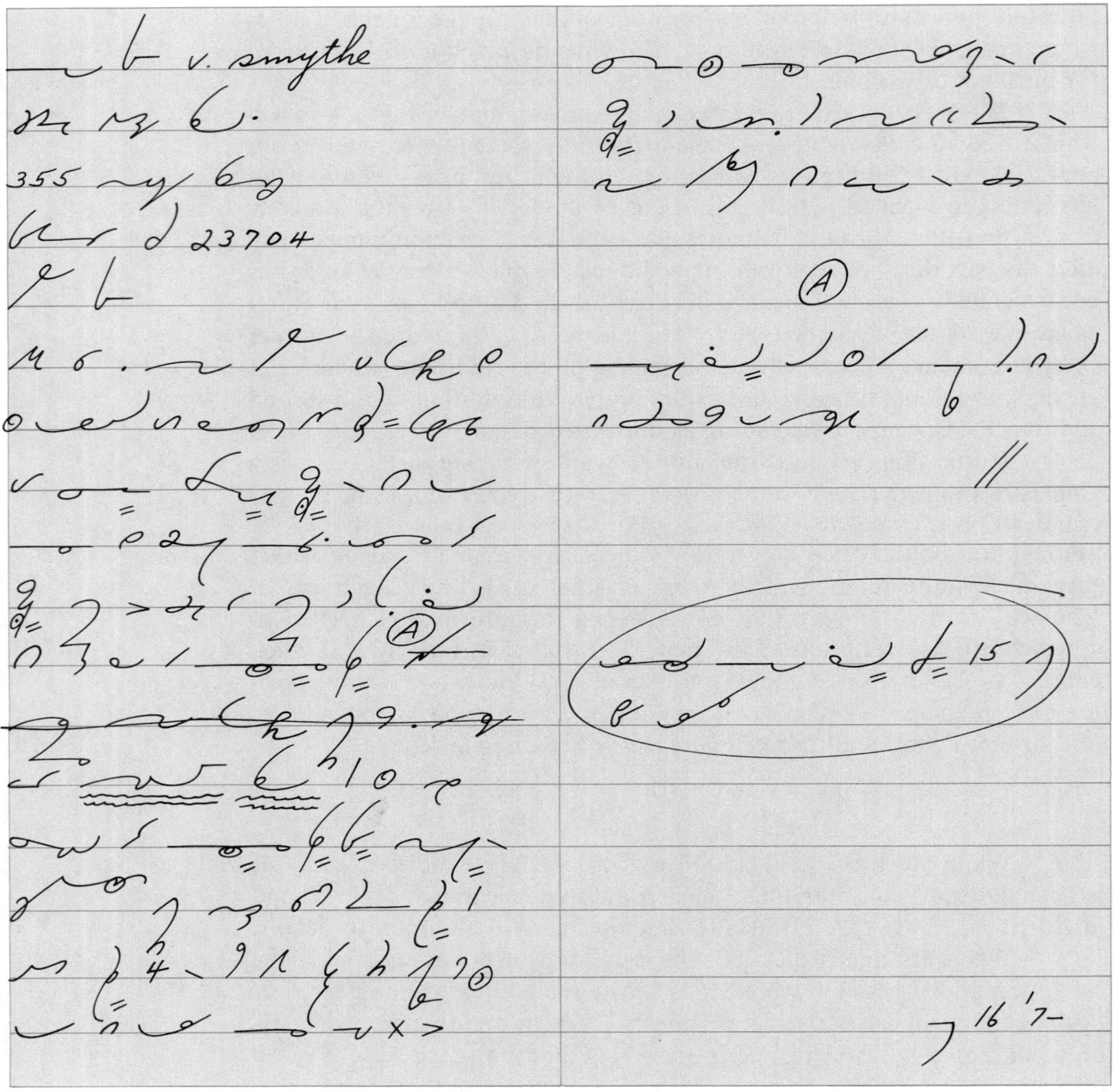

Shorthand notebook page with changes, additions, and instructions marked

When taking a telegram, the secretary must be exceptionally careful to understand the message. The message is usually written in a highly abbreviated fashion, which means that if one word is misunderstood or sent incorrectly the message may be worthless. Also, the secretary needs to

Unit 2 / Dictation and Transcription

understand the urgency of the message, for she may be responsible for determining what kind of service should be used.

Reports often require several drafts. The dictator may prepare a first draft by dictating it to his secretary. At this point, he may not have the complete report clearly in mind, and there may be gaps in the material. The secretary should not become disturbed by this. She will know that when she types the first draft and gives it to her employer, he will be able to fill in the gaps and refine the message he is trying to write.

DEVELOPING YOUR SECRETARIAL QUALITIES

While some of the employer's dictating procedures could be improved, you must remember that you are employed to help him do his work. There may be times when you may make tactful suggestions, but you must be flexible enough in your attitude to pleasantly accept his procedures.

The position of secretary that will be yours is a very responsible one. During dictation, as well as at other times, employers will discuss highly confidential matters with you, using such opportunities to think through ideas that are not yet completely clear in their own minds. You should listen carefully, comment only when asked, and never mention such matters to anyone else.

QUESTIONS

1. What are the basic skills that a secretary must have to take dictation?
2. What does the secretary do when the dictator uses a word that is unfamiliar to her?
3. Why should the secretary have a knowledge of her employer's work?
4. What is the value of attaching related correspondence to incoming mail before it is placed on the executive's desk?
5. Why may a dictator wish not to be interrupted while he is dictating?
6. Why should the secretary respond immediately when she is summoned by her employer?
7. What tools should the secretary take into her employer's office for dictation?
8. What does the secretary do about the work in her typewriter when she is called for dictation?
9. Why is it a good idea to date each day's dictation?
10. Why should a secretary code each item in her shorthand notebook along with each piece of correspondence that is answered by the executive and handed to her?
11. How should the secretary use the pauses or interruptions in dictation?

12. How may an addition that must be inserted in material already dictated be indicated in the secretary's notebook?
13. How may the secretary keep a record of questions that she may want to ask her employer when the dictation is ended?
14. Why is it necessary to be very sure about the message for a telegram?
15. In what way may a report that is dictated differ from a response to a letter?

JUDGMENT

1. A secretary is busy with a rush job for one of the two executives for whom she works. It is late in the afternoon. She is called in for dictation by the other executive.
   What should the secretary do?
2. Mr. Phillips, in dictating a letter to his secretary, asks, "Didn't we send this same information to Mr. Birmingham a couple of weeks ago?" The secretary responds, "Goodness, I cannot remember what we did two weeks ago!"
   What do you think of the secretary's response? What could she have done when Mr. Birmingham's letter arrived?
3. Mr. Haskins, who ordinarily dictates at a rather slow rate, began dictating very rapidly to his secretary, who found this rate beyond her skill. She said to him, "You're going too fast; I'm not getting what you are saying."
   Did the secretary make the right comment to her employer? What do you think she should have done?
4. At the time the secretary is called for dictation, there is no one in the office to take care of incoming calls. Shortly after the executive begins to dictate, the telephone rings.
   What should the secretary do?

PERSONAL QUALITIES

After Virginia Hall opens the mail for her employer, she places it on his desk without reading it. When she is called in for dictation, her employer must stop frequently and ask her to get related correspondence from the file. Her employer sits back while Virginia goes to the file and gets the necessary information. Then she sits and waits while he reads the material before he is ready to dictate.

What improvement could Virginia make in the manner in which she handles the mail for her employer?

LANGUAGE USAGE

Adjectives act as aids to nouns and pronouns by describing or limiting them. Adjectives answer such questions as: *What kind? Which one? Whose? How many?* On a separate sheet of paper, list the adjectives in the following sentences and indicate the question each adjective answers. (Articles, such as *a, an, the*, are considered adjectives, but you may disregard them for this exercise.)

Example: The secretary is sometimes called to the executive's desk when he needs a few items of information in order to answer his correspondence.

    executive's   Whose?
    few   How many?
    his   Whose?

1. An efficient secretary does not delay answering the executive's call.
2. Fewer lines of the notebook will be used if small notes are written.
3. Effective work habits help the secretary take dictation rapidly.
4. The best posture for writing shorthand is with feet flat on the floor, head up, back straight, and arm in a good writing position.
5. The secretary's desk is usually a smaller desk than the executive's.
6. A secretary will do a better job if she pays attention to the major functions she must handle.
7. An alert secretary knows what is happening in her office.
8. Good work is rewarded in the modern office.
9. The promotional ladder for a beginning office worker is known to many workers.
10. When new machines are installed in an office, a secretary must be ready to learn how to use them effectively.

SECRETARIAL WORK

1. Write a short paragraph discussing briefly the reason for each of the practices listed.
   (a) Reading incoming correspondence and attaching correspondence in the files that is related to the incoming correspondence
   (b) Leaving blank three or four lines at the beginning of each new item taken in dictation
   (c) Making notes of questions to be asked at the end of dictation
2. Assume that you are responsible for instructing new stenographers in your company about the manner in which they should take dictation from their new employers. Write a paragraph or two on the advice you would give to help them adjust to the demands of their new jobs.

PART 2 TRANSCRIPTION

Eleanor Dickens' employer, Leonard P. Townsend, is manager of the small appliances division for a large manufacturing company. His job requires the handling of large amounts of correspondence daily, in addition to numerous reports. Therefore, Eleanor takes much dictation that she transcribes quickly and accurately. Eleanor has her desk fully stocked with all the materials she needs for her transcription. She also has reference books, including an up-to-date dictionary, within easy reach.

ORGANIZATION

As a competent secretary you will probably have a time schedule for the day. You will have a certain amount of routine work that must be done if the office is to operate smoothly. Transcription must be fitted into the day's schedule. Because secretarial duties may be different from office to office, it is difficult to say when the transcribing should be done. The time for transcribing depends to some extent upon the time when the dictation is given. As a general rule, most executives like to have their mail ready for signature on the same day that the dictation is given to the secretary.

You will have to keep an efficient work station if you are to do your work quickly and smoothly. Your desk must be kept in good order at all times so that you can easily work on the transcription required. Often-used reference books, including a recent dictionary, should be on your desk and ready for use. You should also have available envelopes, letterheads, carbon paper, second sheets, eraser, eraser shield, stapler, and paper clips before beginning to transcribe.

THE DESK

You should keep the top of your desk clear except for the work you are doing at the time. Everything else is filed away. You should keep a stock of supplies and materials that you will need regularly in the drawers of your desk. When you must send a telegram, for example, you should not find that you are out of forms and must take time to get a supply before you can prepare the telegram. It is a good idea to keep a list on your calendar of supplies that will be needed shortly; and, from time to time, you should go to the supply room to replenish your supplies.

THE TRANSCRIBING PROCESS

As soon as you return to your desk after dictation you will want to begin transcribing any rush items that have been included in the dictation. You should have marked such items so that they are easy to locate.

After taking care of the rush jobs, the other items will be completed. Generally transcription follows the order of dictation, except for rush jobs. You will usually want to go over your notes before you begin transcribing. This involves looking over the notes for words that must be checked in the dictionary, proper names that need to be checked in files, points of grammar that must be checked in a reference book, facts that are missing and must be supplied before the message can be completed.

Handling such details before transcribing will permit you to give full attention to the typewriting and therefore work with few interruptions.

Typing Letters and Reports

You will want your typewriter in good condition so that your transcription will be attractive and easy to read. You should report any needed

Illus. 2-5

Rush work is handled promptly. Related files are near notebook. Correct position of notebook provides ease in transcribing. Good sitting posture results in increased efficiency.

Ohio National
Life Insurance Company

repairs to the person responsible for maintenance of equipment. To use a typewriter that is not working properly will lower your efficiency.

You will want to keep your typewriter clean. In your routine you must establish a time for cleaning your machine, particularly the type face, so that the letters will be very clear.

With a typewriter that is operating properly, you should be able to work at your best speed. You will want to be sure to set the margin stops and tabulator stops so that the material you are to type will be attractively centered on the page.

Assembling a Carbon Pack. Seldom will you make one copy of the material you are transcribing. Generally carbon copies are necessary. You will want to learn how to handle multiple copies easily and quickly; for this, too, can improve your production rate when you are transcribing your shorthand notes.

To insert the original, carbon sheets, and copy sheets (this collection of material is called a *carbon pack*) quickly, you should use the paper release lever, and slip the pack into the machine with the shiny side of the carbon facing forward. Snap the paper release lever into position, and turn the platen knob to bring the paper into writing position. To aid in the insertion of a thick carbon pack, place the flap of a large envelope over the top of the pack and remove the envelope after the pack has been turned to the position for typewriting.

Some secretaries like to insert carbon sheets in a different way:

1. Arrange letterhead and second sheets and slip them behind the platen. Be sure they are firmly anchored.
2. Flip the pack forward over the front of the typewriter.
3. Turn the last sheet, which is the letterhead, back and insert a piece of carbon, shiny side upward, repeating this until all carbons have been inserted.
4. Turn the platen knob, bringing the papers into typing position.

In handling carbon copies give attention to the following:

1. Never squeeze the assembled sheets together. A thumb print or fingernail scratch on a sheet of carbon paper may spoil the appearance of the carbon copy.
2. Handle the carbon paper carefully so that the carbon is not transferred to the fingers. Keep your fingers free of carbon so that carbon smudges will not be transferred to the original and the carbon copies.

3. If the typewriter feed rolls make marks on the copy sheets, adjust the feed rolls and turn the paper up more slowly, or use carbon paper with a harder finish.
4. To make a large number of carbon copies, use lightweight carbon paper and lightweight paper; otherwise the last several carbon copies may be blurred, smudgy, and illegible.
5. Never use a wrinkled sheet of carbon paper, for it will cause a carbon smudge to appear on the copy.
6. Always keep carbon paper in a flat folder or box away from dust, moisture, and heat.
7. When several sheets of paper and carbon paper are being used in an assembly, clip the sheets of paper and carbon paper together at the top after they have been inserted in the machine. This prevents the copies, especially the last ones, from being wound around the platen of the typewriter.
8. By inserting the carbon paper after inserting the letterhead and onionskin or manifold, you can easily remove all the sheets of carbon paper from the pack without smudging by holding the top of the letterhead and onionskin (no carbon paper reaches the very top line of the pack) while you pull out all the carbon sheets by the small amount that sticks out from the bottom of the pack.

Illus. 2-6

Learning how to quickly assemble a carbon pack will improve your production rate when transcribing.

Administrative Management Society

Part 2 / Transcription

Making Corrections. As a careful typist, you will be very much concerned about the corrections that must be made in your copy. Strikeovers give your work an untidy, careless appearance and should never appear in the finished work of a secretary who strives to do her best. Erasing requires skill. Here is a good erasing procedure to follow:

1. Slide the carriage to the right or left to prevent erasure particles from falling into the machine.
2. Insert a solid metal or plastic shield or a 5" by 3" card directly behind the error in the original. Make certain that it is placed between the original and the first sheet of carbon paper. This protects the carbon copies from smudges.
3. Place a plastic or metal shield with cutouts over the material to be erased. Use of the cutout shield will enable you to erase a single letter of single-spaced copy without smearing other letters or lines. Erase in a circular movement for more than one letter; use up and down motions for one letter.
4. Move the solid shield to behind the first carbon copy and erase that copy, using the cutout shield.

Illus. 2-7

Move the carriage to the side before erasing so that filings do not fall into the mechanism. Use a shield to protect copy that is not to be erased.

5. Continue erasing *all* carbon copies in the pack, moving from front to back of the pack.
6. Check the alignment to be sure you will be typing on the same line as before.
7. Strike the correct key or keys lightly, repeating the stroking until the desired shading is achieved.

There are times when the correction of an error requires that an extra letter or a word be inserted. A letter may be added if the letters are typed in such a way that each one occupies less space than it did before. On some machines, this is done by striking the first letter, then holding the backspacer down slightly and striking the second letter, and continuing in this manner until the complete word has been typed. You may want to practice this skill, called *squeezing*, if you have not as yet perfected it.

At other times, the correction of an error requires that a letter be omitted. A letter may be omitted without spoiling the appearance of the page if the remaining letters are typed in such a way that each one occupies more space than it did before. This is done by striking the first letter, striking the space bar, then depressing the backspacer slightly and holding it in that position while striking the second letter, and continuing this operation until the complete word has been typed. This is called *spreading*.

If you are using an electric typewriter, you may have to use slightly different procedures for spreading and squeezing. On some electric typewriters, you will have to hold the carriage by hand while you type the letters in the correct places. On other electric machines, you will find a half-space key that will aid you in proper placement.

There are other ways of correcting errors. There are available correction fluids and tapes that can be used to cover errors prior to retyping. Directions for the use of these fluids and tapes are given on the labels. In general, a small amount of fluid is applied to the error and allowed to dry; then the correct letters are typed. If tape is used, a small piece of tape is placed over the error and you retype the incorrect letters. The tape covers the incorrect letters with a white film. You then backspace and type the correct letters. Correction fluids and tapes are considered superior to erasing since they avoid the rubbing away of the surface of the paper and the possibility of bits of the eraser falling into the typewriter.

Preparing Blind Carbon Copies. There are times when a carbon copy is to be sent "blind." This means that the original copy is not to indicate the name of the person to whom the carbon is to be sent. After you have completed a letter that includes a blind carbon copy, the simplest procedure is to do the following:

1. Release the paper release lever and remove the original only from your typewriter.
2. Turn the remaining sheets and carbons back to the normal position for carbon copy notations.
3. Type flush with the left-hand margin: bcc: Mr. T. F. Smith.

This notation will then appear on the carbon copy for Mr. Smith and on the file copy. If several carbon copies are made and some are being sent in the regular manner, then the *bcc* reference will be on the copy that is designated blind and the file copy only.

Completing the Transcription

Before you remove the letter or memorandum from the typewriter, you must carefully proofread it. An uncorrected error is inexcusable. You should never be too rushed to check the work you are about to remove from the machine. It is far simpler to correct an error that is found before the papers are removed from the machine than it is to correct the error after the carbon pack has been taken from the machine.

After you have completed the letter and have proofread it carefully, remove it from the machine. Next you type the envelope, attach the enclosures that are to be sent with the letter, and then place the envelope face up with the flap over the top of the letter and enclosures. All special delivery and other rush jobs should be taken to the executive for his signature immediately after they are completed. When he has signed them, you should send them out. Once the rush items have been taken care of, you are free to continue with the other items that must be transcribed.

The other general correspondence and reports should be kept together and taken to the dictator when the entire day's transcription has been completed. If you have more dictation than can be transcribed before the end of the day, you should give the completed items to your employer before the day is over so that the portion of the dictation that is transcribed can be mailed on that day.

Carbon copies of letters may be separated from the letters before they are taken to the dictator for signature, or they may be kept with the letters until the dictator has signed the letters. The latter procedure is simpler if the employer is one who is likely to make changes in letters before signing them, for corrections can be made on all copies with no delay. Changes must be made on all copies, and you will want to be as careful about the way that corrections look on carbon copies as you are about the appearance of the original after the correction. If there are many changes you should retype the letter.

If carbon copies are to be sent to others, you should prepare envelopes for such copies and give them to your employer if he is in the habit of signing or initialing such copies. If the copies are to go out without signature, you will hold such copies aside until the executive has signed the original and it is ready for mailing.

Improving Your Transcribing Skill

You will find that your transcribing skill can be improved a great deal as you gain experience. Take advantage of your experience to become a superior transcriber. Below are some helpful hints that you may want to keep in mind as you strive to become a skillful transcriber.

1. Double-check the spelling of the addressee's name when there is any doubt.
2. Check questions of grammar which come up during transcription in a good reference book.
3. When in doubt about spelling or word division, check the dictionary.
4. Avoid dividing words at the end of two or more consecutive lines.
5. Avoid separating one-letter syllables at the beginning or the end of a word. (For word division, see Appendix C.)
6. Number all pages of a letter except the first.
7. Avoid having only one line of a paragraph dangling at the bottom or top of a page.
8. Get in the habit of circling in your notebook the last word typed whenever an interruption occurs. A glance at the page will be all that is necessary to resume transcribing at the correct point. If this is not done, you may see an outline similar to the last word typed and begin transcribing at that point only to find that a part of the letter has been omitted.
9. Proofread carefully every letter that you transcribe sentence for sentence against your notes.
10. Use good judgment in correcting dictation given. If you feel major changes are necessary, it is wiser to check with the dictator than to assume the responsibility. Since a dictator may resent interruptions to check minor details, you should develop the ability to handle the checking on your own.
11. Develop good transcription rates by continuously working to improve your transcription technique.

Illus. 2-8

A good secretary smoothly "shifts mental gears" when interruptions occur and resumes her work with no loss of efficiency.

AT&T

12. Check on the proper outline for any words that you found hard to read. Improving the writing of your shorthand notes is another way of improving your transcription skill.

Though no secretary is perfect, the secretary who returns letters which can be signed and mailed immediately is a joy to her employer. The personal satisfaction that results from producing correspondence that your employer is proud to mail is well worth the painstaking attention to detail that you give each page you transcribe.

QUESTIONS

1. What skills must the secretary possess to handle transcription efficiently?
2. What materials and supplies should the secretary have at hand in order to work efficiently while transcribing?
3. How does a secretary determine the most appropriate time for transcribing?
4. How does a secretary decide upon the order of transcription of the dictation?
5. What kind of checking should a secretary do before she begins her transcription?
6. What responsibility does a secretary have for keeping her typewriter in good working condition?

7. What is a simple procedure for inserting a carbon pack in the typewriter?
8. At what point should a secretary proofread her work?
9. How should carbon copies be handled when they are to be sent to people outside the company?
10. If an executive desires a change in one of the letters transcribed, what should a secretary do?
11. What practice should a secretary follow if she wishes to improve her shorthand skill so that she will be able to read her notes more speedily?

JUDGMENT

1. Esther Adams is a secretary who has the habit of waiting until she has used all her supplies before she goes to the stockroom to replenish them. She may be starting to transcribe a letter that must go out immediately when she finds that she has no carbon paper. At this point, she either dashes out to the stock room or to another secretary's desk to get the needed supplies.

    What would you suggest that Esther do in order to avoid such emergency situations?

2. A secretary finds that she must type six and seven copies of much of the material she is transcribing. The carbon paper she is using is a heavy grade; the second sheets are also heavy. Therefore, the last few copies of the pack are generally very light and difficult to read.

    What do you think the secretary should do about this matter?

3. Ruth Hartman is very careful to make corrections on original copies so that they are not obvious; however, she is careless about the way in which she corrects the carbon copies. She says that no one really sees the carbon copy; so she sees no reason to be careful.

    What would you say to her to encourage her to see the value of making neat corrections on all copies?

4. Betty Morris has the habit of holding letters until she has completed all the transcription. This sometimes means that letters dictated on Monday morning are not signed until late Tuesday.

    Is this a good practice? Why?

PERSONAL QUALITIES

Sarah Billows, secretary to Mr. T. F. Sanford, had taken several letters from her employer. She returned to her desk and was beginning to transcribe the first letter when she noticed that her employer had failed to answer the principal question that the correspondent had raised in his letter. Sarah has the information to answer the question.

What do you think Sarah should do in such a situation?

Part 2 / Transcription

LANGUAGE USAGE

Verbs are words that express action or a state of being. They are closely related to subjects and must agree with their subjects in person and in number.

Type each sentence below using the correct verb.

1. The secretary (know, knows) what changes she may (make, makes) in the dictation she has (taked, taken).
2. The secretary must (had, have) her desk and its contents in perfect order if she (is, are) to work efficiently.
3. Many secretaries (prefer, prefers) to keep their desk tops clear except for the work being handled.
4. Dictation (is, are) usually checked before actual transcription (begin, begins).
5. When the secretary (return, returns) to her desk she will (transcribe, transcribes) the rush items first.
6. The secretary (is, are) able to make many copies with the use of carbon paper.
7. After the secretary has (complete, completed) the letter and has (proofread, proofreads) it carefully, she (remove, removes) it from her typewriter.
8. The carbon copies of a letter (is, are) separated from the letter.
9. Uncorrected errors in a transcript (is, are) inexcusable.
10. The secretary (avoid, avoids) dividing words at the end of two or more consecutive lines.

SECRETARIAL WORK

1. List the steps you would follow in erasing an error on several copies. Be prepared to demonstrate the procedure.
2. A newly employed secretary is having more than the usual amount of difficulty with her carbon copies when she transcribes her shorthand notes. She has trouble with (a) smudges on carbon copies, (b) realigning after making corrections, and (c) cutting certain letters and punctuation marks through the original copy. Briefly outline the steps you would take to help her overcome her difficulties.
3. Assume that you are taking dictation from Miss Sterns. Record the following in your shorthand notebook.

    Be sure to send a blind copy of this letter to Mr. Murphy. Dear Mr. Swift: Your plans for the interior of the New Orleans airport are very interesting. You have combined efficiency with local traditions in a pleasing manner. I have carefully reviewed your plans and have just a few questions that I have listed on the copy. When do you think we can get together to make final decisions about placing orders? Inasmuch as the building schedule has been interrupted, we have slightly more time for planning. Sincerely yours,

PART 3 — DICTATING AND TRANSCRIBING MACHINES

Jean Moran is a very good secretary who takes much dictation from her employer. She also uses transcribing equipment since her employer, who is the executive vice-president of a large chemical company, spends a considerable amount of time traveling. When he is traveling, he takes a small portable dictating unit with him and uses it frequently. His dictation is mailed to Jean, who transcribes it. She will either sign the correspondence or hold it for his signature, depending on his instructions.

KINDS OF DICTATION AND TRANSCRIPTION EQUIPMENT

As a secretary you must be able to take dictation in shorthand, but you may have an employer who uses a machine for recording dictation from time to time. The extent to which executives use machines for dictation depends on the nature of their work, the time at which they choose to dictate, and their preference for the way in which their dictation is to be recorded. The use of dictating machines continues to increase. The fact that you can be at work on another secretarial task while your employer is dictating on a machine means that the cost of dictating each letter is less. A secretary's time is far more costly than that of the machine. Furthermore, you will generally work regular hours. Executives often work after hours, and it is convenient to have equipment available for recording drafts of reports and letters. Executives also spend much time traveling; and, to continue to handle their communications, they frequently use dictating machines to prepare discs, tapes, or belts that can be easily mailed to the office for transcription.

To accommodate these varied uses, equipment is available in portable units, in single units, and in remote control network systems.

Portable Units

The small transistorized units provide an executive with the equipment he needs to dictate in comfort at home, in his car, or on a trip. In fact, several airlines provide portable machines for businessmen who desire to dictate while on a flight. There is also a service that provides a dictating machine at the departure point of a flight or at a hotel. The discs on which the executive has dictated can be transcribed by a local branch office of his company or can be mailed back to his own secretary.

Illus. 2-9

Portable dictating equipment enables an executive to dictate anywhere anytime.

Dictaphone Corporation

Standard Units

Separate machines for dictation or transcription are available with a variety of features and with different types of recording devices. The executive has one machine on his desk for dictating, and the secretary has a different machine on her desk for transcribing. Combination units are also available and are popular in offices where limited use is made of such equipment. A combination unit is one that performs both the dictating and the transcribing functions. Inasmuch as only one person can use such a unit at one time, the work must be carefully planned so that a secretary will not need to postpone her transcription because the machine is requested once again by the executive.

Remote Control Systems

Networks of equipment provide a way for executives throughout a company to use the services of a central dictation and transcription facility. An executive may have only to push a simple fingertip control to begin his dictation. In other instances, the executive dials a special number on his regular telephone and is connected to a machine that is ready to record what he says. There are many variations of networks available. For example, it is possible to have connections at several locations so that an executive at a branch office is able to call to the home office in another town and dictate on a machine. Furthermore, there are systems that allow the use of a regular outside telephone to call into a company where the dictating machines are available.

In a company where a network system has been installed, executives tend to use the service as a supplement to that provided by their secretaries. When their secretaries have unusually heavy workloads, the executives use the central service so that their secretaries need not transcribe the dictation. Stenographers in the central office prepare the transcription and return it to the executives' offices for signature.

THE SECRETARY'S RESPONSIBILITY

Your executive's dictating and transcribing units should always be ready for use; therefore, from time to time you will want to check the machines to see that they are working properly. To continue to use a machine that is in need of repair is to work inefficiently. You must also see that there is an adequate supply of belts, discs, tapes, or cassettes on hand.

Dictating Skill Needed

As a secretary you may not be called upon to dictate. However, as your competence and responsibilities increase, you may be required to dictate routine correspondence that will be transcribed by other stenographers. Therefore, you will want to know what the good techniques for machine dictation are.

A hand microphone is usually used to record dictation on a machine in the office, or an instrument resembling a telephone is used to record dictation in a central transcription room. The operation of the hand microphone varies slightly with the different models. Dictation machines all follow a basic pattern of providing a bar for starting and stopping the dictation. There are usually labeled keys or buttons for repeating a few words of the dictation, for indicating corrections, and for showing the length of each dictated letter.

To begin dictating, set the tape (or belt) in motion by a slight pressure on the starter bar. Hold the microphone just a few inches from your lips. Keep the tape (or belt) in motion only when actually dictating. If you are interrupted or if you need time to think, stop the machine.

Some manufacturers furnish desk microphones which may be used in place of the hand mouthpiece. The use of the hand mouthpiece is better when the machine is to be used in open offices or in places that are somewhat noisy or not too private. The desk microphone is used in private and quiet offices. The desk microphone is available with either hand or foot control for starting or stopping the machine. The foot control on the desk microphone frees both hands for making notes or for handling papers needed to dictate the reply.

The dictating unit will not only record but will also play back the dictation that has been completed. Thus you may have the machine repeat your dictation for you at any point.

Special instructions to the transcriber may be dictated along with the regular dictation. Greater efficiency can be developed, however, by using a system of marks covering some of the routine instructions, including stating the number of carbon copies desired or indicating a rush letter. These marks may be made on a strip of scaled paper called an *indicator slip*, which is placed in a special holder attached to most dictating models. The marks referring to a particular letter are written or cut into the part of the indicator slip that is directly in front of the dictating machine. The beginning and the ending of a letter are also marked on this indicator slip in order to give the transcriber the opportunity to judge the length of the letter and to plan its placement on the letterhead. When either the dictation is finished or the record is filled, the tape or disc and its accompanying indicator slip are removed from the machine. The record and the indicator slip, along with the files, are then delivered or sent to the person who is to transcribe the dictation.

Illus. 2-10

Indicator slip

Dictating Suggestions

Efficient machine transcription depends to a large extent upon the quality of the dictation. The following five hints for improving machine dictation were prepared by Gray Dictation Systems:

1. Relax — be natural — you're talking to another person.
2. Hold the microphone two to three inches from your lips and speak directly into it.
3. Until it is a habit, be careful in the use of the start-stop control so that you don't lose the first or last part of your dictation.
4. Have a mental outline of what you want to say, and say it clearly in a conversational tone at normal speed.
5. To help the transcriber, tell her the number of copies before you dictate a letter, indicate paragraphs, and pronounce unusual names with special care or spell them out.

Transcribing

If your secretarial duties include machine transcription, you have many of the same problems that are encountered in transcribing from shorthand notes. The chief difference is that, in machine transcription, you must depend upon your hearing.

Most transcribing machines are equipped with ear pieces or headsets that either fit into the ears or rest gently against the ears. You place the dictated record on the transcribing machine, then place the indicator slip in the slot provided for it, and proceed to transcribe.

For ease in the operation of the transcribing machine, adjust the controls to suit your particular needs. The speed control, the volume control, and the tone control are all adjustable.

The indicator slip which accompanies each recording should serve as a guide for efficient transcription. You should listen to the corrections and special instructions before beginning to type from the recording. Then note the length of each letter as it is marked on the slip and set the margin stops and the vertical spacing on the typewriter for the correct placement of the letter on the letterhead.

At first, transcription is usually performed by starting the machine, listening for a few words, a phrase, or a sentence, stopping the machine, typewriting the words, starting the machine again, listening for a few more words, and so on until each letter (or other material dictated) has been transcribed.

Illus. 2-11

Dictating equipment is timesaving. It is the practical solution for handling heavy workloads. It releases both employer and secretary for more important duties.

IBM Corporation

As skill increases, you should be able to type without interruption. It is then unnecessary to stop the transcribing machine to backspace to relisten to the dictation. You will be able to stop and start the transcribing machine without pausing in your typing.

The rate of machine transcription can be increased and the number of time-consuming errors can be reduced if the following suggestions of experienced transcribers are adopted:

1. Listen to the corrections and special instructions *before* transcribing any of the dictated material.
2. Use the indicator slip as a guide for the proper placement of material to be transcribed.
3. Be sure that you understand the meaning of the dictation before typing so that you will avoid
   (a) errors in grammar
   (b) errors in punctuation
   (c) errors in spelling
   (d) confusion of homonyms, such as *bare* for *bear*
4. Develop the power to carry dictation in your mind in order to avoid the overuse of the repeat key.
5. Develop the skill of an expert — keep the typewriter moving, but stop the transcribing unit. Listen to one phrase ahead of your typewriting.
6. Use the parts of the typewriter to advantage, especially the tabulator and the variable line spacer.

QUESTIONS

1. What are the advantages of machine dictation over shorthand dictation?
2. Under what circumstances would a portable dictation unit be advantageous?
3. What is a disadvantage of having only the combination unit dictating-transcribing machine?
4. How do executives use voice recording machines today?
5. What is the main advantage of a foot control over a hand control on a desk microphone?
6. How may the dictator give special instructions to the secretary?
7. How should the secretary use the indicator slip?
8. Give four hints for improving machine dictation.
9. How may the secretary judge the length of a letter dictated on a dictating machine?
10. List five suggestions which will make the use of machine transcription more efficient.

JUDGMENT

1. Discuss why a secretary who can take dictation by another means should also learn to transcribe dictation from a machine.
2. In what way does the use of dictating and transcribing machines lead to a saving for an employer?
3. Should a transcribing machine operator be as well qualified as a secretary who transcribes letters from shorthand notes?
4. Whenever Mr. Adams dictates, he fails to prepare an indicator slip. How would you ask him to remember to prepare one for you?

PERSONAL QUALITIES

Virginia Hall has been appointed secretary to Mr. James Murray, the chief purchasing agent, referred to as "Mumbling Jim" by the other secretaries. He dictates slowly in a very low voice, but he mumbles and swallows his words. Virginia asks him to repeat the words and phrases she can't understand, something he is always willing to do.

Recently he has been using a dictating machine for his dictation after office hours, but it takes Virginia twice as long to transcribe the recorded dictation. Even then she is not always sure that she has transcribed correctly.

Virginia has received a pamphlet called *Ten Commandments for Dictators* from a dictating machine company which she has placed on Mr. Murray's desk. He cannot understand why it was left on his desk; he considers himself an excellent dictator.

What do you think of Virginia's action? Should she tell Mr. Murray that his dictation could be improved?

LANGUAGE USAGE

Type each of the following sentences using the correct verb.

1. Dictating and transcribing machines (is, are) used extensively to record and transcribe dictation in business offices where there (is, are) a heavy volume of correspondence.
2. The handling of correspondence (is, are) aided by the use of dictating and transcribing machines.
3. Either you are to use the dictating machine or I (am, are).
4. Neither the tape nor the belt (is, are) usable on a home style record player.
5. The outstanding advantage of dictating machines (is, are) that the secretary need not be present during the dictation.
6. The combination dictation and transcription model (is, are) used by only one person at a time — the dictator or the secretary.
7. The general manager, as well as his assistant, (is, are) making plans to tour the plant.
8. Each tape, belt, and disc (is, are) to be transcribed promptly.
9. The dictator and not the machine (are, is) usually at fault.
10. The board of directors of this corporation (want, wants) its meetings recorded on tape.

SECRETARIAL WORK

If dictating and transcribing machines are available, dictate the following letter on a machine and then transcribe it. This letter contains several errors which you should correct as you dictate and transcribe.

If dictating and transcribing machines are not available make the corrections needed and type the letter.

Mr. Edward H. Richardson, Richardson Engineering Company, 1420 Hickory Drive, Richmond, Vir. 23222 Dear Mr. Richardson (¶1) We have just introduced our latest portable dictating machine, the EXECUTIVE. You will be satisfied with no other machine once you have tried the EXECUTIVE. (¶2) The portable dictating machine for the busy business man is not a new idea. Our EXECUTIVE with it's small overall dimensions and lightweight battery are new concepts. Our new battery will outlast any other battery on the market today. (¶3) We would like you to use the EXECUTIVE for two weeks on a trail basis. Take it with you where ever you go. We will even furnish you with two free cassettes for recording your important dictation. If at the end of the trial period you do not believe that the EXECUTIVE is the best portable recording machine made, simply return it to us. (¶4) If you would like to experiment with the EXECUTIVE, please call our office at 947-8340. We shall deliver your EXECUTIVE and cassettes immediately. Sincerly yours Michael J. Desmond Sales Manager

Unit 3 THE MAILABLE LETTER

Part 1. Letter Placement and Styles
     2. Parts of the Letter
     3. Stationery

The secretary must know all the possible parts of a business letter and the different styles that can be used. She must understand how to arrange a letter so that it will present a pleasing appearance to the reader and get his interest.

VOCABULARY BUILDER

A vocabulary of truth and simplicity will be of service throughout life.

Winston S. Churchill

horizontal
adjective: parallel to a base line; level

p. 66 The complimentary close begins at the **horizontal** center of the page.

eliminate
verb: to get rid of; to expel; to set aside as unimportant

p. 66 The simplified style **eliminates** the salutation and the complimentary close.

estimate
verb: to appraise; to judge the value or worth of something

p. 68 A letter placement table such as that shown . . . will help you **estimate** the spacing for letters.

omit
verb: to leave out or to leave unmentioned; to fail to perform or make use of

p. 69 . . . **Omitting** the names that appear in the letterhead.

influence
verb: to affect or alter by indirect means

p. 73 The letterhead may **influence** the placement of letters on the page for balance.

specific
adjective: falling into a named category; characteristic of or peculiar to something; accurate; precise

p. 75 There are times when a letter is addressed to a company, but a **specific** person should see the letter.

emphasize
verb: to stress; to give importance to; to give special consideration

p. 76 The writer of a letter may wish to use a subject line as a way of . . . **emphasizing** the key topic of the letter.

detract
verb: to speak ill of; to take away something

p. 89 . . . , a poor quality paper may **detract** so much from the attractiveness of a letter or make erasing so difficult. . . .

dignified
adjective: worthy; distinctive; esteemed; honored

p. 90 Usually the simpler the letterhead the more **dignified** is the appearance.

facilitate
verb: to make easier

p. 91 Some firms use several different colors of paper for carbon copies to **facilitate** the identification of different types of letters in the files.

PART 1 — LETTER PLACEMENT AND STYLES

Sharee Nance recently read an article by The Dartnell Corporation reporting that the average cost of a business letter is $3.19. Sharee read that each letter requires time on the part of the dictator and the secretary. In addition, office costs, such as space, equipment, and lighting, must be added to the cost of the letter. Finally, there is the cost of the paper, envelopes, and other supplies used to produce attractive letters. Sharee's employer is willing to pay the cost of a letter, for he knows that each letter represents the company and is a very important type of communication.

After reading the article Sharee promises herself that she will produce attractive letters — letters that quietly but clearly show that she and her company are efficient.

THE FIRST IMPRESSION

The recipient or addressee of a letter (the person who receives the letter) sees the total letter on the sheet of paper and forms an impression before he begins to read the message. A well-placed letter with clean, even type will make a very good first impression. Such a letter will encourage the recipient to read the letter with the care that your employer would like his letter to receive. A poorly typewritten, carelessly placed letter may fail to get the attention it deserves. It is your responsibility as the secretary to judge each letter you typewrite in a critical fashion and with this question in mind: How will this letter look to the receiver?

A letter gives a good first impression if:

1. Margins, indentations, and spacing are pleasing to the eye.
2. Parts of the letter are correctly placed according to the style selected.
3. There are no obvious erasures and no strikeovers.
4. It is clean — has no smudges or fingermarks.
5. Type is even and clear.

LETTER STYLES

You will be told the letter style that is used in the office where you work. Many companies use a standard style throughout their offices; in other companies, the person dictating the letters will decide the style to be used. The following is a discussion of the letter styles used in business offices today.

Modified Block Style

With the modified block style of letter (Letters A and B on page 67 and the model letter on page 77), the date is typed beginning at the horizontal center of the page. The inside address is blocked at the left margin. The first lines of the paragraphs may be indented (Letter A), or they may be blocked (Letter B). The complimentary close begins at the horizontal center of the page. Businesses use the modified block style more than any other.

Block Style

In the block style (Letter C on page 67) all lines of the letter begin at the left margin. Because the letter can be typed without using tabular stops, it is easy to type. It is a modern style and is gaining in popularity in many offices.

Simplified Style

The simplified style (Letter D on page 67) eliminates the salutation and the complimentary close. All lines begin at the left margin. This style, which is the easiest to type, was introduced and is promoted by the Administrative Management Society. This organization reports that you can save 10.7 percent of the cost of preparing a letter by using this style.

LETTER PUNCTUATION

The most commonly used styles of punctuation are open and mixed. The open style, which is gaining in popularity, leaves out punctuation marks at the ends of the special lines (Letters B and C). In the mixed style of punctuation, a colon is typed after the salutation and a comma after the complimentary close (Letter A).

MARGINS AND SPACING

Placement of a letter on a sheet of letterhead paper is a skill that the good secretary develops with experience. With practice you will be able to balance properly each letter you type and you will not need to retype

Letter A

CONSOLIDATED STEEL COMPANY
PITTSBURGH, PA 15218   412-275-5690

September 29, 197-

Mr. David W. Griffin, Manager
Admiral Steel Products Company
179 Moore Street
Brooklyn, NY 11206

Dear Mr. Griffin:

   Thank you for your order for 12 steel racks of commercial heavy weight, size 12" x 36" x 75". We are pleased to have this order from you.

   A large shipment of these racks is on its way from our factory. It should reach us within a few days. We are, therefore, holding your order until our shipment arrives. Unless we hear from you to the contrary, we shall assume that this action is satisfactory. We shall ship the racks as soon as they arrive.

   The enclosed booklet on steel shelving may be of interest to you. Let us know if we can serve you further.

                              Sincerely yours,

                              James C. Davis
                              James C. Davis, Manager
                              Order Department

ra
Enclosure

Letter A
Modified block style, mixed punctuation, indented paragraphs

Letter B

Office of William R. Biel
ATTORNEY AT LAW
601 TIMES BUILDING   BALTIMORE, MD   21202   301-967-9198

October 23, 197-

Miss Mary Jane Harris
Secretary, Business Club
Thomas Jefferson High School
Baltimore, MD 21212

Dear Mary Jane

I am glad to accept your invitation to meet with the Thomas Jefferson High School Business Club. Thank you very much for giving me a choice of three dates. I would prefer to be with you on March 20 at 2:30 p.m.

I understand from what you told me over the telephone that you would like me to speak on office procedures and practices. I shall be very happy to do so. Within the next week or ten days I shall send you the exact title of my remarks so that you will be able to include that item of information in your program.

May I suggest that I talk for approximately twenty minutes so that about half of the time will be available for the question and answer period that you would like to have.

It will be good to return to the school where I received my own training. I am looking forward with pleasure to your meeting of March 20.

                              Very truly yours

                              William R. Biel
                              William R. Biel

da

Letter B
Modified block style, open punctuation, blocked paragraphs

Letter C

STANDARD METALS PRODUCTS, INC.   SMP
2901 Brunswick Place
Trenton, NJ 08608
609-911-4000

September 5, 197-

AIRMAIL

Stanley Powers Company
8311 Whitehall Avenue
St. Louis, MO 63114

Gentlemen

This letter will confirm our telephone conversation of yesterday afternoon. We shall appreciate your sending us information on surplus raw materials for electronics that you have available for sale.

We are particularly interested right now in cold rolled steel and pretinned nickel silver. We are interested, also, in coils of extra tough hard copper.

Keep us in mind when additional lots of materials for electronics become available. We are suppliers for South American outlets and are in constant need of all types of electronic materials.

Yours very truly

Foster Palmer
Foster Palmer, Manager
Purchasing Department

jm

Letter C
Block style, open punctuation

Letter D

PEMBERTON PRODUCTS, INC.
371 Ashdale Avenue   Minneapolis, MN 55426

May 17, 197-

Mr. William S. Scott, Manager
Four Seasons Cruises, Inc.
178 Fifth Avenue
New York, NY 10010

AMS SIMPLIFIED LETTER

This letter is written in the style recommended by the Administrative Management Society. The formal salutation and complimentary close are omitted. These are not the only changes that have been made, however. Other improvements are given below:

1. The extreme left block format is used.
2. A subject heading is used and should be typed in capitals a triple space below the address.
3. Paragraphs are blocked (no indentations).
4. The writer's name and title are typed in capitals at the left margin at least three blank lines below the body of the letter.
5. The initials of the typist are typed at the left a double space below the writer's name.

Please show this letter to the correspondents in your company. You will find that its use reduces your letter-writing costs.

William C. Kane
WILLIAM C. KANE, PRESIDENT

tm

Letter D
Simplified style

Illus. 3-1   Four business letter styles

Part 1 / Letter Placement and Styles   67

letters because the placement is not balanced. You will develop the skill needed to judge whether a letter is short, average, or long from the amount of space you used in taking your shorthand notes or from the indicator slip if the dictation was recorded on a machine.

Usually the best arrangement is when the side margins are even and the bottom margin is slightly wider than the side margins. In some business offices, however, a standard length for the typewritten line is used for all business letters. The secretary then varies the spacing between the letterhead or top edge of the paper and the date line according to the length of the letter. See the model letter on page 77 if you need to review the parts of a letter.

A letter placement table such as that shown below will help you estimate the spacing for letters. This placement table is for letters typed on 8½″ × 11″ paper and is easy to follow.

Illus. 3-2

LETTER PLACEMENT TABLE

(1) Actual Words in Body of Letter*	(2) Letter Length	(3) Width of Side Margins	(4) Type Date on Line**
Up to 100	Short	2″	20
101–150	Medium {1	1½″	18
151–200	2	1½″	16
201–250	3	1½″	14
251–300	4}	1½″	12
301–350	Long	1″	12
More than 350	Two-Page	1″	12

*Actual Words in Body of Letter represents the complete words — not the average five-stroke words used to measure typing speed.
**Count lines from top edge of paper.

To judge letter placement from shorthand notes:

1. Estimate the number of words in the letter.
    (a) Estimate the number of shorthand outlines you write on each line: for example, six outlines on each line of your notebook.
    (b) Count the number of lines of shorthand notes for the letter: for example, 31 lines in your notebook.
    (c) Multiply the number of lines of shorthand notes by the number of outlines on each line: for example, 31 × 6 = 186.

2. Determine the width of the side margins from the Letter Placement Table: for example, 186 words (Column 1 of the Letter Placement Table) means the letter is of medium length (Column 2) and the side margins (Column 3) should be 1½" wide.
3. Determine the date line from the Letter Placement Table: for example, the date for a letter with 186 words should be typed on Line 16 (Column 4).

As you become experienced and gain confidence, you will be able to estimate the correct placement for letters without counting shorthand outlines or the number of lines used in your notebook.

SIMPLIFYING THE TYPEWRITING OF LETTERS

Many office managers attempt to reduce the cost of letters in one or more of these ways:

1. Using open punctuation. Eliminating marks of punctuation after the salutation and complimentary close is clearly a timesaving feature of open punctuation.
2. Omitting names that appear in the letterhead. For example, there is no need to typewrite the name of the company below the complimentary close if it appears in the letterhead. Also, the typewritten name and title of the dictator need not appear in the closing lines if they are in the letterhead.
3. Typewriting letters in block or simplified style. These letters can be typed faster than other letter styles because every line is started at the left margin and the tabular key is not used. In addition, in the simplified letter the salutation and complimentary close are omitted.
4. Using a standard line length for all letters. When the length of letters varies, a secretary can save time by establishing a standard line length and varying the distance between the letterhead and the date and between the complimentary close and the reference initials. Some offices use a six-inch line for all letters, and the skillful secretary can make each letter attractive with this standardization.

INTEROFFICE MEMORANDUMS

In the office in which you will be employed, you may type many short business notes or reports on forms called interoffice memorandums.

Part 1 / Letter Placement and Styles

These memorandums remain within the organization itself. They are brief and to the point because their only purpose is to communicate with other members of the organization quickly and clearly. The chief advantage of these forms is that they can be typed quickly. Titles (*Mr., Mrs., Dr.,* etc.), the salutation, the complimentary close, and the formal signature are usually omitted.

The forms, with the heading *Interoffice Memorandum,* may be printed on half sheets or whole sheets of paper, which generally is a less expensive paper than the company letterhead. The printed words *To, From, Date,* and *Subject,* with enough writing space after each of them, may be included in the heading of the form. Usually the company name also appears on the interoffice memorandum.

APEX CORPORATION   **INTEROFFICE MEMORANDUM**

To: Gary Keyton   **Date:** October 21, 197–

From: Stan Pruitt   **Subject:** Interoffice Memos

Start the interoffice memo a double space below the typewritten heading material and block it at the left margin.

Since the writer's name is in the heading there is no need to type it at the end of the message. The typist's initials are placed a double space below the message. All end-of-letter notations such as the typist's initials and carbon copy information are typed as they are in letters.

cm

cc Jim Hereford

Illus. 3-3

You should double-space after the last line of the heading and the first line of the message. Short messages of not more than five lines may be typed double space; longer messages should be typed single space. Reference initials should be typed at the left margin a double space below the last line of the message. When enclosures are sent with a memorandum, the enclosure notation should be typed a double space below the reference initials.

An interoffice memorandum is often sent to a number of people within the organization. In such cases carbon copies may be used. The names of all who are to receive copies, however, should be listed on the original and on all carbon copies. Another practice is to type the original and one carbon file copy with the names of the recipients. The original, with any special enclosures, is sent to the first person on the list. When he is finished with it, he draws a line through his name and sends the memorandum along to the next person on the list. This is repeated until all the interested persons have seen it. This practice is most satisfactory when there is an enclosure or an attachment with the interoffice memorandum that is either too long or too difficult to reproduce.

QUESTIONS

1. To determine the costs of letters in an office, what expenses must you include?
2. What will the recipient notice first when he receives a letter?
3. How does the modified block style differ from the block style?
4. Why is the block style letter easy to type?
5. What are the features of the simplified style of letter?
6. How does mixed punctuation differ from open punctuation?
7. Why is a standard line length considered a timesaving technique?
8. How do you determine letter placement from shorthand notes?
9. How would you determine the placement of a letter that has 155 words?
10. What is the major advantage of writing a short business note or report in the form of an interoffice memorandum?

JUDGMENT

1. In what ways can an efficient secretary assist in keeping the costs of letters at a minimum?
2. Why do you think the secretary should try to have each letter correctly placed the first time it is typed?
3. How will you know which letter style to use on your first job?

PERSONAL QUALITIES

Sally Mason has just been hired as secretary to Mr. Jennings and Mr. Felty. She has been typing Mr. Jennings' letters in block style with open punctuation and Mr. Felty's letters in the modified block style with mixed punctuation because the previous secretary told Sally this is the way they seemed to prefer the letters. Sally believes the blocked style with open punctuation is best but is not sure she should mention this to Mr. Felty.

What should Sally do?

Part 1 / Letter Placement and Styles

LANGUAGE USAGE

An adverb is a word that modifies a verb, an adjective, or another adverb. An adverb answers the questions *how? when? where? how much? how little? to what degree? in what manner?*
Examples: She speaks French *fluently*. (Modifies verb *speaks*)
         A *very* high wall surrounded the house. (Modifies adjective *high*)
         You drive *too* recklessly. (*Too* modifies adverb *recklessly*. *Recklessly* modifies verb *drive*.)

List the adverbs in the following sentences. In a second column list the words they modify.

1. We found the dollar bill here.
2. The letter was almost completed.
3. Joan types letters more neatly than Betty.
4. Yesterday the company team played the league champions.
5. The longest line in the letter was four inches wide.
6. Her employer did not go home.
7. All the letters are very long.
8. The lawyer looked carefully at the evidence.
9. The secretary had too much to do.
10. Quietly and efficiently she worked on the letters until she completed them.

SECRETARIAL WORK

1. Assume that you are a secretary who writes approximately five characters to a shorthand line. You have taken three letters from your employer. Their lengths are indicated below. For each letter decide the side margins you would use, and on what line you would type the date.

    (a) Letter No. 1 is 15 shorthand lines in length.
    (b) Letter No. 2 is 20 shorthand lines in length.
    (c) Letter No. 3 is 40 shorthand lines in length.

2. *Letter in Modified Block Form* — Compose a brief letter in which you describe the modified block form. Type the letter, addressing it to your teacher, in modified block form. Use mixed punctuation and blocked paragraphs.

3. *Letter in Block Form* — Compose a brief letter in which you describe the block form. Type the letter, addressing it to your teacher, in block form. Use open punctuation.

4. *Letter in Simplified Form* — Compose a brief letter in which you describe the simplified form. Type the letter, addressing it to your teacher, in simplified form.

PART 2 PARTS OF THE LETTER

After Kay Niemeyer started her new secretarial position, she read in the office manual that the proper styling of each letter requires careful attention to many details. How well Kay takes care of these details will help determine the kind of impression her letters will make when they are read by the persons who receive the letters. Kay decided to study parts of letters so that she would be able to type them almost without thinking about them. She would then be able to concentrate on the content of the letter and become a more valuable secretary to her employer.

THE LETTERHEAD

The letterhead (Item 1, page 77) is important because it gives the first impression that a company wishes to make on the recipient of the letter. For example, notice the industrial, "big business" impression of the Consolidated Steel Company letterhead, which is Letter A on page 67, in comparison with the individual, personal impression of Letter B, the lawyer's letterhead, on the same page.

The letterhead may influence the placement of letters on the page for balance. A letterhead should be easy to read, attractive, and representative of the company that sends it.

DATE

The date on a letter (Item 2, page 77) is very important because it tells the sender and the recipient when the letter was typed. It helps the sender and the addressee identify a particular letter if several letters have been written by the sender to the same person. You must date every letter you typewrite. The date line contains the name of the month written in full, the date, and the year. Abbreviated forms of the date, such as 11/13/7- or 11-13-7-, never should be used in letters.

In the modified block style letter the date is typed at the horizontal center of the page (Letter A, page 67), and for the block style the date is typed starting at the left margin (Letter C, page 67).

INSIDE ADDRESS

The inside address (Item 3, page 77) is typed three blank lines below the date at the left margin. The inside address is a complete reference for filing the carbon copy in the sender's office. It also gives complete information as to whom the letter is directed at the recipient company, since often the envelope with the address on it is thrown away when the letter is opened. The inside address should contain the name, title (when appropriate), and the complete address of the person or the company to whom the letter is to be sent.

Abbreviations should be used sparingly because they give a somewhat careless appearance to the letter and because they can increase the difficulty of reading.

Name and Company Lines

The name of the person and the company should be typed to conform exactly with the style used by the person and the company receiving the letter. For example, if you were typing a letter to a man who writes his name *Edward R. Voiers* you would not type his name *E. R. Voiers*.

Official Titles

When a person's official title is included in the address, it may be placed on either the first or second line. If the title is placed on the first line, it is separated from the person's name by a comma. Since either placement is correct, you should choose the one that will give better balance to the length of the lines in the address.

Street Address Line

When the name of the street is a number from one to ten inclusive, the street name is spelled out (367 Second Avenue or 381 Tenth Street); figures are used for street names that are numbers above ten. When a street is identified by figures, the house number is separated from the street number by a hyphen with a space on either side, 157 – 179th Street. If the street number is preceded by *East*, *West*, *North*, or *South*, however, the hyphen is not necessary; for example, 589 South 117th Street.

City, State, and ZIP Code Line

The name of the city is separated from the name of the state by a comma.

The United States Postal Service has designated two-letter abbreviations for states to be used with the ZIP (Zone Improvement Plan) Code. A list of two-letter state abbreviations can be found on page 632 in Appendix D. These approved abbreviations are written in all capital letters and without periods. Use of the ZIP Code reduces mailing costs and speeds mail deliveries by using automated equipment.

The Zip Code number should be typed on the same line as the city and state with one or two spaces after the state and with no mark of punctuation between the state and ZIP Code number.

Forms for addresses are:

```
Mr. William F. Wells, Vice-President
The American Copying Company
3546 Broad Street
Philadelphia, PA 19140

Mr. James A. Satterfield
President, Consultants Limited
465 Avenue of the Americas
New York, NY 10011
```

ATTENTION LINE

There are times when a letter is addressed to a company, but a specific person in the company should see the letter. In such a case, an attention line is typed a double space below the inside address. Even though companies use attention lines, there is actually very little reason for them. If a letter is to be directed to an individual, his name should be placed at the beginning of the inside address. When there is an attention line the salutation agrees with the company name on the first line of the inside address rather than with the attention line.

```
Almond Construction Company
321 Forbes Boulevard
Pittsburgh, PA 15222

Attention Mr. Whitney T. Drews

Gentlemen:
```

SALUTATION

The salutation (Item 4, page 77) is a greeting to the addressee, the person to whom the letter is written. It is typed a double space below the address or attention line. The body of the letter begins a double space below the salutation. A salutation may be as informal as *Dear Joe* or as formal as *Sir*.

The salutations shown at the top of page 76 are arranged from the least formal to the most formal. Notice the capitalization used in each.

For Men	*For Women*
Dear John	Dear Jane
My dear John	My dear Jane
Dear Mr. Simon	Dear Mrs. (Miss) Whitman
My dear Mr. Simon	My dear Mrs. (Miss) Whitman
Dear Sir	Dear Madam
Sir	Madam

For a Corporation   *For a Firm of Women*
Gentlemen   Ladies

For a Firm of Men   *For a Firm of Men and Women*
Gentlemen   Gentlemen
                             Ladies and Gentlemen
                             My dear Mrs. Smith and Mr. Jones

SUBJECT LINE

The writer of a letter may wish to use a subject line (Item 5, page 77) as a way of headlining or emphasizing the key topic of the letter. When a subject line is used, type it a double space below the salutation with a double space below the subject line. The topic may be preceded by the word *Subject*, although there is a trend away from this. The subject line may be typed even with the left margin or centered on the page.

BODY

A double space follows the salutation before you begin the body of the letter (Item 6, page 77). Single spacing is always used for the body of the letter except for very short messages. Be sure to paragraph the body of the letter so that it will be easy to read. Use double spacing between paragraphs to give the letter a more attractive appearance.

Keep the right margin as even as possible and about as wide as the left margin. You can do this by setting the right margin stop from five to eight spaces beyond the point where you want the line to end, so that the bell will ring just before the space where the line ends. You will still have space to complete a short word or add a hyphen for a word that must be hyphenated before the carriage stops moving.

THE SECOND PAGE

On letters of more than one page, each page except the first is numbered. The heading for the second and following pages should include (1) the name of the addressee as it appears on page one, (2) the page number, and (3) the date. Two styles of headings are the block form and the spread form; however, the block form is easier to type, since there is no need for centering or backspacing.

1. Printed Letterhead	1	**ANDIKE MACHINE CO.** 2811 Paxton Avenue Austin, TX 78212 512-281-1816	
2. Date		2 May 19, 197-	3 blank lines
3. Inside Address	3	Mr. James A. Gordon 3421 - 58th Street Austin, TX 78212	1 blank line
4. Salutation	4	Dear Mr. Gordon	1 blank line
5. Subject		5 The Business Letter	1 blank line

6. Body	6	Thank you for your letter of May 14 in which you asked for the guidelines that we follow in preparing business correspondence. In our firm we strive to write attractive and convincing business letters with a minimum of expense.
		
		We use a letter that is generally accepted in business and requires little time and effort to prepare. Here are some guides to aid you in making your letters more effective.
		
		  1. Use open punctuation.
		
		  2. Use modified block style. (You may prefer extreme block style. This means that the date, complimentary close, signature, and title of the dictator will start at the left margin.)
		
		  3. When in doubt about the parts of a business letter, use this letter as a reference.
		
		We hope that this information will assist you in making your correspondence more effective. Please let us know if we can help you further.
			1 blank line

7. Complimentary Close	7	Sincerely	
8. Signature	8	*Kenneth H. Rhodes*	3 blank lines
9. Typed Name 10. Title	9 10	Kenneth H. Rhodes Office Manager	1 blank line
11. Reference Initials	11	ht	1 blank line
12. Enclosure Notation	12	Enclosure	1 blank line
13. Carbon Copy Notation	13	cc Mr. Wayne B. Monroe	1 blank line
14. Postscript	14	You will discover that the ability to write effective letters is a valuable business asset.	

Model letter, modified block style,
open punctuation, blocked paragraphs

Illus. 3-4

One of the following forms may be used at the top of the second and succeeding pages:

Block Form

```
Mr. Arthur C. Marcuso
Page 2
June 16, 197-
```

Spread Form

Mr. Arthur C. Marcuso   2   June 16, 197-

The space between the top of the second sheet and the heading should be about an inch (6 line spaces). Two blank lines should be left between the second-page heading and the body of the letter. Type at least two lines of the paragraph at the bottom of the first page, and carry over at least two lines of a paragraph to the top of the second page.

For the second page use plain bond paper of the same quality as the first-page letterhead.

COMPLIMENTARY CLOSE

The complimentary close (Item 7, page 77), which is written on the second line below the body of the letter, is the *good-bye* of the letter. The complimentary close and the date start at the same horizontal point on the page. In the block style (See Letter C, page 67), the date and complimentary close begin at the left margin. In the modified block style (See Letter A, page 67), they begin at the horizontal center of the page. Only the first word of the complimentary close is capitalized.

Complimentary Closings

Business Letters

Yours truly	Yours sincerely
Yours very truly	Sincerely yours
Very truly yours	Very sincerely yours
	Yours very sincerely

Formal Letters

Respectfully yours   Yours respectfully

Friendly Letters

| Cordially yours | Yours sincerely |
| Yours cordially | Sincerely yours |

SIGNATURE, TYPED NAME, AND TITLE

Your employer signs his name (Item 8, page 77) between the complimentary close and his typed name (Item 9, page 77). The typed name overcomes problems caused by a poorly written signature. The dictator's name is typed four lines below the complimentary close.

    Yours truly

    M. O. Thomas

    M. O. Thomas, Vice-President

Sometimes the name of the company is typed as part of the signature. In that case the company's name is typed in all capital letters on the second line below the complimentary close. The name of the dictator is typed four lines below the company name. When both the name of the dictator and his official title (Item 10, page 77) are used, the title may be typed on the same line as his name or on the line below the typed name.

    Very truly yours

    UNION TRUCKING AND STORAGE CO.

    Frederick W. Pendleton

    Frederick W. Pendleton
    Purchasing Agent

When you type your employer's name, you should not use his personal title before the name, such as *Mr.* or *Dr.* For a woman, however, type her legal name (this means her own first name, middle initial, and married last name) and place *Miss* or *Mrs.* before it. The title *Miss* or *Mrs.* may be typed either with or without parentheses.

Signature of an Unmarried Woman	Signature of a Married Woman or Widow
Yours sincerely,	Very truly yours
Eva M. Kelly	*Alice B. Canter*
Miss Eva M. Kelly	Mrs. Alice B. Canter
or	or
(Miss) Eva M. Kelly	(Mrs) Alice B. Canter

If a woman wants to be known by her married name by using her husband's first name and middle initial (for example, Mrs. Dwight D. Eisenhower), she can sign her legal name and place her married name below in parentheses.

Part 2 / Parts of the Letter

Signature of a Married Woman

Very truly yours

Elaine E. Brooks
(Mrs. John Brooks)

Mrs. Elaine E. Brooks

Your employer may not be available to sign a letter that must be mailed and he may ask you to sign his name and mail the letter. If you are requested to do this, be sure to initial the signature.

Very truly yours,

Robert E. Maxwell

Robert E. Maxwell   *R. H.*

You may write a letter over your own signature for your employer in such cases as making a reservation or an appointment, canceling a reservation or an appointment, and sending your employer's regrets at his inability to attend a function.

Very truly yours

Sharon Bryant

Secretary to Lawrence R. Nelson

You must be sure that each letter is signed, either by your employer or yourself, before you fold it and insert it in an envelope for mailing.

REFERENCE INITIALS

To indicate who typed the letter, place your initials (Item 11, page 77) in lower case letters a double space below the typed name even with the left margin. Sometimes you will see the initials of the dictator before the secretary's initials; but this is unnecessary work, since everyone knows who dictated the letter from the typed name below the signature.

ENCLOSURE NOTATIONS

An enclosure is anything placed in the envelope with the letter. Any enclosure you send should be noted at the end of the letter. This is a reminder to you to be sure to include the enclosure. It is also a service to the addressee who can quickly check to see if the material is included in the envelope. The enclosure notation (Item 12, page 77) should be typed at the left margin two lines below the reference initials. One enclosure is indicated by the word *Enclosure*. More than one enclosure is indicated by the correct figure typed after the word *Enclosures*. More than one enclosure may also be indicated by the word *Enclosures* typed on one line, followed by a list of the enclosures, each enclosure being listed on a separate line and indented five spaces from the left margin. Typical enclosure notations are:

```
Enclosure        Enclosures 2        Enclosures
                                       Price List
                                       Circular
                                       Sample X-14
```

SEPARATE COVER NOTATIONS

When the letter refers to items sent under separate cover — that is, in another envelope or package and not included with the letter — you should type the proper notation at the left margin two lines below the last enclosure line, or two lines below the reference initial line if there are no enclosures. One item sent under separate cover is indicated by the words *Separate Cover*. Two or more separate cover items are usually indicated by the correct figure typed after the words *Separate Cover*. In some offices the means of transportation used for sending the separate cover material is indicated. If it is desired, the nature of the item or items may be indicated in the same manner as enclosure items. Typical separate cover notations are:

```
            Separate Cover 2
            Separate Cover—Express
            Separate Cover—Mail
                Price List C12
```

MAILING NOTATION

When a special postal service, such as registered mail or special delivery, is to be used, a mailing notation to that effect may be typed in all capital letters even with the left margin either (a) two lines below the last line of typing or (b) between the date line and the first line of the inside address with a blank line above and below. (See Letter C, page 67.) Some firms type mailing notations only on carbon copies. Some firms make no notation at all.

CARBON COPY NOTATIONS

When you prepare a carbon copy for the information of a person other than the addressee of the letter, the notation *cc* (Item 13, page 77),

Illus. 3-5
Addressed envelopes for business letters

followed by the name of that person, is typed at the left margin two lines below the last line of typing. If it is not desirable for the addressee to know that a carbon copy has been sent to someone else, the reference notation *bc* (blind copy) or *bcc* (blind carbon copy) should be typed with the name of the recipient on all carbon copies, but not on the original letter. Blind copy notations are typed in the usual position for noting carbon copy distribution. To save time the notation may be typed before the letter is removed from the machine by placing a card or piece of paper over the notation position on the original copy.

Unit 3 / The MAILABLE Letter

POSTSCRIPT

Sometimes your employer will dictate a postscript to a letter. A postscript (Item 14, page 77) is a short message that is typed on the second line below all other notations. It may be preceded by the abbreviation *PS*, but the modern trend is to type it in the same form as any paragraph in the letter.

The postscript is sometimes used to take care of a detail omitted from the letter by mistake. It is often used, however, to emphasize a special point by setting it apart from the rest of the letter.

ADDRESSING THE ENVELOPE

If the letter is to be handled efficiently by the postal clerks, it is very important that the address on the envelope be accurate and easily read. Type the address single spaced on the envelope exactly the same as the inside address of the letter.

An attention line should be typed immediately below the name of the company in the address. Special notations, such as HOLD FOR ARRIVAL and PLEASE FORWARD, are typed in all capital letters a triple space below the return address. Mailing notations, such as SPECIAL DELIVERY and REGISTERED MAIL, are typed in capital letters below the stamp. Airmail envelopes should be used for airmail letters; or, if not available, the word AIRMAIL is typed in capital letters below the stamp. Note illustrations of typed envelopes on page 82.

Illus. 3-6

Special notations should be accurate and easily read to insure efficient postal service.

Ohio National Life Insurance Company

QUESTIONS

1. Why is the date on a letter important?
2. Where are two possible places on a horizontal line for typewriting the date?
3. Why is the address of the recipient typed in a letter?
4. Where are two places the title of the recipient may be typed in the address?
5. What does ZIP mean, and why is it used?
6. What salutation is generally used for a corporation?
7. What is the purpose of a subject line?
8. Where does the subject line appear in a letter?
9. Where does the body of a letter begin?
10. Why is the block heading easier to type than the spread heading on the second page of a letter?
11. Where are two places on a horizontal line for typing the complimentary close?
12. What are reference initials? Where are they typed?
13. Why should there be a notation for enclosures?
14. When is a postscript used?
15. How does a typist indicate that a letter is to be held for arrival of the recipient?

JUDGMENT

1. With the exception of state names, why are abbreviations avoided in letters and on envelopes?
2. Why do you believe a secretary should initial a signature which she wrote for her employer?
3. Why should a woman use *Miss* or *Mrs.* in her signature, yet a man should never precede his signature with *Mr.*?

PERSONAL QUALITIES

Sally Quinn is a stenographer in a stenographic pool. She spends most of the day transcribing letters. Although there is a supervisor in the pool, there is very little supervision of the workers. Sally finds that she must retype practically every letter because when she finishes one, she finds that it is not placed properly on the page. She knows that she should not have to do this, and she feels very uncomfortable about how well she is doing her job. She realizes that she could do twice as much as she presently does. However, no one else seems to be paying any attention to her, and she has not been told that her production is low.

If you were Sally, what would you do at this point?

LANGUAGE USAGE

A preposition is a connecting word which shows the relation of a noun or pronoun to some other word in the sentence.
Example: Be confident *of* success when you become a secretary.

Type each sentence below, choosing the preposition which you believe is correct.

1. The executive went (in, into) the mail room to see if a letter he needed had been received.
2. The secretary must choose (between, among) two positions for the subject line of a letter.
3. A good secretary does not become angry (with, at) her employer.
4. The address on the envelope should be (like, as) the inside address in the letter.
5. The secretary should be careful (and, to) type the special lines of a letter correctly.
6. (Inside, Inside of) the room the temperature was 80.
7. Keep (off, off of) the grass.
8. This book is different (from, than) that which you have.
9. (Between, Among) salutations for business letters some are more formal than others.
10. Her new office desk was identical (with, to) the one she had chosen from the catalog.

SECRETARIAL WORK

1. The following exercises may be completed on one sheet of paper in the following manner: top half of front page, Exercise (a); bottom half of front page, Exercise (b); top half of back page, Exercise (c); bottom of back page, Exercise (d).
   (a) Your employer dictates a letter to the McConnell Engineering Company, 296 Walnut Street, Denver, Colorado 80204. The letter is to be delivered to Mr. Thomas Hamilton of that firm. Type the date, inside address, and salutation.
   (b) Type the appropriate salutation for a business letter to each of the following:
   (1) Mr. J. Sommers
   (2) Miss Nancy Hall
   (3) Patricia Trent and Jane Taylor
   (4) John Myers and Mary Standley
   (c) Type an appropriate heading for the second page of a letter written to Mr. F. M. Randall on May 16, 197–.
   (d) C. W. Graham, president of the Graham Advertising Agency, has dictated a letter to be sent to a long-time client. Type a suitable complimentary close, typewritten company name, dictator's name and official title, and your reference initials. There will be two enclosures.
2. In the following problems prepare one carbon copy and type the address on an envelope if the necessary supplies are available. If envelopes are typed, attach them to the letters in the same manner described on page 50.

(a) *Letter in Block Style* — Type the letter in the illustration on page 77 in block style with open punctuation.

(b) *Two-Page Letter* — Type the following letter in modified block style with blocked paragraphs and open punctuation. The sign ¶ means *paragraph*.

June 29, 197–, Mr. Earl F. Sawyer, Manager, Harold Dean Manufacturing Company, 928 Harrison Building, 1258 Columbus Drive, Los Angeles, California 90012.

Dear Mr. Sawyer Irritated customers . . . lost orders . . . tied-up lines . . . delays and misunderstandings . . . garbled messages . . . excessive phone bills . . . wasted sales effort. These are some of the costly results of the poor telephone practices so common today in business. (¶) But they don't have to be common in *your* business. You can make sure *all* your calls — incoming and outgoing — are handled courteously, efficiently, and economically by using our unique training program, BETTER BUSINESS BY TELEPHONE. (¶) And right now, as a new subscriber, you will receive a free bonus portfolio of past issues describing correct telephone techniques such as

— The 15 rules of telephone courtesy that *everyone* should follow.
— Why no secretary should *ever* use the blunt question "Who's calling?"
— How to build sales and goodwill when taking telephone orders.
— What to say — and what *not* to say — in handling complaint calls.
— Why so many executives now make and take their own telephone calls.
— The six ways to save time — and money — on all telephone calls.
— Why *new employees* need telephone training — and how to give it.
— How to handle the caller who doesn't want to give his name.
— *Why* and *how* to use the telephone to collect past due accounts.
— How to turn more of your telephone *inquiries* into actual *sales*.

(¶) BETTER BUSINESS BY TELEPHONE has already helped more than 16,000 companies, of every size and type, make more effective use of their telephones. Included are one-man-and-a-girl offices — and such companies as Du Pont, American Airlines, Ford, Sears Roebuck, General Electric, Arthur Murray Studios, *The Wall Street Journal*, etc. (¶) BETTER BUSINESS BY

TELEPHONE will help you with every phase of your telephone operation, from handling routine calls to planning a complete telephone sales campaign. (¶) Regular twice monthly bulletins bring you the latest in tested telephone techniques . . . case histories showing how other progressive companies are solving telephone problems and making the most of telephone opportunities . . . hints on time- and money-saving procedures . . . ideas that spark your own thinking on how you can make your company's telephone contacts a sales and public relations *asset* rather than a liability. (¶) Along with the bulletins for management, you get regular twice monthly *Fone-Talks* for employees . . . all *Special Reports* and *Supplements* as issued . . . easy access to all past issues that may help you . . . and unlimited use of our *free mail consultation service* on your individual telephone problems. And your subscription starts with a "Telephone Improvement Kit" which shows you exactly how to make the best possible use of our material. (¶) As a BETTER BUSINESS BY TELEPHONE subscriber, you'll have everything you need to make your company's handling of the telephone as good as that of any company in the country . . . and to *keep* it that way. And you'll quickly see why we receive such comments as this from Harvard C. Wood, President, H. C. Wood, Inc., Lansdowne, Pa.: (¶) "I have a warm feeling toward your organization because I feel you are rendering a splendid service to those businessmen who want to use the telephone effectively and efficiently." (¶) You'll find full information on rates on the enclosed order form. Just tell us how many copies of each bulletin you will need to cover your department heads and key employees. We'll do the rest. Sincerely yours, Arthur Downing, Manager, Customer Service.

PART 3 STATIONERY

Ruth Franks has been working for the Pruett Steel Company for only a very short time and notices that many different kinds of stationery are used. In her school business courses students used only one kind of stationery. Mrs. Donna Schaeffer, the administrative assistant, explains to Ruth that the paper used for typing letters is important because the quality of the paper and the design of the letterhead will impress the recipient when he opens the letter. The quality of the paper and the style of the letterhead should be correct both for the kind of business and for the position held in the business by your employer. For example, the letterhead of a department store will be different from the letterhead of a steel manufacturing company. Correspondence sent from the president's office is on better quality paper than that used in the purchasing department.

USING OFFICE STATIONERY

Different types of office stationery can affect the quality of the typing on the paper.

1. *Finish:* A smooth finish will help give clear-cut typed copy, while a rough finish may make the type difficult to read.
2. *Quality:* High quality papers are easier to correct and have less tendency to leave erasure marks than is the case with low quality papers.
3. *Weight:* Very lightweight or thin paper will wrinkle and tear easily, while very heavy paper may be difficult to fold.
4. *Color:* While white is a satisfactory and appropriate color and is always in good taste, the use of a color appropriate to the nature of the business can sometimes be used very effectively. It is usually more difficult to erase on colored paper than it is to erase on white paper.

Type of Paper Commonly Used

Bond paper, which was originally used for printing bonds, is most frequently used for business letters because it takes a typed impression clearly. It is firm and strong so that erasing is relatively easy. It is quite attractive in appearance, and it is more permanent than many types of paper. Bond paper may be purchased in various qualities ranging from inexpensive sulphite bond (wood content) to bond of 100 percent rag content. The best qualities are usually watermarked with a design or name.

Paper comes in a number of weights such as 9, 13, 16, 20, and 24 pounds. The paper most widely used is the 20-pound weight. The weight of bond paper is based on the weight of a ream (500 sheets) measuring 17″ × 22″—four times the size of a standard letterhead. When the paper is cut into four equal parts, a ream of 20-pound paper in 8½″ × 11″ letterheads weighs five pounds.

It is generally considered false economy to use a poor quality letterhead paper. The difference in cost between poor quality paper and good quality paper is very slight.

Furthermore, a poor quality paper may detract so much from the attractiveness of a letter or may make erasing so difficult that it defeats the purpose of a letter that is otherwise in excellent form.

The second and succeeding pages of a letter are typed on paper without a letterhead but of the same quality and size as that on which the letterhead is printed.

Size of Paper

Letter paper may be obtained in a variety of sizes, but the following are most commonly used:

8½″ × 11″	Business or Regular
8″ × 10½″	Government
7¼″ × 10½″	Executive or Monarch
5½″ × 8½″	Baronial

The business or regular size, 8½″ × 11″, is the most widely used size for ordinary business correspondence. Legal size paper, which is 8½″ × 13″, is used for summaries, reports, briefs, and other legal papers but not for ordinary business correspondence. The executive or monarch size is used almost exclusively by executives and professional men who have their individual stationery for business or personal use.

The baronial size may be used for very short business letters; however, since there is a tendency to misplace or misfile it, its use is limited in most business firms.

The Letterhead

Quite commonly the printed letterhead includes the name of the firm, the mailing address, the telephone number, and, if it is not indicated in the name of the firm, the nature of the business. The branch or department, the name and the title of the official using the stationery, the address of the chief office of the company, the location of branch offices, and the cable address are sometimes included. There is a trend, however, to eliminate such information as the slogan, the trademark, names of the officers, and lists of products. Usually the simpler the letterhead the more dignified is the appearance.

The return address on the envelope should harmonize with the letterhead. It is placed in the upper left corner of the envelope.

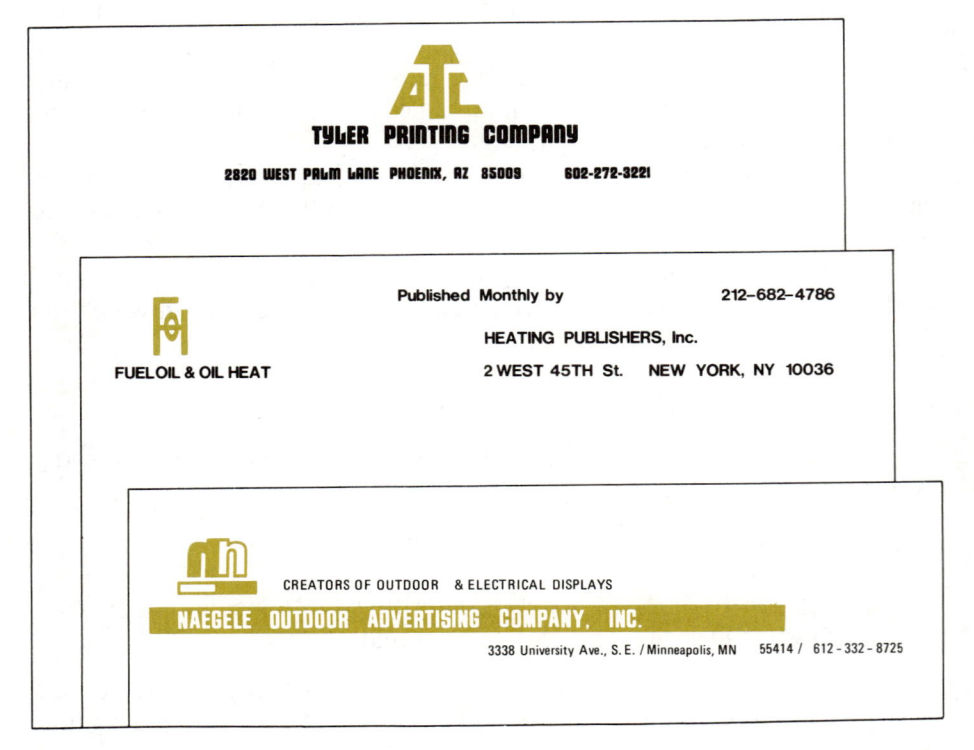

Illus. 3-7
Typical letterheads

Paper for Carbon Copies

Paper for carbon copies, usually known as onionskin, manifold, or second sheets, is ordinarily much thinner than letterhead paper. The thin paper is best because you can type several carbon copies. A suitable paper for carbon copies is one that is thin but strong with a firm surface so that the carbon impression will be clear.

Some firms use several different colors of paper for carbon copies to facilitate the identification of different types of letters in the files. For example, the carbon copies for ordinary correspondence may be on yellow paper, those for acknowledgment of orders may be on white paper, and those for collection letters may be on blue paper. Also, different colors of carbon copies are made when it is customary to prepare two or more copies for separate filing. For example, if a branch office makes two carbon copies — one for its own files and one for the home office files — the distribution of the copies may be easier if different colors are used.

For a two-page letter, both sides of the copy sheet may be used. This method reduces the amount of paper and avoids crowding files. When this is done the first page of the carbon copy is reversed and turned upside down so that the second page heading is directly behind the last lines of the first page. Although a letter written on two sides of a thin sheet is not quite so readable as it would be if separate sheets were used, it is usually readable enough for a file copy. A carbon copy of the reply is sometimes typed directly on the back of a letter to keep related correspondence together and to save filing space.

ENVELOPES

There are many sizes of business envelopes in general use. Two sizes are used more than any others:

Small, also called No. 6¾, or commercial (6½″ × 3⅝″)
Large, also called No. 10, or legal (9½″ × 4⅛″)

The large envelope is used for one- and two-page letters and for letters with enclosures. The small envelope is always used with half-size letterheads and sometimes with one-page letters. Other sizes of envelopes may be used for special purposes, but a firm tries to avoid having a large supply of odd-size envelopes.

Envelopes should match the letterhead sheet in weight, finish, and color. If the envelopes and the letterheads are purchased at the same time and from the same company differences in paper stock are avoided.

In addition to standard envelopes, there are two other types designed for special purposes: window and business reply envelopes.

Window Envelope

Window envelopes are used in business so that you don't have to address envelopes. The address on the letter, statement, or invoice shows through the window. Their use not only saves time but prevents letters being put into wrong envelopes.

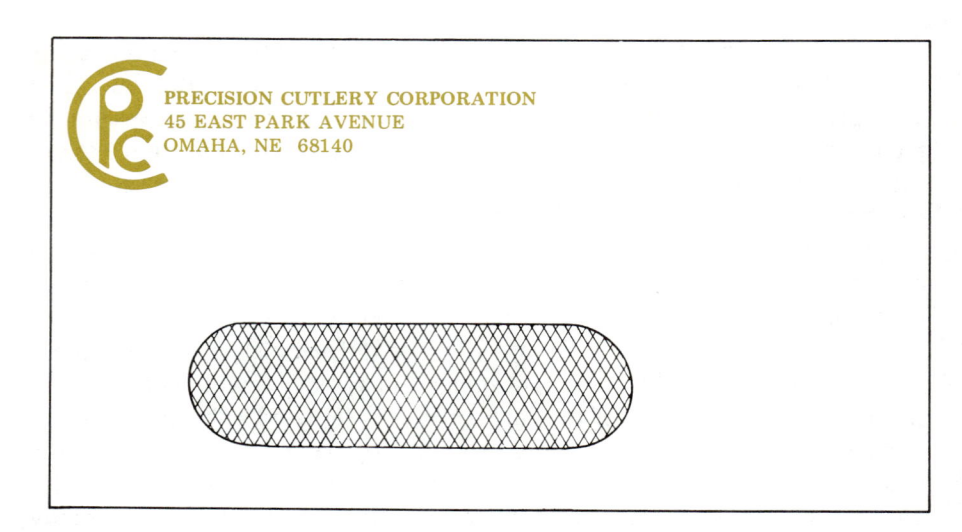

Illus. 3-8
Window envelope

PRECISION CUTLERY CORPORATION
45 EAST PARK AVENUE
OMAHA, NE 68140

The address must be written so that it can be seen through the window after the letter or bill is folded. Some businesses have a mark printed on their stationery to show the location for the address. The first few letters should be checked to see whether they are correctly folded to show through the window. The method of folding the letter or bill for the window envelope is different from the method of folding used for an ordinary envelope. Methods of folding letters are described in Unit 7, Part 2, under "Outgoing Mail."

Business Reply Envelope and Card

Your company can get a business reply permit from the post office. This lets you enclose a special business reply envelope or card that the addressee may return without paying postage. The post office collects postage from your company when it receives the returned envelopes and cards.

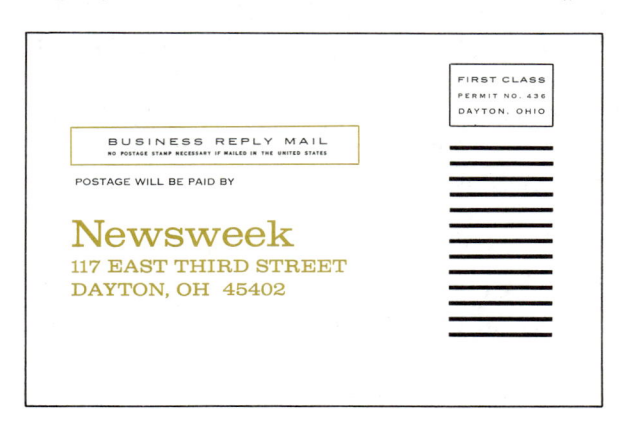

Illus. 3-9
Business reply card

FIRST CLASS
PERMIT NO. 436
DAYTON, OHIO

BUSINESS REPLY MAIL
NO POSTAGE STAMP NECESSARY IF MAILED IN THE UNITED STATES

POSTAGE WILL BE PAID BY

Newsweek
117 EAST THIRD STREET
DAYTON, OH 45402

Unit 3 / The Mailable Letter

Such envelopes and cards are frequently used when a firm is sending out correspondence to which replies are invited such as sales literature inviting inquiries from prospective customers. The amount collected for a business reply envelope or card is two cents more than the ordinary postage. A business reply envelope that is enclosed in a No. 6¾ envelope should be of slightly smaller size, such as No. 6¼. Likewise, a No. 9 business reply envelope should be used for an enclosure in a No. 10 envelope.

QUESTIONS

1. What should you consider when office stationery is to be selected?
2. Why should you use a high quality paper for letters?
3. When should a company choose colored paper for its correspondence?
4. What is the regular size of paper for letters?
5. What kind of information is generally a part of a letterhead?
6. Why is a thin paper generally chosen for carbon copies?
7. For what reason would a firm use several different colors of paper for carbon copies?
8. What are the two most common sizes of business envelopes?
9. Why are window envelopes sometimes used?
10. When is the postage for business reply cards and envelopes collected?

JUDGMENT

1. Why do you think the president of a company might have a special type stationery?
2. Why should the second page of a long letter be typed on paper of the same quality as the letterhead?
3. Why are both sides of the carbon copy sheet used on a two-page letter?

PERSONAL QUALITIES

Cathy's first day as a secretary was a busy one. Her employer, Mr. Billings, dictated several letters which he wanted typed immediately. After looking over the completed work, Mr. Billings returned to Cathy a carbon copy of one letter with the notation, "I sent out the original of this letter because it was a rush item, but will you please try to improve your erasures."

Cathy was bewildered! She wanted to produce good work, but she was uncertain about what kinds of erasures were acceptable or unacceptable.

What should Cathy do?

LANGUAGE USAGE

A conjunction is a word that connects other words, phrases, or clauses. Conjunctions can be *coordinate* or *subordinate*. In this part we will present coordinate conjunctions. In Unit 9,

Part 5, we will present subordinate conjunctions. A coordinate conjunction is independent; it connects equal elements in a sentence. Some coordinate conjunctions are *and*, *but*, and *for*.

Example: Her employer is out of town, *and* she is out of her office. . . . *and* is a coordinate conjunction, which connects the independent clause, *she is out of her office*.

On a separate sheet of paper list the coordinate conjunctions in the following sentences.

1. She and Mary were working on the report.
2. She does not type, neither does she take dictation.
3. He hurried to his desk and picked up the ringing telephone.
4. Slowly and accurately Mary gave him the message.
5. With pain in his heart but with a smile on his lips, he walked toward the conference room.

SECRETARIAL WORK

1. *Letter in Modified Block Form* — Type the letter in the illustration on page 77 in modified block style with indented paragraphs. Use mixed punctuation.
2. *Letter in Modified Block Form* — Type the following letter in modified block style with mixed punctuation. Make one carbon copy.

October 10, 197– Dr. Cyril J. Small 410 Grant Street White Plains, New York 10604.

Dear Dr. Small Subject: Location for Dental Office Thank you for your inquiry about a possible location for a dental office in Englewood, New Jersey. We are glad to be able to tell you that we are soon going to start the construction of eight apartment houses that will provide for 124 families. These apartments will be located on Chestnut Street, just outside the main business district. Any one of the first floor apartments in these buildings would be admirably suited for a dentist's or a physician's office. The rents are reasonable, and the floor plans are unusually well designed. (¶) We have already rented some of the apartments and expect that by the time construction is completed practically all apartments will be rented. Since many of these families will move to Englewood from other communities, they will undoubtedly wish to use the professional services of a dentist. (¶) We are enclosing a floor plan of one of the apartments that we believe could be particularly well adapted to your purposes. We should be glad to discuss this with you whenever it is convenient. Will you come to our office and talk this matter over; or may we ask our Mr. Williams, who is in charge of renting this property, to call on you sometime soon? Very truly yours HAWLEY, HAYES & MILLER Norman C. Hayes, President Enclosure

Unit 4 SECRETARIAL LETTER WRITING

Part 1. Key Skills
  2. Letters Composed by Secretaries

The secretary is often asked to write letters for her executive. When she performs this function, she must remember that she is acting as the direct representative of her firm to the public.

VOCABULARY BUILDER

Language is part of a man's character.
Francis Bacon

thorough
    adjective: carried through to completion; marked by full description; careful about detail

p. 97   To complete such tasks successfully you must have command of basic writing skills as well as possess a **thorough** understanding of the company for which you work.

precise
    adjective: exactly or sharply defined or stated; strictly conforming to rule or convention

p. 98   There are certain words that are frequently used in business which convey **precise** meanings.

trite
    adjective: hackneyed from too much use; stale; meaningless from overuse

p. 98   Words that add nothing to understanding and **trite** expressions reduce the effectiveness of business writing.

analyses
    noun: plural of *analysis*; a separation of a whole into its parts; an examination of the elements of something complex

p. 99   Are there to be **analyses** of shifts in percentages of sales?

transition
    noun: passage from one state, or stage, or place to another; a change

preceding
    adjective: previous; prior; former; immediately before in time or place

p. 103   The first sentence in a paragraph is a signal of the content of the paragraph, or it provides a **transition** from the message of the **preceding** paragraph.

edit
    verb: to assemble by cutting and rearranging; to direct the publication of

p. 104   Initially you may need to compose each letter in your shorthand notebook . . . and **edit** it before you type it.

delegate
    verb: to entrust to another

p. 107   While others **delegate** the writing of correspondence to secretaries, only a few **delegate** to the extent that Mr. Osmond does.

commitment
    noun: an agreement or pledge to do something in the future; something pledged; a state of being obligated

p. 107   You need make no **commitment** in such responses.

alternative
    adjective: offering or expressing a choice between two things, or plans, or courses, or propositions

p. 117   Often form letters are written with **alternative** paragraphs so that the secretary has a choice. . . .

PART 1 KEY SKILLS

Carole Langley is secretary to Mr. Thomas Sanford, one of the vice-presidents of a large food distributing company. Carole has learned a great deal about her company's business in the two years that she has worked for executives in several different offices of the company. Mr. Sanford receives much correspondence, and he likes it answered immediately. Carole has been given responsibility for handling much of the routine correspondence on her own and she signs her employer's name since he feels he need not read through her answers. Also, Carole composes many letters after brief instructions from Mr. Sanford. For example, Mr. Sanford will say to Carole, "The only information that we have about dairy product sales in the Southwest is in the report that Jim Sullivan prepared last month. Will you get that information and write a letter to Bill Young?" or "Just write to Joe Fellows that I shall be unable to attend the meeting in Chicago in late November." It is clear that such brief decisions require much less time than is needed to dictate the full letter to Carole. Carole takes the notes she has recorded and writes letters that Mr. Sanford signs.

The modern business office is an important communications center for the organization it serves. Secretaries are often given a variety of writing tasks ranging from answering routine request letters to preparing detailed reports after collecting the information needed for the report. To complete such tasks successfully you must have command of basic writing skills as well as possess a thorough understanding of the company for which you work. In addition, there are some general rules for writing letters that will aid you in producing high quality messages.

KNOWLEDGE OF ENGLISH GRAMMAR

From your study of English, you have developed basic skill in using the written word accurately. You may feel that a review would be helpful, and you will find such review in Appendix A. Also, you will continue to have the opportunity to recall your knowledge of language usage through the exercises included at the end of each part of this book.

VOCABULARY OF BUSINESS CORRESPONDENCE

There are certain words that are frequently used in business which convey precise meanings. During your studies you have developed an understanding of many of these commonly used business terms. Think about their meanings and their proper use in correspondence. You will find a listing of often used business words in books such as *Word Division Manual: The Fifteen Thousand Most Used Words in Business Communication*.[1] Check your dictionary when you find a word that is unfamiliar to you.

Words that have precise meanings are generally considered the best words in business communication. The writer wants his message to be understood as he intended it to be understood. Misunderstandings can cause delays in completing transactions. A line of poetry may convey a wide range of meanings to various readers. Inasmuch as poetry is an art form, such varied meanings are indeed acceptable. The goal of business writing, though, is to have each sentence mean the same thing to all who read it.

Words that add nothing to understanding and trite expressions reduce the effectiveness of business writing. Such expressions conceal the message from the reader who must read through excess words and mentally cancel them out to learn the intended message. You should be careful to avoid trite usage in your writing.

Common, but not the best	**All that is necessary**
end result	result
true facts	facts
integral part	part
grave emergency	emergency
inaugurate a change	begin
finalize	end or complete
because of circumstances beyond our control, . . .	We have not . . .
At an early date . . .	Soon (or provide a specific date)
Attached hereto you will find	Attached is
Enclosed please find	The (clipping) is enclosed
It affords us great pleasure to . . .	It is a pleasure
Thank you in advance	We shall appreciate
Would you kindly send . . .	Please send . . .

---

[1] J. E. Silverthorn and Devern J. Perry (2d ed.; Cincinnati: South-Western Publishing Co., 1970).

Unit 4 / Secretarial Letter Writing

Secretaries who are skillful in the use of language are invaluable in maintaining high quality written communications in their companies. An illustration of poor use of language is:

> We did not believe that 561 instances in a total of 2,500 were sufficient to demand high priority; but we believe, nevertheless, that that problem is of prime importance.

What does the writer wish to say? Will the reader be left confused? Will the reader wonder how important the problem is to the writer? If something does not demand high priority, how can it be of prime importance? What does *prime* mean if it doesn't mean *first*?

PLANNING YOUR MESSAGE

You will need to know clearly what your message is to be. If you are uncertain, it is unlikely that the recipient will get an understandable letter or report. Keeping the following questions in mind will help you handle your writing assignments properly.

Is Your Understanding of the Letter Correct?

You must understand thoroughly what the message is to say. If you are answering a letter, you will want to read the letter you received with attention to those details that you must include in your response. A question to keep in mind while you read the letter is: What does the writer want to know? You may wish to write brief notes of the points that require a response. Checking your understanding assures you that you will cover all the details in your message.

If you are writing a letter or report that was requested by your employer, be sure that you know clearly the reason for the message and what it is to convey. If, for example, your employer says, "Please draft a brief report on sales for the Western Region for the last year," you will need to know answers to questions such as:

Are the sales to be shown weekly? semimonthly? monthly?
Are the sales representatives to be indicated?
Are there to be analyses of shifts in percentages of sales?
For what period are the sales to be recorded? the calendar
   year? the fiscal year?

Is Your Information Accurate and Current?

You should never assume that the information you had for a former piece of correspondence is accurate for the present. Prices change, policies shift, and progress continues.

Illus. 4-1

An effective business report or letter requires that information be checked carefully.

National Cash Register Company

Most written communications require specific details. You can never *assume* that you know those details. You will always check the most reliable sources for information. Failure to get the most recent information may make it necessary to write further letters of explanation and often create embarrassing situations for a company. For example, if a secretary includes in a letter a price for a product, assuming that the last price she had was the correct one, she may learn later that there has been a price increase. In the meantime the recipient of her information may have placed an order based on the price the secretary quoted. The company may decide that it will honor the price quoted inasmuch as the customer was responding to recently received information. This means that the payment is less than it should be. However, to have informed the customer that the price quoted was inaccurate may have led to ill will between the company and the customer.

Is Your Language Appropriate and Clear?

The rules of language usage with which you have become acquainted in your English classes are very important to you as you compose letters. Be aware of the words you choose and of the phrases you select. You want them to be sensible and helpful in conveying your message to the reader. Words chosen should be natural for the occasion. If the writer and the reader know each other well, the tone of the letter may be informal. However, if the writer knows a third person will read the letter, the tone of the letter may be more formal. Circumstances will alter the tone of the message. In many, if not most, of the messages you will write you should assume a somewhat neutral role; the letter should convey the needed information in a straightforward fashion. The recipient gets no impression of the personality of the writer. For example, if you are responding to a request for a new bulletin, you may write the following:

> Enclosed is the bulletin which you requested. We hope that you will find it of interest. If we can provide additional details, please write to us.

You should not write

> Gee, does it make us happy to know that you want our bulletin, which is enclosed. We think it is a dandy, and we know you will feel the same. Read it quickly and completely and then if you find that you have some unanswered questions, drop us a line!

You will want to be careful that your written language conveys the tone that is appropriate for your letters. There are many so-called everyday expressions that are satisfactory for use in speaking, but do not convey meaning accurately if used in writing. What words in the illustration above do you feel are inappropriate for a business letter?

Simple words should be chosen when they accurately convey your meaning. Long, pompous-sounding words can detract from the clarity of your message. For example:

use simple, direct words: *a careful review was made*
not pompous words: *a studious analysis was undertaken*

use simple, direct words: *another house was found*
not pompous words: *a substitute abode was uncovered*

Is Your Message Courteous?

In person-to-person meetings it is possible to convey courtesy in several ways — in your manner of looking at the person, in your tone of voice, in your general responsiveness. Letters have only words and these must be chosen skillfully if the recipient is to feel the response is gracious and courteous. You will want to read your letter while thinking of the recipient and imagining how the message will seem to him. Authorities on letter writing underscore the need for the *you* approach in writing good letters. The *you* approach merely means that the letter writer has an understanding of his reader's possible responses to the message.

Not a courteous statement: You promised to send us the material by the 15th; it is the 16th and we have not yet received it. You have broken your promise.

A courteous statement: We have not yet received the material that you promised to send us by the 15th. Is it enroute? If it is not, can you let us know when we may expect to receive it?

Is Your Message Complete?

This step is a two-sided consideration. A letter must contain all information requested; at the same time a letter should contain no unnecessary information. Recipients ordinarily do not enjoy reading paragraph after paragraph of material that is of no interest to them. Two questions to guide you in checking completeness are:

Have all the writer's questions been clearly answered?
Is there any information here that does not belong in the message?

THE STRUCTURE OF THE MESSAGE

The message reflects a structure from the first sentence to the last. There are many variations in structure, but all messages should answer *yes* to these questions:

Is Your Opening Appropriate?

Written communications must capture the attention of the recipient. The opening sentence should tell the reader why you are writing. In general, the point of the message should be clear very early in the first paragraph. However, there are times when there must be some background material presented before the point of the message will make sense to the reader. In such cases it is important that the opening sentence be of sufficient interest to hold the attention of the recipient until he reaches the reason for the letter.

Is Your Message Divided by Paragraphs?

Rules for paragraphing are flexible. Paragraphing provides a means of subdividing your message into meaningful units that aid the recipient in reading the message and in grasping the various points. The first sentence in a paragraph is a signal of the content of the paragraph, or it provides a transition from the message of the preceding paragraph.

Is Your Message Presented Logically?

For a clear understanding of the letter, the information in it should be planned and developed logically. To write a paragraph that cannot be understood until a later paragraph is read is to be thoughtless of the reader. Your message should unfold: It should provide the information in such a way that the reader will understand your message without having to reread it. For example, to begin a letter *I will be happy to meet you in San Francisco on May 15* can be confusing if the original letter requested a meeting in Salt Lake City on April 14. The recipient immediately wonders: What about my request for a meeting on April 14? Didn't he get my letter? If the recipient reads on, he may find in a later paragraph a reference to the writer's inability to be in Salt Lake City.

ORGANIZING YOUR WRITING TASKS

You will want to develop a procedure for handling your writing tasks so that you are efficient. Assume that you have read the mail and have set aside the letters that you will take care of yourself. The following steps may aid you in writing the answers quickly:

1. Read each of the letters, making notes on the letter itself or in your shorthand notebook indicating the points to be made in your response.
2. Make a list of all the information and enclosures you will need. As you gather the information you need, check each item off your list. Make a note of any items you cannot find.

Illus. 4-2

Developing efficiency in handling writing tasks assures your employer's confidence in your work.

3. Begin to write your answers. Initially you may need to compose each letter in your shorthand notebook (preferably in shorthand) and edit it before you type it. After you have gained some experience you will find that you will be able to compose your letters directly at the typewriter by merely reading the letter to be answered and looking at the brief notes you have made.
4. Read each letter before you remove it from your typewriter to be sure that it is complete as well as typed accurately.
5. Sign the letters on your own or for your employer or leave them for his signature. You will learn from your employer which letters you are to answer with your signature, which you are to answer for him and sign his signature, and which you are to answer for him but leave on his desk for his signature. The pattern that your employer uses is a personal choice and you will learn what it is.

Employers differ in how they assign the task of handling correspondence. Some like a secretary to do much of the writing, but they want to see all the letters and sign them so that they are fully aware of the nature and extent of correspondence. Others merely want to know which correspondence the secretary has handled so that they have a general idea of what is happening. They feel no need for the detailed information that reading each letter would provide.

QUESTIONS

1. Which kinds of messages may a secretary be requested to write?
2. What should a secretary know about commonly used business words?
3. What is likely to be the impression on the reader of a letter that has spelling and grammatical errors in it?
4. What is a *trite expression*?
5. Why should a secretary avoid trite expressions in writing messages?
6. Why does a secretary check her understanding of the contents of the letter she is to answer?
7. Why is up-to-date information important when answering a letter?
8. What is meant by a *neutral role* for a secretary writing for her employer?
9. How is the tone of a letter reflected?
10. Why must a message be presented in a logical order?

JUDGMENT

1. How will a secretary know which of the letters she writes should be signed by her employer?
2. How may a secretary become acquainted with her employer's style of writing?
3. How does a secretary check the accuracy of her information?
4. How does a secretary improve her writing vocabulary?
5. Why is the *you* attitude important in business correspondence?

PERSONAL QUALITIES

Mr. Fred Carlin, chief metallurgist of the Allied Foundry, has asked Evelyn Palmer, his secretary, to compose a reply to a letter received from the Personnel Department of the Case Engineering Company. The Case firm has requested information about an applicant for employment as a metallurgist, John T. Dean, who was discharged by Mr. Carlin because of careless work and costly mistakes in casting metals. Evelyn checked on the facts of Dean's employment and cause for discharge. This is the body of the letter Evelyn composed, signed, and sent to the Case Engineering Company:

John T. Dean was employed by us from January 15 to August 13 of this year as a metallurgist.

He was discharged because of careless work and costly mistakes in casting metals which involved the loss of a great deal of money for our firm.

If there is anything else you would like to know about Mr. Dean, don't hesitate to write us.

Is this the kind of letter that a secretary should have written on her own?

If you had been responsible for composing the letter for your employer, in what ways would your letter have differed from that of Evelyn Palmer?

LANGUAGE USAGE

The apostrophe is used (1) to show the possessive case of nouns, (2) to show omission or contraction, (3) to form some plurals. Type the sentences given below and insert apostrophes where needed.
Example: Marys typewriter should be repaired.
Correct: Mary's (possessive case) typewriter should be repaired.

1. Its not clear what is to be done with these materials.
2. The 1960s were called the Soaring Sixties.
3. Why did she type the *2s* and *8s* so lightly?
4. The Oxfords visit was an unexpected pleasure.
5. The report of the mens group will be ready by noon tomorrow.
6. Lawrences work in this course is below average.

Part 1 / Key Skills

7. The printing for this firm is done by Jones and Williams print shop.
8. Is Sallys aunt going with her to Europe?
9. When *ands* and *thes* are used in titles, they should not be capitalized.
10. Watertowns young people find the schools very exciting.

SECRETARIAL WORK

1. Each of the following letter portions has at least one of the faults of letter composition discussed in this part. Read each item carefully to determine what is wrong; then rewrite it as you think it should be written.

    (a) In regard to the motors these are being shipped from Madeira today addressed to you at your office and have somebody there to receive the shipment because it must be signed for and will you be sure to acknowledge by letter to me.

    (b) In reply to your letter of July 10, we wish to advise that an examination of our records shows that your insurance policy is still in force.

    (c) If you would specify more carefully on your orders that you want the latest models, it would save us a lot of trouble and expense.

    (d) If you will send me a big order right away, it will help me to win a prize in the contest that our company is conducting and you will receive merchandise that is superior in quality at no higher price than you have been paying other dealers.

    (e) We need the measurements of the windows in figuring the size these draperies should be. These figures are necessary so that we can make the draperies the correct size.

    (f) Hoping it will be possible for you to give us your decision on this matter by Friday, we are . . .

    (g) We are enclosing our check for $306.98 in full payment of invoice for $327.55 less return of $12.50 and discount of $6.27. (There is an error of $1.80 on the invoice.)

    (h) We want to tell you that we find your new publication extremely interesting.

2. Bring to class an actual business letter consisting of several paragraphs that you consider below average. Evaluate the letter. Write your specific criticisms; then rewrite the letter. Be prepared to make a report on this exercise to the class.

3. Bring to class an actual business letter that you consider satisfactory. List the characteristics of the letter that make it effective.

PART 2 — LETTERS COMPOSED BY SECRETARIES

Dorothy Alexander is Mr. R. E. Osmond's secretary. She has learned that her employer prefers that she reply to as much of his correspondence as possible. During the last year she has assumed increasing responsibility for the correspondence. She has learned to fully understand Mr. Osmond's style of writing. She realizes that Mr. Osmond is not a typical executive. While others delegate the writing of correspondence to secretaries, only a few delegate to the extent that Mr. Osmond does. The situation pleases Dorothy, for not only is she a competent letter writer but she finds this task enjoyable.

LETTERS OF ACKNOWLEDGMENT

Many executives follow the practice of responding to letters as soon as they are received. When your executive is away from his office he may expect you to reply to letters. You need make no commitment in such responses. A letter of acknowledgment need say only that the letter has been received and that it will be called to the executive's attention when he returns. You may want to include the date of his return in the letter.

A typical letter of acknowledgment signed by the secretary is

Dear Mr. Reeder

  Your letter to Mr. Preston inviting him to participate in your fall seminar on October 5 and 6 has been received. Unfortunately Mr. Preston is out of the office and will not return until January 20. Your letter will be brought to his attention at that time.

  I hope this delay will cause you no inconvenience.

             Sincerely yours

             Theresa Thomas

             Mrs. Theresa Thomas
             Secretary to Mr. Preston

LETTERS OF APPOINTMENT

    Frequent trips to other cities involve planning for appointments with people whom your executive would like to see. Your executive will often give you the facts and expect you to compose a gracious request for an appointment. Appointment letters should give the purpose as well as the time, date, and place of the appointment. The person granting the appointment frequently sets the time. Sometimes, however, an appointment may be set at the convenience of the person seeking the appointment.

    Here is an illustration of an appointment letter:

Dear Mr. Conn

    While Mr. Preston is attending the National Dairy Show in Chicago during the week of April 15, he would like an opportunity to talk with you about your new equipment. Will it be possible for you to meet him in his suite at 4 p.m. on Tuesday, April 16? He will be staying at the Palmer House in downtown Chicago.

                        Sincerely yours

                        Theresa Thomas

                        Mrs. Theresa Thomas
                        Secretary to Mr. Preston

    You may frequently write a letter confirming an appointment after you have checked the date and time with your employer.

    An example of a confirmation letter follows:

Dear Mr. Preston

    It will be a pleasure for Mr. Conn to meet you at 4 p.m. on April 16 in your suite at the Palmer House in Chicago. At that time he will have information about our new equipment.

                        Sincerely yours

                        Eileen Ryan

                        Miss Eileen Ryan
                        Secretary to Mr. Conn

Illus. 4-3

A secretary should always check her employer's schedule before writing a letter confirming an appointment.

Shaw-Walker

LETTERS MAKING RESERVATIONS

While most reservations are made by telephone, many are still made by letter. A request for a reservation should include the name and business affiliation of your employer, the accommodations desired, and the time of departure if a travel reservation, or the time of arrival if a hotel reservation.

Gentlemen

Please reserve a drawing room on your train, <u>The Limited</u>, leaving Denver for Salt Lake City at 10 a.m. on Sunday, December 12, for Mr. Harry A. Wilson, General Sales Manager of the Empire Tape Recording Corporation. The ticket will be called for on Monday, December 6.

Please confirm this reservation.

Yours very truly

Ruth M. Brown

Miss Ruth M. Brown
Secretary to Mr. Wilson

For a hotel reservation:

Gentlemen

Please reserve a single room for T. L. Preston, President of the National Dairy Association, for the night of November 13. He plans to arrive at your hotel about 9 p.m. and will be leaving at noon on November 14.

We shall appreciate your confirmation of this reservation.

Yours very truly

Theresa Thomas

Mrs. Theresa Thomas
Secretary to Mr. Preston

LETTERS REGARDING MEETINGS

Often your executive will give you full responsibility for writing to members of committees, of which he serves as chairman, informing them of forthcoming meetings.

An illustration of such a notice follows:

Dear Mr. Landers.

The first meeting of the Finance Committee of the Girl Scouts of the U.S.A. will be held on Tuesday evening, October 13, at 7:30 in Room 1203A in the National Headquarters Offices here in New York.

Within a few days Mr. Preston will be sending you a copy of the proposed budget. He is looking forward to seeing you on the 13th.

Sincerely yours

Theresa Thomas

Mrs. Theresa Thomas
Secretary to Mr. Preston

You will sometimes assume responsibility for acknowledging a letter concerning a meeting. You should first check the matter with your employer (he may have some personal or business appointments that are unknown to you) so that you can inform the person who has sent the notice whether your employer will be present. Such a letter follows:

Dear Mr. Preston

    Mr. Landers has received your letter about the first meeting for this year of the Finance Committee. He must be present at a business conference in Los Angeles on October 13 and 14 and, unfortunately, will be unable to attend the Finance Committee meeting. However, he is planning to send you a memorandum of his reactions to the proposed budget.

                  Yours sincerely

                  Marianne T. Cook

                  Mrs. Marianne T. Cook
                  Secretary to Mr. Landers

LETTERS OF TRANSMITTAL

    From time to time your executive will ask you to send materials to other persons. As secretary to a lawyer, for example, you would routinely mail contracts, deeds, mortgages, and other legal documents. If you were the secretary to an executive who appears before public groups you might be asked to send copies of speeches, which have been reprinted, to those who request them. When you are asked to send such items, you should send a brief letter of transmittal. A carbon copy of the letter is then kept in the files as a permanent record of the mailing of the enclosures.

    Illustrations of such letters that you may write are as follows:

Dear Professor Lanlow

    Two copies of the address Mr. Preston delivered before the Association for the Advancement of Management are enclosed.

    We are happy to send these to you. If you should need additional copies for classroom use, please let us know.

                    Sincerely yours

                  Theresa Thomas

                  Mrs. Theresa Thomas
                  Secretary to Mr. Preston

Dear Mr. Manning

    The contracts have been completed and are enclosed. There are small red checks at all points where your clients' signatures should appear.

    Mr. Preston will look forward to receiving these contracts within a week.

                            Sincerely yours

                            Theresa Thomas

                            Mrs. Theresa Thomas
                            Secretary to Mr. Preston

Enclosures

Illus. 4-4

A reliable secretary who relieves her employer of correspondence details is a valuable asset to him and to the company.

FOLLOW-UP LETTERS

Your employer may ask you to send a letter concerning a matter that has not yet been taken care of. You will find most of the details needed for the follow-up letter in the carbon copy of the first letter that was sent. The date of the first letter is given, and most of the contents are restated. You may enclose a copy of the original letter.

Dear Mr. Fisher

On November 3 we asked you to submit an estimate of the cost of modernizing the lighting in our new offices on Third Avenue which we expect to occupy on February 1. We have not received the estimate, and we cannot go ahead with the other work until we hear from you.

If you are still interested in the contract, will you please submit your estimate on or before December 21.

                    Sincerely yours

                    T. L. Preston

                    T. L. Preston

Dear Mr. Stanton

On October 14 we sent you a letter in which we asked if you might be able to meet with our sales representatives from the Eastern Region to discuss the topic, "Helping a Customer Become Acquainted with a New Product." As of today we have not heard from you. Our program will go to press shortly, and we should like to list all participants on it. A copy of our earlier letter giving all the details of the meeting is enclosed.

We hope that we shall have the pleasure of hearing from you shortly.

                    Sincerely yours

                    T. L. Preston

                    T. L. Preston

THANK YOU LETTERS

You may be expected to handle thank you letters that are sent somewhat regularly on receipt of certain publications or information. Thank you letters should express your appreciation sincerely and simply.

Dear Mr. Hanley

Thank you for your letter concerning Miss Susan Renslow whom we are considering for a position on our staff.

We appreciate your generous and helpful consideration.

Sincerely yours

T. L. Preston

T. L. Preston

Dear Mr. Letner

Your contribution to last week's seminar of our junior executive group was greatly appreciated by all the participants. Discussion among the group continues to include points you raised in your opening remarks.

The participants and I are most grateful for your generous and helpful cooperation. We thank you.

Yours sincerely

T. L. Preston

T. L. Preston

REMITTANCE LETTERS

Many remittances, especially checks (frequently voucher checks), are self-explanatory and require no letter of remittance. This is especially true when payment is for an invoice or monthly bill. When a remittance is for an unusual payment, a remittance letter should be sent. The letter should indicate the purpose of the payment, the amount, and the form in which it is sent: check, draft, or money order. It should also include any necessary explanation. A remittance letter should include an enclosure notation. The notation is typed two spaces below the reference initials.

An illustration of a remittance letter follows:

Gentlemen

    Our check for $255.93, in payment of Invoice 3960, is enclosed. We have deducted $43.38 from the original amount of the invoice to cover the cost of goods we returned to you.

                Yours very truly

                S. E. Walker

                S. E. Walker, Treasurer

ve

Enclosure
    Check 696 for $255.93

LETTERS OF INQUIRY

    A letter of inquiry seeks information. Since specific information is desired, the letter must be worded clearly. Questions must be asked in such a way that their meaning cannot be misunderstood. If it is necessary to get data on a complex subject or problem, a series of numbered questions should be asked. Follow this plan when you are composing a detailed letter of inquiry:

1. Give the subject of your inquiry at the beginning of the letter.
2. Give the reason for your inquiry and explain why the letter was addressed to the reader.
3. Add explanatory material that may be of help to the reader, such as specific details, definitions, dates, and descriptions.
4. End the letter courteously. Avoid stock phrases, such as, *Thanking you in advance* . . . or *Awaiting your reply, we remain* . . . . Instead, use *Any assistance you may give us will be greatly appreciated* or *We shall appreciate any assistance you give us.*

    When the answer to a letter of inquiry will be a favor to you, enclose a stamped self-addressed envelope of convenient size.

    A brief paragraph on a business letterhead and the signature may be all that is necessary for a good letter of inquiry.

Gentlemen

    Sometime ago you published a booklet entitled <u>An Office Manager's Guide for the Selection of New Office Equipment</u>. This booklet should be helpful in selecting equipment for our new branch office in Fargo. If it is still available, will you please send us a copy. Thank you.

                          Very truly yours

                          P T Gaines

                          P. T. Gaines
                          Purchasing Department

    The answer to a letter of inquiry should be brief, adequate in covering all the questions asked, and courteous. An illustration follows:

Dear Mr. Gaines

    The booklet you requested, <u>An Office Manager's Guide for the Selection of New Office Equipment</u>, has just been reprinted. A copy is being mailed to you with our compliments.

    Your interest in this booklet is appreciated. We hope it will prove helpful to you in selecting office equipment for your new branch office in Fargo.

                          Yours sincerely

                          S. M. Landes

                          S. M. Landes
                          Marketing Department

    You should answer a letter of inquiry promptly. Promptness is a matter of courtesy and affords a real opportunity to build goodwill. A reply that leaves the business office the day the inquiry is received is certain to gain respect for the company.

LETTERS ORDERING GOODS OR SERVICES

    A letter written to purchase goods or services is an order letter. The order should be clear, specific, and complete. Misunderstanding means delay and inconvenience to both firms.

Usually every order for goods will show the following information: quantity, price, catalog number (if there is one), destination of shipment, method of shipment, desired delivery date (this determines the method of shipment to some degree), and the method of payment.

Order blanks are often distributed to regular customers by the seller. It is common practice, however, for business firms to print their own order forms. The use of these forms reduces the chances of making mistakes or omitting required information in ordering goods and does away with the need for writing order letters.

An illustration of a letter ordering goods is given below.

```
Gentlemen

   We would like to place an order for the
following item:

One 2' x 3' visual magnetic control board in
   dark green, MCB-279-70-DG, at $49.50

   Our Check 363 is enclosed.  We would ap-
preciate your sending us a copy of your
latest brochure that provides information on
letter styles.

   Your prompt handling of this order will
be appreciated.

                     Very truly yours

                     Talcott Barnes

                     Talcott Barnes
                     Office Manager
```

FORM LETTERS

In many offices some kinds of letters are written over and over again and it is, therefore, economical to compose letters that can be used in response to similar requests. Secretaries often build their own files of form letters and organize a coding system so that they can quickly locate an appropriate letter. Often form letters are written with alternative paragraphs so that the secretary has a choice and can thus select the paragraph that is most appropriate for a particular recipient.

Letters acknowledging orders, sending out requested information, requesting references for prospective employees, and thanking companies or individuals for references are just a few of the instances where form letters are likely to be useful. Illustrations of form letter paragraph inserts follow.

Prospective Customer

1. It was a pleasure to talk with you when you visited our booth at the recent _____ Convention. The material that we promised to mail you is enclosed.

2. We are asking _____ who represents our company in your city to call you and arrange an appointment at your convenience, as you requested.

3. If you should like further information about our products, feel free to write to us; or you may call _____, our representative in your city. His telephone number is _____.

Requesting Reference

_____ has applied for a position with our company and has given your name as a reference. We would appreciate your completing the attached form and returning it in the enclosed self-addressed stamped envelope. There is space for any additional comments you may wish to make.

Thank you for your courtesy in responding to this request.

QUESTIONS

1. For what reason might a secretary acknowledge a letter in her employer's absence?
2. What must the secretary cover in a letter of appointment?
3. What must the secretary keep in mind in writing a letter making a reservation for a hotel room for her employer?
4. What is a letter of transmittal?
5. How may a carbon copy of a letter be used in following up a matter that has not been completed?
6. What is the secretary attempting to convey in a thank you letter that she writes?
7. What points should the secretary keep in mind as she composes a letter of inquiry?
8. Why is promptness important in a letter of inquiry?
9. What does an order letter include?
10. What should a remittance letter include?
11. Why are form letters used in a business office?
12. What are some types of inquiries that can be handled by form letters?

JUDGMENT

1. Why should the secretary be noncommittal in a letter of acknowledgment?
2. Why does the secretary file a copy of a letter of transmittal?
3. "Every letter is a sales letter." Do you agree with this statement? Why?
4. Why is it important to word a letter of inquiry clearly?
5. In general, when does a secretary compose her own letters rather than have them dictated to her?

PERSONAL QUALITIES

Joan Sellers opens the mail and reads a letter inviting her employer to a luncheon meeting on Wednesday of the following week. She notes that it is from a group before which he has spoken on earlier occasions. She checks his calendar and finds that he is free for luncheon on the date of the meeting. She writes a letter accepting the invitation. The next day Mr. Manning, her employer, is looking over his calendar for the next week; he notes this luncheon engagement and asks Joan about it. After he hears about the meeting he says, "I don't have time to attend such a meeting." She or her employer will have to write another letter.

What should Joan have done before she wrote a response to the invitation? What can Joan do now?

LANGUAGE USAGE

On a separate sheet of paper type each of the following sentences inserting the punctuation marks needed.

1. Secretaries compose letters memorandums and reports for their employers.
2. However it is common for businesses to design and duplicate their own forms for intercompany use.
3. Doris has developed form letters for general inquiries requests for brochures and orders for standard products.
4. Will Schedule C give me last years production as well as sales?
5. When a rough draft is required a secretary is able to type at a very fast rate.
6. A letter in which an item is ordered should be clear specific and complete.
7. Many remittances such as checks and money orders are self-explanatory and they require no letter of remittance.
8. She is ordering six copies of the booklet *Planning for Wise Use of Time*.
9. Is March 15 April 4 or April 20 the best date for our next meeting?
10. When the secretary sends out a requested bulletin she should write a brief letter of transmittal.

SECRETARIAL WORK

1. Write a letter to a company manufacturing dictating and transcribing equipment asking for information on the models available and the prices of the models. Prepare your specifications on the basis of information in Unit 2, Part 3, on voice recording and transcribing machines.

2. An order has been received for three copies of *Walden* by Thoreau. Your bookstore carries editions by Modern Library, Inc.; Peter Pauper Press; and Doubleday & Company, Inc. You don't know which edition the customer wishes. Write a letter to the customer requesting the missing information.

3. Your employer, Mr. T. F. Franklin, has received a letter asking him to make the keynote address, "The Future of Our Industry," at the annual meeting of the Cement Industry Association. Mr. Franklin is out of the country for a month. What kind of letter should you write? Write it.

4. Assume that you are employed by Mr. Arthur J. Randolph, General Manager of the Randolph Office Equipment and Supply Company, 39 Broad Street, Newark, New Jersey 07104. All letters written in this office are in block form with open punctuation.

   (a) Write a letter to the Robel Paper Company, 495 Grove Street, Buffalo, New York 14216, asking them to quote prices and terms on 250 reams of bond paper and to submit samples. Your letter should specify weight, size, color, and finish you desire. (If you are in doubt about these items, refer to Part 3 of Unit 3.) Make two carbon copies of the letter.

   (b) Write a letter to the Chicago Equipment Manufacturing Corporation, 140 Congress Street, Chicago, Illinois 60605, ordering the following merchandise:

6 quires	Mimeograph Stencils #960, 8½" x 18", blue, $3.75 each	
6 boxes	Ditto Master Units, #24-1011, 8½" x 11", $6.40 each	
20 cans	Spirit Fluid, #24-2010, 1 gallon, $2.70 each	

   Make two carbon copies.

Unit 5 SECRETARIAL TYPEWRITING

Part 1. Preparing Business Reports
2. Parts of Business Reports
3. Financial Statements and Reports
4. Legal Papers, Minutes, and Resolutions

The secretary can be of great assistance to her employer when he is preparing a business report. She will aid in the researching, writing, and revising, and will be responsible for typing a flawless final draft.

VOCABULARY BUILDER

In language clarity is everything.
Confucius

collate
verb: to collect, compare carefully in order to verify and arrange in order

p. 124   You **collate** pages of the report.

deletion
noun: something destroyed or wiped out, especially by blotting out, cutting out, or erasing

p. 125   X out typing errors and **deletions** in the first draft instead of taking time to erase them.

alignment
noun: the proper positioning or state of adjustment of parts in relation to each other

p. 131   The periods in the leaders should be in vertical **alignment** also.

inverted
adjective: turned inside out or upside down

p. 138   With a long title the **inverted** pyramid style may be used. . . .

reveal
verb: to uncover; to make known; to divulge

p. 152   A look at the financial reports of several companies would . . . **reveal** some minor differences in style.

document
noun: an official or original paper relied upon as the basis, proof, or support of something; a writing conveying information

p. 161   There are various kinds of legal papers, or **documents** — contracts, wills, deeds, leases, affidavits, powers of attorney.

capacity
noun: the ability to hold, store, receive, or accommodate

p. 164   In large offices one of the secretaries usually acts in this **capacity**.

validity
noun: having legal force; having objective truth or generally accepted authority; something that is sound

p. 165   He may . . . prove its (last will) **validity** to the court for the purpose of carrying out its provisions.

participate
verb: share; take part in; to possess something of the nature of a person, thing, or quality

p. 170   . . . you should identify the discussion with the names of those who **participate**.

corollary
noun: something that naturally follows; a result; an immediate inference from a proved proposition

p. 171   The special committee on **Corollary** Information reported that the average work week. . . .

PART 1 PREPARING BUSINESS REPORTS

Mr. David R. Singer, who is one of the founders of the management consulting firm of Michaels, Singer & Smith, spends a great deal of his time preparing reports for other businesses. A management consulting firm tries to assist other businesses in operating more efficiently. Jan Allison, Mr. Singer's new secretary, knows that much of the work that he must take home is to finish his reports. Jan knows that she will be valuable to Mr. Singer if she can assist him in preparing his reports. With *extra* effort, she can help him produce superior reports.

IMPORTANCE OF REPORTS

As a business becomes larger, it is more and more difficult to communicate with employees in person and have face-to-face discussions. Business reports make it possible to present much information to others in the company. As a secretary, you will probably type many reports; and, as you gain experience, you may be asked to help gather information to be used in reports.

Illus. 5-1
Gathering information for a business report is often a secretarial responsibility.

Ohio National Life Insurance Company

A business report may be only one page or a long, formal report of more than fifty pages. Some reports are sent to personnel within the company and others are duplicated and sent to people outside the company.

STEPS IN REPORT WRITING

There is no *one* set way to write a report; there are many ways. However, in drafting and revising a business report you and your employer will usually take these steps:

1. He develops a broad idea of the problem to be covered in the report.
2. He prepares either a sketchy or a detailed outline of the contents.
3. He composes the first draft. He may write the entire draft in longhand; he may record it on a dictating machine; or he may dictate it directly to you.
4. You type the first draft in rough draft form.
5. He reorganizes and edits the first draft for content, wording, and sentence structure (usually with your help).
6. You type a second draft of the report.
7. He edits the second draft to insure the best presentation of the contents.
8. You type the report in its final form.
9. You double-check each page for accuracy, particularly accuracy of figures.
10. You collate pages of the report.

The Outline

After the problem to be covered in the report has been determined, your employer prepares an outline.

An outline may be written in complete sentence form or in topical form. *Topical form* means that the topics or headings of the parts of the report are listed. Parallel construction should be used; that is, if one part of the outline is in sentence form, the next part should be a sentence, too. Words, phrases, and sentences should not be mixed throughout the outline. No main heading or subheading should stand alone. For every Roman numeral "I," there should be a Roman numeral "II"; for every letter "A," a letter "B"; for every Arabic "1," an Arabic "2."

In the outline illustrated, each identifying number or letter is followed by a period and two spaces and begins just below the first word of the previous line.

```
               An Outline of a Report on

            PUNCHED CARD DATA PROCESSING OPERATIONS


    I.  Introduction

        A.  Purpose
            1.  To review present operations
            2.  To develop an improved system
        B.  Approach
            1.  To make detailed studies of present equipment
            2.  To prepare flow charts of present operations
                a.  Accounting department
                b.  Payroll department
                c.  Purchasing department

    II. Proposed system

        A.  Staff requirements
            1.  To retrain present personnel
            2.  To employ systems manager
        B.  Equipment requirements
            1.  To study rental costs of additional machines
            2.  To study other costs
                a.  Auxiliary equipment
                b.  Additional cards and tapes
            3.  To study additional wiring costs
```

Illus. 5-2   A topical outline of a report

The Rough Draft

A rough draft is your employer's first attempt to get his thoughts down on paper where they can be edited and improved. The draft may be revised and retyped many times; therefore, you will find the following ten suggestions helpful:

1. Use typing paper strong enough to withstand erasing easily. Do not use manifold paper or expensive letterhead paper.
2. Type double or triple space so that the changes can be clearly marked and easily seen and followed.
3. Allow ample margins (1½ to 2 inches) at the top, bottom, and on both sides of each page to provide enough room for corrections.
4. *X* out typing errors and deletions in the first draft instead of taking time to erase them.
5. A carbon copy should be made in case the original is misplaced. You may also wish to have an extra copy to cut up when reorganizing the material.
6. Number each page in the draft in its proper sequence. Also assign a number to each successive revision of a draft and type the date on it.

7. Type a long insertion on a separate sheet of paper and give it a corresponding page number and letter. For example, the first insertion to be included on page 8 should be numbered "8A" and clearly marked "Insert 8A" at the point where it is to be inserted.
8. Type quoted matter of four lines or more single spaced and indent it in the same form as it will appear in the final draft.
9. Type footnotes single spaced at the bottom of the page, on a separate sheet, or, preferably, insert them in this manner immediately after the reference in the text but separated from the text by solid lines:

---

[1]James R. Meehan, Mary Ellen Oliverio, and William R. Pasewark, <u>Secretarial Office Procedures</u> (8th ed.; Cincinnati: South-Western Publishing Co., 1972), p. 152.

---

10. Keep all rough drafts in a file folder until the final draft has been approved. Your employer may decide to include words, phrases, and sentences deleted from previous drafts in the final draft of his report.

Illus. 5-3
Technical projects often require preliminary work prior to making a report.

National Cash Register Company

Proofreaders' Marks

Proofreaders' marks are used to indicate corrections and revisions in rough drafts of business reports because they are clearly understood and easily followed. Their use greatly reduces the chance of error in the retyping of a draft. Standard proofreaders' marks, as they are indicated in a rough draft and corrected in the text, are shown below. You will need to know their meanings to type rough drafts of business documents efficiently.

Typing the Report

The final draft of a business report should be typed on white bond paper (8½" x 11" in size) of good quality, preferably of 20-pound substance. The body of the report, except for footnotes and long quotations, should be double-spaced. The report should be typed so that it is attractive and easy to read. The typing line should be 6 to 6½ inches long: 60–65 pica spaces or 72–78 elite type spaces.

PROOFREADERS' MARKS

Mark in Margin	Meaning of Mark	Correction or Change Marked in Text	Corrected or Changed Copy
∧	caret; indicates insertion is to be made	If you are interested ∧ we	If you are interested, we
⌒	close up	on the pay roll	on the payroll
≡ or caps	capitalize	Mutual life of New York	Mutual Life of New York
¶	new paragraph	two or more lines. ¶ One caution	two or more lines. One caution
]	move to right	centered over the]columns and then typed	centered over the columns and then typed
[	move to left	cc: Joseph H. Morrow [Gerald A. Porter [Allen A. Smith	cc: Joseph H. Morrow Gerald A. Porter Allen A. Smith
tr or ∽	transpose	monthly be∽fits	monthly benefits
ℐ	take out; delete	We wished you	We wish you
stet	leave it as it was originally	commencing starting next month	starting next month

Illus. 5-4 Proofreaders' marks

Part 1 / Preparing Business Reports

The margins for typed reports are determined by the binding. If the following table of margins for unbound, side-bound, and top-bound reports is carefully followed, the report will be attractive.

MARGINS FOR TYPING BUSINESS REPORTS

Margins	Unbound	Side Bound	Top Bound
Top margin			
First page	2 inches	2 inches	2½ inches
All other pages	1 inch	1 inch	1½ inches
Side margins			
Left	1 inch	1½ inches	1 inch
Right	1 inch	1 inch	1 inch
Bottom margin	1 inch	1 inch	1 inch

Illus. 5-5

Illus. 5-6
Rough draft report with proofreaders' marks

```
                    CHAPTER 11  III
                    PROPOSED SYSTEM IN PRINCIPLE

                                  outlined
    stet        The system discussed below would eliminate the need for
             all punched card installations in any of the branch offices.
     ͜       This would virtually eliminate the need for over time during
             the peak season.  It would also provide weekly reports of the
             expenses and remaining balances in all branches.  An improved
             method for planning and controlling the work is outlined to
    caps ¶   enable the computer center to handle this system. ¶Savings
             under the proposed system are estimated at about $26,000
             annually.  The system anticipates continued growth in the
         ⌐ ∧ ∧  size of Palmer Products and contemplates that∧ in the future∧
             other processing functions will be added to those now pro-
             cessed by the Computer Center.
                 The following procedures are recommended for developing
                                              obtaining
    stet     branch office budgets, for ordering all goods and services,
             for processing payments, and for preparing budgetary reports.
             The Budget Office would consolidate all funds for each branch
     tr      office, regardless of the source, into single line amounts for
             each of the various items in order to facilitate control over
             expenditures.  The line items would differ among branches,
             depending on what the largest items were.  Many branches,
                                                 ∧
      ⌒      however, would require most of the following line items:
             personal services, supplies,
```

Unit 5 / Secretarial Typewriting

A light pencil mark about 1½" from the bottom edge of the page will alert you that you have but one line left to type at the bottom of the page. Be sure to erase this pencil mark when you are proofreading your final copy.

It may be helpful to use a guide sheet such as the illustration below. On a plain sheet of paper, make rulings with very dark ink to show the left and right margins. Numbering the horizontal lines on the right edge of the page is useful in allowing space for footnotes. The guide sheet is placed behind the original copy in the typewriter and followed for proper placement.

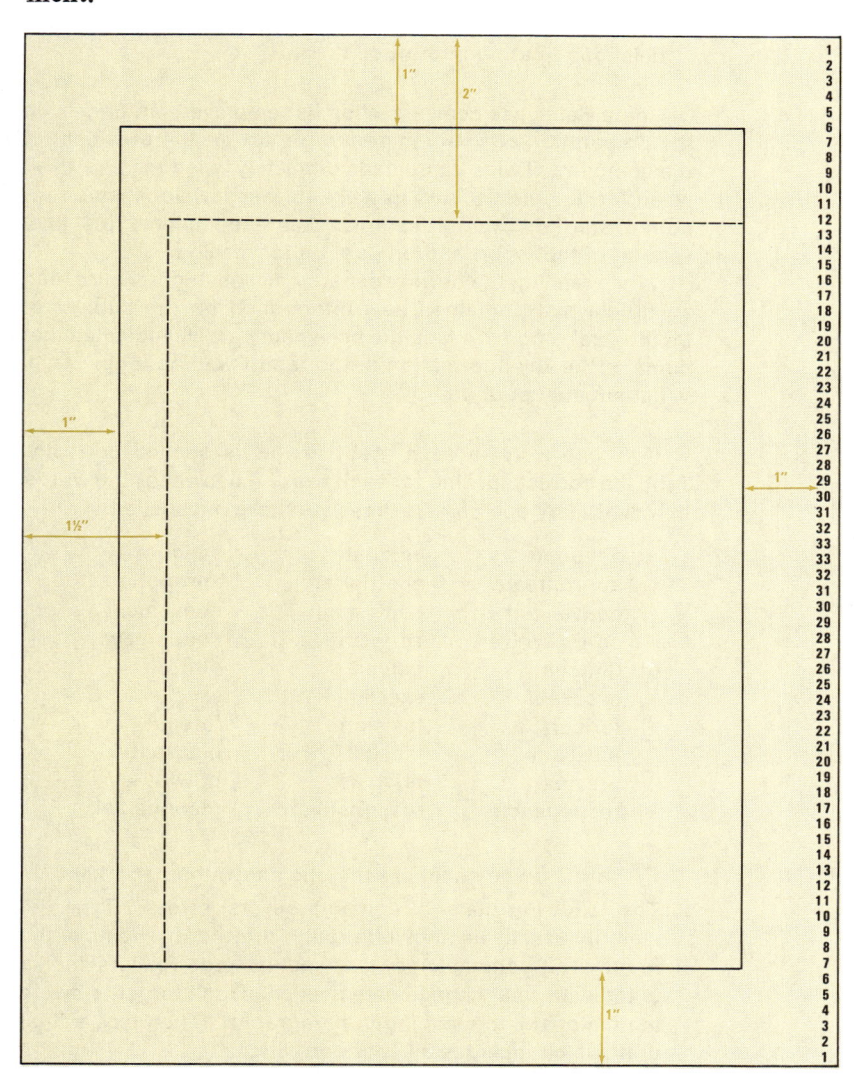

Illus. 5-7
Guide sheet for reports

QUESTIONS

1. What are a secretary's responsibilities in the preparation of business reports and manuscripts?
2. What is the difference between preparing an outline in sentence form and preparing one in topical form?
3. What are the advantages of using proofreaders' marks to show corrections in reports and manuscripts?
4. What determines the margins of typed reports?
5. How can a guide sheet help you in typing a report?

JUDGMENT

1. What advantage does a written report have over direct oral communication?
2. Why is a secretary permitted to *X* out typing errors and deletions in a rough draft of a report?

PERSONAL QUALITIES

Laura Bates has been assisting her employer, Mr. Engels, in the preparation of a very important report for the president of the company. Twice Laura had completely typed the final draft when Mr. Engels decided to make further revisions which required starting over. Yesterday Laura completed the final version of the report and prepared it for mailing.

While reading the newspaper at home last night, Laura read an article that contained new information on the subject of Mr. Engels' report. In fact, the newspaper article indicated that some of the key information in the report was no longer true. What should Laura do?

LANGUAGE USAGE

Only one word in each group below is spelled correctly. Type the correct spelling for each word. Then check the words in a dictionary and correct those you have misspelled.

adequate	adiquate	adequat
appropreate	appropriate	aproppriate
conveneint	conveniant	convenient
co-operative	cooperative	cooperetive
difficult	dificult	difficalt
excellant	excelent	excellent
foriegn	forreign	foreign
pleasant	plesant	pleasent
previus	privious	previous
responsable	responsible	responsibel

SECRETARIAL WORK

1. Prepare a guide sheet like the one shown on page 129.
2. The following material contains several errors. Type the material exactly as shown in rough draft form. Remove the rough draft from the typewriter and use proofreaders' marks to indicate what changes are needed. Don't forget to divide the material into meaningful paragraphs. Then type a final draft which includes all your corrections.

THE SECRETARYS' RESPONSIBILITIES FOR BUSINESS REPORTS

The secertary has many responsibilities in preparing business reports. Once her executive has decided on the subject of the report, she must aid him in gathering facts. In order to gather all the neccessary information she must know how to use the library. Some sources she should check is newspapers, periodicles, and books on that particular subject. After her employer has developed the first draft of the report she must edit it with care. This cannot be done with out a dictionery. When she is ready to type the final draft the secretary should gather all of the supplys she will need. She will need a high quality paper for the original and a lower quality paper for any carbon copies. The carbon paper she uses will depend on her typewriter and the number of copeis to be made. Great care must be taken with her typewriter to be sure that the keys are clean and that it has a new ribbon. Careful erasing is a must. No one should be able to tell that a corection has been made. If the carbon copies are to be sent outside the office corrections on them should also be made with care. The completed report should be proofread with care. No uncorrected errors can be permited in the finished report. This may mean retyping different pages or even the entire report but the effort will be worthwhile. The completed report must be a work of which both the secretary and her employer can be proud.

PART 2 PARTS OF BUSINESS REPORTS

Jan Allison, the secretary to Mr. David R. Singer, devotes a large part of her day to working on business reports. After being with the firm of Michaels, Singer & Smith for only a short time, Jan realized that all business reports can be divided into several particular parts. Although each part serves a different purpose, each is important. Jan knows that if a business report is to be effective the information must be gathered carefully, it must be logically presented, and it must be accurately and attractively typed.

PARTS OF A REPORT

A long and detailed business report may contain a dozen, more or less, specific parts which are classified under three main headings: the introductory parts, the body of the report, and the supplementary parts. Before binding, they are arranged in this order:

A. Introductory Parts
1. Cover
2. Title page
3. Preface or letter of transmittal
4. Table of contents
5. List of tables, charts, and illustrations
6. Summary

B. Body of the Report
1. Introduction
2. Main body or text
3. Conclusions and recommendations

C. Supplementary Parts
1. Appendix
2. Bibliography
3. Index

The body of the report must be developed first; so it is usually typed first. Then the supplementary parts and the introductory parts of the report are typed.

The Cover

The cover should contain this information: the title of the report, the name of the person submitting it, and the date it was submitted.

The Title Page

The items of information that usually appear on the title page are the title of the report, the name of the author, the date, and the place of preparation. Sometimes reports include the name of the person (with his title) for whom the report was prepared.

```
              DATA PROCESSING OPERATIONS
                 PALMER PRODUCTS, INC.




                           For
             William L. Henderson, Vice-President






                           By
                 Michaels, Singer & Smith
                  Management Consultants
                     708 Market Street
                 San Francisco, CA  94102
                       415-621-6693


                    November 14, 197-
```

Illus. 5-8
Title page of a report

Part 2 / Parts of Business Reports 133

Numbering Pages

Small Roman numerals (ii, iii, iv, etc.) are used to number the pages of the introductory parts of the report. The title page is considered as page "i" but no number is typed on it. The numbers are centered and typed one-half inch from the bottom of the page, and they are not followed by periods or any other punctuation.

Arabic numerals, without punctuation, are used to number the pages in the rest of the report. They begin with "1" and run consecutively throughout the report. The number on the first page of each section is centered and typed one-half inch from the bottom of the page. The pages that follow are numbered one-half inch from the top and even with the right margin. If the report is to be top bound, all page numbers are placed at the bottom of the page.

It is wise to number all pages at the same time after the entire report has been typed. If you type the numbers on the pages as you type the report and a rather long change has to be made, you will then have to renumber all pages following the change. Before page numbers are typed, they can be written in pencil on the first carbon copy, which will assist in keeping the pages in numerical order.

Headings

You will choose from several types of headings to improve the appearance of the typed matter and to indicate the relationship of its parts. Headings make a report easier to read and understand. If the material is well organized, the headings and subheadings will serve as a basic outline for the report.

Main Headings. Main headings are usually centered on the page and typed in all capital letters. A main heading is normally followed by a triple space.

Subheadings. There are basically two kinds of subheadings — side headings and paragraph headings.

Side Headings. Side headings are used to indicate major divisions of the main topic. They are typed even with the left margin with the main words starting with a capital letter. Side headings are followed by a double space. They may also be underlined.

Paragraph Headings. If the copy needs to be divided further, paragraph headings may be used. Paragraph headings are indented and underlined. Usually the main words of the heading are capitalized, and the heading is followed by a period.

> CHAPTER VIII
>
> FINANCIAL IMPLICATIONS
>
> The proposed changes in the data processing system would result in substantial financial savings. An initial outlay of $6,500 would be required to get the proper equipment needed to perform all the functions of the consolidated operation. In spite of the initial outlay, however, it is estimated that the proposed system will save about $26,000 annually.
>
> Projected Savings
>
> By consolidating the data processing operations in the home office and eliminating the punched card installations in the branch offices, cost savings will accrue in many areas. The major areas where cost savings can be expected are equipment rentals, personnel, mailing, floor space, and storage.
>
> <u>Equipment Rentals</u>. At the present time, each of the five branch offices is equipped with four punched card machines. The annual cost of renting each of these machines is $960. Since these machines would not be utilized in the proposed system, the gross annual savings in rental cost would be $19,200.

Illus. 5-9
A typed page of a report with headings and subheadings

Preface or Letter of Transmittal

The purpose of the preface or letter of transmittal, illustrated on page 136, is to interest the reader and encourage him to read the entire report. The preface or letter of transmittal is written in a less formal and more personal style than the body of the report.

The preface or letter of transmittal usually will contain the following information:

1. The name of the person or organization that asked that the report be prepared.
2. The main purpose of the report.
3. The scope, or extent of coverage, of the report.
4. Acknowledgments of assistance in the preparation of the report.

Illus. 5-10

MICHAELS, SINGER & SMITH

708 Market Street   Management Consultants

San Francisco, CA 94102   415-621-6693

November 14, 197-

Mr. William L. Henderson
Vice-President
Palmer Products, Inc.
555 Madison Avenue
New York, NY 10022

Dear Mr. Henderson

Accompanying this letter is the report covering our study of data processing operations at Palmer Products, Inc. The report proposes a new data processing system for your firm--first in principle and then in detail-- and suggests a plan of action.

The system proposed would eliminate the need for a punched card installation in any of your branch offices and would provide you with weekly reports of the expenditures and remaining funds in all your branches.

We estimate that annual savings of $26,000 would result from installing a new system. An initial outlay, however, of about $6,500 would be required for the new equipment which we are recommending.

We were materially assisted in our study by the cooperation of your staff and the others we interviewed. We would be pleased to discuss the contents of this report with you after you have had an opportunity to review it.

Sincerely yours

David R. Singer

David R. Singer

rkm

Letter of transmittal

TABLE OF CONTENTS

	Page
Letter of Transmittal..................	ii
Table of Contents.....................	iii
List of Tables	iv
Summary...............................	v

Chapter

I.	Introduction.......................	1
II.	Present Data Processing Activities..	5
III.	Proposed System in Principle........	11
IV.	Staffing Recommendations............	16
V.	Equipment Recommendations...........	20
VI.	Other Mechanized Operations.........	24
VII.	Plan of Action......................	28
VIII.	Financial Implications..............	33
IX.	Conclusions and Recommendations.....	38
	Bibliography........................	45

Table of contents

If a separate summary is not included in the report, usually it is included in the letter.

Table of Contents

The table of contents, shown on page 136, gives an overview of the material covered in the report by listing the main topics or chapter titles with their page numbers. The heading, *Table of Contents*, should be centered two inches from the top of the page and typed entirely in capital letters. Double spacing is used before the titles of chapters or main topics, and single spacing in all other instances. All important words in the chapter or main topic title should be capitalized. Each chapter should be preceded by its number which is typed in Roman numerals and followed by a period and two spaces. The Roman numerals should be lined up with the periods directly beneath each other. Leaders (periods and spaces alternated) should extend across the page from each title to guide the reader in finding the page number at the right.

The periods in the leaders should be in vertical alignment also. This can be done easily by typing all periods at even numbers on the typewriter line scale. Before it is finally typed, the table of contents should be checked for correctness of titles and accuracy of page numbers.

List of Tables

The heading *List of Tables*, like all other main headings, is centered two inches from the top of the page and typed entirely in capital letters. The table numbers are typed in Arabic numerals followed by a period and two spaces. The first letter of every important word in the title of a table is typed with a capital letter. Leaders extend from the title to the Arabic page numbers at the right. Lists of charts and other illustrations are typed in the same form as the *List of Tables*.

Summary

The summary of the report is written after the entire report is completed. It gives the reader a quick overview that saves his time and makes it easier for him to understand the detailed statements contained in the body of the report.

Body of the Report

The division headings in the body of the report should be the same as the titles that appear in the table of contents. Each division should begin on a new page with the word *Chapter* or *Section* centered two inches from the top of the page. It should be typed entirely in capital letters and followed by a chapter or section number typed in large Roman numerals. The title of the chapter or section is centered two line spaces below and also typed in capital letters. A very long title should be broken into two or more lines and divided at the point where the thought in the title changes. With a long title the inverted pyramid style may be used — the top line longer than the second, and the second line longer than the third. Three line spaces should be left between the title and the first paragraph of the report.

Quoted Material

Material from other sources is frequently quoted in a business report to increase the effectiveness of the writer's point of view. All direct quotations should be typed exactly as they are written in the quoted source — in wording, spelling, punctuation, and paragraphing.

1. A brief quotation of fewer than four lines is typed in the text and enclosed with quotation marks.
2. A quotation of four lines or more is started on a new line and typed on shorter, single-spaced lines — indented from both the left and right margins. No quotation marks are used.
3. A quotation of several paragraphs need not be indented, but a quotation mark should precede each paragraph and should follow the final word of the last quoted paragraph.
4. A quotation within a quotation (an inside quotation) is enclosed with single quotation marks. The apostrophe is usually used to indicate a single quotation in typed material.
5. Omissions in a quotation are shown by typing an ellipsis — three spaced periods for an omission within a sentence or between sentences, four periods for an omission at the end of a sentence.

Permission should be obtained to quote copyrighted material if it is to be widely distributed in duplicated reports or printed manuscripts. Material may be quoted from government publications without permission.

Footnotes

Footnotes refer the reader to information outside the text of a report. They are inserted to acknowledge and identify the source of the quoted information, to support points made by the author, to provide additional material for the reader, or to elaborate on the meaning within

> CHAPTER III
> PROPOSED SYSTEM IN PRINCIPLE
>
> The system outlined below would eliminate the need for all punched card installations in any of the branch offices. This would virtually eliminate the need for overtime during the peak season. It would also provide weekly reports of the expenses and remaining balances in all branches. An improved method for planning and controlling the work is outlined to enable the Computer Center to handle this system.
>
> Savings under the proposed system are estimated at about $26,000 annually. The system anticipates continued growth in the size of Palmer Products and contemplates that, in the future, other processing functions will be added to those now processed by the Computer Center.
>
> The following procedures are recommended for developing branch office budgets, for ordering all goods and services, for processing payments, and for preparing budgetary reports. The Budget Office would consolidate all funds for each branch office, regardless of the source, into single line amounts for each of the various items in order to facilitate control over expenditures. The line items would differ among branches, depending on what the largest expense items were. Many branches, however, would require the following line items: personal services, supplies,

Illus. 5-11 A typed page of a report

the text. The Arabic number of a footnote is typed in the text just after the statement to be documented but slightly above the line of writing. For raised numbers, the platen is turned toward the typist a half space before the number is typed. The footnote itself, if it is the first reference to a particular work, should identify the author and the title of the work referred to, give facts about the publication of the work and the copyright date, and cite a specific page reference.

Later references to the same source need not repeat all these details; only *ibid.*, the abbreviation for *ibidem* (meaning in the same place), and the page number are used when references to the same work follow each other. The author's name, *op. cit.*, the abbreviation for *opere citato* (meaning in the work cited), and the page number are used when a previous reference has been made to the same source but other references are between. The author's name and *loc. cit.*, the abbreviation for *loco citato* (meaning in the same place), are used to refer to the same passage in a reference previously cited.

The footnotes below show the use of *ibid.*, *op. cit.*, and *loc. cit.*

---

[1]H. Webster Johnson, How to Use the Business Library (3rd ed.; Cincinnati: South-Western Publishing Co., 1964), p. 148.

[2]Robert R. Aurner and Paul S. Burtness, Effective English for Business Communications (6th ed.; Cincinnati: South-Western Publishing Co., 1970), pp. 537-592.

[3]Ibid., p. 646.

[4]Johnson, op. cit., pp. 142-146.

[5]Aurner and Burtness, loc. cit.

Footnotes should be typed according to the following guides:

1. They are separated from the text by a short, solid horizontal line of 15 pica or 18 elite spaces typed with the underscore key a line below the last line of the text.
2. The first line of the first footnote is typed two lines below the short horizontal line. It is indented the same number of spaces as the paragraphs in the report. The succeeding lines of the footnote begin at the left margin.
3. The reference number, which corresponds with the footnote number in the text, is also typed slightly above the line of writing. It is typed without punctuation or a space between it and the first word of the footnote.
4. All footnotes are typed single space. A double space is used between footnotes.
5. Footnotes are usually numbered in sequence on each page throughout a report or manuscript.

Conclusions and Recommendations

The conclusions are the results of what has been presented in the report. The recommendations contain the writer's suggestions about action that should be taken as a result of the conclusions.

Appendix

The text of a long report or a manuscript may be followed by an appendix; it is omitted in a short report. It usually contains extra reference material not easily included in the text. The appendix may also include tables containing complete original data, general reference tables, and other materials which will help to interpret and to add interest in the report.

Bibliography

All documentary sources (written material) referred to in a business report — books, articles, and periodicals — should be included in the bibliography. It should also include all the references consulted which had worthwhile information related to the report. The references listed in the bibliography should be arranged in alphabetical order by authors, by editors, or by titles if the authors' names are not available. Examples of references in a bibliography follow:

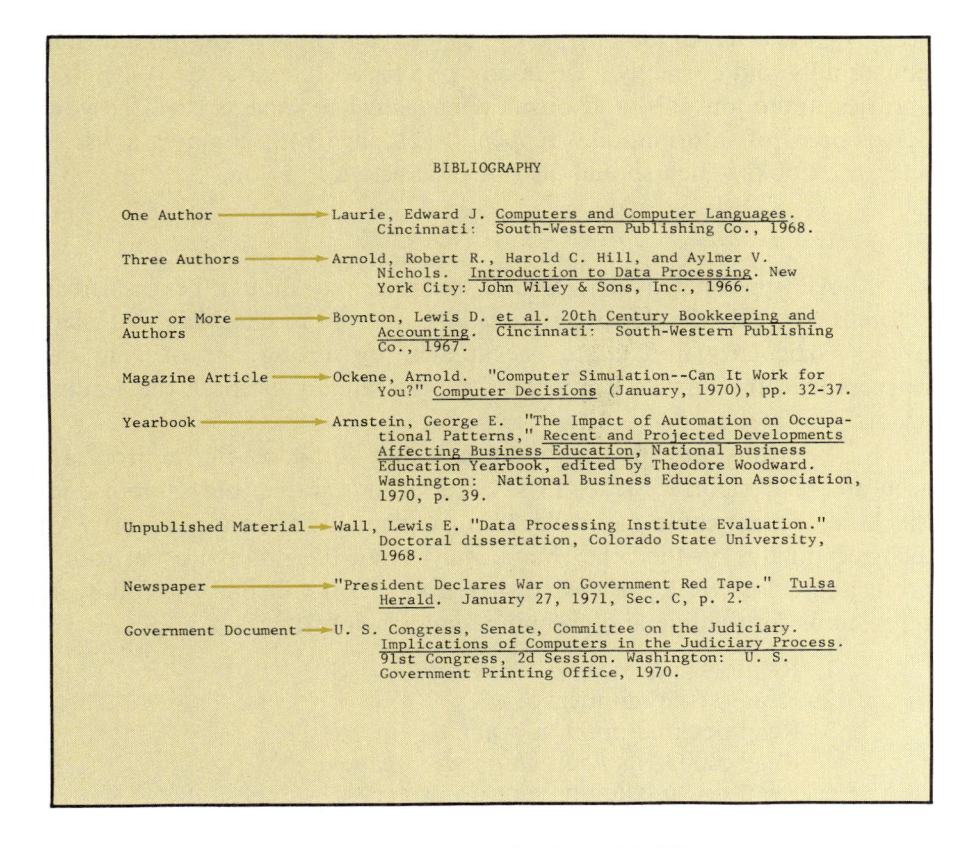

```
                        BIBLIOGRAPHY

One Author ─────────► Laurie, Edward J. Computers and Computer Languages.
                        Cincinnati: South-Western Publishing Co., 1968.

Three Authors ──────► Arnold, Robert R., Harold C. Hill, and Aylmer V.
                        Nichols. Introduction to Data Processing. New
                        York City: John Wiley & Sons, Inc., 1966.

Four or More ───────► Boynton, Lewis D. et al. 20th Century Bookkeeping and
Authors                 Accounting. Cincinnati: South-Western Publishing
                        Co., 1967.

Magazine Article ───► Ockene, Arnold. "Computer Simulation--Can It Work for
                        You?" Computer Decisions (January, 1970), pp. 32-37.

Yearbook ───────────► Arnstein, George E. "The Impact of Automation on Occupa-
                        tional Patterns," Recent and Projected Developments
                        Affecting Business Education, National Business
                        Education Yearbook, edited by Theodore Woodward.
                        Washington: National Business Education Association,
                        1970, p. 39.

Unpublished Material► Wall, Lewis E. "Data Processing Institute Evaluation."
                        Doctoral dissertation, Colorado State University,
                        1968.

Newspaper ──────────► "President Declares War on Government Red Tape." Tulsa
                        Herald. January 27, 1971, Sec. C, p. 2.

Government Document► U. S. Congress, Senate, Committee on the Judiciary.
                        Implications of Computers in the Judiciary Process.
                        91st Congress, 2d Session. Washington: U. S.
                        Government Printing Office, 1970.
```

Illus. 5-12   Examples of bibliographical forms

GATHERING INFORMATION

Your employer may not have all the information that is needed to complete either the footnotes or the bibliography. He may have only a little information to give you such as, "I think the title of the book is *Business Organization and Management* and the author is Tyler, but I'm not sure." Of course, he may not remember the author's first name or even how to spell his name. As for the newspaper article he referred to, all he may remember is that it was in the *Times* last week. The rest is up to you.

There is even more to it than that. Very often in quoting material your employer may not correctly remember each word; he may not have the exact statistics, nor the dates. This, too, is your responsibility. After checking the original sources, you make the changes that are necessary without annoying your employer with such details.

You may have to check reference books such as the *Reader's Guide to Periodical Literature*, *The New York Times Index*, and *The World Almanac*. In compiling reports or writing manuscripts, you will need to know what to look for, where to look, and how to get the information rapidly and correctly. Company purchased reference books, public libraries, trade journals, and business and local newspapers will be your best sources of information. Appendix G, page 648, contains a list of reference books which should also be of assistance to you.

PROOFREADING

All typewritten reports and manuscripts should be proofread before they are duplicated or printed. The text can be checked most effectively, particularly if it contains statistics, by having one of your co-workers read the original copy aloud to you while you check the reading against the final copy.

You must also be absolutely sure that all figures in the proof are accurate. An incorrect letter in a word is undesirable, but seldom does this kind of error cause the reader to misunderstand the entire report. An incorrect figure, on the other hand, may mean the difference between a profit and a loss on a business transaction. You will find the following suggestions for reading and checking figures helpful:

1. Read 2948 as *two nine four eight*.
2. Read 0 (the number) as *oh*.
3. Read decimal point as *point*.
4. Read .00032 as *point oh oh oh three two*.
5. Read down columns, not up or across.
6. Verify totals by addition. This is a double check on the original and on the copy.

The names of persons, places, and other proper nouns should be spelled by the reader, at least the first time that they appear in the copy, in order to avoid errors.

QUESTIONS

1. What are the three main parts of a business report?
2. List the items of information usually given on the title page of a report.
3. Give the two kinds of numerals used to number the pages of a report or a manuscript, and indicate where each kind is used.
4. What is the purpose of a letter of transmittal?
5. Why is the summary of a report placed after the table of contents and before the body of the report?
6. Why are materials from other sources quoted in business reports and manuscripts?
7. What information is contained in a footnote?

JUDGMENT

1. Discuss the reference books and handbooks that you might use to aid you in editing a rough draft for content, wording, and sentence structure.
2. Why are footnotes sometimes used in a business report?
3. Why would a bibliography be included in a report?
4. What is the purpose of proofreading? Give three suggestions for proofreading figures.

PERSONAL QUALITIES

Barbara is a part-time employee working at Mr. Jones's office during the summer. It is time for the Monthly Production Report to be typed, and Mr. Jones has given Barbara the necessary information to complete the final copy. Barbara is uncertain about the style she is to use.

What action should Barbara take before attempting to type the final report?

LANGUAGE USAGE

Four easy rules must be kept in mind if you are to use question marks correctly.

A. A question mark follows a direct question — a period an indirect question, usually introduced by *whether* or *if*.

Examples: Is the Table of Contents typed?
He asked if the Table of Contents had been typed.

B. In a series, if emphasis is desired, a question mark may follow each question.

Example: Where is the Preface? the Table of Contents? the List of Tables? the Appendix?

C. A question mark may be used inside parentheses to indicate doubt.

   Example: The report will be sent to the president, the treasurer, the secretary(?), the sales manager, and four salesmen.

D. A question mark is placed inside or outside the second quotation mark, depending on content.

   Examples: The employer asked, "Who typed the material on research and development?"
   Who typed "Research and Development"?

Type the following sentences on a separate sheet of paper and insert question marks where necessary. Supply any other punctuation marks that are needed.

1. The new secretary asked whether she should place the date on the title page of the report.
2. What happened to the cover the summary the conclusions the bibliography.
3. The treasurer then said who prepared the sales figures for the month of March.
4. The sales manager reported that 1957, 1963, 1967, and 1698 had been the company's best years.
5. Who typed the "Summary of Last Ten Years of Operations."
6. The president asked if you must leave early who will finish this job.
7. Was the footnote placed correctly on the page she asked the new employee.
8. When business reports quote material from other sources should quotation marks be used.
9. Was the information accurate her employer questioned before he read the report.
10. If I should leave early Mary said who will prepare the monthly production report.

SECRETARIAL WORK

1. Type the following five items of information in the form of a title page for a report:
   (a) Title: RESEARCH REPORT ON NEW PRODUCTS AND DEVELOPMENTS.
   (b) For: Thomas B. Carleton, President of the Smith Paper Company
   (c) By: Walter A. Starr, Director of Research and Development
   (d) At: Chester, Pennsylvania
   (e) On: November 30, 197–

2. Type the following TABLE OF CONTENTS with appropriate margins on a single page:

	Page
Letter of Transmittal	ii
Table of Contents	iii
List of Tables	iv
List of Charts	v

Chapter

I.	Introduction	1
	Prices	2
	Outlook	3
	Earnings and Dividends	4
	Employment	5
II.	Directors and Officers	6
III.	Statement of Earnings	7
IV.	Balance Sheet	8
V.	Comparative Balance Sheets	9
VI.	Accountants' Certificate	10
VII.	Property, Plant, and Equipment	11
VIII.	Inventories and Investments	13
IX.	Disposition of Income	15
X.	Research and Development	16

3. Type the following paragraphs in manuscript form with indented paragraph headings.

   Incorporating an Established Business. Owners of sole proprietorships or persons doing business as a partnership may wish to incorporate the business and continue its operations as a corporation. In such a case, the same type of information is provided in the application for a charter as that provided when a corporation is formed to promote a new business. Each subscriber to the capital stock of the corporation indicates on the subscription list the number of shares of stock subscribed and the method of paying the subscription when the charter has been granted. The owner or owners of the established business usually take stock in payment for their interest in the business.

   Goodwill. Frequently the incorporators of a corporation being formed to continue the operations of an established business will agree to pay the owner of the established business more than the value of his proprietary interest in the assets of the business as shown by the balance sheet. This excess value is known as goodwill. The incorporators agree to pay more for the assets of the business than the owner's proprietary interest because the owner has an established trade, and the customers he has served will continue as customers of the corporation.

4. Type the following letter of transmittal in block form with open punctuation (current date):

   Mr. Thomas B. Carleton President Smith Paper Company Chester, Pennsylvania 12055 Dear Mr. Carleton (¶1) The report which accompanies this letter covers the research on new products and the development of new markets for the Smith Paper Company. (¶2) Our employees made dramatic progress last year in developing new products and new markets which will contribute importantly to the Company's future growth. Some of the new products are shown elsewhere in this report; still others — not yet ready for the market — are in various stages of development. Our research and development expenses for last year were almost 25 percent greater than the previous year. After very careful study of the long-range opportunities open to us through research in the physical sciences and in marketing — as well as gains to be made in mechanical development — we think it is safe to say that our total budgets for these important activities will probably be increased by as much as 50 percent over the next three years. (¶3) Smith employees at all levels are committed to a policy of improving the quality of our products and continuing the war against waste and inefficiency in every form. The credit for what we consider to be a truly remarkable achievement in research and development by the Smith Paper Company belongs not only to the Research Division but to all the men and women employed by the Company. Sincerely yours Walter A. Starr Director of Research and Development

5. Type the following page from an annual report to the stockholders. The page is to be typed double space with margins set for binding at the side. The heading is *Research and Development*.

    The Corporation's long-standing emphasis on research and development continues to be directed to new products, to improved products, and to more economical processes and equipment. These activities, located at Yorktown Heights, New York, are conducted to assure the future success of the Corporation. The organization is composed of separate groups with personnel well trained in scientific fields related to the Corporation's business, that is, in chemistry, in physics, in engineering, and in textile technology. Each group has adequate up-to-date facilities and equipment to do modern research in fields of expanding technology. (¶) The combination of the various technical talents at one location enables groups to conduct coordinated research on new fibers and packaging films — and basic or exploratory research directed toward the discovery of new products. Through research the competitive position of fiberglass tires has been improved by developing a method of processing fiberglass so that it is flexible and strong. As a result of this development, passenger car tires have been made even more durable under difficult road conditions.

PART 3 FINANCIAL STATEMENTS AND REPORTS

As one of three secretaries at Standard Products, during the last ten months Jennifer Craig has had the opportunity to perform many different kinds of secretarial tasks. She has appreciated this opportunity since she realizes that, through new experiences with increasingly difficult tasks, she can grow in her job. Also, she enjoys the challenge of new and more important work. Today her boss, Mr. Howard Jackson, laid some rough draft accounting reports on her desk and said: "Jennifer, you've been doing quite well on the statistical material I have given you to type. Do you think you can do as well on financial statements?" Noticing Jennifer's anxious expression, Mr. Jackson said, "Mary probably has typed many of these reports, since she has worked in an accounting office. Get her to give you some of the details. These reports are important; so take your time and make sure they are accurate!"

If we tuned in on Jennifer's thoughts after Mr. Jackson left her desk, we would probably notice her thinking through such comments as these: What is this income statement? And this balance sheet? Why are they so important? I know how to plan for tabulations. What else do I need to know so that I can type these reports to please Mr. Jackson?

UNDERSTANDING FINANCIAL STATEMENTS

A business, like an individual, at times, needs a checkup. An individual reports to his family doctor to get a check on his physical condition. After examining the patient thoroughly, the doctor analyzes his findings and locates the cause of any physical problem the patient may have. The doctor is then able to prescribe medication for the problem.

Those who manage a business can discover the financial health of a business by studying reports called *financial statements*. The two reports common to all types of businesses which furnish the information necessary for management to determine the financial health of a business are the *balance sheet* and the *income statement*.

Balance Sheet

A balance sheet, like a physical examination, reveals whether a business is healthy on a particular date. Analysis of the three main parts shown in the balance sheet on page 150 enables management to tell whether, on a specific date, the business is well or sick. These three parts are (1) *assets* (what the business owns), (2) *liabilities* (what the business owes), and (3) *proprietorship* (the owner's share of the business). The proprietorship part tells what the business is worth, or assets minus liabilities.

On every balance sheet, the total assets always equal the total liabilities plus the proprietorship ($A = L + P$). The form of the balance sheet should make this basic bookkeeping equation obvious to the reader. Double lines typed beneath the figure representing *Total Assets* and beneath the figure representing *Total Liabilities and Proprietorship* attract the reader's attention so that he can see at a glance that the figures are equal.

Income Statement

The income statement shows the financial progress of the business. It shows how successful, or unsuccessful, a business has been during the period stated in the heading of the report: for example, "For the Year Ended December 31, 197–." Success is measured in terms of net income, or net profit. A *net profit* results when the income is greater than the expenses. A *net loss* occurs when the opposite happens.

Below the heading, the income statement shows in convenient form the income of the business, the cost of merchandise sold, the expenses, and the net income, or net loss, that resulted from the operation of the business during the fiscal period. The *fiscal period* is the time covered by the financial statement.

Some employers require that income statements include a column to show the percentage that each item listed is of net sales. For example, the income statement on page 151 shows that Merchandise Inventory, January 1, is 10 percent of sales; that Gross Profit is 13.9 percent; and that Net Income after Deducting Federal Income Taxes is 1.4 percent.

The double lines beneath the last dollar amount listed on page 151 make the Net Income after Deducting Federal Income Taxes of $28,594 immediately noticeable to the reader. Since this is the most important figure on the income statement, the emphasis is justified. By studying the remaining figures in the same column, the reader can understand why and how the profit or loss occurred. For more detailed information, the student may study the remaining columns on the report.

PRODUCING TYPEWRITTEN FINANCIAL STATEMENTS

You will have several major responsibilities in producing final copies of the financial statements. If the statements are to be correct and pleasing in appearance, careful study and planning are necessary before you begin to type.

Study Previous Reports

Before you type any financial statements for your employer, it is a good idea to examine earlier copies of income statements and balance sheets in the company files. Because businessmen compare new financial statements with previous ones, they usually prefer that the same general form be followed year after year.

Check Accuracy of Calculations

With a calculating machine, check to make sure that the addition and subtraction shown on the rough draft submitted for typing are correct. It is also wise to verify, by machine, the accuracy of the addition and subtraction of the figures typed on the final typewritten product. This checks the typing accuracy of numbers.

Illus. 5-13
Careful study and planning are necessary to produce correct and attractive financial statements.

National Cash Register Company

Part 3 / Financial Statements and Reports

STANDARD PRODUCTS
Balance Sheet
December 31, 197-

Assets

Current Assets:
Cash...............................		$ 31,534
Notes Receivable...................		26,120
Accounts Receivable................	$96,500	
Less Allowance for Bad Debts....	1,900	94,600
Merchandise Inventory..............		232,600
Store Supplies.....................		4,817
Office Supplies....................		154
Prepaid Insurance..................		209
Total Current Assets...............		

Total Current Assets: $390,034

Fixed Assets:
Store Equipment....................	$27,000	
Less Allow. for Depr.--Store Equip.	8,860	$ 18,140
Delivery Equipment.................	$20,000	
Less Allow. for Depr.--Del. Equip..	5,940	14,060
Office Equipment...................	$ 8,000	
Less Allow. for Depr.--Off. Equip..	4,200	3,800
Buildings..........................	$75,000	
Less Allow. for Depr.--Buildings...	21,600	53,400
Land...............................		20,000
Total Fixed Assets.................		109,400

Total Assets.......................... $499,434

Liabilities

Current Liabilities:
Notes Payable......................	$ 40,900
Accounts Payable...................	71,614
Employees Income Taxes Payable.....	1,490
FICA Taxes Payable.................	435
State Unemployment Taxes Payable...	147
Federal Unemployment Taxes Payable.	930
Federal Income Taxes Payable.......	19,518

Total Current Liabilities............ $135,034

Long-Term Liabilities:
  Mortgage Payable (20-year, 5%)......   65,000

Total Liabilities.................... $200,034

Proprietorship

Capital Stock......................	$250,000
Retained Earnings..................	49,400
Total Proprietorship...............	299,400
Total Liabilities and Proprietorship.....	$499,434

Illus. 5-14   A balance sheet

STANDARD PRODUCTS
Income Statement
For Year Ended December 31, 197-

				% of Net Sales
Income from Sales:				
Sales...		$2,111,755		100.6
Less: Sales Returns and Allowances......	$ 5,642			
Discount on Sales.................	6,113	11,755		.6
Net Sales...............................			$2,100,000	100.0
Cost of Merchandise Sold:				
Merchandise Inventory, January 1, 197-..		$ 209,800		10.0
Purchases............................	$2,288,650			
Less: Purchases Ret. & Allow....$152,900				
Discount on Purchases..... 304,850	457,750			
Net Purchases........................		1,830,900		87.2
Cost of Merchandise Available for Sale..		$2,040,700		97.2
Less Merchandise Inventory, Dec. 31,197-		232,600		11.1
Cost of Merchandise Sold..............			1,808,100	86.1
Gross Profit on Sales....................			$ 291,900	13.9
Operating Expenses:				
Selling Expenses:				
Delivery Expense.......................	$ 20,573			1.0
Depreciation of Delivery Equipment....	4,813			.2
Depreciation of Store Equipment.......	2,420			.1
Miscellaneous Selling Expense.........	6,294			.3
Sales Salary Expense..................	112,894			5.4
Store Supplies Expense................	15,117			.7
Total Selling Expenses...............		$ 162,111		7.7
Administrative Expenses:				
Bad Debts Expense.....................	$ 1,100			.1
Depreciation of Buildings.............	3,000			.1
Depreciation of Office Equipment......	932			*
FICA Taxes............................	5,800			.3
Federal Unemployment Taxes............	930			*
Insurance Expense.....................	2,037			.1
Miscellaneous Administrative Expense..	3,195			.2
Office Salary Expense.................	58,403			2.8
Office Supplies Expense...............	1,951			.1
State Unemployment Taxes..............	3,139			.1
Total Administrative Expenses.........		80,487		3.8
Total Operating Expenses..................			242,598	11.6
Net Income from Operations...............			$ 49,302	2.3
Other Income:				
Interest Income........................		$ 940		*
Other Expense:				
Interest Expense.......................		2,130		.1
Net Subtraction...........................			1,190	.1
Net Income before Deducting Federal Income Taxes			$ 48,112	2.3
Less Federal Income Taxes.................			19,518	.9
Net Income after Deducting Federal Income Taxes			$ 28,594	1.4

*Percent is less than .1

Illus. 5-15   An income statement

Type the Financial Statements

A look at the financial reports of several companies would show many similarities, but no doubt would reveal some minor differences in style. Points of similarity might include the following:

1. *Use of descriptive titles to introduce groups of similar accounts.* For example, in the balance sheet on page 150, assets which, during the normal course of business operations, will be converted to cash are listed under the title Current Assets. Notice that the first letter of the first word and important words in these introductory titles is capitalized.

2. *Indentations from the left to indicate subdivisions of larger units of information.* In the income statement on page 151, the depth of the horizontal indentations before Selling Expenses and Administrative Expenses indicates that both types of expenses are of equal importance; also that both are subdivisions of a larger grouping labeled Operating Expenses. The additional depth of indentation before Delivery Expense shows that it is a subdivision of Selling Expenses.

3. *Listing of important figures in the last column to the right on the financial statement.* A busy executive can get a good overview of the important parts of the balance sheet on page 150 by reading only the figures listed in the last column at the right.

4. *Use of commas in the amount columns to separate each three digits, beginning to the left of the decimal point.* For example, in the income statement on page 151, the Sales figure is $2,111,755.

5. *Vertical alignment of the decimal point in a column of figures.* Also, when one or more of the items in the amount columns indicate cents, every entry in any column should contain a decimal. For example:

$2,550.42
350.00
1,670.90
80.00

6. *A single line extending the width of the longest item in the column, typed beneath the last figure, to indicate addition or subtraction.*

7. *Double lines typed beneath a figure to identify the final figure in a column.*

8. *Use of leaders (a line of either spaced or unspaced periods) to guide the reader's eye from the explanation column to the first column of amounts.* Leaders are especially necessary when the items in the explanation column vary widely in the amount of horizontal space used or when, on single spaced copy, there is so much space between the explanation column and the first amount column that the reader may lose his place as he reads across. Leaders should be aligned vertically on either even or odd spaces on the typewriter scale and should end at the same horizontal point.

9. *Information given in the heading of the financial statement.* Answers to each of the questions, Who?, What?, When?, should be given on separate lines in that order. The balance sheet should answer the question, When?, with a specific date; the income statement will answer it with a phrase which identifies the fiscal period covered.

10. *Use of the dollar sign with the first figure listed vertically in each amount column.* In the balance sheet on page 150, notice that in the first column the Accounts Receivable figure ($96,500) includes a dollar sign. The same is true of the Cash figure ($31,534) in the second column, and the Total Current Assets figure ($390,034) in the third column. Be sure to use a dollar sign with every figure which has double lines typed directly beneath it.

The important guideline to apply for minor points of style is to *be consistent*. Apply the test of consistency when making decisions related to the following points:

1. *Vertical spacing.*

    In deciding whether to single-space or double-space within a financial statement, consider:

    (a) Length of statement relative to the amount of vertical space available. The common practice is to avoid, if possible, two-page financial statements.

    (b) Ease of reading. Those who analyze financial statements are normally top-management people who have many demands on their time, attention, and efforts. Blank vertical lines scattered among single-spaced copy attract attention; therefore, use them for emphasizing especially important figures.

2. *Capitalization*
   (a) In the heading. Some businessmen prefer that the entire heading of financial statements be typed in all capitals; others require all capitals for only the name of the business. The current trend seems to be away from the practice of using all capitals for every word in the heading of a financial statement.
   (b) In the explanation column. Common practice is to capitalize the first letter of the first word and each important word included in the explanation column. (This practice is followed in both the income statement on page 151 and the balance sheet on page 150.) However, some businessmen prefer that only the first character of an account title be capitalized: for example, Accounts payable.

3. *Colon*

   A colon following a title is used to introduce like accounts (for example, on the income statement a colon following Income from Sales:). The colon indicates that a listing follows.

4. *Indentations*

   The depth of the indentations depends on the amount of horizontal space available in relation to the number of horizontal spaces needed to type the necessary columns across the page. The important thing to remember is that units of equal importance (such as Selling Expenses and Administrative Expenses on the income statement on page 151) should be indented the same number of spaces.

5. *Abbreviations*

   Since two-line entries in the explanation column are commonly avoided (because they interfere with readability), abbreviations within financial statements are acceptable. However, an abbreviation assigned to any one word (such as "Allow." for "Allowance") should be consistently used in the same financial statement. (See the balance sheet on page 150.)

Proofread the Final Product

Proofreading is easier, faster, and more accurate if the person reading the final typewritten product does not have to glance back and forth from the original to the copy being proofread. Either (1) ask another worker in the office to help — choose one who is particularly good at noticing details, or (2) dictate from the original copy onto a dictating machine and then check the final draft as you listen carefully to the recording.

The oral reader should be careful to indicate all capitalization, punctuation, use of dollar signs in figure columns, underscores, blank vertical spacing, and depth of indentations. Unless emphasized orally, these are details which are likely to be overlooked by the proofreader.

A common technique for proofreading columns of dollar amounts is to read down the columns, rather than across the columns.

File Carbon Copy of Final Draft

Before filing, on the copy write the name of the person responsible for the original preparation of the financial statement. Some businessmen require that the rough draft original submitted to the typist be filed along with the carbon copy of the final typewritten product.

ANNUAL REPORTS OF CORPORATIONS

As a means of informing interested persons such as investors, creditors, and prospective investors and creditors, large corporations, at the end of each fiscal year, prepare for distribution well-illustrated complete reports about business activities. An annual report usually contains a letter to the shareholders from the president of the corporation accompanied by a statistical report of the highlights of the year, a description of newly developed products and recently acquired markets, and a number of financial reports with supporting schedules. Ordinarily the financial statements include a statement of income and a balance sheet.

Probably the most widely read table in the annual report is the one which shows a comparison of important figures for the present year with those of the previous year. The table labeled "Highlights of the Year," on page 156, is such a comparative table. Topics included in this illustration are usually found in other comparative reports.

Much of the supporting information, such as a report on the amount of sales in the different territories, is presented in columnar form. Other information, such as the distribution of the sales dollar or the increase or decrease in annual sales, is often better presented by graphs.

Two of the most common types of graphs may include typewritten information: the line graph and the circle graph (see page 156). Two details relative to typing on a graph are especially important:

    1. Center titles of graphs over the diagram and type it in all capital letters.

2. Center horizontally and vertically any typewritten material within the boundaries of the space to which the typewritten material applies. (See "Raw Materials and Other Expenses 56¢" typed inside the large part of the circle graph in Illus. 5-18.)

Illus. 5-16
Portion of a tabular report

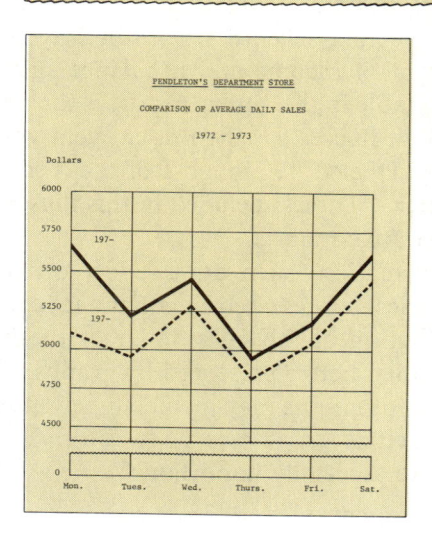

H I G H L I G H T S O F T H E Y E A R

	This Year	Last Year
Net Sales.....................	$239,000,000	$219,000,000
Net Earnings.................	14,000,000	9,800,000
Net Earnings per Share........	$2.95	$2.06
Dividends per Share...........	2.00	2.00
Expenditures for Plant and Equipment.................	4,300,000	5,300,000
Capital Invested in Business at the End of the Year.....	293,700,000	288,800,000
Book Value per Share..........	$61.81	$60.93
Number of Shares Outstanding..	4,751,995	4,738,805
Number of Shareholders........	25,600	27,000
Number of Employees...........	12,800	13,400

Illus. 5-17   Line graph

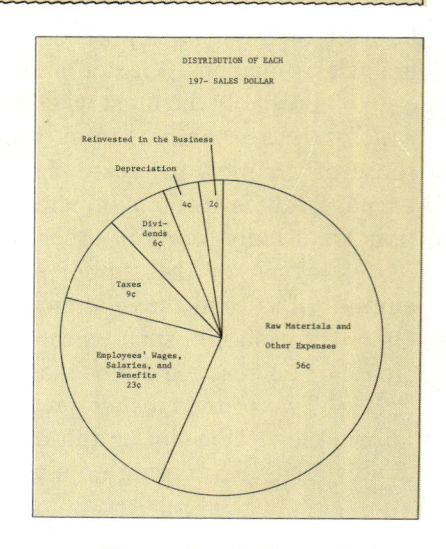

Illus. 5-18   Circle graph

156   Unit 5 / Secretarial Typewriting

QUESTIONS

1. Name three kinds of information contained in a balance sheet.
2. What basic bookkeeping equation should be obvious to one looking at a typed balance sheet?
3. What is the purpose of the income statement?
4. What is *net profit*?
5. Why do businessmen ordinarily prefer that the secretary type financial statements using the same basic form, or design, year after year?
6. Of what use is a calculating machine to the secretary who has been asked to type a financial statement?
7. What is the purpose of leaders extending from the explanation column to the first column of figures?
8. What questions are answered by the heading of a balance sheet and income statement?
9. What is the most important guideline to remember when making a decision on typing style?
10. Of what significance are depths of indentation from the left margin on financial statements?

JUDGMENT

1. Some believe that the person who typed the final copy of the financial statement should proofread while a second person reads orally from the original. Others believe that the person who typed the final copy should be the oral reader and a second person, one unfamiliar with the task, should do the proofreading on the final copy. Which is your choice and why?
2. To what extent should a secretary take it upon herself to redesign the form and style of financial statements?

PERSONAL QUALITIES

After she graduated from high school, Roberta Butler was employed by an export-import firm as a stenographer. She was responsible for typing all the financial statements and reports. When she was interviewed for the position, she was specifically told that her immediate superior would be Miss Hayes, the transcription supervisor.

Roberta became quite disturbed when Tina Davis, the stenographer at the next desk, gave her instructions about the typing of the financial statements, because Tina's instructions conflicted with those given by Miss Hayes.

Every afternoon Tina gave Roberta some of her own work. Tina said that she had too much work, but she was often away from her desk talking with other girls in the office.

Should Roberta have told Miss Hayes that Tina gave her conflicting instructions? Suppose Roberta did not tell Miss Hayes. How could she have handled the situation by herself?

Part 3 / Financial Statements and Reports

LANGUAGE USAGE

A few of the more important comma usages follow:

A. To set off a nonrestrictive phrase or subordinate clause. (A phrase or clause is nonrestrictive if the main clause in the sentence expresses a complete thought when the nonrestrictive phrase or clause is omitted.)

B. To set off phrases or expressions at the beginning of a sentence when they are loosely connected with the rest of the sentence.

C. To set off parenthetical words, clauses, or phrases.

D. To set off words and phrases used in apposition.

E. To separate two or more adjectives if they both precede or follow the noun they modify, provided each adjective modifies the noun alone.

On a separate sheet of paper type the following sentences and insert commas where needed.

1. Mr. Holbrook who is now in Europe will send you a cable soon.
2. Generally speaking a telegram will receive more attention than a letter.
3. An ancient developmental typewriter was the only machine available.
4. Miss Elder my secretary should be here presently.
5. You may therefore draw this conclusion.
6. Neat accurate financial statements however difficult to type are worth the effort.
7. The accountant Edward Caldwell and the manager William Camp studied the income statement before calling the treasurer.
8. Current assets and fixed assets current liabilities and long-term liabilities capital stock and retained earnings are terms you will find on a balance sheet.
9. Her employer said that even though it would take time she had to find the error in the column.
10. The balance sheet showed that the financial condition of the company was not healthy not profitable not optimistic.
11. Miss Brooks the auditor designed the graph.
12. An error on the graph even though minor destroyed its effectiveness.

SECRETARIAL WORK

1. Prepare a balance sheet dated December 31 of this year for the Watson-Vaughn Company using the information beginning at the top of page 159.

Current Assets: Cash $29,290; Notes Receivable $10,340; Accounts Receivable $92,300, Less Allowance for Bad Debts $1,500; Merchandise Inventory $194,320; Store Supplies $6,127; Office Supplies $538; Prepaid Insurance $369; Total Current Assets $331,784.

Fixed Assets: Store Equipment $21,400, Less Allowance for Depreciation of Store Equipment $4,310; Delivery Equipment $25,000, Less Allowance for Depreciation of Delivery Equipment $4,100; Office Equipment $7,300, Less Allowance for Depreciation of Office Equipment $2,500; Total Fixed Assets $42,790.

Total Assets: $374,574.

Current Liabilities: Notes Payable $8,000; Accounts Payable $24,000; Employees Income Taxes Payable $1,200; FICA Taxes Payable $539; State Unemployment Taxes Payable $152; Federal Unemployment Taxes Payable $1,300; Federal Income Taxes Payable $20,412; Total Current Liabilities $55,603.

Long-Term Liabilities: Mortgage Payable (20-year, 5%) $55,000.

Total Liabilities: $110,603.

Capital Stock $238,000; Retained Earnings $25,971; Total Proprietorship $263,971.

Total Liabilities and Proprietorship: $374,574.

Be certain to check the calculations with a calculating machine.

2. Prepare an income statement for the Allison Cosmetics Company for the year ended December 31 of this year with the following information:

Income from Sales: Sales $3,250,850; Less Sales Returns and Allowances $6,420; Less Discount on Sales $8,750; Net Sales $3,235,680.

Cost of Merchandise Sold: Merchandise Inventory (January 1) $350,000; Purchases $3,540,600; Less Purchases Returns and Allowances $190,200; Less Discount on Purchases $540,700; Net Purchases $2,809,700; Cost of Merchandise Available for Sale $3,159,700; Less Merchandise Inventory (December 31) $420,000; Cost of Merchandise Sold $2,739,700. Gross Profit on Sales $495,980.

Operating Expenses: Selling Expenses: Delivery Expense $28,500; Depreciation of Delivery Equipment $6,200; Depreciation of Store Equipment $3,600; Miscellaneous Selling Expense $8,300; Sales Salary Expense $132,500; Store Supplies Expense $20,400; Total Selling Expenses $199,500. Administrative Expenses: Bad Debts Expense $2,100; Depreciation of Buildings $4,500; Depreciation of Office Equipment $1,500; FICA Taxes $6,600; Federal Unemployment

Taxes $1,300; Insurance Expense $3,900; Miscellaneous Administrative Expense $4,800; Office Salary Expense $72,700; Office Supplies Expense $2,400; State Unemployment Taxes $4,300; Total Administrative Expenses $104,100; Total Operating Expenses $303,600.

Net Income from Operations $192,380.

Other Income: Interest Income $1,400.

Other Expense: Interest Expense $3,300; Net Subtraction $1,900.

Net Income before Deducting Federal Income Taxes $190,480.

Less Federal Income Taxes $91,430.

Net Income after Deducting Federal Income Taxes $99,050.

PART 4 LEGAL PAPERS, MINUTES, AND RESOLUTIONS

"Please type the architect's contract so that Mr. Brown can take it with him on the 11 o'clock flight," may be your employer's request. Or he may say, "Please fill out the Baldwin lease so that we can mail it this afternoon." So, you, the secretary, in a manufacturing or service firm, may find yourself busy typing legal forms. The amount of legal work you will do as a secretary will vary in different offices. If you are employed by an attorney or in the legal department of a large firm, you may devote most of your time to the drafting, typing, and proofreading of legal papers. If you are employed by a real estate firm, an insurance company, or a bank, you may spend almost half your time preparing legal documents. In other types of offices, however, the legal work that you will be asked to do may be limited to the occasional typing of a legal form. As a future secretary you should be familiar with the preparation and purpose of the more widely used legal papers.

LEGAL PAPERS

There are various kinds of legal papers, or documents — contracts, wills, deeds, leases, affidavits, powers of attorney. Some may be typewritten by the secretary; others are printed and merely require filling in various blanks to complete them. Some require the services of a notary public; others require witnesses only. You will at some time or other be called upon to type or complete a legal document.

Typewritten Legal Papers

Legal documents may be typed on standard 8½" x 11" paper; however most are typed on legal size paper which is 8½ inches wide and may vary from 13 to 15 inches in length. This paper may have printed left and right margin lines. The left margin rule is usually a double line; the right margin, a single line. In typing material on legal paper with printed margin rules, you should set the margin stops on your typewriter so that the margins of the typewritten material will be at least two spaces within the printed margin lines. If paper without printed margin rules is used for typing a legal paper, you should allow a 1½-inch left margin and a ½-inch right margin. Minimum margins of 2 inches at the top and 1 inch at the bottom are usually allowed. You should prepare enough carbon copies of all legal papers so that each person interested in the paper will have a copy, including at least one copy for the lawyer and one for the court record. An example of a typewritten legal document is shown on page 167. Note particularly the space between the printed margin lines and the left and right margins of the typewritten material, the spacing (triple spacing between the title and the first line, double spacing thereafter), the use of all capitals for certain words in the contract, the punctuation, and the arrangement of the closing lines.

Spacing. Typewritten legal documents are usually double-spaced, but you may single-space some of them, including wills and affidavits (a sworn statement in writing made under oath).

A type of legal paper may be purchased with consecutive numbers printed down the page at the left of the printed left margin line. The number "1" is approximately two inches from the top edge and indicates the position of the typewritten title. The other numbers indicate the positions of the typewritten lines of material and make possible easy reference to any particular part of the legal paper when its contents are under discussion. If the legal paper used does not contain these printed numbers, and if your employer wants to have them on the completed document, it will be a simple matter for you to type them as you type the document.

Erasures. Because a legal paper states the rights or privileges and duties or obligations of the parties who sign it, and later may be submitted in a court of law as evidence, you should prepare each paper accurately and proofread it carefully. You may erase and correct some errors in typing legal papers; others may not be corrected. If the error and erasure affect only one or two letters in a relatively unimportant word, you may erase and make the correction. If, on the other hand, the error you make involves a word which might be important to the meaning of that part of the contract — substituting the word *may* for *must*, for example — or, if an error involves an amount of money, name, or date, the erasure should not be made but the complete paper should be retyped. In some cases, however, such corrections may be made if the corrected paper is initialed by all parties. If you are in doubt, you should ask your employer if it is necessary to retype the legal paper or if it is permissible to erase and correct the error.

Numbers, Dates, and Titles. Quantities in legal documents are usually written in both words and figures, as follows:

A scholarship of one thousand dollars ($1,000)
Under the terms of the will he will receive five thousand (5,000) dollars
A twenty- (20) year mortgage
Fifty (50) shares of Woolworth common stock
Five (5) percent interest

Dates are written in several forms. No one form, however, is more legal than another; therefore, there is no reason why you should not type a date in a legal form as you would type it in a letter. Variations are:

On this, the third day of November, 19—
This 16th day of June in the year 19—
This sixteenth day of June, in the year of our Lord, one thousand nine hundred and seventy-two

Personal titles — Mr., Mrs., Miss — are not used with names in legal documents. Professional titles — Dr., Prof. — are not ordinarily used either.

Printed Legal Forms

Legal documents may be prepared by typing the necessary information on a printed legal form. Standard forms for bills of sale, deeds, leases, mortgages, and wills may be purchased in stationery stores. However, important legal documents, even though they are on a printed form, should be checked by a lawyer.

When typing on printed legal forms, if the item of information that is filled in is important, such as a sum of money, the space that remains on either side of the item after it is typed should be filled in with hyphens. This eliminates the possibility of figures, letters, or words being added later to change the meaning of the typewritten insertion.

The same margins used for the printed matter should be used for the typewritten matter. When carbon copies are prepared, the position of the printed matter on each copy must be checked carefully so that the typewritten additions will appear in the proper places on all copies. Unless this check is made, the typewritten matter on a carbon copy may be written over some of the printed matter, and the copy may be illegible.

Notarized Legal Papers

Many legal documents are notarized. This means a signed statement is added by a notary public (a public official authorized by the state) to show that the paper has been signed in the notary's presence and that the signers have sworn that they are the same persons referred to in the document. The statement by the notary public usually is typed at the bottom of the same paper on which the legal document is typed. It may be typed on a separate page, however, if there is no room for it on the page that contains the legal material.

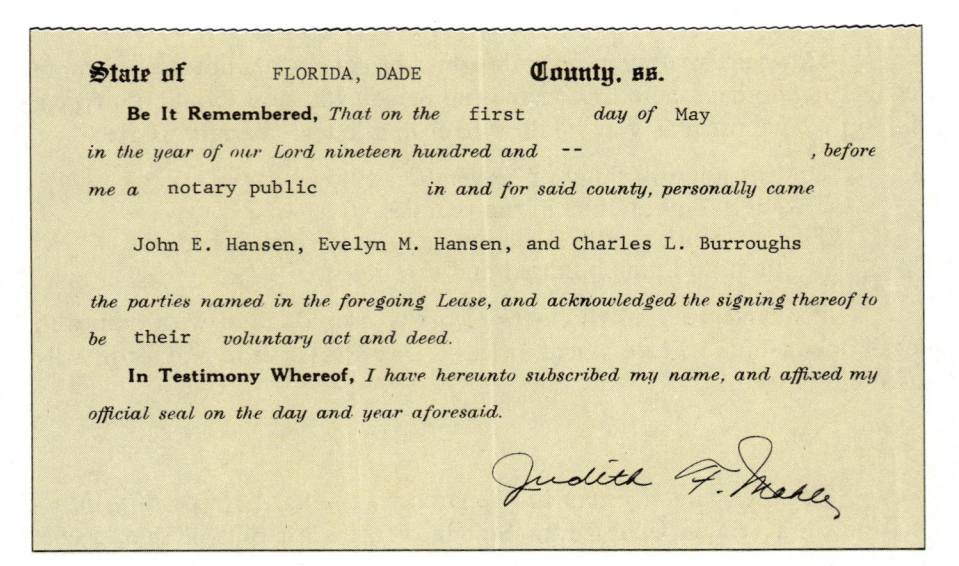

Illus. 5-19
Statement of a notary public

State of FLORIDA, DADE **County. ss.**

Be It Remembered, *That on the* first *day of* May *in the year of our Lord nineteen hundred and* -- *, before me a* notary public *in and for said county, personally came* John E. Hansen, Evelyn M. Hansen, and Charles L. Burroughs *the parties named in the foregoing Lease, and acknowledged the signing thereof to be* their *voluntary act and deed.*

In Testimony Whereof, *I have hereunto subscribed my name, and affixed my official seal on the day and year aforesaid.*

Judith F. Mahle

Do not be surprised if your employer wishes you to become a notary public. In large offices one of the secretaries usually acts in this capacity. In an office building containing a number of small offices, a secretary employed in one of them may act as a notary public for all offices in the building.

The laws for becoming a notary public differ in the various states. In many states an application accompanied by statements that show that the applicant is a citizen and a resident of the state, of the required age, and of good character is submitted to the governor's office. If the application is granted, the notary public secures a notary's seal, which is a metal, hand-operated instrument that embosses on a legal paper the design of a seal containing the name of the notary. A notary's commission is for a limited period of time, usually for two years, but it may be renewed.

Typical Legal Documents

A discussion of a simple contract, a will, a deed, a lease, an affidavit, and a power of attorney — legal papers that are frequently prepared in a business office — will explain the typing problems in preparing legal papers.

Simple Contract. A *contract* is an agreement that can be enforced at law. It creates legal rights and responsibilities. It may be either oral or written; however, some contracts, such as those for the purchase of real estate, must be in writing. Before you type a contract, you should check to see that it includes the following essential information:

1. The date and the place of the agreement
2. The names of the parties entering into the agreement
3. The purpose of the contract
4. The duties of each party
5. The money, services, or goods given in consideration of the contract
6. The time period
7. The signatures of all the parties

The illustration on page 168 shows parts of a simple contract prepared on legal paper with printed margin lines.

Will. A *will* is a legal document in which a person provides for the distribution of his property after his death. The person who makes the will is the *testator* (man) or *testatrix* (woman). He may designate an *executor* (man) or *executrix* (woman) to probate his will, that is, prove its validity to the court for the purpose of carrying out its provisions. Making a will is a technical matter and should be entrusted only to a qualified attorney. Illustration 5–21 on page 167 shows a properly prepared and correctly typed will.

Deed. A *deed* is a formal written instrument by which title to real property is transferred from one person to another. All the details of the transaction should be approved by a lawyer before it is registered with the proper government agency.

Lease. A *lease* is a contract by which one party gives to another the use of real or personal property for a fixed price. This relationship exists when one person, the *lessee*, under an express or implied agreement, is given possession and control of the property of another, the *lessor*. The amount given by the lessee is called *rent* (for real property) or *consideration* (for personal property).

The lease shown on page 166 illustrates the typing problems involved in completing a printed form for a legal document. Observe where typewritten material has been inserted, the method of indicating the amount in words and figures, and the completion of certain words by adding letters that keep the sentences containing those words consistently in plural form.

This Lease Witnesseth:

THAT John E. Hansen and Evelyn M. Hansen, husband and wife,
HEREBY LEASE TO Charles L. Burroughs
the premises situate in the City *of* Miami *in the County of* Dade *and State of* Florida *described as follows:*

Building to be used as a restaurant located at 232 Collins Avenue, Miami, Florida

with the appurtenances thereto, for the term of ten (10) years *commencing* June 1, *19* 72 *at a rental of* Two hundred fifty (250) *dollars per* month *, payable* monthly.

SAID LESSEE AGREE s *to pay said rent, unless said premises shall be destroyed or rendered untenantable by fire or other unavoidable accident; to not commit or suffer waste; to not use said premises for any unlawful purpose; to not assign this lease, or underlet said premises, or any part thereof, or permit the sale of* his *interest herein by legal process, without the written consent of said lessor* S*; to not use said premises or any part thereof in violation of any law relating to intoxicating liquors; and at the expiration of this lease, to surrender said premises in as good condition as they now are, or may be put by said lessor* S*, reasonable wear and unavoidable casualties, condemnation or appropriation excepted. Upon nonpayment of any of said rent for* thirty *days, after it shall become due, and without demand made therefor; or if said lessee or any assignee of this lease shall make an assignment for the benefit of his creditors; or if proceedings in bankruptcy shall be instituted by or against lessee or any assignee; or if a receiver or trustee be appointed for the property of the lessee or any assignee; or if this lease by operation of law pass to any person or persons; or if said lessee or any assignee shall fail to keep any of the other covenants of this lease, it shall be lawful for said lessor* s, their *heirs or assigns, into said premises to reenter, and the same to have again, repossess and enjoy, as in* their *first and former estate; and thereupon this lease and everything herein contained on the said lessor* s '*behalf to be done and performed, shall cease, determine, and be utterly void*

SAID LESSOR S AGREE *(said lessee having performed* his *obligations under this lease) that said lessee shall quietly hold and occupy said premises during said term without any hindrance or molestation by said lessor* s, their *heir or any person lawfully claiming under them.*

Signed this first *day of* May *A. D. 19* 72

IN THE PRESENCE OF:

Louis K. Whitfield   *John E. Hansen*
Robert R. Crowell   *Evelyn M. Hansen*
                            Charles L. Burroughs

Illus. 5-20
Lease

Two-inch top margin for all pages

Testator's name in all capital letters

Double spacing

Copy typed within marginal rules

LAST WILL AND TESTAMENT OF WILLIAM H. STEWART

  I, WILLIAM H. STEWART, a resident of the City of Trenton, State of New Jersey, declare this to be my Last Will and Testament, and revoke all former Wills and Codicils.

  FIRST: I declare that I am married, and wife's name is MARJORIE DAVIS STEWART; I have two children now living, DAVID H. STEWART and STEPHEN C. STEWART.

  SECOND: I direct that my just debts and funeral expenses be paid.

  THIRD: I give, devise, and bequeath to my wife, MARJORIE DAVIS STEWART, all the rest of my estate both real and personal and wheresoever situated, which I may own or have the right to dispose of at the time of my decease.

  FOURTH: I appoint as Executrix of my Will my wife, MARJORIE DAVIS STEWART, to serve without bond. In the event she is unable or unwilling to serve, or to complete such service as Executrix, then it is my wish that HOWARD PATTON, a long-time friend of mine, shall be appointed as Executor.

  This Will and Testament is subscribed by me on the eighth day of December, 1972, at Trenton, New Jersey.

William H. Stewart

  The foregoing instrument, consisting of one page, was subscribed on the date which it bears, by the testator, WILLIAM H. STEWART, and at the time of subscribing was declared by him to be his Last Will and Testament; and we, at the testator's request and in his presence and in the presence of each other, have signed such instrument as witnesses.

Ida M. Turner   residing at   703 Bunker Hill Avenue, Trenton, New Jersey

Anne Hemmerle   residing at   513 New York Avenue, Elizabeth, New Jersey

One-inch bottom margin

First page not numbered

Illus. 5-21
The format of a will

Part 4 / Legal Papers, Minutes, and Resolutions   167

Affidavit. An *affidavit* is a written statement made under oath that the facts set forth are sworn to be true and correct. It must be sworn to before a proper official, such as a judge, justice of the peace, or a notary.

AGENCY CONTRACT

This agreement, made and entered into on this, the fifth day of June, 19--, by and between THE JOSLYN MANUFACTURING COMPANY, a corporation of Muncie, Indiana, the party of the first part, and ROBERT M. BERGOLD, of Dallas, Texas, the party of the second part,

WITNESSETH: That, whereas, the party of the first part is about to open a branch office to be located in Dallas, Texas, for the sale of its products, the said party of the first part hereby engages the services of Robert M. Bergold, the party of the second part, as manager of that office.

The party of the first part hereby agrees to pay the

first part from time to time.

IN WITNESS WHEREOF, The parties have hereunto affixed their hands and seals on the day and in the year first above written.

THE JOSLYN MANUFACTURING COMPANY

Witnesses:

G. M. Van Pelter   *Francis P. Burnett* (Seal)
                       President
                       Party of the First Part

Ken A. Maclin

                       Robert M. Bergold (Seal)
                       Party of the Second Part

Illus. 5-22
Parts of a legal document typed on legal paper

Power of Attorney. A *power of attorney* is a legal instrument authorizing one person to act as the attorney or agent of the grantor. An executive may give an experienced secretary his power of attorney — the power to act for him. It may authorize his secretary to sign checks and other legal documents for him. The power of attorney specifies the acts which the agent is authorized to perform for the principal. It may be granted for an indefinite period, for a specific period, or for a specific purpose only. It must be signed by the principal and should be notarized.

Illus. 5-23
Preparing a conference room for an executive meeting is often the secretary's responsibility.

MINUTES

In our busy business world, with an executive's responsibility covering a wide range of activities, with the need for interchange of ideas, for mutual understandings, for decision-making based not on one man's point of view but on many, meetings are frequent and necessary. What you do in planning and in taking minutes can improve the effectiveness of a meeting. If you are called upon to take and transcribe minutes regularly, a knowledge of parliamentary procedure will be most helpful. This can be acquired by reading either *Robert's Rules of Order*, the standard guide for presiding officers and parliamentarians, or *Standard Code for Parliamentary Procedure*, by Sturgis.

Minutes are the official records of meetings and show the action taken in them. The minutes of a meeting should be a clear, concise presentation of factual information, properly arranged. Since minutes are frequently used for reference, every detail included in them should be complete and accurate.

The planning for a committee meeting, conference, or official meeting is usually done by the chairman's secretary. If you are the chairman's secretary, you will be expected to reserve the meeting room and to notify the members well in advance of each meeting. In addition, you will be responsible for getting paper and pencils for each member of the committee, getting material from the files which might be needed in the meeting, having water and glasses available, and providing for any coffee or refreshments which might be served.

Each member should receive an *agenda* which is a schedule of business to be covered at the meeting. You will also be expected to take and transcribe the minutes of many of the meetings called by your employer. As a general rule, the minutes are edited for omissions and corrections by the chairman before they are distributed to the members.

Gathering Information for Minutes

If you are asked to take the minutes of a meeting, you should have the following information before the meeting starts: the name of the organization, the place, the date, the time of the meeting, and the agenda. You should know, or obtain, the names of those who should attend the meeting. With such a list you can quickly check attendance, and thereby know the names of those present and absent.

You should have available at the meeting the minutes of the previous meetings, particularly those of the last meeting, and any figures, letters, bulletins, reports, and legal papers that might be referred to during the meeting. This foresight on your part will help to keep the meeting running smoothly. The presiding officer or committee chairman may suggest to you the data that should be available at the meeting. Under no circumstances should you leave the meeting to obtain information unless the chairman asks you to do so.

As the meeting progresses, you should take down in shorthand the points that you think are of importance and interest, and, insofar as possible, you should identify the discussion with the names of those who participate. The names of those who make and second each motion should be recorded. Motions and resolutions, whether passed or not, should be taken and transcribed word for word because future proceedings are often governed by the interpretation placed on the wording.

MINUTES OF THE MEETING

of the

E X E C U T I V E   B O A R D

Administrative Management Society

Time and Place of Meeting   The regular monthly meeting of the Executive Board was held on Friday, October 31, 19--, in the conference room of the Pierson Mailing Company. The meeting was called to order at 5:30 p.m. by the President, Robert C. Ellis.

Attendance   Present were Virginia E. Allen, Robert C. Ellis, Henry A. Foster, Eleanor J. Gage, Helen E. Henderson, Martha M. Lester, James P. Sullivan, and Henry J. Townsend.

Approval of Minutes   The minutes of the September 30 meeting, which had been mailed to all the members of the Board, were approved.

Treasurer's Report   The Treasurer, Henry A. Foster, reported a balance on hand on October 24 of $1,536.75. A statement for $168.75 from the Standard Printing Company was presented. A motion was made by Virginia A. Allen and seconded by Martha M. Lester to accept the Treasurer's report and authorize payment of the statement from Standard Printing Company. The motion was carried.

Report of Standing Committee   Miss Allen reported for the Publicity Committee. She said that the release on the Salary Report had been prepared and would be given to the press on November 15.

Report of Special Committee   The special committee on Corollary Information reported that the average work week had been reduced from 40 hours to 37½ hours and that two firms had a basic work week of less than 35 hours. Only one firm reported a work week of over 40 hours.

Unfinished Business   The Secretary submitted two additional estimates for the cost of tabulating the Salary Report. A motion was made by James P. Sullivan and seconded by Henry J. Townsend to accept the bid of $125 submitted by the Reynolds Company. The motion was put to a vote and carried.

New Business   Mr. Foster moved that the cost of the Salary Report for nonmembers be increased to $5. The motion was seconded by Robert C. Ellis. The motion was voted on and carried.

Date of Next Meeting   The next meeting of the Board will be held on Friday, November 28, in Parlor A of the Statler Hotel.

Adjournment   On motion of Robert C. Ellis, seconded by Martha M. Lester, it was voted to adjourn the meeting at 6:45 p.m.

Helen E. Henderson

Helen E. Henderson
Recording Secretary

Illus. 5-24   Minutes of a meeting

Typing the Minutes

The completeness of the typed minutes depends upon the formality of the meeting. The minutes of an informal meeting are brief and cover only the essential points; the minutes of a formal meeting are typed in detail according to a routine pattern. In most sets of minutes, the following points are covered:

1. Name of the group, committee, organization, or business.
2. Time, date, and place of the meeting, and whether it is a regular meeting or a special meeting.
3. Names of the presiding officer, secretary, and those present (also those absent if that can be determined). In the case of a meeting of a large organization, only the number of members present need be recorded to indicate that there was a *quorum* (the minimum number of members necessary for conducting the business of the group).
4. Reading of the minutes of the previous meeting, and the approval, amendment, or correction of those minutes.
5. Reports of the committees or persons who previously were assigned special duties: for example, Treasurer's report, reports of standing committees, and reports of special committees.
6. Unfinished business and the action taken on it.
7. New business, the discussion, and the action taken.
8. Time, date, and place of the next meeting.
9. Time of adjournment.
10. Signature of the secretary or one responsible for the minutes.

Correcting the Minutes

When the minutes are being typed, they should be corrected, even rewritten if necessary, to be certain that they are as nearly perfect as possible when they are read at the next meeting. At the meeting it is sometimes necessary to make corrections in the minutes. If only a few words are affected, lines may be drawn through the incorrect words and the proper insertions made above them. If more than a few words are affected, lines may be drawn through the sentences or paragraphs to be corrected and the corrections written on a new page. The page number of the corrections should be indicated on the original minutes. The minutes should not be rewritten after they have been read and approved at the meeting.

Illus. 5-25
Above average accuracy is required in typing legal documents and minutes.

Kelly Services

RESOLUTIONS

During a meeting, you may be given the responsibility of preparing a resolution. Resolutions are written to express appreciation, to do honor, to indicate action, to express regret, to offer congratulations, to commemorate, or to present a program of action.

WHEREAS and *RESOLVED*, which are characteristic introductory terms in formal resolutions, are typed in capital letters. The first word after *WHEREAS* is not capitalized unless it is a proper name. No comma follows *WHEREAS* unless one is necessary to make the sentence clear. *RESOLVED* or *RESOLVED further* is usually followed by a comma and the first word after it is capitalized.

Some resolutions are less formal. In an informal resolution the terms *WHEREAS*, *RESOLVED*, and *Therefore be it* are eliminated, and the facts or events leading up to the resolution are stated simply and directly. For example, "The following resolution was unanimously adopted:

The Trustees of Martin College accept with thanks the sum of $25,000 representing a gift from the friends and colleagues of the late Harriet Simons for the establishment of the *Harriet Simons Scholarship Fund*. The income from the invested principal is to be used to assist able and needy high school graduates who have selected Martin College for their undergraduate studies. The Fund is to be administered by the Dean of Students."

Part 4 / Legal Papers, Minutes, and Resolutions

QUESTIONS

1. In what ways does legal paper differ from paper used in business?
2. What are the minimum margins usually allowed on typewritten legal paper?
3. What is the advantage of using legal paper on which the lines are numbered?
4. What type of error may be erased and corrected in a legal paper?
5. How are quantities usually written in legal papers?
6. How should words be filled in on a printed legal form?
7. What is meant by the term *notarized*?
8. What are *minutes*?
9. Why must every detail in the minutes be accurate and complete?
10. What is an *agenda*?
11. What information should the secretary have before the meeting starts?
12. What should the secretary bring with her to the meeting?
13. In what divisions are minutes usually arranged, and what specific points are covered?
14. How may the minutes be corrected?
15. What is the purpose of a resolution?

JUDGMENT

1. Is a typing error in a legal paper more serious than a similar error in an important business letter?
2. Why is it an advantage for the secretary in an office to be a notary public?
3. Why do you believe a secretary should not leave a meeting, even during a discussion, unless she is instructed to do so?
4. What should the secretary do if a resolution or a motion is presented in such a way that she is not able to take it down verbatim? What procedure might she use to avoid this difficulty?
5. What should the secretary do if she does not know the name of the person making or seconding a motion and she has been instructed to keep a record of the names of such persons?
6. To what extent should the secretary be familiar with the rules of parliamentary procedure for conducting meetings?

PERSONAL QUALITIES

Rosa was busy with her usual work when her employer, Mr. Adams, asked her to type a contract at once so that it could be signed by Mr. Lara and Mr. Cook who were waiting in his office. When proofreading the contract later Rosa found an error in the amount of money. What should she do?

LANGUAGE USAGE

Three more uses of the comma are:
A. To separate long coordinate clauses that are joined by the conjunctions *and, but, for, neither, nor,* and *or.* The comma is placed before the conjunction.
B. To set off a subordinate clause preceding a main clause.
C. To separate words, phrases, or clauses in a series. A comma precedes the last item in the series.

Type the following sentences on a separate sheet of paper and insert commas where necessary.

1. After the lease was typed the attorney presented copies to all who had signed the document.
2. After she had typed the contract the deed the will and the power of attorney the secretary decided to go to lunch.
3. Although in some cases erasures may be made in legal documents it is better if there are none.
4. The secretary offered to work overtime to complete the affidavit but her employer said it was not necessary.
5. Law firms use printed legal forms whenever possible for this saves much secretarial typing.
6. While the jury was out the lawyer and his client remained in the courtroom.
7. Neither the attorney nor his client agreed with the decision but the judge considered the will valid.
8. After he made his decision he would not change the terms of the contract.
9. The client would not sign the power of attorney as the lawyer had worded it.
10. Since her employer specialized in criminal law laws that dealt only with crime were of great interest to her.

SECRETARIAL WORK

1. From the following brief notes compose the minutes for a meeting of the Holten High School Business Club. Then carefully edit and type the minutes in the correct format.

    Regular meeting — Business Club — Room 26 — 3:15 p.m — November 17, 197–.

    James Ingram, pres., in charge. All members present. Minutes read — approved.

    Inez Carson, treas. — cash balance, $42.75.

    Mildred Pearce, chairman of membership com. — Sam Nugent and David Engle applied for membership — eligible — pd. dues.

    Sally Seymour, ch. of special events com., considering project for raising money — annual school carnival. Recommended exhibit of old and modern office equipment — tickets 25 cents. Discussion — feeling exhibit would not produce enough revenue. Motion by Donna Thomas — club sponsor booth at carnival — ice cream and candy. Motion seconded — Lawrence Steele — vote 26 for, 14 against.

Charles Becker, ch. of program com. — introduced Miss Phyllis Chapman, former student and grad. of dept. — talked on "How My Secretarial Training in School Helped Me in My First Job."

Date of next meeting — Dec. 15 at 3:15 p.m. — Room 26. Motion made by Maureen Stretch and seconded by Jerry Boyle — meeting adjourned at 4:30 p.m.

2. Type the following power of attorney on legal paper, making one carbon copy. Use the current date. If ruled legal paper is not available, rule in ink the necessary vertical lines on regular 8½" x 11" paper.

NOTE: *A power of attorney is a formal written document used for the appointment of an agent.*

Know All Men by These Presents, That I, Ernest W. Dunn, of the city of Beverly, county of Essex, state of Massachusetts, have made, constituted, and appointed, and by these presents do make, constitute, and appoint, Merrill J. Martin, of the city of Salem, county of Essex, state of Massachusetts, my true and lawful attorney, for me and in my name, place, and stead, to sign my name to any and all checks drawn on the First National Bank against my deposits in the same, for the purchase of the property situated at the corner of State Avenue and Congress Street, known as the Randolph property; and I hereby ratify and confirm all that my said agent or attorney will lawfully do, or cause to be done, in connection with this purchase. (¶) IN WITNESS WHEREOF, I have hereunto set my hand and seal this_____ day of _____ in the year of our Lord one thousand nine hundred and_____.

_____

Witnesses:

_____

_____

State of Massachusetts ⎱ ss.
County of Essex ⎰

The above signed authority, Ernest W. Dunn, personally appeared before me on the _____ day of _____ in the year of our Lord one thousand nine hundred and _____, and in due form acknowledged the attached instrument to be his act and deed and declared that it may be recorded as such.

(SEAL)

_____
Notary Public

3. If printed forms for a warranty deed are available, complete an original copy and one carbon copy of that form by adding those parts of the following information that are printed in italic type. Use the current date.

If printed forms are not available, type an original copy and one carbon copy of all parts of the following warranty deed.

KNOW ALL MEN BY THESE PRESENTS:

That I, William W. Fredericks, of Rochester, in the county of Strafford and state of New Hampshire for and in consideration of the sum of *One Dollar and other valuable consideration* to *me* in hand before the delivery hereof, well and truly paid by *James McGuire, of said Rochester*, the receipt whereof *I* do hereby acknowledge have granted, bargained and sold, and by these presents do give, grant, sell, alien, enfeoff, convey and confirm unto the said *James McGuire, his* heirs and assigns, forever, *a certain tract of land situated in Wakefield, in the county of Carroll and state of New Hampshire, on the easterly side of Route 16, so-called, the same being the highway from Wakefield to North Wakefield, bounded as follows:*

Beginning on the easterly sideline of said highway at a stone wall at land formerly of B. Hull, thence by said wall easterly and thence northerly by wall and by stakes and stones and by trees marked "line" to land formerly of M. C. Denicore at Blake field, so-called; thence easterly by said field to land formerly of John C. Peak and the Peter Carroll lot, so-called, formerly owned by John W. Matthews; thence southerly by said Carroll lot to the Peter Carroll place, as it was once called; thence westerly by said Carroll lot and George L. Williams lot, as it was once called, to the aforesaid highway; thence northerly by said highway to the bounds begun at, the same containing forty (40) acres, more or less.

For title reference see deed of Edward Daniels to Albert Swain dated July 30, 1914, recorded Carroll County Records, Book 160, Page 306, the grantor hereof having obtained his title by devise under the will of the late Albert Swain, see Carroll County Probate Records.

To have and to hold the said premises, with all the privileges and appurtenances to the same belonging, to *him* the said *James McGuire* and *his* heirs and assigns, to *their* and *their* only proper use and benefit forever, and *I* the said *William W. Fredericks* and *my* heirs, executors and administrators do hereby covenant, grant and agree, to and with the said *James McGuire* and *his* heirs and assigns, that until the delivery hereof *I am* the lawful owner of the said premises, and *am* seized and possessed thereof in *my* own right in fee simple; and have full power and lawful authority to grant and convey the same in manner aforesaid; that the premises are free and clear from all and every incumbrance whatsoever, except _____ and that *I* and *my* heirs, executors and administrators, shall and will **WARRANT** and **DEFEND** the same to the said *James McGuire* and *his* heirs and assigns, against the lawful claims and demands of any person or persons whomsoever.

And I, *Josephine Fredericks*, wife of the said *William W. Fredericks*, in consideration aforesaid, do hereby relinquish my right of dower in the before mentioned premises.

And we, and each of us, do hereby release, discharge and waive all such rights of exemption from attachment and levy or sale on execution, and such other rights whatsoever in said premises, and in each and every part thereof, as our Family Homestead, as are reserved, or secured to us, or either of us, by Chapter 260, Revised Laws of the State of New Hampshire, or by any other statute or statutes of said State.

IN WITNESS WHEREOF, *we* have hereunto set *our* hands and seals this *23rd* day of *January* A. D. 197–.

_____

_____

STATE OF NEW HAMPSHIRE
County of *Strafford*

On this *23rd* day of *January* 197–, before me, the undersigned officer, personally appeared *William W. Fredericks and Josephine Fredericks* known to me (or satisfactorily proven) to be the persons whose names *are* subscribed to the within instrument and acknowledged that *they* executed the same for the purposes therein contained.

IN WITNESS WHEREOF, I hereunto set my hand and official seal.

(SEAL)

_____

                        Title of Officer

Unit 6 PROCESSING DATA

Part 1. How Data Is Processed
   2. Computing and Recording Machines
   3. Business Forms

The secretary as an assistant to an executive is constantly gathering and using information or data. Many machines, from the adding machine to the computer, are available to help her.

VOCABULARY BUILDER

> *O this learning,*
> *what a thing it is!*
>   **Shakespeare**

routine..........................
adjective: commonplace; of, relating to, or in accordance with established procedure

manipulating.......................
verb: treating or operating with the hands or by mechanical means especially with skill

sophisticated.......................
adjective: highly complicated; complex (as in instruments); worldly wise; knowing

retain..............................
verb: to hold back; to restrain; to keep in possession or use

computations.......................
noun: calculation; a system of reckoning; a method of estimating or accounting

sequence...........................
noun: a continuous or connected series; continuity of progression

distinguish.........................
verb: to mark as separate or different; to separate into kinds, classes, or categories; to single out

compile............................
verb: to collect into a volume; to compose out of materials from other documents

statistical.........................
adjective: dealing with the collection, analysis, interpretation, and presentation of masses of numerical data

authentic..........................
adjective: worthy of acceptance or belief; trustworthy; genuine

p. 181   Some of the **routine** tasks usually performed by a secretary are now performed by machines.

p. 182   Business data processing means **manipulating** words, numbers, and symbols about business transactions to provide useful information.

p. 183   The processing of numbers, words, and symbols has progressed ... to **sophisticated** electronic computers.

p. 187   Also the computer will **retain** the information for future reference.

p. 193   Some of the duties you may perform using a calculator are checking a report containing **computations**, figuring the payroll, preparing financial. . . .

p. 200   The operator must strike the proper keys in the correct **sequence**.

p. 206   Can you **distinguish** between a well-designed and a poorly designed business form?

p. 206   You may copy information and **compile statistical** data from business forms, and you will surely be expected to check, sort, and file forms.

p. 207   A statement, for example, should be prepared on a firm's statement form to prove that the request for payment is **authentic**.

PART 1 — HOW DATA IS PROCESSED

Susan Love is a secretary to Mr. Ted Cass, Sales Manager for Black's Paper Company, which sells paper to hundreds of local businesses. Black's Paper Company has modern electronic equipment to prepare the different kinds of reports and summaries needed by the business. Quite often Susan must talk with the people working in the Data Processing Department to get additional information about the company's records. Susan is surprised at how often she has to ask what certain words mean. The data processing personnel use such terms as *source document, input, output*, and *data*; and Susan is not always sure what they mean. She realizes she has much to learn about data processing and how it is used in business. As a competent secretary Susan needs at least a general understanding of data processing.

THE SECRETARY PROCESSES DATA

The increasing use of electronic data processing equipment in the modern office has changed office procedures and office work. The secretary's work has been changed in many instances also. Some of the routine tasks usually performed by a secretary are now performed by machines. For example, many companies now have their monthly financial statements prepared through the use of electronic data processing equipment. This frees the secretary to perform more of the administrative duties of an office.

As a secretary today, you must be familiar with the vocabulary of data processing. You may be directly involved with the data processing department; and, to communicate effectively, you must be familiar with the most common words used by the people in the data processing department.

You probably will not be concerned with actually operating electronic data processing equipment, although you may operate mechanical data processing machines such as calculators. Your job may involve getting the data to be processed and using the information after it has been processed. This means you must know the many uses of the records and reports provided by the data processing department.

Your job as a secretary may also involve determining what information is necessary and what is not necessary for your employer to read. This will mean using your own judgment not only to determine *what* information your employer should receive but also to decide *how* it should be presented, so that it will take the least amount of time for your employer to read and understand. The use of data processing equipment can make your job more important by freeing you from routine tasks and allowing you to perform more challenging duties.

Illus. 6-1
A *competent* secretary must exercise *good* judgment in presenting *useful* information to her employer.

Wilson Jones Company
Division of Swingline, Inc.

WHAT IS BUSINESS DATA PROCESSING?

Data simply means the words (invoice, balances), numbers (382, 4½), and symbols (#, %) that businesses use in order to make decisions. *Processing* means arranging the data in a series of steps in an organized manner. When the words, numbers, and symbols are organized so that they have meaning, the result is called *information*. *Data processing*, therefore, is arranging words, numbers, and symbols to provide information. *Business data processing* means manipulating words, numbers, and symbols about business transactions to provide useful information.

Whether you realize it or not, you are constantly processing data mentally. Suppose a friend asks you to go to a movie. In deciding if you should or should not go, you are processing data. Some of your data would be the cost of the movie and how much money you have, the length of the movie and how much time you have available, the distance from your home to the theater, the different means of transportation, and whether you believe you would enjoy the movie. In order to give your friend your answer, you must first process all your data. Although business decisions usually involve more important matters, the procedures used are similar.

Data by itself is often meaningless. For example, if twenty sales invoices arrived in your office, it would be impossible to know the total dollar amount of sales by simply looking at the twenty separate invoices. The data must be added together to arrive at a total. This adding of numbers is processing data. The report which results from the processing can be useful to your employer in making many very important decisions about the business.

Data about business transactions is collected, processed, and reported to provide people in the company with information. The data needed by a business will depend upon many factors, such as the size and type of business. The information needed by the owner of a small service station would not be the same as that needed by the executive of a large steel corporation. The more complex the operation of a firm the more different types of information it needs. The method for processing data will depend on such factors as the amount and kind of data and the time and money available for processing the data.

Some people think that data processing is a recent development. The term *data processing* is new, but the activity is not new. The processing of numbers, words, and symbols has progressed from manual methods through several stages to sophisticated electronic computers.

THE NEED FOR PROCESSED DATA

Data is needed for two major reasons — internal use (within the company) and external use (outside the company). Information is used internally to perform the daily activities of the business and to plan the future of the business.

External information is provided to stockholders (owners of the business), government agencies, unions, customers, suppliers, and creditors. Some information serves several purposes. Payroll records, for example, give internal information for payment of salaries and also external information for financial reports to the government and unions.

METHODS OF PROCESSING DATA

Data may be processed by manual, mechanical, tabulating, or electronic means. There are similarities among these methods as well as differences.

Processing Data Manually

The human mind was the earliest means of processing data. When a person hears or sees data, this becomes information to be stored in the brain. The brain is the processor which performs the operations upon the data. The information that results can be in the form of the written or spoken word, or both.

Let's say you are asked to process an order. With the manual method of processing data, you would write a sales slip giving data, such as date, customer's name, customer's address, terms, quantity, and other vital information. The other records such as the invoice, journal entry, ledger, and customer's statement would be copied in handwriting.

It is easy to make errors in routine work, such as copying data from one form to another. The speed and accuracy with which the data is processed is comparatively low; and, for large volumes of work, the cost to process each document is relatively high.

New York Telephone Company

Illus. 6-2   Manual means of processing data

Unit 6 / Processing Data

Processing Data Mechanically

When the intelligence of the secretary is combined with the speed and accuracy of machines, an efficient system can be formed. Office equipment such as calculating machines, typewriters, and bookkeeping machines (see Part 2 of this unit) are combined to perform several operations.

If you were processing a sale using the mechanical means of processing data, you would probably handwrite the sales slip but you would perform the calculations by using an electronic calculator. By using a bookkeeping machine, the journal and ledger entries could be posted and the customer's statement prepared. Thus, you would combine your intelligence with the speed and accuracy of machines to form a mechanical data processing system.

Processing Data by a Tabulating (Punched Card) System

Compared with the manual and mechanical system of data processing, tabulating equipment handles large volumes of data with greater speed and accuracy at a relatively lower cost. The punched card tabulating system consists of the *card punch, verifier, sorter, collator, interpreter, reproducer,* and *accounting machine.* Some of these machines are illustrated in Part 2 of this Unit.

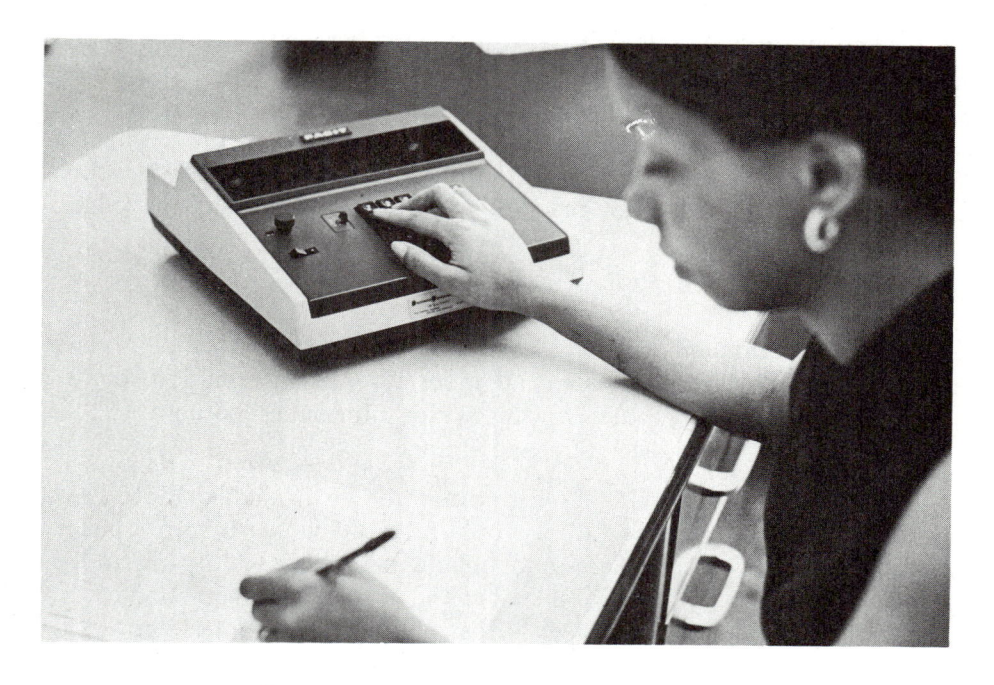

Illus. 6-3   Mechanical means of processing data

Part 1 / How Data Is Processed

Illus. 6-4 Tabulating means of processing data

If you processed a sale by the tabulating method, you would handwrite or typewrite the sales slip. It would provide the information needed to process the data by the tabulating method. The sales slip data would be punched into a punched card and verified, or checked, for accuracy. The holes punched into the card give the information in the form of a code that can be understood by the card punch machines. The punched cards would be processed by machine to produce the journal, the ledger, and the statement.

Processing Data by an Electronic (Computer) System

The computer plays a vital role in the lives of all people today. The business world needs faster and more accurate information for decision-making. The computer can supply this information because of three main features — speed, accuracy, and storage.

Speed. If you were asked to multiply two 10-digit numbers, say 3,575,212,134 by 2,456,754,137, it would be a difficult task with a pencil and paper. This would be an impossible task if you tried to perform the calculations mentally and to remember the original numbers along with the answer for future reference. Most electronic computers, however, could do this calculation along with storing the results in a few *nanoseconds* (a nanosecond is equal to one billionth of a second).

Illus. 6-5   Electronic means of processing data

Accuracy. Accuracy is very important in all businesses. When large numbers of items are processed, it is easy to make errors. In using computers, however, errors can be reduced because the information is verified before it is put into the computer. The computer then follows the same instructions each time without getting tired or bored. Human beings become tired and bored when doing repetitious work and, as a result, make errors.

Storage. Many different types of data can be stored in a computer. Usually the data to be processed and the instructions for processing the data are stored in the computer by using magnetic drums, tapes, or disks. The computer is able to find this data very quickly when it is needed.

Let's say that you are asked to supply a sales slip for the processing of a sale using electronic data processing equipment. You may either handwrite or type this sales slip. Information from the sales slip is then punched into data cards to be processed by the computer. The processing, or manipulation, of the data is performed by a list of instructions to the computer called a *program*. The computer consists of several units which will be discussed in Part 2 of this unit. The computer can prepare the invoice, journal entry, ledger entry, and statement for the customer. Also the computer will retain the information for future reference.

The human mind is an adaptable but very unreliable processor of information. Human beings, however, are needed to handle situations where judgment is required. Electronic data processing combines the talents of people who are slow, inaccurate, and intelligent with computers which are fast, accurate, and not intelligent. Combining the advantages of the human mind and the electronic computer gives the businessman an efficient system of providing information for decision-making.

THE DATA PROCESSING CYCLE

Before a final report is prepared, the data to be used in the report must follow a series of steps called the data processing cycle. The steps in the data processing cycle are (1) origin, (2) input, (3) processing, and (4) output.

Step 1 — Origin of Data

Origin means the beginning or start of something. In business the information to be processed originates in a variety of business papers. The business papers used to record data for the first time are called *source documents*. For example, when you go to a store to buy a record player on a charge account, the sales clerk fills out a sales slip with your name and address, telephone number, description of the item you bought, and the price. Writing this information on the sales slip is the origin of data about your purchase of the record player. Other source documents may include invoices, time cards, or checks.

Step 2 — Input of Data

In Step 2 the data from the source document is recorded in such form that it can be easily manipulated, or processed. If the information is to be processed manually, this step may involve putting the information about your sale in a Sales Journal so that the store can get a total sales figure for the month. If the information is to be processed automatically by electronic equipment, this step may involve punching the data from the source document onto cards or tapes so that it can be processed on electronic equipment. The information is punched into a card or tape by using a card punch, illustrated on page 200.

Step 3 — Processing of Data

The next step is to actually process the data. This may involve classifying, calculating, or summarizing the data. When you purchased your record player, the information concerning the sale was written on a sales slip. The information on the sales slip is processed (added, subtracted, multiplied, divided, or summarized) to prepare a monthly bill for you and to provide reports, such as the Monthly Sales Report, needed to run the business efficiently. The different machines used to process the data will be discussed in Part 2 of this Unit.

Step 4 — Output of Data

The final step in the data processing cycle is the output of data. In this step the information that has been processed is organized and arranged in a usable form. The output document may take a variety of forms. Quite often it is a statement, an invoice, or a report. The output from your purchase of a record player may include a monthly bill to you and a sales report for the store. When data is processed electronically, the output may be another punched card rather than a written report. You are familiar with the monthly utility bill you receive at your home; it is usually in the form of a punched card. This punched card can then be processed automatically when it is returned to the company with payment.

FLOW CHART SYMBOLS

The steps in the data processing cycle can also be shown using a flow chart, which is a diagram of how something moves or flows in a business. Some of the symbols and their meanings in a flow chart are:

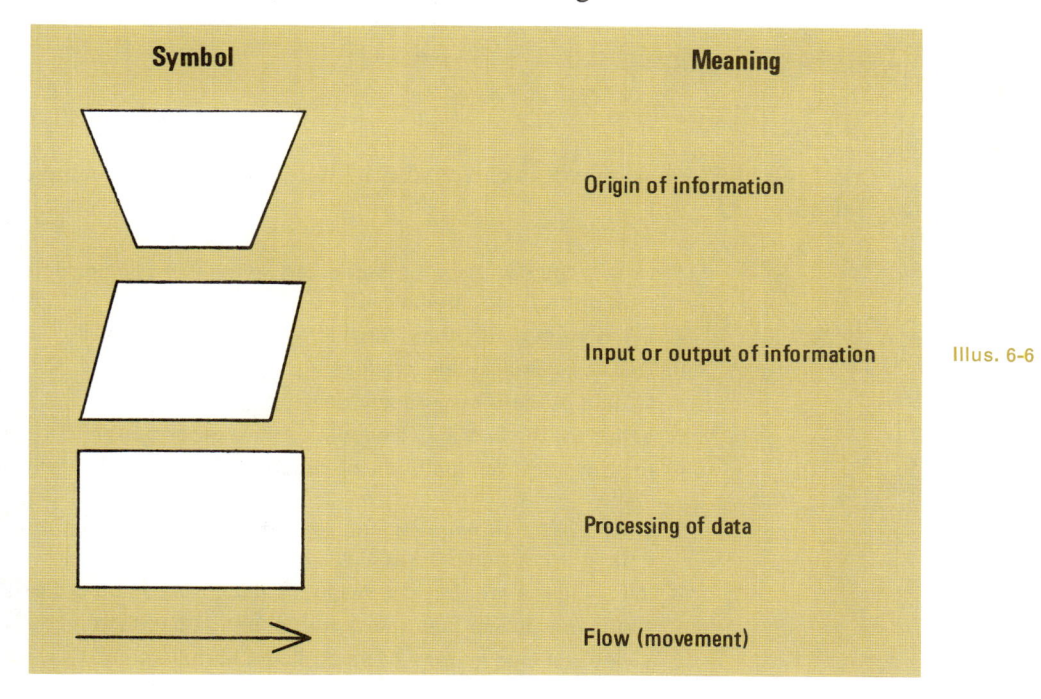

Symbol	Meaning
trapezoid	Origin of information
parallelogram	Input or output of information
rectangle	Processing of data
arrow	Flow (movement)

Illus. 6-6

Part 1 / How Data Is Processed

These symbols are used to describe the process without using words. Using flow chart symbols, the four steps in the data processing cycle could be represented like this:

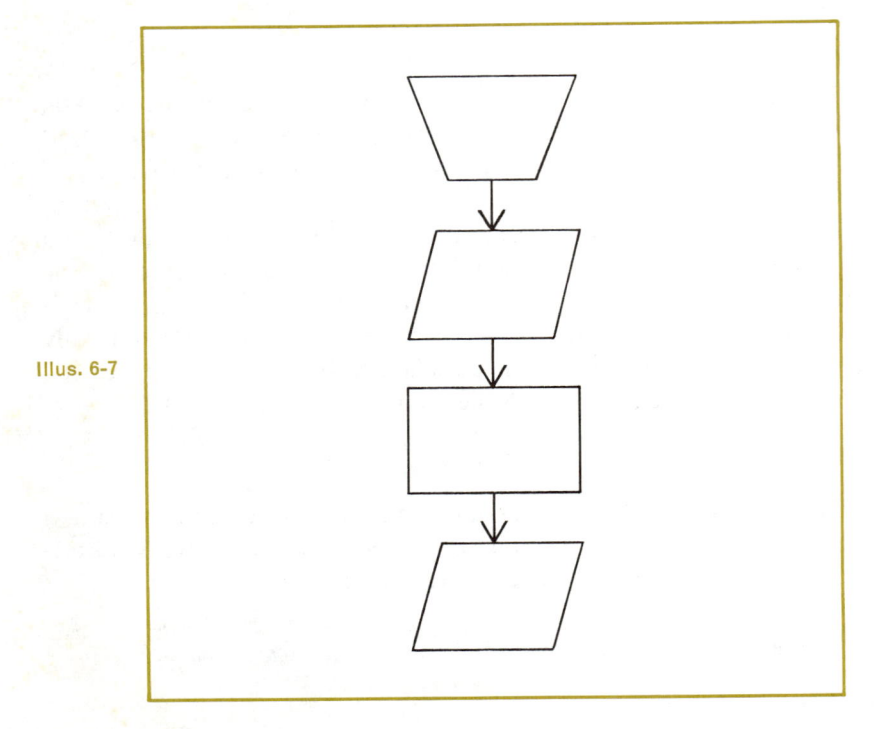

Illus. 6-7

Using flow chart symbols can save time because fewer words have to be used.

QUESTIONS

1. How is the secretary's job affected by the use of electronic data processing equipment?
2. What must a secretary know about data processing?
3. Define business data processing.
4. Is data processing a recent development?
5. What are the two major needs for data processing?
6. Identify the four methods of processing data and briefly explain each.
7. What are the three main features of the computer when the data is processed by the electronic system?
8. What are the four basic steps in the data processing cycle?
9. Name four forms that an output document can take.
10. What is the advantage of using flow chart symbols?

JUDGMENT

1. Sue, a secretary said, "I don't need to know anything about data processing. I'm a secretary." Do you agree with Sue?
2. Jodi was awed by electronic data processing. What can Jodi do to learn more about modern data processing?
3. Do you think all businesses should use electronic data processing? Explain why or why not.

PERSONAL QUALITIES

Mildred Wright is now employed as a stenographer in the stenographic pool of the Allied Insurance Company. Many of the letters and reports that Mildred types contain statistical material.

The company is having an electronic data processing system installed. Mildred is asked if she would care to attend a key punch school maintained by the manufacturer for one week to master the numeric keyboard of the keypunch machine. She is told that, while she may continue as a stenographer, her chances for advancement are somewhat limited by the need for secretaries in the other departments. On the other hand, if she becomes an efficient operator of the key punch machine, her chances of being promoted to a secretarial position in the new Data Processing Department are very good.

Should Mildred continue as a stenographer, or should she accept the offer to train on a key punch machine?

LANGUAGE USAGE

1. Quotation marks are used to enclose the beginning and end of a *direct* quotation.

    Example: The Rev. W. A. Nance, Chaplain for Holiday Inns, Inc., said, "The ability to speak in several languages is valuable; the ability to keep your mouth shut in one is priceless."

2. Quotation marks are used to set off quotations that are *built into* a sentence.

    Example: His letter said that there are "several languages used in data processing" and that he "intends to master all of them."

3. Quotation marks are used to set off a specific part of a complete work. (The title of the complete work is put in italics.)

    Example: "Processing Data," which is Unit 6, will be found in *Secretarial Office Procedures*.

Type the sentences below on a separate sheet of paper and correctly insert the quotation marks.

1. On page 183 the author states the term *data processing* is new, but the activity is not new.
2. In his letter he wrote that speed, accuracy, and storage are features of a computer; and then he went on to explain that computers can store a vast amount of information.

3. Touch-Operated, Ten-Key Electronic Calculator is the title of a section in the fourth edition of *Office Machines Course*.
4. The teacher told the students that they should maintain a neat work area and also that they should always clear the machine before starting the solution to a problem.
5. The first sentence under Flow Chart Symbols says the steps in the data processing cycle can also be shown using a flow chart, which is a diagram of how something moves or flows in a business.

SECRETARIAL WORK

1. Visit a local company that uses electronic data processing and write a report on your visit. Include in your report the advantages and disadvantages of electronic data processing to the firm and your reaction to the employee's acceptance of the system.
2. The following letter was received from a customer complaining about an error made by a computer on his monthly statement.

    Gentlemen:

    I am again returning this statement to you because it is incorrect. As I told you last month, I did not purchase the lawn chair charged to me on May 19; yet it has not been subtracted from my account.

    Will you please tell your computer to straighten this out? I will pay the bill as soon as this correction is made.

    Sincerely yours,

    Charles Townsend

    As soon as you check the complaint you discover that an error was made when writing the account number so that the computer charged the lawn chair to the wrong account.

    (a) Write a letter explaining the situation to Mr. Townsend at 2304 Grove Street, N.E., Salem, OR 97303.
    (b) Was the error the computer's fault?
    (c) How does an error like this affect customer relations?
    (d) What can be done to prevent errors like this from happening again?

PART 2 COMPUTING AND RECORDING MACHINES

After Jo Ann graduated from high school, she began working for the Dowell Company. The Dowell Company did not, at that time, have any modern data processing equipment. However, as their business grew, they installed several of the latest data processing machines to handle their increased payroll and accounts receivable records. Jo Ann was fascinated by how fast the machines worked. She learned many interesting facts about the new data processing machines, such as the electronic calculator, bookkeeping machines, card punch, sorter, and verifier. Do you know how each of these machines is used in business today?

You may have to check columns of figures, discounts, or percentages for a report or a letter that your employer has dictated. It may also be your responsibility, in a small office, to handle payrolls for several departments, sales analyses, financial statements, and expense reports. These business records contain many calculations that can be easily and accurately produced with the aid of an office machine. Computing and recording machines have been installed in modern business offices to handle the ever-increasing volume of paper work. You will frequently work with processed records when you are employed as a secretary, and you should have a clear understanding of the operation of the major data processing machines.

CALCULATING MACHINES

There is a variety of calculating machines that you may use as a secretary. The amount of work you do on a calculator will depend on the business in which you are working. Some of the duties you may perform using a calculator are checking a report containing computations, figuring the payroll, preparing financial statements, and budget and expense reports. You need to be aware of the types of calculators available and the uses of each.

Electronic Calculators

The electronic calculator is the most modern of all the calculators and is replacing many of the other types of calculators. Many models do not have any moving parts and are completely silent. They compute very rapidly.

Illus. 6-8   Marchant electronic calculator

Illus. 6-9   Friden electronic calculator

Some electronic calculators indicate the computation by lighted figures in a window directly above the keyboard; others display the computation on a television-like screen. Models are available that will perform every kind of computation that is normally needed in a business office.

Ten-Key Listing Machine

As the name implies, a ten-key machine has only ten figure keys on the keyboard. Amounts are entered on the keyboard and printed on the paper tape in the order in which they are read. Each figure key, including the 0, or cipher key, is depressed separately. For example, to list $50.60 you would depress the 5, 0, 6, and 0 keys and then depress the motor bar.

Remington Rand

Illus. 6-10   Ten-key listing machine

Because the machine has only ten figure keys, all within easy reach, you will be able to enter amounts on the keyboard without looking at the keys after a few hours of instruction. Touch operation will increase your production rate and greatly reduce your chances of omitting amounts or transposing figures in an amount.

Ten-key listing machines are used primarily for addition and subtraction.

You will use the ten-key listing machine to check figures in reports and financial statements much more quickly and accurately than if you had to do this task manually.

Printing Calculator

If your work demands much multiplication and division, you will want to use a printing calculator. The printing calculator is used extensively as an all-purpose calculator. It is preferred by some office workers, particularly accountants, because the tapes can be forwarded with the source material from which the computations were made. All printing calculators have ten-figure keyboards and, like the other ten-key machines,

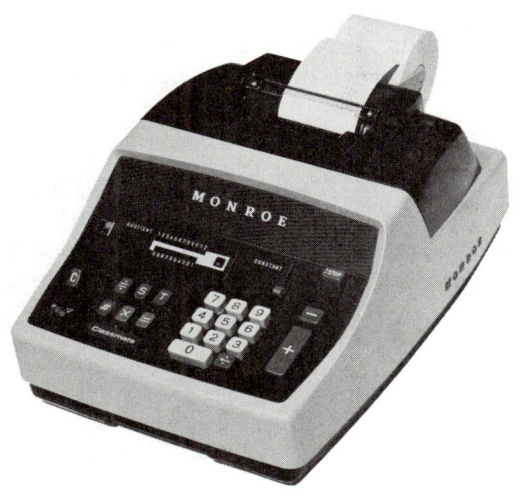

Monroe

Illus. 6-11   Printing calculator

can be operated by touch. You may use the printing calculator to figure extensions on bills to be paid by your firm, to figure commissions or salaries for hourly employees, and to perform many other tasks.

Full-Keyboard Listing Machine

A full-keyboard machine will have from five to twenty columns of keys ranging in ascending order from 1 to 9. You will see that there are

Part 2 / Computing and Recording Machines

no *0* keys on the keyboard; zeros are printed automatically. The full-keyboard listing machine is used primarily for addition and subtraction.

Illus. 6-12
Full-keyboard listing machine

Remington Rand

Some listing machines have movable carriages which will hold statement and ledger cards. If you worked in a small company, you would be able to do your billing work on the listing machine itself.

Rotary Calculators

You may use a rotary calculator for multiplying and dividing numbers with many digits. You can use decimal markers on the keyboard and in the answer dials to guide you in recording amounts with decimals. Rotary calculators are used for many business and engineering problems.

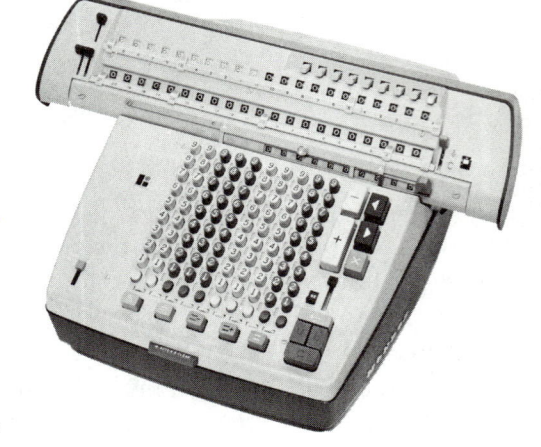

Illus. 6-13
Rotary calculator

Monroe

CASH REGISTERS

The cash register has been widely used in business to process data. It can be used to record a transaction and also to give a receipt to the customer. Special cash registers are available that also show the correct change due a customer.

The cash register records all cash sales, charge sales, receipts on account, or paid-out items on an audit tape. At the end of each day, the audit tape is used to determine whether the amount of cash in the cash register drawer agrees with the cash amount on the tape.

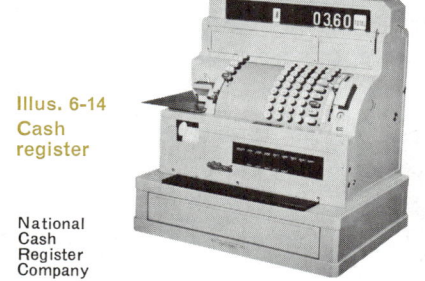

Illus. 6-14
Cash register

National Cash Register Company

```
529.38 Ca
147.06 Ch
 58.21 Re
121.90 Pd
```

Illus. 6-15
Audit tape

BOOKKEEPING MACHINES

Bookkeeping machines are also known as *billing* machines or *accounting* machines. The main advantages of bookkeeping machines are

National Cash Register Company

Illus. 6-16   Bookkeeping machine

Part 2 / Computing and Recording Machines

their ability to tabulate from one position to another and to print at high speeds. Such reports as statements, invoices, and checks can be prepared on a bookkeeping machine much more rapidly and accurately than they can be handwritten. Bookkeeping machines can perform addition; subtraction; and, with a special attachment, multiplication and division.

Bookkeeping machines are particularly valuable to you when you have to repeat the data many times.

INTEGRATED DATA PROCESSING MACHINES

Integrated data processing, or IDP as it is called, is a system based on the ability of office machines to transfer information to other machines automatically. Punched paper tape serves as the medium for automatically transferring the data from one machine to another.

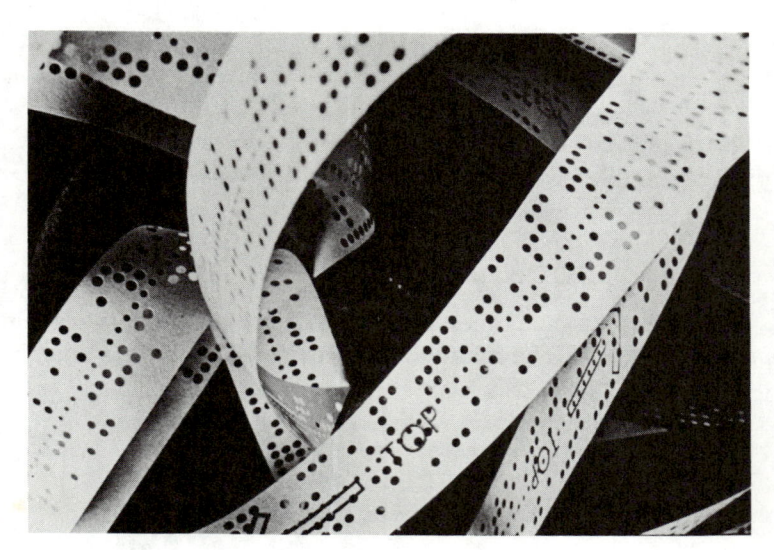

AT&T

Illus. 6-17 Punched tape

Flexowriter

The Flexowriter, an automatic writing machine, is a key instrument in integrated data processing. As you type on it, a punched paper tape containing the information is produced simultaneously. The purpose of the machine is to produce a punched tape of the information so that it can be processed on other machines in the integrated data processing system. Other machines in the system can read the tape and produce typed invoices and other business papers from it at the rate of 100 words a minute or more.

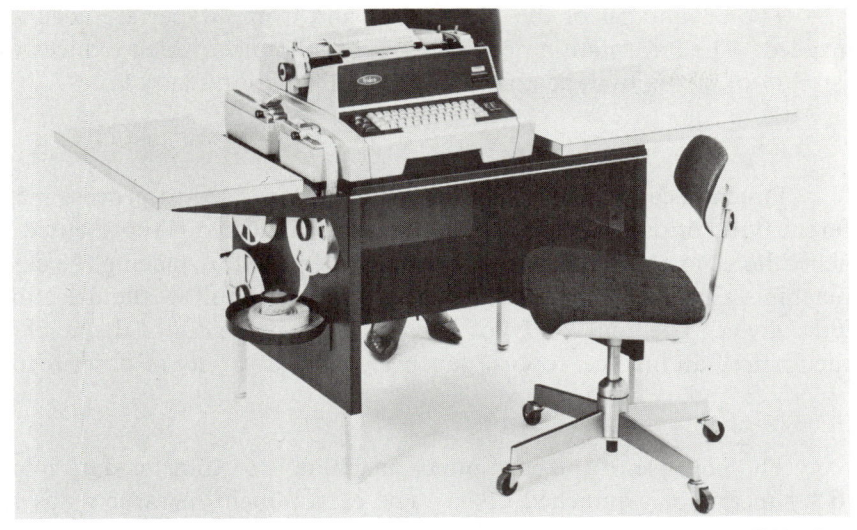

Illus. 6-18
Flexowriter

Friden, Inc.

Some Flexowriters produce edge-punched cards instead of tapes. They perform the same function as the tape, but, because the cards can be kept in files, they are more convenient to handle.

Computyper

You may take the tape from the Flexowriter and put it on the Computyper. The Computyper adds, subtracts, or multiplies the figures on the tape and produces a typed invoice, statement, or other business paper.

Illus. 6-19
Computyper

Friden, Inc.

Part 2 / Computing and Recording Machines 199

The advantages of the Flexowriter and Computyper are accuracy and speed. The information needed is typed only once, which reduces the possibility of errors by repeating the same information many times.

PUNCHED CARD DATA PROCESSING MACHINES

Punched card data processing machines are used to process many different types of data. The information to be processed is represented by punched holes in cards. The information is processed by placing the cards in machines that can read the holes in the cards and follow the directions that are given. The final results of the processing come out of the machine in the form of an invoice, report, paycheck, or in a variety of other forms.

Card Punch Machine

The purpose of the card punch machine is to transfer data into a card by means of a punched code. The card punch operator reads the

IBM Corporation

Illus. 6-20   Card punch machine

source document and depresses keys that punch holes in the cards. The holes represent numbers, letters, and symbols as illustrated in the card below. The machine automatically feeds, positions, and ejects each card. The operator must strike the proper keys in the correct sequence.

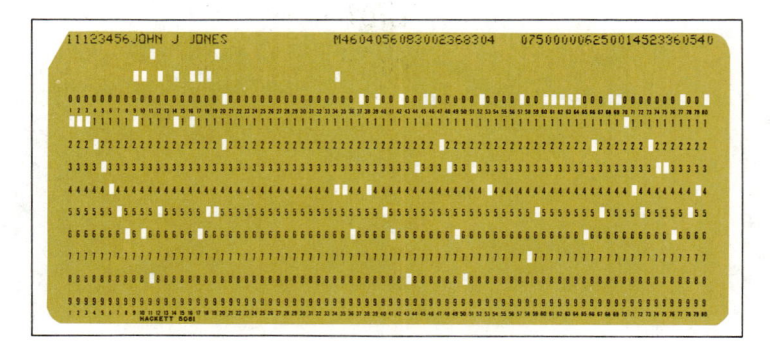

Illus. 6-21   Punch card

Unit 6 / Processing Data

Verifier

Since accuracy is so essential, card verifying is necessary to check original card punching. A different operator usually verifies the original punching by striking the keys of a verifier while reading from the same source of information used to punch the cards. The verifying machine

Illus. 6-22   Card verifier

compares the key struck with the hole already punched in the column on the card. A difference causes the machine to stop, indicating a difference between the two operations.

Sorter

Imagine sorting from 800 to 1,000 cards a minute with complete accuracy! This is one of the outstanding advantages of the punched card system. After the punched cards have been verified, they are sorted into

Illus. 6-23   Sorter

numeric or alphabetic order according to the information that has been punched in them. Payroll cards, for example, may be sorted alphabetically according to the last and given names of the employees or numerically according to their time card numbers.

Tabulator

After the cards have been sorted, they are fed through a tabulator to transcribe and print automatically the information punched in the cards. The tabulator will print names and other descriptive information from a group of cards, add or subtract punched amounts, and print totals and

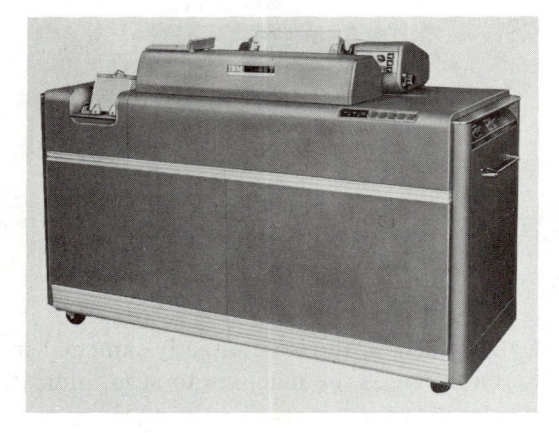

IBM Corporation

Illus. 6-24   Tabulator

grand totals only, without listing either the descriptive information or the separate amounts punched into the individual cards. Tabulating machines operate at speeds ranging from 100 to 150 cards a minute depending upon the type of machine used.

COMPUTERS

Computers are associated with electronic data processing — the processing of records with electronic systems. A typical electronic data processing system uses three groups of linked devices or machines to perform the related steps in an operation.

Input Unit

The input devices are used to enter instructions and data into the storage section of the system. The information to be placed in the computer may be recorded on punched cards, paper tape, or magnetic tape.

Central Processing Unit

The central processing unit includes

1. The *storage section* which stores data, instructions, final results, historical data, master records, and any other information that can be advantageously stored within the computer.

IBM Corporation

Illus. 6-25
The electronic system

2. The *process section* which manipulates the data. Computing — addition, subtraction, multiplication, and division — is performed here.

3. The *control section* which could be called the nerve center of the data processing system. It receives each instruction of the program and analyzes it to determine the operation to be performed. The movement of data into or out of storage is supervised by the control section. It controls the actual execution of the operation. It monitors and supervises the flow of data within the system. It notifies the operator when attention is required.

Output Unit

The output devices are used to take the results of the processing out of the system. The output devices usually reproduce the information on punched cards or in printed form on wide continuous forms.

Part 2 / Computing and Recording Machines

By having a knowledge of the ways data can be processed in an office, you are better prepared to perform your job as a secretary in a modern office.

QUESTIONS

1. Under what circumstances might the secretary use calculating machines?
2. What are the special features of an electronic calculator?
3. What is one of the chief advantages of a ten-key listing machine?
4. How is an audit tape used?
5. What are the main advantages of bookkeeping machines?
6. How is a Flexowriter used?
7. What is the purpose of a Computyper?
8. What are the four basic punched-card machines and for what is each used?
9. Explain how the verifier is used.
10. What are the three units in an electronic data processing system?

JUDGMENT

1. Why are business firms changing to data processing systems?
2. What is the effect of electronic data processing on office employment?

PERSONAL QUALITIES

You have recently been employed by the Gordon Insurance Agency. There are four other secretaries in the office. Adair, the secretary with the most seniority, has been asked to assist you in learning how to operate an electronic calculator. Adair resents having to spend her time teaching you and, as a result, often speaks sharply to you. What can you do to help decrease the tension in this situation? Is a willingness to help others a necessary trait for a good secretary?

LANGUAGE USAGE

Using the suffixes *able* and *ible*, convert the following words into adjectives. Type both the root word and the adjective.

Examples: *Root Word*   *Adjective*
    predict   predictable
    defense   defensible

1. present
2. knowledge
3. resist
4. verify
5. charge
6. accept
7. change
8. prevent
9. notice
10. manage

SECRETARIAL WORK

1. Visit one or more offices in your community to find out what adding and calculating machines are being used. Also find out what particular kinds of jobs are being done on the various machines. If possible, request some of the business forms that are used in connection with these jobs. Prepare a typewritten report on your visit, attaching the forms collected. Be prepared to make an oral presentation to the class.

2. Write to one or more manufacturers of adding and calculating machines asking for literature on their machines. Use this material for a bulletin board display.

3. If calculating machines are available to you, use one of the machines to do the following problem. If calculating machines are not available, do the problem manually.

   You purchase the following items from the Harris Office Supply Company:

		Total Due
15 boxes	Fluid Masters @ $2.46	$36.90
7 reams	Duplicating Paper @ $2.06	15.42
3 boxes	Carbon Paper @ $1.74	5.22
4 boxes	Envelopes @ $1.22	5.88
25	Pens @ $.20	4.00
6	Typewriter Ribbons @ $1.18	7.08
		$74.47

   (a) Carefully check each item to make sure all extensions and totals are correct. On a separate sheet of paper indicate any corrections and the correct total.

   (b) Harris Office Supply Company gives you a 2 percent discount if you pay your bill within ten days. What would be the total amount you should pay Harris Office Supply Company if you paid the bill within the ten days?

PART 3   BUSINESS FORMS

Tina Bruno has worked as a secretary to Mr. Don Brown for two years. Just recently she took a night course in secretarial training at the local college to increase her efficiency in her job. In this course she learned about business forms and how they should be designed. She was able to apply this knowledge on her job by making suggestions for improvements in several of the company's business forms. Do you know the **advantages** of having a well-designed business form? **Can you distinguish between a well-designed and a poorly designed business form?**

    Almost every operation in a business depends upon some type of business form on which data is processed. You and all office employees will work with business forms. Each of these forms should have a specific name and a specific purpose. When merchandise is bought, a purchase order is made out; when a sale is made, many forms are made out to record the complete transaction. When an automobile is produced, numerous forms are used along every step of its manufacture and sale. Forms are needed to record, process, and transmit the information and instructions required for business transactions in all kinds of businesses — from small, local establishments to large, nationally known corporations.

    What part will you, the secretary, have in handling business forms? Of course, how much or how little you do with business forms will depend on the size of the office and the type of work in which your employer is engaged. As a secretarial office worker, you may fill out a handwritten form occasionally, but you will probably spend much more time preparing typewritten forms. You may also use a calculating machine along with the typewriter to complete forms containing computations. You may copy information and compile statistical data from business forms, and you will surely be expected to check, sort, and file forms.

PURPOSE OF BUSINESS FORMS

    A business form is a printed slip of paper on which information can be recorded. Many business forms are used as source documents for the data processing cycle.

The printed information on a form — the firm name, address, telephone number, payment terms, shipping conditions — eliminates the need for recopying this information on every document. For efficient handling, the most important information on the form, whether it be the name, invoice number, amount, or due date, should be printed where it can be read easily and filed accurately.

Another way to reduce the need for recopying data is to make multiple copies. When the data is needed by several people, the use of carbon paper saves time, reduces cost, and increases accuracy. Multicopy forms and carbonless paper are also used to make several copies of a business form.

Each section of a business form should serve a specific purpose. The heading shows that the form is a genuine document issued by a business firm. A statement, for example, should be prepared on a firm's statement form to prove that the request for payment is authentic. The printed name of the form will indicate its purpose: a purchase order (authority to buy); an invoice (bill of sale); and a statement (a request for payment).

The column headings will indicate what is to be done. For example, if an earnings record shows the gross earnings of each employee in one column and the payroll deductions in the following columns, you would be expected to subtract the deductions from the gross earnings and record the differences in the *net earnings* column for each employee. You would also be expected to add all columns and record the totals in the spaces provided at the bottom of the earnings record.

FORM DESIGN

You may not only work with business forms but may also be requested to make suggestions for the design of a new form. Business forms to be filled in on typewriters and other office machines should be designed to take advantage of the spacing and tabular mechanisms of the machines. For example, if a form is to be filled in on a typewriter, the horizontal lines should be one sixth or one third of an inch apart to permit continuous single or double spaced typewriting and to make it unnecessary to use the variable line spacer. Insofar as possible, horizontal and vertical lines should not be used on business forms, especially lines for names and addresses and the traditional vertical line to separate dollars and cents in the amount columns. These lines merely add to the time spent in setting up the proper tab stops or in typing on lines. The name and address are usually typed within a specific area on the form to permit the use of a window envelope. Correct and incorrect forms are illustrated at the top of page 208.

Right	Wrong
S	S
O .	O _____
L .	L _____
D .	D _____
.	
T	T _____
O	O _____

Illus. 6-26

Forms should be printed so that as many lines as possible start at an aligned left margin and at all tabular stops:

	Marginal Stop	*Tabular Stop*
Right	Consigned to Destination Route	Order No. Invoice No. Invoice Date
Wrong	Consigned to _____ Destination _____ Route _____	Order No. _____ Invoice No. _____ Invoice Date _____

Illus. 6-27

To minimize tabulating, spacing for boxed information should be aligned with spacing for columns, as in this example:

Margin Stop	Tab Stop	Tab Stop	Tab Stop	Tab Stop	Tab Stop
Date Entered		Ship Via	Salesman	Cust. No.	Dept. No.
Dec. 15, 197-		Truck	DWB	1732	AQ-32
Quantity Ordered	Quantity Shipped	Description		Unit Price	Amount
147	147	Radio, 77K3180		1.38	202.86
50	50	Tubes, 813R47		1.75	87.50

Illus. 6-28

Ample space should be allowed at the top, bottom, and sides of the forms to permit binding, perforating, and stapling.

When business forms are used as source documents for transferring data to punched cards, the information that must be punched on the cards should appear in the same order on the business form. This will speed up the card punching process because the card punch operator can read and punch the information in sequence.

FORMS FOR PURCHASING

The purchasing and receiving of goods are important operations in any business enterprise. In large organizations these operations are handled by separate departments; in small organizations they are handled by purchasing and receiving clerks and occasionally by secretaries. For example, secretaries are often given the responsibility for purchasing needed office supplies. Whether the buying is done through a department head, by a purchasing agent, by a purchasing clerk, or by a secretary, the aim is the same — to secure for the firm the needed material and equipment of the desired quality at the most reasonable price. The reputation of the seller for honest dealing and prompt delivery is an important factor to be considered in deciding where major purchases should be made.

The purchasing procedure is a well-planned office routine in which each step is determined by the work that precedes it. The purchasing procedure follows this sequence: requesting the goods needed, obtaining quotations on the cost of the goods needed, preparing a purchase order, checking the incoming shipment, and adjusting any damage or claim.

Purchase Requisition

Most of the work of the purchasing department involves the purchasing of goods and services for a firm. The *purchase requisition* is used to inform the purchasing agent or some other authorized buyer for the firm what specific items should be purchased. For example, if you are working for a large business and need bond paper for your office, you will prepare a purchase requisition for the purchasing department. The purchasing department will then get the paper you need.

You will find that the purchase requisition requires such information as the current date, the date the goods are needed, and a detailed description of the goods requested which includes the trade name, catalog number, quantity to be ordered, and the price of each item, if it is known. It may also indicate the name and address of a firm from which the goods may be purchased. You must get all this information before completing this form.

electronic research co.
32 Foster Rd. Long Beach, CA 90805   Area Code 213 891-8393

PURCHASE REQUISITION

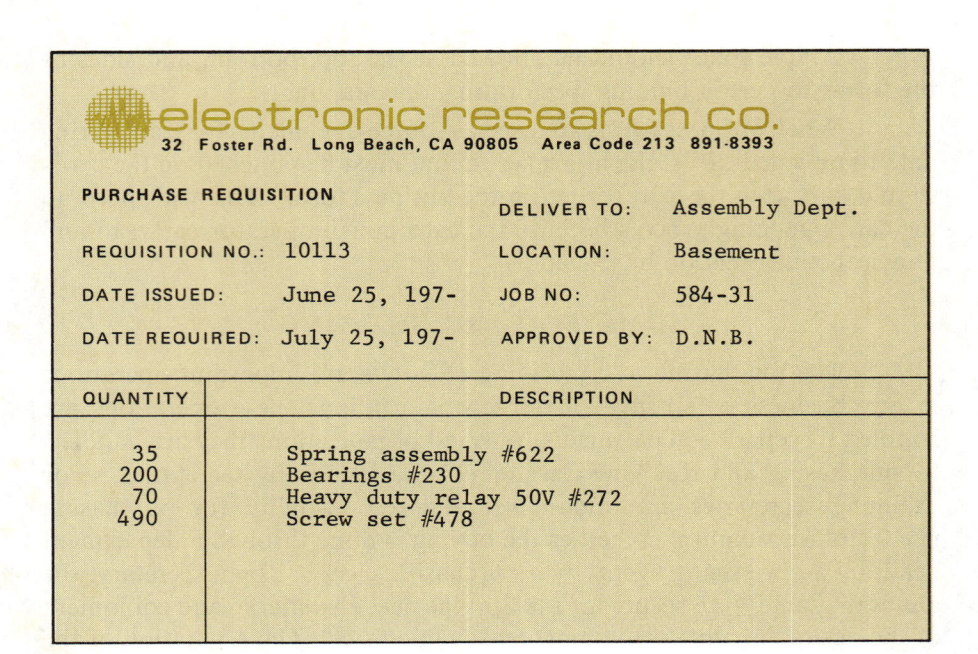

REQUISITION NO.: 10113	DELIVER TO: Assembly Dept.
DATE ISSUED: June 25, 197-	LOCATION: Basement
DATE REQUIRED: July 25, 197-	JOB NO: 584-31
	APPROVED BY: D.N.B.

QUANTITY	DESCRIPTION
35	Spring assembly #622
200	Bearings #230
70	Heavy duty relay 50V #272
490	Screw set #478

Illus. 6-29
Purchase requisition

You usually should prepare two copies of a purchase requisition. You send the original copy (after it has been signed by your employer) to the purchasing agent and keep the duplicate in your files. If you are employed by a large organization, you may be required to prepare additional copies of each purchase requisition so that they may be available for the auditing department or other departments.

Purchase Order

The goods you requisitioned may be ordered in a number of ways: by writing an order letter, by sending a telegram, by making a telephone call, by giving an order to a salesman, by filling out and mailing an order blank that is included as part of a catalog, or by filling out a *purchase order* that has been especially designed for the purpose. Most firms prefer to use purchase orders which they mail to the business from which they order goods (the vendors) because the purchase order is a written record for future references. If the goods are urgently needed by your executive, you can order them by telephone or telegraph; but a confirming purchase order to cover the transaction is prepared and mailed to the vendor later.

electronic research co.
32 Foster Rd.   Long Beach, CA 90805   Area Code 213 891-8393

PURCHASE ORDER

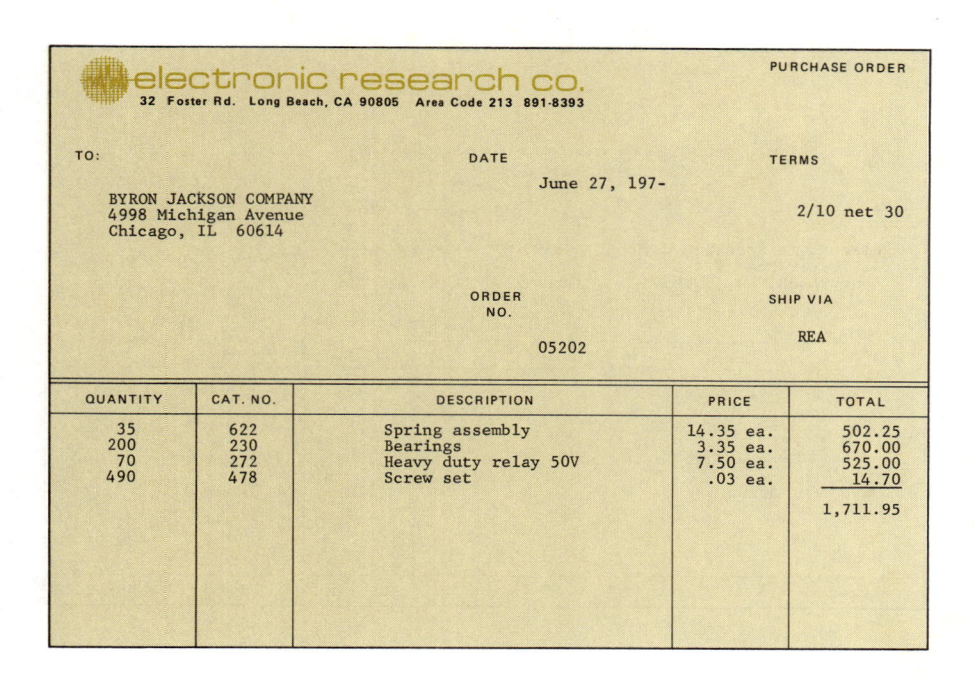

TO:
BYRON JACKSON COMPANY
4998 Michigan Avenue
Chicago, IL 60614

DATE: June 27, 197-

TERMS: 2/10 net 30

ORDER NO. 05202

SHIP VIA: REA

QUANTITY	CAT. NO.	DESCRIPTION	PRICE	TOTAL
35	622	Spring assembly	14.35 ea.	502.25
200	230	Bearings	3.35 ea.	670.00
70	272	Heavy duty relay 50V	7.50 ea.	525.00
490	478	Screw set	.03 ea.	14.70
				1,711.95

Illus. 6-30
Purchase order

You will usually prepare four or more copies of printed purchase orders, because several departments in the firm will need a copy of each purchase order. The purchase order includes the name, address, and telephone number of the firm issuing the order, the date of issue, the name and address of the vendor, the purchase order number, shipping instructions, and terms of payment. It also includes the quantity, the stock number, description of the product, single unit price, and extended total figures.

Purchase Invoice

When the vendor ships the merchandise you ordered, he usually mails an invoice to your firm on the same day. The invoice is known to the vendor as a *sales invoice* and to the buyer, your firm, as a *purchase invoice*. An invoice usually includes the current date, the name and address of the vendor, the name and address of the purchaser, the invoice number, the vendor's order number, the purchaser's order number, the terms of payment, the method of shipment, the quantity of each item, a description of each item, the stock number, the unit price, the extensions, and the total. It may also show trade discounts and other deductions allowed the purchaser by the vendor.

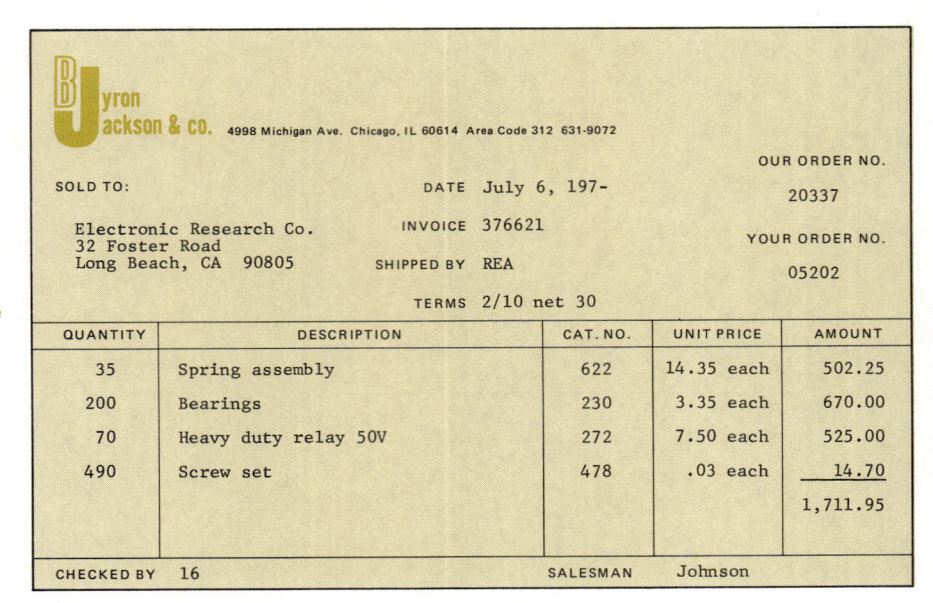

Illus. 6-31
Purchase invoice

Byron Jackson & Co.
4998 Michigan Ave. Chicago, IL 60614 Area Code 312 631-9072

SOLD TO:

Electronic Research Co.
32 Foster Road
Long Beach, CA 90805

DATE July 6, 197-
INVOICE 376621
SHIPPED BY REA
TERMS 2/10 net 30

OUR ORDER NO. 20337
YOUR ORDER NO. 05202

QUANTITY	DESCRIPTION	CAT. NO.	UNIT PRICE	AMOUNT
35	Spring assembly	622	14.35 each	502.25
200	Bearings	230	3.35 each	670.00
70	Heavy duty relay 50V	272	7.50 each	525.00
490	Screw set	478	.03 each	14.70
				1,711.95

CHECKED BY 16   SALESMAN Johnson

In a large firm incoming purchase invoices are usually handled by the purchasing department. As a rule only one copy is received, although some firms request additional copies. If you work in a small firm, you may be responsible for checking the purchase invoices against the terms and conditions of the purchase order to be sure that they agree.

FORMS FOR SELLING

Recording the data directly connected with the sale of merchandise or services is also one of the key operations of any business enterprise. The sales forms on which the data is recorded vary with the size and type of business, but all firms use a sales order form. Department stores and other retail stores also use "layaway" order forms, installment order forms, and sales books.

As a secretary, you should understand the sales procedures followed by modern business firms and the purpose of each of the standard sales forms because much of your dictation may deal with sales. If you are employed in a sales department or by a small firm, you may be expected to prepare and process sales forms.

Sales Order

When a purchase order is received by the vendor, a sales order form is prepared. A *sales order* form is used by most firms to record the sale of merchandise. It provides space for the name and address of the customer, the customer's order number, the seller's invoice number, the terms of payment, the shipping instructions, the number of items, a description of each item, and the unit price. The sales order usually lists any special instructions or conditions and the trade discounts allowed.

Credit Memorandum

Some customers will return merchandise for one reason or another. Your firm, too, may return merchandise delivered too late to be of value; merchandise of the wrong kind, style, or color; or merchandise received in a damaged condition. There may be other reasons why customers do not wish to keep the goods. In most instances, after the customer informs the seller about the situation, the customer will be instructed to return the merchandise. In some cases, it may be more advantageous to make a special allowance to the customer to cover the loss if he keeps the merchandise rather than returns it.

When merchandise is returned or when an allowance is granted to a customer, a *credit memorandum* is issued. This credit memorandum is very much like an invoice and carries about the same information that appears on an invoice. At least two copies are made — one for the customer to whom the credit memorandum is issued and the other for the accounting department to be used in crediting the customer's account for the amount of the returned goods or of the allowance.

Illus. 6-32
Credit memorandum

Part 3 / Business Forms

CREDIT APPROVAL

When the order is received without an accompanying payment in full, it must be approved by the credit department before the merchandise is packed and shipped. The credit department may approve the shipment of the goods on the terms your firm suggests; but, for a firm with a poor credit reputation, it may decide that the goods should be shipped COD (Collect on Delivery). When the latter procedure is recommended, and the terms are different from the credit terms suggested by the buyer, you may be required to write to the customer tactfully informing him of the situation and asking him whether the goods should be shipped under the vendor's terms. This is another duty sometimes performed by the secretary.

BILLING

When the order is shipped to your firm, the bill or invoice is mailed. This vital operation of a business enterprise is commonly known as *billing*, but in some firms is called *invoicing*.

Your firm may not receive all bills at the end of the month. Some companies may bill you on the fourteenth, others on the twenty-first. This procedure is called *cycle billing*. Many department stores and public utilities, including telephone companies and gas and electric companies, have divided their lists of customers and now send out bills on different dates in the month, rather than send out all bills at the end of the month. This makes it possible for the billing departments to work steadily, to avoid peak loads, and to send out bills when completed. Companies may divide customer lists alphabetically, by districts, or by sales territories.

Preparing the Invoice

Every well-organized business establishes a definite procedure for preparing invoices. This procedure may differ with the number of invoices prepared by each concern. A small number of invoices may be prepared on typewriters, a large number on special billing machines, and a very large volume of invoices with integrated data processing equipment.

Most invoices prepared on billing machines or integrated data processing equipment are typed on continuous multiple forms. These forms are printed on continuous strips of paper with perforations between each set of forms. The forms can be separated at the perforation.

Calculating and Checking Invoices

All invoices should be checked for accuracy before they are mailed to the customers. The checking should be done by someone other than the

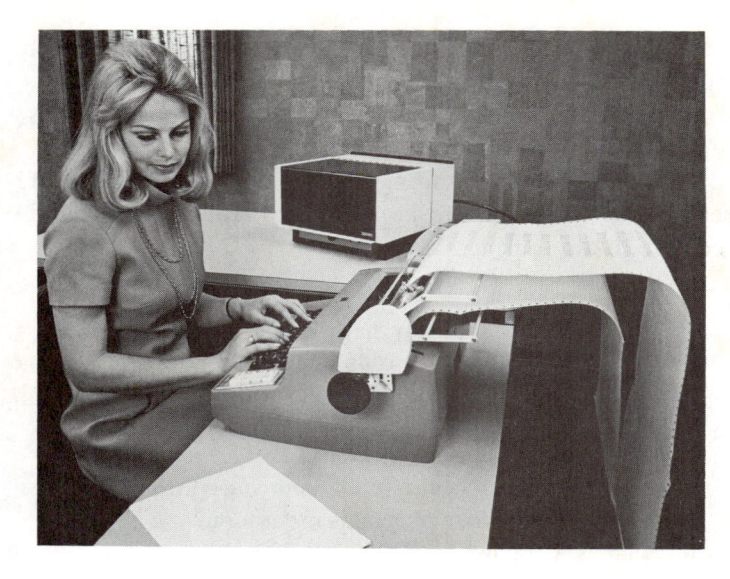

Illus. 6-33
Continuous forms

Qantel Corporation

person who actually prepared the invoice. The extensions can be checked with a desk calculator or by checking the items against precomputed tables. A *precomputed table* is one that lists the items that might be sold and in other columns the prices charged for the various units, such as a dozen, a gross, or a case.

Statements

At regular intervals, usually monthly, you must send each customer a *statement* of his account. The statement shows the amount the customer owed at the beginning of the month, the charges and payments made during the month, and the balance owed at the end of the month.

		STATEMENT OF ACCOUNT		
Byron Jackson & Co. 4998 Michigan Ave. Chicago, IL 60614 Area Code 312 631-9072				
TO Electronic Research Co. 32 Foster Road Long Beach, CA 90805		DATE July 31, 197-		
DATE	ITEMS	DEBITS	CREDITS	BALANCE DUE
July 6	Our Invoice 376621	1,711.95		
July 22	Credit Memo 722		45.00	1,666.95

Illus. 6-34
Statement

Part 3 / Business Forms   215

Statements are usually prepared on bookkeeping machines, punched card tabulating machines, and other data processing equipment, depending upon the size of the business. However, in a small business this may be the responsibility of the secretary.

Your knowledge and understanding of these key operations of purchasing and selling will enable you to be a more capable assistant and partner to the executive in any business.

QUESTIONS

1. Why should a secretary have a knowledge of business forms that are used in buying and selling?
2. Why is form design so important to the office worker? How is it related to the use of the typewriter?
3. What is the purpose of a purchase order?
4. What information is shown on a purchase invoice?
5. What is the purpose of a sales order form?
6. When is a credit memorandum issued?
7. What is the purpose of credit approval?
8. What is the advantage of cycle billing?
9. Customers' bills should be checked for accuracy before they are sent out. What is the best way to do this?
10. What information is shown on a statement?

JUDGMENT

1. Do you think that the purchasing and sales departments are equally important in a business?
2. Would the purchasing department of a bank be as important as the purchasing department of a manufacturing concern? Why or why not?
3. Do you think it necessary that all purchases or sales be confirmed either by use of a filled-in form or by letter? Why or why not would you recommend this practice?

PERSONAL QUALITIES

Mary Young, secretary to Dr. Allan Brooks, a very prominent dentist, types and mails out the monthly bills.

Unfortunately, the bills are rarely mailed out before the tenth of each month. If the statements were mailed out earlier, payments would be made sooner.

Mary feels that she could get out the statements earlier if she were permitted to use a new form. The present form contains horizontal lines for the name and address of each patient, but the lines do not agree with the vertical spacing on the typewriter, and the variable line spacer must be used to move from one line to another.

If you were Mary, what recommendation would you make for redesigning the statement? How would you convince the dentist of the value of a change in statement form?

LANGUAGE USAGE

Several of the words listed below are misspelled. Type the entire list giving the correct spelling for each word.

1. appreciation
2. includeed
3. industral
4. guarantee
5. government
6. jugment
7. neccessary
8. percentage
9. specefications
10. services
11. satisfactary
12. submitted
13. therfore
14. warehouse
15. scheduled
16. reccommendation
17. property
18. provisions
19. offecer
20. oblegation

SECRETARIAL WORK

1. If blank business forms are not available for this and the following problems, use plain paper, and type the information that is ordinarily printed on such forms as shown in the illustrations in this part.

   Type invoices in duplicate for the following sales made by the National Furniture Company, 1440 Jefferson Avenue, Forest Hills, New York 12068, on December 3, 197–, terms 2/10, net 30 days. The quantities and unit prices are given; you are to make all extensions and calculate the totals.

   (a) The Howard Supply Co., 426 Edwards Road, Trenton, New Jersey 08603:

      9 Four Drawer Filing Cabinets, Standard Finish, Style 1805. Price: $85.10 each
      15 Counter Height (3 drawer) Filing Cabinets, Standard Finish, Style 1855. Price: $64.25 each
      84 Frames for Pendaflex File Folders, Style 812. Price: $1.35 each

   (b) The Kramer Publishing Company, 784 Carter Street, Unionville, Connecticut 06085:

      8 Bookcases, open, 52 3/8" x 37 1/2" x 15", Style 1597, Grained Finish. Price: $43.55 each
      2 Single Pedestal Desks, 60" x 30", Style 15021-S1, Custom Finish. Price: $114.75 each
      28 Desk Trays, Letter Size, Style 032. Price: $2.05 each
      2 Side Arm Office Chairs, Style 198, Custom Finish. Price: $50.95 each

2. Type credit memorandums in duplicate for the following credits allowed customers on January 14 by the Modern Furniture Company, Coral Gables, Florida 33926:

   (a) Mr. J. B. Young, 1462 Alhambra Circle, Coral Gables, Florida 33926:

      1 Captain's Chair $55.00
      1 Night Table $39.50

Part 3 / Business Forms

(b) Mrs. Ellen Baker, 3714 Ponce de Leon Boulevard, Coral Gables, Florida 33926:

    2 Arm Chairs at $99.50 each
    1 End Table $35.00

3. Type monthly statements of account in duplicate to be sent to the following customers of Haines and Williams, wholesale grocers, Knoxville, Tennessee 37903, May 1, 197–:

   (a) Robert L. Wilkins, 2580 Moorman Avenue, Knoxville, Tennessee 37905:

Date	Code	Division	Charges	Credits
April 1	C-111	83	142.80	
6	C-113	83	129.65	
10	R-201	90		142.80
15	R-212	90		4.95
21	C-119	83	18.50	

   (b) Anthony M. Upshaw, 501 Klotter Street, Athens, Tennessee 37303:

Date	Code	Division	Charges	Credits
April 15	C-151	83	39.20	
26	R-171	90		39.20
28	C-155	83	14.95	

4. Type the following purchase order as instructed. (If you do not have a blank purchase order, type one similar to the illustration on page 211.)

   Purchase Order 2274 from:

     MELROSE CORPORATION
     7600 Talman Avenue
     Melrose Park, Illinois 60161

   to:

     Gordon Brothers
     1200 State Street
     Chicago, Illinois 60605

   Date: December 20, 197–; Terms 2/10, net 30 days

   Ship Via: ICRR

        4 Legal Size Filing Cabinets, List price $84.50 each
        8 Letter Size Filing Cabinets, List price $75.50 each
        6 Adjustable Posture Chairs, List price $42.50 each

Unit 7 MAILING AND SHIPPING SERVICES

Part 1. Incoming Mail
    2. Outgoing Mail
    3. Air and Surface Shipping

The secretary has many responsibilities related to the proper handling of both incoming and outgoing mail. She will quickly process the incoming mail so that her employer can respond to matters of importance without delay. She understands the different mailing services and their advantages.

VOCABULARY BUILDER

systematically.....................
    adverb: in an organized or established manner; methodically

verify..............................
    verb: to confirm; to check the truth, accuracy, or reality of

devise.............................
    verb: to form in the mind; arrange the plan of; prepare; think out; create

efficiency.........................
    noun: quality that produces the most effective service; state of possessing skill for performance of a job

destination........................
    noun: a place which is set for the end of a journey or to which something is sent

processing........................
    verb: to lead toward an end by a series of actions or operations; to subject to special treatment

extravagance.....................
    noun: an instance of excess; an excessive outlay of money; something that exceeds the limits of reason or necessity

affixed............................
    verb: fastened; attached in any way; added (as a signature)

perishable........................
    adjective: likely to become spoiled, ruined, or destroyed

modes............................
    noun: particular forms or varieties of something

Be brief, for no discourse can please when too long.
                        Cervantes

p. 221   You can be of great help to him as you process his mail . . . and arrange it **systematically** before giving it to him for his action.

p. 225   If no letter, statement, or invoice comes with the check, **verify** the amount with the file copy of the bill.

p. 226   . . . you may **devise** and duplicate referral slips that will save both your employer's and your time in getting information to his associates. . . .

p. 234   You can save time and increase your **efficiency** this way.

p. 236   The ZIP Code is a five-digit number that identifies the **destination** of a piece of mail.

p. 237   . . . the following rules will help to speed the **processing** of your outgoing mail.

p. 238   He estimates that **extravagance** adds at least 10 percent to the annual cost of all domestic mailing.

p. 240   When a first-class letter is enclosed, its postage is added to the parcel postage and **affixed** on the outside of the package.

p. 253   Almost all types of goods, including machine parts, **perishable** foods, printed materials, and flowers, are moved by air express.

p. 256   All carriers in all **modes** of transportation provide tracing services.

PART 1 INCOMING MAIL

Lorraine D'Orsay is secretary to a manufacturer's representative for several product lines. There are three girls in the office. Besides Lorraine there is an order clerk, who processes the orders; and a general clerk who operates the teletype machine, answers the telephone, and prepares the outgoing mail. All the incoming mail is placed on Lorraine's desk. As she opens each piece of mail she carefully checks to see that everything has been removed before throwing the envelope away. As it comes out of the envelope all mail is kept together and placed face down on her desk. Lorraine then time stamps each individual piece of mail. Her time stamp indicates the month, day, year, and time of arrival. She then reads and makes mental notes of the incoming mail. Orders are placed in one stack to her left to be checked and approved by her employer. Magazines, advertising, and other sales promotional mail are placed in a second stack to her right. Correspondence is placed in the center stack. Before giving the correspondence to her employer, Lorraine reads all letters except those marked Personal or Confidential. The files are pulled on those that are replies and the latest letter is placed on the top and stapled to the file.

The United States Postal Service presently handles about 86 billion pieces of mail every year. One of your first and most interesting duties as a secretary will be to assist your employer in handling his ever-increasing volume of mail. You can be of great help to him if you process his mail efficiently as it arrives and arrange it systematically before giving it to him for his action.

The system of handling the mail will depend upon the size and type of business in which you are employed. In a large office the incoming mail is opened, sorted, and distributed by the mail department. In a small office, you will be expected to open, read, and sort all the incoming mail.

OPENING THE MAIL

When the volume of incoming mail is very large, the letters are opened in the mail department with an automatic mail opener. It trims a narrow strip off one edge of each envelope. The amount taken off is so small that there is little risk that the contents will be damaged. In order to reduce the chances of cutting the contents, the envelopes may be jogged on the table before they are placed in the opener so that the contents will fall away from the edge that is to be trimmed.

Illus. 7-1
Electrically operated letter opener

Pitney Bowes

In the mail room the mail is sorted by departments. A sorting tray, with a separate compartment for each department, is used for this purpose. After the mail has been sorted, it is delivered by a mail clerk or a messenger. Usually mail is delivered several times a day, the first mail of the day being the heaviest.

When the mail reaches your employer's office, you should put aside the letters that can be answered or handled without being referred to your employer. Give them your attention when you have some free time. This type of mail includes the communications that can be answered with form letters, circulars, advertisements, and routine reports. Requests for catalogs or price lists, for example, can be handled in this manner. However, your employer may wish to see even these in order to be aware of all inquiries that are received. He will later turn them over to you for handling. You request the mail department (usually by filling in a company form for that purpose) to send the catalog or price list immediately and note on the letter that it has been mailed. This will make it much easier for your employer to answer his important mail.

If you open the mail in your office, use a letter opener or a paper knife. If you should cut a letter or an enclosure as you are opening an envelope, use transparent mending tape to put it together again.

After you have opened the envelopes, remove the letters and other enclosures carefully. Look at each letter and its enclosures as soon as they are removed and attach the enclosures to the letter. If an enclosure is missing, you should note the omission in the margin of the letter. You may be expected to make up a special memorandum and keep it on file if the missing enclosure is a check, a money order, cash, or stamps.

Keep the envelopes until you have examined each letter for the signature and the address. If either is missing on the letter, attach the envelope to the letter. Sometimes a check is received with no other means of identification except the envelope in which it was mailed. If the date of the letter is different from the postmark, keep the envelope. Sometimes the envelope of an important document is stapled to the document because the date of mailing may prove to be of some importance. If, after you have thrown away the envelope, you notice that the return address is not printed or typed on a letter, you may be able to find the address in a telephone directory, a city directory, or in the correspondence files. Once in a while you may make an error by opening a personal or confidential letter. If this happens place the letter back in the envelope and write on the outside "Sorry — opened by mistake," and add your initials. Don't let this happen too frequently, however. Personal mail should remain personal and should be delivered to the executive's desk unopened.

Dating the Mail

After you have checked the incoming mail for enclosures, return addresses, and signatures, mark it with the date and time. You can do this with a pen or pencil, a rubber stamp, or a time stamp machine.

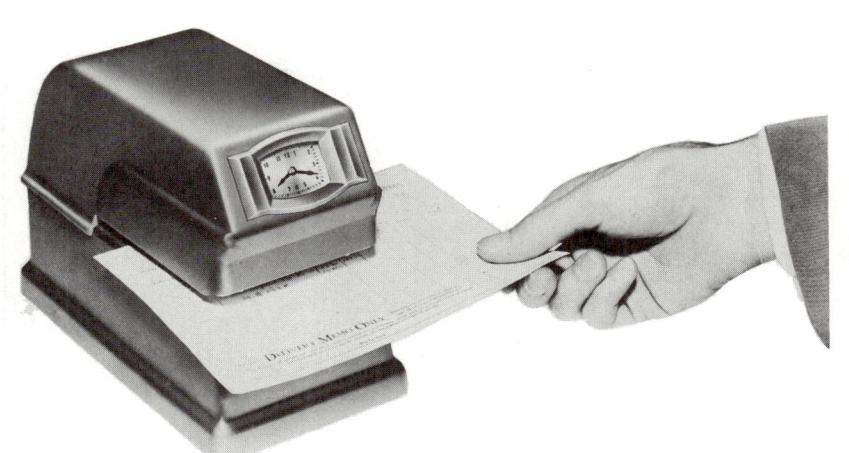

Illus. 7-2
Time stamp

This time stamp prints the year, month, day, hour, and minute of receipt and dispatch of letters, telegrams, and other documents.

IBM Corporation

Part 1 / Incoming Mail

Underlining and Annotating

If your employer prefers, you may further assist him in handling his correspondence by underlining and annotating. Good judgment is necessary here, however, since a letter that has too many markings may cause annoyance to an executive.

First of all, as you read, you should underline the key words and phrases in the letter. This will help him to get a clear understanding of the letter rapidly. It will also give you a complete understanding of the contents of each letter.

Secondly, as you read, find out the answers to questions and problems that your employer will need to know before answering a particular letter. Write the answers and comments in the margins of the letter in clearly worded, legible handwriting. This is called *annotating.* For example, if an order is addressed to your employer, check with the credit department and the shipping department to see if and when the order can be shipped. Then write the information on the letter so that your employer will have it when he dictates the acknowledgment of the order. The notation can simply be: *Credit satisfactory, stock on hand for immediate shipment.*

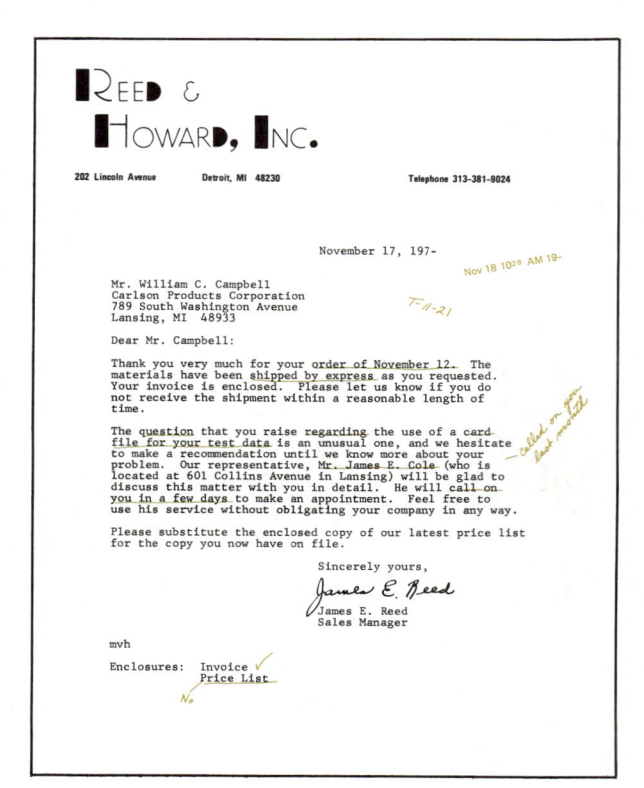

Illus. 7-3
Annotated and date-stamped letter

A request for payment is an important piece of incoming mail that you must handle carefully. Make sure that the bill has not already been paid and then check the accuracy of every item and every amount before placing it on your employer's desk for payment. Your employer will have a great deal of confidence in you when he realizes that the figures that reach him through the incoming mail are accurate or that you have noted any errors.

A letter containing a check should also be handled with extreme care. You should immediately compare the amount of the enclosed check with the amount mentioned in the letter. If no letter, statement, or invoice comes with the check, verify the amount with the file copy of the bill. If it is the policy of your firm to turn all checks received over to the cashier immediately, write the amount of the check and the date it was received in the margin before giving the letter to your employer.

Another problem that you will meet is the rerouting of letters addressed to your employer but actually related to someone else's work. In this case, just write the correct name above that of your employer; but let him see it before sending it to the proper person or department. He may want to add a covering note.

Attaching Related Materials

Photocopies or carbon copies of previous correspondence, reports, and other related information will be of great assistance to your employer in answering his mail. They may be attached to the incoming mail or placed where your employer can get them easily if he needs them when he is dictating the replies.

Illus. 7-4
A secretary checks incoming mail very carefully before presenting it to her employer.

Ohio National Life Insurance Company

Organizing Correspondence

When annotating has been completed and all attachments have been added, the mail should be placed on your employer's desk or in his incoming mail basket.

The mail should be arranged according to your employer's preference. He may prefer to read his important business mail first, or he may wish to read his unopened personal and confidential mail first. As a general rule, you should arrange the mail in the order of its importance. The following arrangement is usually satisfactory:

1. Unopened personal and confidential letters
2. Airmail
3. Business letters of special importance to your employer
4. Letters containing checks or money orders
5. Other business letters
6. Letters containing orders
7. Letters containing bills, invoices, or other requests for payment
8. Advertisements
9. Newspapers and magazines

Special delivery letters and registered mail are usually not delivered along with the regular mail. They should be handled promptly upon receipt and brought to your employer's attention quickly. If a special delivery letter or a registered letter should come to your desk along with the regular mail, you should process it immediately and turn it over to your employer without delay.

PHOTOCOPYING MAIL

Very often a letter addressed to an executive should be read not only by him but by one or more other executives or assistants. Photocopies of such letters are sent to the proper persons in the organization for immediate action. A photocopy for each person who should see the correspondence should be clipped to the letter and the names of the persons to whom you are suggesting that the photocopies be sent should be listed at the bottom of the original copy. Your employer may want to add to the list or he may decide to reduce it. He may wish to write instructions on the photocopies so that his orders will be carried out promptly.

REFERRING AND ROUTING MAIL

Correspondence is frequently referred to an executive's associates or assistants for an answer. If one is not already available, you may devise and duplicate referral slips that will save both your employer's time and your time in getting information to his associates and requesting the necessary action from them. When you refer correspondence, reports, or other business documents to someone else, be sure to keep a record of the transfer in a notebook. Otherwise you may lose track of very important business papers. The record should include the date it was sent, the name of the person to whom it was sent, the subject, the action to be taken, and the date when you expect to follow up if a follow-up should be necessary.

Illus. 7-5
Referral slip

This check-off slip saves the executive's time in distributing mail to his associates and assistants and in requesting their responses.

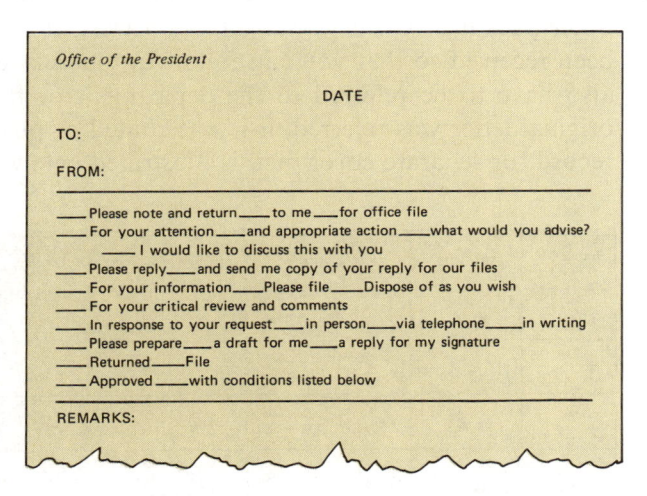

```
Office of the President
                                    DATE
TO:
FROM:
____ Please note and return ____ to me ____ for office file
____ For your attention ____ and appropriate action ____ what would you advise?
        ____ I would like to discuss this with you
____ Please reply ____ and send me copy of your reply for our files
____ For your information ____ Please file ____ Dispose of as you wish
____ For your critical review and comments
____ In response to your request ____ in person ____ via telephone ____ in writing
____ Please prepare ____ a draft for me ____ a reply for my signature
____ Returned ____ File
____ Approved ____ with conditions listed below

REMARKS:
```

Some correspondence and often important articles in trade magazines are to be read by others. Many firms use either a rubber stamp or a duplicated routing slip with the names of all the departments or executives

```
Please read the attached material and pass
it on to the persons indicated.

                        Date         Date
Refer to:             Received    Passed on
W. N. Ames            _____    _____
M. P. Conrad          _____    _____
N. A. Davis           _____    _____
P. F. Evans           _____    _____
C. X. Hill            _____    _____
F. J. Klein           _____    _____
S. D. Larsen          _____    _____
P. J. Murtagh         _____    _____
N. W. Nelson          _____    _____
J. L. Peterson        _____    _____
J. W. Robinson        _____    _____
G. A. Simpson         _____    _____

Return to:
```

Illus. 7-6
Routing slip

One of these slips is attached to each piece of mail that should be distributed to others. The names of those who are not to receive it are crossed off.

Part 1 / Incoming Mail   227

of the firm to whom the material is to be sent. Either you or your employer should check the names of the persons who are to receive and pass on the material.

SPECIAL MEMORANDUMS

As you read certain letters, you will notice promises of materials that are being sent under separate cover. To be sure that you receive them, it will often be desirable for you to keep a record of mail expected in another package. Check at least twice a week to see which items have not been received so that you can follow up on delayed mail. This mail will also have to be referred to the department or the person to whom the original letter was referred, if it was routed or photocopied. One type of record for separate cover mail is illustrated below.

Illus. 7-7
Register of expected mail

The register shows that the first four items have been received and the last item has not yet arrived.

Date of Entry	Article	From Whom	Date Sent	Department	Individual	Date Received
3-12	Catalog	A. H. Martin & Co	3-11	Purchasing		3-14
3-14	Book	F. Stevens	3-12	Advertising		3-18
3-18	Tickets	G. H. Simms	3-15		P. L. Martin	3-21
3-20	Folders	Kimball Bros	3-18	Filing		3-23
3-22	Catalog	Bryce & Maye	3-20	Purchasing		

Because of its special importance, you may find it necessary to keep a record of the receipt of mail that is insured, special delivery, or registered. Use a form similar to the one illustrated below.

Illus. 7-8
Register of insured, special delivery, and registered mail

Received		From Whom		For	Kind of Mail Received
Date	Time	Name	Address	Department or Individual	
10-1	8:15 a.m.	R. J. Walker	New York City	Accounting	Registered
10-1	9:20 a.m.	Mrs. V. Jones	Denver, Colo	O. Miller	Insured
10-2	2:15 p.m.	Art Shop, Inc.	Chicago, Ill.	Sales	Special Delivery

228   Unit 7 / Mailing and Shipping Services

QUESTIONS

1. Why should every secretary, regardless of the size of her office, know the best ways of handling incoming mail?
2. If you were opening incoming mail with an electrically operated letter opener, how would you avoid cutting the contents of the envelopes?
3. Why should the secretary inspect the enclosed contents of every letter as soon as they are removed from the envelope? For what specific enclosures should all secretaries look?
4. A letter is received but the enclosure is missing. What should the secretary do?
5. Under what circumstances is it desirable to attach the envelope to the contents of a piece of mail?
6. Why are letters time stamped upon their receipt?
7. What do you do when you annotate mail?
8. What is a satisfactory order of importance for most executives' mail?
9. Give an example of a piece of mail that should be photocopied for circulation and another that should be routed.
10. A letter is received in which reference is made to a package coming under separate cover. How can a secretary remind herself to look for the package in a later delivery?

JUDGMENT

1. Under what circumstances is incoming mail likely to be opened by hand? by machine?
2. Your employer, the office manager in a medium size company, has learned that there are many difficulties and problems in handling incoming mail. He has asked you, his secretary, to study the situation and report your findings to him. You have found the following practices prevailing throughout the company.
   (a) The mail is opened by hand by the receptionist who also handles the switchboard. When the mail is too heavy for her to take care of by herself, she receives help from any of the stenographers in the office who happen not to be busy.
   (b) Enclosures that are referred to in letters frequently are not with the letters that are distributed to the various executives. The executives are, therefore, uncertain whether the enclosures have been received or whether they have been received and separated from the letters.
   (c) Often a letter is not answered until sometime after it is received, but the executives do not know whether the delay is in their own offices or whether the letter has not been delivered to them promptly.

(d) Before an order is filled, it is handled by the credit department, the sales department, and the order department. In some instances, it goes first to one department and in other instances first to another department, according to where the mail clerk is going first.

After studying your report the office manager asks you for suggestions for eliminating these difficulties. What methods for solving these problems would you suggest?

PERSONAL QUALITIES

Edna Larsen, secretary to the comptroller, opens and reads her employer's mail every morning before placing it on his desk for reply. After opening and reading a letter from the president of the company questioning some of the comptroller's financial practices, she notices that the envelope is clearly marked CONFIDENTIAL.

How would you handle this situation if you were Edna?

LANGUAGE USAGE

Semicolons are used to punctuate complex elements in a sentence. Below are three uses of the semicolon:

A. Between independent clauses not joined by a conjunction
   Example: Confidential mail is confidential; it should not be opened by a mail clerk or by a secretary.

B. Before a conjunction joining two independent clauses when one clause (or both) has internal punctuation
   Example: Considered daily, the cash savings in the mail department represent only a small amount; but, considered over a period of years, they amount to several thousand dollars.

C. After each independent clause in a series when one (or more) has internal punctuation
   Example: The secretary removed the letter from the envelope; she checked the enclosures against the list at the bottom of the letter; and then she placed a paper clip on the letter, the price list, the booklet, and the sample.

Punctuate the sentences below based on the three semicolon rules you have reviewed above.

1. The mail clerk was dating the mail the secretary was transcribing the dictation two executives were discussing the forthcoming sales meeting when suddenly the air conditioner went off the elevators stopped and the lights went out.

2. The office manager told the new secretary that the rubber stamp would show the year the month the date and the time of arrival of the letter but the secretary did not know if she should stamp the front or the reverse side of the letterhead.

3. Advertising materials should be kept on the left orders should be kept on the right correspondence should be kept

in the center unopened personal and confidential mail should be handed to your employer immediately checks and other enclosures should be attached to correspondence.

4. In most offices correspondence is stamped orders are stamped invoices are stamped including both copies if they are sent in duplicate new price lists are stamped and brought to the employer's attention advertising material as a rule is not stamped.

5. The secretary placed the annotated correspondence on her boss's desk he reviewed it quickly and told her to answer the inquiries as soon as possible.

SECRETARIAL WORK

1. Compose and type an interoffice memorandum to one of your classmates instructing her how the company for which you both work wishes incoming mail handled. Her responsibility will be to date stamp the mail and route it. All orders will be directed to the order department. Correspondence regarding credit will be sent to the credit department. Personal and confidential mail will not be opened but will be directed to the addressee. Inquiries concerning products will be sent to the sales department. Checks and correspondence related to payment of bills will be sent to the accounting department. Make your instructions clear regarding handling of enclosures. The only time she will underline or annotate or write on any letter is in the event an enclosure is not with the mail. Correspondence addressed to individuals in the firm will be routed directly to them. Tell her under which circumstances an envelope will be attached to the correspondence when it is passed on to the department or individual addressee. Give her instructions as to what action she should take regarding special delivery mail.

2. You are the secretary to Mr. John Roman, the head of the Purchasing Department of the Fabric Division of the Fifth Avenue Ladies Apparel Company in your city. Recently he directed a letter to a fabric manufacturer requesting swatches of a new polyester material in all colors. A letter has been received in response to his inquiry, but the swatch booklet was not enclosed. Compose a follow-up letter to Mr. Ralph Holmes, Polyester Division, Hilton-Dracket Fabric Manufacturing Company, 2300 Euclid Avenue, Fort Wayne, Indiana 46803. Use a modified block style letter with mixed punctuation. Advise Mr. Holmes that the swatch booklet was not enclosed in his letter. Mr. Roman is out of the city. Compose the letter under his name and title of Chief Purchasing Agent. Sign the letter with his name, but put your initials under the signature to indicate that you have signed the letter. Make one carbon copy.

Part 1 / Incoming Mail

PART 2 OUTGOING MAIL

"Penny, along with the regular mail today, there are a few special items. Send the letter to Al Dauten in Seattle airmail. The signed contracts on the Wirmel agreement should be sent registered mail with a return receipt requested. Also, send these samples back to the Research Department in Newark by parcel post and insure them for $50." As an experienced secretary, Penny Green knows the different kinds of mailing services and how to use them.

A complete listing of postal services with the details for their use can be found in the Postal Service Manual of the United States. Postal services and rates are changed from time to time; therefore, it is important that you have an up-to-date copy of the Postal Service Manual in your office. It may be purchased from the Superintendent of Documents, United States Government Printing Office, Washington, D.C. 20402.

You should be able to select the proper mailing service for all the different types of outgoing mail. For instance, a letter may be sent by special delivery to insure prompt delivery, by airmail if it is to go a great distance, or by certified or registered mail if it contains valuable papers. A fee for special delivery or for special handling may be added to fourth-class mail to insure the prompt delivery of parcel post packages. For a small fee, a return receipt, which is proof that an item has been received, may be requested when using insured, certified, or registered mail.

HANDLING OUTGOING MAIL

The system of handling outgoing mail, like the system of handling incoming mail, depends upon the size and the type of business in which you are employed. In a small office the secretary usually is responsible for all the details connected with outgoing mail. In a large office the mail is collected from each department several times throughout the day by a messenger or a mail clerk and taken to the mailing department where it is sealed and stacked near the *postage meter*, which is a machine that automatically prints the amount of postage, the postmark, and the mailing date on the envelope.

Folding and Inserting Letters

Folding a business letter properly is not a difficult process, but care should be taken that the creases are straight and that they are made without harming the neatness of the letter. Paper, 8½" x 11", to be inserted in an ordinary — No. 6 — envelope (6½" x 3⅝") is folded and inserted as follows:

Illus. 7-9

With letter face up on desk, fold bottom up to ½ inch from top.

Fold right third to left.

Fold left third to ½ inch from last crease.

Insert last creased edge first.

Only two folds are necessary if the letter is to be placed in a large — No. 10 — envelope (9½" x 4⅛"):

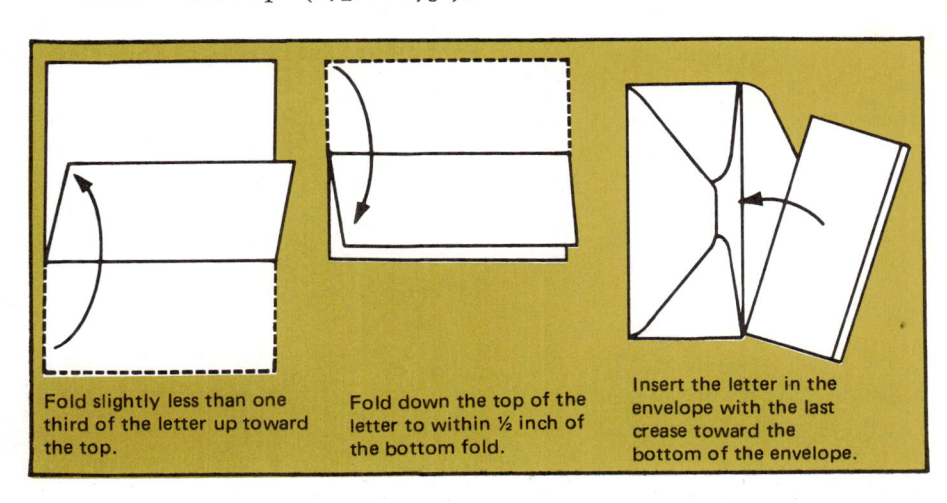

Illus. 7-10

Fold slightly less than one third of the letter up toward the top.

Fold down the top of the letter to within ½ inch of the bottom fold.

Insert the letter in the envelope with the last crease toward the bottom of the envelope.

A letter should be inserted in an envelope in such a way that it will be in a normal reading position when it is removed from the envelope and unfolded. The enclosures that accompany the letter should be folded

Part 2 / Outgoing Mail　　233

with the letter or inserted so that they will come out of the envelope at the same time the letter is removed.

For a large No. 10 window envelope, 8½″ x 11″ letter sheets are folded as shown below:

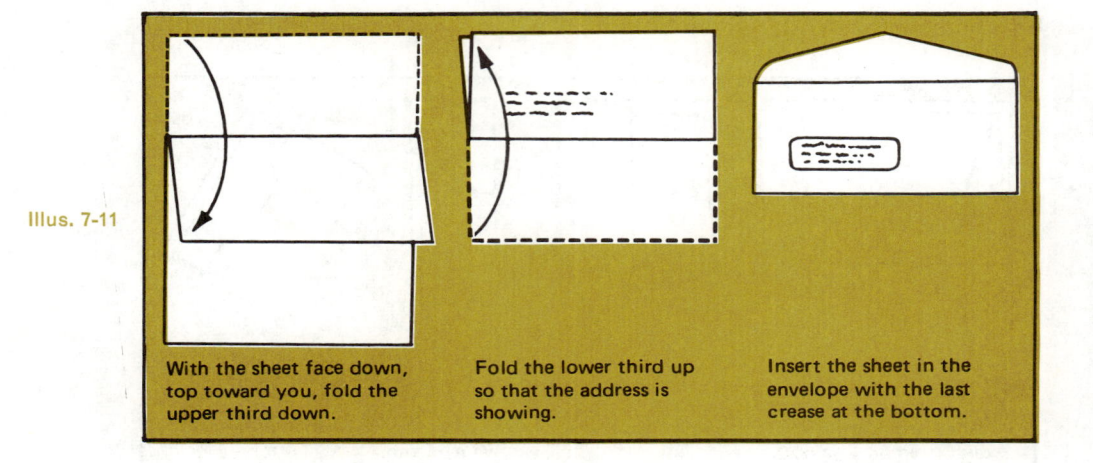

Illus. 7-11

With the sheet face down, top toward you, fold the upper third down.

Fold the lower third up so that the address is showing.

Insert the sheet in the envelope with the last crease at the bottom.

Small No. 6 window envelopes are also available; they are used mostly for bills or statements that are designed to fit with only a single fold.

Sealing Envelopes

If you should have to seal a large number of envelopes without the use of a sealing machine, spread about ten envelopes on a table, address down, flap open, one on top of the other with the gummed edges showing. Brush over the gummed edges with a moist sponge or a moistener to soften the glue so that the flaps can be closed quickly and sealed. When sealing, start with the top envelope, the one nearest you, and work down to the first one placed on the table.

Stamps

You may also put postage stamps on rapidly by arranging six to eight envelopes on top of each other, showing just the upper right part of each one. Moisten the strip of stamps with a damp sponge and put on one stamp after the other. You can save time and increase your efficiency this way.

Postage stamps may be purchased in sheet, booklet, or coil form. The bound booklets of stamps are preferred for personal and home use; business firms find it better to work with the 100-stamp sheets or the coiled

234   Unit 7 / Mailing and Shipping Services

stamps. Coiled stamps are often used in business because they can be quickly placed on envelopes and packages and because they are less likely to be lost or damaged than are individual stamps.

Precanceled Stamps and Envelopes

For an advertising campaign your employer may wish to use precanceled stamps or precanceled stamped envelopes. Their use reduces the time and cost of handling mail. Precanceled stamps and envelopes are purchased from the post office with the cancellation lines already stamped on them. When the sorted mail is returned to the post office, it is not necessary for the letters to go through the canceling machine again. Therefore, the mail is dispatched more quickly. Precanceled stamps and envelopes cannot be used for first-class mail.

Stamped Envelopes and Cards

Another means of saving your time is through the use of stamped envelopes of different denominations which may be purchased in various sizes — singly or in quantity lots. The return address will be printed on them by the post office for a small fee if the envelopes are purchased in quantity lots.

First-class postal cards may be purchased in single or double form. The double form is used when a reply is requested on the attached card. Airmail postal cards are also available, but only in the single form.

If you are left with spoiled stamped envelopes and cards (if uncanceled), you may exchange them for stamps, stamped envelopes, or postal cards. You may also obtain an exchange on stamps if you happen to buy the wrong denomination.

Metered Mail

The most efficient device you can use to put postage on any class of mail is the postage meter machine. This machine prints the postmark and the proper amount of postage on each piece of mail. The imprint of a fully automatic metering machine may also carry a slogan or a line or two of advertising, such as IT'S SMART TO BE THRIFTY, next to the postmark. Metered mail is neither canceled nor postmarked at the post office; therefore, it is processed and dispatched quickly.

The meter of the postage machine is set at the post office for the amount paid at the time. The meter registers the amount of postage used on each piece of mail, the amount of postage remaining in the meter, and the number of pieces that have passed through the machine. The meter locks when the amount paid for has been used; it is then necessary to take it to the post office again to pay for more postage. Additional postage should be bought before the meter locks. You will find the postage meter very easy to operate, and it will save you a great deal of time.

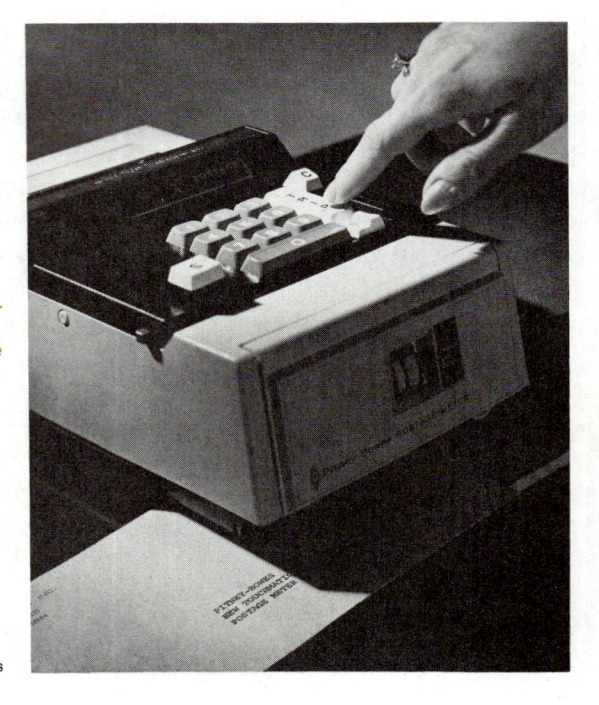

Illus. 7-12
In this desk-model postage meter the amount of postage for each envelope is set by depressing the correct keys. After the envelope is inserted in the machine and the trip bar is depressed, the postage is printed on the envelope.

Pitney Bowes

ZIP Codes

To assure prompt delivery of your mail always use ZIP Codes. Their use increases the speed, accuracy, and quality of *all* mail service. The ZIP Code is a five-digit number that identifies the destination of a piece of mail. For instance:

9	45	77
Area	Sectional Center or Large City	Local Zone

The *9* identifies one of ten large areas made up of three or more states into which the entire country has been divided. The next two figures, *45*, represent the sectional center or large city within that area. And, finally, the *77* represents the local delivery zone within that city or sectional center.

The code should appear on the last line of *both* the envelope address and the return address following the city and state. One or two spaces should be left between the last letter of the state and the first digit of the code. The address should be typed in block form:

Fisher Division
The Simmons Company
2350 Washington Avenue
San Leandro, CA 94577

All Zip Codes can be found in the *National Zip Code Directory*.

OPTICAL CHARACTER READER (OCR)

The post office is installing Optical Character Readers, electronic equipment which will speed up the mail. This equipment can read printed or typewritten addresses and sort letters with speed and accuracy.

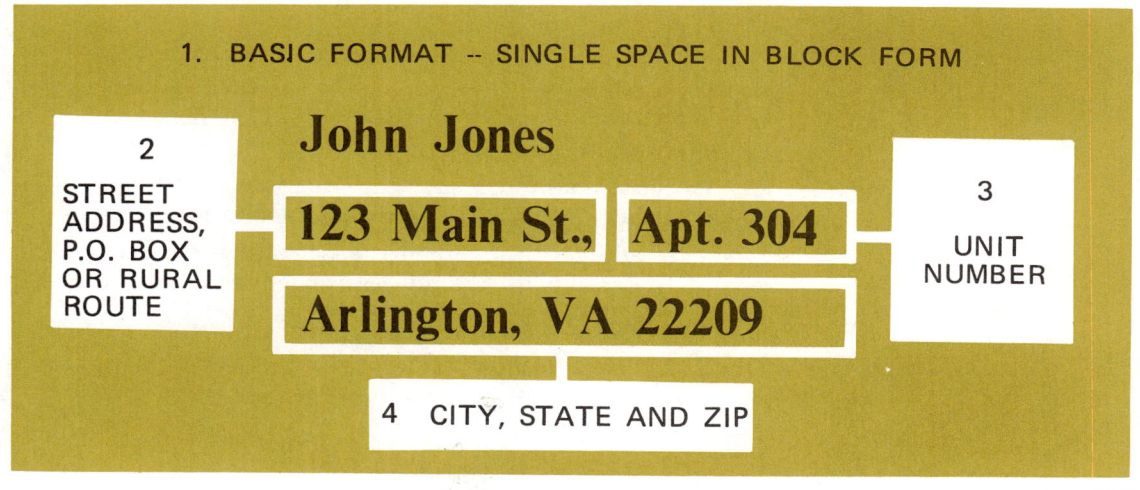

1. BASIC FORMAT -- SINGLE SPACE IN BLOCK FORM

2 STREET ADDRESS, P.O. BOX OR RURAL ROUTE

John Jones
123 Main St., Apt. 304
Arlington, VA 22209

3 UNIT NUMBER

4 CITY, STATE AND ZIP

Illus. 7-13

Even if your post office does not have OCR equipment yet, the following rules will help to speed the processing of your outgoing mail.

1. *The Basic Format.* The address should be typed single space in block form.
2. *Street Address*, *P.O. Box*, or *Rural Route*. These should be shown on the line immediately above the City, State, and ZIP Code.
3. *Unit Number.* Mail addressed to occupants of a multi-unit building should include the number of the apartment, room, suite, or other unit. The unit number should appear immediately after the street address on the same line — never above, below, nor in front of the street address.
4. *City*, *State*, and *ZIP Code.* They should appear in that order on the bottom line of the address.

ITEMS TO CHECK BEFORE MAILING LETTERS

Before mailing your outgoing correspondence, check each letter first to be sure that:

1. Any enclosures noted at the bottom of the letter are actually enclosed in the envelope.
2. Numbers, such as order numbers, referred to in the correspondence are correct.
3. Carbon copies for others are prepared for mailing.
4. Your initials appear below your employer's signature on any letter you have signed for him.

Then check each envelope to be sure that

1. The address on the envelope agrees with the inside address of the letter.
2. The ZIP Code is typed on the last line of *both* the envelope address and the return address.
3. Any special notations, such as Registered, Special Delivery, and Airmail, have been noted on the envelope.
4. The typed address on a label for a package to be sent separately agrees with the address on the envelope.

Finally, to skip one sorting operation at the post office, separate and identify the *Local* and the *Out-of-Town* mail. Free self-sticking, wrap-around labels are available from most post offices.

DOMESTIC MAIL SERVICE

Domestic mail is that sent within the United States, its territories and possessions, Army-Air Force (APO) and Navy (FPO) post offices, and also mail for delivery to the United Nations, New York City. You can speed the mail delivery and reduce the cost of mailing if you use the right mailing service at the right time. A United States Postal Service official states that millions of dollars are wasted each year because of the general lack of knowledge of postal services. He estimates that extravagance adds at least 10 percent to the annual cost of all domestic mailing. You can always get up-to-date postal information free of charge at the Information window of your local post office.

CLASSES OF DOMESTIC MAIL

Your employer will expect you to know the different kinds of domestic mail most widely used by business firms. The six kinds of domestic mail listed on page 239 will be considered separately.

1. First-class mail — letters, postal cards, and postcards
2. Second-class mail — newspapers and periodicals
3. Third-class mail — circulars and other miscellaneous printed matter
4. Fourth-class mail — parcel post
5. Airmail
6. Mixed classes of mail

First-Class Mail

First-class mail is usually sealed letters only; however, the following mail must also be sent first class:

1. All matter sealed against postal inspection
2. Postal cards (cards sold by the post office with stamps imprinted on them) and postcards (privately purchased mailing cards on which stamps are put)
3. Business reply cards and envelopes
4. Matter, partly in written form, such as statements of account, checks, punched cards, and filled-in forms
5. Other matter in written form, such as typewritten reports and documents

Second-Class Mail

In today's news-conscious world, certain newspapers and magazines are sent at second-class rates of postage which are lower than parcel post or third class. Authorization to publishers and news agents to mail at bulk second-class rates must be obtained from the Postal Service.

Third-Class Mail

What is third-class mail? Almost every day you receive in your own home circulars and advertisements that have been sent through the mails at third-class rates. This mail is used for materials that cannot be classified as first- or second-class mail and that weigh less than 16 ounces. The same material in parcels weighing 16 ounces and over is considered fourth-class mail. The following may be sent by third-class mail service:

1. Circulars, books, catalogs, and other printed matter
2. Merchandise samples

Envelopes may be sealed if marked *Third Class* anywhere on the envelope. In the absence of such a marking, sealed envelopes will be subject to first-class mail rates.

Fourth-Class Mail (Parcel Post)

Fourth-class mail is also known as parcel post. It includes merchandise, printed matter, and all other mailable matter not included in first-, second-, or third-class mail that weighs 16 ounces or more. Parcel post rates are determined according to (1) the weight of the parcel and (2) the distance the parcel is being sent. There are limitations on the weight and size of parcel post packages.

Parcel post packages may be sent sealed or unsealed. Unless it is clearly marked *First Class* a sealed package is usually treated as parcel post by the postal sorters regardless of the amount of postage paid.

Airmail

The swiftest means of sending mail a distance of 200 miles or more is by air. It need not be used for shorter distances because first-class mail is usually delivered within 200 miles as quickly as airmail. Airmail is carried by air and the fastest connecting ground carrier; therefore, the rate is higher than for other domestic mail. It is given the quickest handling in both dispatch and delivery, but it is not given special delivery unless a special delivery fee has been paid in addition to the airmail postage. Stamped airmail envelopes with a red, white, and blue border design may be purchased at any post office. Plain envelopes and regular stamps may also be used for airmail. Should you use an ordinary envelope for airmail, be sure to print or type in capital letters the word *AIRMAIL* below the postage and above the address on the right side of the envelope or paste Airmail labels on the front and back of the envelope. Any matter that is acceptable in domestic surface mail may be sent by airmail with the exception of items that might possibly be damaged by changes in temperature or atmospheric pressure.

Mixed Classes of Mail

Sometimes it is better to send two pieces of mail of different classes together as a single mailing to be sure that they both arrive at the same time. A first-class letter may be attached to the outside of a large envelope or parcel of a different class of mail, or it may be enclosed in a large envelope or parcel. When a first-class letter is *attached*, the postage is affixed to each part separately. When a first-class letter is enclosed, its postage is added to the parcel postage and affixed on the outside of the package. The words *First-Class Mail Enclosed* must be written, typed, or stamped below the postage and above the address. A piece of mixed mail is handled and transported by the post office as mail matter of the class in which the bulky portion falls — not as first-class mail.

INTERNATIONAL MAIL

Mail is now sent to all parts of the world, either by air or surface transportation, in ever-increasing volume. International mail is divided into two general categories — postal union mail and parcel post. Postal union mail is further divided into two groups — *LC* mail and *AO* mail. LC mail (letters and cards) consists of letters, letter packages, and postal cards. AO mail (articles, other) includes printed matter, samples of merchandise, matter for the blind, and small packets.

The postage for letters and postal cards mailed to Canada and Mexico is the same as that for the United States. To all other countries the rates are higher and the weights are limited. Overseas parcel post packages must be packed even more carefully than those for delivery within the continental United States. A *customs declaration* form must be attached to each parcel with an accurate and complete description of its contents.

SPECIAL POSTAL SERVICES

The United States Postal Service also provides many special services, such as:

1. Special Delivery
2. Special Handling
3. Registered Mail
4. Certified Mail
5. Insured Mail
6. COD Service
7. Tracing Mail
8. Recalling Mail

Special Delivery

Special delivery provides the fastest handling and delivery service for any kind of mail. Special delivery mail is handled at the post office of destination with the same promptness given to first-class mail and, in addition, is given immediate delivery (within prescribed hours and distances). The fees charged are in addition to the regular postage. They vary according to the weight of the letter or parcel. The mail must be stamped or marked *Special Delivery*.

Special Handling

On payment of a fee in addition to the regular postage, a parcel labeled *Special Handling* will be given the same prompt handling and delivery service as is given to first-class mail. Special handling parcels are delivered the same way that parcel post is ordinarily delivered — on regularly scheduled trips, not special delivery. The fees are lower than special delivery fees. Special handling services may be used only with parcels sent as third- or fourth-class mail.

Registered Mail

Mail is registered to give protection to valuable and important mail. Money, checks, jewelry, stock certificates, and bonds are included in the valuable items frequently sent by registered mail. Important items include contracts, bills of sale, leases, mortgages, deeds, wills, and vital business records. Registration provides insurance, a receipt for the sender, and proof of delivery. Mail may be registered for insurance up to $10,000 if no other insurance is carried. If other insurance is carried, postal insurance liability is limited to a maximum of $1,000. All classes of mail may be registered provided the first-class or airmail rate is paid.

Before your mail will be accepted for registration, you must

1. Seal it. Masked tape or transparent tape cannot be used to seal registered mail.
2. Have the complete names and addresses of *both* the sender and the addressee on the mail.
3. Declare the *full* value of the mail to the postal clerk.

You will be given a receipt showing that the post office has accepted the registered mail for transmittal and delivery. For an additional fee you may obtain a *return receipt* to prove that the registered mail has been delivered.

Certified Mail

If your mail has no value of its own (such as a letter, a bill, or an important notice) and yet you want proof of mailing and delivery, you may find it less expensive to send it by *Certified Mail*. It provides a receipt for the sender and a record of delivery. No insurance coverage is provided for certified mail.

Insured Mail

Third- or fourth-class mail, or airmail containing third- or fourth-class matter, may be insured for up to $200 against loss or damage. A receipt is issued for insured mail. It should be kept on file until the insured mail has arrived in satisfactory condition. If an insured parcel is lost or damaged, the post office will reimburse you for the value of the merchandise or the amount for which it was insured, whichever is the smaller.

COD Service

Merchandise may be sent to a purchaser COD, that is, *collect on delivery*, if the shipment is based on an order by the buyer or on an agreement between sender and addressee. The seller may obtain COD service by paying a fee in addition to the regular postage. The maximum amount collectible on one package is $200. The total fee varies with the amount to be collected, the weight of the package, and the distance it is to travel.

Tracing Mail

If mail has not been delivered within a reasonable time, you may make a written request to have it traced. The post office will supply you with a form for tracing a piece of mail. Although the post office will cooperate in every possible way, it is almost impossible to trace unregistered, uninsured, or uncertified mail, especially if it does not carry a return address. Consequently, all mail should carry a complete return address and valuable or important mail should be registered, certified, or insured.

Recalling Mail

Once in a great while it may be necessary to recall a piece of mail you have already mailed. This will require prompt action on your part. Go to the post office in your mailing zone to recall a letter mailed to a local address or to the central post office to recall a letter mailed out of town. Fill in Form 1509 (*Sender's Application for Withdrawal of Mail*) and the post office will have the piece of mail returned to you.

AIDS FOR VOLUME MAILING

There are other mailing aids for business firms for use in advertising campaigns and for announcements of new products and services.

Mailing Lists

Many firms keep lists of their customers, prospective customers, subscribers, clients, or others to whom they address mail repeatedly. A firm may use a number of mailing lists for different purposes — for instance, to advertise a new product, to announce a new service, or to institute a new policy. Special mailing lists of all kinds of prospective buyers, both nationwide and regional, can be purchased. One of your secretarial duties may be to develop the mailing list and keep it up to date.

Mailing Lists on File Cards

The names and addresses of a mailing list are frequently kept on 5" x 3" cards that are filed in alphabetic order. These cards may be grouped under various classifications, such as doctors, druggists, jewelers, and stationers. The different groupings may be indicated by colored tabs, or the cards for each group may be filed in separate drawers or compartments in the card file.

The cards may also be filed by subject — the subject that the prospective customer has been interested in or may be interested in later.

Illus. 7-14
File cards in address style and index style for a mailing list

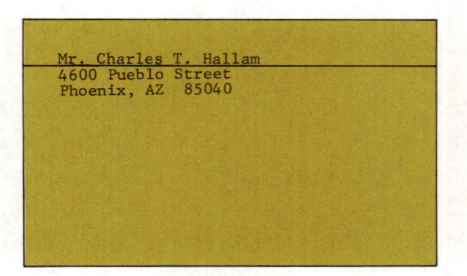

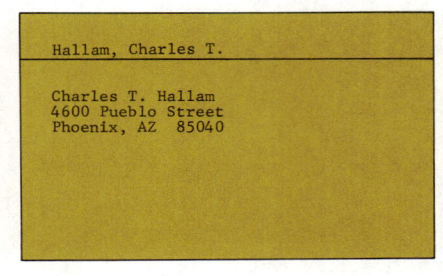

```
Mr. Charles T. Hallam
4600 Pueblo Street
Phoenix, AZ  85040
```

```
Hallam, Charles T.

Charles T. Hallam
4600 Pueblo Street
Phoenix, AZ  85040
```

Up-to-Date Mailing Lists

Unless mailing lists are kept up to date, they soon lose much of their usefulness. The names on all mailing lists are constantly changing as newcomers move into the sales area and others move out. Additions, deletions, and corrections of names and addresses should be made whenever the information is received. You learn of many of the necessary changes in addresses when mail is returned because of nondelivery.

The post office will assist you in maintaining an up-to-date mailing list. It will make corrections on a mailing list or correct individual addresses if requested to do so. For a small fee it will also supply the ZIP Codes for an entire mailing list.

Chain Feeding of Envelopes for a Mailing List

The names and addresses on a mailing list are usually typed on the envelopes if the list is used infrequently. A chain feeding method of inserting and addressing the envelopes will save a great deal of time in typing from the list. The four steps in the widely used front-feed method follow:

1. Stack the envelopes *face down*, with the flaps toward you, at the side of the typewriter.
2. Address the first envelope; then roll it back (toward you) until a half inch shows above the alignment scale.
3. Insert the next envelope from the front, placing it between the first envelope and the cylinder.
4. Turn the cylinder back to remove the first envelope and to position the second one. Continue the "chain" by feeding all envelopes from the front of the cylinder.
5. The envelopes will stack themselves in order at the back of the cylinder. Remove them after about every sixth envelope is typed.

Illus. 7-15
The front-feed method of chain feeding of envelopes

IBM Corporation

Addressing Machines and Addressing Services

You may use an addressing service or, if your office has it, an addressing machine in addressing a large number of envelopes. Because mailing lists are used over and over again, the names and addresses are often stenciled or embossed so that the envelopes can be automatically addressed on an addressing machine. Two widely used styles of addressing machines are the Addressograph, which prints from a metal plate; and the Elliott, which prints from a stencil plate. Also, some businesses are now using their computers for addressing large numbers of envelopes.

The Addressograph. The Addressograph is often used for addressing envelopes and cards for permanent mailing lists. It may also be used to print the inside addresses on letters or to print names, addresses, numbers, and other identifying information on bank statements, monthly bills, time cards, paychecks, dividend checks, and other business forms. The plates can be coded so that an automatic selecting device can be used as the letters are addressed. Classification tabs can be attached to the address plates of a particular mailing list, and the automatic selector will then select and print only these plates without changing the order of any of the plates in the file.

Elliott Addressing Machine. The stencil address plates used in the Elliott addressing machine can be prepared on a typewriter. When a small attachment is used, the small stencil plates are typed in much the same manner as ordinary stencils. The stencil addressing equipment is not often used to print inside addresses on letters or other material that should give the appearance of being completely typed. The plates are, however, often used for mailing lists with frequently changing addresses.

Computer Addressing. Some large firms use their computers for addressing envelopes and cards. The computer can print the addresses directly on the cards and envelopes, or it can print address labels which have an adhesive backing. When adhesive-backed labels are printed, they are then attached to the front of the envelopes.

Illus. 7-16
An addressing machine

Addressograph-Multigraph
Corporation

Outgoing mail, as you can see, may mean one letter to thousands of persons. It may mean first to fourth class and even mixed mail; or it may mean domestic, foreign, and special service mail. Your knowledge and understanding of postal services and effective mail handling can save your employer time and money and can increase the efficiency of his business. Anytime you are faced with an unusual problem involving mailing, call the postmaster or the superintendent of mails at your local post office. He or one of his assistants will furnish the latest official information.

QUESTIONS

1. Why would you use precanceled stamps and envelopes with outgoing mail?
2. What are the advantages of using metered mail?
3. How is payment made for postage used in a postage meter machine?

4. Why are ZIP Codes now used with all classes of mail?
5. What is the function of an Optical Character Reader (OCR)?
6. What are some of the items to be checked in a letter and on the envelope before it is released for outgoing mail?
7. What kind of mail must be sent at the first-class rate?
8. What is included in second-class mail?
9. What is the weight limit of third-class mail?
10. What is the other name for fourth-class mail? How does it differ from other classes of mail?
11. What are the differences between *Special Delivery* and *Special Handling?*
12. List some of the items that you would ordinarily send by *Registered Mail.*
13. What is the maximum amount collectible on a single COD package?
14. What is the purpose of keeping a mailing list?
15. What is the major difference between the Addressograph and the Elliott addressing machines?

JUDGMENT

1. If your employer asked you to mail the following items for him, what mailing service would you use for each and why?
    (a) A stock certificate for fifty shares of American Telephone and Telegraph Company stock
    (b) An important lightweight package containing copies of a speech your employer will deliver at a convention
    (c) A package to the research department of your company containing a sample portion of a product on which a complaint has been filed
    (d) A business letter to be mailed a distance of 1,500 miles
    (e) A business letter to be mailed a distance of 175 miles, but one that should be delivered as quickly as possible
2. In a business office in which you are working (a) several letters are returned because of incorrect and incomplete addresses, and (b) others are delivered with insufficient postage for which the recipients must pay. What would you suggest to correct such occurrences?
3. Suppose that the firm for which you work is considering using a postage meter machine instead of ordinary postage stamps for its outgoing mail. What do you think are the advantages that might come from the use of such a machine? the disadvantages?
4. Postal authorities report that millions of letters and parcels become part of undeliverable *dead letter mail* every year. What can you suggest to avoid having some of your volume mail become dead letter mail?

5. What steps can you take to keep your mailing lists current and correct?

PERSONAL QUALITIES

Just before closing time Mr. Arnold dictated a request for important information to one of the branch managers and asked Mary Reynolds to send it by airmail. In the rush to get it out before 5 o'clock, Mary forgot that the letter was to be sent airmail. The letter was metered and went out at the regular rate.

Five days later Mr. Arnold comments to Mary that he cannot understand why he has not received a reply from the branch manager who is usually very prompt in supplying requested information.

Should Mary explain that the letter was accidentally mailed at the first-class rate and that the branch manager probably has not yet had time to reply, or should she offer no explanation and hope for a reply in the next day's mail?

LANGUAGE USAGE

1. The following terms were taken from Unit 7, Parts 1 and 2. Write the meaning of each term. Consult the text or a standard dictionary if you are not sure of the definition.
   - (a) computer addressing
   - (b) domestic mail
   - (c) LC and AO international mail
   - (d) mailing lists
   - (e) mixed mail
   - (f) postal cards
   - (g) precanceled stamps
   - (h) return receipt
   - (i) tracing mail

2. Type the correct spelling of each of the following words used in mailing:
   - (a) accurate   or acurate
   - (b) applicable   or applicible
   - (c) bulky   or bulkey
   - (d) catagories   or categories
   - (e) cataloges   or catalogs
   - (f) certified   or certefied
   - (g) circulers   or circulars
   - (h) exceding   or exceeding
   - (i) mailible   or mailable
   - (j) prescribed   or perscribed
   - (k) receipt   or reciept
   - (l) transmited   or transmitted
   - (m) underlinning   or underlining

SECRETARIAL WORK

1. Using an 8½″ x 11″ sheet of paper and an ordinary No. 6 envelope, fold the paper as you would a letter and insert it in the envelope.

248   Unit 7 / Mailing and Shipping Services

2. Using three sheets of 8½" x 11" paper and a large No. 10 envelope, fold the three sheets together and insert them in the envelope.

3. Using an 8½" x 11" sheet of paper and a large No. 10 window envelope fold the sheet and insert it in the envelope. (If you do not have a window envelope, fold the sheet as though it would be inserted in a window envelope.)

4. Address envelopes of either 6½" x 3⅝" (No. 6) or 9½" x 4⅛" (No. 10) for the following names and addresses. If envelopes are not available, type the addresses on slips of paper of approximately one of these sizes. You may assume that these names and addresses were taken from the classified directory of New York, N.Y.

   Acme File Company, 30 Warren Street, 10007
   Airport Duplicating Service, 510 East End Avenue, 10028
   American Stationery Company, 59 East 44th Street, 10017
   Apollo Supply Company, 139 Varick Street, 10013
   Buckeye Printing Company, 30 West 59th Street, 10019
   Chase Office Supply Company, 10 West 35th Street, 10001
   City Systems, 59 Ann Street, 10038
   Columbia Stationers, 199 East 14th Street, 10003
   Cosmopolitan Supply Company, 410 West 24th Street, 10011
   Dale Ribbons, 92 Park Avenue, 10016
   Diamond Equipment Company, 210 East 27th Street, 10016
   Duplicating Service, Inc., 10 Park Row, 10038
   Embassy Manufacturing Company, 400 West 59th Street, 10019
   Empire Filing Equipment, 192 Seventh Avenue, 10011
   Equity Equipment, 310 West 46th Street, 10036
   General Equipment Company, 92 Fourth Avenue, 10003
   Globe Service Corporation, 10 East 39th Street, 10016
   Guide Systems, Inc., 179 West 37th Street, 10018
   Howard Stationery Company, 92 John Street, 10038
   Hygrade Desk Company, 129 Fifth Avenue, 10003

5. Your employer, Mr. John Randolph, General Manager of Randolph Office Equipment and Supply Company, has instructed you to order the latest edition of the Postal Service Manual. Inasmuch as you do not have an order form for this purpose, you will write a letter. If necessary, check with the library or the post office to determine the amount of the remittance that should accompany the order.

   Randolph Office Equipment and Supply Company letters are written in modified block form (no paragraph indentations) with mixed punctuation.

PART 3 — AIR AND SURFACE SHIPPING

Marlene Rowat is secretary to the vice-president in charge of sales for a nationwide mail-order house. Since all the orders are received by mail or from the company's distribution outlets in large cities, Marlene must have an above average knowledge of the various shipping methods. Although the actual packaging of the orders is done in the Shipping Department, Marlene has schedules and rates for different ways of shipping at her fingertips. This is necessary for two reasons — first, the customer must pay shipping charges on all orders; therefore, the least expensive method is used. Secondly, if an order is to be rushed — as is often the case at Christmas time — packages must be shipped the fastest way possible, but with shipping cost kept in mind. Marlene is not alone in being aware of shipping costs. Every business must be very aware of this factor, since, in most cases, shipping costs are included in the price of the product; and every company wants to keep its prices as low as possible to meet competition.

"What's the best way to send that package?" your employer may ask. It may be just a small parcel urgently needed by a customer, or it may be a large package of advertising materials. Your employer may consider the speed of delivery to be of much more importance than the cost. Whatever the case may be, you must be familiar with all the available types of ground and air shipping services.

Every business firm uses a number of different shipping services to deliver parcels and to distribute large commodities. As an alert and intelligent secretary, you should be familiar with the advantages of each service. You may be required to decide how small parcels should be sent. You may be called upon to prepare the necessary forms for express and freight shipments for which trains, planes, trucks, and buses are used. Occasionally you may be asked to prepare the forms for tracing a shipment or for filing a claim for goods damaged in transit.

RECENT DEVELOPMENTS IN SHIPPING

With the great increase in volume, the shipping of goods in the United States and Canada has undergone many rapid changes in the past few years. Trucks have replaced trains for a great deal of shipping across the nation, and shipping by air is becoming widespread.

Recent developments in packaging have also aided the shipping process. Lightweight, theft-proof containers are being used in place of heavy wooden crates. In addition, shipping terminals and airports have been equipped with automatic equipment which uses high speed conveyer belts to handle packages of all sizes. Railroad terminal yards have been equipped with automatic switching equipment and closed-circuit TV to save time and shipping costs.

METHODS OF SHIPPING

Goods may be shipped to various points by railway, truck, bus, planes, or by a combination of two or more of these services. Each of these services has its own advantages: some offer faster delivery; some offer a higher degree of safety; some are less expensive; and some are much more convenient for the shipper, for the receiver, or for both. The values of each of these services should be known to the shipper so that he may select the best and the most suitable shipping service.

Shipping Guides

Where can you look for the information you and your employer need about shipping? Various guidebooks are printed to assist you in selecting the method of shipment that is best for each shipment. There are several guides which are widely used in business offices and which you will find very helpful.

The United States Postal Service Manual gives complete information about all classes of mail.

The Express and Parcel Post Comparative Rate Guide gives a complete list of all express stations and the comparative charges between express and parcel post shipments.

Leonard's Guide gives rates and routings for freight, express, and parcel post.

Parcel Post

Also called fourth-class mail, parcel post is a method of transporting goods that is used most often when small items are to be shipped to widely scattered places. Some details of parcel post service are discussed in connection with the classes of mail in Unit 7, Part 2. Parcel post shipments are handled by the United States Postal Service. The cost of sending a package parcel post depends on the weight of the package and the distance it is to travel.

Air Parcel Post

When speed is important in the delivery of a package, you will probably send the parcel by air. The delivery time can be greatly reduced by using air parcel post. The rates are higher than for ordinary parcel post. Increasingly, air parcel post is being used to carry merchandise to distant and isolated places. This is especially true for Hawaii and Alaska and other areas where surface travel is slow.

REA Express

A telephone call to the nearest REA Express office will bring an express truck to your door to pick up packages of all kinds and sizes. This is a very fast and convenient way to ship packages. Delivery is usually made directly to the home or office of the addressee. The cost of shipping depends upon the weight of the shipment and the distance it has to travel.

Illus. 7-17
Signing receipts for delivery of packages may be a secretary's responsibility.

REA Express

Air Express

You will find air express the swiftest method of commercial transportation. This service includes shipping by air to all parts of the United

States and to most foreign countries. Air express shipments receive special pick-up and delivery service. Almost all types of goods, including machine parts, perishable foods, printed materials, and flowers, are moved by air express. Small packages or shipments may be placed on regular passenger planes. Large or bulky shipments are usually sent by special air freight cargo planes.

Bus Express

Most bus lines throughout the country offer package express service. This is a particularly useful service when destination points are located where there is no airport and when speed of delivery is important. Many points receive same day delivery — many within a few hours — which may be even faster than air service. Frequent and direct bus trips between the cities and the fact that terminals are usually located in business districts account for the speed of handling and delivery.

Illus. 7-18
Business depends upon the services of specialized carriers of small packages.

United Parcel Service

United Parcel Service

United Parcel Service is a specialized carrier of small packages that weigh no more than 50 pounds. Its rates are competitive with parcel

Part 3 / Air and Surface Shipping

post. The service is provided over most of the nation. It offers shippers many services which are not available from parcel post, including pickup of packages at the shipper's place of business.

Truck Transportation

Another shipping service which your employer may use is truck transportation. The truck is the best type of local transportation available. Arrangements can easily be made with a trucking company to make regular calls at your place of business to pick up and deliver goods. Truck transportation is also available for long-distance hauls. Some long-distance truck firms offer overnight service to insure the prompt delivery of goods.

Railway Freight Service

For shipping bulky articles and goods for which the speed of delivery is not important, railway freight service is often used. The cost of shipping by rail is lower than the cost of shipping by truck or any other method.

Illus. 7-19
Railway freight is often used when speed of delivery is not important.

Union Pacific Railroad

MARKING GOODS FOR SHIPMENT

Whether goods are shipped by freight, express, parcel post, or some other way, it is important to the prompt movement and proper delivery of shipments that the goods be marked correctly. The rules of the carriers require that the shipper mark each package plainly, legibly, and durably. In marking shipments, the following rules should be observed in order to insure the proper delivery of packages:

1. The addressee's name and address must be shown.
2. The word *From* should precede the name and address of the shipper. This explanation is of great assistance to both the shipper and the carrier if the shipment gets lost, is unclaimed, or is refused by the addressee.
3. Packages containing articles easily broken should be marked *Fragile* or *Handle with Care*. Packages containing merchandise that is perishable, such as fruit, should be marked *Perishable*.
4. Marking should be done with a brush, stencil, crayon, or rubber stamp. If lettered by hand, a good clear style of lettering should be used. Labels should be prepared on a typewriter and fastened securely to the packages.

Illus. 7-20
Proper packaging is important if merchandise is to withstand rough handling in shipping and storage and reach its destination undamaged.

Administrative Management Society

PACKAGING

Goods for shipment must be packaged properly if they are to be delivered without damage. It is the responsibility of the shipper to properly package the item for shipment. The item to be shipped, the method of transportation to be used, and the distance to be traveled will be the determining factors in packaging. The decision on a damage claim is often decided on the basis of how well the goods have been packaged.

TRACING

It may be necessary to trace a shipment if the goods are not delivered within a reasonable time. All carriers in all modes of transportation provide tracing services. Information required to trace a shipment is:

1. Shipper's name and address
2. Name and address of the person to whom the goods were shipped
3. Shipping date
4. Quantity of packages involved
5. Shipping receipt
6. Routing used

CLAIM FOR LOSS

You submit a claim to the transportation company for a total or partial loss if the shipment is not delivered, if it is totally or partially destroyed, or if it is delivered in a damaged condition. Claims for loss are presented by either the shipper or the addressee, depending upon who owns the goods.

QUESTIONS

1. Why should a secretary have some understanding about the methods of shipping goods?
2. What are some of the more recent developments in shipping services?
3. What shipping guides are commonly used in business offices?
4. What are the advantages of REA Express?
5. What are the advantages of air express?
6. What are some of the advantages of United Parcel Service?
7. What are some of the rules you should follow in marking goods for shipment?

JUDGMENT

1. How will you ship a small parcel to a customer in a large city 1,500 miles away if the parcel is needed quickly?
2. How will you ship a small carton of merchandise to a customer in a suburb ten miles away if the merchandise is needed within the next few days?
3. How will you ship a package to a customer in a town along a major highway about 200 miles away if the town has no airfield and is 50 miles from the nearest railroad station?
4. When would you recommend that a shipment of merchandise be made by air rather than railroad?
5. When would you recommend that a parcel be shipped by air parcel post instead of by ordinary parcel post?

PERSONAL QUALITIES

Mr. Howard C. Patton, an executive of a large brokerage firm in New York City, asked his new secretary, Jeanette Wilson, to photocopy the entire file folder of a client with a large account. The client had moved to Hawaii; so Jeanette was also asked to wrap the photocopies and mail them by air parcel post to the manager of the firm's branch in Honolulu.

Two weeks later Mr. Patton received a telephone call from the manager of the Honolulu branch. He said that the records had not been received. However, much to his embarrassment, the client had already called but he could not suggest investments because he had no record of the customer's holdings.

Mr. Patton then learned that Jeanette had delayed mailing the photocopies because she said that she did not have the time to wrap them. Furthermore, she felt that it was not her job as a secretary to wrap and mail packages. When she finally had them ready, she mailed them by ordinary parcel post.

What do you think of Jeanette's attitude with regard to the wrapping and mailing of packages? What was wrong with shipping the records by ordinary parcel post? If you were in Mr. Patton's place, what would you do?

LANGUAGE USAGE

Adjectives are used to indicate an increasing or decreasing degree of quality, quantity, or manner. The three degrees of comparison are positive, comparative, and superlative.

Example:	*Positive*	*Comparative*	*Superlative*
	light	lighter	lightest
	useful	more (less) useful	most (least) useful

On a separate sheet of paper list the adjectives in the sentences below and indicate which degree of comparison is used.

1. The secretary called the trucking firm and asked that a small pick-up truck stop at the office to pick up the package.
2. Of all the merchants on Fifth Avenue, Mr. Clay had the prettiest window display.
3. The dispatcher's list contained three bulky pickups which the small pick-up truck could not hold.
4. The package was wrapped less securely than it should have been.
5. The typewriter, the books, the calculator, the stove, and the produce had to be crated carefully before shipment to either a close or far destination.
6. A larger box could not be found.
7. The driver spoke most softly even though the anger showed on his face.
8. Of the two secretaries, she wrote the more legibly.
9. Companies demand prompt movement and proper delivery of their shipments.

10. The building contained much ventilation, more light, and the most space of any of the warehouses they examined.

SECRETARIAL WORK

1. Make a study of the following shipping services available in your community and be prepared to report your findings orally to the class and in writing to your teacher:
   (a) REA Express Service
   (b) Bus Express
   (c) United Parcel Service
   (d) Truck Service
   (e) Railway Freight Service
2. What transportation service would you suggest for shipping the following from your local community:
   (a) A standard manual typewriter to a college you are entering 100 miles away
   (b) The 24 volumes of the *Encyclopaedia Britannica* to a relative 500 miles away
   (c) An electronic desk calculator weighing 30 pounds to a branch office 50 miles away
   (d) An electric stove weighing 300 pounds to your employer's home 10 miles out of town
   (e) Twenty cases of produce to a market 70 miles away

Unit 8 THE SECRETARY AND THE PUBLIC

Part 1. Greeting Callers
   2. Good Language Usage

The secretary personally greets all visitors to her executive's office. It is her duty to make visitors feel that they are welcome. By her appearance, manner, and speech she tries to convey the manner in which the office functions.

VOCABULARY BUILDER

affiliates
noun: associates (as members of a club or organization)

transacted
verb: completed; carried on (as business); performed

maintains
verb: keeps in an existing state; preserves; provides for

tactfully
adverb: smoothly; artfully; graciously; skillfully

preliminary
adjective: preceding the main discourse or business; introductory

hospitable
adjective: given to a generous and cordial reception of guests

disrupted
adjective: broken apart; broken down

tolerant
adjective: forbearing; charitable; liberal; unprejudiced; patient; broad-minded

colloquial
adjective: characteristic of familiar or informal conversation; dialect of a local or regional nature

distorted
adjective: twisted out of the true meaning or proportion; twisted out of a natural, normal, or original shape or form

---

What grace is to the body good sense is to the mind
La Rochefoucauld

p. 261 ... a travel agency with **affiliates** in fifty different countries.

p. 261 While much business is **transacted** by telephone and letter, there continue to be many person-to-person meetings.

p. 262 The secretary **maintains** a calendar of appointments and visitors.

p. 262 The secretary handles cancellations — either by her employer or by a caller — quickly and **tactfully**.

p. 264 ... the record for a particular day sometimes includes reminders of appointments and conferences for the following few days that require **preliminary** work by the executive.

p. 267 In greeting a caller who is unfamiliar you should be **hospitable** and helpful.

p. 270 While you attempt to schedule appointments for the length of time that seems correct, there will be times when the schedule will be **disrupted**.

p. 278 ... you will find that people are **tolerant** of differences. ...

p. 280 Often these **colloquial** words and expressions lend ease and naturalness to what is said; however, they must be used with care.

p. 281 Overuse of the hands, unnatural use of the eyes, **distorted** facial expressions will detract from what your voice and language are trying to convey.

PART 1 GREETING CALLERS

Vickie Royal is secretary to Mr. Anthony Bodoni, who is Director of Community Affairs of Pagano International, a travel agency with affiliates in fifty different countries. Vickie works in the New York City office, which is the headquarters for the Western Hemisphere. She greets and talks with people from all parts of the world. While most visitors write or call ahead of time to make appointments, there are many times when someone arrives unexpectedly because of changes in schedules. For example, Mr. Jannesen who had an appointment to see Mr. Bodoni on Thursday arrived on Tuesday afternoon. He told Vickie that his plans had changed and he was leaving for Copenhagen on Wednesday afternoon instead of Thursday night. It was extremely important that he see Mr. Bodoni before he left. Vickie, who is skillful in handling such emergencies, was able to reschedule the appointment. Mr. Bodoni knows how valuable his secretary is; for countless visitors tell him about the gracious, intelligent aid they receive from Vickie; and he finds in his international travels that clients always inquire about Vickie.

PERSON-TO-PERSON MEETINGS

While much business is transacted by telephone and letter, there continue to be many person-to-person meetings. Executives meet with customers and other businessmen individually and in groups. They have conferences with other executives and with company employees. In addition, many companies participate in civic activities. Community leaders visit and meet with executives in their offices. Acquaintances and friends may come to the office for business-related reasons or for brief, friendly visits. Members of executives' families may stop by from time to time.

THE RESPONSIBILITIES OF THE SECRETARY

While a receptionist is usually the first person callers meet when they arrive at the office, as an executive's secretary you will be *his* official hostess. In this role you must be aware of office etiquette. While customs vary from office to office, there are some general practices that are observed in most offices.

1. The secretary schedules appointments for her employer.
2. The secretary maintains a calendar of appointments and visitors.
3. The secretary reminds her employer of his appointments.
4. The secretary handles cancellations — either by her employer or by a caller — quickly and tactfully.
5. The secretary makes arrangements for special facilities if conferences are not to be in the executive's office.
6. The secretary courteously assists all visitors, including those who have not made an appointment.
7. The secretary keeps a record of all callers where this is required and maintains up-to-date card files.
8. The secretary remains calm if a caller is difficult and continues to be courteous and helpful.
9. The secretary keeps a visitor informed if a delay occurs, and she makes the waiting period as pleasant as possible.
10. The secretary takes care of beverages and food if refreshments are offered visitors at coffee break time.
11. The secretary aids her employer in maintaining the schedule planned for each day.
12. The secretary keeps her employer informed if it is necessary for her to leave her desk.

Scheduling Appointments

In some offices executives will see no one from outside the organization without an appointment. In other offices executives will make no specific appointments but will see people if it is convenient. In still other offices executives reserve part of each day for scheduled appointments and a part for unscheduled appointments.

Some executives prefer to approve every appointment, which means that you must check each request before you can confirm it. It may be more practical, however, for you to make the appointments after you fully understand the time that is available. Generally an executive will discuss his weekly plans early on Monday and then review them briefly each morning so that you have up-to-date information on the executive's plans.

You will receive requests for appointments in many different ways. There will be callers who request appointments in person; there will be telephone calls from people wanting appointments; and there will be letters requesting appointments. All such requests should receive immediate attention.

Ohio National Life Insurance Company

Illus. 8-1
The secretary often uses the telephone for scheduling appointments for her employer.

If the appointment is requested in person, after recording it on your calendar, you should record on a small card the details of the appointment so that the caller will have a record of his appointment. When the appointment is requested by telephone, you should be sure to state very clearly the details of the appointment. Also, when an appointment is requested by letter, the return letter should be complete concerning the date, time, and office location. If the person writing is unfamiliar with the general location of the office, it is thoughtful to enclose a map with directions to the office clearly marked.

Maintaining a Calendar

You must be sure to get full details about each caller who is requesting an appointment for the first time. These details aid the executive in knowing the nature of business to be transacted at the time of the appointment. Also, if there arises a need to change the date of the appointment or to talk with the person prior to his visit, you will know where to call or write to the individual. Your records on each caller should include full name, address, telephone number, and the organization with which the caller is associated. Also, there must be recorded the date and the exact time of the appointment; the name of the executive with whom the appointment is made, in case you make appointments for more than one executive; and the amount of time to be set aside.

Part 1 / Greeting Callers

The details of appointments may be noted on an ordinary desk calendar if the number of appointments for each day is limited. If there are many appointments each day, a ruled schedule form is commonly used. The appointment record should include the executive's appointments away from the office. Many executives have their secretaries keep reminder calendars of a personal nature, such as luncheons with friends or medical appointments.

It is common for the executive, as well as the secretary, to maintain a calendar. In such instances, it will be necessary for you to check your employer's calendar frequently to be sure that there are no conflicts with appointments. All appointments which the executive makes on his own should be recorded on your calendar so that you have a complete list of all business and personal engagements. You are also responsible for adding the appointments you have made to the executive's calendar so that he is fully aware of what is to take place each day.

Reminding the Employer

It is a common practice for the secretary to place a copy of the record of appointments for the day on her employer's desk early each morning. Along with the record, there should be any related business papers or materials that will be useful during the meetings. In addition, the record for a particular day sometimes includes reminders of appointments and conferences for the following few days that require preliminary work by the executive.

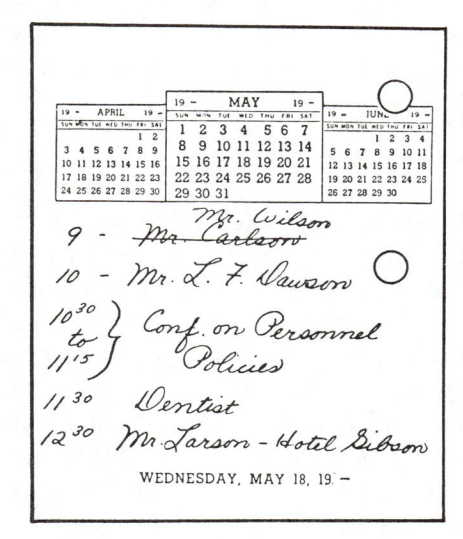

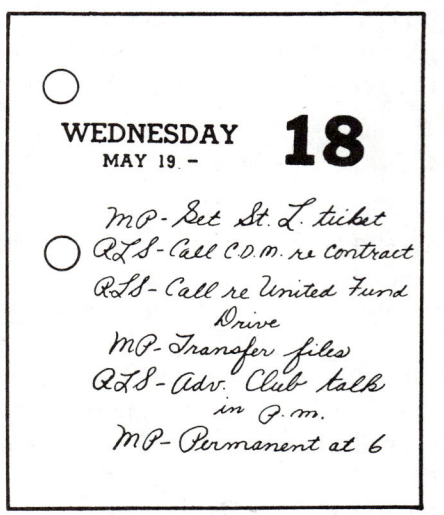

Illus. 8-2   Calendar pad appointment record

Unit 8 / The Secretary and the Public

Canceling Appointments

From time to time, appointments must be canceled. When a caller finds he cannot keep a scheduled appointment, he may telephone and request a change. You should handle such a request as graciously as you handled the original request.

There are times when the executive must cancel an appointment. As soon as you know that an appointment cannot be kept, you should notify the other person so that only minimum inconvenience will result. If the executive is sure about his future schedule, you may be able to suggest some future dates for another appointment which will be convenient for your employer and also for the individual requesting the appointment.

Once in a while an appointment will not be canceled until very near the scheduled time, which means that the caller will arrive at the executive's office only to learn that the appointment is canceled or postponed. In such circumstances you must be very tactful and considerate toward the caller. If someone else can assume the absent executive's role, efforts should be made to arrange for that person to talk with the caller. This procedure will often avoid inconvenience to the caller and create goodwill for your firm.

APPOINTMENTS
WEDNESDAY, MAY 18, 19--

Time	Engagements	Memorandums
9:00	Mr. Wilson	Call C. D. Moore re Contract
9:30		
10:00	Mrs. L. F. Dawson	Call Mr. Calhoun re United Fund Drive
10:30	Conference on Personnel Policies	
11:00		
11:30	Dr. Campbell	
12:00		
12:30	Lunch—DDL—Gibson	Work on Adv. Club talk

Illus. 8-3   Appointment schedule

Arranging for Facilities

There are many times when a conference brings together more people than can meet conveniently in the executive's office. In such instances you must be sure there is an appropriate place for the meeting. If there is a conference room in the office where you and your executive work, you will probably have to make arrangements to use it.

Shortly before the time of the meeting, you should check to be sure that the room is open; that the furniture is arranged satisfactorily; that water and glasses are on the table; and that pads, pencils, and other materials that will be needed are in place.

Assisting Callers

The people who come to your office are important to your organization. You must understand this, and your manner must reflect your concern with helping callers. Consider the attitude conveyed by the secretary in the following example:

> Jane is busy typing a letter when Mr. Lorman, who has a 10 a.m. appointment with her employer, enters the office. Mr. Lorman is from out of town and wrote for the appointment. The last time he was in the office was about nine months ago. Jane — preoccupied — looks up and, continuing to type, says,
>
> Jane: "Oh, hi, Mr. Lorman. Will you see if Mr. Sattler is free? I'm busy trying to get this letter finished."
>
> Mr. Lorman: (embarrassed by such casual treatment): "Yes, of course. Will I find Mr. Sattler in his office?"
>
> Jane: "I think so. It's the one over there." (Jane points vaguely to the right.)

What is Jane's attitude toward callers?

Now let us assume that the call was handled in this manner:

> Jane is busy typing a letter when Mr. Lorman enters the office for his 10 a.m. appointment. She stops typing immediately and graciously greets Mr. Lorman:
>
> Jane: "Good morning, Mr. Lorman. How nice it is to see you again. Mr. Sattler is expecting you. Did you have a good flight from Denver?"
>
> Mr. Lorman: "Hello. It's good to see you, Jane. My flight was fine, and I'm glad to be here again."
>
> Jane: Please have a seat, and I'll check to see if Mr. Sattler is free now. It is just a minute before 10."

What impression does Jane give by her behavior in this instance? In the second example, the secretary presented a friendly, helpful

Illus. 8-4
Even if she is interrupted momentarily the secretary should not neglect the caller in any way.

attitude toward the caller. He will have a positive opinion of the organization. He was expected, recognized, and treated graciously. The secretary gave him her full attention until he was guided into the executive's office. Contrast this impression with that which could result from the behavior in the first example. The visitor was not given any hint that he was expected, even though he was called by name which was only a minimum courtesy. The caller could easily have believed that he was unwanted and was interrupting the secretary, since she did not even stop typing — in fact, she continued her work while she motioned him toward the executive's office where the *caller* had to determine if the executive was ready to see him. It is extremely discourteous to let a caller enter an executive's office alone. If the executive is on the telephone or has someone in his office, the caller will be embarrassed at entering unannounced. The secretary's behavior in the first instance was rude and ill-mannered. The caller will remember this office only as being impolite, unfriendly, and disrespectful toward a visitor!

In greeting callers who have appointments you should indicate your knowledge of the appointment and your genuine interest in seeing that the visitor is given assistance.

In greeting a caller who is unfamiliar you should be hospitable and helpful. You should determine the purpose of the caller's visit and assist him by making an appointment or by referring him to someone who can help him. Notice the manner in which Cynthia handled this stranger:

Cynthia: "Good morning. May I help you?"

Caller: "Yes, I am Richard Nichols, of the Intercontinental Transportation Services. I would like very much to see Mr. Bellows about the services we can provide for your international sales meeting next year."

Cynthia: "I am sure Mr. Bellows will be interested in what you have to offer, but, unfortunately, he is in a meeting and has appointments scheduled throughout the day. Would it be convenient for you to come in on Friday or next Tuesday?"

Mr. Nichols: "No, I will be out of town for the next week."

Cynthia: "Could you send him a letter with descriptive brochures? As you realize, Mr. Bellows would be particularly interested in the cost of your services and what you provide."

Mr. Nichols: "Yes, I could write a letter and possibly I could talk with him when I return from London."

Cynthia: "Fine. Your letter will receive attention, and Mr. Bellows will call your office if he wishes further information. I will note on the letter that you were in the office today."

Mr. Nichols: "Thank you very much."

In this instance the secretary knew that Mr. Bellows was gathering information about travel services that were available, and she knew that he would want this additional information. She, however, did not reveal any information to Mr. Nichols, which was a wise omission on her part. Secretaries do not reveal the company's business concerns without being told to do so by their employers.

Recording Callers

In some companies a record is kept of all callers. If you have all the information from having recorded it at the time the appointment was made, you may merely confirm the accuracy of the material you have in your card file. If you are talking with a caller without an appointment, you will ask him for the information after you have greeted him courteously. If the caller has a business card, you may find that it contains all the information you need. Or you may prefer to staple the business card to a 5" x 3" card and record below the business card any additional information needed.

In offices where a card file of callers is maintained, you will want to review it from time to time so that it contains only the names of current callers. Notes of dates of appointments and purpose of visit and similar details are sometimes written on the back of the cards for reference purposes. This card file enables you to recall earlier visits and, therefore, to greet returning callers more appropriately.

Handling Difficult Callers

Once in a while an unfamiliar caller may be a difficult caller who will require a firm response. The difficult caller may refuse to indicate why he is there, but he continues to insist that he must see the executive *immediately*. He may speak discourteously and appear angry. It is important that you remain calm in such a situation. You should continue to be helpful as you seek to get information about the purpose of his visit. Generally such a caller responds to kindness and will eventually tell his name and the purpose of his call. He may have a good reason for seeing the executive. If the executive is in and available, you may proceed as you would with any unscheduled appointment. If the executive is not available, you might suggest that the caller write a letter explaining the situation that he wants to discuss. It might be appropriate to invite the caller to sit down and write his letter immediately. After such courteous treatment, the caller will leave feeling satisfied about his visit.

Callers who refuse to give their names and remain firm about not revealing the nature of their business should not be admitted to the executive's office. In such situations you must remain courteous but firm!

Handling Delays

Sometimes callers must wait to see the executive. They may arrive too early. The executive may have taken more time than was scheduled for earlier appointments. Emergencies may have arisen. In such cases waiting is unavoidable. You should try to make the delay as pleasant as possible. If you know the length of the delay, you may indicate this to the caller. If you are not certain you may say:

> "I'm sorry, but Mr. Cannon is still in a meeting. I am not sure how long the meeting will last, but possibly it will end shortly. Mr. Cannon knows you were expected at eleven and he will not want to keep you waiting."

or

> "Mr. Cannon tells me that the meeting should be ended in about ten minutes. He apologizes for this delay and will see you as quickly as possible."

When the executive is ready to see the next caller, you may walk into the office with the caller and say, "Here is Mr. Smith." If the caller is unacquainted with the executive, you will want to introduce the caller in a friendly, gracious manner. Any one of the following is considered a proper introduction:

> "Mrs. Ableson, may I present Mr. Cannon?"
>
> "Mrs. Ableson, may I introduce Mr. Cannon? Mrs. Ableson is from International Communications."
>
> "Mr. Cannon, this is Mr. Dawson, of Denon Electronics."
>
> "Mr. Cannon, Mr. Dawson, Vice-President of Denon Electronics."

Handling Refreshments

Coffee breaks are customary in business offices, and often visitors who are in the office at coffee break time are invited to have something to drink and eat. You will want to find out the custom of your employer; however, it is not unusual for a secretary to quietly and briefly interrupt a conference that is likely to last through the morning or afternoon coffee time to inquire about refreshments for the visitor and her employer. After you know what is wanted, get it quickly and take it into your employer's office or conference room quietly and without any comment.

Maintaining the Schedule

While you attempt to schedule appointments for the length of time that seems correct, there will be times when the schedule will be disrupted. A caller has a longer, more complicated matter to discuss than had been anticipated; the executive is interrupted with important telephone calls which prolong the conference; callers arrive late; or numerous other situations, many of them unavoidable, require adjustments throughout the day.

Generally executives appreciate the assistance of their secretaries in keeping the schedule moving smoothly. For example, some executives follow a policy of having the secretary inform them of the next appointment about five minutes before the scheduled end of the appointment underway. Arlene, the secretary to a man who sees people for many hours most days, uses this procedure which her employer likes:

> Walking quietly to the door of Mr. Beacon's office, Arlene will wait for a slight pause in the conversation and then say, "Mr. Beacon, Mr. Deane, who has an appointment with you in approximately five minutes, has arrived."
>
> Mr. Beacon's response usually is, "Thank you. We will be finishing our discussion very shortly." However, there are times when Mr. Beacon will respond, "Arlene, will you apologize to Mr. Deane for keeping him waiting, but we must continue this conversation for about fifteen more minutes."

Leaving the Desk

If you find that you must be away while your employer is talking with someone, you should tell a co-worker how long you will be away and where you may be reached. If there is no one else in the area, it may be appropriate to slip a note to the executive so that he knows that your desk is unattended. He then will be able to be alert to the arrival of the next appointment or of unexpected persons. Executives often call on their secretaries to get materials that are needed at a conference. If you leave your desk without informing your employer, his search for you may be embarrassing and time-consuming.

QUESTIONS

1. For what purposes are person-to-person meetings held in business offices?
2. If an executive wants to approve every appointment made, how will his secretary handle a request for an appointment?
3. Why would a secretary give the person requesting an appointment in person a card indicating the date and time and location of his scheduled appointment?
4. Why should the secretary get information about a telephone caller who is making his first appointment?
5. Why is it necessary for the secretary to record on her calendar the appointments that the executive made on his own?
6. Why would a secretary give the executive reminders of appointments that are forthcoming in the next day or two?
7. For what purposes would the secretary check a conference room before a scheduled meeting of her employer and a group of visitors?
8. What attitude should the secretary strive to convey to callers?
9. What kind of information might a secretary keep in a card file record of callers?
10. Explain briefly how the secretary might handle a difficult caller?

JUDGMENT

1. Your employer calls you into his office to tell you that he must leave town at noon instead of at 6 p.m. as originally scheduled. You note that he has three appointments for the afternoon. What would you do about these appointments?
2. An out-of-town caller comes to see your employer without an appointment. Your employer has set aside certain morning hours to receive callers. It is now afternoon. The caller says that he is leaving town that night. What would you do?
3. Two callers appear for 3 p.m. appointments. One is listed on your calendar; the other is not. The one that is not listed

Part 1 / Greeting Callers

was apparently made by the employer when he met the caller at a downtown restaurant earlier in the week. What will you do about this matter?
4. Your employer has a crowded appointment schedule for the afternoon. Shortly before 2:30 a caller appears who says he must see your employer for a few minutes immediately. At the time there is someone in the office with your employer and a person waiting to see him at 2:30. What would you do?
5. A caller asks to see your employer. However, he refuses to give you his name or to indicate the purpose of his visit. What would you do?

PERSONAL QUALITIES

Jane was asked to relieve one of the secretaries while she went on an errand for her employer, Mr. Smith. While the secretary was away, a caller appeared who wanted to see Mr. Smith. The caller did not have an appointment; but, since Mr. Smith was in his office alone, Jane pointed out the office and told the caller to walk right in.

After fifteen minutes the caller left, and shortly afterwards Mr. Smith stormed out of his office and angrily said to Jane, "Why did you let that man in my office? Don't you know that I don't see callers during the morning hours? I reserve the morning hours for reading and answering correspondence."

What was wrong with the way Jane handled this situation? In what way could she have avoided the annoyance caused Mr. Smith?

LANGUAGE USAGE

For each of the following responses made by a secretary, indicate whether you think the response is appropriate or inappropriate. If inappropriate, rewrite the response so that it is appropriate.

1. Jane: (Talking to a fellow executive of her employer) "Why would you think you could just walk in and see Mr. Sanders? He is a busy man and you have worked here long enough to know that."
2. Grace: "Good morning. May I help you?"
3. Frieda: "Oh, I don't know how long Mr. Evans will be in this conference because the man with him is one who talks on and on."
4. Alice: "I am very sorry, but Mr. Jaynes' schedule is crowded this morning. Would it be convenient for you to see him this afternoon?"
5. Marianne: "Mr. Waters cannot see you, but I know he hasn't purchased the conference table yet, and I think you might be able to convince him that your table is best. Do you want to see him tomorrow?"

6. Connie: "Do you-all want coffee or what?"
7. Joan: "I will make an appointment for you to see Mr. Henley, but you can't have more than 15 minutes."
8. Carol: "Mr. Wilson, I am very sorry that Mr. Richards will be unable to keep his appointment with you at 10 tomorrow morning. He has been called out of town and will not be back until Friday evening. Is there some time next week that would be convenient for you?"
9. Susan: "Mr. Winters, do you realize that this conference is a half hour longer than you expected it to be?"
10. Betty: "Oh, you do have an appointment! I guess I forgot all about it."

SECRETARIAL WORK

1. The Modernaire Cosmetics Company has its executive offices in Dubuque, Iowa. Mr. Carl Ashton is Vice-President in charge of promotional activities. The following events occur during the course of one morning:

    (a) Mrs. Suzy Walls, a fashion editor for a popular magazine, arrives at 9:20 for an appointment at 9:30.

    (b) At 10 the receptionist calls you to tell you that a Mr. Lower is in the lobby requesting an appointment with Mr. Ashton. Mr. Lower has a very interesting display that can be adapted for use by Modernaire cosmetics, particularly for a forthcoming exhibition in which Modernaire will participate. It will take about fifteen minutes to set up and demonstrate the display.

    (c) At 11 the Personnel Manager calls you to tell you that a young lady, who has majored in art in college and who has some very good samples of her work with her, has just come in to apply for a position in sales promotion. You know that Mr. Ashton is searching for just such an employee. The young woman must leave for New York City in the afternoon and will not return for two weeks.

    (d) Mrs. Ashton, your employer's wife, comes in at 11:50. She and Mr. Ashton have a luncheon engagement at noon. Someone is in Mr. Ashton's office when she arrives.

    Consider how you would handle each of these situations. Be prepared to act as either the secretary or the caller before your class. Also, be prepared to evaluate the manner in which your classmates handle each of the situations.

2. You have made the following appointments for your employer, Mr. Burns, for Thursday, November 15. The date preceding each item is the date on which each appointment for November 15 was made:

November 1 — A 9:30 appointment is scheduled for Mr. T. F. Ford, who wrote requesting a morning appointment on the 15th.

November 6 — Mr. Sherwood, a close business associate of Mr. Burns, calls to see if Mr. Burns can meet him for lunch at the Essex Club on the 15th at 12. You check with Mr. Burns; his answer is yes.

November 8 — Mr. Wells of the Sales Department, calls to schedule a meeting for four company officials and himself in Mr. Burns' office at 11 on the morning of the 15th. This will last a half hour.

November 9 — Mr. Burns asks you to call Mr. T. Myers, of a local advertising agency, to see if Mr. Myers can come to the office at 2 on the 15th. Mr. Myers is free to come.

November 12 — Mr. Burns asks you to make appointments with two of his staff for Thursday. He would like to see Mr. Cansler at 3:15 and Mr. Derwood at 3:30.

November 14 — Mr. A. R. Jackson calls from another town to see if he can talk with Mr. Burns for a few minutes early the next morning. You schedule an appointment for 9.

November 14 — Mr. Ford's secretary calls to cancel the appointment at 9:30 tomorrow, inasmuch as Mr. Ford will be unable to arrive as early as scheduled. He would like a late afternoon appointment. An appointment is scheduled for 4 p.m.

November 14 — Mr. B. H. Mellon calls to see if he can have an appointment tomorrow morning with Mr. Burns. A 30-minute meeting is scheduled for 9:30.

November 14 — Mr. Burns asks you to check on an appointment at 10 the next day with Miss Jennie Gales of Personnel. She is free to come.

November 14 — Mr. Jack Colman of the Advertising Department calls to see if he can talk with Mr. Burns the next day. An appointment is scheduled for 3 p.m.

Record your employer's appointments for November 15, in the order in which they were made, on a form similar to that illustrated on page 264. Then type a copy of these appointments for Mr. Burns on a form similar to that illustrated on page 265.

PART 2   GOOD LANGUAGE USAGE

Sandy Dunnigan is secretary to the personnel manager of a large food products company. Sandy frequently meets the public. She screens all incoming telephone calls for her employer. She assists applicants in completing application blanks. She conducts tours through the company. Sandy enjoys her work, and her employer depends upon her to handle many tasks.

Mr. Fitzgerald, the personnel manager, is fond of saying, "Sandy is a charming young woman with an excellent command of the English language. Her voice is pleasing to the ear, her conversation is warm and natural, and her choice of words is always well suited to the occasion."

YOUR PERSONALITY

When you look up from your work to greet a caller it is your total appearance and personality that the visitor sees. Your poise, your self-confidence, your gestures, your voice, your hairstyle, your dress, your speech — all combine to make an impression on the caller. The competent secretary moves quietly and gracefully as she greets a visitor. She dresses attractively and appropriately. Her voice is pleasant; her words are well chosen and softly spoken.

While it is possible to "learn how to act," such learning is not enough. Most people can quickly tell when someone is acting and when she is being herself. What you should seek is the deep, natural desire to behave properly towards others. It is not enough to be friendly toward a caller; an attitude of friendliness can be assumed for the moment. But a cordial reception and a sincere interest result in a friendly behavior which stems from a warm personality.

The secretary who courteously calls a visitor by name and appears interested in him and then completely forgets him for 45 minutes has fully destroyed the initial impression. When she returns to the visitor's lounge and says, "Oh, my goodness! I forgot all about your being here!" her thoughtlessness is evident. If the secretary really cares about her employer's visitors and is concerned about them, she does not forget them.

YOUR APPEARANCE

You have learned from experience the style of clothing that is comfortable and attractive for you. As a secretary, you will want to dress so that your attire is appropriate for the business in which you work. Organizations, in very much the same way as individuals, have "personalities"; and employee dress varies considerably. For example, a young secretary working for a new film-producing firm in the loft of an old building would not dress the same as a young secretary working for a bank in the heart of a downtown financial district.

You will want your appearance to reflect your personality and convey to the visitor the kind of person you are.

YOUR MANNERS

The accepted way of behaving in a variety of situations is what we mean by *manners*. As a child you were taught the manners for talking to those older than you, the manners that were expected in a store, or at a meeting. So, too, in the business office there is a code of etiquette that the secretary knows well and uses naturally and with graciousness.

The secretary knows how to greet people, how to introduce her employer to a visitor who is a stranger, and how to create an atmosphere of friendliness and helpfulness.

When you greet an office visitor you must temporarily shift from the work you are doing to give full attention to the person who has come to your desk. To appear annoyed at a visitor who interrupts your work — even if it is a rush assignment — is unbecoming behavior. Good manners require you to be calm and fully attentive to the visitor, for you know that your duty to your employer's guests is just as important as the many other tasks that you perform.

YOUR SPEECH HABITS

Your speech habits are a very important part of your total personality. Your speech habits reflect *you*. Even on the telephone they reveal your personality, your physical appearance, your manners. You want to be sure, then, that they serve you most favorably. You may have developed speech habits that are annoying to others. Therefore, you will want to spend some time in understanding how you speak and in eliminating unpleasant speech habits.

Proper pronunciation, good enunciation, careful choice of words — all contribute to effectiveness in your speech. The secretary who wants to be fully qualified for her position will strive to develop and improve her speech habits.

Illus. 8-5
Your voice and your speech habits, even on the telephone, reveal your personality, your appearance, and your manners.

AT&T

Expressing Ideas

Have you ever heard the comment, "I know what I want to say, but I don't know how to say it"? An effective speaker is one who thinks well and who is able to outline mentally what he wishes to say. If ideas are worth presenting, they deserve careful and thorough attention before they are shared with others.

In a business office it is extremely important that what is said is clearly understood. Misunderstandings can cause problems between people. What you say should mean clearly what you intend it to mean. When speaking with someone, have you ever said, "Oh, you didn't understand what I meant . . . "? Making this comment indicates that your thoughts were not clearly expressed.

Ideas should be expressed in such a way that

1. The speaker conveys what is on his mind.
2. The listener understands what the speaker is saying.
3. The speaker and listener can make progress in their conversation.

Voice

A voice that is pleasant is a valuable asset in the business office. A pleasant voice is one that does not distract from the message being spoken; that is, the listener concentrates on *what* is said not *how* it is said.

Part 2 / Good Language Usage

Your voice is not separate from the rest of your body. It will reflect the quality of both your physical and mental health. If you are not feeling well, for example, you will generally convey the feeling of discomfort through your voice. On the other hand, if you are in excellent health, your sense of well-being is reflected in your voice. Are you able to determine how happy your friends are by the tone of their voices? Do you know what happens to your voice when you are fatigued?

Become aware of your voice. Does the way you speak need improvement? Do you talk too rapidly? too slowly? too softly? too loudly? Are you happy with the pitch of your voice? Can you speak easily and without straining your voice? These are just some of the questions that you will want to think about as you become aware of your own voice.

A common weakness of female voices is their tendency to be relatively high pitched. When you are tense your voice tends to become higher pitched. It is then strained, and words are produced only with heightened effort. The final effect is not attractive to the listener.

Because of the great amount of speaking that a secretary must do during her working days, it is extremely important that you learn to use your voice effectively. The most effective use of your voice will also produce the most pleasing voice for your listeners.

Pronunciation

It will be to your advantage to adopt the pronunciation of words most readily understood and accepted in the office and community where you work and live. It is sometimes difficult to find an acceptable standard of pronunciation inasmuch as standards differ from place to place. What is acceptable pronunciation in Boston may not be acceptable in Atlanta. Speech authorities say that you should attempt to follow the usage of the educated people of the community. Of course, if you should be working in a community that is in a different part of the country from where you grew up, you will find that people are tolerant of differences they will find in your pronunciation. In fact, to immediately attempt to imitate the speech of a new area is to make your speech sound affected. To say that your speech is *affected* means that you are attempting to speak in a manner that is unfamiliar to you. A young lady from Atlanta who is working in Boston will not be able to assume the pronunciation of the new city without sounding affected. Most people find such assumed speech patterns unattractive.

You will, however, want to guard against pronunciation errors that are caused by careless speech habits. Some of these are listed at the top of the next page.

		FAULTY		CORRECT
Dropping the sound of *g* in words ending in *ing*	—	*workin'* *goin'* *typin'*	for for for	*working* *going* *typing*
Dropping the sound of *r* in words ending in *r*	—	*fatha* *numba*	for for	*father* *number*
Adding the sound of *r* when it is not called for	—	*idear* *Cubar*	for for	*idea* *Cuba*
Using the wrong vowel sound	—	*fur* *fell* *git* *Toosday*	for for for for	*for* *fill* *get* *Tuesday*
Substituting one syllable for another	—	*chimley* *punkin* *libery*	for for for	*chimney* *pumpkin* *library*

As you know, the dictionary will aid you when you are uncertain of the pronunciation of a word. Consult it when you are unfamiliar with the correct pronunciation of a word that you wish to use.

Enunciation

The term *enunciation* means the precision with which you pronounce each word. It is important that you develop correct enunciation so that you always will be understood. Two of the most common errors in enunciation are running words together and the failure to sound all the syllables of a word. *Didya* for *did you*, *gimme* for *give me*, *whatchagonna* for *what are you going to*, *uster* for *used to*, *lemme* for *let me* are examples.

There are many words in the English language that are very similar to at least one other word. It is important that such words be enunciated clearly if the listener is to grasp the word intended. Words of this nature include the following:

ascend	irrelevant
assent	irreverent
cease	picture
seize	pitcher
council	sense
counsel	since
descend	statue
descent	stature
eminent	statute
imminent	track
incidents	tract
incidence	while
attack	wild
attach	wile
immigration	worth
emigration	work
	word

Part 2 / Good Language Usage

Diction

The use, choice, and arrangement of words is known as *diction*. Good diction is an asset in the modern business office. If you are to speak properly, you must choose words that are recognized as correct by authorities in the American language. You must choose words that will be acceptable to the people you address and will lead to a favorable response.

Colloquial Words and Expressions

As you know, the spoken language of a society is constantly changing. There always will be at a given time certain words and expressions that are considered satisfactory for informal communication but are not appropriate for more formal situations, such as communication in the business office. Often these colloquial words and expressions lend ease and naturalness to what is said; however, they must be used with care. Seldom are they as appropriate as the accepted words that convey the same meaning. Some examples are:

COLLOQUIAL	PREFERRED
around for *about*	I will leave the office *about* (not *around*) five o'clock.
contact for *get in touch with* or *call* or *talk with*	I will *call* (not *contact*) Mr. Jones when I arrive in Chicago tomorrow.
post for *informed*	Please be sure to keep Mr. Pearson *informed* (not *posted*) of your progress.
wait on for *wait for*	Will you be able to *wait for* (not *wait on*) Mr. Ray tonight?

Slang

Although colloquialisms are sometimes acceptable, slang is out of place in a business office. Slang is made up of widely used current terms which have a forced meaning such as *to get with it* meaning *to cooperate* or *dig this* meaning *understand this*. Words or expressions of this type are contrary to good language usage.

The wide usage of certain slang words and phrases, such as *on the ball* or *to miss the boat*, have caused them to lose some of the undesirable quality that they had in the past; however, their usage in the business office should be very much limited. A vocabulary made up of *swell*, *lousy*, *guy*, and other slang is an indication of a very weak English background.

Mannerisms

People use more than their voices when they utter words to convey thoughts. They use eyes, facial expressions, hand and arm gestures, and,

Illus. 8-6
Your eyes, your face, your smile, your hand and arm gestures — all assist you in communicating with others.

Wilson Jones Company
Division of Swingline, Inc.

at times, their whole body to express their thoughts. The proper use of facial expressions and gestures can help a person communicate. However, improper use of expressions and gestures can be highly distracting. Overuse of the hands, unnatural use of the eyes, distorted facial expressions will detract from what your voice and language are trying to convey. It is well to study your mannerisms, your voice, your speech so that you may eliminate any habits that may be offensive to your business associates or personal friends.

Courtesy

In communicating with others in a business office you must recognize the need to be courteous. Courtesy requires that you be a good listener. To "do all the talking" is seldom if ever the appropriate thing to do. Furthermore, interrupting a person who is talking is highly discourteous. For example, if you must enter your employer's office to give him information that he has requested for a conference that is under way, you should wait quietly at the door until there is an appropriate pause in the conversation and he signals you that you have his attention.

Courtesy requires that you give attention to the person you are addressing or to the person who is talking with you. To talk with one person while you are looking at another person or at another part of the

Part 2 / Good Language Usage

room is discourteous. Effective public speakers are those who can establish "eye contact" with their audiences. Then the listeners feel that the speaker is talking to them personally. So it is in a two-way conversation. To talk directly with someone by looking at him is to convey to the listener that you are talking with him.

Effective oral communication, which will be an important part of your secretarial duties, will improve if you give attention to what you say and how you say it.

QUESTIONS

1. If a secretary learns how she should act toward callers, it really doesn't matter how she feels about people. Do you agree with this comment? Explain your answer.
2. How should a secretary judge the manner in which she should dress for the company in which she works?
3. Describe the manner of the secretary at the moment a caller approaches her desk.
4. If you find it difficult to explain what you mean, what should you do?
5. What is a "clearly presented idea"?
6. What is meant when someone says, "Your voice reflects your emotions"?
7. What generally causes a voice to be too high pitched?
8. Give an illustration of a careless speech habit.
9. Give an illustration of words that require careful enunciation so that misunderstandings do not arise.
10. Why should you avoid the use of slang in the business office?
11. How can you convey to another person the fact that you are a good listener?
12. Why is speech courtesy important to a secretary?

JUDGMENT

1. Sally is an extremely efficient secretary. In fact, she is constantly figuring out ways of doing two things at one time. She prides herself on being able to type while she carries on a conversation. She likes to get a great deal of work done, and she feels that callers are impressed if they find her working at top speed. They don't mind, she believes, if she continues typing or talking on the telephone and merely says, "Yes?" in recognition of their presence.

    What is your reaction to Sally's view of how she should work?

2. Betsy is a young woman with a habit of ending all her sentences with "uh." For example, she might say: "Shall we go downtown on Saturday, uh?" or "I am looking forward to the next class, uh." She and some friends began using the "uh"

at the end of all sentences when they were young; and, while the others gave up the habit, Betsy continues it.

What should Betsy do about this speech mannerism?

PERSONAL QUALITIES

Betty Sands is executive secretary to Mr. Edward Zaneville, President of the Smith Iron Works Company. As executive secretary, Betty handles confidential matters. One day a junior executive, Mr. Tanner, said to Betty, "Someone was in my office this morning, and he told me that our company is moving out of town. I haven't heard anything about it. Is this true, Betty?"

"Mr. Tanner," said Betty, "I have no information for *you* on this matter. I would suggest that you forget about it. Why do you listen to such rumors?"

Mr. Tanner became very angry and, as he hurried out of the office, said, "Well, I have other sources for finding out what I want to know."

Did Betty handle the situation in the most effective way? Did Mr. Tanner behave appropriately? What should Betty do next?

LANGUAGE USAGE

Homonyms are words that are pronounced alike but are different in meaning. The pairs of words below include some that are homonyms and some words that are often incorrectly pronounced as though they were homonyms. Those pairs that are not homonyms require careful pronunciation so that the difference in the words is clear to the listener. Use a dictionary to check the pronunciation of each pair of words, as well as the meaning of each word. Then write a sentence using each word correctly. Indicate which pairs are homonyms.

1. affect
   effect
2. precedent
   president
3. profit
   prophet
4. residence
   residents
5. sight
   site
6. statue
   statute
7. than
   then
8. waist
   waste
9. weather
   whether
10. work
    worth

SECRETARIAL WORK

1. Make a list of words and expressions that you have heard that illustrate slurring or improper sounding of syllables. What suggestions would you make to eliminate these habits?
2. Make a list of slang words and expressions that you hear daily. Opposite each word or expression write its meaning.

3. What are some mannerisms that you have observed that you believe detract from the attractiveness of a person?
4. If a tape recorder is available, make a recording of the following:

   (a) Read a paragraph from a textbook.
   (b) Discuss with one of your classmates the responsibilities that the secretary has when she meets the public.
   (c) Explain to a classmate the manner in which callers are to be treated in a business office.

   Listen to your own voice and write your reactions to it. As you listen pay attention to your ability to express ideas; your voice; your pronunciation, enunciation, and diction; and your use of colloquial and slang words and phrases.

Unit 9 TELEPHONE AND TELEGRAPH SERVICES

Part 1. Receiving Calls
2. Placing Calls
3. Special Telephone Equipment
4. Special Communications Services
5. Domestic and International Telegraph Services

The secretary makes constant use of the telephone while conducting business for her executive. To be of most aid, she must know how to handle and record incoming calls and how to make outgoing calls. The secretary also must be competent in sending telegraphic messages.

VOCABULARY BUILDER

Enthusiasm is the most beautiful word on earth.
Christian Morgenstern

irritating
    adjective: tending to produce physical displeasure; something that arouses anger or impatience

monotonous
    adjective: uniform, unvarying, same, tedious, tiresome

category
    noun: class, group, classification

economical
    adjective: given to thrift; frugal; sparing; operating with little waste or at a saving

rotary
    adjective: turning on an axis like a wheel

formerly
    adverb: in time past

conference
    noun: formal interchange of views; a consultation; a meeting

transmitted
    verb: sent or transferred from one person or place to another; to send out a signal either by radio waves or over a wire

indicate
    verb: to point out or point to with more or less exactness

confusion
    noun: disorder; chaos; lack of clearness or distinctness; disarranged

p. 288   A high-pitched voice tends to become shrill and **irritating**.

p. 288   A **monotonous** voice sounds indifferent because it is flat and lacks spirit.

p. 300   Government agencies are listed under three **categories**. . . .

p. 306   What is the quickest and most **economical** type of long-distance telephone call?

p. 311   Touch-tone telephones have buttons instead of the **rotary** dial.

p. 311   Button telephones have almost completely replaced the two or three individual telephones that were **formerly** found on the busy executive's desk.

p. 318   "Eve, set up a **conference** call for 2 p.m. with Howard Walsh in Chicago, Mark Ross in Boston, Earle Carter in Denver, and Arthur Mann in Dallas."

p. 320   A teletype . . . operates on the same principle as a telephone except that the typewritten, rather than the spoken, word is **transmitted**.

p. 329   **Indicate** whether the message is sent paid, collect, or charge.

p. 330   Such words should be spelled out to the operator to avoid **confusion**.

PART 1   RECEIVING CALLS

> Diane Roberts is secretary to Mr. Keller, Vice-President in charge of the Planning Department for the Northern Construction Company. When Mr. Keller is away from his desk or doesn't wish to be disturbed, Diane must answer all his incoming telephone calls. She knows the work of the Planning Department, and she has a very pleasant telephone voice. Through experience, Diane has learned to handle Mr. Keller's incoming calls properly.

Can you imagine working in an office that has no telephone? Of course not! It would be impossible for today's business to run smoothly and efficiently without the rapid communication that is made possible with telephones. In fact, telephones have become so important to business that they are used in about 90 percent of all business transactions.

Using the telephone will be an important part of your secretarial career. You will be asked to make and receive all types of telephone calls. With each call you will be representing your company. The impression you give over the telephone will reflect — positively or negatively — on the people for whom you work. Therefore, it is important that you understand the proper techniques for using the telephone.

TELEPHONE PERSONALITY

Developing your telephone personality will require careful thought and effort. Since the caller will not be able to see you, you will not be able to rely on good grooming or on an attractive appearance to create a favorable impression. The only image of you that your caller has comes from your voice, your speech, your vocabulary, and your manner. You should try to improve the attractiveness of each. If you speak with a friendly smile in your voice, you will create a favorable impression of your company.

Voice

A voice can convey a spirit of interest, alertness, courtesy, and helpfulness over the telephone; or it can reflect an attitude of indifference, impatience, or inattention. It is often true that it is not what is said but the way it is said that really counts in a telephone conversation. A pleasant voice is much nicer to listen to than one which is loud, harsh, or shrill. You can improve your voice if you think and speak with a smile. Try to think of the caller as a person — not just as an unknown voice — who needs your help. You can have the *voice with a smile* if you talk with callers in a pleasant manner. Here are some suggestions to improve your telephone voice:

Illus. 9-1
The voice with a smile gives the caller a favorable impression.

AT&T

1. *Speak clearly*. A normal tone of voice — neither too loud nor too soft — carries best over the telephone.
2. *Use a low-pitched voice*. A low-pitched voice carries better over the telephone and is kinder to your listener's ear. A high-pitched voice tends to become shrill and irritating.
3. *Use voice inflection*. The rise and fall of your voice not only get your thoughts across but also add personality to your voice. A monotonous voice sounds indifferent because it is flat and lacks spirit.

Speech

Your speech habits are just as important as your voice: a pleasant voice makes you easy to listen to; good speech habits make you easy to understand. You should pronounce words clearly and correctly so that callers understand what you are saying. It is important that callers hear your message correctly.

Below are some suggestions for good telephone speech.

Illus. 9-2
Good speech habits convey efficiency to the caller.

AT&T

1. *Speak carefully.* Distinct speech is essential, since the listener can neither read your lips nor see your expression. Be careful to pronounce each word clearly; don't mumble or slur syllables.
2. *Talk at a proper pace.* A moderate rate of speech is easily understood, but the pace should be related to the ideas you are expressing. You should give some information more slowly: for example, technical information, lists, information the listener is writing down, numbers, names, and foreign or unusual words.

3. *Use emphasis with words.* The stress or emphasis placed on words, or groups of words, may change the meaning of what you are saying.

Vocabulary

Your ideas should be stated simply with descriptive words when they are needed. Technical, awkward, and unnecessarily lengthy words may confuse the other person and may require an explanation or may even cause a misunderstanding.

Be careful not to use language which will offend the listener or create a bad impression of the company you represent. Avoid trite words, phrases, and slang expressions. *Yes* sounds much better than *Yeah* or *OK*.

Courtesy

Courtesy is just as important in a telephone call as it is in a face-to-face conversation, but too often callers complain about secretaries who rudely interrupt them, who do not listen carefully, or who give them "the run-around." A secretary with a good telephone manner is always courteous, sincere, understanding, and helpful to callers.

INCOMING CALLS

As part of your secretarial duties you will probably answer many of your executive's incoming calls. Some executives want their secretaries to answer all their incoming calls. Other executives prefer to answer their own calls but expect the secretary to handle calls when they are busy or away from their desks.

Answer Promptly

You should answer all incoming calls promptly and pleasantly. No one likes to wait; furthermore, you have no way of knowing who is calling — it may be a very important call. In fact, no matter who is calling, if he thought enough of your business to make a call, you must give him prompt attention. The telephone should be answered on the first ring.

As you reach for the receiver, reach for your notebook. You must be ready to take notes immediately. *You should hold the mouthpiece about an inch from your lips* and speak directly into the telephone in a normal conversational tone of voice.

Identify Yourself

A telephone conversation cannot really begin until the caller knows that he has reached the right number. You should always identify yourself and your firm, office, or department immediately. Never answer by saying "Hello" or "Yes?" — these greetings add nothing to the identification.

If you answer an outside line, give your firm's name, followed by your name, as "Northern Construction Company, Miss Roberts." If your company has a switchboard, your operator has already identified the company; and you may answer your employer's telephone by saying, "Mr. Keller's office, Miss Roberts." When answering an office extension in a department, identify the department and give your name — "Planning Department, Miss Roberts."

Screening Calls

One of your most important duties as a secretary may be to screen your employer's incoming telephone calls when he is away from his office, has someone with him, or is talking on another line. Explain why your employer cannot talk, and, if possible, suggest another way in which you can help the caller, such as:

> Mr. White, Mr. Keller is attending a committee meeting. Is there anything I can do to help you?
> Mr. White, Mr. Keller is in conference. Would you care to talk to his assistant, Mr. Goetz?

Illus. 9-3

"May I say who's calling, so I can find out if he's in, or not?"

Newspaper Enterprise Association

Giving Information

You must be very careful when giving information if your employer is not available for telephone calls. For instance, a reply such as "Mr. Keller left for Minneapolis this morning" may be just enough information to let a competitor know that Mr. Keller is interested enough in a certain construction contract to make a personal trip to the construction site. Unless you are absolutely sure that your employer would want others to have the information, do not give out specific details over the telephone to outside callers.

Say	*Rather than*
He is out of the city. May I ask him to call you when he returns on Monday?	He was called to New York to help close the Jones contract.
He is not at his desk. May I take a message?	He is discussing the merger with the comptroller.
He will be in tomorrow morning. May I ask him to call you then?	He is at the Bonnie Brook Country Club.

Getting Information

Some telephone callers do not care to give their names; others prefer not to say why they are calling. You will frequently have to find out *who* is calling and, if the name does not help you, *why* he is calling. Try to get the information as tactfully as possible by using an appropriate response, such as:

> Mr. Keller has a visitor at the moment. If you will give me your name and telephone number, I will ask him to call you just as soon as he is free.
> Mr. Keller is not at his desk just now. May I give him a message for you?
> Mr. Keller is talking on another line. May I help you?

If you must ask a direct question to get the information, state it as a request rather than as a demand: "May I tell Mr. Keller who is calling?"

Taking Messages Accurately

A pad of forms for recording the details of incoming telephone calls should always be kept on your desk next to the telephone to take messages when your employer is out. When your employer returns he can use the messages to return the calls, a practice which promotes better customer relations. It is very important, therefore, that you record all the details of every message accurately.

Illus. 9-4
A secretary should always be prepared for any notes she may wish to record of telephone conversations.

AT&T

The message, written clearly, should include

1. The exact time of the call and the date
2. The name of the caller and his company (check the spelling of any unusual name)
3. The telephone number, the caller's extension, and area code, if it's a long-distance call (check the number)
4. The details of the message
5. The initials of the person who wrote the message

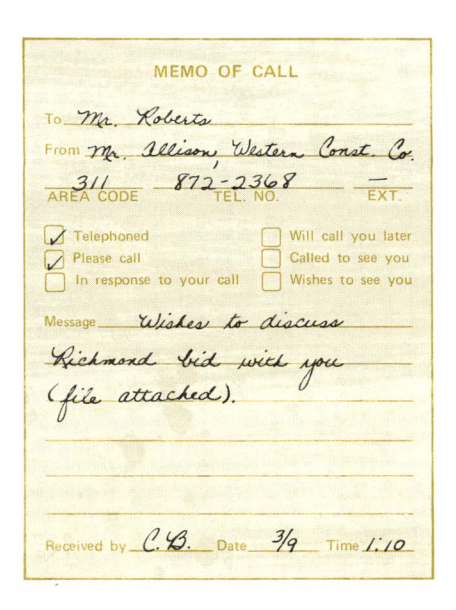

MEMO OF CALL

To *Mr. Roberts*
From *Mr. Allison, Western Const. Co.*
311   *872-2368*   —
AREA CODE   TEL. NO.   EXT.

☑ Telephoned   ☐ Will call you later
☑ Please call   ☐ Called to see you
☐ In response to your call   ☐ Wishes to see you

Message *Wishes to discuss Richmond bid with you (file attached).*

Received by *C.B.* Date *3/9* Time *1:10*

Illus. 9-5
Memo of call

Part 1 / Receiving Calls   293

Transferring Calls

Sometimes you will have to transfer a call to another extension or number. Calls are usually transferred when the caller has reached a wrong extension, when the caller wishes to speak with someone else, or when the caller's request can be handled better by someone else. Tell the caller why the transfer is necessary, and be sure that the call is being transferred to the proper person. In these instances you may say to the caller:

> I am sorry; you have reached the wrong extension. What extension were you calling? . . . I can transfer your call. Just a minute, please.
> I shall be glad to transfer your call to Mr. Williams. His extension is 2368. Just a minute, please.
> Mr. Young has all the information on that matter. May I transfer your call to him?

To transfer a call you should push down and release the receiver button of the telephone *slowly*. This action flashes a signal light on the switchboard which will attract the operator's attention. After the operator answers your signal, you might say, "Please transfer this call to Mr. Williams," or, "Please place this call on Extension 2368."

If you are disconnected during a call made *to* you, hang up, but try to keep your line free to receive the call back. If you placed the call, signal the operator and ask her to place the call again; or, if you dialed the call, dial it again. If you dialed a long-distance call, dial *O* for Operator and explain that you were disconnected.

Automatic Answering and Recording Set

A telephone answering and recording set called *Code-a-phone* will automatically answer the telephone and record a message after business hours or during the regular business hours if there is nobody to answer the telephone. Here is how it works. Before the executive leaves the office for the day he dictates a message to the set: for example,

> This is John Keller speaking. You are listening to a recording of my voice. If it is important, you may reach me at 701-555-2579. When you hear the tone you can record a message for me if you would like to do so. Thank you.

At the first opportunity either the executive or his secretary can play back the messages recorded by the callers.

Telephone Answering Service

With a telephone answering service you know that all your calls will be answered when you are unable to receive them personally. The telephone answering service operator takes your calls for you and relays the messages to you or your business associates. The names of firms that supply telephone answering service are listed in the Yellow Pages.

TERMINATING CALLS

Try to leave a favorable impression by ending each telephone conversation in a friendly, unhurried manner. It is very bad manners to end a call by hanging up abruptly. As the conversation ends, thank the caller for his call with an appropriate remark such as:

> Thank you very much for calling, Mr. Ames.
> Thank you for your message. I'll ask Mr. Keller to telephone you as soon as he returns.
> Thank you for the information. I'll give it to Mr. Keller.

Be sure to say "Good-bye." After the caller has hung up, replace the receiver *gently*.

PERSONAL TELEPHONE CALLS

The policy of using a business telephone for personal calls varies in different offices. Some firms permit a limited number of personal calls; others permit none at all. However, all firms oppose the overuse of a business telephone for personal calls. Callers who wish to discuss personal matters with you during business hours should be politely discouraged. Personal calls should be made only when they are necessary.

TELEPHONE TIPS

In the business office you will meet many people for the first time over the telephone. Here are some telephone tips to help you make that first impression a favorable one.

1. Answer calls properly by
    (a) Answering at the end of the first ring
    (b) Identifying yourself properly
    (c) Identifying the answered phone properly
    (d) Noting all appropriate information
    (e) Letting the caller end the conversation
2. Always be courteous by
    (a) Greeting all callers pleasantly
    (b) Listening attentively
    (c) Responding appropriately
    (d) Using the caller's name
    (e) Apologizing for any delays or errors

3. Project a pleasing personality by
    (a) Acting naturally
    (b) Being friendly
    (c) Showing interest in the caller
    (d) Speaking expressively
    (e) Displaying alertness
4. Transfer calls with care by
    (a) Being very tactful
    (b) Explaining to the caller why the transfer is necessary
    (c) Signaling the switchboard attendant
    (d) Giving the attendant the proper name and the correct extension number
    (e) Hanging up the receiver *gently*

QUESTIONS

1. On what does *telephone personality* rely?
2. Give several suggestions for improving telephone speech habits.
3. How should you identify yourself when answering a business call?
4. What information should be recorded when taking a telephone message?
5. How can calls be transferred?
6. What is the best way to terminate telephone calls?
7. Discuss the use and the abuse of the office telephone for personal phone calls.

JUDGMENT

1. Your employer is very busy and wants to be interrupted by as few telephone calls as possible. How would you know which calls to answer yourself and which calls to refer to your employer?
2. The secretary to the office manager of a business buys almost all the office supplies. Therefore, some calls coming to the office are for the office manager and some are for the secretary. What should the secretary say when she answers the telephone?

PERSONAL QUALITIES

The Plant Planning Division of the Midland Manufacturing Company has two secretaries — Alice Bennett, the senior secretary, and Betsy Evans, the junior secretary. Betsy is stationed in the outer office and also serves as the receptionist for the division. The division has two telephone extensions — 621-2368 and 621-2369. Betsy spends about 15 to 30 minutes on the telephone every morning talking about personal matters and office gossip with her co-workers in other offices.

After one prolonged conversation devoted mainly to office gossip, Alice speaks to Betsy. She tells her that she has been tying up an office telephone with personal chatter when she should be devoting her time to pertinent office business.

Betsy responds by pointing out that (a) Shirley Clinton, of the Payroll Department, had called her — she had not called Shirley — and (b) while she has been using Extension 2368 the other extension, 2369, was still available for calls.

Was Alice correct in speaking to Betsy about her prolonged telephone conversation with Shirley? Do you approve or disapprove of Betsy's responses? Give your reasons for your approval or disapproval.

LANGUAGE USAGE

Below are three simple rules for helping you correctly add *ing* endings to verbs.

1. An *e* is usually dropped before the *ing*.
   Example: hope   hoping
             prove   proving
2. Before adding *ing*, *ie* is changed to *y*.
   Example: die   dying
             lie   lying
3. When the final syllable contains a long vowel, the *ing* will be preceded by a single consonant.
   Example: conceal   concea*l*ing

   When the final syllable contains a short vowel, the *ing* will be preceded by a double consonant. (However, in recent years usage has been tending toward only a single consonant. It is, therefore, wise to check your dictionary for the preferred usage.)

   Example: program   progra*mm*ing or progra*m*ing
             cancel   cance*l*ing or cance*ll*ing

On a separate sheet of paper, type the following words using the correct *ing* ending. When in doubt check the dictionary for correct usage.

    1. advise   11. occupy
    2. apply   12. occur
    3. argue   13. plan
    4. balance   14. put
    5. continue   15. study
    6. dictate   16. tie
    7. dine   17. transcribe
    8. drop   18. transfer
    9. label   19. type
  10. manage   20. verify

SECRETARIAL WORK

1. The following telephone calls were received on March 5, 197–, while the persons called were out of the office. Prepare a report of each call on a form similar to that shown in the illustration on page 293.

    (a) William C. Adams, of Chicago, called Alfred Rogers at 10:30 a.m. regarding Order R-325-C. Mr. Adams' telephone number is 312-891-3456. He will call again at 2:00.

    (b) Mrs. James Arthur called Mr. Arthur (her husband) at 12:30 p.m.

    (c) Mr. James Linden, of Philadelphia, called William Spencer at 11:45. He said that he had received Order 10256 but had not received Order 10245, which had been placed a week before Order 10256. His telephone number is 215-922-8230.

    (d) Earl Kramer called Alfred Rogers at 4:15. He will meet Mr. Rogers at 5:30 at the club.

2. Certain words and hackneyed expressions used in telephone conversations have little relationship to modern telephone manners. The following trite and outdated telephone usage is still heard too frequently. Reword and type courteous sentences or questions for each.

    (a) Please put Mr. Davis on the phone.
    (b) He's tied up now. Can I have him call you back?
    (c) He's engaged at the moment. Hold the line.
    (d) OK, I'll have him call you back.
    (e) Who do you want to talk to?
    (f) What do you want to talk to him about?
    (g) I'll put Mr. White on the wire.
    (h) I'll have to hang up now.
    (i) Hello, Miss Ames, National Slippers.
    (j) Put the receiver on the hook.[1]

---

[1] There is no hook anymore — it's a cradle.

PART 2 PLACING CALLS

Mr. James Bunker, the Credit Manager of Artcraft Camera Company, places most of his outgoing local calls himself. However, when he wants to make a long-distance call, he has his secretary, Gayle Kerr, place the call. Gayle understands fully the different kinds of long-distance services that are available, and she knows which service will be best in terms of speed and cost for each call.

OUTGOING CALLS

More and more executives are saving telephone time by answering and placing their own telephone calls. However, you may be expected to make your own telephone calls and to place calls for your employer. In order to make calls courteously and efficiently, you should have a fairly clear idea of the purpose of each call before you make it. You may find it wise to make a list of the points you wish to cover before making an important call. Be sure that your employer is free to talk before you place a call for him, for when you say, "This is Mr. Bunker's secretary. Mr. Bunker would like to speak with Mr. Hardy," you may be speaking with Mr. Hardy.

USING TELEPHONE DIRECTORIES CORRECTLY

Before making calls you should know how to get information from telephone directories quickly and how to operate the telephone properly. Three different telephone directories may be consulted to make outgoing calls: your own personal directory of frequently called persons and firms, the Telephone Directory (the White Pages), and the Yellow Pages.

Be sure you have the correct number before making a call. If you are not sure of the number, refer to a telephone directory to avoid possible delay and embarrassment. If you cannot find a number you want to call in the directory, call an information operator. For numbers in your own area, call Information by dialing the number listed in the front of the Telephone Directory. To reach an out-of-town information operator, dial the proper area code, then 555-1212. The number 555-1212 is the nationwide information number.

Personal Telephone Directory

An up-to-date list of frequently called local and out-of-town telephone numbers will save you and your employer a great deal of telephoning time. Booklets to be used as personal telephone directories can be obtained from most telephone companies. For the small firm or office, an "automatic finder" can be used. By moving the indicator to the correct letter of the alphabet, you can reach the desired page immediately. A large personal listing can be kept more easily on cards in a revolving visible file on your desk.

The Alphabetical Directory

The names of subscribers are listed alphabetically in this directory. Individual names and firm names are easily located, unless the spelling of a name is unusual, and then it is cross-referenced as:

>   Gray   — See also Grey
>   Hoffman — See also Hoffmann, Hofmann
>   Rees   — See also Reis, Reiss, Riess

For the convenience of their customers or clients, business and professional people often list their home numbers directly below their business listings: for example,

>   Banks Jacob groc 4740 ReistwRd..............271-3469
>   Res 3516 VaAv...........................271-4092

It is often necessary to call government agencies to request information or to get answers to questions which are constantly arising about government regulations. Government agencies are listed under three categories:

>   Federal agencies under United
>   States Government..............U.S. Government
>   Agriculture Dept of
>   Labor Dept of
>
>   State agencies under state
>   government....................North Dakota State of
>   Employment Service
>   Highway Dept
>
>   County and municipal agencies
>   under local governments.........Minneapolis City of
>   Education Board of
>   Fire Dept
>   Police Dept

The first few pages of the alphabetical directory contain useful information including instructions for making emergency calls, local and long-distance calls, service calls (repair, assistance, etc.) and special calls (overseas, conference, collect, etc.). In addition, area codes for the United States and Canada, sample rates, and telephone company business office addresses and telephone numbers are listed.

The Yellow Pages

The Yellow Pages are used when you wish to find out quickly where you may obtain a particular product or service. The names, addresses, and telephone numbers of business subscribers are listed alphabetically under the name of the product or service. Many business organizations use advertising space and artistic displays to tell their customers about the organization's operations, including brands carried, hours, and services. Nationally advertised or trademarked products may be listed with the names, addresses, and telephone numbers of most of the local dealers arranged alphabetically under a word or trademark design.

Illus. 9-6
The efficient secretary knows that the Yellow Pages will provide quick, accurate information.

AT&T

Part 2 / Placing Calls 301

For instance, your employer may ask you to reorder master sets and copy paper for the A. B. Dick spirit duplicator. Under the heading, "Duplicating Machines & Supplies," the A•B•DICK trademark is displayed. Many local dealers are listed below "*WHERE TO BUY THEM.*"

At another time your employer may ask you to call a certified public accountant named Smith who has an office on North Fifth Street. Since there are so many Smiths listed in the alphabetical section, it will be much easier to refer to the heading in the Yellow Pages "Accountants — Certified Public" to find this particular Mr. Smith.

Smith R R 209 N 5........................721-2626

PLACING LONG-DISTANCE CALLS

When you are a secretary you will often be asked to place long-distance calls for your executive. The two most generally used types of out-of-town calls are *station-to-station* and *person-to-person* calls.

Station-to-Station Calls

A station-to-station call is made to a certain telephone number. Make this type of call if you are willing to talk with anyone who may answer the telephone or if you are fairly certain the person with whom your employer wishes to speak is within easy reach of his telephone.

Person-to-Person Calls

When you wish to speak with a particular person in a large company, place a person-to-person call. A person-to-person call is directed to a specific person, room number, extension number, or department. Make this type of call only if you wish to talk with a particular person or if you are not sure he is within reach of his telephone. You must have assistance from a telephone operator to place a person-to-person call.

Direct Distance Dialing (DDD)

Direct distance dialing is a method of placing all station-to-station calls and some person-to-person calls by using the dial on your telephone. No assistance is needed from the operator in order to complete the call. The front pages of the Telephone Directory provide complete directions for direct distance dialing.

Station-to-Station DDD. In order to use direct distance dialing in making a station-to-station call, in many areas you must first dial the number *1*, which is a prefix code that will give you a long-distance line.

Illus. 9-7
A secretary should always have her shorthand book available when placing outgoing calls for any notes that she may wish to record.

AT&T

Next you dial the three number area code which represents the area of the country you are calling. Area codes are required when calling from one area to another. In those areas of the country where the prefix code is not required, you simply dial the three digit area code to get a long-distance line. Finally, you dial the seven digits of the particular telephone number you wish to reach. For example, suppose you were in Cincinnati and wished to call the Alhambra Book Store in New York City, whose telephone number is 360-8437. You would dial 1-212-360-8437.

> 1 is the prefix code to get a long-distance line.
> 212 is the area code for New York City.
> 360-8437 is the telephone number of the Alhambra Book Store.

Person-to-Person with DDD. In more and more cities it is also possible to use direct distance dialing for person-to-person calls. You must first dial a special prefix code. This special prefix code signals the telephone company's computer that you wish to make a person-to-person call with DDD. You then dial the area code and the particular telephone number. The operator will come on the line and ask for the name of the person you are calling. When that person answers, the operator notes the start of the call. This is required for billing purposes.

Person-to-Person without DDD. If you cannot dial the person-to-person call directly, you dial the operator and ask her to place the call for you. Place the call with the operator in this order: area code, telephone number, and the name of the person with whom you wish to speak. For example, you should say, "I'm making a personal call to Area Code 311 and the number is 341-8912. I would like to speak with Mr. James Gordon." Remain at the telephone until your call is completed or until you receive a report from the operator. If your call cannot be completed at the time it is placed, try it later.

Time Factor

It is important that you be aware of the time differences across the country. The United States is divided into four standard time zones: Eastern, Central, Mountain, and Pacific. Each zone is one hour earlier than the zone immediately to the east of it. When it is 3 p.m. Eastern Standard Time, it is 2 p.m. in the Central zone, 1 p.m. in the Mountain zone, and noon in the Pacific zone. Because of time differences, you must remember not to call Los Angeles from New York City before 12 noon because it is only 9 a.m. in California, or New York from California after

Illus. 9-8
Map of telephone area codes and time zones

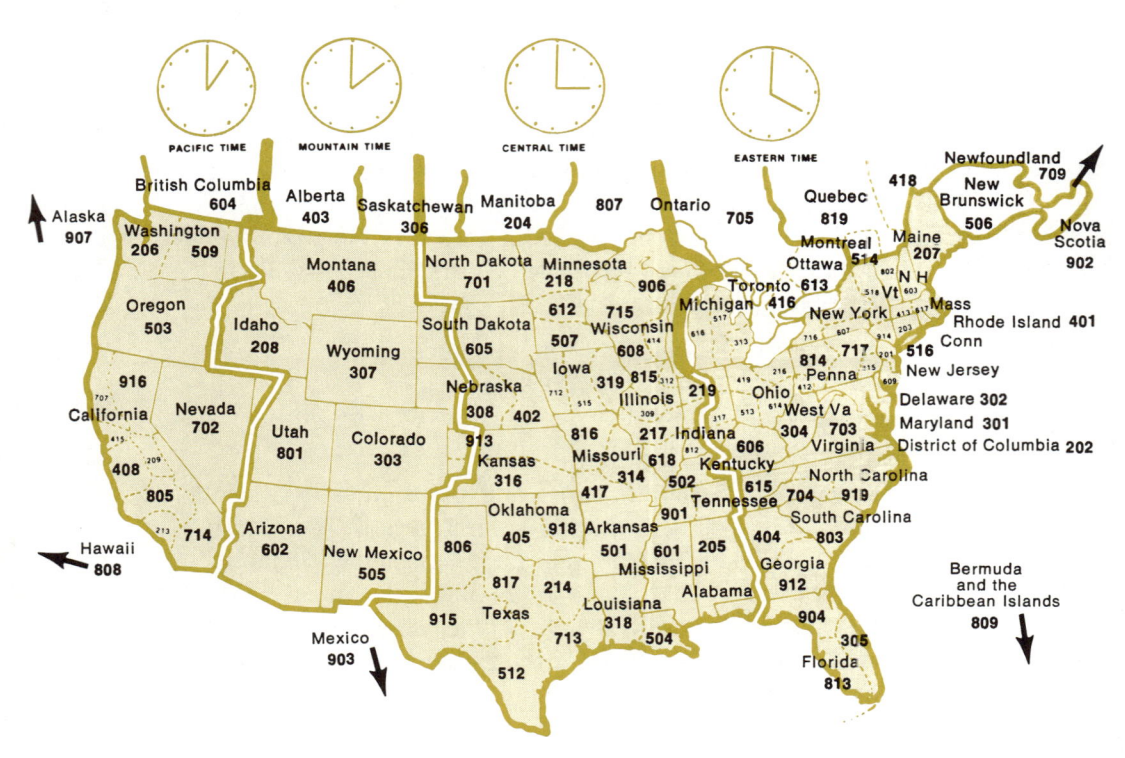

Unit 9 / Telephone and Telegraph Services

2 p.m. because it is then after 5 p.m. in New York and the office you wish to call is likely to be closed.

THE COST OF TELEPHONE SERVICE

The cost of telephone service is determined by the kinds of equipment the business has and the ways in which the equipment is used.

Cost for Local Calls

Businesses are charged in many different ways for their telephone service. In most communities the business is charged a basic rate for its telephone service, and it then can make as many local calls as it wishes. In a few large cities you are allowed a certain number of calls for a base rate and are charged for each extra call.

Costs for Long-Distance Calls

Charges are made for all out-of-town telephone calls or calls made beyond the local service area. The amount of the charge depends upon the distance, the type of call, the time of day or night that the call is made, and the length of the conversation. As a secretary you should know when it is advisable to make each type of call and the relative costs of the calls.

The cost of a station-to-station call is about 30 percent less than the cost of a person-to-person call because a call can be made to a particular number in much less time than a call to a particular person. The cost of all long-distance calls you dial yourself is lower than calls for which you need assistance from the operator.

The rates for long-distance calls are based on an initial charge for three minutes. Lower rates are in effect between 5 p.m. and 8 a.m. on weekdays. These lower rates also apply all day on Saturdays, Sundays, and holidays.

TELEPHONE TIPS

Whether in your business office or in your own home you can place long-distance telephone calls more effectively by

1. Planning your conversation before placing the call
2. Checking the area code and the number before placing the call
3. Giving the person you are calling time to answer
4. Identifying yourself properly and giving the reason for the call
5. Thanking the person you called for helping you

QUESTIONS

1. What information would you put in your employer's personal telephone directory?
2. Under what circumstances would you use the alphabetic telephone directory?
3. When would you most likely use the Yellow Pages?
4. Under what set of circumstances would you recommend the placing of a person-to-person long-distance call?
5. What is direct distance dialing, and how is it used?
6. What information should you furnish the operator when you make a person-to-person long-distance call if direct dialing is not used?
7. What is the quickest and most economical type of long-distance telephone call?

JUDGMENT

1. Your employer asks you to get a certain customer on the telephone. Should you connect him as soon as someone answers the company's telephone, or should you wait until the particular person your employer wishes to speak with is put on the telephone?
2. You sometimes place calls for your employer. Most of these calls go to the same firms. How should you be prepared so that you can make these calls quickly?
3. Charles Allen, a traveling salesman, makes the long-distance calls described in the following paragraphs. What type of service should he use in each case?
   (a) Mr. Allen wishes to telephone his home as inexpensively as possible.
   (b) A customer asks for information about a special contract. It is necessary for Mr. Allen to talk personally with the general manager to get this information.
   (c) Mr. Allen receives an order from a customer who asks that the order be telephoned to the company at once.
   (d) Mr. Allen calls the office to get prices on a new item.

PERSONAL QUALITIES

Barbara Washington places most of the calls for her employer, the purchasing agent, Mr. Thomas Downs. Because Mr. Downs spends most of his business day on the telephone with sales representatives, Barbara tries to save his time by not putting Mr. Downs on the telephone until she has the other party on the line.

One Monday morning she is asked to call the executive vice-president, Mr. Bertram Moore. When he is told that Mr. Downs is calling he picks up the receiver and says, "Yes, Tom, what can I do for you." Barbara responds by saying, "I'll put Mr. Downs right on, Mr. Moore." Mr. Moore is visibly annoyed and says, "Tell Mr. Downs I haven't got time to wait for him," and hangs up.

Barbara feels that she has caused Mr. Downs unnecessary difficulty with his superior when she was only trying to help him. Discuss ways in which Barbara should place calls to Mr. Downs' superiors in the future.

LANGUAGE USAGE

The following 20 words are spelled both correctly and incorrectly. On a sheet of paper type the correct spelling of each word.

1. appropriate	appropriete
2. assocciates	associates
3. assurance	assurrance
4. brusquely	brusquelly
5. convay	convey
6. courtious	courteous
7. conversationel	conversational
8. dialing	dailing
9. economical	econemical
10. efficeint	efficient
11. frequently	frequintly
12. monotoneous	monotonous
13. overseas	over seas
14. preferance	preference
15. specific	spicefic
16. techneques	techniques
17. transfering	transferring
18. terminating	terminateing
19. unnecessary	unnecessery
20. vocabulery	vocabulary

SECRETARIAL WORK

1. Using your telephone book, look up and list the telephone numbers for
   (a) All emergency call telephone numbers for the fire department, police department, doctor, ambulance, state police, and Federal Bureau of Investigation
   (b) Telephone service calls — business office, repair service
   (c) A large business firm in the community
   (d) One of the banks in the community
   (e) The area codes for New York City, Chicago, Los Angeles, and Philadelphia
2. The questions below require the use of the Yellow Pages.
   (a) If you knew the address of a doctor but not his name, would you look in the Yellow Pages for his name under "Doctors" or under "Physicians & Surgeons (M.D.)"?

(b) How are lawyers listed in the Yellow Pages — under "Attorneys" or under "Lawyers"?
(c) If you were to order typewriter ribbons by telephone, under what heading in the Yellow Pages would you look for a firm selling typewriter ribbons?
(d) Suppose you work in a one-man office and are missing telephone calls (and business) because your telephone is unattended when your employer is traveling and you are out of the office. What service is listed in the Yellow Pages that you could recommend to your employer to remedy the situation?
3. Use the Telephone Directory to type an alphabetical list of names, addresses, and telephone numbers of ten business firms in your area that might employ you after you graduate.

PART 3 SPECIAL TELEPHONE EQUIPMENT

Mary Martinez is secretary to the president of a medium-sized company. She has had many years of experience as a secretary in small, medium-sized, and large companies. During her years of secretarial service she has on many occasions been willing and gracious during emergencies in assisting at telephone operations. As a result she has learned the many and various types of telephone communications that today are standard equipment in many offices. Her employers through the years have learned to depend on her and to admire her ability and efficiency in using all kinds of telephone equipment to its greatest advantage.

Telephone companies provide special equipment to meet the special needs of every business. All telephone equipment has the same basic purpose: to make rapid oral communication possible. As a secretary, you will be expected to use different kinds of telephone equipment.

SWITCHBOARD

Most businesses have a private business exchange (PBX) or switchboard to aid in handling telephone calls.

A PBX system has three main functions:

1. To receive incoming calls
2. To place outgoing calls
3. To make calls between offices within the business

Usually companies have special switchboard operators. Sometimes, however, secretaries are asked to fill in at the switchboard at the noon hour or at other times during the day.

Cord Switchboard

Cord switchboards are used in large businesses where many telephone lines are needed. The switchboard operator receives all incoming calls, makes the connection for interoffice calls, and either places outgoing calls or provides the outside line to dial the call.

Cordless Switchboard

There are many kinds of cordless switchboards. Usually companies that do not have a great volume of telephone calls will use a cordless board. A full-time operator is not needed since incoming calls can usually be made to any extension number and employees can place their own outgoing calls. The operator will normally answer only those calls that are of a general nature.

Illus. 9-9
A cordless switchboard has many applications in a modern office. It does not require a full-time operator.

AT&T

Call Director

The call director permits you to answer many lines from one location. You can also transfer calls and make outside calls. If your executive wishes, he can both make and receive calls without your help.

Illus. 9-10
In a busy office a Call Director is a time-saver for both executive and secretary.

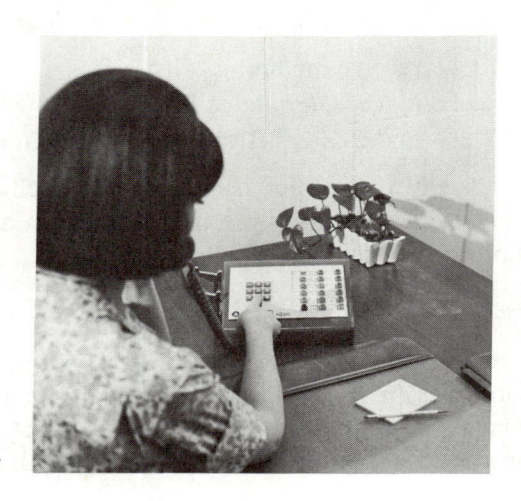

AT&T

TOUCH-TONE TELEPHONE

Touch-tone telephones have buttons instead of the rotary dial. Listen for the dial tone; then push the numbered buttons for the telephone number. As each button is pushed you will hear a tone.

Touch-tone calling systems are being installed in all major cities and are available to both home and business users. The advantage of this calling system is the increased speed in dialing. In more and more firms touch-tone buttons are also being used to send data to computers.

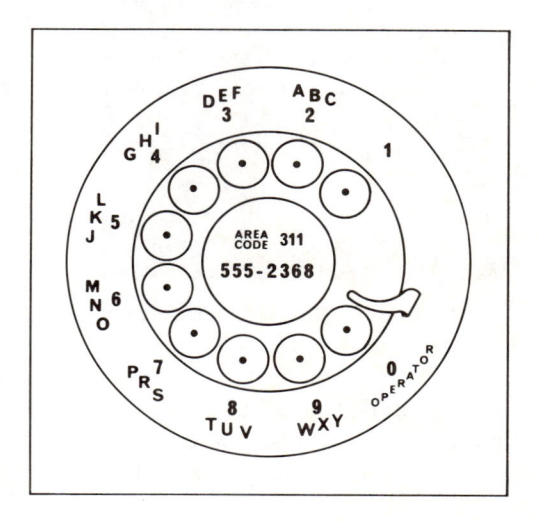

Illus. 9-11
Dial telephone

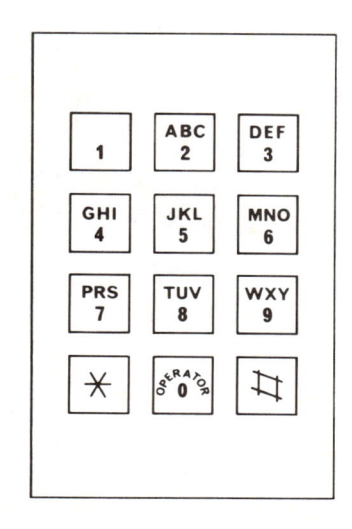

Illus. 9-12
Touch-tone telephone

BUTTON TELEPHONE

Button telephones have almost completely replaced the two or three individual telephones that were formerly found on the busy executive's desk. A button telephone may have anywhere from one to six buttons along the base of the instrument, but the six-button variety is most commonly used.

Arrangement of the Buttons

The buttons on a six-button telephone should be arranged and labeled in this order:

1. The *hold* button is the button on the left side of the telephone. When it is depressed you will be able to hold a call while you make or answer another call. The first caller is then *unable to overhear your second conversation.*

Illus. 9-13
This six-button telephone enables a secretary to handle more than one call on her extension.

AT&T

Button 1	Button 2	Button 3	Button 4	Button 5	Button 6
Hold	2368	2369	2370	2371	2372

The hold button does not remain depressed but returns to normal when you release it. However, if you do not use it before pressing another button to accept a second call, the first call will be cut off.

2. The pick-up buttons, Buttons 2, 3, 4, 5, and 6, are used to make and receive outside calls. A line will be connected when you depress the correct button.

Operating a Button Telephone

A number of calls can be handled on a push-button telephone at the same time. The steps in the receiving and handling of two incoming calls follow:

1. Depress the *pick-up* button connected with the ringing line before lifting the receiver. (Pick-up buttons usually light up when in use.)
2. If a call comes in while you are talking on another line, excuse yourself, depress the *hold* button, then depress the pick-up button connected with the ringing line and answer it.
3. When the second call is completed, return to the first call by depressing the button for that line.

Custom-made arrangements, designed to meet the special needs of a particular office, may be found on the job. For instance, a *signal* button, frequently a buzzer, may be used to signal a secretary.

SPEAKERPHONE

You need not pick up the receiver at all when you use the Speakerphone. When a call comes in, you press a button and talk as you would to a visitor in your office. The caller's voice comes from a small loudspeaker on your desk. The volume of the loudspeaker can be adjusted to suit your desires. Your own voice is picked up by a microphone sensitive enough to hear your voice anywhere in your office or all the voices in an office conference. You can talk and listen with both hands free to take notes or to look up records. When you want to make a private call, you can pick up the receiver and your Speakerphone automatically becomes a regular telephone again.

AUTOMATIC DIALING TELEPHONES

There are several automatic dialing telephones commonly used in business offices. Automatic dialing telephones save a great deal of telephoning time, and they eliminate the possibility of dialing a wrong number.

Card Dialer

The Card Dialer uses small plastic cards for numbers you expect to call frequently. They should be coded and placed in the storage area in the unit. To place a call, you insert the proper card in the dial slot, lift the receiver, and when you hear the dial tone, press the start bar.

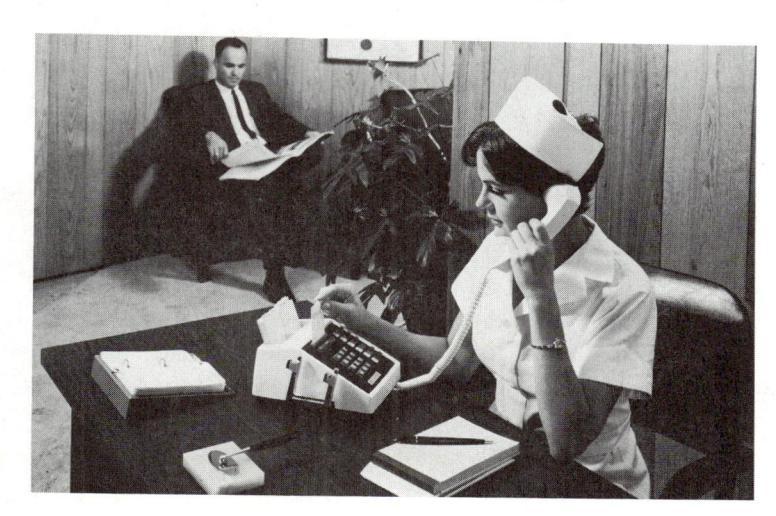

Illus. 9-14
A Card Dialer is useful to the secretary who places volume calls. It is fast, efficient, and reliable.

AT&T

Part 3 / Special Telephone Equipment

Magicall

The Magicall magnetic tape dialer is also used to save dialing time. The names and telephone numbers of frequently called parties are listed on a magnetic tape. After a name has been brought into position on the "scanner," it can be dialed automatically from the stored telephone number on the magnetic tape by simply pushing the start bar. Up to 1,000 telephone numbers can be stored in the memory of the Magicall.

Call-A-Matic

The Call-A-Matic is a touch-tone automatic dialer. It is a combination of a six-button touch-tone telephone and a magnetic tape dialer with a storage for up to 500 telephone numbers.

Illus. 9-15
The Call-A-Matic tape dialer is another telephone feature that can save valuable executive and secretarial time.

AT&T

PICTUREPHONE

The Picturephone is a new kind of telephone equipment — it lets you see the person you are talking to and he sees you. The Picturephone is rather expensive, but it may prove to be a valuable aid to business firms. Conferences and sales demonstrations can be conducted over the Picturephone. This, of course, will save a great deal of time and expense. The Picturephone is being introduced gradually — first in Pittsburgh, then in Chicago, Washington, Detroit, Cleveland, Newark, and Philadelphia. In the beginning it will be available in business areas only, and calls can be made to other firms in the area.

Illus. 9-16
Many business uses are predicted for the Picturephone.

AT&T

BELLBOY

The Bell System provides a personal signaling service called the Bellboy. The Bellboy is actually a pocket radio receiver with a 40-mile radius that, by means of a tone signal, alerts the carrier to call his office or home for a message. Your employer may put this small receiver in his pocket whenever he is going to be away from his office telephone. When you wish to contact him you dial his Bellboy number just as you would call any regular telephone number. This sends out a signal from radio transmitters located throughout the local coverage area. The signal is picked up at once on his Bellboy receiver, and he can call you from any telephone.

MOBILE TELEPHONE

This radio telephone provides your employer with a listed number for his car that is part of the nationwide dial network. He can make and receive calls from his car just as he would from his office telephone. It helps him avoid the risk of missing important calls while he is on the road and provides him with a way to handle emergencies more efficiently.

More than 25,000 customers now use mobile telephones. They are installed in trucks, buses, planes, trains, and taxicabs, as well as in private automobiles.

QUESTIONS

1. What do the initials *PBX* mean?
2. What are the two advantages of the Speakerphone over the regular telephone?
3. How can the use of the Magicall save telephoning time?
4. What type of communications system is a Bellboy?
5. Why would an employer install a mobile telephone in his car?

JUDGMENT

1. Discuss the probable business uses of the Picturephone.
2. Discuss the advantages of a touch-tone telephone over the traditional rotary dial telephone.

PERSONAL QUALITIES

Claire Rogers and Ann Brown fill in as relief switchboard operators during the noon hour. Claire handles a call in this fashion: "Mr. Smith's extension is busy." After about 15 seconds she says, "Still busy." When the extension is free she says, "I'll ring him now."

Ann handles a similar call in this fashion: "Mr. Clark's extension is busy. Will you wait, please?" After about 15 seconds she says, "Mr. Clark is still busy." When the extension is free she says, "You may have Mr. Clark's extension now. Thank you for waiting."

Which of the two approaches to the handling of a delayed call is more likely to make a favorable impression on the caller? Why?

LANGUAGE USAGE

On page 72 it was stated that an adverb is a word that modifies a verb, an adjective, or another adverb. An adverb, like a descriptive adjective, may also be used in comparisons.

Examples: Sheila types *fast*. (Positive adverb *fast* modifies verb *types*.)

Sheila types *faster* than the other girls. (Comparative adverb *faster* modifies verb *types*.)

Sheila responded *most* happily. (Superlative adverb *most* modifies adverb *happily*.)

On a sheet of paper list the adverbs in the following sentences and tell the words they modify.

1. Joan was merely trying to be kind to the caller, but the visitor misunderstood her.
2. The secretary was most gracious, but Mr. Smith said that he could wait no longer.
3. Mr. Brown canceled the appointment immediately.
4. Mr. Phillips called and said that he would arrive sooner than he expected.
5. With a little more tact, the secretary could have soothed the customer's feelings.
6. Not all secretaries are as efficient as Elaine.

7. His tire was almost flat by the time he arrived for his appointment.
8. She was less inclined to make the trip after she heard the weather predictions.
9. The farther he traveled the worse conditions became.
10. Her warm smile and sincere interest in people were very valuable assets.

SECRETARIAL WORK Prepare an office telephone directory for John Carl Warner and Associates, a firm of architects and planning consultants, from the following list of officers and associates. Arrange the names of the 25 officials in alphabetical order before typing them with their respective titles and home telephone numbers. Type the last name of each official first — in solid capitals.

Name	Title	Home Telephone Number
John Carl Warner	President	566-0101
Carl T. Warner	Executive Vice-President	542-3481
Martin C. Hunter	Vice-President	764-5244
Leonard T. Hart	Vice-President	562-8796
James J. Carroll	Secretary	241-2442
Arthur D. Brown, Jr.	Treasurer	231-2633
Donald R. Stewart	Project Manager	891-7350
Joseph C. Margolo	Systems Manager	764-1121
Emery Hirschman	Personnel Director	732-4575
Eugene C. Davis	Construction Supervisor	231-9367
Jean Wiley	Interior Designer	441-8452
Wallace D. Russell	Comptroller	681-3794
Walter E. Nelson	Office Manager	764-1985
Arthur A. Schiller	Construction Supervisor	562-5521
Josef Ausubel	Chief Draftsman	231-4872
David C. Palmer	Project Manager	764-3363
Walter J. Roberts, Jr.	Transportation Engineer	871-5046
Thomas M. White	Public Relations Director	231-0785
Wayburn Evans	Chief of Shop Drawings	541-6914
Lisa T. Guthrie	Landscape Designer	764-2658
Thomas F. O'Brien	Construction Supervisor	231-1479
Ralph T. Spencer	Project Manager	831-0837
Lawrence A. Adams	Construction Supervisor	321-7525
Joseph A. McMurray	Estimator	922-8240
William C. Peterson	Construction Supervisor	771-3313

PART 4 SPECIAL COMMUNICATIONS SERVICES

"Eve, set up a conference call for 2 p.m. with Howard Walsh in Chicago, Mark Ross in Boston, Earle Carter in Denver, and Arthur Mann in Dallas. Would you also ask Joseph Hummell and Ronald Sigler if they would come to my office for the conference?" These instructions were given to Eve Craft by her employer, Mr. Clifford Pickens. Because of her understanding of special long-distance services available, Eve had no difficulty in setting up the conference.

Conference calls are just one of many special long-distance services provided by the telephone company. These rapid services include both oral and written communications.

SPECIAL LONG-DISTANCE CALLS

Now let us take a look at the special long-distance services with which you should become familiar. These services include collect calls, credit card calls, conference calls, wide area telephone service, and overseas telephone calls. Before placing these calls, check the front pages of the Telephone Directory for instructions. Usually you dial "0 Operator."

Collect Calls

If you want the charges reversed — if you want the station or the person you are calling to pay the charges — notify the operator when you place the call. This gives the station or person you are calling an opportunity to accept or refuse the call before the connection is made. The charges may be reversed on both station-to-station and person-to-person calls.

Credit Card Calls

Many business executives have credit cards from the telephone company that allow them to charge long-distance calls. Credit card telephone service provides a convenient way to make long-distance calls when traveling. If your executive should ever ask you to place a credit card call for him, he will give you his card. You should call the long-distance operator and tell her that you wish to place a credit card call. You should then give her the credit card number, the area code, and the telephone number you are calling. The charges for the call will be billed to your executive's account.

Conference Calls

A conference call is a telephone call that enables several persons at different locations to talk to each other at the same time. As many as ten locations can be connected for a conference call. To arrange such a call you should give the operator the names, telephone numbers, and locations of the persons to be connected for the call. Be certain to give the exact time that the call is to be put through. Then be certain that your employer is ready to receive this call!

Wide Area Telephone Service (WATS)

Some of the telephone lines into the company for which you work may be called "WATS" lines, and some phones may be called "WATS" phones. This means that the firm offers its customers, without charge, Wide Area Telephone Service. Firms that use this service believe that, if they offer their customers this free service, they will get more business. Many hotel and motel chains use WATS service in order to make it easier for their customers to make room reservations.

The WATS phones or lines are used only for making and receiving station-to-station long-distance calls. To determine whether the company you wish to call offers this service, dial Area Code 800 and then 555-1212. The 800 is the standard area code for all WATS lines, and the 555-1212 is for operator assistance.

Overseas Telephone Calls

Underseas cables, satellites, and radio now make it possible to telephone 200 countries and areas overseas. Most calls are operator dialed. To place an overseas call or to obtain additional information, see the front pages of the local Telephone Directory. You usually dial "0 Operator."

Some typical weekday station-to-station rates for the first three minutes from any point in the United States are: to the United Kingdom, $5.40; to Hawaii $5.70; to France and Italy $6.75; to Israel and Vietnam $9.00. The person-to-person weekday rates for the first three minutes to the same areas are considerably higher — to the United Kingdom $9.60; to Hawaii $9.50; to France, Italy, Israel, and Vietnam $12.00.

TELETYPEWRITER SERVICE

"Jean, will you send a message to our New Orleans plant requesting information on the carload shipment of insulation board to Lumbermen's Supply Company in Columbus that was promised for delivery on January 15?" A few minutes later Jean entered Mr. Robertson's office in Dayton, Ohio, with a teletype message reading:

```
AMCO   TWX 410-345-7890   JAN 14   MSG 12
ATTN   JOHN ROBERTSON SALES

LUMBERMEN'S ORDER B-70581 SHPD GULF MOBILE &

OHIO--PENN CENTRAL JAN. 7 CAR SPOTTED PENN

CENTRAL SIDING COL O JAN 14 10:30 AM

JAMES FERGUSON
```

A teletype is a typewriter-like machine which operates on the same principle as a telephone except that the typewritten, rather than the spoken, word is transmitted. Messages typed on the standard typewriter keyboard of a teletypewriter are transmitted and reproduced as they are

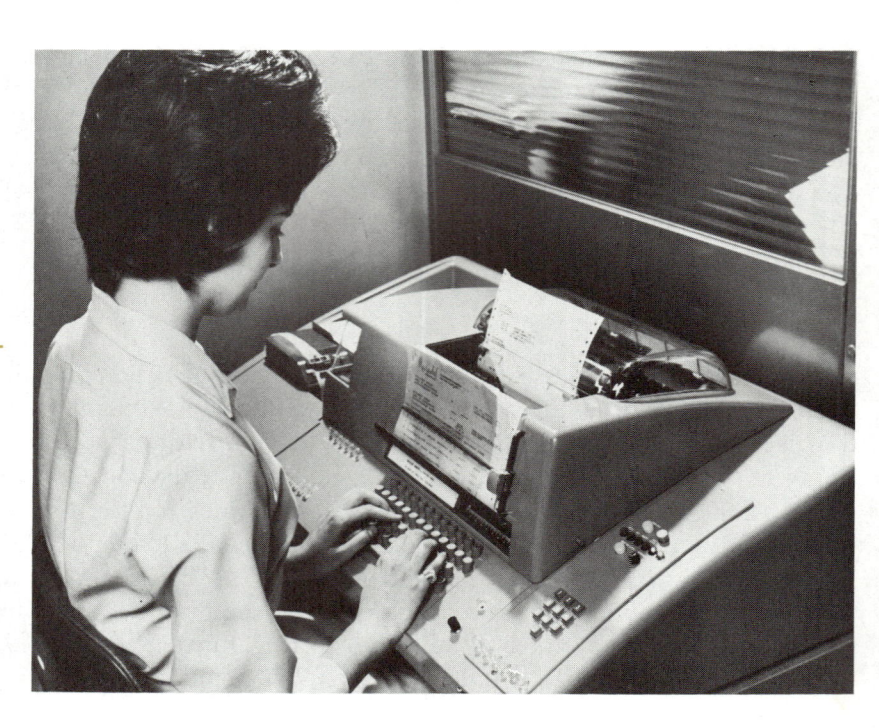

Illus. 9-17
District office teletype operator transmits order by tape directly to manufacturing plant in distant city.

Teletype Corporation

320   Unit 9 / Telephone and Telegraph Services

typed. A message may be reproduced on a single machine or on many machines, depending on the kind of service the business wants. Teletype equipment is often used for communication between offices of the same firm and between offices of different firms when speed is an important factor and when a written record of the message is desired. Usually a special operator will send and receive the teletyped messages. Sometimes, however, secretaries are asked to sit in for the regular operators.

There are two basic types of teletype service — teletypewriter exchange service and teletypewriter private line service.

Teletypewriter Exchange Service (TWX)

Teletypewriter exchange service (TWX) operates through a Western Union service. Each subscriber has a teletypewriter number and is furnished with a directory of all teletypewriter subscribers in the United States.

Before sending a message, the teletype operator signals the TWX equipment she is calling and types the exchange and the number she wishes to reach. After the connection has been made and the called unit is ready to receive, the teletype operator types her message. As the sending operator types the message, the receiving machine instantly copies it. The rates for teletyped messages are much lower than the rates for station-to-station telephone calls.

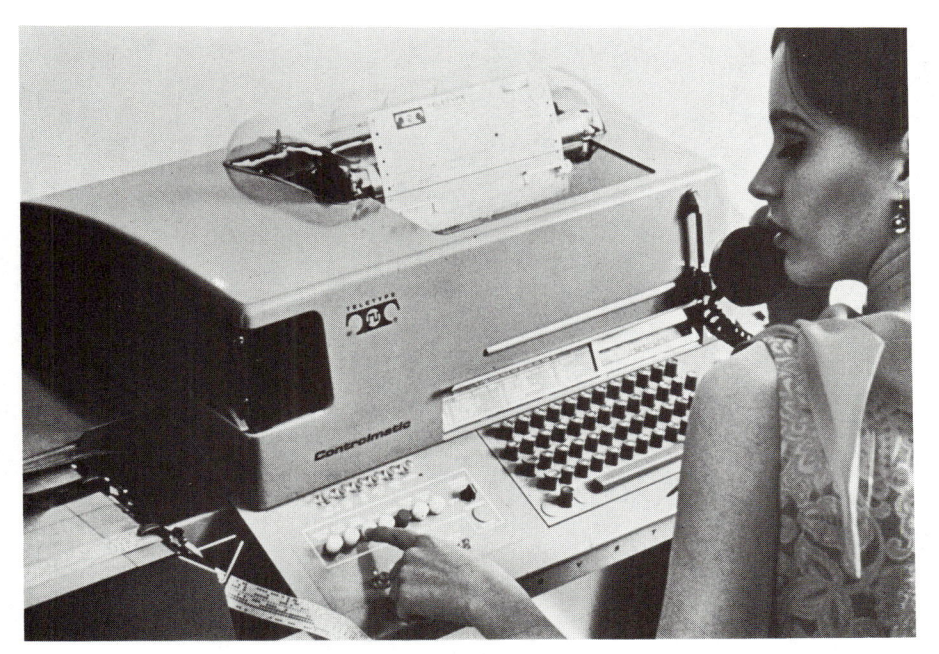

Illus. 9-18
Plant operator depresses start button transferring district office order from tape to hard copy.

Teletype Corporation

Part 4 / Special Communications Services

321

Teletypewriter Private Line Service (TWPL)

Teletypewriter private line service (TWPL) or leased wire service messages do not go through a central Western Union office. The machines are connected by direct wires. They are used for interoffice communications by firms with a number of branch offices and plants throughout the country.

Data-Phone Service

Data-phone service provides the means for sending payrolls, inventories, sales figures, and other business data from one location to another rapidly. Data-phones can handle data prepared on punched cards, paper tape, or magnetic tape. Machine signals from the punched cards or tape are converted into tones that are sent over regular telephone lines. The Data-phone at the receiving offices changes the transmitted tones back into whatever is required: punched cards, paper tape, or magnetic tape.

Data-phone sets are capable of transmitting at speeds of up to 4,500 words per minute. The charge for this service is the same as it would be for a regular long-distance call.

Illus. 9-19 District office secretary sends monthly territory sales figures to home office by Data-phone.

AT&T

QUESTIONS

1. What would be an advantage to the executive of using a credit card to make a long-distance call?
2. What is a conference call? How would you set up a conference call for your executive?
3. Why do businesses provide WATS lines for their customers?
4. What is a teletype? From a business standpoint, what advantage does it have over a telephone?
5. What are three types of business data transmitted frequently by Data-phones?

JUDGMENT

1. The number of overseas telephone calls from the United States has increased from 11,750 calls in 1927 to more than 19,500,000 in 1969. Discuss the reasons for this tremendous increase in overseas calls.
2. Consider the types of business firms that might use a teletypewriter installation advantageously.

PERSONAL QUALITIES

One day when Louise Hills came back from lunch early, she overheard Rosalind Robinson, another secretary, placing a long-distance call to her mother. Louise was very startled when she heard Rosalind give her employer's telephone credit card number to the operator. Later when Louise asked Rosalind about the use of her employer's credit card, Rosalind replied, "I had to call my mother right away. I'll tell Mr. Jenkins about it later and pay him for the call."

What do you think of Rosalind's actions? How do you think Mr. Jenkins will react when he is told?

LANGUAGE USAGE

Here are seven sets of words that are frequently misused. Type the sentences on a separate sheet of paper using the correct word that applies in each instance.

1. *Don't* and *Doesn't*
    (a) He (don't, doesn't) seem to mind when we use his phone.
    (b) It (don't, doesn't) take long to file a telegram.
2. *Like* and *As*
    (a) It tastes good (like, as) a steak should.
    (b) (Like, As) Maine goes, so goes the nation.
3. *Lie* and *Lay*
    (a) Now I (lay, lie) down my burden.
    (b) The typed letters (lay, lie) on his desk.
4. *Sit* and *Set*
    (a) We (sit, sat) for hours waiting for the test to be given.
    (b) Cares (sit, set) heavily upon the manager.

5. *Can* and *May*
   (a) (May, Can) we tell you about the other types of files in our office?
   (b) (May, Can) you type as well in an emergency?
6. *Affect* and *Effect*.
   (a) What was the (affect, effect) of the announcement?
   (b) The drop in the stock market may have a telling (affect, effect) on employment opportunities.
7. *Raise* and *Rise*.
   (a) Let me (rise, raise) the window for you.
   (b) Price (raises, rises) were announced by the automobile manufacturers.

SECRETARIAL WORK

Select a member of the Secretarial Office Procedures class to work with you in placing and taking this typical service call. One of you should be prepared to make the call and the other prepared to answer it. Use a Teletrainer or a telephone if either is available. If neither is available, simulate the call.

Information for the Caller

Assume that you are a secretary preparing a statistical report in the Advertising Department of an air conditioner manufacturer. The electronic calculator you have been using to verify the figures in the report has broken down, and you are asked to call a serviceman. You will need to know the make and model of the calculator before placing the call. Use the Yellow Pages to find the name and telephone number of manufacturers under the heading: *Adding & Calculating Machines*. If the Yellow Pages in your telephone directory do not list office machines service, use the following information:

Adding & Calculating Machines & Supplies
   Monroe — Sales, Service, and Rental.........555-2368

Information for the Receiver

Assume that you are the secretary taking the service call for the Monroe Calculator Company. When the call comes in from the Advertising Department, verify the information about the machine, the address of the air conditioner manufacturer, and the room number and floor of the Advertising Department. Tell the caller approximately when to expect the serviceman.

As other members of your class make and answer the service call, evaluate their telephone techniques under the following headings:

1. Placing and Beginning the Call
2. Development of the Call
3. Closing the Call
4. Telephone Personality

PART 5 | DOMESTIC AND INTERNATIONAL TELEGRAPH SERVICES

"Joy, Al Stevens and I just reached an agreement on the phone of our purchase of the Little Rock property. Let's send him a written confirmation. Make the telegram read: This will confirm our verbal agreement of July 8, 197–, in which we, Arcade Products, Inc., agree to purchase your property at 1807 Beech Street, Little Rock, Arkansas, for $82,000. Payment to be made as follows: $10,000 by July 15, 197–; remainder by date of occupancy, September 1, 197–. Please confirm if these facts agree with your understanding of our statement." Joy Parsons realizes that great care must be taken to insure the accuracy of this message. Joy also knows that with a message of this importance she will have the telegraph company report back when it has delivered the message.

DOMESTIC TELEGRAPH SERVICE

When you want to send the most rapid *written* communication send a telegram. It can be sent from coast to coast and is usually delivered in a few minutes. You can be sure, too, of getting attention because a telegram carries with it a note of urgency and importance.

Technological progress during the past 30 years has produced a vast chain of high-speed telegraph message centers throughout the United States, Canada, and Mexico. Hundreds of thousands of telegraph messages and money orders are sent over Western Union wires every business day. Most of these messages relate to business transactions: buying and selling merchandise, buying and selling stocks and bonds, making reservations, or sending money.

A telegram can be sent a distance of 1,500 miles and delivered in less than an hour, while the average business letter would spend over a full day en route, even if it were sent by airmail.

After you are employed in an office you will probably be expected to know when to send a telegram and which type of service to use. You may also be expected to know how to compose telegrams and how to get your messages to the telegraph office in the shortest time.

Selecting the Service

The telegraph company provides two different types of message service. Messages are sent and delivered according to the type of service used. Some are sent and delivered immediately; others are sent during the night and delivered early during the following morning. The two types of service are the

     (1) Full-rate telegram
     (2) Overnight telegram

Full-Rate Telegram. When there is great urgency about the message or when speed in having the message received is important, you will send the full-rate telegram. A full-rate telegram, usually referred to simply as a telegram, is the faster type of telegraph service. The message is sent immediately at any time during the day or night, and, if it is received during business hours, it is telephoned or delivered to the addressee at once. If it is received after business hours, it is relayed to the addressee as soon as possible. Although it is the more expensive type of service, it is used most frequently by businessmen because of the speed with which it is sent and delivered. The basic charge is made for a message of 15 words or less; a small charge is made for each additional word in the message.

Overnight Telegram. An overnight telegram is more economical than a fast full-rate telegram but it is a slower type of telegraph service. It will be accepted by the telegraph office any time up to midnight for delivery the following morning. The basic charge is for a minimum of 100 words. Additional words are charged at the rate of 1 to 1½ cents a word. It is used mostly for messages of considerable length such as business proposals, progress reports, and detailed instructions.

Counting the Chargeable Words

Since the cost of a telegram is based on a minimum number of words in the message plus an additional charge for extra words, it is important that you know how to count the chargeable words. The following summarizes the rules for counting words:

1. One address and one signature are free.
2. The punctuation marks below are sent as written but are not counted or charged for.

  . (period or decimal point)   - (hyphen)
  , (comma)   () (parentheses)
  : (colon)   ? (question mark)
  ; (semicolon)   "" (quotation marks)
  — (dash)   ' (apostrophe)

3. Figures are counted as one word for every five characters. With figures the decimal point, the comma, and the dash are considered as punctuation marks and not counted.

    34,785 (five figures with comma as punctuation)............................1 word
    378,534 (six figures with comma as punctuation)............................2 words
    4.333 (four figures with decimal point as punctuation)...................... 1 word
    10—160 (five figures with dash as punctuation). 1 word

4. The following special characters may be sent and charged for at the rate of one word for each five characters: $, &, # (number or pounds), "(inches or seconds), '(feet or minutes), / (fraction mark).

The percent sign is transmitted as o/o and counts as three characters.

    83.33% (four figures and % — decimal point as punctuation)..................2 words
    $44.50 (four figures and $ — decimal point as punctuation)..................1 word
    $450.25 (five figures and $ — decimal point as punctuation)....................2 words
    #4,960 (four figures and # — comma as punctuation)....................1 word

5. The special characters ¢ (cents), @ (at), and ° (degree) cannot be transmitted. They are written out and sent as words.

6. Dictionary words from the English, German, French, Italian, Dutch, Portuguese, Spanish, and Latin languages are counted as one word each, regardless of length. Nondictionary words and words from all other languages are counted as one word for every five characters.

7. Geographic names are counted according to the number of individual words contained in them even when they are written without spaces.

    ST. LOUIS ....2 words
    ST.LOUIS ....2 words
    NEW YORK CITY ....3 words
    NORTH DAKOTA ....2 words
    FARGO, N. D. ....3 words

8. Abbreviations of single words are counted as full words.

9. Common abbreviations are counted as one word for every five characters. Spaces between the abbreviations increase the word count. Periods are considered punctuation and are not counted.

NYC .... 1 word
N. Y. C. .... 3 words
COD .... 1 word
FOB .... 1 word
a.m. .... 1 word

10. Initials in names are counted as separate words. A last name with a prefix, such as "Du" in DuBois, does not count as a separate word if it is not followed by a space. Initials, when separated by spaces, are counted as separate words, but when written together are counted at the rate of one word for each five letters

JOHN F. KELLER...................... 3 words
JAMES O'DONNELL.................... 2 words
CARL VAN TIL........................ 3 words
RALPH DUMONT....................... 2 words
J. J. WILLIAMS...................... 3 words
W.A.R. DAVIS....................... 2 words

Preparing a Telegram

You must prepare a telegram carefully if it is to be delivered without delay and if it is to be understood by the one who receives it. The secret of a well-worded telegram is to state your message as clearly and briefly as possible. The suggestions shown on pages 329 and 330 should be kept in mind in preparing a telegram.

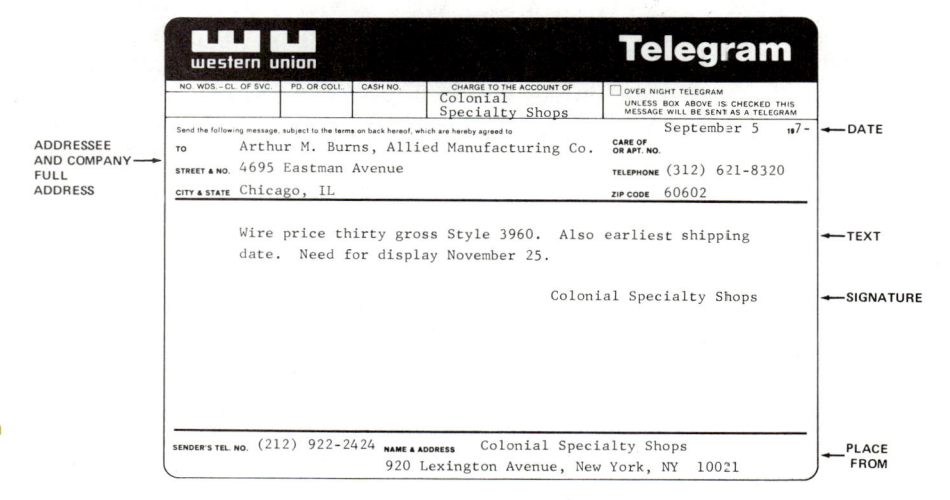

Illus. 9-20
Full-rate telegram
Every telegram should include all the elements shown in the full-rate telegram.

1. *Use Western Union telegram blanks.* You can obtain pads of telegram blanks free of charge at any Western Union office.
2. *Type three copies of the telegram.* Ordinarily the original goes to the telegraph company, the second copy to the correspondence file, and the third to the addressee so that he can check to see that the message was transmitted correctly.
3. *Type the message with capital and lower case letters.* The message should be double spaced. Do not divide a word at the end of a line.
4. *Indicate whether the message is sent paid, collect, or charge.* If it is to be charged, indicate the account below the heading, CHARGE TO THE ACCOUNT OF.
5. *Indicate the type of service desired.* Type an "X" in the box before Over Night Telegram at the upper right of the blank if you want to send an overnight telegram. Unless the box is checked the message will be sent as a full-rate telegram.
6. *Type the date.*
7. *Type the full name of the addressee.*
8. *Type the complete address and telephone number of the addressee.* Whenever possible give the office number. Spell out such words as *North* and *South*. Do not use suffixes with street numbers (34 not 34th Street).

Illus. 9-21
Overnight telegram

Part 5 / Domestic and International Telegraph Services

9. *Write the message clearly and include punctuation.* The use of punctuation marks makes the message clearer. There is no extra charge for them.
10. *Include your address and telephone number.* After the signature type the sender's telephone number, name, and address. This is important if hotel or travel reservations are requested.

Filing a Telegram

How can you file a telegraphic message? When it is filed, a message is turned over to Western Union for transmission and delivery. A message can be filed in any one of seven different ways:

1. *Over the Counter.* A prepared message can be taken to a Western Union office or a message can be written at the counter.
2. *Over the Telephone.* A telegram can be filed over the telephone. When a message is telephoned to a Western Union office care must be taken to be sure that names and unusual words are transmitted accurately. Such words should be spelled out to the operator to avoid confusion.
3. *Tie Line Service.* Tie lines are used when the firm sends and receives a large number of telegrams. A tie line is a system of direct wires between the business and the telegraph company.
4. *Facsimile Service.* A handwritten or typewritten message can be transmitted from a business office on a *Desk-Fax,* a small, desk-sized machine that can both

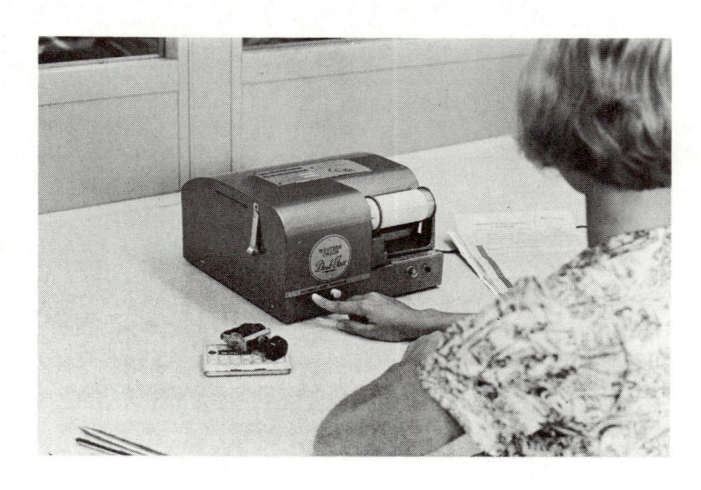

Illus. 9-22
Desk-Fax

send and receive an exact copy. The message is placed on the cylinder of the machine, and the outgoing button is pressed. An electronic eye then scans the message and flashes an exact copy of it to a similar machine at the nearest high-speed telegraph center, which in turn flashes it to its destination. The Desk-Fax also receives telegrams by the same process with equal speed and simplicity.[1]

5. *Teleprinter Service.* A telegraphic message can be sent on a specially installed printing machine with a keyboard like a teletypewriter. This machine is called a teleprinter. As the message is typed in a business office on the teleprinter, it is being recorded on a tape or message form in the telegraph office. The message is transferred immediately to a telegraph line and transmitted to its destination.

6. *Telex.* The dial-a-wire service, called Telex, permits users to dial other subscribers instantly, regardless of distance. This two-way customer-to-customer teleprinter service links major cities in the United States and also serves many countries in other parts of the world.

7. *Private Wire Systems.* Many telegraph users, with a large volume of communications, require private telegraph systems of their own. Such private networks are built, installed, and maintained for businesses by Western Union. A system may extend hundreds, or even thousands, of miles and connect a company's offices and plants in as few or as many as a hundred cities.

One of the new and growing developments in the business world is electronic data processing (see Unit 6) — the use of machines to speed the processing of vast amounts of paper work. Since it is necessary to quickly gather sales, payroll, inventory, shipping, and other data from distant cities and branch offices for processing at a central point, many business firms use a private wire system.

Western Union has developed private wire systems, called *data communication,* that, in addition to handling business messages, will also transmit data, either in punched card or tape form ready for instant processing at the destination by business machines and computers.

---

[1]Because of technological improvements in other services, which make more rapid communications possible, Western Union began phasing out Desk-Fax service in the fall of 1971.

Cash, Charge, and Collect Service

Telegraph service may be paid for in any one of four ways:

1. With cash at the time the message is sent. Cash may be required of an infrequent telegraph user.
2. Through business charge accounts. Charge accounts are carried by the telegraph company, particularly for large firms that send many telegrams every business day. These accounts are billed on a monthly basis.
3. Through telephone subscribers' accounts. An individual may send a telegram from a telephone or from a Western Union office and have it charged to his telephone bill.
4. By the person receiving the message. A message may be sent collect. This means that the receiver of the telegram pays for it upon delivery. To send a telegram collect, type the word *Collect* beneath the heading PD OR COLL. at the top of the blank.

Telegraphic Money Orders

One of the quickest and safest ways for you to send money is to send a telegraphic money order. The amount to be sent is turned over to the telegraph office together with the name and address of the recipient and any accompanying message. There is a charge for sending the money order and a slight additional charge for any accompanying message. You will be given a receipt for the amount of money sent.

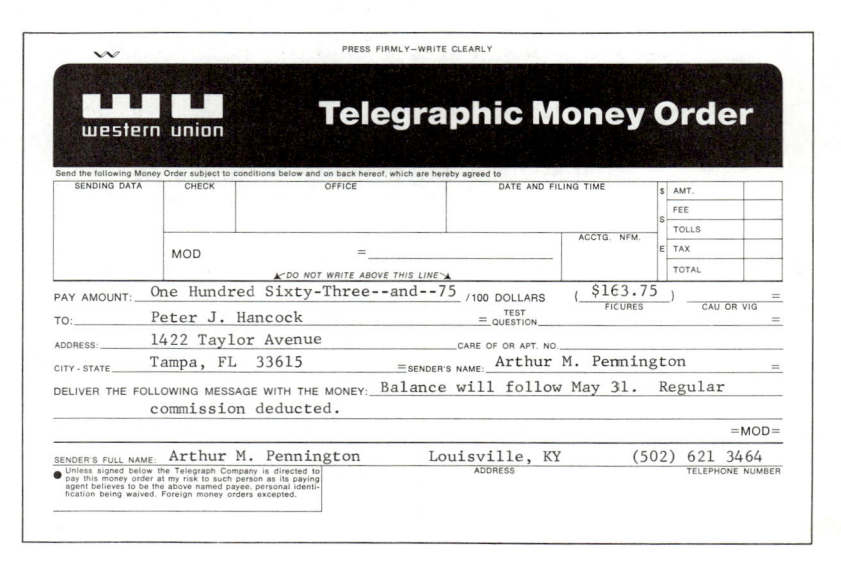

Illus. 9-23
Telegraphic money order

332   Unit 9 / Telephone and Telegraph Services

The recipient's telegraph office notifies him when the money order arrives; however, he must furnish evidence of his identity before the money is given to him.

Delivery of Telegrams

A telegraphic message may be delivered in any one of five ways:

1. *By messenger.* The message may be delivered in a sealed envelope by a Western Union messenger.
2. *By telephone.* The telephone is often used instead of the messenger for speed and convenience, especially when the addressee is located at a distance from the telegraph office. The Western Union operator will mail a copy of a telephoned message to the addressee upon request at no extra charge.
3. *By teleprinter.* This machine, described under "Filing a Telegram" on page 331, automatically receives and prints messages.
4. *By facsimile.* Facsimile copies of messages are received by Desk-Fax users.
5. *By mailgram.* A new electronic mail service developed by Western Union and the United States Postal Service enables companies in New York City to deliver 100-word messages anywhere in the continental United States for about one third the cost of a 15-word telegram. Mailgrams may be called in, delivered, or sent via Telex to a Western Union office. They are delivered in special envelopes the next business day by a regular letter carrier.

If the telegraph company fails to deliver a message or makes an error in the transmission of the message, it is liable for damages. The limits of liability are stated on the back of each telegraph blank.

Special Telegram Services

When messages are of a legal nature or of serious concern to both sender and recipient, two additional services are available.

Repeat Back. At the time the message is filed with the telegraph company, you may decide that the message is important enough to need special attention. For example, the message may contain figures, names to be published, or dates. For an additional charge, a message may be repeated back from its destination to the sending office to be checked for possible errors. If errors are discovered, the corrected message is then sent at no additional charge. *Repeat Back* must be typed at the top of the telegraph blank if this additional service is desired.

Report Delivery. Occasionally written evidence of the time of delivery and the address of the person or firm to whom the telegram was delivered is considered necessary. To get this additional information, you must pay the cost of a return telegram and type *Report Delivery* or *Report Delivery and Address* at the top of the telegraph blank. These words of instruction are counted and charged for.

Differences in Time Zones

A branch office in Seattle wishes to contact your office in Miami. It is 5 p.m. in Seattle. It is a long message which will be reported at a branch meeting on the following afternoon. The secretary in Seattle wisely sends it as an overnight telegram. You will receive it when you arrive at work the next day. If a telegram is to be sent any great distance east or west, the secretary must be aware of the difference in time between the sending office and the receiving office to decide upon the correct service. A home office located on the East Coast is opened and closed three hours earlier than a branch office in San Francisco; a telegram sent anytime after 2 p.m. from a branch office on the West Coast would not arrive in a Boston home office until after closing hours. The message could be sent more economically as an overnight telegram for delivery the following morning. In dealing with telegraphic services, you will be expected to know the different time zones and the present time in each of them.

INTERNATIONAL TELEGRAPH SERVICE

More and more businesses are opening branches in foreign countries. This means that international communications are becoming very important. Cablegrams may be sent to foreign countries by means of cables under the seas and by radio.

Kinds of Service

International telegraph service and domestic telegraph service are similar. There are three types of international telegraph service: *Full-Rate* (FR) messages, *Cable Letters* (LT), and *Ship Radiograms*.

Full-Rate Messages (FR). A full-rate message is the fastest and most expensive type of overseas service. It is transmitted and delivered as quickly as possible. It may be written in any language that can be expressed in letters of ordinary type, or it can be written in code. A minimum charge is made for a message of seven words or less.

Cable Letters (LT). A cable letter, or letter telegram, is transmitted during the night and delivered at its destination the following morning. The message must be written in plain language, not code. A minimum charge is made for a message of 22 words or less. The cost is only one half that charged for full-rate messages.

Ship Radiograms. Plain language or code may be used in sending radiograms to and from ships at sea. A minimum charge is made for a message of seven words or less.

Code Messages

Cablegrams and radiograms are much more expensive than domestic telegrams. Not only are the rates higher but many more words are counted and charged for. In order to reduce the cost of overseas messages, many firms send their messages in code. One five letter code word may be used in place of a common phrase that would normally take four or five words. For example, the code word *ODFUF* may be used in place of the statement, "Please cable at once," and only one word would be charged for instead of four.

You count chargeable words for international messages in about the same way that you do for domestic telegrams. The major differences are

1. Each word in the address is counted and charged for.
2. Code words are counted as five letters to the word.
3. Each punctuation mark is counted as one word.
4. Special symbols, such as ¢, $, and #, must be spelled out because they cannot be transmitted.

Cable Code Addresses

Because each word in the address is counted as a chargeable word, firms that have a great many international messages often use a single code word as the business's cable address. The following shows the regular address and the cable code address of Mutual Books, Inc., of the Philippines.

Regular Address	*Cable Code Address*
Mutual Books, Inc. 465-A A-Mabini Shaw Boulevard Mandaluyong, Rizal Philippines	Mubinc

Part 5 / Domestic and International Telegraph Services

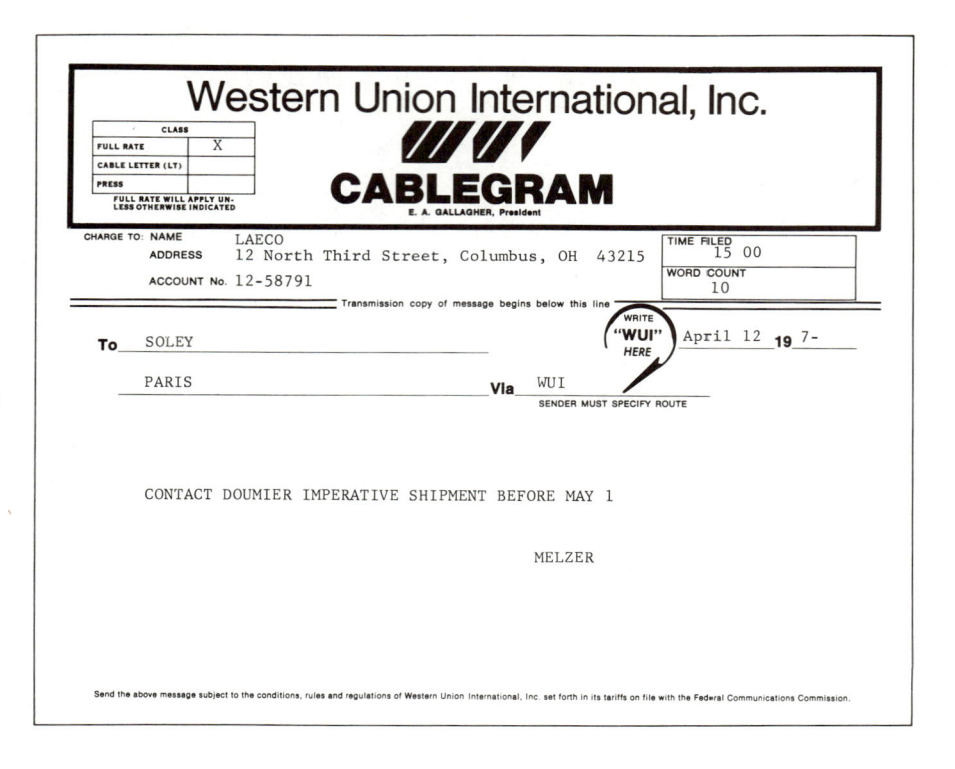

Illus. 9-24
A full-rate cable

```
                    Western Union International, Inc.
        CLASS
FULL RATE      X                  WUI
CABLE LETTER (LT)
PRESS                        CABLEGRAM
FULL RATE WILL APPLY UN-       E. A. GALLAGHER, President
LESS OTHERWISE INDICATED

CHARGE TO: NAME    LAECO                              TIME FILED
           ADDRESS 12 North Third Street, Columbus, OH 43215   15 00
           ACCOUNT No. 12-58791                       WORD COUNT
                                                         10
                    Transmission copy of message begins below this line
                                                  WRITE
   To    SOLEY                                    "WUI"    April 12  19 7-
                                                  HERE
         PARIS                           Via      WUI
                                         SENDER MUST SPECIFY ROUTE


         CONTACT DOUMIER IMPERATIVE SHIPMENT BEFORE MAY 1

                                                  MELZER
```

There is a small annual charge for registering the cable address with the telegraph company.

Differences in Time

Time differences will determine, in part, the service you choose. If you work in an office that has a heavy volume of overseas communications, be sure you have a chart of the time zones around the world.

QUESTIONS

1. What are two types of domestic telegraph service?
2. Give the essential features of each class of domestic service and the relative cost of each.
3. What punctuation marks are sent without charge?
4. How are figures counted in telegrams?
5. What suggestions should be followed in preparing a telegram?
6. What are some of the ways in which telegrams may be filed?
7. In what four ways may telegraph service be paid for?
8. How is money sent by telegraph?
9. How may telegrams be delivered?

10. What is meant by a repeat back message? Is there a charge for such service?
11. In what way is a knowledge of time zones important when sending telegrams?
12. Name and describe the various international telegraph services.
13. What is an advantage of a code message?
14. Describe a cable code address.

JUDGMENT

1. At 4:30 p.m., in Philadelphia, Pennsylvania, you are instructed to send a 17-word telegram to a customer in Denver, Colorado. It is important that the message be delivered as quickly as possible. Which type of service should you use?
2. At 3 p.m., in Portland, Oregon, you are instructed to send a 30-word telegram to the home office in Boston, Massachusetts. The office in Boston closes at 5 p.m. The message should be delivered as quickly as possible. Which type of service should you use?
3. How many telegram words are in each of the following combinations?

   (a) $1,925.50   (d) C. A. Van Dyke
   (b) $50.00   (e) COD
   (c) New Jersey   (f) FOB

4. Under what conditions do you think a telegraphic money order would most likely be used by an office?
5. The executive for whom you work wants to send a message to a business associate who has left by ship for a vacation in London. What communication service should be used?

PERSONAL QUALITIES

Mr. Edward Collins telephones his New York office from a hotel in Chicago at noon. The call is collect because his wallet with currency, travelers' checks, and credit cards has been either mislaid or stolen. In any event he needs $200, and he needs it immediately. His secretary promises to send the money at once, but later realizes that in the excitement Mr. Collins failed to indicate how the money should be sent.

The secretary sends the money in the form of a cashier's check in a special delivery airmail letter.

What method of sending the money could the secretary have used?

If you were the secretary, what would you have done?

LANGUAGE USAGE

A conjunction is a word that connects other words, phrases, or clauses. Conjunctions may be *coordinate* or *subordinate*. In Unit 3, Part 3, coordinate conjunctions were presented.

A *subordinate* conjunction is dependent in that it connects unequal elements in a sentence.

Example: The secretary rushed to her desk *when* the telephone rang. . . . *when* is a subordinate conjunction, which connects the subordinate clause, *the telephone rang*.

Type the following sentences and underline the subordinate conjunctions.

1. You will not type attractive letters unless you plan carefully.
2. Although the secretary was with the company two years, her employer was not pleased with her work.
3. She made a file for the conference so that everything would be in one place.
4. The typist studied shorthand because she wanted to learn to take dictation.
5. Don't leave before you pay your dues.

SECRETARIAL WORK

In each of the following problems compose the message and select the kind of message to be sent. Type the messages and make two carbons.

1. At 10 a.m., on October 15, 197–, your employer, Thomas A. Evans, Office Manager of the Davis Advertising Agency, San Francisco, California, asks you to send a telegram to the Sheraton Hotel in St. Louis, Missouri, reserving a single room at $18.50 for the night of October 17, 197–. He will arrive at the Sheraton at about 8 p.m. on the 17th. Ask the hotel to wire confirmation immediately. The message is to be charged to the company. It must be delivered as quickly as possible.

2. At 4:30 p.m., on December 10, 197–, you are asked to send a telegram for H. R. Harris, President of the Harris Construction Company, El Paso, Texas, to the Warner Manufacturing Company, Pittsburgh, Pennsylvania, whose office closes at 5 p.m. Ask them to cancel Order 8675 of December 9. Tell them that a letter will follow the telegram.

3. On February 4, 197–, your employer, Mr. E. O. Colby, asks you to prepare a telegraphic money order form for $125 to be sent to the firm's sales representative, Sam D. Browning, at the Hotel Dennis in Atlantic City, New Jersey. You are to include a message informing Mr. Browning that a special sales meeting has been scheduled for February 25 at the Statler Hotel in Boston.

4. Your employer has plane reservations on TWA Flight 204 from O'Hare Airport on Tuesday, March 17. The flight is scheduled to arrive at John F. Kennedy International Airport in New York City at 4 p.m. Eastern Standard Time. He wants the Long Island manager to meet him at the airport.

Unit 10 COPYING AND DUPLICATING

Part 1. Copying and Reproducing Machines
    2. Duplicating Machines

The secretary is often requested to make several copies of business papers. She must decide whether she should use a copying machine, a stencil duplicator, a fluid duplicator, or an offset machine. Without a knowledge of each of these processes, she cannot make intelligent decisions.

VOCABULARY BUILDER

complicated..........................
  adjective: difficult to analyze, understand, or explain; complex

visible...............................
  adjective: capable of being seen; exposed to view; apparent

manually.............................
  adverb: of, relating to, or involving the hands; worked by hand

versatile.............................
  adjective: changing; turning with ease from one thing to another; having many uses or applications

absorbent...........................
  adjective: spongelike

deposits.............................
  verb: places, especially for safekeeping; settles; adheres

accumulate..........................
  verb: to heap up or pile up; to amass; to collect; to increase in quantity or number

pliant...............................
  adjective: flexible and springy; something easily bent or folded

multiple.............................
  adjective: consisting of, including, or involving more than one; many; various

factors..............................
  noun: causes that actively contribute to the production of a result; goods or services used in the process of production

---

Clarity is the supreme politeness of him who wields a pen.
  Jean Henri Fabre

p. 341 This can be important when the item to be reproduced is a **complicated** drawing or illustration.

p. 342 Corrections, if you make them properly on the original, are not **visible** on the copy.

p. 345 At specific points in the letter, the machine stops automatically to allow you to **manually** type in information that will vary from letter to letter.

p. 350 It is a very dependable and **versatile** machine.

p. 350 It prints best on **absorbent**, rough finished paper of any color.

p. 357 Pressure on the face of the master with a typewriter or writing instrument **deposits** a carbon image on the back of the master sheet in. . . .

p. 358 Clean the type well, giving extra attention to type faces where ink is likely to **accumulate**, such as *e, a, w, g, o*.

p. 358 If your typewriter does not have a smooth, medium hard platen, place a sheet of heavy paper or **pliant** plastic behind the carbon sheet. . . .

p. 362 In your office there is frequently a need for **multiple** copies.

p. 362 What **factors** should be considered in deciding which method of duplication would best fit your needs?

PART 1 — COPYING AND REPRODUCING MACHINES

Mr. Garza told Annette Bella, his secretary, to use her own judgment as much as possible so that he doesn't have to take the time to give complete instructions for all her work. Frequently Mr. Garza will ask Annette to prepare copies of letters and other material to send to the company's branch offices, but he will not always tell her what kind of copier or duplicating machine to use. Annette has learned about copiers and duplicating machines in school and uses her knowledge to decide how to prepare the messages.

COPIERS

Your employer will often ask you to make copies of business papers. The fastest way to make a copy is by using a copying machine, sometimes called a photocopying machine. Copying machines have been in growing demand in recent years and are now standard equipment in most offices. Some offices will have more than one copier. There may be a floor model which is used when many copies are needed. In addition, you may have a small model on a desk or table near you on which you can make several copies when necessary.

Copiers have an advantage over other methods of duplication because a copy can be prepared from an original paper without preparing a stencil or a master. Copies can be prepared at the rate of one a second on some machines, and some copiers will enlarge or reduce the material during the copying process.

Features of Copiers

Copiers have the following features:

1. Exact copies of an original can be produced. This can be important when the item to be reproduced is a complicated drawing or illustration.
2. They can be used when one or several copies are needed, although combination copier-duplicator equipment will reproduce an unlimited number of copies.

3. They are inexpensive when only a few copies are made from the original. Quite often companies record how much customers owe them on ledger cards. At the end of the month the ledger cards are reproduced on a copier, and the copy is sent to the customer as a monthly statement.
4. Copiers are easy to operate. You simply set the dial for the number of copies desired and insert the original in the copier. The original is scanned by the machine and copied. The copy of the original then comes out of the machine. All colors are reproduced in black.
5. Some models prepare transparencies that can be projected on a screen. These may be used by your employer to illustrate an important point in a business meeting.
6. Some models prepare offset mats. You can place these mats on an offset machine and reproduce the item in large numbers.

Types of Copiers

There are many types of copying machines, but you will probably use the electrostatic and infrared most frequently in the office.

Electrostatic. The electrostatic copier is probably used more than any other in the office. It produces dark black copy that can look very much like the original. Corrections, if you make them properly on the original, are not visible on the copy.

Illus. 10-1
Electrostatic copier

You can make copies at the rate of one a second on some machines. You can also enlarge or reduce copies on some models during the copying process. For many models you will not need special paper for this process. This process is frequently called "Xerox," the brand name of one of the companies that makes this type of copier.

Infrared. An infrared copier can make copies in as little as five seconds. With this machine you must use a special paper, which is very thin and is available only in an off-white color. It will not copy all colors, particularly red, blue, and green. You can prepare offset mats and fluid masters on the infrared copier. Sometimes this process is called "Thermofax," the brand name of a company that makes this type of copier.

Answering Correspondence

Your employer may sometimes use copiers for answering letters, as shown on page 344. Handwritten notations are made on the original letter and it is then copied. The letter is mailed back to the sender, and the copy is placed in the office files. This saves your employer's time; he does not have to dictate an answer to the letter. You will not have to type an answer; so your time is saved also. Both the letter and the reply are on one sheet; so filing space is saved.

Since this method of answering letters is somewhat informal, it is used when corresponding with persons who know each other quite well or when the subject of the letter requires an immediate reply.

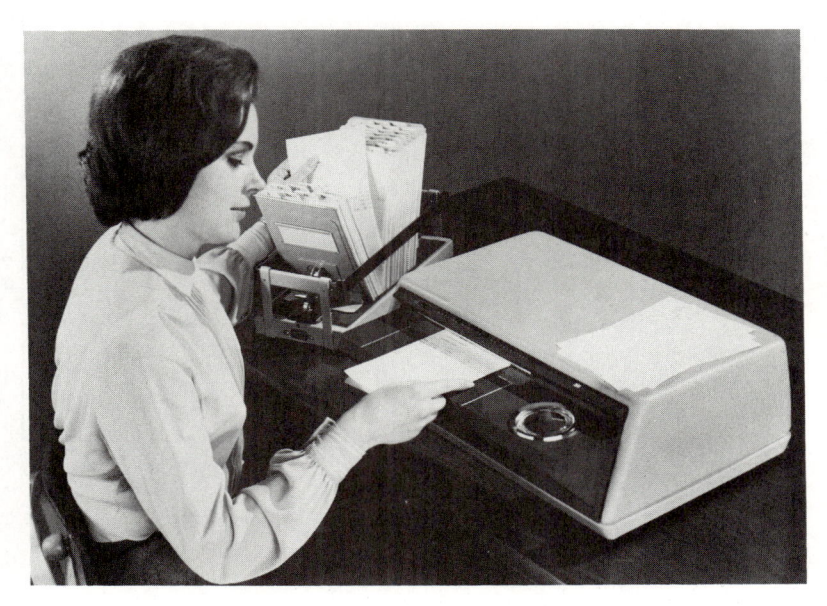

Illus. 10-2
A desk model infrared copier can be used to reproduce ledger cards which then become monthly statements.

Administrative Management Society

Part 1 / Copying and Reproducing Machines

Standard Supply Company 4422 North Seventh Street Dallas, TX 75208

December 10, 197-

Mr. J. W. Stauffer, Sales Manager
The Arnold Products Company
23 North Redd Street
Roanoke, VA 24014

Your Invoice 31336

Dear Jerry

    On November 14 we ordered 12 cases of AA batteries on our Purchase Order 2986. On November 20 we received your invoice showing that the batteries were shipped on November 18.

    We received 10 cases of the batteries on November 25. As yet we have not received the other two cases. Will you please let me know immediately if the additional batteries were placed on back order or if they were shipped separately?

    Also, we need about 250 additional advertising sheets on the tape players for distribution to our customers.

    Thank you.

Sincerely

John

John Mendes
Manager

st

[Handwritten notations:]
Sorry, John; our error; 2 cases placed on back order
Shipping today by separate package

Illus. 10-3

Copy of letter with notations

AUTOMATIC TYPEWRITERS

Sometimes your employer may wish to send the same letter to many different people. He may not want the recipients to know that they are receiving copies of the letter. If the copies are prepared on a copying machine or duplicator, it will be rather obvious that they are not originals. When your employer wants original copies for a large number of people, you can use an automatic typewriter.

The automatic typewriter produces original typewritten form letters in large quantities. The automatically typed letters are individually typed so that they do not look like form letters. They are used to give the recipient a favorable impression; however, this is the most expensive way to reproduce large quantities of an item.

To use the automatic typewriter, you first prepare a master copy of the letter on paper tape, magnetic tape, or cards, depending on the machine you are using. After the master copy has been prepared, you simply place the tape or card on the typewriter, insert paper in the machine, and push the button to start the typing. The machine will automatically type the letter. At specific points in the letter, the machine stops automatically to allow you to manually type in information that will vary from letter to letter. For example, you might have automatic stops to allow you to insert the date, inside address, salutation, or other special information. Some automatic typewriters also have an attachment for embossing the signature on each letter.

Illus. 10-4
An automatic typewriter stops to permit the operator to insert information.

Part 1 / Copying and Reproducing Machines

COLLATORS

Any time you have a duplication job of two pages or more, you must collate it — that is, the pages must be assembled in proper order and fastened into sets. The simplest method of collating is to place the copies of each page in individual stacks on a table, then lift the top page from each stack until a complete set is assembled. This method, however, is both tiring and time-consuming.

Sometimes you may use a rotating circular table. With this device, you place individual stacks of papers in proper sequence along the edge of the table. As the table rotates, you simply take the top sheet from each stack as it passes your fixed position.

Mechanical collating machines are often used in offices where there is a great deal of duplicating and collating. The pages of a duplicated job are stacked in separate compartments of the collator. A rubber-tipped metal rod rests on each stack and pushes a page out of each compartment as the foot control is depressed. The pages are gathered in sets and criss-crossed for stapling or binding after each depression of the foot control. Available also are automatic collators that mechanically gather the pages together and bind them into sets.

QUESTIONS

1. What is the advantage of a copier over a duplicating machine?
2. List four features of copiers.
3. When would you use a copier to answer a letter?
4. What is one advantage of automatic typewriters?
5. Describe the simplest method of collating.

JUDGMENT

1. What are two office situations in which a copying machine may be used?
2. Your employer is considering the purchase of a copying machine. What facts can you present to help him in making his decision?

PERSONAL QUALITIES

A new copying machine has been installed in the personnel department to reduce copying expense. The director of personnel has decided that it would be more efficient to have just one person in the department operate the machine and control the supplies; and he has asked Mary Sherwood, a new employee, to assume this responsibility.

Immediately after the machine is installed, Mr. Yates, the chief clerk in the payroll department, asks Mary to make a copy of a newspaper clipping covering an account of a naval battle of World War II. Mr. Yates is interested in naval history and considers himself an authority in this field. Mary graciously made the copy of the clipping for Mr. Yates. Since that time he has brought in an ever-increasing number of clippings, photographs, and diagrams of naval battles to be reproduced on the copying device.

The photocopying paper costs more than five cents a sheet. If Mary continues to do all of Mr. Yates's work, she will use up her copy paper stock in half the expected time. Sensing that a difficult or embarrassing time lies ahead, Mary wonders what she should do.

What courses of action could Mary take? Which course of action would you take? Why?

LANGUAGE USAGE

The word *get* is one of the most overworked terms in the English language. In the sentences below, substitute a word that will improve the sentence by eliminating the *get* construction. (Do not rewrite or rephrase the sentence.)

1. *Get* a reservation for me at the Sheraton Hotel in San Francisco for the night of August 14, late arrival.
2. *Get* me on a flight leaving about 4 or 4:30 Monday afternoon for Kansas City.
3. We ought to *get* a new file cabinet to replace the one in Mr. Smith's office.
4. The office staff was well pleased when everyone *got* a new desk.
5. Her employer *got* upset when she was late for work the third time last week.
6. He *got* control of the company through purchase of the stock.
7. Little time is needed to *get* to the railroad station.
8. He *got* that increase in salary justly.
9. The St. Louis office *got* the award for selling the most subscriptions.
10. He *got* the information, but with great difficulty.

SECRETARIAL WORK

1. The following material is to be reproduced on an office copier. Type the copy in an attractive style.

    PROGRAM FOR THE SEVENTH ANNUAL BUSINESS EDUCATION CONFERENCE

    WEDNESDAY, July 6, 197–. 12:00 noon — Registration. Conference Lounge, Student Union Building, East Wing, 2:00 p.m. — First Session, Baldwin Auditorium: Speaker, Dr. Robert G. Ball, Central Teachers College, Pittsburgh, Pennsylvania, "A Changing, Progressing Business Education." 2:45 p.m. — Intermission. 3:00 p.m. — Speaker, Mr. Henry Reynolds, Philadelphia Public Schools, Philadelphia, Pennsylvania, "Curricular Problems in Business

Education As Viewed by a Supervisor of Business Education"; Speaker, Miss Marilyn Donnell, Illinois Junior College, Chicago, Illinois, "Answering the Needs of Today's Business World." 4:15 p.m. — Forum: Moderator, Dr. T. J. Collins, Department of Business Education, Eastern Academy, Newark, New Jersey; Discussants, Dr. Robert G. Ball, Mr. Henry Reynolds, Miss Marilyn Donnell. 6:45 p.m. — Dinner, State Room, Student Union Building, East Wing: Presiding, Mrs. Edith R. Jones, Department of Business Education, Southern University, Atlanta, Georgia; Speaker, Dr. K. T. Lerner, Director of Business Education, Ohio Western College, Toledo, Ohio.

2. Type a guide copy of the following report to the stockholders of the Wakefield Gypsum Company. Use your best judgment in planning the layout of the guide copy. Correct all errors and make the layout as attractive as possible. The report is to be photocopied.

To the stockholders —

Profits for the first nine months and the third quarter of this year, compared with corresponding periods of last year, were as follows —

	this year		last year	
	Amount	Per share	Amount	Per share
9 months Consolidated Companies;				
Profit before income taxes..................	$13,894,371	$4.86	$12,474,298	$4.36
Less United States and Foreign Taxes on Income.........	7,030,558	2.46	6,405,100	2.24
Profit after income taxes..	6,863,813	$2.40	6,069,198	$2.12
Dividends from *Subsidiaries* NOT CONSOLIDATED..	$84,725	.03	188,140	.07
3rd Quarter Consolidated Companies;				
Profit before Income Taxes	4,808,157	$1.68	$4,407,167	$1.54
Less United states and foreign Taxes on Income................	2,469,175	.86	2,253,296	.79
PROFIT AFTER INCOME TAXES................	$2,338,982	$.82	$2,153,871	$.75
Dividends from SUBSIDIARIES NOT CONSOLIDATED...............	22,887.00	.01	71,199.00	.03
NET Income.............	$2,361,869	$.83	$2,225,070	.78

PART 2 DUPLICATING MACHINES

"Marcia, here is the program for the company's awards dinner next week. We will need two hundred copies." Marcia often receives instructions such as these from her boss. It is Marcia's responsibility to decide which duplicating process to use. The business in which she works has stencil, fluid, and offset duplicating equipment. Each of these processes has its advantages. Marcia must know which process will be best for each job that her employer gives her.

Duplicating machines have been standard equipment in offices for many years. Where there is a need for many copies, duplicating equipment can meet the demand. In many large offices there is a central duplicating department. When you need many copies of a business paper, you send detailed instructions to the duplicating department, along with a master or stencil. The central duplicating department then makes the copies. In a small office you may be responsible for the entire operation. You will have to cut the stencil or master and operate the equipment. Some types

Illus. 10-5
The secretary often uses a stencil duplicator when many copies are needed.

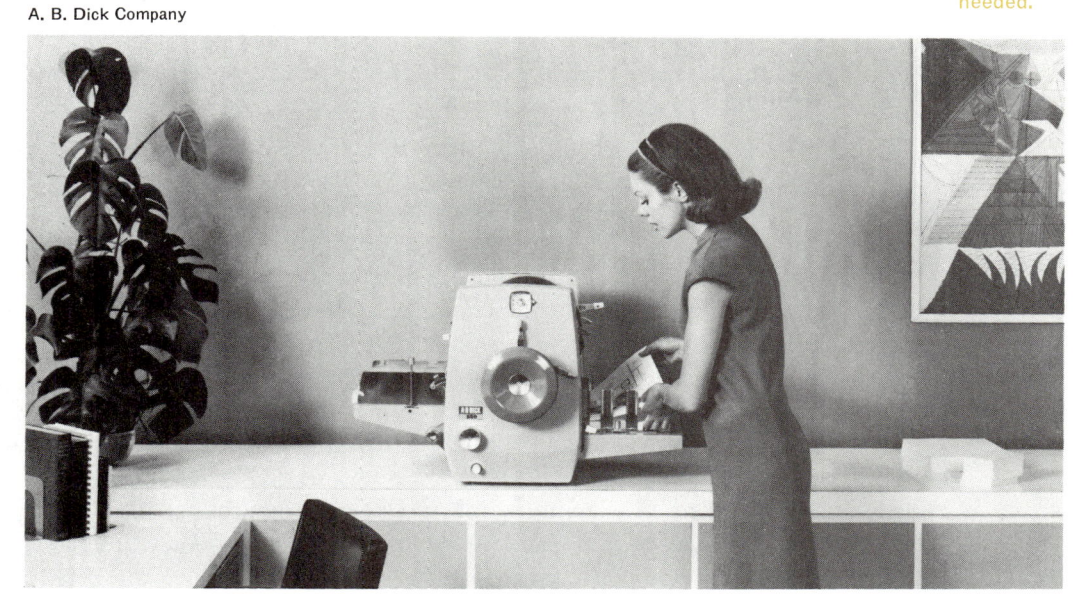

A. B. Dick Company

Part 2 / Duplicating Machines 349

of duplicators are very simple to operate; others require skilled operators. Copying machines are sometimes used to make the master copy for duplicating equipment, thus reducing the time you must take to type a master.

STENCIL DUPLICATING

You are likely to find in an office a stencil duplicating, or mimeograph, machine. It is a very dependable and versatile machine. You should know how to prepare stencils and how to operate the duplicator.

Features of Stencil Duplication

The stencil duplicator has the following features:

1. It is used when up to 10,000 copies are needed.
2. Copies are inexpensive for long runs and comparatively expensive for short runs.
3. Compared with the fluid duplicator, copies are of better quality; compared with the offset duplicator, copies are of poorer quality.
4. It is not too difficult to cut a stencil or to operate the duplicator.
5. Illustrations can be traced onto the stencil or manufactured insets may be purchased and used.
6. It can be used to reproduce color.
7. Stencils can be stored and used again when more copies of that item are needed.
8. It prints best on absorbent, rough finished paper of any color.

Principles of Stencil Duplication

The four elements necessary for the stencil duplication process are stencil, ink, copy paper, and the stencil duplicator. A stencil is prepared by pushing aside the wax coating on the fibrous stencil sheet with a typewriter key or a stylus. This is called *cutting a stencil* or *stencilization*. The stencil sheet is then placed on the stencil duplicator. Duplication occurs when ink flows through the openings made by the typewriter keys and comes in contact with the copy paper being fed through the machine.

Probably you will use a standard stencil more than any other type. By looking at the illustration on page 352, you can see that stencils are designed to aid you in placing properly the material to be duplicated. Following the guidelines and numerals shown will insure attractively positioned copies.

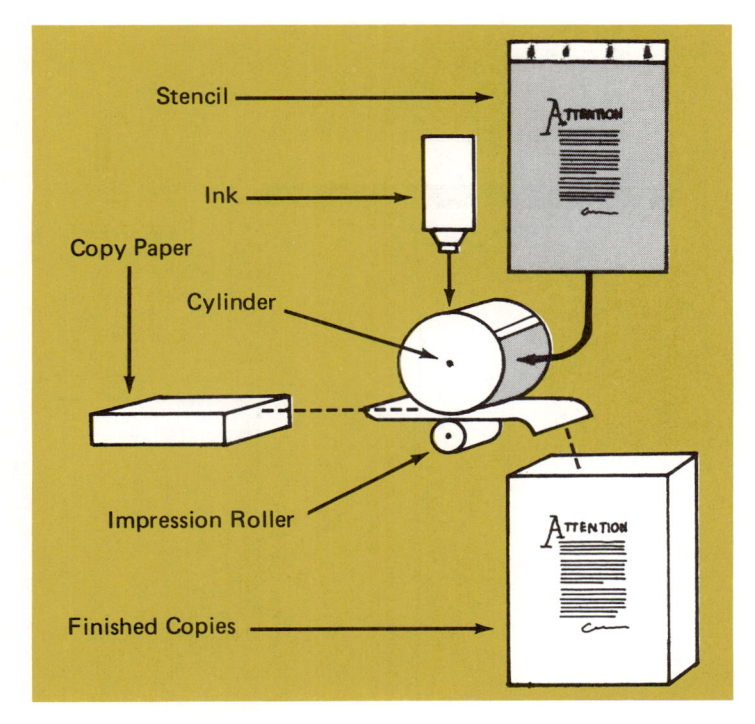

Illus. 10-6
Stencil duplication

A. B. Dick Company

Typing a Stencil

These are the steps that you should follow in typing a stencil:

1. *PREPARE THE GUIDE COPY.* To assure proper positioning on the stencil sheet, you should type the material to be put on the stencil on ordinary typing paper first. (Be sure to use the same size paper that will be used to run off the duplicated copies.) Remember that you must plan to stay within the boundary lines on the stencil sheet. As you gain experience in preparing a stencil, it usually will be unnecessary to prepare a guide copy unless the job is difficult.

2. *PREPARE THE TYPEWRITER.* Shift the ribbon control to "stencil" position. This disengages the ribbon and allows the type face to strike the stencil sheet directly.

    Clean the type. A type face covered with ink deposits from the ribbon can interfere with the "cutting" process.

    Move the paper bail rollers so that they are just outside the boundary markings on the stencil sheet.

Part 2 / Duplicating Machines 351

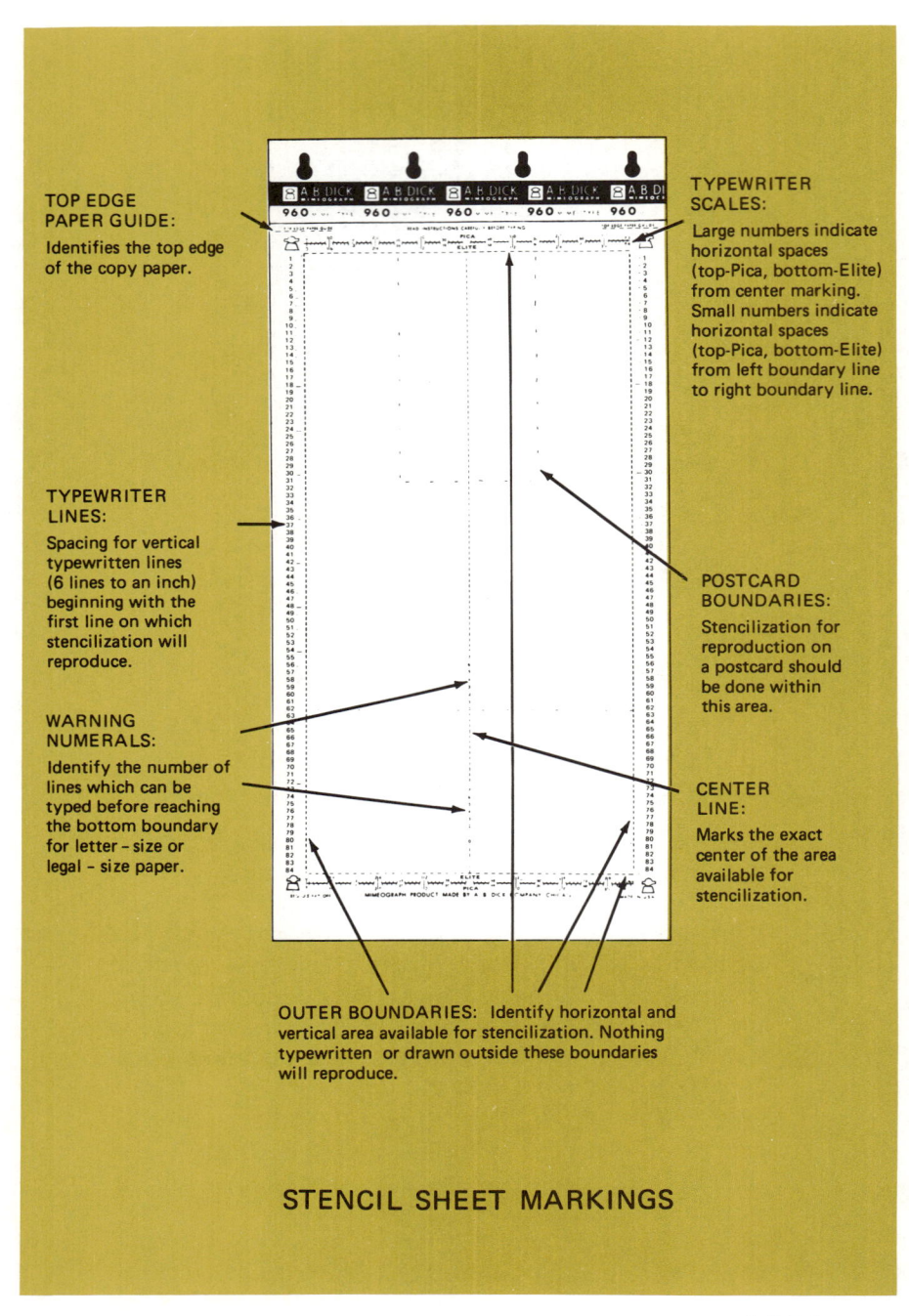

TOP EDGE PAPER GUIDE: Identifies the top edge of the copy paper.

TYPEWRITER LINES: Spacing for vertical typewritten lines (6 lines to an inch) beginning with the first line on which stencilization will reproduce.

WARNING NUMERALS: Identify the number of lines which can be typed before reaching the bottom boundary for letter – size or legal – size paper.

TYPEWRITER SCALES: Large numbers indicate horizontal spaces (top-Pica, bottom-Elite) from center marking. Small numbers indicate horizontal spaces (top-Pica, bottom-Elite) from left boundary line to right boundary line.

POSTCARD BOUNDARIES: Stencilization for reproduction on a postcard should be done within this area.

CENTER LINE: Marks the exact center of the area available for stencilization.

OUTER BOUNDARIES: Identify horizontal and vertical area available for stencilization. Nothing typewritten or drawn outside these boundaries will reproduce.

STENCIL SHEET MARKINGS

A. B. Dick Company

Illus. 10-7   Stencil sheet markings

3. *PREPARE THE STENCIL.* If the stencil has a protective sheet, remove it. Place the guide copy directly beneath the stencil sheet, making sure that the top edge of the guide copy is aligned with the top edge paper guide marking on the stencil sheet. Since you can see through the stencil sheet, it is easy to check the position of the guide copy beneath. Mark the stencil sheet with dots of correction fluid to aid in positioning the material when the stencil sheet is inserted in the typewriter. Remove the guide copy and lay it aside. Place the cellophane film over the stencil sheet and smooth it down. This film helps make the copy sharper. Insert the cushion sheet between the stencil sheet and the backing sheet.

4. *INSERT THE STENCIL IN THE TYPEWRITER.* With the backing sheet next to the platen, carefully roll the stencil into the typewriter, taking care to avoid wrinkling the stencil sheet. Straighten the stencil in the same manner that you would an ordinary sheet of typing paper. (Disengage the paper release, match top and bottom right corners and top and bottom left corners. Engage the paper release.)

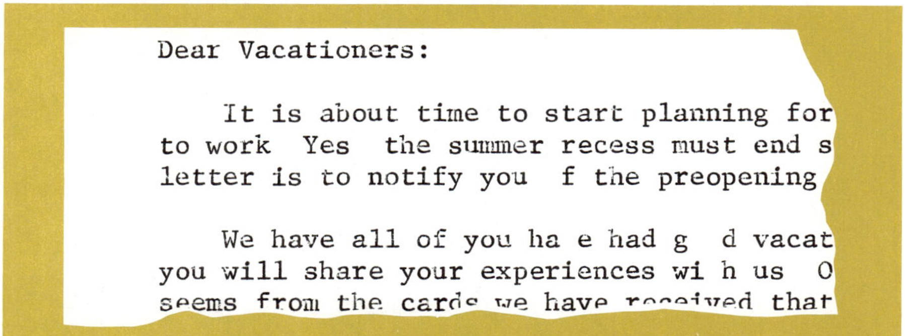

Illus. 10-8
A poorly cut stencil

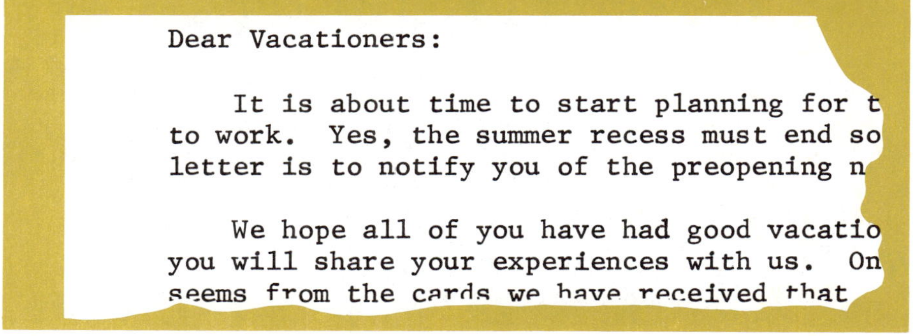

Illus. 10-9
A correctly cut stencil

A. B. Dick Company

Part 2 / Duplicating Machines

5. *TYPE THE STENCIL.* An electric typewriter automatically gives the even pressure needed for typing a stencil. If a manual typewriter is used, however, you will probably obtain better results if you type a little slower than your usual rate. Strike with greater force those letters and special characters that have a large printing surface, such as *M, W, E, A, $, #, &,* and *@,* so that the entire typeface area will cut through the stencil. Strike with less force letters and punctuation marks having small sharp printing surfaces, such as *c* and *o,* the comma, and the period.

6. *CORRECT ERRORS IMMEDIATELY AFTER THEY ARE MADE.* Lift the paper bail; turn the stencil up several lines so that you may work at the point the typing error occurred. If a film covers the stencil sheet, pull it loose from the top of the stencil assembly and lay it over the front of the typewriter. (The correction must be made on the stencil sheet itself.) Correct the error by lightly rubbing a rounded object

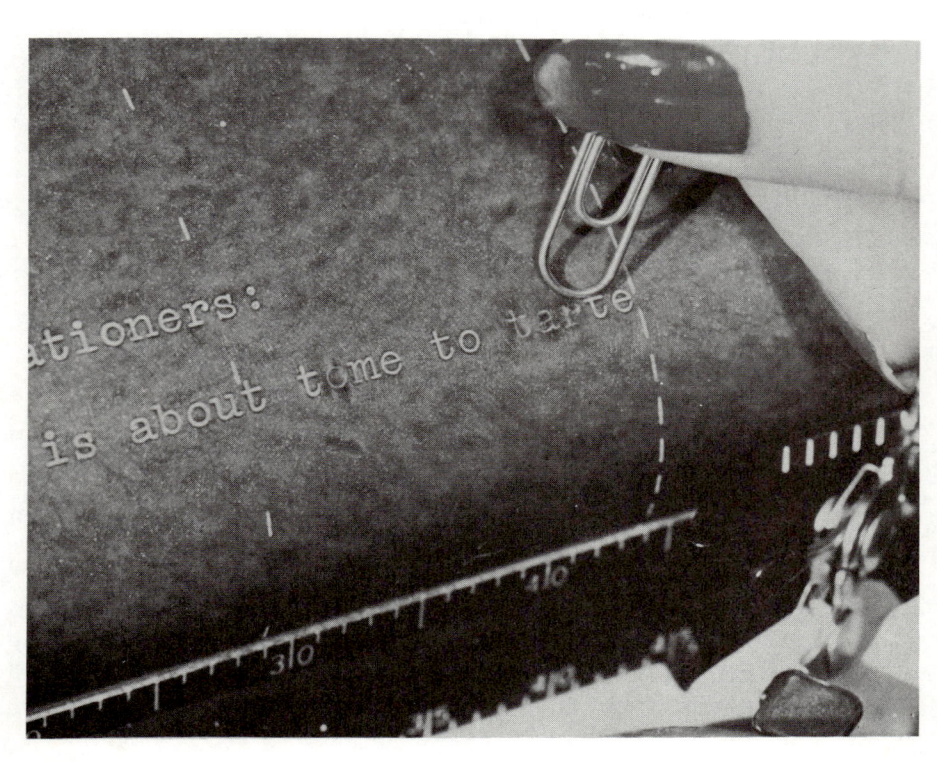

Illus. 10-10
Burnishing to correct an error

A. B. Dick Company

Unit 10 / Copying and Duplicating

such as a paper clip or a glass rod burnisher in a circular motion over the error. This corrects the error by smoothing a small amount of the surrounding stencil coating over the error.

Replace the coating to the area with a single upward stroke for each character from the brush of a bottle of stencil correction fluid, a chemical compound which is about the same as the stencil coating itself. Before applying fluid, be sure to remove the excess liquid from the correction brush. Only a thin coating is needed.

Replace the brush quickly; tighten the cap on the bottle. This prevents the fluid from becoming dry and thick. Allow 30 to 60 seconds for the fluid on the correction area to dry.

Roll the stencil back to typing position and then type the correction, using a stroke slightly heavier than normal. An extremely heavy stroke may cut too deeply into the weakened stencil fiber.

Illus. 10-11
Replace stencil coating with correction fluid

A. B. Dick Company

Part 2 / Duplicating Machines

7. *PROOFREAD.* Always proofread carefully and make corrections before removing the stencil from the typewriter. If you discover an error after the stencil has been removed, you must realign the stencil in the typewriter in the same position as when the copy was first typed.
8. *REMOVE THE STENCIL FROM THE TYPEWRITER.* To avoid wrinkling or damaging the stencil sheet, be sure to disengage the paper release before attempting to remove the stencil.

Duplicating

Detailed instructions of operation may be obtained from the manufacturer of the machine. Some machines have step-by-step directions attached to the duplicator. Since these instructions are designed for a particular machine, it is wise to study them carefully before attempting to duplicate copies.

FLUID DUPLICATING

You will probably find that the fluid duplicating process is the easiest to learn. When many copies are needed but the quality of the copies is not of great importance, you should probably use a fluid duplicator.

Features of Fluid Duplication

Fluid duplicators have the following features:

1. They are used when up to 200 copies are needed; although, with a well-typed master and careful operation of the duplicator, as many as 300 copies can be made from one master.
2. This is probably the least expensive duplicating process for about 10 to 30 copies.
3. It is easy to prepare a master and easy to operate the duplicator.
4. Copies are not as attractive as most other duplicating methods.
5. Several colors can be duplicated.
6. They print best on smooth-finished, glossy paper of any color.
7. The masters can be saved to be used again.
8. The purple dye from the master soils your hands very easily.

9. Handwriting and artwork can be produced easily and quickly.
10. They are used mostly for interoffice communications such as notices of meetings, informal reports, safety rules, and company activities.

Principles of Fluid Duplication

The five elements necessary for fluid duplication are a master sheet, carbon sheet, copy paper, fluid, and the fluid duplicator.

A master sheet is placed over the carbon side of a carbon sheet. Pressure on the face of the master with a typewriter or writing instrument deposits a carbon image on the back of the master sheet in reverse image.

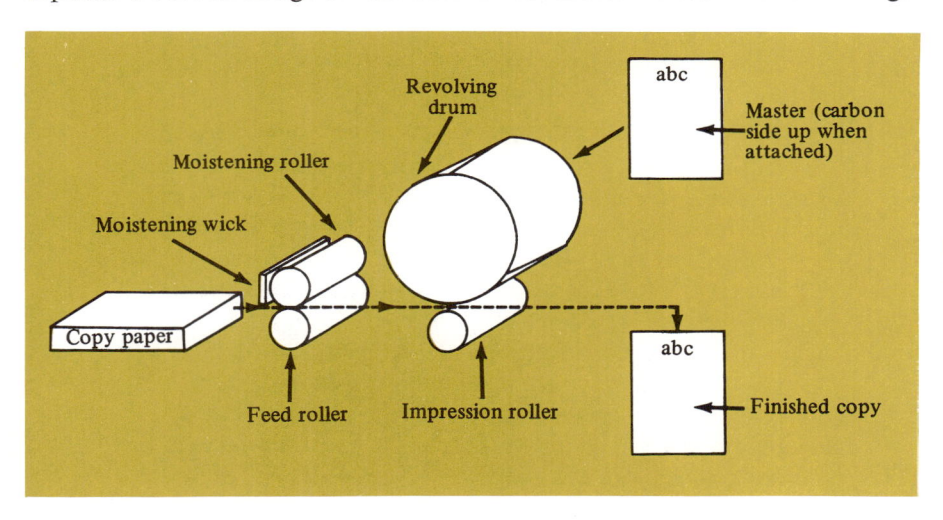

Illus. 10-12
Fluid duplicator

A. B. Dick Company

The master sheet is placed on the cylinder of the fluid duplicator. As the cylinder rotates, the master comes in contact with a sheet of copy paper which has been moistened with an alcohol-like fluid as the paper enters the duplicator. The fluid causes a very light coating of carbon to transfer from the master sheet to the copy paper.

Preparing a Master

You will have best results when preparing a typewritten master by following these instructions:

1. *PLAN THE PLACEMENT OF THE COPY ON THE MASTER.* Leave at least one-half inch blank at the top or bottom of the master. This allows space for the master to be clamped onto the cylinder (either end of the master can be attached to the cylinder).

2. *PREPARE THE TYPEWRITER.* Clean the type well, giving extra attention to type faces where ink is likely to accumulate, such as *e, a, w, g, o.*

3. *INSERT THE SET IN THE TYPEWRITER.* The *set* refers to the sheet of master paper and the sheet of carbon. The open end of the master should be inserted first in the typewriter so that you can make corrections on the master without separating the master sheet from the carbon sheet. As you see it in your typewriter, the white master sheet is nearest you; the carbon is next, carbon side toward you. Be sure to remove the tissue sheet between the master sheet and the carbon sheet before inserting it in the typewriter. If your typewriter does not have a smooth, medium hard platen, place a sheet of heavy paper or pliant plastic behind the carbon sheet to serve as a backing sheet.

4. *TYPE THE MASTER.* An electric typewriter automatically gives the even pressure needed for typing a master. If a manual typewriter is used, you will probably obtain better results if you type a little slower than your usual rate. The carbon will be deposited on the back of the sheet on which you type, thus making a reverse reading copy.

   Because of the positioning of the materials in the typewriter, typing results in a positive ribbon image on the front of the master sheet, which makes proofreading easy, and a reverse reading carbon image on the back of the master sheet.

5. *CORRECT ERRORS.* If corrections are necessary, make them according to the information which follows:

   When you type a master copy, your typing simply puts carbon deposits on the back of the master sheet. When you make an error, you have carbon where you do not want it. Be sure to make the correction on the carbon deposit side of the master sheet.

   To correct an error (as in a misspelled word), you must first eliminate the error. The best procedure for this is to lightly scrape off the unwanted carbon deposit with a razor blade or knife or cover the error with correction tape. After the error has been removed, you are ready to type the correction.

   However, remembering that *fluid carbon paper can be used only once*, and that you have used the carbon at that point where you typed the error, you must provide some new carbon there. So, insert a slip of fresh carbon (cut from the bottom of the carbon sheet or from another carbon sheet) under the master at the point where you must type the correction; after you type the correction, remove the extra carbon slip before going on.

6. *PROOFREAD.* Always proofread and make corrections before removing the master from the typewriter.

7. *DISENGAGE THE PAPER RELEASE AND REMOVE THE SET FROM THE TYPEWRITER.* Carefully separate the master sheet from the carbon sheet, and discard the carbon sheet. Cover the carbon side of the master copy with the tissue sheet to protect it until it is attached to the machine for duplicating.

Illus. 10-13
Fluid master in the typewriter

Bell & Howell

OFFSET DUPLICATING

If your employer wants a large number of copies of a business paper and the quality of reproduction is very important, the job should be done on an offset duplicator. Copies made on an offset duplicator are of a much finer quality than those made on a stencil or fluid duplicator.

Features of Offset Duplication

Offset duplication has the following features:

1. Copies of excellent quality are produced. The copy looks like the type on the page of this book.
2. Many thousands of copies can be produced from a master.
3. Cost is moderate for short runs and inexpensive for long runs.
4. Masters are easily prepared, but machine operation is difficult.
5. Copies can be produced in many colors.
6. Many copies can be produced quickly.
7. Copies can be printed on a variety of weights, sizes, colors, and quality of paper.

It is quite unlikely that you will operate an offset duplicator. A skilled operator is needed to run these machines. Usually both the operators and the machines will be found in the central duplicating department. You, however, may have to prepare the offset masters for the material to be duplicated.

Illus. 10-14
Offset duplicator

A. B. Dick Company

Preparing Offset Masters

Preparing a paper master with the use of a typewriter or special writing tools is a simple process.

1. *PREPARE TYPEWRITER.* Type faces should be clean and feed rolls and platen free of ink smudges and deposits. You should use typewriter ribbons of carbon plastic, carbon paper, or special grease fabric because they are receptive to the special offset ink.

    Move the paper bail rollers outside the lined left and right boundary markings on the master to prevent the rollers from smearing the type. Avoid using too much hand cream when handling a master. Greasy deposits on the master will pick up ink during duplication.

2. *INSERT MASTER.* Insert the master so that the markings on it face you. Guide markings on paper masters include a top edge paper guide, center markings for both 8″ and 8½″ wide paper, and warning numerals for use when nearing the bottom of 11″ and 14″ long paper.

3. *TYPE MASTER.* Use an even touch in typing, firm enough to deposit a uniformly dark image. A too heavy touch results in embossing on the reserve side of the master. Avoid embossing since the embossed letters may be pressed beyond the reach of the ink roller, resulting in hollow-looking letters. Set the pressure control on an electric typewriter to the lowest position where all characters will print.

4. *CORRECTING ERRORS.* A very soft, nongreasy eraser must be used. Special offset erasers produce best results.

    Erase the image very lightly with a "lifting" motion. It is necessary only to remove the greasy deposit. It is not necessary to remove the ghost image left since this image will not reproduce. The slick finish on the master should not be damaged. Keep the eraser clean by frequently rubbing it on a piece of clean paper.

Photo-Offset Masters

There are two types of offset duplicating masters: paper masters and metal masters (sometimes referred to as aluminum plates). Short-run, medium-run, and long-run masters may be purchased. Up to 5,000 copies can be obtained from a single long-run paper master, but 25,000 or more copies can be run from an aluminum plate. The short-run paper masters are the least expensive; the aluminum plates are most expensive.

ELECTRONIC STENCIL OR MASTER MAKERS

The firm for which you will work may have a machine that will make offset masters, fluid masters, and stencils for you. With these machines, the original copy is wrapped around one cylinder and an offset master, a fluid master, or a stencil is wrapped around another cylinder. When the machine is started, the original copy is exactly reproduced on the master or stencil in a matter of minutes. The process is faster than the manual typing of masters or stencils. Also, it completely eliminates the need for proofreading the master or stencil because an exact copy is produced, whether it is an engineer's drawing, a complicated tabulation, a detailed business form, or an interoffice communication.

QUESTIONS

1. What is another name for a stencil duplicating machine?
2. What are some of the features of stencil duplication?
3. How is the typewriter prepared for typing a stencil?
4. Describe how to make corrections on a stencil.
5. Why should you proofread a stencil before you remove it from the typewriter?
6. List four of the most important features of the fluid duplicator.
7. Why should you leave at least one-half inch blank space at the top or bottom of the fluid master?
8. Describe how the fluid master set is inserted in the typewriter.
9. Describe how to make a correction on a fluid master.
10. What are two special features of the offset process which make it superior to either stencil or fluid duplicating?

JUDGMENT

1. In your office there is frequently a need for multiple copies. What factors should be considered in deciding which method of duplication would best fit your needs?
2. Many operators of the special types of duplicating machines learn the method of operation on the job. What then are the advantages, if any, of becoming familiar with these machines while in school?

PERSONAL QUALITIES

You work in the office of an insurance company that has a duplicator used by nine of the employees. It seems that the machine is frequently out of order when you want to use it. On several occasions you notice that the machine controls have not been turned off when you must use the machine. Also, there always seems to be a great deal of waste copies around the machine because users are not getting good copies all the time. This seems to be a case of "everyone's responsibility is no one's responsibility." What should you do?

LANGUAGE USAGE

Type the correct spelling of each of the following words:

1. secede — seceed — sesede
2. exceed — excede — exsede
3. procede — proceed — prosede
4. intersede — interceed — intercede
5. preceed — precede — presede
6. sucess — succes — success
7. sensible — sensable — sensibel
8. independent — independant — independint
9. responsable — responsible — responseble
10. comittee — commitee — committee

SECRETARIAL WORK

1. The following announcement is to be reproduced on a stencil duplicator and sent to all the salesmen in the field. Type the stencil. If stencils are not available, type the announcement on plain paper.

   To all company salesmen:

   Because of rising costs it will be necessary to increase prices on canned fruits. The new prices indicated below will go into effect on the first day of next month.

Stock Numbers	Name	Present Price (Case)	New Price (Case)
CF 27	Sliced Apples	6.18	6.48
CF 28	Applesauce	5.10	5.45
CF 31	Fruit Cocktail	8.04	8.55
CF 36	Peaches (Halves)	6.22	6.53
CF 38	Peaches (Sliced)	6.15	6.45
CF 41	Pears (Halves)	8.15	8.60
CF 45	Pineapple (Sliced)	7.56	8.04
CF 50	Pineapple (Crushed)	6.14	6.45

2. The material shown below and at the top of page 364 is to be reproduced on a fluid duplicator. Type the material in tabular form on a fluid duplicating master. Rule the form. If fluid masters are not available, use plain paper.

   Comparison of Estimated and Actual Expenses.

   Last year:

   Sales Salaries: Estimated, $7,000.00; Actual, $7,118.00
   Office Salaries: Estimated, $7,500.00; Actual, $7,556.00
   Delivery Expense: Estimated, $1,600.00; Actual, $1,591.05
   Advertising: Estimated, $300.00; Actual, $312.95
   Rent: Estimated, $1,500.00; Actual, $1,500.00
   Supplies: Estimated, $300.00; Actual, $287.60
   Insurance: Estimated, $2,100.00; Actual, $2,100.00
   Depreciation: Estimated, $500.00; Actual, $521.16
   Miscellaneous: Estimated, $350.00; Actual, $357.35

This year:

Sales Salaries: Estimated, $7,500.00; Actual, $7,439.00
Office Salaries: Estimated, $7,800.00; Actual $7,780.00
Delivery Expense: Estimated, $1,650.00; Actual, $1,612.45
Advertising: Estimated, $350.00; Actual, $365.75
Rent: Estimated, $1,500.00; Actual, $1,500.00
Supplies: Estimated, $350.00; Actual, $342.75
Insurance: Estimated, $2,250.00; Actual, $2,250.00
Depreciation: Estimated, $550.00; Actual, $565.32
Miscellaneous: Estimated, $400.00, Actual, $392.40

Unit 11 BUSINESS FILING

Part 1. Records Control
    2. Alphabetic Filing Rules for Names of Individuals
    3. Alphabetic Filing Rules for Business Firms and Other Organizations
    4. Filing Equipment and Supplies for Correspondence

The secretary controls the records and files within her office. Unless she knows and understands the rules of filing, she will not be able to find papers needed by her executive when they are requested.

VOCABULARY BUILDER

> *Teach thy tongue to say, "I do not know."*
> **Talmud**

neglected ....
    adjective: given little attention or respect; disregarded; left undone or unattended to especially through carelessness

prospective ....
    adjective: relating to or effective in the future; expected

procedure ....
    noun: a particular way of accomplishing something or acting

assumes ....
    verb: takes; receives; takes to or upon oneself

vertical ....
    adjective: upright

lateral ....
    adjective: situated on, directed toward, or coming from the side

maximum ....
    adjective: the greatest quantity or value attainable

logically ....
    adverb: in accordance with inferences reasonably drawn from events or circumstances

consistency ....
    noun: agreement or harmony of parts or features to one another or a whole

accessories ....
    noun: a thing of secondary importance; an object or device not essential in itself

p. 370   Filing is one of the most important — yet one of the most **neglected** — duties performed by most office workers.

p. 371   To find the names of customers and **prospective** customers in the parts of the country in which they are located, some offices maintain geographic files.

p. 379   When you have identical names in filing, they are indexed by the usual **procedure**; but the filing....

p. 380   When a woman marries, the only part of her husband's name that she legally **assumes** is his last name.

p. 406   The typical pull-out drawer file cabinet — the **vertical** file — is used in most business offices.

p. 407   Because of the increasing number of records that must be kept in expensive office space, many organizations are now using **lateral** ... files.

p. 408   Units that are seven or eight shelves high provide the **maximum** amount of filing area for the floor space....

p. 412   Miscellaneous folders should be examined often so that individual and special folders may be prepared to expand the filing system **logically**.

p. 413   **Consistency** in typing captions on labels is important.

p. 415   In addition to filing cabinets, guides, and folders, there are many **accessories** that will make your filing job easier.

PART 11 RECORDS CONTROL

"Carol, get me the files on the Jenkins contract. Mr. Jenkins is on the phone with a question." Mr. Ashburn knows that his secretary, Carol Hirsch, will find the contract and bring it to him within just a few minutes. In addition to her other fine qualities, Carol understands the importance of being able to file business papers properly and of being able to *find* them quickly when they are needed.

Compare Carol with the girl who thought to herself: Where is it? I know I put that letter away carefully so that I could find it quickly — but where? These were the thoughts that raced through the mind of a secretary as she searched nervously for the letter for which her boss was impatiently waiting. *If only she had filed it correctly in the first place!* Don't let this happen to you!

Illus. 11-1
File it correctly so that it can be found quickly!

Remington Rand

Part 1 / Records Control 367

In our high-speed "computer age" it might surprise you to learn that paper work must accompany every business action. Even a telephone call may require papers to place an order, report on a shipment, or make a payment. The information contained in these papers forms the basis for a variety of decisions and moves the business forward.

All the records which you will file will be important to the continued successful operation of your firm. The records become part of the *memory* of the organization. Not only do the records provide a history of the business, but they also provide a basis for future decisions. In today's business offices, important decisions are based upon available up-to-date information. The risks are too great for an executive's decisions to be based upon guesses or hunches.

The proper care of records is also important to every family. Everyone has records to keep — insurance policies, appliance guarantees, bills, receipts, apartment leases. Those who do not keep these personal records in order soon see their insurance policies lapse because the premiums have not been paid; service cannot be obtained when an appliance breaks down because the guarantee cannot be found; bills become overdue; or an item is charged for twice because the receipt from the first payment cannot be found.

RECORDS CONTROL

Every important record, whether it belongs to the nation's largest business or to its smallest, must be stored where it can be found when needed. The regular way in which a business keeps track of its records and correspondence is called *records control*. Since business information is created and spread about in so many different ways, a records control program plays an important role in providing the "business intelligence" of any firm for which you may work.

Four main areas with which records control is concerned are:

1. *Files Management* — Developing effective information (or filing) systems, deciding upon the particular type of equipment and supplies needed for each of the systems, and controlling and improving the different systems.
2. *Information Retrieval* — Developing effective and rapid methods of retrieving, or finding, filed information.
3. *Records Protection* — Deciding what the vital records of a firm are and developing a program for protecting them. (*Vital* records are the important papers of a business that are needed to continue operating after a fire or some other disaster.)

4. *Records Retention and Disposition* — Determining which records should be kept, where they should be kept and for how long; deciding when and how outdated records should be destroyed.

FILES KEPT BY THE SECRETARY

As a secretary, you will be responsible for keeping your employer's business records in an orderly fashion. You may be expected to decide which material should be filed, where it should be filed, and how it should be filed. A great deal of mail that is addressed to your employer (advertisements, announcements, and other third-class mail) need not be filed at all. When you are first employed, a brief discussion of the files with your employer should prove helpful in deciding which material should be thrown away and how the material to be filed should be classified. Most large firms have a records retention schedule which can help you classify materials as to their importance. In addition to the regular business files of your office, your employer may ask you to keep a separate file of his personal correspondence which may include records of his civic and professional activities.

CENTRAL FILES

Many firms find it economical to maintain a central file of all materials that may be needed by different departments or by the entire organization. It is also possible that a large department within an organization, such as the purchasing department, may centralize its own files.

Because the file clerks in a central file department are well-trained specialists and are properly supervised, faster and better filing service is possible. A central file department eliminates the keeping of duplicate copies of material and makes for more efficient use of filing equipment and filing floor space. The central file department should always serve as an active information file — not just as a place for filing old and unneeded records. As a secretary, you will work with the central file department. You will have to decide which material must be filed in central files and which material should be kept in your own office. You will also have to know how to call for information kept in the central files.

FILING

What is filing? *Filing* is a system of arranging and storing business papers in a neat, orderly, and efficient manner so that they can be located easily and quickly when they are wanted.

Filing is one of the *most important* — yet one of the most neglected — duties performed by most office workers. Errors in filing may appear to be funny in cartoons, but they are costly and embarrassing in a business office. Your employer doesn't expect to have to wait for filed copies of his correspondence or other business papers.

In order to *find* material efficiently, you must follow standard rules and procedures of filing. Not only must you know the rules of filing and apply them but you must also keep your files up to date by giving some part of every day to filing. Otherwise you may get so far behind that you will have to search through the files and then the unfiled material on your desk when you are asked to produce information.

SYSTEMS OF FILING

The most important reason for having a filing system is so that you can locate information quickly. Filing systems should be developed around the way records are called for, or the way they are used.

Alphabetic Name Files

Since most business records are referred to by the name of a firm, these names determine the type of filing system that will be used. This system of filing, known as an *alphabetic file,* is the most widely used in business. When you look for a firm name in a telephone directory, you are using this system.

Illus. 11-2
Alphabetic name file

The Globe-Wernicke Systems Co.

370 Unit 11 / Business Filing

Alphabetic Subject Files

Another filing system found in most business offices is an *alphabetic subject file*. The Yellow Pages of a telephone directory are arranged in alphabetic subject file order. Under the letter *E* in the Yellow Pages you will find such subject headings as Employment Agencies, Employment Contractors — Temporary Help, Employment Counselors, and Employment Service. Most offices have both an alphabetic company name file and also a subject file.

Geographic Files

To find the names of customers and prospective customers in the parts of the country in which they are located, some offices maintain geographic files. A geographic file may be set up according to the name of a state and then be further subdivided by the sales territories within the state, or by cities, towns, or counties. Sales offices and magazine publishers are two users of geographic filing systems.

Numeric Files

Since some business papers are identified by number rather than by name, numeric files are frequently used. Life insurance companies file their policies by the policy number. However, in addition to the main numeric file, an alphabetic file by the names of all policyholders (listing their policy numbers as well) is also kept on cards or on computer tape for fast retrieval.

Chronological Files

Another basic filing system is the chronological file, a file maintained in the order of time according to the year, month, and day. For example, an automobile insurance company would keep a chronological file showing the exact day of the year on which each automobile owner's insurance policy expires. This helps the company prepare and mail a new policy to each owner before his current automobile insurance expires.

To help your employer plan his day, you would also use a chronological file. These files are kept for daily appointments, conferences, and other important business engagements. A desk calendar is one form of chronological filing. Other chronological files of unfinished, pending, or follow-up work may be kept in a *tickler file*, a file arranged according to the days of the month. Since it is almost impossible to remember everything that must be done on a given business day, a chronological file should be developed and checked daily so that proper action may be taken at the right time.

THE CARE OF RECORDS

For business purposes, records are classified in four general groups: vital, important, useful, and nonessential. All records considered essential to the operation and growth of an organization, such as the financial statements, legal papers, and tax records, are classified as *vital records*. At least 43 percent of the business firms that lose their vital records in a fire, flood, or tornado are forced to go out of business. These records should be protected by microfilming them and storing the microfilm in a fireproof cabinet, or by photocopying them and filing the copies in another location.

Now let us consider the next two classifications: important and useful records. *Important records* are those which could be replaced, such as personnel records, but only at great expense. These records should also receive a degree of protection because of their confidential nature. *Useful records*, such as the records of accounts payable, are those which can be replaced — but with some delay and inconvenience. They should be kept in regular file cabinets.

Finally, we must be concerned with nonessential records. *Nonessential records*, such as press releases, are those which soon outlive their usefulness — perhaps some of them should never have been filed in the first place. They should be destroyed to save valuable file space and floor space. Records management experts estimate that over 40 percent of the material in active office files is nonessential and can be safely destroyed in short order — or immediately — without any embarrassment or inconvenience to anyone.

Illus. 11-3
The proper care of records is necessary. These records survived a scorching fire because of careful storage in fireproof files.

Shaw-Walker

RECORDS CONTROL AND THE SECRETARY

Much of your secretarial time will be taken up by matters related to records control. When you are typing a letter, you are preparing a record (the carbon copy) for the files. When you are reading and deciding what to do with incoming mail, you are preparing materials for filing. The result of almost *all* your secretarial duties will be placed in the files.

To be most effective as an assistant to your executive, you must thoroughly understand business filing and records control procedures. These procedures and the supplies and equipment with which you will be working are covered in the parts that follow.

QUESTIONS
1. Why do business firms keep records?
2. Name and describe four main areas of records control and management.
3. Define the term *filing*.
4. Name five systems of filing.
5. Give an example of a *vital* record. An *important* record. A *useful* record.

JUDGMENT
1. What problems could a business have if it did not have an orderly way of storing and finding important business papers?
2. If you work in a business that has a central file department with filing specialists to take care of the records of the business, why will it still be necessary for you to have a knowledge of filing and records control?

PERSONAL QUALITIES

Sheila Baker, a recent high school graduate, accepted her first full-time position as a stenographer in the purchasing department of a very large company. During her first two weeks of work, the woman supervisor of the department acquainted her with the department's operations. The supervisor also explained the tasks and duties for which Sheila alone would be responsible.

After introducing Sheila to her co-workers and giving her an overview of the purchasing department and what it does, Mrs. Williams, the supervisor, explained to Sheila the filing system used in the department. Sheila was then given several correspondence files to read and prepare for filing. While having lunch with several of the girls in the department, Sheila commented that she didn't know if she would stay on this job or not. "After all," she said, "I accepted this position to be a stenographer, not a file clerk."

Is Sheila correct in having doubts about her new position? Could the supervisor have chosen another way of teaching Sheila the basics of her job? How can reading correspondence and preparing it for filing help a new employee?

LANGUAGE USAGE

On a sheet of paper list the words in Column 1. Then write the number of the definition for each word from Column 2.

Example:

(a) retrieval   (3) act or process of recovering or finding

Column 1
- (a) retrieval
- (b) manually
- (c) retention
- (d) disposition
- (e) chronological
- (f) essential
- (g) inconvenience
- (h) document
- (i) capacity
- (j) client
- (k) embarrassment

Column 2
- (1) not suitable, unfit
- (2) confusion or distress of thought, speech, or action
- (3) act or process of recovering or finding
- (4) act of ordering or arranging in an orderly way
- (5) relating to or involving the hands
- (6) a maximum measure of content or output
- (7) arranged by date or by order of occurrence
- (8) official paper; writing conveying information
- (9) a person who engages the professional services of another
- (10) act of keeping in possession or use
- (11) belonging to the nature of things

SECRETARIAL WORK

You have just accepted a position with the City Haul Trucking Company, Inc., 105 Grand Boulevard, South, St. Louis, Missouri 63103, which just began operations a month ago. This company picks up local parcels — small and medium sized — for delivery to large interstate trucking companies. Since St. Louis is a connecting point between the eastern and western sections of the country, it will be necessary to have a filing system which incorporates many features. Files will have to be set up for accounts payable and accounts receivable, purchases, receipts, costs of truck maintenance, payroll, personnel, correspondence, records of daily pickups and daily deliveries, and claim files for lost or damaged parcels.

Consult the Yellow Pages of your local telephone directory under Filing Equipment, Systems & Supplies, and then compose and type letters to be sent to at least two companies explaining your problem, requesting information, literature, and the assistance of one of their representatives.

PART 2 — ALPHABETIC FILING RULES FOR NAMES OF INDIVIDUALS

> When Diane Grollman was hired as the secretary to Mr. Walter Stalder, she was surprised to be told that one error in filing could cost as much as $92. Diane quickly realized that if she was going to be valuable to Mr. Stalder she would have to recall and use all the filing rules that she had learned in school. Diane's care in filing and knowledge of proper procedures have made it possible for her to work without having misfiled one item in over two years.

A filing system is costly to set up and maintain. Therefore, if the system you use is to be worth this high cost, the information in it must be available when it is needed. This means that business correspondence and other filed materials must be arranged in an exact and established order.

FILING RULES

Every filing method makes use of filing rules. Only if you know the standard rules for filing, and apply them the same way every time, can you find the filed materials quickly when they are needed.

The most widely used method of filing is based on the alphabet; however, because of difficulties involved in indexing some materials or because of the great volume of materials filed, other filing methods have been developed. These are numeric, geographic, and subject filing.

In certain cases, where more specialized filing procedures are used, you will need on-the-job training to fully understand these methods. By following one set of filing rules and recognizing the importance of records control, you will be of great assistance to your employer and play an important role in the successful operation of your office. Since every business, regardless of its size, uses one or more alphabetic filing method, it is important that you learn the rules for alphabetic filing.

ALPHABETIC INDEXING FOR INDIVIDUALS

The first step in filing procedures is *indexing*. When you arrange names for filing purposes, you are indexing. The rules for alphabetic indexing begin at the top of page 376.

1. Personal Names

When you consider the name Walter B. Anderson, each word and each initial or abbreviation is a separate *indexing unit*. Thus, you have three indexing units. The units of an individual's name are considered in this order: (a) last name, or surname; (b) first name, initial, or abbreviation; (c) middle name, initial, or abbreviation. Therefore *Anderson* is the first indexing unit, *Walter* is the second, and *B.* is the third. (In the examples, the names are in alphabetic order.)

```
Anderson, Walter B.      | 72

Walter B. Anderson
575 Crane Road
Middletown, NY 10940
```

INDEX ORDER OF UNITS

Names	Unit 1	Unit 2	Unit 3
Walter B. Anderson	Anderson	Walter	B.
Henry David Brown	Brown	Henry	David
Edward J. Cox	Cox	Edward	J.
A. B. Davis	Davis	A.	B.

2. Surnames (Last Names)

When the last names of individuals are different, the alphabetic order is determined by the last names alone. *The letter that determines the order of any two names is the first letter that is different in the two names.* In the following lists the underlined letter in each last name determines the alphabetic order of that name when compared with the preceding name. Note that when one last name is the same as the first part of a longer last name, the shorter name goes before the longer. This is often called the *nothing before something* rule of filing order.

Last Names	Last Names	Last Names
Hall	Hoffman	Johns
Hill	Hoffmann	Johnston
Hull	Hofmann	Johnstone

3. Last Names Containing Prefixes

A last name containing a prefix is considered as one indexing unit. The common prefixes include *D', De, Del, du, Fitz, La, Mac, Mc, O', Van, Von,* and *Von der.* Spacing between the prefix and the rest of the last name, or capitalization of the prefix makes no difference when indexing. Note that the prefixes *Mac* and *Mc* do not go before other names beginning with the letter *M* but are placed in strict alphabetic order.

INDEX ORDER OF UNITS

Names	Unit 1	Unit 2	Unit 3
Frances C. D'Arcy	D'Arcy	Frances	C.
Mario L. Del Favero	Del Favero	Mario	L.
Robert J. du Pont	du Pont	Robert	J.
Malcolm Paul MacDonald	MacDonald	Malcolm	Paul
James J. Manning	Manning	James	J.
Helen C. McConnell	McConnell	Helen	C.
Charles H. Mead	Mead	Charles	H.
Mary M. O'Shea	O'Shea	Mary	M.
Henry T. Van Allan	Van Allan	Henry	T.
Carol A. Van Derbeck	Van Derbeck	Carol	A.
Elsie D. von Koch	von Koch	Elsie	D.

4. Compound Last Names

A compound last name (*Fuller-Smith*, for example) is indexed as two separate units. The hyphen is ignored. In a last name such as *St. Claire*, *St.* is considered to be the first unit (in spelled-out form as *Saint*) and *Claire* the second unit. *St.* is not considered a prefix as in Rule 3 because it is an abbreviation for the word *Saint*. The prefixes in Rule 3 are not abbreviations.

INDEX ORDER OF UNITS

Names	Unit 1	Unit 2	Unit 3
Michael Ross-Harris	Ross(-)	Harris	Michael
Robert J. Ross	Ross	Robert	J.
Allen Ross-Sanders	Ross(-)	Sanders	Allen
George J. Rosse	Rosse	George	J.
Edwin St. Claire	Saint	Claire	Edwin
Gerald St. John	Saint	John	Gerald
Marie T. Satone	Satone	Marie	T.
Harold Twigg-Porter	Twigg(-)	Porter	Harold

5. Given Names (First Names)

When the last names are alike, you consider the first names in determining the alphabetic order. When the last names and the first names are both alike, the middle names determine the alphabetic order, as illustrated at the top of page 378.

INDEX ORDER OF UNITS

Names	Unit 1	Unit 2	Unit 3
William A. Smith	Smith	William	A.
Winifred C. Smith	Smith	Winifred	C.
Walter Clark Thompson	Thompson	Walter	Clark
Walter Crane Thompson	Thompson	Walter	Crane

6. Initials and Abbreviated First or Middle Names

A first initial is considered an indexing unit and goes before all names that begin with the same letter. An abbreviated first or middle name (*Wm.* for *William*, for example) is usually treated as if it were spelled in full. Originally a nickname — *Bob* for *Robert*, *Larry* for *Lawrence*, etc. — was always indexed as if written in full. Recently, however, many names formerly considered nicknames have become given names. Unless the first name is thought to be a nickname — *Tom* for *Thomas* — it should be indexed as written.

INDEX ORDER OF UNITS

Names	Unit 1	Unit 2	Unit 3
R. Robert Brogan	Brogan	R.	Robert
Robt. R. Brogan	Brogan	Robert	R.
Robert Richard Brogan	Brogan	Robert	Richard
Sam F. Brogan	Brogan	Sam	F.
Sam'l George Brogan	Brogan	Samuel	George

7. Unusual Names

When you can't decide which part of a name (usually a foreign name) is the last name, the last part of the name as written should be considered the last name. This type of name is often cross-referenced as explained on page 395.

INDEX ORDER OF UNITS

Names	Unit 1	Unit 2	Unit 3
Juan Maria Mallendez	Mallendez	Juan	Maria
Boyd Nelson	Nelson	Boyd	
Arthur Patrick	Patrick	Arthur	
Lee Kuan Yew	Yew	Lee	Kuan
Geza Zsak	Zsak	Geza	

8. Identical Personal Names

When you have identical names in filing, they are indexed by the usual procedure; but the filing order is determined by the parts of the address as follows:

(a) Town or City Name
(b) State Name
(c) Street Name
(d) House Number (in numeric order)

INDEX ORDER OF UNITS

IDENTIFYING ELEMENTS
(another way to determine alphabetic order when the names are the same)

Names	Unit 1	Unit 2	Unit 3	City	State	Street	House Number
Charles G. Grant 145 Beach Street Kingston, IL 60145	Grant	Charles	G.	Kingston	Illinois	Beach	145
Charles G. Grant 204 Pearl Street Kingston, NY 12401	Grant	Charles	G.	Kingston	New York	Pearl	204
Charles G. Grant 177 State Street Kingston, NY 12401	Grant	Charles	G.	Kingston	New York	State	177
Charles G. Grant 350 State Street Kingston, NY 12401	Grant	Charles	G.	Kingston	New York	State	350

9. Seniority in Identical Names

A term indicating seniority, such as *Senior* or *Junior*, or *II* (*Second*) or *III* (*Third*), is not considered an indexing unit. The term is used as an identifying element in determining the alphabetic order for filing purposes.

INDEX ORDER OF UNITS **IDENTIFYING ELEMENTS**

Names	Unit 1	Unit 2	Seniority Titles
John Young	Young	John	
John Young, IV	Young	John	(Fourth)
John Young, Jr.	Young	John	(Junior)
John Young, Sr.	Young	John	(Senior)
John Young, III	Young	John	(Third)

10. Titles

(a) A personal or professional title or degree is usually not considered in filing, but it is put in parentheses at the end of the name.

(b) When a religious or foreign title is followed by a first name only, it is indexed as written.

INDEX ORDER OF UNITS

Names	Unit 1	Unit 2	Unit 3
(a)			
Dr. Alfred G. Brown	Brown	Alfred	G. (Dr.)
Arthur E. Brown, M.D.	Brown	Arthur	E. (M.D.)
Raymond C. Ellis, Ph.D.	Ellis	Raymond	C. (Ph.D.)
Mme. Jeannine Patou	Patou	Jeannine (Mme.)	
Mayor John J. Ryan	Ryan	John	J. (Mayor)
Lieut. Earl T. Stewart	Stewart	Earl	T. (Lieutenant)
Senator Ralph Williams	Williams	Ralph (Senator)	
(b)			
Brother Andrew	Brother	Andrew	
Father Henry	Father	Henry	
King George	King	George	
Lady Anabel	Lady	Anabel	
Prince Philip	Prince	Philip	
Princess Margaret	Princess	Margaret	
Sister Mary Martha	Sister	Mary	Martha

11. Names of Married Women

If it is known, the legal name of a married woman should be used rather than her husband's name. When a woman marries, the only part of her husband's name that she legally assumes is his last name. Her legal name includes either (a) her first name, her maiden last name, and her husband's last name, or (b) her first name, her middle name, and her husband's last name. In other words, a married woman's legal name could be *Mrs. Jane Foster Burke* or *Mrs. Jane Melinda Burke* but not *Mrs. Marvin J. Burke.*

The title *Mrs.* is put in parentheses after the name but *it is not considered in filing.* Her husband's name is given in parentheses below her legal name.

INDEX ORDER OF UNITS

Names	Unit 1	Unit 2	Unit 3
Mrs. Thomas (Mary Parker) Smith (Mrs. Thomas Smith)	Smith,	Mary	Parker (Mrs.)
Mrs. Theodore Smith	Smith,	Theodore (Mrs.)	
Mrs. Frank (Evelyn Marie) Zeller (Mrs. Frank Zeller)	Zeller,	Evelyn	Marie (Mrs.)

QUESTIONS

1. How many indexing units are there in the name *Gerald V. Wilcox*?
2. What is meant by the *nothing before something* rule?
3. How is an abbreviated first name like *Benj.* treated?
4. Is *Van Der Veer* considered one, two, or three filing units?
5. If two people have last names that are alike, what will determine the order in which their names are indexed?
6. Is the city or state considered first when filing identical names?
7. Which is the correct order for indexing *Jr., Sr., III, IV,* or *Fourth, Junior, Senior, Third*?
8. What is done about the *Dr.* in *Dr. James B. Moulton*?
9. How are religious and foreign titles treated in indexing?
10. What is the legal name of a married woman?

JUDGMENT

1. What confusion might be caused if last names containing a prefix were not treated as one unit?
2. Why are foreign names often difficult to index?

PERSONAL QUALITIES

Betty Kirshner is secretary to the vice-president in charge of legal matters for a manufacturing company. She handles much correspondence and other legal papers for her employer. All the files are maintained in separate confidential files in his office. She is often interrupted by telephone calls and executives and others who must see her boss personally. Her day is so busy that she finds it difficult to take care of her filing duties.

If you were Betty what would you do to keep control of the files for which you are responsible?

LANGUAGE USAGE

A good practice is not to use a capital unless a rule exists for its use. Four basic rules of capitalization are:

A. Capitalize the first word of a sentence.
   Example: He asked if we were ready to go.
B. Capitalize the first word of a direct quotation.
   Example: He asked, "Are you ready to go?"

C. Capitalize proper nouns and adjectives.
   Example: Beaumont High School   Mexican music
D. Capitalize the important words of titles
   Example: *A Short History of the English People*

Type the following sentences on a separate sheet of paper using capitalization wherever necessary

1. a condensed version of his new novel will appear in the march issue of the reader's digest.
2. the new york firm had all its vital records on microfilm stored underground at a secret location in altoona, pennsylvania.
3. when he was in independence, missouri, he visited the truman library.
4. when she opened the drawer marked contracts and agreements, she was surprised at the number of files it contained.
5. dean lindsey told his secretary to file the volume entitled an inquiry into the nature of certain nineteenth century pamphlets in the school library.

SECRETARIAL WORK

In completing the following filing exercise, you will need one hundred 5" x 3" filing cards, or plain paper cut to about that size. (When the dimensions of a card are mentioned, the first number indicates the width of the bottom edge, and the second number indicates the depth. With a 5" by 3" card, the 5" means that the bottom edge is 5 inches wide, and the 3" means that the card is 3 inches in depth. Normally, however, these cards are referred to as 3" by 5" cards.)

(a) Type each of the following names in index form at the upper left-hand side of a card.
(b) Type the number of each name in the upper right corner of the card. (These numbers will aid in checking the answers.)
(c) After the names have been properly indexed and typed, together with their respective numbers, arrange the cards in alphabetic order.

1. Dr. Herman G. Hofmann
2. Salvatore L'Abbate
3. Joan Neuhaus
4. Shirley M. Schecter
5. Mrs. Adele C. Welsh
6. Mrs. Minnie B. Ballau
7. Ernest Sanford Black
8. Lloyd C. Carpenter
9. Thomas F. Corey
10. David E. Forbes-Watkins
11. Harry D. Van Tassell
12. Stanley Schechter
13. Arthur Neuhaus
14. Henry M. Kaufmann
15. George A. Heinemann
16. Vicki Forbes
17. Maryalice Corey
18. Mrs. Evelyn M. Cannon
19. Sidney J. Bernstein
20. Albert Theron Baldwin
21. Hartzell P. Angell
22. Mrs. Bessie Berkowitz
23. Joseph A. Colombo
24. Mrs. Agnes F. Burns
25. John A. Farrell
26. Arnold H. Hansen-Sturm
27. Arthur Jacobs
28. Robert L. Michalson

29. Viggo Rambusch
30. W. Anthony Ullman
31. E. Cooper Taylor
32. Nicholas Rambone
33. James D. McLean
34. C. Albert Jacob, Jr.
35. Rev. Herbert W. Hansen
36. John Farrell
37. Paul G. Clarke, Jr.
38. Gino Borsesi
39. Thomas L. D. Berg
40. Bette P. Albert, M.D.
41. Robert S. Hackett
42. Olaf Ellison
43. Mrs. Evelyn E. Clarke
44. Charles W. Borman
45. Thomas L. Beckett, Ph.D.
46. Norman J. Abrams, D.D.S.
47. Mrs. Sharon Ennis
48. Edwin C. McDonald, Jr.
49. Alfred H. Phillips
50. Anthony Y. Szu-Tu
51. Julia B. Fee
52. N. R. Heinneman
53. Julia Ann Kaufman
54. Kazan Michel
55. William St. John
56. Seymour C. Ullmann
57. Patrick Colombo
58. George L. Cady
59. Marvin T. Bernstein
60. Mrs. Lillian M. Backer
61. David B. Bandler, Jr.
62. Malcolm Carpenter, M.D.
63. Mrs. J. Black
64. D. Howard Daniels
65. Maxine Friedman
66. Richard D. Hoffman
67. Annette C. LaBelle
68. Arabelle J. O'Brien, M.D.
69. Madelyn Russell Segal
70. Harold A. Welch
71. Richard D. Zirker
72. Mrs. Gladys Smythe
73. James F. O'Neill
74. R. O. Ennis
75. James A. Gilmartin
76. Thomas M. Ellis
77. Samuel H. Clark
78. Robert D. Block
79. Edward J. Barrett
80. Albert V. Marcus
81. Joseph Lloyd Barnett
82. Samuel Clark
83. A. Marvin Gillman, M.D.
84. Leo J. Madden, D.D.S.
85. William M. Smith
86. Gloria Younger
87. Dr. William Bloch
88. A. V. Danielson
89. Harry A. Humphries
90. Carol Philipps
91. Barbara Ann Barken
92. Wilford R. Young
93. Joseph E. Black
94. Irving T. Siegel
95. James E. Clark, Jr.
96. William J. O'Neil
97. Malcolm MacDonald
98. Harry S. Humphreys
99. Louis M. Friedmann
100. Henry L. Daniels

PART 3 ALPHABETIC FILING RULES FOR BUSINESS FIRMS AND OTHER ORGANIZATIONS

Judy Melvin was the first secretary Mr. Howard Bivens hired when he started Ambex Paper Products six months ago. She is amazed at the number of different organizations — business firms, government agencies, religious bodies, schools, newspaper and magazine publishing companies — that call on Ambex for its products. Judy has spent a great deal of time establishing the filing system. Mr. Bivens depends completely on Judy to see that the files are up to date at all times. With the help of a records consultant, Judy has assumed complete supervision of the filing system and is gradually becoming expert in alphabetizing. The filing system Judy established is truly a pleasure with which to work.

ALPHABETIC INDEXING FOR BUSINESS FIRMS AND OTHER ORGANIZATIONS

The alphabetic indexing rules presented in Part 2 are also used in filing for business firms and other organizations. Businesses, however, can sometimes present special indexing problems. A mastery of the following rules should give you the confidence you need when you have to file materials for other than names of individuals.

12. Business or Firm Names

The following rules determine the indexing of a business or firm name:

(a) As a general rule, the units in a firm name are indexed in the order in which they are written. The word *and* is not considered an indexing unit.

(b) When a firm name includes the full name of a person, the person's last name is considered as the first indexing unit, his given name or first initial as the second unit, his middle name or initial as the third; and the rest of the firm name is then considered.

(c) Occasionally a business name contains the name of a person (for example, *Arthur Murray* or *Fanny Farmer*) who is so well known that it would confuse most people if the name were to be transposed. In such cases, the name is indexed as it is popularly known and cross-referenced. For example, *Fanny Farmer Candy Shops, Inc.*, would be cross-referenced as *Farmer, Fanny Candy Shops, Inc.*

(d) The name of a hotel or motel is usually indexed in the order in which it is written. However, if the word *Hotel* or *Motel* appears first, it is transposed to allow the most clearly identifying word to become the first indexing unit (for example, *Hotel McKitrick* is indexed as *McKitrick Hotel*).

INDEX ORDER OF UNITS

Names	Unit 1	Unit 2	Unit 3	Unit 4
Ames Art Shop	Ames	Art	Shop	
Hotel Ames	Ames	Hotel		
Brown and Son Realty Co.	Brown (and)	Son	Realty	Company
Campbell Soup Company, Inc.	Campbell	Soup	Company	Incorporated
Citizens National Bank	Citizens	National	Bank	
John Hancock Mutual Life Insurance Co.	John	Hancock	Mutual	Life
John H. Kramer Shoe Repair Shop	Kramer	John	H.	Shoe
Michigan Savings and Loan Co.	Michigan	Savings (and)	Loan	Company
Modern Tile Store	Modern	Tile	Store	
Montgomery Ward and Company	Montgomery	Ward (and)	Company	
Motel Morris Gift Shoppe	Morris	Motel	Gift	Shoppe
L. Morrison Moss Supply Co.	Moss	L.	Morrison	Supply
Singer Wallpaper and Paint Company	Singer	Wallpaper (and)	Paint	Company

13. Alphabetic Order of Business or Firm Names

The first units of firm names determine the alphabetic order when those units are different. The second units determine alphabetic order when the first units are alike. The third units determine alphabetic order when the first and second units are alike.

INDEX ORDER OF UNITS

Names	Unit 1	Unit 2	Unit 3	Unit 4
Gunn Printing Company	Gunn	Printing	Company	
Gunn Radio Shop	Gunn	Radio	Shop	
Hess Beauty Shoppe	Hess	Beauty	Shoppe	
Mary Hess Beauty Salon	Hess	Mary	Beauty	Salon
Hess Specialty Shop	Hess	Specialty	Shop	
Irwin Shoe Distributors	Irwin	Shoe	Distributors	
Irwin Shoe Mart	Irwin	Shoe	Mart	

14. Articles, Prepositions, and Conjunctions

(a) The articles (*a*, *an*, *the*); prepositions (*of*, *on*, *for*, *by*, etc.); and conjunctions (*and*, *&*, *or*) are *not* considered as indexing units and should be put in parentheses.

(b) However, when a preposition is the first word in a business name (as in *At Home Bakery* or *In Town Motel*), the preposition is treated as the first indexing unit.

INDEX ORDER OF UNITS

Names	Unit 1	Unit 2	Unit 3	Unit 4
L. S. Andrews & Co.	Andrews	L.	S. (&)	Company
A Bit of Scotland	Bit (of)	Scotland (A)		
By the Sea Inn	By (the)	Sea	Inn	
First National Bank of Cincinnati	First	National	Bank (of)	Cincinnati
The House of Design	House (of)	Design (The)		
In Between Book Store	In	Between	Book	Store

Illus. 11-4
Five-drawer file systems are replacing four-drawer systems in effecting space-saving economies.

Humble Oil & Refining Company

15. Abbreviations

An abbreviation in a firm name is indexed as if it were spelled in full. Single-letter abbreviations are also indexed as though spelled in full. If the meaning of the abbreviation is not *definitely* known, however, the name should be indexed as it is written.

INDEX ORDER OF UNITS

Names	Unit 1	Unit 2	Unit 3	Unit 4
Amer. Paper Co.	American	Paper	Company	
Ft. Lee Stores, Inc.	Fort	Lee	Stores	Incorporated
Penn Central R.R.	Penn	Central	Railroad	
St. Vincent's Hosp.	Saint	Vincent's	Hospital	
U.S. Rubber Co.	United	States	Rubber	Company
YWCA	Young	Women's	Christian	Association

16. Single Letters

When a firm's name is made up of single letters, each letter is considered as a separate indexing unit. The spacing between the single letters is not considered in indexing. Firm names made up of single letters are filed before words beginning with the same letter because of the *nothing before something* rule.

INDEX ORDER OF UNITS

Names	Unit 1	Unit 2	Unit 3	Unit 4
A & A Auto Parts	A (&)	A	Auto	Parts
ABC Printers	A	B	C	Printers
A C Cleaners	A	C	Cleaners	
A–Z Dry Cleaners	A (–)	Z	Dry	Cleaners
Acme Rug Co.	Acme	Rug	Company	
WNBC	W	N	B	C
X-Cel Advertising Service	X (-)	Cel	Advertising	Service

17. Hyphenated and Compound Names and Words

    (a) Hyphenated firm names are indexed as if they were separate words; thus, they are separate indexing units (for example, *Allis-Chalmers*).

    (b) Each part of a hyphenated "coined" word (such as *The Do-It-Ur-Self Shop*) is considered to be a separate indexing unit.

(c) A single word written with a hyphen (a word containing a prefix, such as *anti-*, *co-*, *inter-*, *mid-*, *pan-*, *trans-*, *tri-*) is filed as one indexing unit.

INDEX ORDER OF UNITS

Names	Unit 1	Unit 2	Unit 3	Unit 4
(a)				
McGraw-Edison Company	McGraw(-)	Edison	Company	
Shaw-Walker	Shaw(-)	Walker		
Stokens-Van Buren, Inc.	Stokens(-)	Van Buren	Incorporated	
(b)				
Bar-B-Q Drive-Inn	Bar(-)	B(-)	Q	Drive(-)
C-Thru Window Company	C(-)	Thru	Window	Company
Econ-O-Me Cleaners	Econ(-)	O(-)	Me	Cleaners
(c)				
Inter-State Truckers Assoc.	Inter-State	Truckers	Association	
Mid-City Garage	Mid-City	Garage		
Pan-American Insurance Co.	Pan-American	Insurance	Company	

18. Two Words Considered as One

If separate words in a firm's name are often considered or written as one word, these words as a group should be treated as one indexing unit. The use of a hyphen or spacing is of no indexing significance. This rule does away with the separating of similar names in the files. Examples of such words include *airport, carload, crossroads, downtown, eastside, goodwill, halfway, mainland, railroad, seaboard,* and points of the compass words, such as *northeast, northwest, southeast,* and *southeastern.*

INDEX ORDER OF UNITS

Names	Unit 1	Unit 2
Down Town Garage	Down Town	Garage
Good Will Agency	Good Will	Agency
The Half-Way Restaurant	Half-Way	Restaurant (The)
North Eastern Airlines	North Eastern	Airlines

19. Titles in Business Names

(a) A title *in a business name* is treated as a separate unit and is indexed in the order in which it is written.
(b) The titles *Mr.* and *Mrs.* are indexed as written *rather than* spelled in full.

INDEX ORDER OF UNITS

Names	Unit 1	Unit 2	Unit 3	Unit 4
Dr. Posner Shoe Co., Inc.	Doctor	Posner	Shoe	Company
Madame Adrienne French Cleaners	Madame	Adrienne	French	Cleaners
Mr. Foster's Shops	Mr.	Foster's	Shops	
Sir Michael, Ltd.	Sir	Michael	Limited	

20. Compound Geographic Names

Compound geographic names containing two English words (such as *New York*) are treated as two separate indexing units, but compound names written as one word (such as *Lakewood*) are considered as one indexing unit.

INDEX ORDER OF UNITS

Names	Unit 1	Unit 2	Unit 3	Unit 4
Ft. Wayne Finance Co.	Fort	Wayne	Finance	Company
New Jersey Thruway Res't	New	Jersey	Thruway	Restaurant
Newport Knitting Co.	Newport	Knitting	Company	
St. Louis Post Dispatch	Saint	Louis	Post	Dispatch

21. Numbers

A number in a business name is treated as though written in full and is considered one indexing unit (regardless of the length or number of digits). In order to use a smaller number of letters to indicate a number, four-digit numbers are written in hundreds and five-digit numbers are written in thousands. For example, the four-digit number *1,250* would be written *twelve hundred fifty* instead of *one thousand two hundred fifty*. The five-digit number *10,010* would be written *ten thousand ten*.

INDEX ORDER OF UNITS

Names	Unit 1	Unit 2	Unit 3	Unit 4
A-1 Envelope Co.	A(-)	One	Envelope	Company
40 Winks Motel	Forty	Winks	Motel	
42nd Street Playhouse	Forty-second	Street	Playhouse	
40,000 Investment Association	Forty Thousand	Investment	Association	
The 400 Cake Shop	Four Hundred	Cake	Shop (The)	
4th Federal Loan Co.	Fourth	Federal	Loan	Company

Part 3 / Alphabetic Filing Rules

22. Foreign Names

(a) Each separately written word in a compound foreign name is considered as a separate indexing unit. The words *San* and *Santa* mean *Saint* and are, therefore, indexed separately.

(b) A foreign prefix is combined with the word that follows it and is indexed as one filing unit (as explained in Rule 3, Part 2, page 376).

(c) Unusual foreign names are indexed as written.

INDEX ORDER OF UNITS

Names	Unit 1	Unit 2	Unit 3	Unit 4
(a) Mesa Verde Distributors	Mesa	Verde	Distributors	
Puerto Rico Travel Bureau	Puerto	Rico	Travel	Bureau
San Francisco Chronicle	San	Francisco	Chronicle	
Terre Haute City Service	Terre	Haute	City	Service
(b) Du Bois Fence & Garden Co.	Du Bois	Fence (&)	Garden	Company
LaBelle Formal Wear Shops	LaBelle	Formal	Wear	Shops
Las Vegas Convention Bureau	Las Vegas	Convention	Bureau	
Los Angeles Wholesale Institute	Los Angeles	Wholesale	Institute	
(c) Ambulancias Hispano Mexicana	Ambulancias	Hispano	Mexicana	
Iino Kauin Kaisha Imports	Iino	Kauin	Kaisha	Imports
Mohamed Esber, Cia	Mohamed	Esber	Cia	

23. Possessives

The *apostrophe s* (*'s*), the singular possessive, is *not* considered in filing. An *s apostrophe* (*s'*), the plural possessive, *is* considered as part of the word. Very simply, consider all letters to be in the indexing unit up to the apostrophe; drop those after it.

INDEX ORDER OF UNITS

Names	Unit 1	Unit 2	Unit 3	Unit 4
Brook's Jewelry Store	Brook('s)	Jewelry	Store	
Brooks' Brothers Clothing	Brooks'	Brothers	Clothing	
Paul's Limousine Service	Paul('s)	Limousine	Service	
Pauls' Real Estate Agency	Pauls'	Real	Estate	Agency

24. Identical Business Names

(a) Identical names of two or more businesses are arranged in alphabetical order according to the names of the cities in the addresses. The name of the state is disregarded unless the towns have the same name.

(b) If several branches of one business are located in the same city, the names of those branches are arranged alphabetically or numerically by streets. If more than one branch is located on the same street in the same city, the names are arranged according to the numeric order of the building numbers. Names of buildings are not considered unless street names are not given.

	INDEX ORDER OF UNITS			IDENTIFYING ELEMENTS			
Names	**Unit 1**	**Unit 2**	**Unit 3**	**City**	**State**	**Street**	**House Number**
(a) Office Supplies Company Akron, Ohio	Office	Supplies	Company	Akron	Ohio		
Office Supplies Company Canton, Ohio	Office	Supplies	Company	Canton	Ohio		
Office Supplies Company Lansing, Michigan	Office	Supplies	Company	Lansing	Michigan		
(b) National Food Market 225 Main Street Columbus, Ohio	National	Food	Market	Columbus	Ohio	Main	225
National Food Market 187 Prospect Street Columbus, Ohio	National	Food	Market	Columbus	Ohio	Prospect	187
National Food Market United Building 341 Stone Drive Columbus, Ohio	National	Food	Market	Columbus	Ohio	Stone	341
National Food Market 722 Stone Drive Columbus, Ohio	National	Food	Market	Columbus	Ohio	Stone	722
National Food Market Young Building Columbus, Ohio	National	Food	Market	Columbus	Ohio	Young	

25. Churches, Synagogues, and Other Organizations

(a) The name of a church or synagogue is indexed in the order in which it is written unless some other word in the name more clearly identifies the organization.

INDEX ORDER OF UNITS

Names	Unit 1	Unit 2	Unit 3
First Baptist Church	Baptist	Church	First
The Chapel at Brown & Vine	Chapel (at)	Brown (&)	Vine (The)
Congregation of Moses	Congregation (of)	Moses	
Trinity Lutheran Church	Lutheran	Church	Trinity
St. Paul's Church	Saint	Paul's	Church

(b) The name of a club or any other organization is indexed according to the most clearly identifying unit in its name. For example, the most clearly identifying unit in *The Ancient Order of Mariners* is *Mariners*.

INDEX ORDER OF UNITS

Names	Unit 1	Unit 2	Unit 3
Fraternal Order of Eagles	Eagles	Fraternal	Order (of)
Loyal Order of Moose	Moose	Loyal	Order (of)
Local 200, Retail Store Employees Union	Retail	Store	Employees
Rotary Club	Rotary	Club	

26. Schools

(a) The names of elementary and secondary schools are indexed first according to the name of the city in which the schools are located, and then by the most distinctive word in the name.

INDEX ORDER OF UNITS

Names	Unit 1	Unit 2	Unit 3	Unit 4
Indian Prairie School, Kalamazoo, Michigan	Kalamazoo	Indian	Prairie	School
Oakwood Elementary School, Kalamazoo, Michigan	Kalamazoo	Oakwood	Elementary	School
Oakwood Junior High, Kalamazoo, Michigan	Kalamazoo	Oakwood	Junior	High
Pershing School Portage, Michigan	Portage	Pershing	School	

(b) The names of colleges or universities are indexed according to the most clearly identifying word in the name.

INDEX ORDER OF UNITS

Names	Unit 1	Unit 2	Unit 3
Albany Business Col.	Albany	Business	College
Indiana Business School	Indiana	Business	School
Iowa State University	Iowa	State	University
University of Iowa	Iowa	University (of)	
Northwestern University	Northwestern	University	
Slippery Rock State College	Slippery	Rock	State

27. Newspapers and Magazines

(a) The name of a newspaper is indexed in the order in which it is written unless the city of publication does not appear in its name. In that case, the name of the city is inserted before the name of the newspaper.

INDEX ORDER OF UNITS

Names	Unit 1	Unit 2	Unit 3	Unit 4
The Canton Herald	Canton	Herald (The)		
The Journal Gazette Ft. Wayne, Indiana	Fort	Wayne	Journal	Gazette (The)
The New York Times	New	York	Times (The)	
The Wall Street Journal, New York, NY	New	York	Wall	Street

(b) The name of a magazine is indexed in the order in which the name is written. A cross-reference may be made listing the publisher, as described on page 395.

INDEX ORDER OF UNITS

Names	Unit 1	Unit 2	Unit 3
Administrative Management	Administrative	Management	
Harvard Business Review	Harvard	Business	Review
The Office	Office (The)		
Reader's Digest	Reader's	Digest	

28. Federal Government Offices

The names of all federal government agencies and offices are indexed under United States Government. They are indexed as shown at the top of page 394.

Part 3 / Alphabetic Filing Rules   393

(a) United States Government
(b) Name of the department
(c) Name of the bureau
(d) Name of the division or subdivision
(e) Location of the office
(f) Title of official, if given

```
District Director
Internal Revenue Service
Indianapolis, Indiana  46204
```

would be indexed

```
United States Government
    Treasury (Department of)
    Internal Revenue Service
    Indianapolis
    District Director
```

Names	INDEX ORDER OF UNITS

District Director
Agricultural Research Service
Federal Building
Tallahassee, Florida 33602
	United States Government
	   Agriculture (Department of)
	   Agricultural Research Service
	   Tallahassee
	   District Director

Bureau of International Commerce
U.S. Department of Commerce
Philadelphia, Pennsylvania 19108
	United States Government
	   Commerce (Department of)
	   International Commerce (Bureau of)
	   Philadelphia

Division of Employment Statistics
Bureau of Labor Statistics
U.S. Department of Labor
Cleveland, Ohio 44199
	United States Government
	   Labor (Department of)
	   Labor Statistics (Bureau of)
	   Employment Statistics (Division of)
	   Cleveland

Customs Service
U.S. Department of the Treasury
San Francisco, California 94102
	United States Government
	   Treasury (Department of the)
	   Customs Service
	   San Francisco

Data Processing Center
Veterans Administration
St. Paul, Minnesota 55511
	United States Government
	   Veterans Administration
	   Data Processing Center
	   St. Paul

(Note: Rule 28 also applies to foreign government names.)

29. Other Political Subdivisions

The names of other political subdivisions — state, county, city, or town government — are indexed according to

(a) Geographic name of the subdivision, such as *New Jersey, State* (*of*); *Westchester, County* (*of*); or *Philadelphia, City* (*of*)
(b) Name of department, board, or office
(c) Location of the office
(d) Title of the official, if it is given

INDEX ORDER OF UNITS

Names	Unit 1	Unit 2	Unit 3	Unit 4
Police Department 　Alliance, Ohio	Alliance	City (of)	Police	Department
Clinton Co. Park Commission 　Dubuque, Iowa	Clinton	County (of)	Park	Commission
Municipal Public Works Div. 　Lancaster, Pa.	Lancaster	City (of)	Public	Works
State Health Department 　Columbus, Ohio	Ohio	State (of)	Health	Department

30. Subjects

Sometimes it is better to file materials according to subject rather than under the name of the person or business. The reason for this is that the subject may be more important than the name of the person or business. Applications for employment are examples of this type of indexing. The applications are of major importance; the names of the applicants are of secondary importance.

INDEX ORDER OF UNITS

Names	Unit 1	Unit 2	Unit 3	Unit 4
C. J. Browning (Advertiser)	Advertisers:	Browning	C.	J.
R. M. Smith (Advertiser)	Advertisers:	Smith	R.	M.
H. L. Kramer (Application)	Applications:	Kramer	H.	L.
Jack Myer (Application)	Applications:	Myer	Jack	
J. Frank Smith (Application)	Applications:	Smith	J.	Frank

CROSS-REFERENCING

What will you do when a letter or other material to be filed could be asked for by more than one name? Examples are firm names that consist of two or more surnames, the names of married women, and the names of magazines. You may look for the name according to an indexing order that is not shown on the piece of correspondence or on the file card. For example, you may remember only the name *Goodman* in the firm name *Bergdorf-Goodman*; you may not remember a married woman's legal name — you may remember only that her husband's name is *Thomas Devine*; or you may remember the name of a magazine, *Life*, but not the name of the publisher, *Time, Inc.*

In such instances, a cross-reference sheet should be filled out and filed under the other title. It should indicate where the material is actually

Part 3 / Alphabetic Filing Rules

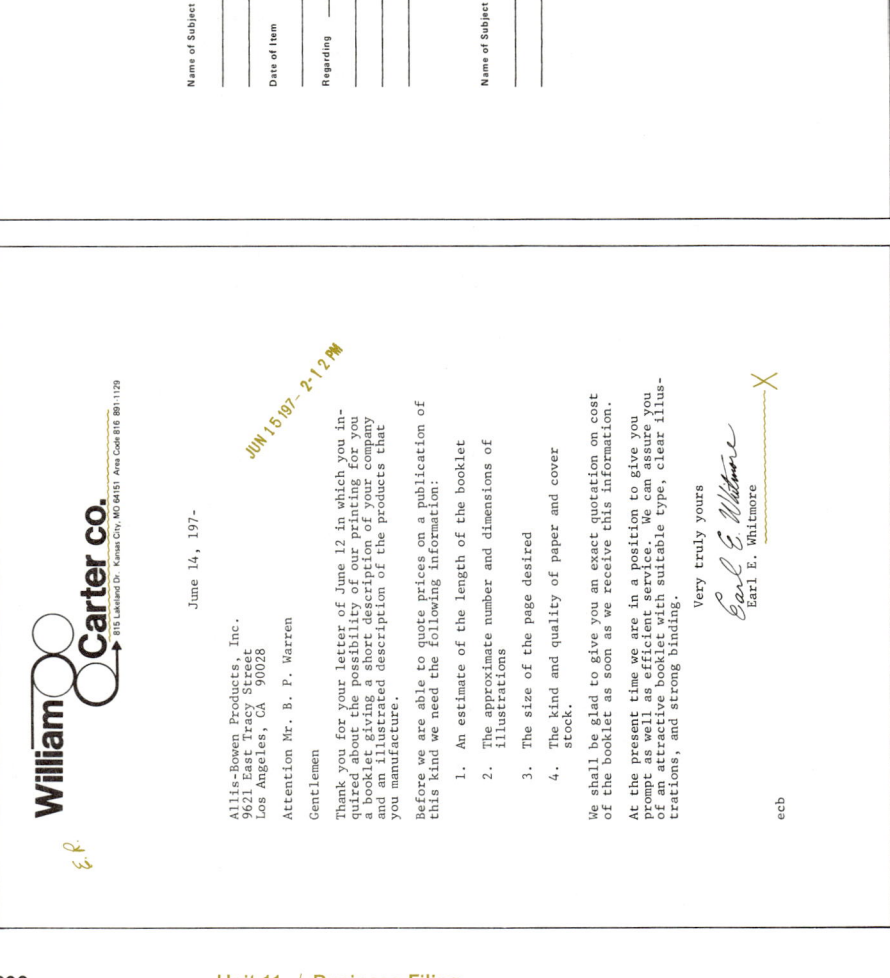

William Carter Co.
815 Lakeland Dr. Kansas City, MO 64151 Area Code 816 891-1129

E.R.

June 14, 197-

JUN 15 197- – 2-12 PM

Allis-Bowen Products, Inc.
9621 East Tracy Street
Los Angeles, CA 90028

Attention Mr. B. P. Warren

Gentlemen

Thank you for your letter of June 12 in which you inquired about the possibility of our printing for you a booklet giving a short description of your company and an illustrated description of the products that you manufacture.

Before we are able to quote prices on a publication of this kind we need the following information:

1. An estimate of the length of the booklet
2. The approximate number and dimensions of illustrations
3. The size of the page desired
4. The kind and quality of paper and cover stock.

We shall be glad to give you an exact quotation on cost of the booklet as soon as we receive this information.

At the present time we are in a position to give you prompt as well as efficient service. We can assure you of an attractive booklet with suitable type, clear illustrations, and strong binding.

Very truly yours

Earl E. Whitmore ─────X

ecb

Illus. 11-5
Coded letter

CROSS-REFERENCE SHEET

Name of Subject ____ Whitmore, Earl E.
                     Kansas City, MO 64151

Date of Item ____ June 14, 197-

Regarding ____ Request for further information as basis for quotation on printing a booklet

SEE

Name of Subject ____ Carter, William, Company
                     815 Lakeland Drive
                     Kansas City, MO 64151

Illus. 11-6
Cross-reference sheet

The line drawn under the name *Carter Co.* in the letterhead above indicates the name under which the letter should be filed. The line drawn under the name *Whitmore*, which is extended into the margin and marked with an "x," indicates that the letter may be called for by Whitmore's name rather than by the name of the company. Consequently, the cross-reference sheet above was prepared and should be filed under the name *Whitmore, Earl E.* (The notation *ER* is a release mark, which indicates that the paper is ready to be filed. *June 15 . . . 2-12 PM* is a time stamp indicating when the letter was received.)

filed. If a photocopying machine is available, it is more efficient to make a photocopy than to fill out a cross-reference sheet. The photocopy should then be filed under the other title.

Although cross-referencing is important for locating filed information quickly, care should be taken in deciding which records really need to be cross-referenced. Too much cross-referencing takes a lot of time and a lot of space. Too little cross-referencing will cause needless and costly delays in getting important information.

Cross-Reference for a Company Known by More than One Name

If the name of a firm is *Rogers-Turner Food Mart*, the original piece of correspondence should be indexed as it is written. You should, however, make a cross-reference card or sheet for the second name in the title. Consequently, if you remember only the second name, *Turner*, you will find on the cross-reference for *Turner* "See Rogers-Turner Food Mart."

Cross-Reference for the Name of a Married Woman

You will file the original piece of correspondence for a married woman under her legal name, that is, her given first name, her maiden last name, and her husband's last name. Her husband's given name might be cross-referenced to find the filed piece of correspondence faster. If the legal name of a married women is *Mrs. Dorothy Lee Hall*, this name should be indexed on the original piece of correspondence; and a cross-reference card or sheet based on her husband's name should be prepared.

```
Hall, Dorothy Lee (Mrs.)

Mrs. Raymond C. Hall
1230 Fifth Street
Marion, IA. 52302
```

Illus. 11-7

```
Hall, Raymond C. (Mrs.)

See Hall, Dorothy Lee (Mrs.)
```

Illus. 11-8

QUESTIONS

1. In what order are the units of a business name considered for filing purposes?
2. What is done when units of an individual name are included in a firm name?
3. How are the words *and*, *of*, and *for* treated in indexing?
4. In a firm name what differences are made in indexing between two words combined with a hyphen and a single

word containing a hyphen — for example, *Walker-Gordon Mills, Inc.*, and *Mid-Hudson Electric Co.*?
5. What are the rules for geographic names?
6. State simply the rule for indexing possessive words.
7. Give examples of subject titles that would be used in preference to the names of the persons or businesses that are concerned.
8. What is a cross-reference card?
9. What is the advantage of using photocopies as cross-reference copies?
10. Give two examples of types of names that are frequently cross-referenced.

JUDGMENT

1. Why is each word in a geographic name usually treated as a separate indexing unit?
2. For what purposes other than filing may a secretary make use of the rules for alphabetic indexing?

PERSONAL QUALITIES

Louise Allen has been with the Lily Soap Company since it was started over thirty years ago. She developed the filing system for the firm and is now supervisor of the central files. Her filing procedures are used in all the executive offices so that materials sent to the central files can be filed and found quickly.

She has her own fixed ideas about filing rules; for instance, the customers' names beginning with *Mac* and *Mc* are placed ahead of all the other names in the *M* section of the alphabetic files. This is but one of the variations in alphabetic filing at the Lily Soap Company.

New employees are confused because the system is so different from the rules of filing they have been taught. They waste much time and energy filing and finding correspondence. Louise is not willing to accept any suggestions for change, claiming that the system has been operating successfully for over thirty years.

If you were to be employed as a secretary at the Lily Soap Company, how would you attempt to reconcile the differences between company practice and the filing rules you learned in school? How would you plan to get along with Louise?

LANGUAGE USAGE

On a separate sheet of paper write the plural form of each of the following business words. After you have written the plural forms, check your answers in a dictionary.

1. attorney
2. belief
3. business
4. chief clerk
5. city
6. company
7. delivery
8. prefix
9. salesman
10. secretary
11. series
12. statistic
13. studio
14. trade-in
15. youth

SECRETARIAL WORK

1. In each of the following names of individuals select the *first* indexing unit.

    (a) R. Harold Dana
    (b) Hubert Smith-Johnson, Jr.
    (c) Lois J. McDowell
    (d) Veronica Blake
    (e) Father Francis
    (f) Chairman Frank Simpson
    (g) Mrs. John Hanson
    (h) President Walter C. Schott
    (i) T. J. Fairleigh, News Commentator
    (j) Attorney Edward K. Wilcox

2. In each of the following business names select the *second* indexing unit.

    (a) The Holden Paper Company
    (b) Woodward & Lothrop Department Store
    (c) A to Z Cleaning Service
    (d) Trans-Canada Air Lines
    (e) North West Wholesale Furriers
    (f) Tommy Tucker's Toys
    (g) Johnson-Hardin Produce Company
    (h) San Bruno Public Warehouse
    (i) A-1 Window Washers
    (j) St. Louis Pharmaceuticals, Inc.

3. In each of the following names select the *first* indexing unit.

    (a) Provident Bank & Trust Company of Cleveland
    (b) Michigan State University
    (c) National Association of Life Underwriters
    (d) Exchange Club
    (e) St. Gertrude's Church
    (f) University of Cincinnati
    (g) Disabled American Veterans
    (h) Camden Savings and Loan
    (i) Yale Alumni Association
    (j) Miss Hall's Preparatory School for Girls

4. Is the order of the names in each of the following pairs correct? Type the pairs of names on a separate sheet of paper. Make any corrections in indexing order that are necessary.

    (a) H. M. Jones
    Henry M. Jonas
    (b) Carl O'Bannon
    J. B. Obannon
    (c) Mrs. Rena Lawson Carter
    Harold Lawson-Carter
    (d) Professor Walter Hampton
    Walter Charles Hampton

(e) George Carpenter, II
George Carpenter, III
(f) Sister Julia
Julia Sisson
(g) Ernest V. Mellon, Sr.
Ernest V. Mellon, Jr.
(h) Dr. Frank Tarkington
Frank D. Tarkington
(i) Francine the Florist
Francis J. Flanagan
(j) Charlie's Place
Charlie Porter, Plumbing

5. Indicate the order in which the parts of the following titles are considered in indexing.
   (a) Board of Education
   Hamilton County, Oregon
   (b) Pennsylvania State Department of Highways
   (c) Central Trust Company of Delaware
   (d) Department of Public Welfare
   City of Minneapolis, Minnesota
   (e) Phillips & Woods (Real Estate)
   (f) Division of Unemployment Compensation
   Ohio State Employment Service
   (g) Oakwood First National Bank
   (h) M. Meredith Weatherby (Application for Employment)
   (i) The Gerald Gerrard Gun Shop
   (j) The War College
   U.S. Department of Defense

6. Arrange the following names in correct alphabetic order in each group.

   Group 1
   (a) H. Duncan McCampbell
   (b) Mack Campbell
   (c) The Campbell Soup Company
   (d) J. C. MacCampbell

   Group 2
   (a) Martin and Ulberg
   (b) Martin C. Ulberg
   (c) Martin-Ulberg, Inc.
   (d) K. Martin Ulberg, M.D.

   Group 3
   (a) Rosewood Delicatessen
   (b) Olde Rosewood Tea Shoppe
   (c) Rose Wood (Mrs.)
   (d) Roselawn Public Library

Group 4

(a) Five Corners Car Wash
(b) Five-Corners Creamery
(c) Five O'Clock Shop
(d) 15th Avenue Apartments

Group 5

(a) Williams Ave. Brake Service
(b) William's Coiffures
(c) Williams' Sons (Brokers)
(d) Williamson Heater Company

Group 6

(a) La Maisonette
(b) Lamson & Towers Advertising
(c) Lamps & Lighting, Inc.
(d) Laap Brothers Furniture

Group 7

(a) 2 in 1 Cleaning Service
(b) 22d Street Theater
(c) Twenty-One (Restaurant)
(d) Twosome Dance Club

Group 8

(a) Mrs. J. C. (Barbara) Sands
(b) Santa Barbara Police Dept.
(c) St. Barnaby's Episcopal Church
(d) Barbara St. John

Group 9

(a) Boy Scouts of America
(b) Boy's Scouting Club
(c) Boy and Bike Shop
(d) Boys' and Dads' Day Committee

Group 10

(a) J. & L. Fruit Market
(b) Jones & Laughlin Steel
(c) J. L. Jones, Jr.
(d) J. L. Jones, Sr.

Group 11

(a) Southern Railway
(b) South Boston Beanery
(c) South Western Printing Company
(d) Rachael W. Souther

Group 12

(a) Black's
(b) Blacks'
(c) Blacks' Super Market
(d) S. Black & Son

Group 13

(a) K-P Kitchenware
(b) Kennedy-Porter Fencing
(c) Arthur P. Kennedy
(d) P. Kennedy Arthur

Group 14

(a) St. Joseph's Orphanage
(b) St. Joseph (Missouri) Railroad Depot
(c) San Jose Growers' Assn.
(d) Sanjor Coffee House

7. In completing this exercise you will need 50 5" x 3" file cards or plain paper cut to about that size.

(a) Type each of the following names in index form at the top of a card. Type the number of each name in the upper right corner of the card. (These numbers will aid in checking the answers.) Type the name and address below the indexed name. (See illustration on page 376.)
(b) After the names, numbers, and addresses have been typed, arrange the cards alphabetically.
(c) Save these cards for use in assignments in Unit 12.

(1) Janitrol Heating Service, 6602 No. Clark St., Chicago, IL 60626
(2) Kitty's Korner Kitchen, Cooper Bldg., Marietta, OH 45750
(3) Mlle. Jeanette Cecil Sagan, 3 Rue de la Pais, Paris, France
(4) Janitor Supplies & Equipment Co., 9 W. 7th St., Akron, OH 44314
(5) Robert P. Van der Meer, 221 Watervliet St., Detroit, MI 48217
(6) Jerome Labelson, Apt. 3B, 60 Sutton Place, South, New York, NY 10022
(7) Williams & Williams, Tax Consultants, Suite 12, Statler Hotel, Cleveland, OH 44141
(8) Jasper J. Seaman, Chalfonte Hall, Campus Station, Durham, NC 27707
(9) Meyer Lufkin & Son, Commercial Bldg., 9th & Walnut, Omaha, NE 68108
(10) Meyer, E. Jones & Millikin Co., 210 N. State St., Albany, NY 12210
(11) Youman & Garties Mfg. Company, 316 Spring St., N.W., Atlanta, GA 30308
(12) The World-Telegram News, Dallas, TX 78421
(13) Raymond J. Vandermeer, 3920 Alamo Drive, Houston, TX 77007
(14) Mid Way Service Station, Junction State Routes 7 & 9, Osburn, ID 83849

(15) Ringling Bros.-Barnum & Bailey Circus, Winter Headquarters, Sarasota, FL 33580
(16) Greenstone Zion Reform Temple, Cor. Reading & Vine Sts., Greenstone, PA 17227
(17) William's U-Fix-It Shop, 4920 Carthage Rd., Richmond, VA 23223
(18) Seamen's Rest, 60 Front St., New Orleans, LA 70130
(19) Wati Rajhma, Room 2100, United Nations Secretariat, New York, NY 10017
(20) Oberhelman Bros. Flooring, Inc., 420 Vine St., Seattle, WA 98121
(21) P. M. Diners' Clubhouse, 22 Regent St., Louisville, KY 40218
(22) Society for the Sightless, 1404 K St., N.W., Washington, D.C. 20005
(23) J. & K. Seaman Hauling Line, 160 N. First St., Ottumwa, IA 52501
(24) 29th Street Mission, 13 - 29th St., San Francisco, CA 94110
(25) La Belle Dresses, 18 Circle Drive, Rogers, CT 06263
(26) Rosenswig's Dept. Store, 6920 Appletree Rd., Wilmington, DE 19810
(27) R. & L. Benjamin & Company, 14 West Decatur St., Ft. Smith, AR 72901
(28) Mayor Michael O'Berne, City Hall, Baltimore, MD 21202
(29) Midway Seafood House, 3109 Collins Ave., Miami Beach, FL 33839
(30) Boy's Hobby Shop, 1010 Pacific Blvd., Portland, OR 97220
(31) Automatic Food Dispenser Co., 112 High St., Colorado Springs, CO 80904
(32) Automatic Food Dispenser Co., 19th & Ewald Sts., Camden, NJ 08105
(33) Automatic Food Dispenser Co., Camden, OH 45311
(34) Boys' Hobby Haven, 730 Pine St., St. Joseph, MO 64504
(35) Lufkin Central Savings Society, 9 So. Main St., Lufkin, TX 75901
(36) Rosen's Fresh Fruit Market, 1403 La Cienega St., Los Angeles, CA 90035
(37) Kitty-Kat Products, Ashport, TN 38003
(38) Long Island Railroad, 69–75 Rockefeller Plaza, New York, NY 10020
(39) Adolph G. Meier Lumber Co., First St. at B. & O. R.R., Columbus, OH 43201
(40) Dr. John W. Barnhart, 22 Medical Arts Bldg., Oak Park, IL 60403

(41) John Barnhart, 635 Capitol Ave., Springfield, IL 62701
(42) Drury Hill Farms, Inc., Box 10, Route 4, Drury, PA 18222
(43) Carthage Mills, Inc., Springvale, GA 31788
(44) Police Department, Drury, PA 18222
(45) P. M. Dinersman Company, 1614 Meridian St., Indianapolis, IN 42625
(46) Branford & Branford Co., Artesia, MS 39736
(47) Branford, Branford and Branford, Attorneys, Union Life Bldg., St. Louis, MO 63155
(48) Olde Seaport Inn, Front and Plum Sts., Alexandria, VA 22313
(49) John L. Barnhart, Sr., 2226 Washington Avenue, Fargo, ND 58102
(50) Ninety and Ninth Apartments, 90th St. at 9th Ave., New York, NY 10024

PART 4 FILING EQUIPMENT AND SUPPLIES FOR CORRESPONDENCE

> The following conversation took place between James Dobson, a lawyer, and his secretary, Lucille Ruebel.
>
> "Lucille, why are all of our contracts folded in the middle? I would like to be able to give our clients a copy that hasn't been creased."
>
> "Mr. Dobson, there really isn't much choice with our filing equipment. The drawers aren't wide enough to take legal papers unless they are folded. Yet we have to put prepared contracts in the files in order to protect them until the client picks them up. If you would like, I'll be glad to see what filing equipment is available for the kinds of paper we must store."

Knowing the indexing rules for filing is absolutely necessary. But, unless you have the proper filing equipment and the correct supplies, you will not have an efficient filing system. Don't be like the young secretary who wanted to take an automobile trip. She planned her trip and studied the road maps carefully. When she got into her car, however, it wouldn't start. Her equipment was defective, and so she could not accomplish her purpose. Unless your filing equipment and supplies are correct, your filing system will "break down."

FILING EQUIPMENT

Good tools are necessary if you are to make your filing system work for you. In large offices filing equipment is usually ordered through the purchasing department, and files are available from the supply room. However, in a small office you may make recommendations and assist your employer in purchasing equipment and supplies. This will require careful study to make correct decisions. Whether you work in a large office or a small office, you will be more efficient if you are familiar with the kinds of equipment and supplies that you will be using on your job.

Proper storage of records is necessary in all businesses. The *size* of the material to be filed is the first factor to be considered; the *number of items* to be filed each day is second.

Standard filing cabinets are available for storing the two most common sizes of business records: letter size (8½" x 11") and the legal size (8½" x 13" or 8½" x 14"). Other cabinets are designed to house card files, visible records, punched cards, computer print-outs, blueprints, and other materials.

Vertical Files

The typical pull-out drawer file cabinet — the vertical file — is used in most business offices. Vertical file cabinets are manufactured in two-, three-, four-, and five-drawer units. Two-drawer vertical file cabinets are used beside the desk and contain only the most active records. Three-drawer vertical file cabinets are often referred to as counter-height cabinets. Five-drawer vertical file cabinets are replacing four-drawer units since they occupy the same amount of floor space, but contain an additional drawer.

Office space in the business districts of many large cities is very expensive and may rent for as high as $15 a square foot; so a saving in floor space for filing cabinets can greatly reduce the cost of housing records.

Every business office has correspondence files. Correspondence files consist of letters, telegrams, teletype messages, purchase orders, invoices, memorandums, reports, and interoffice messages. Reading the correspondence files of any company is the easiest way to learn the nature

Illus. 11-9
Three-drawer vertical file cabinets are often referred to as counter-height cabinets.

Kelly Services

of its business and the history of its transactions. Active correspondence files are usually kept in desk-side two-drawer files; while files on completed transactions are kept in three-, four-, or five-drawer files in other areas of the office.

Lateral and Shelf Files

Because of the increasing number of records that must be kept in expensive office space, many organizations are now using lateral and shelf files. The lateral cabinets look a lot like a chest of drawers and are frequently used as area dividers or low partitions. Often the secretary and the executive will have lateral cabinets behind their desks to house the records they refer to constantly such as current correspondence, sales reports, price lists, production reports, trade handbooks, and periodicals of the industry.

In shelf filing, papers are held in folders placed on shelves in an upright position. Some shelf files are built with open shelves (like the shelving of library books); others are equipped with sliding doors to protect the records. Some are equipped with sliding shelves which draw out sidewise, similar in operation to the pull-out drawer in a typical file cabinet.

Illus. 11-10
Often a secretary will have a lateral file behind her desk to house constantly used records.

Oxford Pendaflex Corporation

Part 4 / Filing Equipment and Supplies

Units that are seven or eight shelves high provide the maximum amount of filing area for the floor space while keeping the records within reach. While much floor space can be saved by using shelf files, many records management consultants believe that individual records cannot be filed or found as quickly as in vertical files, particularly when sliding doors are used to protect the shelf files. They believe shelf filing is most effective for storing records that are not frequently requested.

In addition to the standard filing equipment mentioned here, there is a great deal of specialized filing equipment that is used in microfilming and in the data processing field which is described and illustrated in Part 4 of Unit 12. You will usually be most concerned with vertical files and lateral files since your files should contain only materials that are called for frequently. Shelf files and special files are usually found in the central filing department where less frequently called for materials are stored.

Illus. 11-11
Shelf files provide a maximum amount of filing area.

Tab Products Co.

FILING SUPPLIES

Since your secretarial duties will be concerned mostly with alphabetic name and subject files, which are often combined in one system, you should know how to use the tools within a file drawer to their greatest advantage.

Each drawer in a correspondence file contains two different kinds of filing supplies — guides and file folders. The *guides* in an alphabetic correspondence file divide the drawer into alphabetic sections and serve as signposts for quick reference. They also provide support for the folders and their contents.

File folders hold the papers in an upright position in the file drawer. They are made of heavy paper stock and serve as a container to keep papers together.

Guides

Guides are heavy cardboard sheets which are the same size as the folders. Extending over the top of each guide is a tab upon which is marked or printed a notation or title called a *caption*. The caption indicates the alphabetic range of the material filed in folders behind the guide. For example, a guide may carry the caption *A* which would tell the secretary that only material starting with the letter *A* would be found between that guide and the next guide. This tab may be part of the guide itself, or it may be an attached metal or plastic tab. Sets of guides may be purchased with printed letters or combinations of letters and numbers that may be used with any standard filing system. Other guide tabs are blank, and the specific captions are made in the user's office.

Guides may be obtained with a rod projection that extends below the body of the guide. The projection contains a metal eyelet through which a file drawer rod may be run, thus holding the guides in place and preventing the folders from slipping down in the drawer.

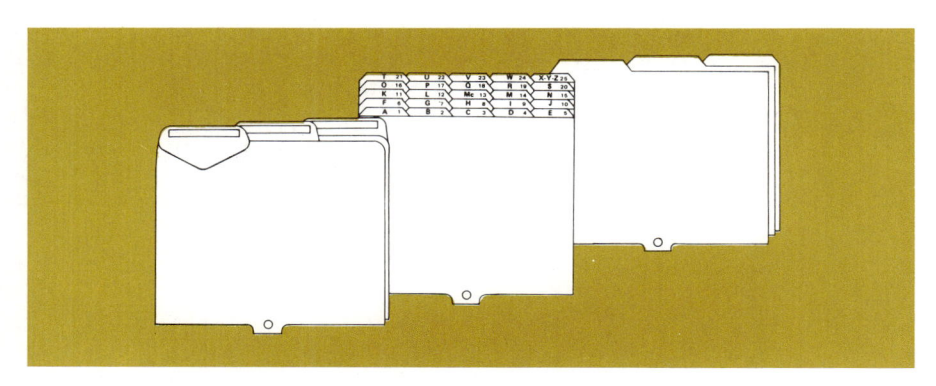

Illus. 11-12
File guides with metal eyelets for projection rods

Kinds of Guides. Guides are classified as primary or secondary. The *primary guides* indicate the major divisions — alphabetic, numeric, subject, geographic, or chronological — into which the filing system is divided. *Secondary guides* (also called auxiliary or special name guides) are subdivisions of the primary guides and are used to highlight certain types of information, for example, to indicate the placement of special folders (such as those for *Advertising* or *Applications*). They are also used to indicate a section of the file in which many folders with the same first indexing unit are placed. For example, if a file contains many individual folders for the name *Brown* behind the primary guide with the caption *B*, a secondary guide with the caption *Brown* might be placed in the file drawer to aid in finding one of the *Brown* folders.

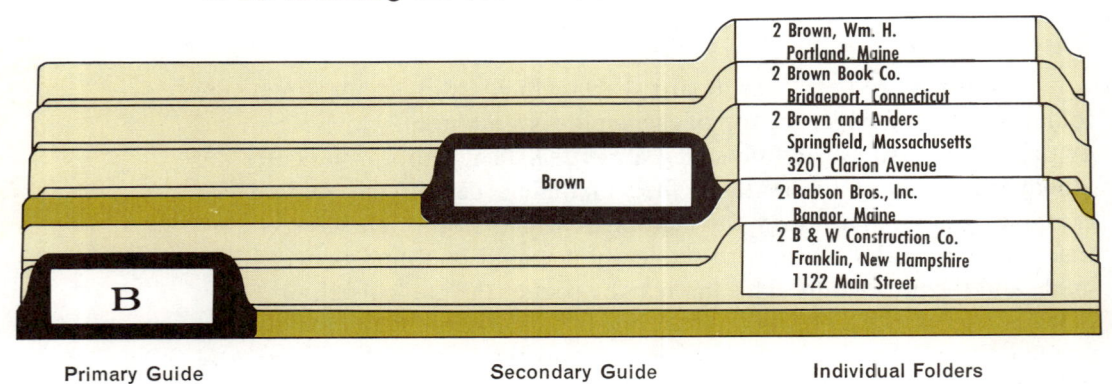

Primary Guide   Secondary Guide   Individual Folders

Illus. 11-13

Number of Guides. If individual folders are to be located quickly, not more than ten should be filed behind any one guide. The number of guides, however, will depend on the actual use of the file and the amount of material in each folder. Anywhere from 15 to 25 guides in each file drawer will help in finding and filing in most filing systems.

CHART SHOWING PRIMARY GUIDE CAPTIONS FOR VARIOUS ALPHABETIC SUBDIVISIONS

10 A-Z	25 A-Z	40 A-Z	60 A-Z	80 A-Z	120 A-Z	160 A-Z	Guide No.
A–B	A	A	A	A	A	A	1
C–D	B	B	Am	Ae	Al	Ai	2
E–G	C	Be	B	An	An	Am	3
H–J	D	Bo	Be	B	Ar	An	4
K–L	E	C	Bi	Bar	B	Ar	5
M	F	Ci	Br	Be	Bar	B	6
N–R	G	Cr	By	Bi	Be	Bam	7
S	H	D	C	Bo	Ben	Bas	8
T–V	I	Di	Ce	Br	Bi	Be	9
W–Z	J	E	Co	Bu	Bo	Ben	10

The Globe-Wernicke Systems Co.

Folders

A folder is made of a sheet of heavy paper that has been folded once so that the back is about one-half inch higher than the front. Folders are larger than the papers they contain so that they protect them. Two standard folder sizes are *letter size* for papers that are 8½" x 11" and *legal size* for papers that are 8½" x 13" or 8½" x 14".

Folders are cut across the top in two ways — so that the back is straight (straight cut) or so that the back has a tab that projects above the top of the folder. Such tabs bear captions that identify the contents of each folder. Tabs vary in width and position. The tabs of a set of folders that are one-half cut are half the width of the folder and have only two positions. *One-third cut* folders have three positions, each tab occupying a third of the width of the folder. Another standard tab is *one-fifth cut* which, as you can see, has five positions. Other folders "hang" from a metal frame placed inside the file drawer.

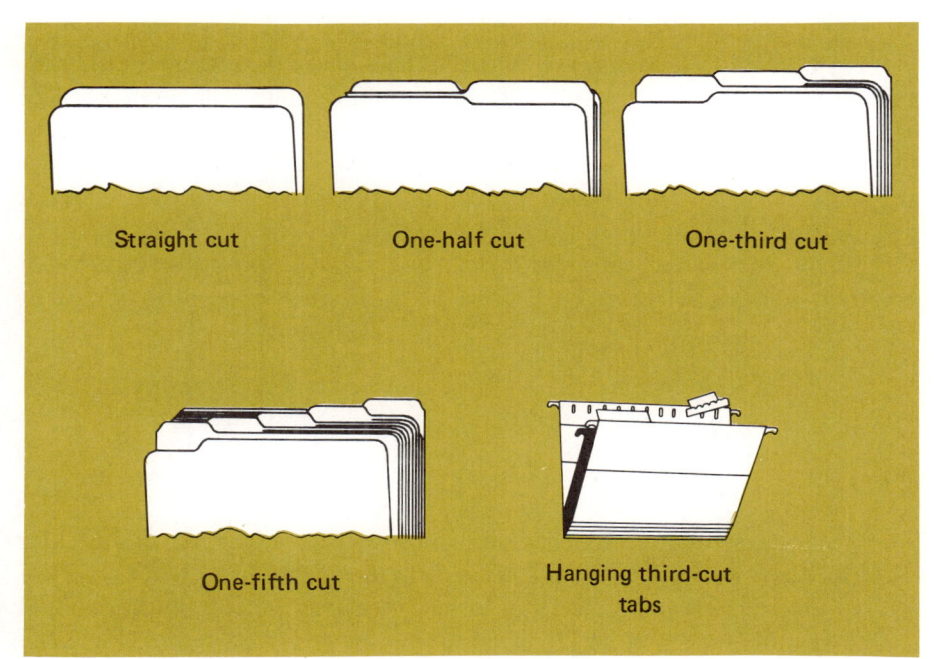

Straight cut   One-half cut   One-third cut

One-fifth cut   Hanging third-cut tabs

Illus. 11-14

Miscellaneous Folders. A miscellaneous folder is kept for every alphabetic primary guide. It is called a *miscellaneous* folder because it contains filed material from more than one person or firm. When there are fewer than six pieces of filed material to, from, or about the same person or firm, these documents are placed in a folder bearing the same caption as the primary guide it serves. For example, if the caption on the primary guide is *B*, the caption on the miscellaneous folders will also be *B*.

Individual Folders. When six pieces of filed material to, from, or about one person or subject have accumulated in the miscellaneous folder, an individual folder for this material is prepared. The caption on the tab of an individual folder identifies the correspondent. Obviously materials will be found faster if they are filed in an individual folder rather than in a miscellaneous folder.

Special Folders. When an organization files a large amount of material that relates to one subject (such as applications for employment) all this related material is placed in a special folder. The caption identifies the subject or the name of the material. A special folder may be prepared to file all identical last names, thus removing them from the miscellaneous folder. For example, all the *Smiths* may be removed from the miscellaneous folder and placed in a special folder, thus permitting material filed under *Smith* to be found faster.

Capacity of Folders. Folders should never become overcrowded. Each separate folder should contain not more than one inch of filed material. Most file folders have *score lines* at the bottom that are used to widen each folder and thereby increase its capacity. When the folder begins to fill up, the first score is creased; as more pieces of filed material are inserted, the remaining scores are creased.

When a folder can hold no more material it should be subdivided into two or more folders. Subdivisions may be made according to date or by subject:

```
        Jones Company              Jones Company
          January-March                 Orders
        Jones Company              Jones Company
          April-June                  Receipts
```

The subdivided folder should be properly identified. *Folder 1* or *Folder 2* does not indicate what is in the folder.

Miscellaneous folders should be examined often so that individual and special folders may be prepared to expand the filing system logically.

Labels

There are two principal kinds of labels for filing — folder labels and file drawer labels. Folder labels come in a variety of colors. Each company has its own system of identifying file folders by the use of color. You will find the use of color in filing a great help in locating particular files in a matter of seconds and thus acts as a money-saving device in keeping costs under control. Drawer labels are usually white.

Folder Labels. The captions on folder labels may be printed or typewritten. It is better if they are typewritten because they can be read more easily.

Consistency in typing captions on labels is important. The captions should always be typed in exact indexing order (*Brown John A* — not *John A. Brown*). Punctuation other than a hyphen or dash is usually omitted. In order to insure uniformity in the files you should type the first letter in the caption at the same point on each label, usually two spaces from the left edge. Type the name on the label so that after the labels have been attached to the folders, the names will appear at the top edge of each tab. For ease in reading, upper and lower case letters should be used. In a subject file, however, the caption of the main subject is sometimes typed in all upper case letters to make it stand out. The subdivision file labels are then typed in upper and lower case.

Labels must be kept in good condition and must be replaced when torn or difficult to read. Hard-to-read or torn labels tend to delay the finding of filed materials.

Illus. 11-15 The captions at the left are inconsistent in their punctuation, capitalization, and placement. Captions may be typed in all capital letters or as shown at the right.

Drawer Labels. Drawer labels are used to identify the contents of each file drawer. To locate filed material quickly, the labels must be specific, easily read, and up to date. The information should appear on the drawer as illustrated at the top of page 414.

Illus. 11-16

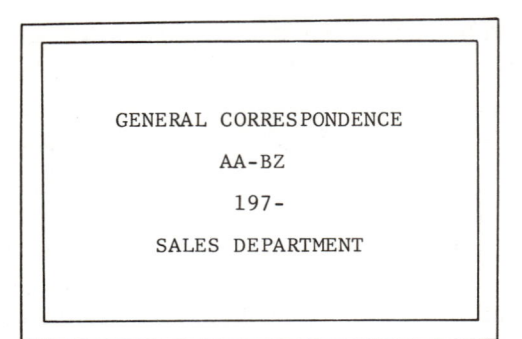

```
GENERAL CORRESPONDENCE
        AA-BZ
        197-
    SALES DEPARTMENT
```

Line 1 — Description
     2 — Index
     3 — Year
     4 — Unit or department

When the contents of a cabinet are changed in any way, the drawer label must be corrected immediately.

POSITIONS OF GUIDES AND FOLDERS

Since the tabs on guides and folders take up only part of the space available, they may appear in several positions. In any filing system, the tabs in each position should be of the same width. Specific positions should be reserved for each type of guide and folder. When guide positions are made with regard to the position of the folders, the filing system becomes well organized. An example of this is an alphabetic system in which four filing positions are used.

Illus. 11-17

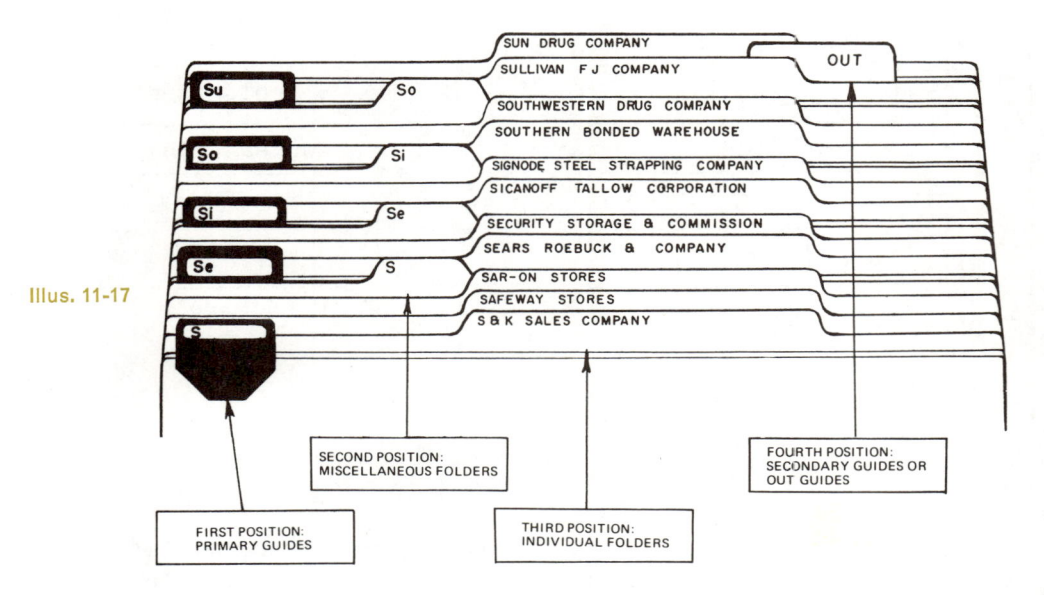

Guides and folders shown:
- Su / So — SUN DRUG COMPANY, SULLIVAN F J COMPANY, SOUTHWESTERN DRUG COMPANY, SOUTHERN BONDED WAREHOUSE
- So / Si — SIGNODE STEEL STRAPPING COMPANY, SICANOFF TALLOW CORPORATION
- Si / Se — SECURITY STORAGE & COMMISSION, SEARS ROEBUCK & COMPANY
- Se / S — SAR-ON STORES, SAFEWAY STORES
- S — S & K SALES COMPANY
- OUT

FIRST POSITION: PRIMARY GUIDES
SECOND POSITION: MISCELLANEOUS FOLDERS
THIRD POSITION: INDIVIDUAL FOLDERS
FOURTH POSITION: SECONDARY GUIDES OR OUT GUIDES

1. First position: Reserved for primary guides indicating the major divisions of the system.

Unit 11 / Business Filing

2. Second position: Reserved for miscellaneous folders. Miscellaneous folders carry the same caption as the primary guides and are placed at the end of each category, *immediately in front of the next primary guide.*

3. Third position: Reserved for individual folders filed directly behind the primary guides.

4. Fourth position: Reserved for secondary guides or out guides. (An out guide is put in the file to indicate that a folder has been borrowed.)

FILING ACCESSORIES

In addition to filing cabinets, guides, and folders, there are many accessories that will make your filing job easier. Some of these are a table or desk to be used when arranging material for the files, file boxes or baskets into which material is placed, and a sorter for arranging papers before they are filed.

QUESTIONS

1. Why would a five-drawer vertical file be preferred to a four-drawer file?
2. What are the three different types of folders that will be found behind any particular guide in a file drawer?
3. What is a miscellaneous folder, and where is it placed in relation to the primary guide and the other folders?
4. What information should a drawer label contain?
5. What is the purpose of an out guide?

JUDGMENT

Princess Helena of Greece recently opened a branch of her cosmetics firm in the United States. Kathy Cushing has just been hired as secretary to Mrs. Peggy Cummings who will head the United States operations.

In addition to the other divisions of the United States branch, there will be a research division for developing new cosmetics. Cosmetic formulas are guarded very carefully. One of Kathy's most important responsibilities is maintaining the highly confidential files of newly developed products. These files are locked when not in use.

Recently at lunch a fellow employee asked Kathy about the ingredients in a new face powder. The girl asking for the information said that her doctor needed to know the ingredients in order to perform an allergy test on her. What should Kathy do?

PERSONAL QUALITIES

Jean Fowler is employed in the Central Records Department of the Adams Electric Company. When Bill Stone, one of the young men in the Accounting Department, phones for information about invoices and other records, he always identifies himself as J. B. Adams, President of the company. Jean has become well aware of the fact that he is joking and usually gives him a smart answer.

One day Jean received a telephone call from a man who identified himself as J. B. Adams. Thinking that the caller was the alleged humorist in the Accounting Department, Jean gave him a very smart answer. Her caller proved to be the real but somewhat astonished J. B. Adams, President of the company.

Jean recovered quickly and supplied Mr. Adams with the information he asked for. Later she began to worry about what had happened and about her general conduct in telephone conversations, particularly when dealing with the young man in the Accounting Department.

Should Jean call the President and try to explain her unusual behavior, or should she try to forget the incident and hope the President will forget it too? What recommendations would you make concerning Jean's behavior?

LANGUAGE USAGE

Of the following 20 words, at least ten of them have been misspelled. Type the entire list giving the correct spelling of each misspelled word.

1. accessories
2. chronalogical
3. consistency
4. distroyed
5. efficiency
6. essential
7. facilitate
8. familar
9. guarentees
10. latteral
11. miscellaneous
12. obviously
13. partition
14. primery
15. reciepts
16. refered
17. retrievel
18. secretary
19. similiar
20. verticle

SECRETARIAL WORK

List five or more places where your name is on file indicating in each instance just how it is filed. For example, list how your name is filed for Social Security purposes, for school records, for life insurance, for a charge account, for a driver's license, for a public library card, in a telephone directory.

Unit 12 RECORDS MANAGEMENT

Part 1. Basic Filing Procedures
   2. Charge-Out, Follow-Up, Transfer, and Retention
   3. Numeric, Subject, and Geographic Filing
   4. Special Files and Information Systems

The secretary has a responsibility to her employer and to her firm to thoroughly understand the records management system with which she works. Not only must she know how to file records properly, but she must also be sure that the important records of the business are protected from possible disasters.

VOCABULARY BUILDER

relatively..............................
    adverb: the state of being dependent for existence on or determined in nature, value, or quality by relation to something else

distinctive..............................
    adjective: different; special; unique; particular

manila..............................
    adjective: a strong and durable paper of a brownish or buff color and smooth finish made from Manila (Philippine Islands) hemp

utilized..............................
    verb: made use of; converted to use

adequate..............................
    adjective: sufficient for a specific requirement; lawfully and reasonably sufficient

anticipated..............................
    adjective (or verb): looked forward to; foreseen; expected; visualized

subordinate..............................
    adjective: placed in a lower class or rank; inferior

warrant..............................
    verb: to declare or maintain with certainty; to certify; to assure; to justify

projecting..............................
    adjective: thrown or cast forward; protruding; jutting out

capable..............................
    adjective: having sufficient physical or mental ability

Be sparing of speech, and things will come right of themselves.
                Lao-Tse

p. 421   Although selecting the indexing caption is **relatively** simple in most cases, there are always some records that might be requested in different ways.

p. 421   A cross-reference sheet (usually of a **distinctive** color) is prepared with the name and address. . . .

p. 423   This is a **manila** card the same size as a file folder, with a tab in the same position as those used for individual folders.

p. 438   Inactive records are inexpensively maintained in the center, since all the floor space can be **utilized**. . . .

p. 438   Without **adequate** indexing, protection, and control of these inactive records, all the time and effort spent in the transfer program have been wasted.

p. 441   All the forecasts on **anticipated** expenditures for your department for the coming year will be filed by the subject caption. . . .

p. 448   Secondary guides are used for the **subordinate** titles that are related to the main subjects on the primary. . . .

p. 451   If there is not enough correspondence to **warrant** the use of a separate city folder, the communication is placed in a miscellaneous state folder. . . .

p. 462   These card guides indicate on **projecting** tabs the various alphabetic sections into which the file drawer is divided.

p. 467   Motorized electronic equipment is available that is **capable** of retrieving information stored on microfilm at very high speeds. . . .

PART 1 BASIC FILING PROCEDURES

Audrey Frierson has been the secretary to Mr. Walter Carrelli since he started the Carrelli Air-Conditioning Company a year ago. Audrey, with the help of a filing consultant, set up the filing system in the beginning and has supervised its expansion. When a new employee is hired, Audrey explains the filing procedures that they are to use. Among the many things Audrey stresses are the proper collection, inspection, and cross-referencing of materials to be filed.

Effective filing procedures begin long before any material is actually placed in the files. If they are properly applied, systematic filing procedures will in the long run save you time which you can use to perform other important office duties. But of even greater importance, well-organized and carefully followed filing practices insure the prompt retrieval of filed records.

COLLECTING PAPERS FOR THE FILES

The basic reason for having a filing system is so that you or your employer can find desired information when it is needed. Unless materials are filed promptly and properly, this is not possible.

Correspondence and other business papers that are to be filed should be gathered in an orderly manner. Materials to be filed should be kept in a special basket or tray which is usually marked *File*.

Several times a day you should gather the materials to be filed from both your desk and your employer's. Occasionally it may be necessary to go through the papers on your employer's desk (with his permission, of course) to gather materials that should be filed.

INSPECTING

The next step in the filing process is inspecting each document that is to be filed. During the inspection you should separate those current materials that will go into your or your employer's files from those that will go to the central filing department. In large offices several times a day a messenger collects the papers to be filed in the central files.

During the inspection process you look for a *release mark*, which is your authority to file each letter. This mark indicates that action has been taken on the letter, and it is released for filing. The release mark is usually indicated by the initials of you or your employer. These initials are placed in the upper left corner of the letter.

Since it is assumed that carbon copies are ready to file, they do not bear release marks. Many firms prepare carbon copies on paper with the words FILE COPY printed in large outline letters across the face of the sheet. Frequently colored paper is used for the file copy.

In addition to checking for the release mark, you should examine records for completeness. All correspondence that is clipped together is examined and stapled (if it belongs together) in the upper left corner. The reply is stapled on top of the incoming letter. Paper clips, rubber bands, or straight pins are never placed in the file drawer. Torn papers should be mended at this time.

INDEXING

Although every step in the filing process is important, the indexing step is particularly significant. *Indexing* is the process of determining how a document is to be filed. An incorrect decision at this time may mean a lost letter. At the very least, it means lost time in locating the letter. It is necessary, therefore, to scan or read each letter carefully to determine the *key name* or title that best identifies the material.

The way materials are requested usually determines the way they should be indexed. An incoming letter could be filed under the name appearing on the letterhead, the name of the person signing the letter, the name of a person or business mentioned in the body of the letter, or the subject of the letter. For example, a letter announcing a new fire-resistant filing cabinet would probably be filed under the heading "Office Equipment" in a folder labeled "Filing Cabinets" rather than under the name of the distributor appearing on the letterhead.

Copies of outgoing letters could be filed under the name of the addressee, the name of a person or business mentioned in the letter, or the subject of the letter. If a letter is of a personal nature, it is filed under the name of the person to or by whom it is written, even though the letter may have been written on a company letterhead. If there is any doubt about how a document should be indexed, the person who has released the record for filing should be consulted.

CODING

After the exact indexing order has been chosen, the document is marked or coded. A document may be coded in several different ways. The indexing units may be underlined.

|Acme Dry Cleaning Corporation

R. Robert |Wagner

or the units may be numbered:

      1   2   3   4
Acme Dry Cleaning Corporation

  2   3   1
R. Robert Wagner

If the name or subject does not appear in the letter, it must be written in, preferably in the upper right portion of the paper. All coding is done with a colored pencil. Coding aids in filing the record each time it is removed from the file as it does not need to be reread.

CROSS-REFERENCING

Although selecting the indexing caption is relatively simple in most cases, there are always some records that might be requested in different ways. For example, your firm might receive a letter from a good customer recommending an applicant for a position. Obviously this letter of recommendation should be filed with other records referring to the applicant and would be filed in the applicant's folder in the "Applications" section. It may be well, however, to keep a record of the letter in the customer's folder. The name of the applicant, therefore, is underlined on the letter as the primary indexing unit. The customer's name (of secondary importance in this instance) is also underlined and an X placed at the end of the line in the margin to show that a cross-reference should be made.

A cross-reference sheet (usually of a distinctive color) is prepared with the name and address of the customer, the date of the letter, a brief description of the letter, and where the letter is filed following the "SEE." This cross-reference is then placed in the customer's folder, in its proper date sequence with the other papers, as a record of the letter.

Rather than prepare regular cross-reference sheets, many companies prefer using a photocopy of the original. This speeds retrieval since a complete copy of the record is available at each file point. Do not forget, however, to underline an X on each copy, so that you will know in which folder each is to be filed.

Many hard-to-index documents should be cross-referenced in several places, for this is your one opportunity to think of the number of ways by which material may be requested. Too much cross-referencing

Illus. 12-1   Letter properly released and coded

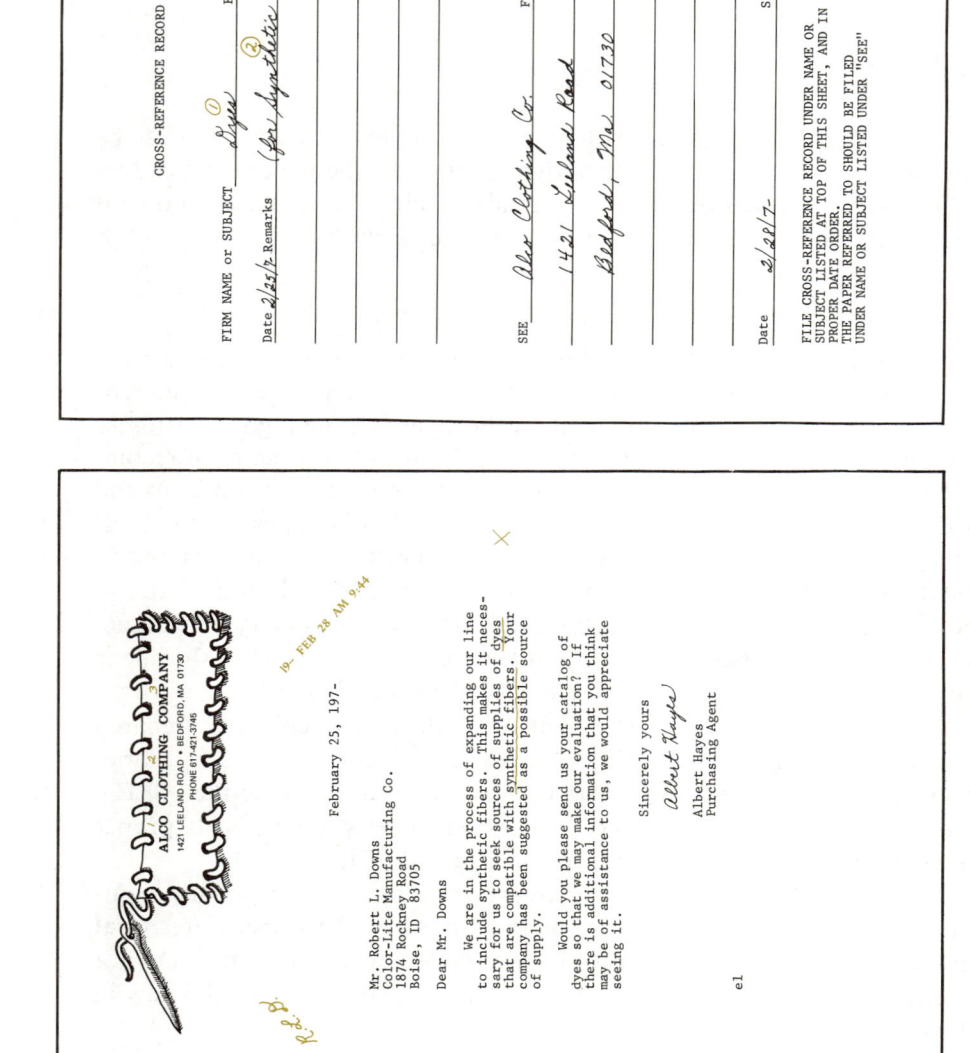

Illus. 12-2   Cross-reference for letter

422   Unit 12 / Records Management

requires considerable time as well as filing space; however, too little cross-referencing may delay retrieval.

If a permanent cross-reference is desired, a cross-reference guide is prepared. This is a manila card the same size as a file folder, with a tab in the same position as those used for individual folders. A situation requiring a permanent cross-reference guide might be as follows: The name of a company with which you do a great deal of business is changed. Another folder is prepared for the new name and all the material is placed in this folder. The old folder is now replaced with a permanent cross-reference guide with the necessary retrieval information on its tab:

Adams and Smith Manufacturing Co.
See Adams and Jones Manufacturing Co.

If a special form is not available, use the back half of the folder as a cross-reference guide by cutting off the front flap of the folder at the score line. The cross-reference guide remains in the file as long as the name or subject is still active. (See page 449 for additional information on cross-referencing.)

SORTING

After the records have been coded and the necessary cross-reference sheets prepared, the material is ready to be sorted. *Sorting* is the process of arranging the records in indexing order before placing them in the folders.

Illus. 12-3
Daily filing time can be greatly reduced by using proper indexing and sorting equipment.

Yawman & Erbe

A. INSPECTING means seeing that the letter has been released for filing. GTF indicates that this letter has been released.

B. INDEXING means determining the key name under which the correspondence should be filed. This letter should be filed under Shipley-Langston Stores.

C. CODING means determining and marking the exact indexing order. The correct order is (1) Shipley (2) Langston (3) Stores.

D. CROSS-REFERENCING means trying to decide if the letter might be requested in some other way. This letter should be cross-referenced under (1) Langston (2) Shipley (3) Stores. The X indicates that it has been cross-referenced.

E. SORTING means arranging all the records in indexing order before placing them in the files. This letter would be sorted under S.

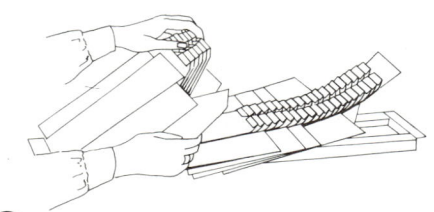

F. PLACING RECORDS IN THE FILES simply means storing the correspondence in the proper place until it is needed.

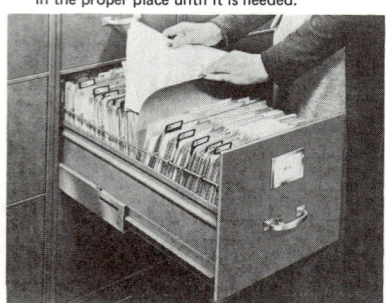

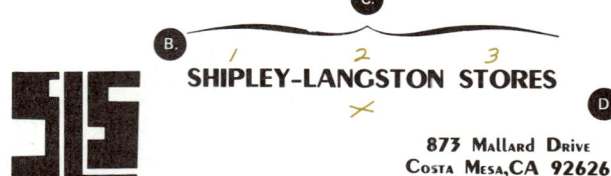

SHIPLEY-LANGSTON STORES
1   2   3

873 Mallard Drive
Costa Mesa, CA 92626
Telephone 714-633-0525

GTF

197- MAR 20 AM 10:45

March 18, 197-

Mrs. Grace T. Froman, President
Foremost Fashions, Inc.
2142 Granada Avenue
San Francisco, CA 94112

Dear Mrs. Froman

You were right! Your spring collection of dresses is the fastest moving line we have ever carried. After being on our racks for only two weeks, about 40 percent of our stock has been sold.

I wish you could be here to listen to our customers' compliments. Being wise shoppers, they realize the versatility, practicality, and economy of your dresses. We have never before witnessed such complete acceptance by the consumer.

We send our congratulations on your success. If the present sales pace continues, you should receive a substantial follow-up order within the next two weeks.

Sincerely yours

George B Verner

George B. Verner
Manager

sv

Illus. 12-4   Basic filing procedure

Sorting serves two important purposes. First, it saves actual filing time. Since the records are in exact indexing order, you are able to move quickly from drawer to drawer, thus saving time and energy for other important tasks. Second, if documents are requested before they are filed, they can be found quickly.

If the volume of filing is high, special sorting trays or compartments should be used. Sorting trays are equipped with alphabetic, numeric, or geographic guides, depending upon the classification system you are using. When you sort materials alphabetically, for example, records beginning with the letter *A* are placed behind an *A* guide; those beginning with *B*, behind a *B* guide, and so on through the alphabet. After the materials have been rough sorted, they are removed from the sorting tray and placed in exact alphabetic order (fine sorting). If the volume of material is low, this same procedure may be followed on your desk top.

PLACING RECORDS IN THE FILE

After the records have been fine sorted they are placed in the files. A systematic routine should always be followed:

1. Locate the proper file drawer by examining drawer labels.
2. Scan the primary guides in the drawer to locate the major alphabetic section desired.
3. Check to see if an individual or special folder has been prepared for this material. If so, file the record here.
4. If no individual or special folder is available for this particular record, file the letter in the miscellaneous folder for the section.

ARRANGING MATERIALS IN FOLDERS

Letters should always be placed in folders with the front of the letter facing the front of the folder and the top of the letter at the left side.

In *individual* folders, letters are arranged according to date, with the *most recent* record in front. In *miscellaneous* folders, documents are arranged alphabetically by name; if there are two or more records for the same individual or company, they are arranged according to date, with the most recent record first. In a *special* folder, the records are arranged alphabetically by name and then by date in each group of names.

TWENTY FILING HINTS

Twenty filing hints recommended by experienced secretaries are given on the following pages.

Part 1 / Basic Filing Procedures 425

1. Be a good housekeeper. Well-organized, carefully administered files encourage accurate filing and rapid retrieval. What is more, you will enjoy filing!
2. Don't foolishly economize on file supplies. Good quality supplies hold up through continued hard use; poor quality supplies soon wear out and hinder the efficiency of the system. Choose the right supplies for the right records with a particular system in mind.
3. Before refiling any folder that has been removed from the files, quickly examine its contents. You may find a lost document by performing this simple procedure. Always "jog" the contents of a folder before returning it to the file.
4. Set aside a definite time each day for filing. Remember: records belong in the file — not in or on desks.
5. Constantly analyze your filing system and recommend ways in which it can be improved. Your employer will appreciate any suggestion for an improved information system. Seek the advice of your office supplies dealer. Constantly review the various business publications. They'll keep you informed on the latest products and new developments in the field of records management.

Illus. 12-5
Don't allow folders to bulge. Bulging folders encourage filing errors.

Oxford Pendaflex Corporation

6. Let color help. Use different color labels for different file years or periods. A well-planned color scheme will aid in prompt filing and retrieving.
7. Keep your system simple. If others must use your files, be certain they understand how the system works, but insist that you do all the filing and refiling. Provide a handy place for them to place the materials they have removed from the files. They will be glad to cooperate — and it will guarantee file accuracy.
8. File the most active records in the most easily reached parts of the file cabinets. Active records belong in the top drawers, less active documents in bottom drawers. This saves both time and energy.
9. Use your filing cabinets only for filing, not for storing office supplies and other items. File only vital records in the special fire-resistant equipment that has been purchased for their protection.
10. Don't allow folders to bulge. Bulging folders encourage filing errors. When necessary, subdivide individual folders into monthly folders. Expand your system by preparing special and individual folders whenever possible.

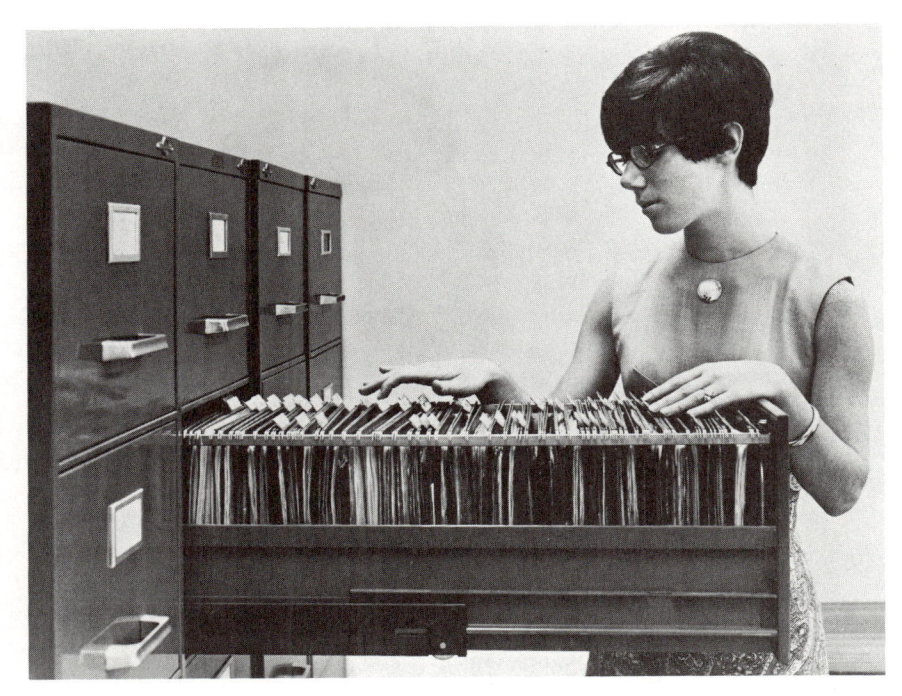

Illus. 12-6
Expand your system by preparing special and individual folders whenever possible.

Oxford Pendaflex Corporation

Part 1 / Basic Filing Procedures

11. Separate records that must be maintained in the files for long periods of time from those of temporary value.
12. If smaller than normal sized documents are placed in file folders, glue or tape them to standard size paper. They will be easier to find.
13. If a particular document was difficult to retrieve, cross-reference it when it is finally found. It will save time when it is requested again.
14. Protect the tabs on guides and folders. Always lift a folder or guide by the side — never by the tab. Replace folder labels as soon as they are difficult to read.
15. Don't fill a file drawer to capacity. Leave at least six inches of working space in each file drawer. It speeds up your work and prevents papers from being torn.
16. To avoid accidents, close a file drawer immediately after using it; and open only one drawer at a time.
17. Use the proper filing tools. A rubber finger helps separate documents; a file shelf makes you more efficient at the file; a file stool conserves your energy (yes, you can file sitting down).
18. Mend all torn documents before placing them in a file folder.
19. Follow a regular program of removing inactive records from the active files.
20. Be certain to follow, without variation, the office procedures that have been established to protect vital records.

QUESTIONS

1. How are letters and other papers gathered together for filing and by whom?
2. Do carbon copies of outgoing letters need release marks?
3. Is *indexing* something that is written?
4. What are the various captions under which incoming letters could be filed?
5. Under what captions may copies of outgoing letters be filed?
6. Under what caption is a personal letter filed?
7. What is coding and how is it done?
8. What is cross-referencing?
9. What is used to establish a permanent cross-reference?
10. How are letters arranged in *individual* folders? in *miscellaneous* folders? in *special* folders?

JUDGMENT

1. Why are indexing and coding so important in filing?
2. It is said that cross-referencing can be overdone. Under what circumstances might this be true?
3. Why is the most recent letter placed in front in an *individual* folder?

PERSONAL QUALITIES

In the office of the Walters Shoe Company, Mr. J. B. Wilkins has received a letter asking for an answer to an earlier letter written by the National Leather Company. The unanswered letter was found in the *special* folder of the National Leather Company. The letter bears the initials JBW as a release-for-filing mark, but Mr. Wilkins says he does not remember initialing the letter. The initials were actually placed there by mistake by Mr. Wilkins' secretary. What should the secretary do in this situation?

LANGUAGE USAGE

All twenty key words listed below are used in filing. After you have studied the example, type the key word and the word or phrase you believe is *nearest in meaning* to the key word.

Example: facilitate — (a) appreciate (b) depreciate (c) *make easier* (d) negotiate

1. *adhere* — (a) to expect (b) to hold closely (c) to part (d) to loosen
2. *appropriate* — (a) approximate (b) apt (c) fitting (d) unsuitable
3. *caption* — (a) finishing stone (b) heading or title (c) rank of captain (d) seizure
4. *comprehensive* — (a) compelling (b) complex (c) extensive (d) limited
5. *consistent* — (a) consonant (b) incompatible (c) incongruous (d) tribunal
6. *conventional* — (a) contrary (b) customary (c) jovial (d) well informed
7. *distinctive* — (a) distasteful (b) sound harsh (c) intemperate (d) individual
8. *document* — (a) a particular principle (b) an established opinion (c) any written item (d) ownership of land
9. *effective* — (a) exhausted of vigor (b) flowing out (c) producing intended results (d) show enthusiasm
10. *identical* — (a) idealistic (b) matching (c) unlike (d) visionary
11. *initial* — (a) beginning (b) concluding (c) inheriting (d) suggesting
12. *legible* — (a) branch of military science (b) multitude (c) valid (d) capable of being read

13. *primary* — (a) humble (b) last (c) main (d) proud
14. *procedure* — (a) a disposition (b) course of action (c) to defer action (d) to progress
15. *propel* — (a) foretell (b) multiply (c) project (d) prove
16. *retention* — (a) silent (b) rejoinder (c) remedy (d) memory
17. *retrieval* — (a) recovery (b) retraction (c) retrenchment (d) retribution
18. *sequence* — (a) separation (b) series (c) seriousness (d) sermon
19. *variation* — (a) deviation (b) sameness (c) truthfulness (d) word for word
20. *vital* — (a) unimportant (b) expendable (c) resounding (d) essential

SECRETARIAL WORK

1. The following letters pertaining to the application of John A. Dillon are filed in the "Applications" folder of the firm where you work. Indicate the order, from front to back, in which the letters should be placed in this folder.
   (a) Henry & Currier Company's March 8 letter of recommendation
   (b) John A. Dillon's March 12 letter stating that he will call on March 15
   (c) Your firm's March 3 letter to Mr. Dillon asking him to come in for an interview
   (d) John A. Dillon's March 18 letter accepting the position
   (e) Your firm's March 5 letter to the Henry & Currier Company asking for information about Mr. John A. Dillon
   (f) Your firm's March 11 letter to Mr. Dillon asking him to come in for a second interview
   (g) Your firm's March 17 letter offering Mr. Dillon a position in the cost accounting department
   (h) John A. Dillon's March 1 letter of application
   (i) Your firm's March 9 letter to Henry & Currier Company thanking them for their cooperation

2. The following letters are filed in the Harvey O. Jackson individual folder. Indicate the order, from front to back, in which the letters should be placed in this folder.
   (a) Harvey O. Jackson's order of April 1
   (b) Your firm's letter of April 8 enclosing the April 6 invoice
   (c) Harvey O. Jackson's letter of April 30 enclosing a check
   (d) A cross-reference sheet dated April 10
   (e) Your firm's letter of May 3 acknowledging the check of April 30
   (f) Your firm's invoice of April 6 for the April 1 order

3. The letters listed on the next page are filed in the "To-Tw" miscellaneous folder. Indicate the order, from front to back, in which the letters should be placed in this folder.

(a) Your firm's letter of September 30 to Arthur Towne, Jr.
(b) The receipted invoice sent to you on September 21 by Albert Town
(c) Towne and Lovitt's order of September 2
(d) Your firm's letter of September 28 to Richard G. Twitchell
(e) Your firm's invoice of September 6 covering the September 2 order from Towne and Lovitt
(f) An advertising circular and letter dated September 14 sent to your employer by H. J. Tweed

4. This is a continuation of the alphabetic indexing exercise begun in Unit 11, Part 3.

   (a) Type the following names in index form on 25 file cards. Type the number in the upper right-hand corner and the name and address below the indexed name as you did in Unit 11, Part 3.
   (b) Integrate these 25 cards in proper filing order with the 50 cards prepared in Unit 11, Part 3.
   (c) Save the cards for the assignment following Unit 12, Part 4.

   (51) X-Cel Paints & Varnishes, 532 Mill St., Pittsburgh, PA 15221
   (52) Theodore C. Haller, 59 E. 10th St., Charleston, WV 25303
   (53) Henry R. Elston, II, 660 N. Michigan Ave., Chicago, IL 60611
   (54) XYZ Electrical Repair Service, 2d and Main Sts., Lexington, KY 40507
   (55) Countess Flora's Dance Academy, Chase Hotel, St. Louis, MO 63166
   (56) Mrs. K. D. Ingles (Hazel Parks), 40 Sheridan Dr., Providence, RI 02909
   (57) Quick Brothers Florists, 6720 Turkey Run Rd., Nashville, TN 37202
   (58) Charles T. Hallam, 4600 Pueblo St., Phoenix, AZ 85041
   (59) Hall-Kramer Printing Co., Inc., 7700 S. Wells St., Chicago, IL 60621
   (60) R. Nelson Forrester, 377 Desert Drive, Reno, NV 89504
   (61) Robert N. Forrest, 781 University Ave., Minneapolis, MN 55413
   (62) Sister Julietta, Sacred Heart Academy, Racine, WI 53401
   (63) William A. Graves, 239 N. Vineyard Drive, Kenosha, WI 53140
   (64) Mrs. Arthur P. Matthews (Helen), 5229 Crest Drive, Cleveland, OH 44121

(65) Town & Country Furniture Co., Town & Country Shop-In, Centerville, IN 47330
(66) U.S. Electrotype Corp., 2101 - 19th St., Long Island City, NY 11105
(67) Prince George Hotel, St. Thomas, Virgin Islands 00801
(68) Les Trois Chats Inn, 48 Henri St., Quebec, Province of Quebec, Canada
(69) 29 Palms Motel, U.S. 60 at First St., Twenty-Nine Palms, CA 92277
(70) Venice Yacht Club, 29 Oceanside Drive, Venice, CA 90291
(71) Mr. Morris Book Store, 6th & Pike Sts., Mt. Morris, IL 61054
(72) State Auditor, Columbus, OH 43216
(73) Hire-the-Handicapped Committee, 30 Le Veque Tower, Denver, CO 80201
(74) Hamilton County SPCA, Colerain & Blue Rock Sts., Cincinnati, OH 45223
(75) Port-au-Prince Imports, Inc., 21 Main St., Gulfport, MS 39501

PART 2 CHARGE-OUT, FOLLOW-UP, TRANSFER, AND RETENTION

After five years of operations, the Nickerson Printing Company has expanded to the point where it needs a central filing system. A new filing clerk has just been hired. Julia Coombs, Mr. Nickerson's secretary, has supervised the files since the company was founded. Until the central files are set up and are being maintained by the new clerk, Julia will continue to oversee the use of the files. Julia knows that it is necessary to maintain the system of charging out files, following up on correspondence, and transferring and storing records. Until the new file clerk learns the system, she will have to look to Julia for guidance.

Records are kept because they contain needed information; filing systems are developed in order to retrieve this information promptly and efficiently. Yet if records are often removed from the files without *charging* them to the borrower, the system will soon become useless. It will certainly not be worth the time, effort, and money that have gone into its development and maintenance.

Since the people who borrow records from the files are busy, they may neglect to return these documents to the files. Although every worker should feel responsible for maintaining an effective office information system, it is your responsibility as a secretary to protect the records placed under your control. Therefore, some type of charge-out and follow-up system must be developed to insure the return of borrowed documents to the files.

CHARGE-OUT

There are times when other executives or secretaries will need materials that are stored in your files. When materials are borrowed from your files, you should prepare a form that identifies the records removed. This form (usually 5″ x 3″ or 6″ x 4″) is known as a *requisition* card and has spaces for a full description of the material borrowed, the name and department of the borrower, the date the material was removed from the file, and the date it is to be returned.

Charge-Out Forms

In addition to the requisition card, four kinds of forms are commonly used when material is taken from the files. They are *out guides, out folders, carrier folders,* and *substitution cards.*

Out Guides. An out guide is a pressboard guide with the word *OUT* printed on its tab. It is placed in the files when an entire folder is borrowed. There are two forms of out guides. One type is ruled on both sides, and the charge information is written directly on the guide. When the folder is returned, the out guide is removed and the charge information crossed out. The guide is then ready for further use.

The other kind of out guide has a pocket into which a requisition card is placed. This form is preferred since it is faster to use and the charge information is usually more legible. The requisition cards may later be used to analyze the activity of the files. A tabulation of the cards will determine how often the files are used and which records are most active.

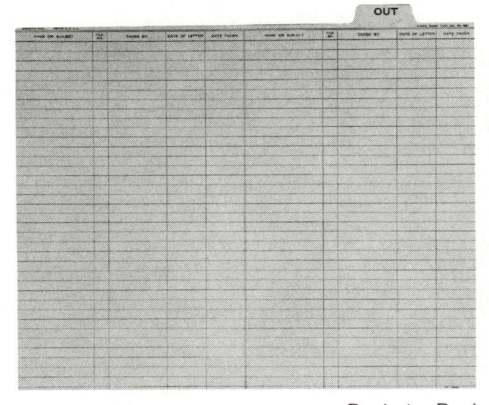

Remington Rand
Illus. 12-7   Ruled out guide

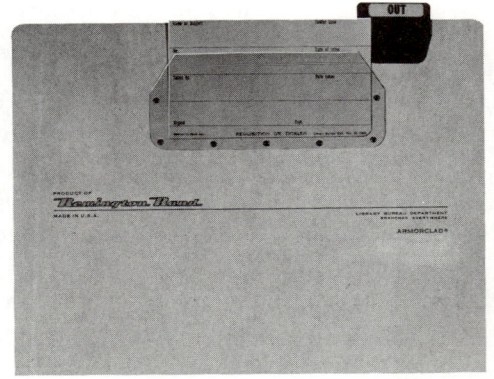

Remington Rand
Illus. 12-8   Out guide with pocket

Out Folders. Some firms prefer using out folders when an entire folder is requested from the files. If additional material reaches the files before the regular folder is returned, it is temporarily filed in the out folder. This material is then filed in the regular folder when it is returned.

Carrier Folder. A carrier folder is useful in reminding the borrower to return records to the files. It is of a different color from the regular folders with the words *RETURN TO FILES* printed on it. The requested material is removed from the regular folder and sent to the borrower in a

434   Unit 12 / Records Management

carrier folder. An out card or guide is placed in the regular folder containing the charge-out information. The regular folder remains in the file to hold any material placed in the file before the carrier folder is returned. A carrier folder saves the regular folder from the wear and tear it would receive when removed from the files.

Substitution Cards. A substitution card is a tabbed card, usually salmon-colored, that is placed in a folder when single documents are borrowed. The word *OUT* is printed on the tab. The charge-out information may be recorded on the card itself or on a requisition form inserted in a pocket of the substitution card. A substitution card is basically the same as an out guide.

Remington Rand
Illus. 12-9   Out folder

Remington Rand
Illus. 12-10   Carrier folder

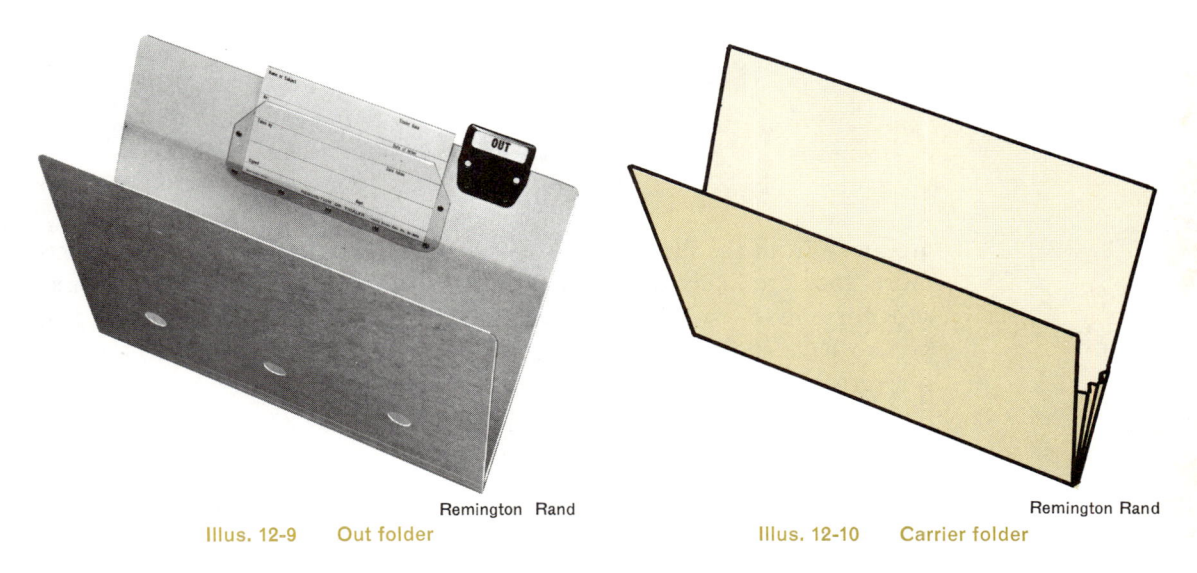

Photocopies

To avoid removing important papers from the files, many firms prepare photocopies of a requested record. When this method is used, the document is removed from the files and copied on a copying machine. The original document is then refiled and the photocopy sent to the borrower with instructions to destroy it after use. This method is generally used when single documents are requested rather than an entire folder.

Length of Charge Time

Borrowed materials are usually used by the borrower immediately and should be returned to the files as soon as possible. The longer records

Illus. 12-11
Requests for files may be made in person, over the phone, or through inter-office mail. No matter what method is used, a form should be prepared that fully identifies the records removed from the files.

Ohio National Life Insurance Company

are away from the files, the more difficult it is to get them back; furthermore, they are likely to be lost or discarded. Most firms charge out records for only one week (with weekly extensions, if found necessary). It is best to have short charge-out periods and prompt follow-up of materials not returned to the files.

FOLLOW-UP

How will you remember to give attention to the many matters that require future attention? Since you should not rely on your memory, you will find it necessary to devise a system that will call your attention to these matters at the exact date when action must be taken. A file that is designed for this purpose is called a *follow-up file* and is arranged in chronological order. Two common follow-up files are the card tickler file and the dated follow-up folder file.

Card Tickler Files

A card tickler file consists of a set of 12 monthly primary guides and 31 daily secondary guides. Important matters to be followed up are recorded on cards and placed behind the appropriate month and day guides in the file. A card tickler file may be used to follow up records that have been borrowed from the files or to follow up other matters that require attention.

Illus. 12-12
Follow-up file

Dated Follow-Up Folders

This file resembles the card tickler file except that a folder is available for each day of the month. Items that require follow-up are placed in the correct day folder, and the folder is then placed behind the appropriate monthly guide. For example, a folder may contain a photocopy of an incoming letter or an extra carbon of an outgoing letter that requests an answer by a certain day. On that particular day you should check to see if an answer to the letter has been received. If not, follow-up action is taken. By using photocopies and extra carbons for follow-up, the correspondence can be filed in its proper place and the official folder is always complete. This procedure saves a great deal of time.

TRANSFER

Office files should contain only those records that are needed to operate efficiently. If inactive or outdated records are never removed from the files, needed information becomes more and more difficult to retain and retrieve. Every organization should adopt a plan of removing inactive documents from the active files by *transferring* these records to a records center.

Removing inactive records from the office files serves three important purposes:

1. Active records can be filed and retrieved quickly.
2. Expensive office space and file equipment are kept at a minimum.

3. Costs are reduced since transferred records are housed in inexpensive file equipment, usually cardboard transfer cases.

It is important to remember that not every document received in an office should be filed; not every document retained in the active file should be transferred.

Transferring File Folders

Records that must be kept for long periods of time should be separated from those of temporary value when placing records in transfer cases. Miscellaneous, special, and individual folders are usually transferred from the active to the inactive files when they are no longer needed. Each transferred folder should be stamped *Transfer File* to prevent it from being returned to the active files should it be requested from the records center. Many firms use different colored folder labels to identify different file periods.

The Records Center

A records center is an important part of any transfer program. This center houses documents no longer needed for daily reference. Records may be stored at the center indefinitely or for a temporary period only. Inactive records are inexpensively maintained in the center, since all the floor space can be utilized (floor to ceiling filing) and inexpensive equipment can be used to house the records.

Documents maintained in the center must be accurately indexed and controlled so that they will be available if requested. Without adequate indexing, protection, and control of these inactive records, all the time and effort spent in the transfer program have been wasted.

RETENTION

Every organization is faced with the problem of how long to retain its records. Because of the growing volume of paper work, many firms have established *record retention schedules*. This schedule identifies the retention value of every record created or received by an organization and determines which records must be retained and for how long. Useless records occupy expensive floor space and costly equipment; they hinder the rapid retrieval of needed information.

While certain documents must be retained permanently, most records created and received in the average business organization have a limited period of usefulness. The National Records Management Council estimates that 95 percent of all corporate paper work over a year old is rarely, if ever, referred to again. Most record authorities estimate that 40 percent of all stored records can be legally destroyed.

Even though every organization must develop its own retention schedule, factors that affect the retention value of business records include:

1. Legal requirements (federal, state, and local)
2. Office use (those records needed to operate on a daily basis)
3. Historical documents
4. Vital records

A retention schedule can be adopted only after a thorough study of the record requirements of a particular organization. Legal counsel should always be sought. Once a schedule is adopted, it must be continually revised to meet changing conditions and needs.

QUESTIONS

1. Why should all materials taken from files be *charged out* to the person taking them?
2. What is a requisition card?
3. What are the two types of out guides? Which is better?
4. What is the difference between an out guide and a substitution card?
5. How is the out folder used?
6. What are the advantages of releasing photocopies rather than original documents from the files?
7. Describe a card tickler file and tell of its use.
8. Why are inactive records removed from the office files?
9. Why should a transferred folder be stamped *Transfer File*?
10. List four factors that affect the retention schedule of business records.

JUDGMENT

The filing department of a certain business is so small that no one person is responsible for the keeping of a record of material borrowed. Each person who needs correspondence from the files removes it from the folders, signs his name in a record book kept for this purpose, and takes the correspondence with him. Can you recommend any improvement in this system?

PERSONAL QUALITIES

Your company has a rule that all materials requisitioned from the files must be returned within 48 hours. One of the company executives has a habit of holding folders for a week or more frequently creating problems in the filing room.

What action could the records supervisor take to try to improve this situation?

LANGUAGE USAGE

Type the following sentences and insert the correct punctuation.

1. Yes she said Ill take the folder with me
2. What are these Xs for
3. Carsons folder contained 20 pieces of correspondence ten of which were retained but the Moore file contained 15 pieces of correspondence all of which were retained
4. Smiths folder was removed early Tuesday morning it should have been returned by Thursday afterroon
5. The supervisor said that out guides substitution cards and out folders are used frequently

SECRETARIAL WORK

1. Type captions on folder labels for each of the following authors, who contributed articles to a recent issue of *The Office*, a magazine of management, equipment, and automation. (If folder labels are not available, type the names on blank sheets of paper approximately 3½" x 1½".)

George H. Harmon	Joe E. Torrence
Arthur L. Ratz	Charles A. Agemian
Jord H. Jordan, Jr.	Denis S. Greensmith
J. A. Mosher	Theodore K. Cobb
Wesley S. Bagby	T. M. Galloway
Thomas G. Morris	E. Philip Kron
Richard I. Tanaka	Patrick R. Gaffney
Frank Plasha	Carl W. Golgart
Bruce I. Blackstone	John H. Dunham
Bernard Goldstein	Robert E. Bennis
G. Peter Ignasiak	Ellsworth H. Morse, Jr.
Clarence E. Franke	K. R. Atkins, Jr.
James D. Parker, Jr.	Donald F. Evans
William W. Newell	Walter M. Carlson

Type the name without punctuation on the lower half of the folder label about two spaces from the left edge, as illustrated.

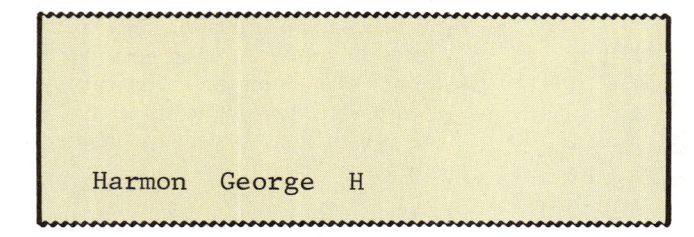

```
Harmon    George    H
```

2. After the names in Problem 1 are indexed in alphabetical order type the list on a single sheet of paper. Center the heading, AUTHORS OF THE JANUARY ISSUE, and type the list in two double spaced columns.

Unit 12 / Records Management

PART 3 — NUMERIC, SUBJECT, AND GEOGRAPHIC FILING

Allison Taylor was recently hired as the secretary to Mr. Harold Skeen, the General Sales Manager for Midwest Appliance Wholesalers, Inc. This company distributes household appliances to all parts of the United States. Allison was asked to work in the filing department for one week so that she could get accustomed to the filing systems used and so that she could get a quick picture of how the business operates. She quickly discovered that in addition to an alphabetic filing system, Midwest Appliances uses a numeric system for stock numbers and orders, a subject system for major appliances, and a geographic system for sales territories.

As a secretary, you will probably be more concerned with alphabetic correspondence filing methods than with numeric, subject, or geographic. To assist your executive properly, however, you may need to understand other filing systems and how they operate. You may be required to request records from a filing department that uses one of the other systems. You may also be required to code correspondence for storage in the central files.

Records must be filed in the manner by which they will be called for — by name, by number, by subject, or by geographic area. When you have correspondence with a customer, you know that it will be filed alphabetically by the company name. However, if your executive asks that copies of the sales reports be sent to the managers of each territory, you will make use of a geographic file. In a purchasing department, you will keep a numeric file by the purchase order number. All the forecasts on anticipated expenditures for your department for the coming year will be filed by the subject caption *Budgets* not under *Controller Jamison*.

NUMERIC FILING

With the widespread use of data processing systems for repetitive and statistical operations in many organizations, numbers have become important in identifying many records in today's businesses. In general, only large systems use numeric filing. Records that are frequently identified by number and filed in a numeric sequence are insurance policies, purchase orders, sales orders, contracts, licenses, customers' charge accounts, bank accounts, and credit card accounts. Many large government agencies such as the Social Security Administration, the Veterans Administration, and state motor vehicle bureaus file their records in numerical order.

Illus. 12-13
Many records are filed in numerical sequence, and many kinds of businesses and government agencies use numerical files.

Oxford Pendaflex Corporation

Since it would be impossible to remember the file number of every business paper, an alphabetic card index of the numerically filed material is maintained by name or by subject as a cross-reference. Numeric filing systems are *indirect* in finding and filing because, in most instances, reference must be made to the alphabetic card index before a document is found or coded.

A numeric file usually consists of three parts:

1. The file itself, in which the documents are filed by an assigned number and in which the guides and folders bear numeric captions.

2. An index card control file, in which names or subject titles are arranged alphabetically.
3. An *accession* book or *register*, in which a record of assigned numbers is kept.

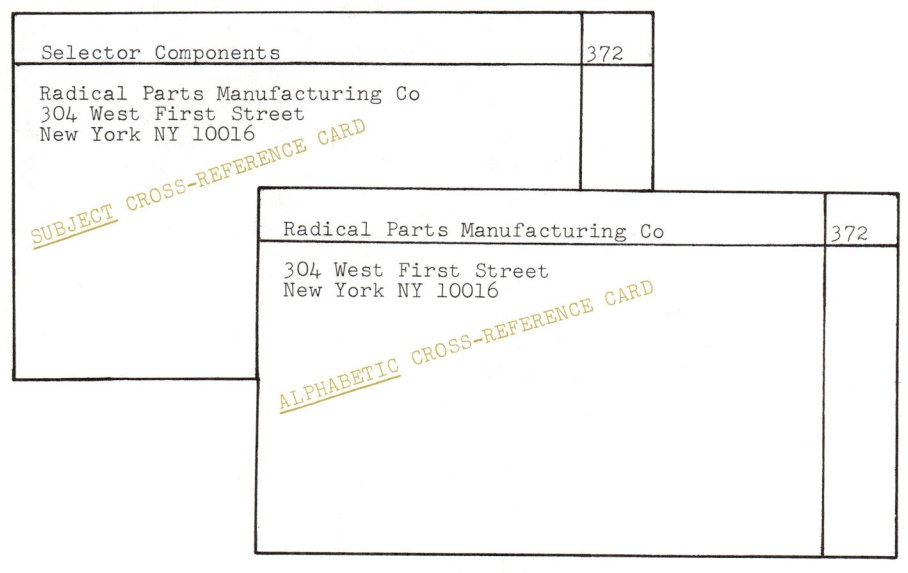

```
┌─────────────────────────────────────────┬──────┐
│ Selector Components                     │ 372  │
│                                         │      │
│ Radical Parts Manufacturing Co          │      │
│ 304 West First Street                   │      │
│ New York NY 10016                       │      │
│                                         │      │
│   SUBJECT CROSS-REFERENCE CARD          │      │
└─────────────────────────────────────────┴──────┘
```

```
┌─────────────────────────────────────────┬──────┐
│ Radical Parts Manufacturing Co          │ 372  │
│                                         │      │
│ 304 West First Street                   │      │
│ New York NY 10016                       │      │
│                                         │      │
│   ALPHABETIC CROSS-REFERENCE CARD       │      │
│                                         │      │
└─────────────────────────────────────────┴──────┘
```

Illus. 12-14   Index control cards

NUMERIC ARRANGEMENTS

There are several arrangements of numbers that may be used in numeric filing:

1. The numbers may be in consecutive order (consecutive number filing).
2. Certain portions of a long number may be used as the first indexing unit (terminal-digit and/or middle-digit filing).
3. The number may be combined with letters of the alphabet (alpha-numeric filing).

Consecutive Number Filing

In this arrangement documents are filed in strict numeric sequence. The number is written in the upper right portion of the paper, and an alphabetic card is typed as a cross-reference to the assigned number. The papers are filed in numerical sequence in folders, and the card is filed alphabetically in the index. Additional papers related to the same subject are checked against the card index and coded with the same number.

Illus. 12-15
Consecutive number file
Documents are filed by number and cross-referenced in alphabetic and subject card files.

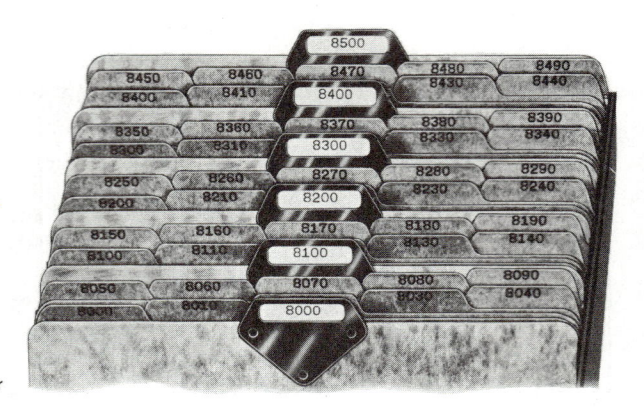

Shaw-Walker

Legal Files. In legal firms a number (for example, 607) is assigned to a client and as additional matters are handled for the same client, they are given a secondary number (607-1 — Will) to separate the new material. An alphabetic cross-reference card is made for each client as well as for each item the legal firm is taking care of for the client. Individual folders are prepared for each and are filed numerically:

    607   John W. Rodgers
    607-1 Will
    607-2 Real Estate Holdings
    607-3 Income Tax Records
    607-4 Insurance

Project and Job Files. Consecutive numeric filing is used for these two types of records primarily because there are related drawings, blueprints, and artwork connected with the correspondence and such material is controlled more easily through a numbering system. Almost always it is necessary to subdivide the correspondence by subject. Drawings will have secondary numbers for parts of the project or job, and dates for revisions of drawings become an important identifying factor. Numbers are obtained from the accession book. The alphabetical card index is an essential key for locating material by name or subject.

Numeric Correspondence Files. Because it is a slow and indirect method, ordinary correspondence today is seldom filed numerically. The need to keep papers confidential is the primary reason for using this system. Numbers are assigned in consecutive order from the accession book, and individual folders are made for each correspondent. All papers for this correspondent are placed in this folder, with the most recent material in the front. An alphabetic index card is made. Neither the accession book nor the card index is available to unauthorized personnel.

Illus. 12-16
Confidential correspondence files which combine numbers and names

Shaw-Walker

Terminal-Digit Filing

Terminal-digit filing is a method of numeric filing based on reading numbers from *right to left*. It is ideal for any large numeric file with five or more digits. In terminal-digit filing, the numbers are assigned in the same manner as for consecutive number filing, but the numbers are read in small groups (00–99) beginning with the terminal (or final) group. It is widely used by banks for depositors' savings accounts, mortgages, and loans; by hospitals for medical case records; and by insurance companies for policyholders' applications.

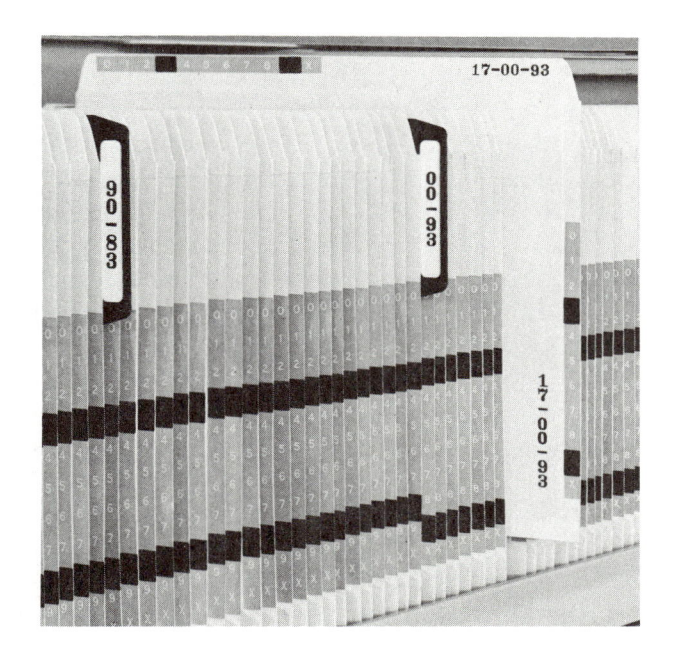

Illus. 12-17
Terminal-digit file
Where individually numbered folders hold records for insurance policies, claims, cases, etc., terminal-digit filing is fast and accurate.

Shaw-Walker

Part 3 / Numeric, Subject, and Geographic Filing   445

In the terminal-digit system, the primary division of the files is based on the last two digits of a number, the secondary division upon the next two digits, and the final division upon the first digits. For example, if you were to look up life insurance policy number 225101, you would read the numbers from right to left in pairs of digits instead of from left to right as whole numbers.

22	51	01
Final	Secondary	Primary

You would first locate the drawer containing those materials or records whose numbers end with 01. Then you would search down the guides in that drawer for the number 51. Lastly, you would file or find the material in proper order behind the number 22. Numbers of fewer than six digits are brought up to that figure by adding zeros to the left of the number.

When even larger numbers are common, they may be broken down for filing in groups of three digits, 000 to 999.

Alpha-Numeric Filing

Banks now identify the checking accounts of their depositors by numbers. In some banks an individual account number is assigned to each depositor according to an *alpha-numeric plan*. This is a method of assigning numbers to accounts in such a way that even with additions and deletions, the accounts filed in numeric sequence will also be in alphabetic sequence. Originally the accounts are arranged in exact alphabetic sequence and assigned account numbers with uniform gaps between numbers to allow for additional accounts. This number is printed with a special magnetic ink on a set of blank checks before the checks are given to the depositor. After a check has been drawn, cashed, and returned to the bank, a machine automatically "reads" the number and charges the account of the depositor. The canceled checks are filed daily in front of check size guides, which usually contain the signature card of the depositor, and are accumulated until the time of the month when the statement and canceled checks for the period are returned to the depositor.

There are other alphabetic-numeric filing systems which are highly specialized and are used in large filing departments with special problems that these systems are designed to solve. Your secretarial duties may indirectly bring you into contact with these various filing systems. Filing personnel who work with alphabetic-numeric systems are given on-the-job training before being assigned to the operation of such systems. On-the-job training is normally necessary because of the differences in the systems.

Guides and Folders Used in Numeric Filing

The type and quantity of supplies used in numeric filing will depend on the arrangement that is used. Individual folders can be made for each number, with the number on the tab, or the number and name typed on a label affixed to the tab. Guides are normally inserted for every ten folders.

SUBJECT FILING

Every organization has materials which are important because of their content rather than because of the person to whom or by whom they are written. For these materials a *subject* filing system is necessary. Since subject filing is generally used in the administrative and executive areas of a business, your secretarial duties should bring you into direct contact with this system of filing. Subjects are placed in alphabetical order, and related subjects may be grouped together. A folder labeled "Applications" with the subheading "Salesmen" is an example. The names of all sales applicants are not easily remembered; therefore, the names are of secondary importance in filing, and the letters should be placed in a special subject folder labeled "Applications — Salesmen." As long as there are only a few subject folders they are filed in a regular alphabetic or numeric system along with the other folders.

Illus. 12-18
A subject file

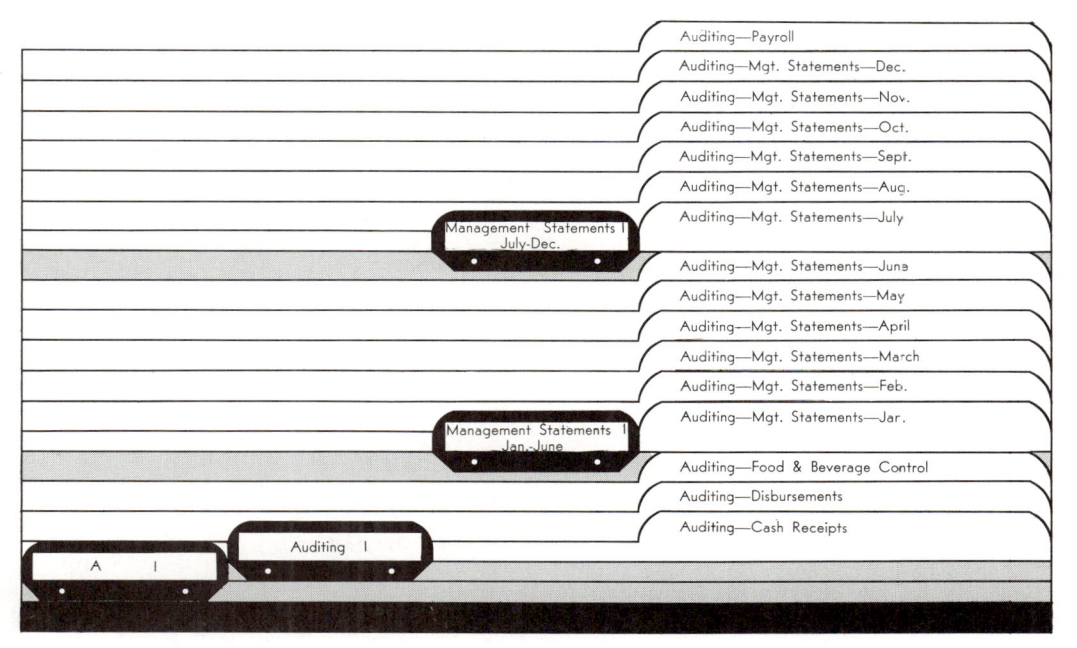

Auditing—Payroll
Auditing—Mgt. Statements—Dec.
Auditing—Mgt. Statements—Nov.
Auditing—Mgt. Statements—Oct.
Auditing—Mgt. Statements—Sept.
Auditing—Mgt. Statements—Aug.
Auditing—Mgt. Statements—July
Management Statements
July-Dec.
Auditing—Mgt. Statements—June
Auditing—Mgt. Statements—May
Auditing—Mgt. Statements—April
Auditing—Mgt. Statements—March
Auditing—Mgt. Statements—Feb.
Auditing—Mgt. Statements—Jan.
Management Statements
Jan.-June
Auditing—Food & Beverage Control
Auditing—Disbursements
Auditing—Cash Receipts
Auditing
A

The following list shows some typical subject filing captions:

Advertising	Finance	Payroll
Applications		Personnel
Associations	Government — Federal	Price Lists
Audit Reports	Government — Municipal	Production
	Government — State	Public Relations
Balance Sheets		
Budgets	Insurance	Real Estate
		Reports
Conferences and Conventions	Legal Matters	Research
Contracts	Maps	Sales
Credits and Collections	Methods and Procedures	Speaking Invitations
	Minutes	Statistical Data
Directors' Meetings	Mortgages	
		Taxes — Federal
Employee Benefits	Operating Overhead	Taxes — Municipal
Equipment & Supplies	Operating Policies	Taxes — State

Guides and Folders Used in Subject Filing

In a subject file you will make use of several different types of guides and folders. The main subject titles are used as captions for primary guides. These serve the same purpose as primary guides in an alphabetic file. Secondary guides are used for the subordinate titles that are related to the main subjects on the primary guides behind which they are placed.

There is a miscellaneous folder for each main subject in which all papers relating to that topic are filed. Individual folders are made for subdivisions of the main subject when sufficient papers (usually six or seven) accumulate for the subtopic. Subdivisions may be made by

Subject:
Safety
    Accident Prevention

Name:
Associations
    American Manufacturers Association

Date Periods:
Production Reports
    January–June, 197–
    July–December, 197–

When individual folders are used in a subject file, they are placed behind the primary or secondary guides that classify the subject matter of the correspondence in those folders. In this way correspondence is doubly identified — by subject, as shown by the guide captions; and by titles, as shown on the folder captions. Main subject and subdivision captions must be shown on each folder tab.

Cross-Reference to a Subject File

An alphabetic cross-reference is necessary in a subject file for maintaining consistency in assigning subjects. Cross-referencing may be done by using a 5″ x 3″ card index, which is very flexible since additions can be made easily. Photocopies and carbon copies may also be used for cross-reference purposes.

Some companies distribute copies of the main subjects of the filing system (and possibly a definition of each) to each department for its use in dictating letters or when requesting materials from the files.

Subject Filing Procedures

In filing by subject, there are six basic steps which you should follow.

Inspecting. Each letter should be checked to see that it has been released for filing.

Indexing. The letter must be read carefully to determine under which subject it should be filed. Thorough familiarity with the outline of subjects and their subdivisions is necessary.

Coding. When the subject of a letter has been determined, the caption is written on the letter in the upper right corner or it is underlined if it appears in the letter.

Cross-Referencing. If more than one subject is involved in a letter — a very frequent occurrence — a cross-reference caption is underlined and an *X* is placed at the end of the line in the margin. An extra carbon copy, a photocopy of the letter, a cross-reference sheet, or a 5″ x 3″ index card should also be prepared.

Sorting. Material is sorted first according to the main subjects and second by the main subdivisions.

Placing Material in Folders. Material that is placed in an individual folder is filed with the latest date in front. If there is no individual folder, the material is filed in the miscellaneous folder for the main subject in alphabetic order according to subdivisions or in date order, latest date to front.

GEOGRAPHIC FILING

If you are using a geographic filing system, geographic location is the prime indexing factor. In the United States, for instance, materials would be arranged alphabetically first by states, then by cities or towns within the states, and finally alphabetically by the names of the correspondents in the cities or towns. A geographic file may also be based upon territories of salesmen, upon cities in a single state, or upon districts or streets for local correspondence.

Typical users of geographic filing systems are publishing houses, mail-order houses, radio and television advertisers, real estate firms, and organizations dealing with a large number of small businesses scattered over a wide area. The personnel in many of these small businesses change frequently; therefore, the name of the individual owner or manager is often less important than the location of the business.

Geographic filing is an indirect method of locating folders for individual correspondents. It is slower to operate since papers must be sorted as many as three times, depending on the geographic arrangement that is selected.

Arrangement of a Geographic File

The primary guides in a geographic filing system bear the names of the largest geographic divisions. The specific arrangement will depend on the needs of the company and the volume of records. For example, a geographic filing system based on states would have each guide tab printed with the name of a state; and all correspondence with people in that state would be filed behind that guide. These state guides are usually arranged alphabetically: thus, Alabama is first, followed by Alaska and the other states in alphabetic order. They could also be arranged by a division of the country into areas, such as "West Coast"; and behind these guides the secondary guides or folders for the states of California, Oregon, and Washington would be filed.

The secondary guides bear the names of the geographic subdivisions. For example, behind each primary state guide there are secondary guides with captions that provide for the alphabetic arrangement of cities and towns within that state.

A geographic file may include several different kinds of folders, such as individual folders, city folders, and state folders. Individual folders in a geographic file are used in the same manner as they are in an alphabetic file. They differ, however, in their captions, because in a geographic file, the caption on an individual folder includes the name of the city and state, as well as the name of the correspondent. The geographic identification should appear on the top line, the correspondent on the second. This arrangement of the captions aids in the correct placement of the folders behind the appropriate state and city guides.

Illus. 12-19
Geographic file

Shaw-Walker

If there is no individual folder for a correspondent, his communication is filed in a city folder. If there is not enough correspondence to warrant the use of a separate city folder, the communication is placed in a miscellaneous state folder at the back of the appropriate state section of the file.

For larger cities, several city folders are sometimes necessary. These are assigned alphabetic captions and placed behind a secondary city guide. For example, five Chicago folders might be used, the first for those Chicago correspondents whose names fall into the alphabetic range of A–C; the second, D–H; the third, I–M; the fourth, N–R; and the fifth, S–Z.

Cross-Reference for Geographic Filing

As in alphabetic filing, there are times when cross-references must be prepared on a letter. The geographic location, the correspondent's name, and other information about the letter are written in the proper spaces on the form.

Card Index

In geographic filing you must know the name of the city and state in which a person or business firm is located to find a letter referring to that correspondent. Because this information is not always known, it is advantageous to keep a card index with a geographic correspondence file. This is usually a 5" x 3" card file, which includes a card for each correspondent giving the name and address of the correspondent. The card index is arranged alphabetically by the names of the correspondents.

Illus. 12-20
Card index

Shaw-Walker

Geographic Filing Procedure

The filing procedure for a geographic file is similar to that for alphabetic filing, except that the state and city are of primary importance in coding and filing. In coding it is desirable to mark on each letter the city and state as well as the name of the correspondent. The location may be circled and the name of the correspondent underlined.

Materials are sorted by geographic units, starting with the key unit for the first sorting and continuing until all the units involved in the filing system have been used. For example, the first sorting might be on the basis of states, the second sorting on the basis of cities or towns, and the final sorting on the basis of correspondents.

Letters are arranged in the folders as follows: (1) in an individual folder by date, (2) in a city folder by the names of the correspondents and then by date, (3) in an alphabetic state folder by the names of cities or towns and then by the names of correspondents according to date. In each case, of course, the most recent letter is placed in front.

SUMMARY OF FILING METHODS

Each filing method has its advantages and disadvantages. On page 453 is a summary of the outstanding features of the four methods.

	ADVANTAGES	DISADVANTAGES
Alphabetic	1. Direct filing and reference. 2. No index required. 3. Records may be grouped by individual or by company name. 4. Simple arrangement by guides, folders, and colors. 5. Easy-to-find miscellaneous records.	1. Possibility of error in filing common names. 2. Related records may be filed in more than one place. 3. Too little or too much cross-referencing.
Numeric	1. Most accurate of all methods. 2. Unlimited expansion. 3. Definite numbers to identify name or subject when requesting files. 4. Uniform system of numbers used in departments of company. 5. Cross-referencing permanent and extensive. 6. Complete index of correspondents and subjects.	1. Requires specialized training. 2. High labor cost. 3. Indirect filing and reference. 4. Miscellaneous records require separate files. 5. Cumbersome index.
Subject	1. Records grouped by subject in technical or statistical files. 2. Unlimited expansion.	1. Extensive cross-referencing necessary. 2. Difficulty in classifying records for filing. 3. Difficulty in filing miscellaneous folders. 4. Necessary use of index in determining subject heading or subdivision.
Geographic	1. Direct filing and reference for geographic area (indirect for individual correspondence). 2. Provision for miscellaneous records. 3. Records grouped by location.	1. Location as well as name required. 2. Triple sorting necessary — by state, by city, by alphabet. 3. Increased labor cost. 4. Increased possibility of error. 5. Reference to card index necessary. 6. Detailed typed descriptions on folder labels. 7. Confusion in miscellaneous files.

Illus. 12-21

COMMERCIAL FILING SYSTEMS

This part would not be complete without a short summary of the more widely used commercial filing systems, which are listed below:

NAME	MANUFACTURED BY
Barkley Color Code	Barkley Corporation
Direct Name	Yawman & Erbe
Ideal Index	Shaw-Walker
Nual Alphabetic	Amberg File & Index Company
Pendaflex	Oxford Pendaflex Corporation
Safeguard	The Globe-Wernicke Systems Co.
Super-Ideal	Shaw-Walker
Tailor-Made	Shaw-Walker
Tel-I-Vision	Smead Manufacturing Company
Variadex and Triple Check Automatic Index	Remington Rand Office Systems Division of Sperry Rand
Verti-Swing	The Globe-Wernicke Systems Co.

Illustrated are the three which you would most likely encounter in a business office. All make generous use of color, of primary and secondary guides, of individual and miscellaneous folders, and all are designed for efficiency and ease of operation.

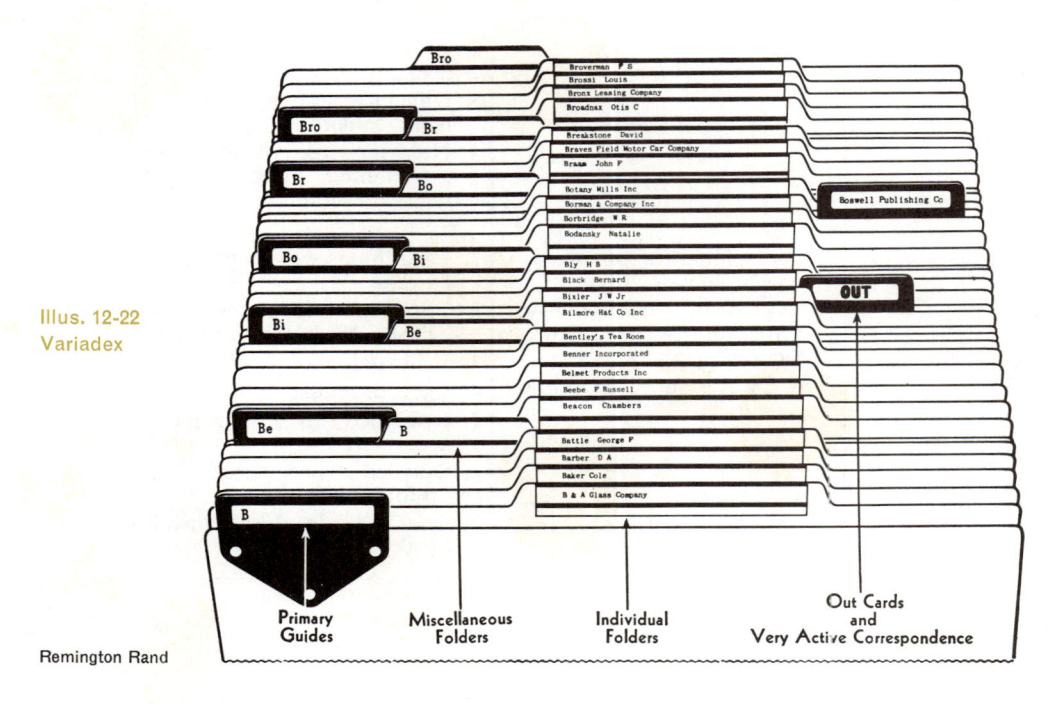

Illus. 12-22
Variadex

Remington Rand

454   Unit 12 / Records Management

Only the basic filing tools have been presented here. When the time comes that you are asked to set up a filing system or improve upon one that is already established in your office, it would be well to visit an office supplies store, study office supply catalogs, and consult with a filing specialist. This will be necessary before you and your employer can make any decisions about the filing system. Filing will be an important part of your secretarial duties. Give thought to selecting the best system for your particular needs.

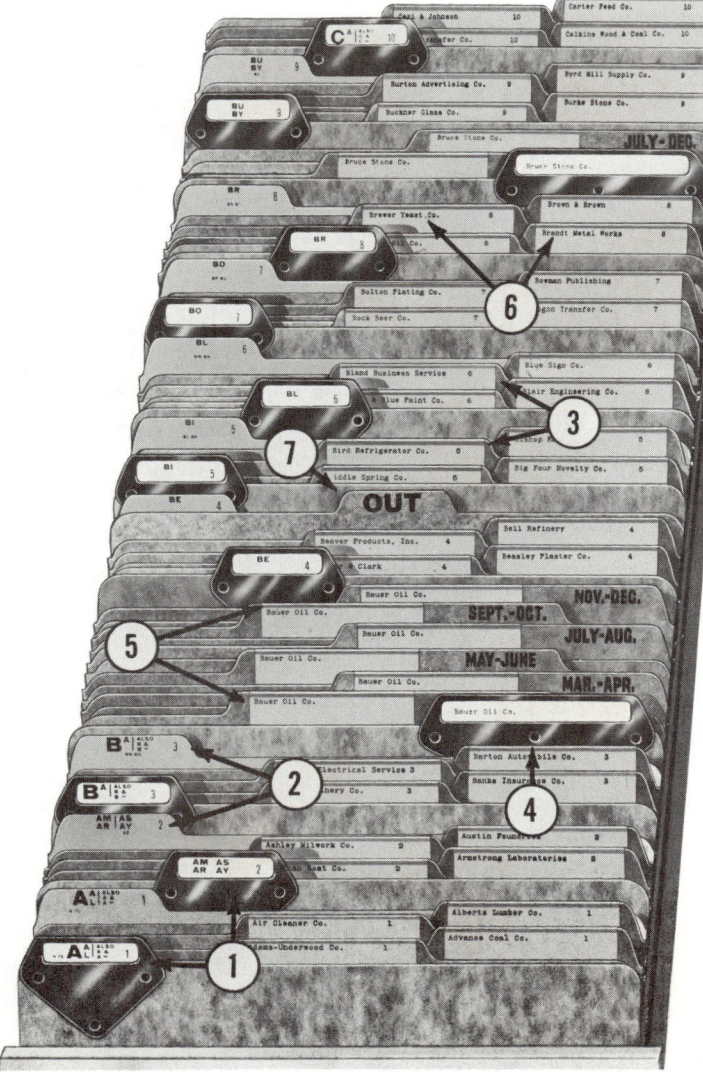

Illus. 12-23
Super-Ideal

Features:

1. Primary guide
2. Miscellaneous alphabetic folder
3. Individual folders
4. Special name guides
5. Date period indivicual folders, wide tab
6. Gummed labels with color strips
7. Out guide

Shaw-Walker

Part 3 / Numeric, Subject, and Geographic Filing 455

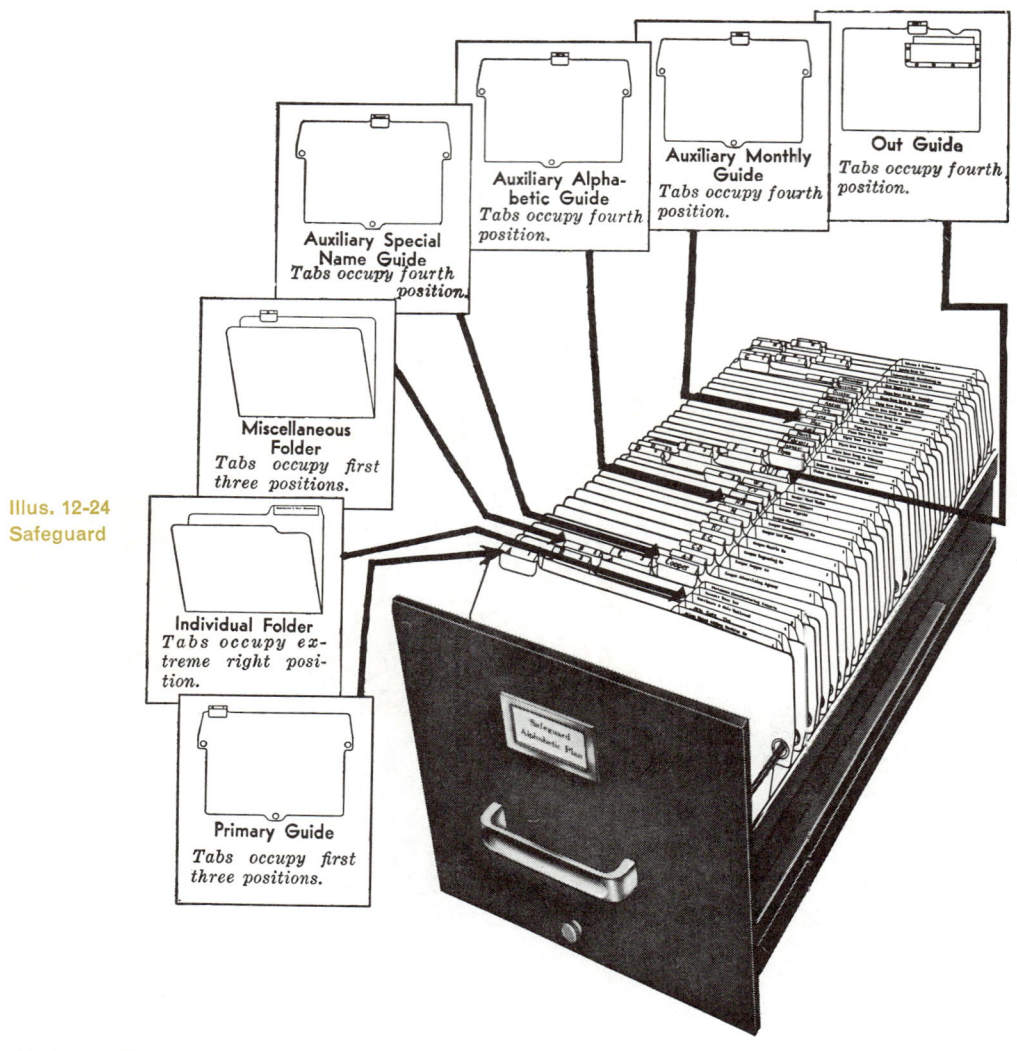

Illus. 12-24
Safeguard

Auxiliary Special Name Guide
Tabs occupy fourth position.

Auxiliary Alphabetic Guide
Tabs occupy fourth position.

Auxiliary Monthly Guide
Tabs occupy fourth position.

Out Guide
Tabs occupy fourth position.

Miscellaneous Folder
Tabs occupy first three positions.

Individual Folder
Tabs occupy extreme right position.

Primary Guide
Tabs occupy first three positions.

The Globe-Wernicke Systems Co.

QUESTIONS

1. Name the three parts of a numeric filing system. What is the purpose of each?
2. How is a number assigned to a correspondent in a numeric file?
3. How is a number assigned to a subject? Give an example.
4. When is a subject filing system used in preference to other methods?
5. What is the major problem in a subject file?
6. How is a letter coded in a subject file?

7. Explain the procedure of cross-referencing in a subject file.
8. What is the basis for geographic filing?
9. What kinds of guides and folders are used with a geographic filing system?
10. When is a folder for a given city opened? for an individual correspondent?
11. What is one method of indicating the essential words in geographic coding?
12. Why is it advantageous to have a card index for a geographic file?
13. With a geographic system, how are materials arranged in an individual folder? in a city folder? in an alphabetic state folder?
14. What are some of the advantages and disadvantages of the numeric system?
15. List three commercial filing systems which you may likely encounter in an office.

JUDGMENT

1. What are the advantages of using numbers as well as subjects for guide and folder captions?
2. How should an office decide whether it ought to arrange its files by name, number, subject, or geographic location?
3. What is a practical situation where terminal-digit filing may promote office efficiency?
4. What steps would you take if your employer were to ask your assistance in setting up a filing system?

PERSONAL QUALITIES

A secretary filing under a subject system must read letters and papers carefully, since they may contain references to more than one subject. Caryl Carson, with whom you work, fails to read the material to be filed, and, as a result, there is much misfiling and improper cross-referencing.

Whenever the chief file clerk corrects her, Caryl becomes impatient and tells the chief clerk the system is stupid and does not make sense.

How would you help Caryl to improve her work habits and to understand the importance of proper operation of the filing system?

LANGUAGE USAGE

The relative pronouns *who* and *whom* are quite frequently misused. When a relative pronoun is the subject of a subordinate clause, *who* is used. When a relative pronoun is the object of a verb or preposition, *whom* is used.

Examples: Sam Davis is the man *who* can do the job.

Grace is the girl *whom* we are hiring.

Type each of the following sentences, inserting the correct usage of *who* or *whom*. If you are unsure of your choice, try substituting *he* for *who* and *him* for *whom* before making your final decision.

1. To _____ did you release the Ames folder?
2. _____ signed the substitution card for the letter?
3. _____ does she know in the central filing department _____ can be of assistance?
4. Since it was not signed, we could not tell from _____ the letter was received.
5. _____ said that six or more letters from one firm should be placed in an individual folder?
6. The personnel officer, _____ I saw yesterday, asked me to come back next week.
7. Now you know _____ should get the promotion.
8. Can Agnes, _____ proofreads so accurately, retype the entire report?
9. _____ shall I talk to about this?
10. _____ decided that the lighting was inadequate for our work?
11. Don't you know _____ called me?
12. He told them _____ we had selected as our chairman.
13. For _____ are you waiting?
14. The matter of _____ shall pay for the delay is still to be decided.
15. Do you understand _____ is in charge of the division and _____ will be responsible for the reports?
16. Was it _____ I thought it was?
17. They also serve _____ only stand and wait.
18. _____ wouldn't enjoy a vacation at this time of the year?
19. With _____ shall I go?
20. Have you noticed _____ is always late?

SECRETARIAL WORK

Type the following twenty business firm names, addresses, and account numbers on 5″ x 3″ cards. File them three ways: (1) alphabetically, (2) geographically, and (3) numerically.

5001 Cobin & Sons, Washington, D.C. 20013
5004 Connell Manufacturing Co., Seattle, Washington 98111
5009 The Cole Manufacturing Co., San Francisco, California 94101
5006 Crawford, Crawford and Croll, Cincinnati, Ohio 45201
5003 Cone, Lambert and Ulysses, Chicago, Illinois 60690
5002 Corn and Frederick, Dallas, Texas 75221

5005 Max Collier & Sons, Tallahassee, Florida 32302
5007 Conwit Tailors, Gainesville, Florida 32601
5008 Cone, Arnold & Co., New York, New York 10001
5010 Cobbs Corporation, Boston, Massachusetts 01432
5019 Conklin Company, Erie, Pennsylvania 16512
5015 Conner Corporation, Cleveland, Ohio 44101
5016 The Samuel Collins Company, St. Louis, Missouri 63177
5013 Colton Company, Boise, Idaho 83707
5012 Conrad & Matthew, Reno, Nevada 89504
5011 Coyne Corporation, Los Angeles, California 90053
5014 Craig & Stanton Corporation, San Luis Obispo, California 93401
5017 Cole & Monford Co., Nashville, Tennessee 37202
5018 Conners Metal Manufacturing, Inc., Cicero, Illinois 60650
5020 Conover & Sterling, Baton Rouge, Louisiana 70821

PART 4 SPECIAL FILES AND INFORMATION SYSTEMS

Carolyn French has been with the Seattle Chemical Company since it was founded eight years ago. For the past three years Carolyn has been secretary to the president, Mr. Norman Bowman. Quite often Mr. Bowman asks Carolyn to obtain information from the company's electronic data processing center. Usually, however, Carolyn can find, in the files near her desk, all the information Mr. Bowman needs for decision-making. Mr. Bowman has often commented, "I can always count on Carolyn to find the information I need — and find it in a hurry!"

CARD FILES

From small to large, practically all offices make use of card files. You may keep a small card file on your desk that contains the names, addresses, and telephone numbers of people whom you call or write to frequently. Secretaries for doctors and dentists usually have card files containing information about patients; teachers often have a card file for each of their classes; libraries, of course, have card catalogs covering all the books in the library. A card file is needed as a cross-reference in numeric, geographic, and subject filing. Card files are used in almost every department in a business firm; shipping, receiving, purchasing, inventory control, personnel records, payroll, and stock records may be maintained on cards.

Cards used in filing are usually 5″ x 3″, 6″ x 4″, or 8″ x 5″. The size selected usually depends upon the amount of information that is needed on the card. The 5″ x 3″ is the most widely used card size.

When typing information on the cards for the files, follow this simple procedure:

1. Type the name in exact indexing order.
2. If the card is not ruled, begin typing on the third line from the top of the card. If the index card is ruled, begin typing above the printed line.
3. Indent two spaces from the left edge of the card and set a margin.

4. Use upper and lower case letters. They are easier to read.
5. Abbreviations may be used since space is limited.
6. Be consistent in style, spacing, capitalization, and punctuation.

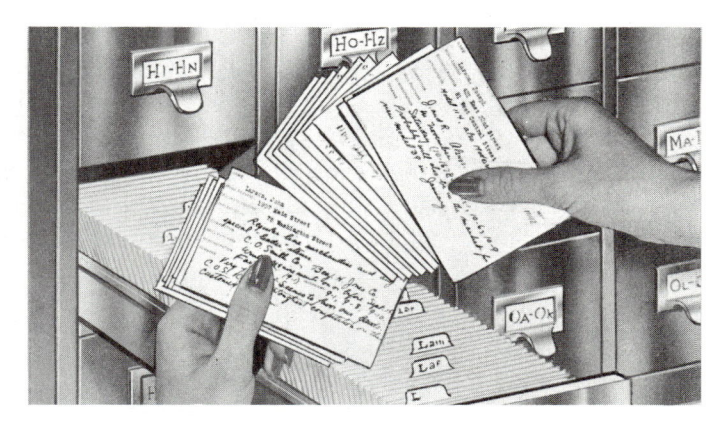

Illus. 12-25
Card files for drawers

Shaw-Walker

Vertical Card Files

These are the types of files in which the card stands on edge, usually the width of the card. Thus, a 5″ x 3″ card rests on the 5-inch edge; the 6″ x 4″ card rests on the 6-inch edge; the 8″ x 5″ card rests on the 8-inch edge. There are, however, exceptions to this; some cards are filed according to the depth of the card. The cards may or may not be ruled, depending upon whether they will be typed or handwritten.

Illus. 12-26
A card file may be an alphabetic, geographic, numeric, or subject file. Card files may contain current records; while storage card files may contain historical and seldom used records. Cards may be easily replaced as the files are closed and put in storage, and substitute current cards are added or rearranged.

Ohio National Life Insurance Company

Just as guides are needed to divide the file drawer to keep the folders in order, it is also necessary to divide the cards in an alphabetic card file into convenient alphabetic sections with a set of *card guides*. These card guides indicate on projecting tabs the various alphabetic sections into which the file drawer is divided. In some cases special primary and secondary guides are used, and color frequently plays an important part.

The notations on the tabs of the guides consist in most cases of letters, such as *Alf, Alli, Alm, Alt, Am, An*; but they may consist of popular surnames such as *Allen, Anderson, Andrews,* as you will notice in the illustration below. They indicate the alphabetic range of the cards filed in each section. The file cards are placed in alphabetic order behind the appropriate guide just as the folders are placed behind the guides in the file drawer.

Illus. 12-27
File cards with guides

Shaw-Walker

Visible Card Files

These are files in which a portion of the card is visible at all times, that portion generally showing the name, department, or product to which

Unit 12 / Records Management

the card record refers. These cards are generally placed in pockets on horizontal trays, or on vertical sheets, or in files that appear in book form. The total card becomes visible as the overlapping cards are raised to provide a view of the whole card.

Illus. 12-28
Visible record card cabinet

Remington Rand

Signals on Visible Records. In addition to cards that are especially printed for use with visible files, small metal or plastic signals are available. These may be placed in various positions on the cards to indicate something important about the record. For example, if a visible file is used for collection records, the signal may indicate that the account is in good standing, or that it is overdue. Some signals may be used to indicate that it is very much overdue or that the firm with the account is no longer to be given credit because of poor standing. These signals are sometimes placed in special positions on the card and frequently are in different colors. For example, blue may indicate a good credit standing, yellow may suggest mildly overdue, orange may mean very much overdue, and red may tell you that no further credit is to be extended.

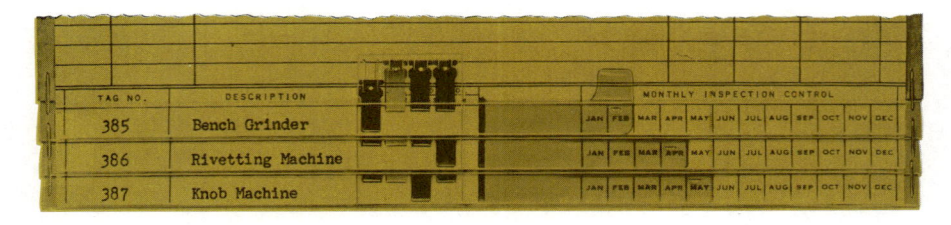

Illus. 12-29
Signals on visible records

Acme Visible Records, Inc.

Reference Visible Systems. These files usually carry only a strip instead of a whole card, the strip containing perhaps a name, address, and telephone number of persons who are called rather often. The strips are usually referred to as visible panels and are generally limited to one or two lines.

Illus. 12-30
Visible panel system for reference records

E. H. Brown Advertising Agency

Rotary Wheel Files

These are cards to be used where quick reference to a large number of cards is needed. Cards used with this type of equipment are punched or cut at the bottom or at the side, depending upon the style of wheel. There are small wheel files for desk-top use and also large rotary motorized equipment that is used when a great deal of information must be available for fingertip retrieval.

Illus. 12-31
Rotary wheel file

Business Efficiency Aids, Inc.

Random Files

In this kind of system, the cards not only have typed or printed information on them, but also are equipped with strips of metal teeth which are attached to the bottom edge of the card. These teeth are cut in relation to magnetic rods that run under the cards. These files are operated by a keyboard, and the depression of certain keys causes one or more cards to be pushed up, thus locating them and making them available

Illus. 12-32
At the touch of the keys this file automatically selects the right card. Valuable time is saved, and delays are avoided.

Acme Visible Records, Inc.

Part 4 / Special Files and Information Systems   465

quickly. This system has the advantage of allowing one card to be identified under one of several possible captions. It is often found in banks, savings and loan associations, and finance companies where fast reference to a customer's file assures prompt service and goodwill.

Elevator Files

This type of file is power driven and is in a sense a multiple card file with trays arranged on shelves which may be brought to the level of the operator by the use of an elevator or power-driven system. The shelves in this kind of a file operate on the same principle as a ferris wheel at an amusement park. The shelves may be wide enough to take four, five, or more trays of 5″ x 3″ cards; and any single machine may include a large number of shelves. The operator pushes a button to move any particular shelf into position. At that point she may work directly on some cards, or she may remove a complete tray of cards and turn them over to someone else to work on.

Illus. 12-33
Elevator files

Ohio National
Life Insurance Company

MICROFILMING

Because of increasing information needs, many businesses are using microfilm as a solution to certain of their information problems. Microfilm is a photographic method of copying records in miniature. Since microfilm cannot be viewed by the naked eye, a machine called a reader or a reader-printer is used. This machine magnifies the microfilm.

Microfilm makes it possible to store vital records and save storage space at the same time. For example, about 3,000 letter-size documents can be photographed on a 100-foot roll of microfilm. The United States Army Rocket Guided Missile Agency "files" over 100,000 engineering drawings in only four feet of floor space. The microfilming process and equipment, however, are very expensive.

Microfilm is widely used as a method of processing, distributing, and retrieving information. Schools, banks, department stores, libraries, government offices, and research centers are among the many users of microfilm.

Duplication and Copying

With the development and refinement of the reader-printer, *hard copies* of information on microfilm are quickly obtained by pressing a button. The term *hard copies* refers to a photocopy of the material on the microfilm. Duplication by microfilm also eliminates time-consuming manual transcribing and also provides error-free copies.

Retrieval

Motorized electronic equipment is available that is capable of retrieving at very high speeds information stored on microfilm and producing hard copies almost immediately. The Social Security Administration, for example, maintains the microfilm records of over 130 million people and can obtain a hard copy of any record in 90 seconds.

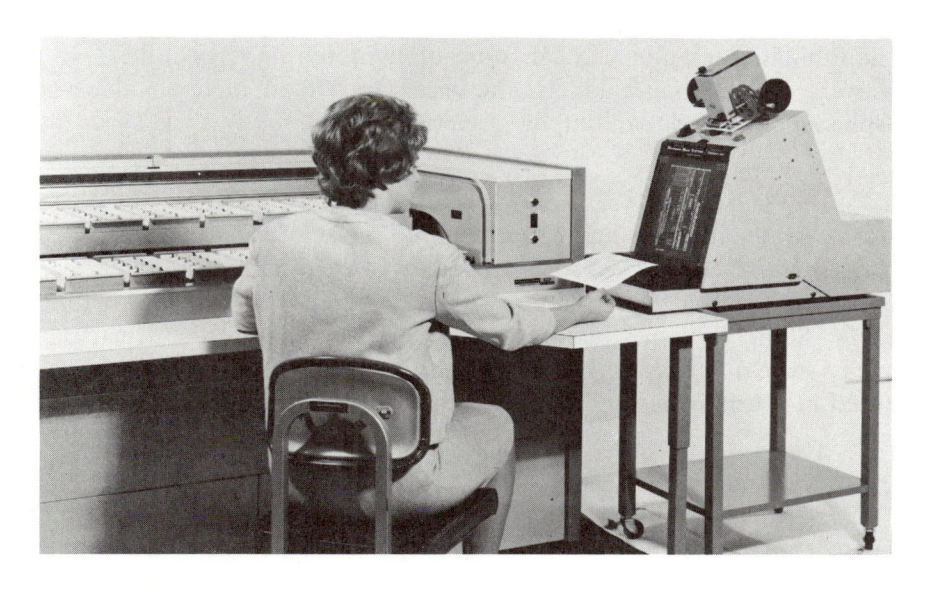

Illus. 12-34
In this typical installation the operator is using a reader-printer to produce a "hard" or paper copy from a microfilmed image. The entire operation from the search to the finished print takes less than a minute.

Remington Rand

Part 4 / Special Files and Information Systems

What to Microfilm

All documents should not be microfilmed. Although documents reduced to microfilm occupy about two percent of the space required by regular records, microfilm should not be used only as a method of saving space, except in unusual situations. Inactive records should be transferred to low-cost record centers after realistic retention periods have been adopted. The expense of microfilm cannot be justified if infrequent use is made of too many office records. In most cases records must be retained for fifteen years or more before it is economical to microfilm only to save space.

ELECTRONIC DATA PROCESSING

Electronic data processing equipment can store more information and retrieve it faster than any other system. Specially trained people handle the equipment for both input and retrieval of data. As a secretary in a data processing department, you would be very much concerned with the equipment and how it is used. As a secretary in any other department, you should be familiar with how the data processing equipment can aid your employer and you. In almost all cases, however, you would need the assistance of the people in the data processing department in order to store or retrieve information.

Tabulating (Punched) Cards

With the tremendous increase in the use of electronic data processing equipment, most companies have extensive tabulating card files. The tabulating or punched cards are often stored in vertical files. In the drawers of the filing cabinets, the cards are stored in removable trays. Alphabetic, numeric, and alpha-numeric indexing systems are used.

Computer Tapes and Disks

Magnetic tapes and disks can hold more information in less space than can punched cards. The tapes and disks are usually stored in fire- and heat-resistant cabinets or safes.

Some electronic data processing equipment uses punched paper tape to store information. The punched paper tapes themselves are usually placed in specially designed folders that contain pockets for the tape.

Retrieval

Retrieval of information stored in a computer is quite rapid. When you request information from a computer, it may print out the information on a continuous sheet of paper or on specially prepared business forms. It is also possible that you may work in a business that has visual display units for retrieving information. With visual display units, the information you request is shown on a television-like screen.

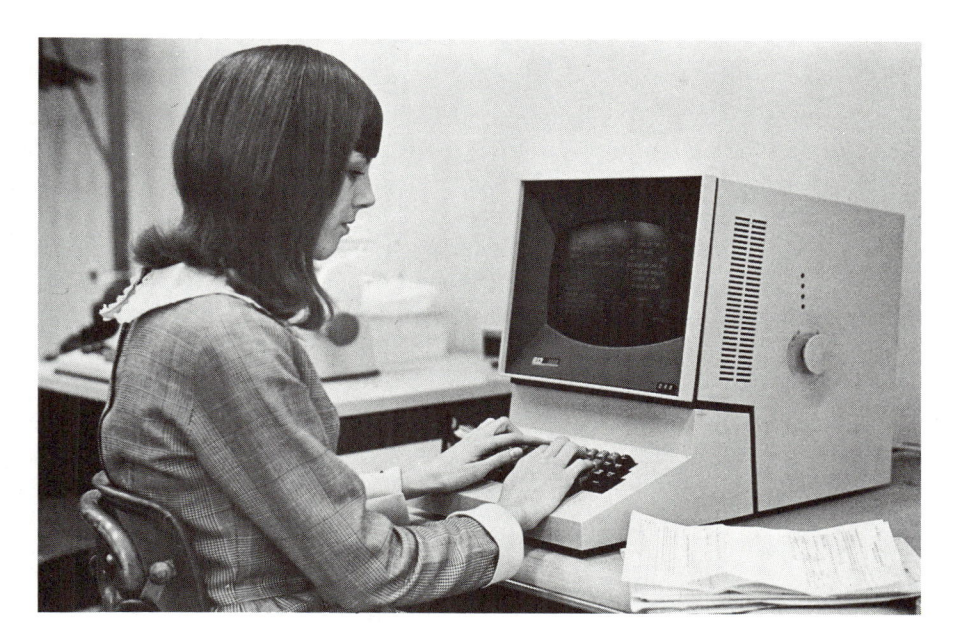

Illus. 12-35
Visual display unit for retrieving information

Ohio National Life Insurance Company

WHICH FILING SYSTEM?

If a filing system is to operate effectively, considerable time must be given to its development. A good filing system cannot be designed casually. The solution to many records management problems is neither simple nor easy. The development of an effective filing — and finding — system must be based on good planning, careful analysis, clear thinking, and sound experience.

Here are some factors that should be considered when developing a filing system:

1. *The record requirements of the office.* What kinds of records are retained? How are these records created or received? What is the total volume of records retained each week, month, or year? What about future expansion of the system?
2. *Using the system.* How are the records requested and used? How active are the records? How long must the records be retained?

Part 4 / Special Files and Information Systems

3. *Storing the records.* What type of classification system should be used? Will a centralized or decentralized file plan be most effective? Where will the inactive records be stored?
4. *Equipment and supplies.* What specific types of equipment and supplies — out of the vast array available — would be most appropriate for this system in this office?

Since every office has different records requirements, a system used in one office is not always suitable for another. Remember that you are storing important information that must be retrieved quickly — you are not merely keeping pieces of paper.

Every filing system should be as simple as possible to use. In addition, the system should be efficient and reliable in providing needed information and also should be economical to operate and maintain.

When an office decides to install a new filing system or to change an old one, three methods may be considered. A qualified person in the office may analyze the particular information requirements and develop an "office-made" system, a system may be purchased from a filing equipment and supplies manufacturer, or a records consultant may be engaged to design a tailor-made filing system to meet the company's particular needs.

QUESTIONS

1. What determines the size of the cards used in card filing?
2. What card size is most widely used in business files?
3. Why are metal or plastic signals used with visible card records?
4. When are cards filed on rotary wheel files?
5. Give one of the advantages of a random file.
6. Give one of the advantages of an elevator file.
7. Other than the great saving in filing space, what are some of the other factors to be taken into consideration before installing a microfilming system?
8. What does the term *hard copies* mean in microfilming systems?
9. Why are magnetic tapes and disks preferred to punched cards in electronic data processing systems?
10. What are four of the factors to be considered in developing a filing system?

JUDGMENT

Discuss how each of the following statements will affect your work as a secretary.

1. The best retention system for *many* records is not to produce the records at all. If a record has a *retention value of only a few days,* it should be *destroyed and not filed.*

2. Considering the marked increase in the cost of labor, equipment, space, and overhead, it has been determined that the cost of retrieving only one misfiled paper may now amount to $92.46.

PERSONAL QUALITIES

Connie Kathman is a secretary in a downtown office of a large manufacturing company. Connie always keeps her files up to date and in good order, and she is able to produce a file within seconds after it is requested. On Saturdays, however, her employer, the manager; the assistant manager; and several traveling representatives for the firm come into the office and catch up on reports and other paper work that they do not have time to handle during the week.

Almost weekly Connie finds misplaced files; files are lost; and, on one occasion, she did not locate a file that her employer needed until after he had left town because the assistant manager had used it and placed the folder in the wrong file.

What should Connie do?

LANGUAGE USAGE

Type each of the following sentences using the correct form of the word in parentheses.

1. We don't have (no, any) more carbon paper.
2. Please (bring, take) that letter here, and I'll photocopy it.
3. Where do the typists place (there, their) initials on the letters?
4. Resort reservations are not (so, as) expensive this summer as they were last summer.
5. Mary (sure, surely) knew her filing rules.
6. (Try to, Try and) picture a more perfect setting.
7. They work (well, good) together.
8. (Leave, Let) me answer the phone, please.
9. (It don't, It doesn't) matter if you are a bit late.
10. Everyone in our class (has, have) seen the filing movie, *It Must Be Somewhere*.
11. You were (very, real) thoughtful to call.
12. They (should of, should have) mailed it sooner.
13. We (differ with, differ from) you on the value of such elaborate planning.
14. Act (as if, like) you were interested in the suggestion.
15. Please (lay, lie) down to rest at the end of the day.

SECRETARIAL WORK

This is the conclusion of the alphabetic indexing exercise begun in Unit 11, Part 3, and continued in Part 1 of this unit.

Prepare your last 25 index cards from the names listed on page 472 and integrate them with the 75 cards you now have from the two previous assignments.

(76) Henry R. Elston, IV, 2728 Germantown Rd., Germantown, PA 19144
(77) Chamber of Commerce, 12th & Olive Sts., Joliet, IL 60433
(78) Chief Engineer, Safety Division, Arkansas State Highway Dept., Ft. Smith, AR 72901
(79) Horace Mann Junior High School, 2500 Euclid Ave., Erie, PA 16511
(80) St. Mark's Episcopal Church, Oakwood, MO 63401
(81) University of New Mexico, Albuquerque, NM 87103
(82) Wm. A. Graves, 1620 N. Vernon Place, Winnetka, IL 60093
(83) Second National Bank, 8th & Race Sts., Spokane, WA 99202
(84) Ye Olde Garden Gate Antiques, 49 W. Elm St., Independence, KS 67301
(85) Security Savings Society, 74 Ohio Ave., Watertown, NY 13601
(86) Vera's Beauty Salon, 29 W. Adams St., Bennington, VT 05201
(87) Jack the Tailor, 536 S. 29th St., Oklahoma City, OK 73129
(88) Downtown Merchants Assn., 1200 Transportation Bldg., Wheeling, WV 26003
(89) Lady Constance Cosmetics, 128 W. 63rd St., New York, NY 10023
(90) Citizens Bank & Trust Co., Manchester, NH 03105
(91) Hartford Water Department, Hartford, CT 06101
(92) U.S. Marshal, Justice Dept., Federal Bldg., Boise, ID 83707
(93) Arnold A. Townley-Jones, 5021 Eastman Blvd., Chicago, IL 60622
(94) Chief Inspector, Food & Drug Administration, Health & Welfare Dept., Post Office Bldg., Butte, MT 59701
(95) United Fine Arts Fund, Terminal Bldg., Dallas, TX 75222
(96) Baldwin-Wallace College, Berea, OH 44017
(97) Harold McArthur & Sons, 4587 Roland Ave., Glendale, CA 91209
(98) MacArthur Sportswear, 688 Jefferson St., Kalamazoo, MI 49007
(99) Bernice L. McAdoo, 3 Alpine Terrace, Trenton, NJ 08610
(100) Perkins-Reynolds Insurance Agency, 200 Nicollet Ave., Minneapolis, MN 55401

Unit 13 TRAVEL

Part 1. Travel Services and Arrangements
   2. Itineraries and Travel Expense Reports

The secretary has increased responsibilities when her employer must travel. She must keep the office operating smoothly while he is gone. She can provide valuable assistance in planning the executive's trips, in making reservations, and in completing expense reports when he returns.

VOCABULARY BUILDER

determine..........................
    verb: to settle or decide by choice of alternatives or possibilities; to obtain definite and firsthand knowledge of; to come to a decision

frequently..........................
    adverb: often; at short intervals

spacious..........................
    adjective: roomy; vast or ample in extent; large or magnificent in scale

reimbursement..........................
    noun: repayment

deserted..........................
    adjective: abandoned; unoccupied; lonely

desolate..........................
    adjective: forsaken; barren; deserted

legitimate..........................
    adjective: genuine; lawful; legal; conforming to recognized principles or accepted rules and standards

exceeded..........................
    adjective: to go beyond a set limit

per diem..........................
    adjective or noun: by the day; for each day

incidental..........................
    adjective: minor items (as of expense) that are not particularized

---

He who knows no foreign language knows nothing of his own.
                        Goethe

p. 477   In order to **determine** which flights go to your employer's destination, you can call the airline.

p. 480   If your employer **frequently** travels between two major cities, he may wish to take an air shuttle flight.

p. 481   If your employer wants sleeping quarters, more **spacious** accommodations, or room to do some work while traveling by train, you should make a....

p. 488   On his return, Anne must assist Mr. Miller in carefully completing expense reports for **reimbursement**....

p. 489   Also, avoid poor connections that would force him to wait in the pre-dawn hours at an almost **deserted** airport to change planes or in a **desolate** railroad station to change trains.

p. 496   Such items as plane and train fares, taxis, tips, meals, and hotel accommodations are considered **legitimate** travel expenses.

p. 498   Some policies allow a fixed daily amount which, if **exceeded**, will not be reimbursed. This is known as a **per diem** rate.

p. 498   He merely is paid a fixed amount extra a day for all his expenses for food, lodging, taxi cab fares, and **incidental** traveling expenses.

PART 1   TRAVEL SERVICES AND ARRANGEMENTS

"Susan, I have to be in Denver next Tuesday at noon for a conference on the McLaurin contract. Will you get me a flight no later than 8:30 Tuesday morning? On Wednesday I want to take a look at our new computer in the San Diego branch. I would like to be there about 11. If you can't get me an early Wednesday morning flight out of Denver, get me something around 5 or 5:30 Tuesday afternoon and make a hotel reservation for me in San Diego Tuesday night. You can get a return flight from San Diego around 5 Wednesday afternoon." Mr. Gordon gives his secretary, Susan Moyer, the responsibility for making his travel arrangements. As an experienced secretary, Susan knows how to make flight and hotel reservations that permit Mr. Gordon to travel with speed and comfort.

Travel by business executives is quite common. In fact, almost all executives have to do some traveling. They have to go to other cities to attend conferences, to meet customers, to learn about new methods of company operations, and to study new projects and equipment.

Business executives often depend upon their secretaries to make travel plans and reservations for them. This may be one of the most interesting parts of your job.

PLANNING A TRIP

When an executive learns that he must go out of town, the trip must be planned in great detail. It is very important for the executive to know when and where he will be and how he will travel. His associates must know where they can get in touch with him at all times.

The details of planning a trip may be taken care of by a special transportation department within the company, by a travel agency, or by the executive and his secretary.

Transportation Departments

Many large companies have special transportation or traffic departments that take care of travel arrangements for their employees.

When an executive tells his secretary that he must go on a business trip, she sends a memorandum with the details to the Transportation Department. Since the Transportation Department is in constant contact with airlines, railroads, and bus companies, it can quickly find the best way for the executive to travel. The Transportation Department also knows which hotels and motels are in the area that the executive intends to visit.

The Transportation Department will give the executive a suggested travel schedule. If the executive approves the schedule, the Transportation Department will then get the necessary tickets and reservations.

Travel Agencies

Sometimes businesses will depend upon travel agencies to make the plans and get the reservations for their traveling executives. This is especially true when an overseas trip is planned. It does not cost the executive or his company anything to use the services of a travel agency. The travel agency collects a fee from the transportation company with which it makes the reservations.

The Secretary

Very often your employer will give you the full responsibility for planning his trips. This is often the case when he does a great deal of traveling.

In order to plan his trips properly, you must find out what your employer's preferences are when he is traveling. Does he prefer to fly? Does he prefer one hotel or motel to another? You must learn the answers to these and many more questions before you can properly plan his trips. He will depend upon your good judgment to arrange an efficient itinerary.

AIR TRAVEL

The fastest way to go from one city to another is to fly. This is why most businessmen prefer air travel, especially for long trips. An executive could have breakfast in Philadelphia, fly to St. Louis for a four-hour conference, and be back in Philadelphia before his office closes for the day.

Air travel does have an element of uncertainty about it, because flights may be delayed or canceled due to bad weather. If your employer must be at his destination at a specific time, he may ask you to make alternative arrangements so that he can travel either by air or by rail. He is more likely, however, to make allowances for delays in departure or arrival by flying during the afternoon of the day before his scheduled appointment and spending the night in a hotel at his destination. This not only insures his prompt arrival but also gives him a fresh start for the appointment.

Classes of Service

Airlines provide two basic classes of service — first class and coach. First-class service costs more than coach, because the first-class passengers are given wider, more comfortable seats at the front of the plane. In addition, the meals provided first-class passengers are usually of a higher quality than those served in the coach section.

Before making a flight reservation for your employer, you must find out what he prefers with regard to service and what your company's policies are. Some companies request that their executives fly coach unless the trip is a long one. If your employer will be flying a long distance, or if he will be traveling during mealtime, or if he has work to do on the plane, it will probably be better for you to make a first-class reservation for him. If he is traveling only a short distance and is flying between mealtimes, he will probably ask that you make a coach reservation for him.

Flight Information

In order to determine which flights go to your employer's destination, you can call the airline. This is the fastest way of getting flight

Illus. 13-1
The fastest way to go from one city to another is to fly.

Pan American World Airways, Inc.

Part 1 / Travel Services and Arrangements   477

information. If, however, your employer has several places he must visit, you may spend quite a bit of time on the telephone.

When a long trip is planned or when several different areas must be visited, it is better to consult the *Official Airline Guide* for the flight information. This book gives information on all flights to all cities by all airlines. It will tell you the time the plane leaves, when it arrives, the cost of the flight, and the kinds of service available. By consulting the *Official Airline Guide*, you can offer your employer several choices of flights. He can then select the one that will best fit his needs.

All airlines publish complete timetables of their flights. They also publish separate schedules for flights between major cities. These schedules for flights between major cities are often printed on small cards that are convenient for the executive to carry or for you to keep in your files.

Airline Reservations

Once the executive has decided which flights will best fit his plans, you must make his flight reservations. Advance reservations are necessary for almost all airline flights. You make the reservations in person at the airport, at the airline ticket office, or at a travel agency. You may also make airline reservations over the telephone.

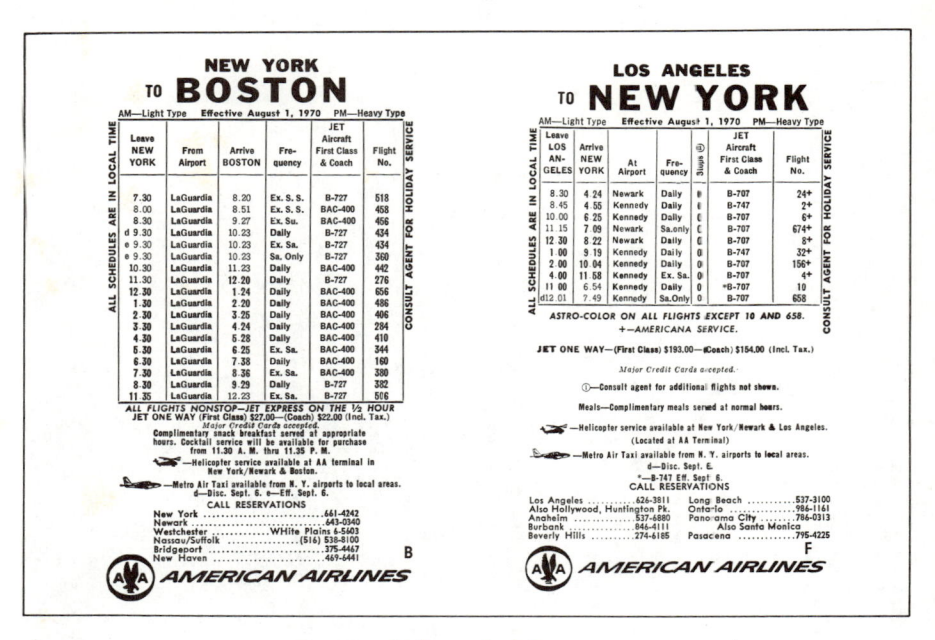

Airline schedules

Illus. 13-2   Illus. 13-3

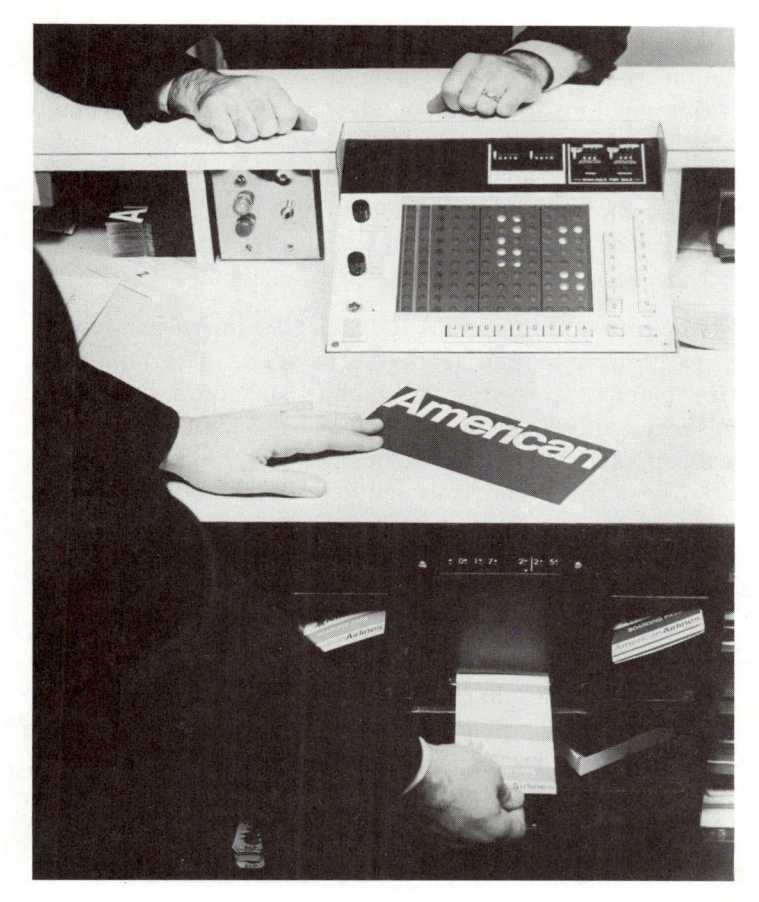

Illus. 13-4
The airline tickets may be picked up at the air terminal as your employer checks in.

American Airlines

When you request a reservation either in person or on the telephone, the airline representative will tell you immediately whether your reservation is confirmed. All major airlines use computers to keep track of how many seats are available for each flight.

Pickup of Tickets

When you make flight reservations, it is most important for you to know when and where to pick up the tickets. They may be picked up before the flight at the airline ticket office, at the air terminal as your employer checks in, or they may be mailed to either his business or home address. Air transportation may be paid for in cash or by check, or it may be charged on some credit cards, one of which is the Universal Air Travel Card. When tickets are mailed, the airline expects a check in payment within 72 hours after they have been received.

Transportation to the Airport

When helping your employer plan his trip, you must remember to allow enough time for him to get to the airport. Airports are usually located a good distance from the center of the city. Sometimes it takes an hour or more to go to the airport. In addition most airlines expect passengers to check in about 30 minutes before flight time.

The executive may drive his personal car to the airport, but most executives prefer to use an airport limousine or a helicopter.

Airport Limousines. Most cities have airport limousines or bus service to carry passengers to and from the airport. The limousines usually leave from major downtown hotels, suburban motels, and airline ticket offices. This service is usually much less expensive than taking a taxi. Limousine services operate on a regular schedule, and you should check the schedule with the airlines for your employer when you help him plan his trip.

Helicopter Service. Many large cities have helicopter service available to carry passengers between the airport and the center of the city, or to suburban areas, and also between airports when there is more than one in a large city. Naturally this is the fastest way to get to the airport. While this service is expensive, it is often less costly than the executive's time spent in traveling 20 to 30 miles in heavy traffic.

Cancellation of Reservations

If, at the last minute, your employer cannot leave on his trip, you should cancel the reservation immediately. Cancellation is possible at any time up to the time of departure. When a flight reservation is canceled, the unused tickets should be returned to the airline as soon as possible for a refund or credit, if a credit card was used to purchase the tickets.

Air Shuttle Flights

If your employer frequently travels between two major cities, he may wish to take an air shuttle flight. These are regularly scheduled flights that travel only in a limited area. For example, there are shuttle flights between New York and Boston. There are also shuttle flights between San Francisco and Los Angeles.

To take a shuttle flight, the executive would go to the proper gate at the airport, get a free boarding pass from a vending machine, fill out the boarding pass, and board the plane. No advance reservations are necessary. After the plane takes off, the stewardess prepares a ticket and collects the fare. A seat is guaranteed to every passenger no matter how many people arrive for a given flight. If one plane is filled, another is brought into service.

TRAIN TRAVEL

Although planes are used more often than trains for long-distance traveling, some businessmen prefer to make overnight train trips to leave the full day free for business appointments. Businessmen sometimes take trains on short intercity trips to save traveling time. There are some high-speed trains that offer very fast service between large cities. The *Metroliner*, for example, covers the 226 miles between New York and Washington in less than three hours. Another advantage of train travel is that railroad stations are usually located in or near the business district. While it may take a great amount of time to go to and from an airport, little time is needed to go to the railroad station.

Your employer may not care to fly. He may prefer to travel by rail, or he may find rail travel more efficient under certain conditions. For example, you may find it necessary during winter months to make reservations for your employer for both air and railroad travel if he must be present at a conference and weather predictions are unfavorable. In that case, if the weather is favorable for flying, he will take the plane and you will cancel his train reservation. If the weather is so bad that planes are grounded, he will take the train and you will cancel his flight reservation.

Classes of Services

Railroads, like airlines, offer different classes of service. The two classes of train service are coach and first class (Pullman or sleeping car).

Coach Accommodations. Reservations need not be made for travel in most coach cars. A regular railroad ticket, which may be purchased at the station window, entitles you to transportation in a coach car. You need not get the ticket in advance; however, reservations are necessary for seats on some special trains, such as the *Metroliner*.

First-Class Accommodations. If your employer wants sleeping quarters, more spacious accommodations, or room to do some work while traveling by train, you should make a first-class or Pullman reservation for him. Reservations for Pullman accommodations are made at the railroad ticket office. The tickets must be picked up and paid for or charged sometime before the scheduled departure time of the train. Naturally first-class accommodations cost more than coach.

Canadian Pacific

Illus. 13-5
First-class accommodations provide room for work or conferences when traveling by train.

Railroad Timetables

Every railroad publishes its own timetables. Timetables tell which trains are available, where they go, and when they leave and arrive. At first, reading a timetable may seem difficult. Every timetable, however, fully explains how it is to be used.

BUS TRAVEL

Businessmen sometimes take buses to make calls in suburban and outlying districts. In regions where no other kind of public transportation is available for intercity travel, bus transportation is convenient and popular. Buses operate on regular schedules from terminals located in or near the business district. Bus transportation is the least expensive means of travel. Fares on all buses are lower than coach fares on railroads and airlines.

AUTOMOBILE TRAVEL

There are many times when businessmen prefer to drive a car to get to their appointments. This is often true for short trips in the local area. Also, an executive who flies into a large city may decide that a rented car will get him to his appointments faster and more economically than any other way. This is especially true when he has many stops to make or if some of his appointments are in small towns or outlying areas. By traveling by automobile, a businessman does not have to plan his appointments according to bus or train schedules.

Rental Services

Rental cars are available at almost every airport. If your employer decides he wants to rent a car at his destination, you may make the reservation at the local branch of the car rental agency. Simply tell the agency when and where the car is wanted. When your employer arrives at his destination, his car will be waiting.

The cost of a rental car is usually determined by two factors — the length of time the car is used and the number of miles it is driven. The charges can be paid for by cash, check, or credit card.

Automobile Clubs

If your employer does a great deal of traveling by car, he will probably be a member of one of the automobile clubs, such as the American Automobile Association (AAA). Among the many services offered by these clubs are routing services, insurance, emergency repair and towing service, and advice on where to stay and where to eat.

Automobile Routing

Planning the route for a proposed automobile trip is not difficult. If your employer does belong to one of the automobile clubs, the club will furnish him with the maps he needs and mark the best route for him to take. Several major oil companies also offer this service.

You and your executive can plan the trip yourselves with the use of a current *Road Atlas* which includes maps of each state and usually Canada and Mexico.

FOREIGN TRAVEL

Trips to foreign countries by American businessmen are quite common. When a trip to another country is planned, the details of the trip should be given well in advance to the Transportation Department or a travel agency. Enough time must be allowed to make all the necessary reservations. Naturally almost all businessmen travel by plane to foreign countries.

Passports

Passports are required for travel in almost all foreign countries except Canada, Mexico, and the Central American countries. If your employer needs a passport, he must apply for it from the Department of State. His application should be completed at least a month before the passport is needed.

Visas

Some countries require foreign travelers to have visas in order to travel in their country. A visa is simply an endorsement on a passport by a representative of the country granting permission to enter the country for a certain purpose and length of time. If your employer's travel plans include a country that requires a visa, it will be obtained from the foreign consulate located in the United States.

Vaccinations

When your executive is planning a trip to a foreign country, remind him that he should be vaccinated against smallpox. Inoculations for other diseases may be necessary, depending upon the countries your executive must visit.

TIME FACTORS IN TRAVEL

When you are assisting your executive in planning a trip, make sure you allow for the differences in time zones and for the time it takes to travel from one place to another. For example, if your employer would be leaving Portland, Oregon, for a 2 p.m. conference in Atlanta, Georgia, he would have to leave Portland no later than 3 a.m. It takes seven hours to fly from Portland to Atlanta. In addition, there is a three-hour difference in time zones. Then, of course, you must allow at least one hour for your executive to get from the airport to the place where the conference is to be held. In this example, it would probably be better for your employer to travel the day before the conference so that he could get a good night's rest.

You must take even greater care when a foreign trip is planned. If your executive is traveling to London, you should see that he is scheduled for a flight that will arrive in London in the early evening. That will give him an opportunity to rest and relax before he has to transact any business.

QUESTIONS

1. If your company has a Transportation Department, what information should you give it when your employer is planning a trip?
2. Why is a travel agency willing to make travel arrangements free of charge?
3. What are some of the factors you should consider when trying to decide whether flight reservations for your executive should be first class or coach?
4. If your employer plans a trip from Racine, Wisconsin, to St. Louis, Missouri, which book would tell you which flights are available?
5. When might your executive prefer to travel by train? by bus? by automobile?

JUDGMENT

1. More businessmen now travel by plane than by train. How do you account for this marked change in the traveling habits of American businessmen?
2. A single company, Greyhound, which began in 1914 in Hibbings, Minnesota, with two employees and a seven-passenger Hupmobile car, now employs 34,000 people to maintain and drive about 5,400 buses. How do you account for this great increase in bus transportation in the United States?

PERSONAL QUALITIES

Grace Butler is employed as secretary to Edward Barrett, a chemist who has recently been appointed Chief of the Science Division. He is an excellent chemist but has had no experience as an office administrator.

Recently he took a business trip to Birmingham, Alabama. He rented a car at the airport but forgot to carry a credit card. He had to leave a $25 cash deposit and had great difficulty getting a personal check cashed. Furthermore, he failed to make any hotel or motel reservations and had to drive 50 extra miles one evening before finding a vacancy along the highway.

Despite all this, he is a dedicated scientist and a wonderful boss. He is scheduled to make two more trips: one to an international science convention in Geneva, Switzerland, and one to San Francisco. He has never been abroad before, nor has he ever been to the West Coast.

Suggest how you might be of help to him in planning both trips.

LANGUAGE USAGE

On a piece of paper type the correct spelling for each of the 20 words that follow and give an appropriate synonym or brief meaning for each word.

Part 1 / Travel Services and Arrangements

Example: reserveations or reservations
Correct spelling — reservations
Synonym or meaning — accommodations

1. alternative or alternetive
2. available or availible
3. cancelation or cancellation
4. conferance or conference
5. destination or destenation
6. efficeint or efficient
7. foriegn or foreign
8. hellicopter or helicopter
9. itinerery or itinerary
10. limousine or limosine
11. memorandum or memorandom
12. perdiction or prediction
13. preferance or preference
14. routing or routeing
15. shuttel or shuttle
16. spaceous or spacious
17. specific or specefic
18. suberban or suburban
19. terminal or terminel
20. time table or timetable

SECRETARIAL WORK

Assume that you are employed by a national sales manager with a home office in Chicago. He plans to make a business trip to New York City where he will stay at the Hotel Commodore at 109 East 42nd Street. During his stay in New York City he hopes to work in an overnight trip to a national business convention in Atlantic City, New Jersey, where his firm will be displaying its products in Convention Hall. While in Atlantic City, he will stay at The Shelburne Hotel at Boardwalk and Michigan Avenue.

For the trip from Chicago to New York he is considering two ways of traveling:

1. A first-class TWA flight from O'Hare Airport to John F. Kennedy International Airport. Flights leave each hour from 7 a.m. through 11 p.m. The flying time from Chicago to New York is less than two hours. The fare is approximately $70.
2. A sleeping car reservation on the Broadway Limited. It leaves Union Station in Chicago at 4:30 p.m. daily and arrives in New York City at 9:50 a.m. the following morning. The fare is approximately $75.

For the trip from New York to Atlantic City he is considering three ways of traveling:

1. Limousine service. The limousine would pick him up at the Commodore Hotel and deliver him to The Shelburne. The traveling time is slightly less than three hours. The fare is $10 each way.
2. Rent-a-car service. The make and model he prefers rents for $15 a day plus 15 cents a mile. The trip is about 100 miles.
3. Nonstop bus service. The traveling time from the Port Authority Bus Terminal on West 42nd Street to the Atlantic City Bus Terminal is 2 hours and 20 minutes. The fare is $4.40 each way.

Consider the two ways of traveling to and from Chicago and the three ways of getting to and from Atlantic City. Indicate the methods of travel you would recommend for each trip. Give your reasons for each recommendation. Among the factors that should be considered are cost, speed, comfort, convenience, frequency of service, and types of accommodations.

PART 2 ITINERARIES AND TRAVEL EXPENSE REPORTS

Anne Bingham is secretary to Mr. Russell C. Miller, an international financier. Mr. Miller's interests and contacts are many and varied. Mr. Miller travels frequently. While he is away, Anne must take care of his mail and keep a daily report of events that will be of interest to him when he returns. Anne must prepare detailed itineraries for all his trips. She or any of his associates must be able to reach him within hours in the event of a national or international crisis that would require purchase or sale of the company's financial holdings. For this reason she must be exceptionally efficient in assisting him in arranging his trips. She must have at her fingertips the latest air, train, and bus schedules. She must also know something about foreign moneys, since Mr. Miller prefers to carry with him a certain amount of foreign currency for taxicab fares, tips, and small purchases in the country in which he is traveling. On his return, Anne must assist Mr. Miller in carefully completing expense reports for reimbursement of his travel expenses by the company and for audit by the Internal Revenue Service, if requested.

Since modern transportation methods permit business executives to travel extensively without being away from their offices for long periods, they travel much more than ever before. How well you help your employer plan his many business trips will determine the success of those trips. You must make reservations for him on different transportation systems and at hotels or motels, and you must help plan and arrange his appointments. Whether your employer travels by air, train, or bus, you must make the necessary arrangements, keep the office operating smoothly while he is away, and assist in the preparation of detailed records of expenses incurred on his business trips.

THE TRIP FOLDER

When your employer tells you that he must take a trip, you should immediately set up a trip folder. Tickets and confirmations of hotel or motel reservations should be attached to or enclosed in the folder. All correspondence related to the trip and reminders of appointments and engagements should be placed in the folder. Also, reports, meeting programs, outlines, notes and/or copies of speeches to be given or other materials to be used on the trip should be included. These should be arranged in the order in which the appointments or engagements are to be kept. A form on which expenses may be recorded should be put in the trip folder.

THE ITINERARY

An *itinerary* is a detailed plan or route to be followed when traveling. It tells your employer, your company, and you where he will go, how he will travel, where he will stay, what he will do, and when he will return. In planning an itinerary you must include the

1. Date, time, and place of departure
2. Transportation accommodations
3. Arrival date, time, and place
4. Hotel or motel accommodations
5. Appointments and engagements

The same steps are taken in preparing the itinerary for every stop until the trip is completed. The transportation tickets and the hotel reservation confirmations should be put with the itinerary. The itinerary, transportation tickets, and hotel confirmations should be placed in the front of the trip folder.

Preparation of Itinerary

When your employer goes on a business trip, he follows the itinerary that you have prepared and, therefore, depends upon your exactness as to time schedules, your attention to the details of reservations, and your care in making proper appointments. Moreover, he depends upon your thoughtful consideration of his comfort and convenience, as well as the speed, quality, and cost of the traveling facilities used. When you plan a trip for your employer for the first time, you should discuss it with him to get a clear idea of his preferences; furthermore, you should get his approval before making any specific reservations. If at all possible, try to avoid scheduling his arrival in a strange city after midnight when most restaurants and other facilities are closed. Also, avoid poor connections that would force him to wait in the predawn hours at an almost deserted airport to change planes or in a desolate railroad station to change trains. Such thoughtless planning may enable him to arrive in a distant city in

                    ITINERARY FOR MR. RUSSELL C. MILLER
              New York, Philadelphia, Baltimore, and Pittsburgh
                           September 16-23, 197-

TUESDAY--September 16   (CLEVELAND TO NEW YORK)

    5:00 p.m.   Leave office for Cleveland-Hopkins Airport

    6:00 p.m.   Leave Cleveland on American Airlines Flight 358
                           (ticket in American Airlines envelope in trip folder).
                           Snacks served in flight.

    7:17 p.m.   Arrive New York, LaGuardia Airport
                           Limousine to East Side Airlines Terminal at 37th Street
                           and First Avenue.
                           Taxicab to the New York Hilton Hotel at Rockefeller
                           Center (confirmation of hotel reservation in trip
                           folder).

    8:30 p.m.   Convention registration and hospitality hour (Empire
                           Room--second floor of the Hilton).

WEDNESDAY--September 17   (CONVENTION IN NEW YORK HILTON)

    All day   Convention meetings, including luncheon and banquet
                           (convention program with tickets for the September 17
                           luncheon and banquet in envelope marked "Convention"
                           in trip folder).

                           Reminders: Try to meet Edward J. Gaynor, Buyer
                                                   General Mills Company
                                                   White Plains, New York

                                                   Robert C. DeValue, Buyer
                                                   National Products Company
                                                   Paramus, New Jersey

THURSDAY--September 18   (CONVENTION IN NEW YORK HILTON)

    Morning   Convention meetings, including luncheon
      and   (ticket for September 18 luncheon in "Convention"
    Afternoon   envelope).

    7:30 p.m.   Dinner with James G. Brugger, buyer for Morgan Invest-
                           ment Co., at the Twenty One Club, 21 West 52nd Street.
                           (Reservations made with Mr. John of 21 Club on Thurs-
                           day, September 10, by phone from Cleveland.)

                           Reminder: Phone Penn Central for reservations for
                           seat on the Metroliner (212) 736-4441 leaving from
                           Pennsylvania Station at 8:30 a.m., Friday, September 19,
                           for Philadelphia.

FRIDAY--September 19   (NEW YORK TO PHILADELPHIA)

    8:15 a.m.   Pick up ticket at Metroliner window in Pennsylvania
                           Station.

    8:30 a.m.   Leave New York on Metroliner.

    9:46 a.m.   Arrive Philadelphia, Penn Central Station at 30th
                           Street. Taxicab to Bellevue-Stratford Hotel (con-
                           firmation of hotel reservation in trip folder).

Illus. 13-6   First page domestic travel itinerary

OVERSEAS ITINERARY FOR MR. RUSSELL C. MILLER
New York, London, and Paris
October 5-19, 197-

Date	Place	Time	ITINERARY	Page 1
October 5	TWA Terminal at Area 4 of John F. Kennedy International Airport	8:00 a.m.	Check in for TWA 747 Superjet Flight 706 departing at 9:00 a.m. for London. You should have with you: TWA first-class tickets, BEA coach tickets, American passport, Vaccination certificate, $500 in the following currency: Travelers' checks for $450, English money 15, French money 15, Single dollar bills 20, $500	
October 5		9:00 a.m.	Leave for London. (Full course meals are served in flight.)	
October 5	Heathrow Airport	8:50 p.m.	Arrive at Heathrow Airport. Show passport. Claim luggage. Clear customs. Taxi into London (fare 2 pounds, 10 shillings--about $6--add 25 percent for tip). Reservations for 7 days at the Savoy (confirmation in trip folder).	
October 6-12	London		Daily conferences with London office management.	
October 13	Heathrow Airport	10:00 a.m.	Leave for Paris on BEA Flight 223.	
October 13	LeBourget Airport	11:10 a.m.	Arrive at LeBourget Airport. Show passport. Claim luggage. Clear customs. Pay airport departure tax of 5 francs (90 cents). Taxi into Paris (fare 20 francs--about $3.60). Reservations for 7 days at the Hotel Bristol (confirmation in trip folder).	
October 13-19	Paris		Daily conferences with Paris office management.	

Illus. 13-7 First page overseas travel itinerary

time for an important early morning conference, but he will not be as alert and refreshed as after a good night's sleep.

Distribution of the Itinerary

You should have handy for quick reference at all times a copy of your employer's itinerary so that important messages and mail can be forwarded to him. Some companies require that copies of itineraries of key men be distributed to other personnel in the organization so that they too are able to get in touch with a key man if it becomes necessary. However, it is most important that you be aware of your employer's location at all times so that he can be reached within minutes, if necessary, should an emergency arise.

It is not unusual for an executive to request his secretary to make an additional copy of his itinerary for his wife while he is traveling.

> Mary is secretary to Mr. Ross, regional manager for a large manufacturing company. Mr. Ross is required to spend 80 percent of his time traveling with his salesmen in the territory under his supervision. Because of differences in time zones, it is not unusual for Mary to receive long-distance business calls at her home after working hours. Therefore, she keeps a copy of Mr. Ross's itinerary alongside her telephone in her apartment for immediate reference in the event a problem arises which needs his personal attention. Mr. Ross is grateful for Mary's special kind of loyalty which has enabled him to solve many problems that would otherwise confront him on Friday afternoon when he returns to his office after being on the road all week.

Illus. 13-8
If an employer travels much of the time it is well for his secretary to keep a copy of his itinerary near her home telephone.

AT&T

SELECTION OF HOTELS AND MOTELS

Which hotel or motel should you choose for your employer? You should choose the one that is most in keeping with the firm's standards. Your employer need not stay at the best hotel in a large city, but he should stay at a *good* hotel or motel. Most companies have lists of hotels and motels where they prefer their executives to stay.

Hotel Directories

Occasionally your employer will be traveling in a part of the country that is completely unfamiliar to him. You can obtain information about accommodations in the area from one of the hotel directories. The most frequently consulted hotel directory is the *Hotel and Motel Red Book*, a directory published annually which lists the hotels and motels that are members of the American Hotel Association. The leading hotels and motels in the United States are classified geographically according to states and are listed alphabetically under the cities in each state; the hotels and motels in Canada are classified according to the cities in the different provinces. The directory also lists the principal hotels and motels in Mexico, the West Indies, Central and South America.

The *Red Book* lists information about each member hotel and motel. It includes the name and address of the hotel or motel, the name of the manager, the telephone number, the range of rates for both single and double rooms with a letter "E" within a circle above them to denote that it is operated on the European plan or an "A" within a circle above the rates to denote the American plan. When a hotel or motel is operated on the European plan, the rate represents the cost of the room only. Under the American plan, the rate includes the cost of meals as well as the cost of the room. Most commercial hotels and motels are operated on the European plan. The location is also indicated with key letters: A — Near Airport; D — Downtown; E — Near Expressway; R — Resort Area; and S — Suburban.

Another valuable aid often used in trip planning is the *Mobil Travel Guide*. In addition to the usual information, the *Mobil Travel Guide* includes a rating system so that you will have an idea of the quality of a hotel, motel, or restaurant at which you are planning to make reservations for your employer.

Making the Reservations

After your employer has decided at which hotel or motel he would like to stay, you may make the reservation by telephone, telegram, or letter, depending upon the amount of time you have. Most large hotel and motel chains have central reservation offices through which you may make instant reservations at any hotel or motel in the entire chain by calling, without charge, a nationally listed number. Your request for reservations should include:

1. The kind of room desired — single room or suite of rooms
2. The type of accommodations — single, double, or twin beds
3. The approximate rate preferred
4. The number of persons in the party
5. The date and approximate time of arrival
6. The date and approximate time of departure
7. A request for confirmation

The reservation confirmations should be included with the transportation tickets and the itinerary in the trip folder so that your employer will have them when he registers at the hotel or motel. In many cities and towns, accommodations are at a premium because so many people are traveling; consequently, having confirmation of the reservation will save your employer much time and trouble at the registration desk.

TRAVEL FUNDS

If your employer's trip is to be lengthy, he probably will not want to carry enough cash to pay all his travel expenses because cash is too easily mislaid or stolen. He may prefer to carry a limited amount of cash for minor expenses and to pay his bills with travelers' checks, a credit card, a letter of credit, or a personal check.

Travelers' Checks

Travelers' checks are sold at express offices, travel agencies, banks, and Western Union offices. The American Express Company travelers' checks are sold in denominations of $10, $20, $50, and $100. They cost one dollar per $100.

The buyer of a travelers' check is required to sign it in the presence of the agent who issues the check. When it is presented for payment, the buyer is required to sign the check again in the presence of the person who cashes it. If the signatures seem to be identical, sufficient identification has been established. Travelers' checks may be cashed at banks, hotels, express and telegraph offices, and other places where travelers frequently make purchases. Since you cannot sign travelers' checks for your employer, you must remind him to pick them up in time for his trip.

Illus. 13-9   Travelers' checks

Travelers' checks have the following advantages:

1. The checks may be cashed easily almost everywhere.
2. The company issuing the check will refund the face value of a lost travelers' check if it has not been signed the second time.
3. The holders of American Express Company travelers' checks may, while they are traveling abroad, use the services of the express offices in other countries for such things as the receipt of personal mail, radiograms, and cablegrams.

Credit Cards

Your employer will also want to carry one or more of the nationally recognized credit cards when he travels, such as *American Express*, *Carte Blanche*, *Master Charge*, *BankAmericard*, or *Diners' Club*. They will be accepted at almost all restaurants, hotels, motels, gift shops, florist shops, and car-rental agencies throughout the United States and Canada. Furthermore, the charge slips and itemized statements furnished by the credit card organizations provide a written record that may be used as proof of items listed on an expense account or to justify certain types of income tax business deductions.

Letters of Credit

On extended business trips or international trips for which a considerable amount of money will be needed, your employer may consider it wise to carry a letter of credit. The cost of exchanging a large amount of money into a letter of credit is considerably less than it would be to change it into travelers' checks.

A letter of credit may be purchased from a bank by depositing the required amount. The letter states that the individual carrying it is entitled to the privilege of getting money from the banks named in the letter of credit up to the amount on deposit in the issuing bank. In using a letter of credit, your employer would apply at one of the named banks; and, after being identified by his signature on an identification card on file at the bank, he would draw a draft against the letter of credit and obtain his money. The bank honoring the draft would endorse the amount on the back of the letter of credit. All endorsements on the back are deducted from the face of the letter of credit to show the exact balance that may still be drawn against it.

Personal Checks

Most hotels, motels, airlines, and railway systems will accept a personal check in payment if the traveler can produce a driver's license or other proper identification. In addition to a signature on the personal check, a driver's license usually lists the motorist's identification number, date of birth, sex, height, and color of eyes.

EXPENSE REPORTS

Part of your responsibility in handling the executive's business trips may be the preparation of a final report of his expenses. Business firms expect executives to submit itemized accounts of travel expenses. Some firms advance funds to traveling executives; others reimburse executives after expense reports have been approved. Such items as plane and train fares, taxis, tips, meals, and hotel accommodations are considered legitimate travel expenses. Firms differ, however, in their policies regarding such items as laundry and entertainment expenses. Your employer may expect you to check his records and receipts and to assist generally in the preparation of his expense reports.

Federal income tax regulations suggest a daily diary of expenses. In it your employer should itemize all his travel and entertainment expenses. You may be called upon to assist your employer in keeping the diary when he returns from a trip and hands you a group of receipts. You will know the exact fares paid for his travel, as the bills for the tickets cross your desk. Most executives will welcome such aid.

The diary should include the date and amount of expenditures for transportation, lodging (place), meal expenses, entertainment expenses (meal costs, place, and receipt if the meal runs above $25, names of persons entertained and indication of business relationship), and tips and telephone calls (daily totals are sufficient.)

WEEKLY TRAVEL EXPENSE REPORT

INSTRUCTIONS FOR COMPLETING THIS REPORT ARE ON THE REVERSE SIDE

FAIRCHILD HILLER

DEPARTURE: HOUR 5:00 PM · PLACE: PLANT ☒ (WHICHEVER IS LATER)
RETURN: HOUR ___ · PLACE: HOME ☐ PLANT ☐ (WHICHEVER IS EARLIER)

NAME: Russell C. Miller
BADGE NUMBER: 742
DEPT. NO.: 31
DATES FROM: 9/16/7-
TO: 9/19/7-

EXPENSE ITEMS / DATE →	SATURDAY	SUNDAY	MONDAY	TUESDAY 9/16	WEDNESDAY 9/17	THURSDAY 9/18	FRIDAY 9/19	TOTALS
1. ROOM				31 00	31 00	31 00	26 00	119 00
2. MEALS & TIPS				8 00	2 50	37 00	14 50	62 00
3. LAUNDRY						4 50		4 50
4. TIPS				2 50	3 50	7 00	4 25	17 25
5. SUB-TOTAL OR PER DIEM				41 50	37 00	79 50	44 75	202 75
6. RAILROAD							12 50	12 50
7. AIRPLANE				39 00				39 00
8. CAR OR BUS								
9. PERSONAL AUTO								
10. TAXI				7 00		3 50	2 50	13 00
11. PARKING								
12. TOLLS								
13. TEL. & TELEGRAMS				1 50	4 75	2 50	4 00	12 75
14.								
15.								
16.								
TOTALS →				89 00	41 75	85 50	63 75	280 00

MILEAGE

FROM (INDICATE PLACE OF DEPARTURE): Cleveland
TO (INDICATE DESTINATION): New York, Philadelphia, Baltimore, Pittsburgh
PURPOSE OF TRIP: Invest. Analysts Convention & Branch office visits
APPLICABLE CHARGE NO.: Executive Travel 31
ACCT. NO.: 8 2 7 4 - 9 9 8 3 - 7 4 2 3 1

REG. ATTACHMENTS:
- LODGING RECEIPT ☐ AMOUNT
- AIRLINE TICKETS ☐ DUE RAD
- RENTAL CAR INV. ☐ DUE EMPLOYEE
- PARKING - TOLL RECEIPT ☐ ADV. REDUCTION
- CONFERENCE RECEIPT ☐ DATE APPLIED

FOR OFFICE USE ONLY

REMARKS: Trip continued to Baltimore and Pittsburgh. See accompanying expense report for Sep. 20-23.

RENTAL CAR MILEAGE BREAKDOWN:

I CERTIFY THE ABOVE EXPENDITURES WERE MADE ON BEHALF OF REPUBLIC AVIATION DIVISION
DATE: 9/25/7-
SIGNED: Russell C. Miller
DEPT. HEAD APPROVAL: Joseph J. Cohen
TREASURY APPROVAL: Harold R. Mason
CHECKED BY: KEB

Fairchild Hiller
Republic Aviation Division

Illus. 13-10 Completed expense report

Part 2 / Itineraries and Travel Expense Reports

Company Travel Policy

Most businesses have a company guide for their employees regarding reimbursement for travel in an official capacity. Travel expenses which the company will approve are usually specified so that the traveling employee will have his reasonable and necessary expenses while on a business trip refunded to him.

This policy will cover such items as which travel expenses are included, which living expenses are allowed, arrangements for travel advances, reporting of expenses, travel insurance coverage, and special arrangements necessary for foreign travel.

Living Expenses. Company policies vary widely in how much and in which way they will reimburse a traveling employee for living expenses. Lodging, meals, tips, telephone calls and telegrams, laundry and valet service, and taxi fares are all living costs. Some policies allow a fixed daily amount which, if exceeded, will not be reimbursed. This is known as a *per diem* rate. For any amount less than the per diem rate the employee does not have to keep detailed records of living expenses. He merely is paid a fixed amount extra a day for all his expenses for food, lodging, taxicab fares, and incidental traveling expenses. The amount depends upon the policy of the firm.

Travel Advances. Most companies grant an employee a cash advance which he picks up at the cashier's office before leaving on a business trip. This is the estimated amount of money it will cost him while he is away from home traveling for the firm. Most of the advance is usually in travelers' checks so that the traveling employee will not have to run the risk of carrying large amounts of cash.

Travel Insurance. Most firms carry travel insurance policies covering all their employees while traveling on company business.

Company Credit Cards. Many firms purchase credit cards for their traveling personnel. The credit card contains the firm name and the employee's name. While traveling, the employee charges most of his expenses on the company credit card. Consequently, a traveling employee is able to travel farther and longer with a smaller advance and fewer travelers' checks.

Checklist for Preparing a Trip

Foresight is a valuable quality in a good secretary. It is especially valuable when she is assisting her employer in preparing for a trip. Before your employer leaves, be sure that all is in order — his transportation tickets, hotel reservations, itinerary, various materials that he will need. Make a duplicate list of all files he is taking with him — one to be kept in the office, the other to be placed in his trip folder.

Your employer should carry with him:

Transportation tickets and reservations
Hotel reservation confirmations
A copy of his itinerary
Financial resources — credit cards, travelers' checks, some cash, his personal checkbook

Your employer's travel folder should contain:

All letters, memorandums, reports, and programs that he will need (It is well to keep copies in the office.)
A list of all files he is carrying
Outlines for or copies of speeches that he will make, if he is to speak
Telephone numbers, reminders of appointments, and separate instructions which he will need but which may not appear on his itinerary

Your employer's brief case should contain:

Sharpened pencils, stamps, stationery, an expense report pad, large and small envelopes (several addressed to you), one or two writing pads (usually the 8½" x 11" yellow legal ruled), paper clips, and a few rubber bands
His travel folder
Files or materials that he will need for work he may wish to do while he is traveling

> Mary Baker is particularly adept at taking care of Mr. Ross's brief case. As soon as he returns to the office she removes all files, his trip folder, his expense account records, the copy of his itinerary, all ticket stubs, hotel and other receipts — in short, the entire contents are removed for proper handling. She then checks his brief case to see that all basic contents are in order for his next trip — sharpened pencils, a fresh supply of stamps, stationery, a new writing pad, a blank expense report pad, a supply of envelopes. The brief case is now ready to receive the necessary materials for his next trip.

WHILE YOUR EMPLOYER TRAVELS

When your employer is traveling you will have to assume responsibility for the smooth operation of his office. You may have many more duties to perform and many more difficult decisions to make during his absence. Your very first duty will be to take care of his daily mail. The most important communications should be brought to his attention while he is away — by telephone, telegram, cablegram, air mail, or special delivery letter. Others you may acknowledge and hold for his attention, and still others you may take care of yourself. He may have you forward the original communications or keep the originals and forward copies. Most businessmen would prefer to have you hold the originals and forward copies rather than risk losing valuable documents in the mails.

Unexpected visitors, certain telephone calls, and important business matters that come up will also be of great interest to your employer. He may have you send him a brief summary of them, or he may prefer that you keep a file folder with a summary of them for his personal examination when he returns. Obviously, you will also keep a complete list of all appointments, meetings, and conferences which you have scheduled for him during his absence.

QUESTIONS

1. What should be included in a trip folder?
2. What is an itinerary, and what must it include?
3. To what extent should your employer's preferences, comfort, and convenience be taken into consideration in preparing his itinerary for a business trip?
4. What information is given in the *Hotel and Motel Red Book* about the hotels and motels that belong to the American Hotel Association?
5. What is the difference between the European and the American plan of operating hotels and motels, and how is it indicated in the *Hotel and Motel Red Book*?
6. List at least six items of information that you would give in order to make a satisfactory reservation at a hotel.
7. Why would your employer prefer to carry travelers' checks on an extended business trip rather than large amounts of cash?
8. What are the advantages of using a credit card on a business trip?
9. What is a letter of credit, and how is it obtained?
10. When a hotel cashier is asked to cash a personal check, why would he prefer to see a driver's license instead of a Social Security card?
11. Why should a trip diary be kept? What items should be covered in it?
12. What is a travel advance, and how is it obtained?

JUDGMENT

1. Assume that your employer is going on an extended business trip. Under what circumstances would you recommend that he carry:

(a) Travelers' checks
(b) Personal checks
(c) A credit card
(d) A letter of credit

PERSONAL QUALITIES

Mr. Walton is leaving on a two-week trip to the West Coast to visit the various branches of the company. His secretary, Betty Simpson, has carefully worked out his air transportation, hotel reservations, and appointments.

Two days before scheduled departure, Mr. Walton changes his plans for one day and throws the whole itinerary out of balance. Marjorie Foss, a stenographer in the office, thinks Mr. Walton is inconsiderate, but sees that Betty has two courses of action open to her:
(a) Make the changes in the itinerary, or
(b) Leave the itinerary as it was originally planned and let her employer work out his own changes.

What would you do if you were in Betty's place? What must Marjorie learn before she moves from her stenographer's position to that of a secretary?

LANGUAGE USAGE

The following sentences contain commonly misused terms. On a separate sheet of paper type each sentence using the correct form of each word.

1. The secretary (accepted, excepted) the invitation to the dinner meeting in her employer's name, since he was out of the city.
2. Her employer told her before he left that it would be (all right, alright) to do this.
3. Mr. Jones was (all ready, already) committed to give the breakfast address at the meeting when the program director asked him to be the (principle, principal) speaker at the final dinner meeting.
4. Although the president of the company was (reared, raised) in France, his travels in America made him a (real, very) enthusiastic baseball fan.
5. When Mr. Lower did not (appear, show up) in time to address the convention, the chairman became alarmed and telephoned the former's office.
6. Mr. Wilson was a dark (complexioned, complected) man who was recognized by the olive green suitcase he carried.
7. (All together, Altogether) ninety persons were on the airplane when it left the Kansas City airport.
8. Although the weather (affected, effected) his past football injury, it did not prevent the executive from making many business trips.
9. The (farther, further) he was away from the office the more (likely, liable) he was to call his secretary at any time.

10. The motel was (luxurious, luxuriant) but the noise from the swimming pool (in back of, behind) his room (irritated, aggravated) him.
11. Although there was (much, lots of) work to be done in preparation for the trip, Mr. Hill's secretary gladly worked overtime.
12. There was agreement (between, among) the four officers of the company that traveling was necessary if the company was not to (lose, loose) money.
13. Although her employer was in poor physical (shape, condition), he was no different (from, than) the other executives when they exercised in the gymnasium.

SECRETARIAL WORK

1: Write a letter to the Sheraton-Plaza Hotel, Copley Square, Boston, Massachusetts 02116, making a reservation for your employer, Horace O. Ransom, who is comptroller of of the Maxwell Manufacturing Company, 292 Peachtree Street, N.E., Atlanta, Georgia 30308. Mr. Ransom wants a single room. The rate should be approximately $25 a day. He will arrive in Boston at about 6 p.m. on Friday, May 14, and plans to leave about 3 p.m. on Monday, May 17. Type the letter in modified block style with open punctuation. Mr. Ransom will sign the letter. Type an original and one carbon copy.

2. Your employer, Mr. J. C. Kimball, must make a trip from Los Angeles to New Orleans in order to attend the National Underwriters Convention. He will leave from Los Angeles International Airport on Sunday, April 4, at 3 p.m. PST aboard National Airlines Flight 86 which arrives in New Orleans at 8:20 p.m. CST. Dinner will be served on the flight. From the airport, he will take the airport limousine to the Jung Hotel, which is the headquarters for the convention. He will attend the opening session of the convention at noon on Monday, speak at a meeting on Tuesday at 10:15 a.m., attend a Rotary Club luncheon at 12:30 p.m. on Wednesday, visit a new office building — The Prudential Building — on Thursday at 9:30 a.m. where he will spend the day, and attend the convention banquet on Thursday at 6:30 p.m. On Friday he will attend the morning session only. He will leave New Orleans at 12:30 p.m. CST on National Airlines Flight 39 which arrives in Los Angeles at 2:03 p.m. PST. Lunch will be served on the flight.
   (a) Write for hotel reservations at the Jung Hotel, 1500 Canal Street, New Orleans LA 70140 for Mr. Kimball. The rate should be about $20 per day.
   (b) Type an itinerary with three carbon copies for Mr. Kimball.

Unit 14 SECRETARIAL ACCOUNTING

Part 1. Petty Cash — Handwritten
    2. The Checkbook and the Bank
    3. Making Cash Payments
    4. Income Tax Procedures

The secretary is often entrusted with making small cash payments from the petty cash fund, and sometimes with making payments by check. To do this, she should understand banks and the many services they can provide. Needless to say, she must be completely honest and trustworthy.

VOCABULARY BUILDER

*He said little,
but to the purpose.*
Cabell

originally
adverb: of or relating to the beginning; initially

conscientious
adjective: governed by or conforming to the dictates of conscience; careful; upright

specimens
noun: an item or part typical of a group or whole; a sample

reconcile
verb: to restore to harmony; adjust; settle

confidential
adjective: private; secret

deducted
verb: taken away from; subtracted

designate
verb: to point out the location of; to make known directly; to specify

obscurity
noun: the state of being concealed or hidden, covered up or remote

appositive
noun: a grammatical construction in which two nouns referring to the same person or thing stand in the same relation to the rest of a sentence.

periodic
adjective: occurring at regular intervals; consisting of or containing a series of repeated stages

p. 506   The sum should equal the amount **originally** set aside for the fund.

p. 509   Like all other skills, good handwriting cannot be retained long without **conscientious** practice.

p. 510   . . . (b) Look at other **specimens** of his handwriting which may be of help to her?

p. 513   Among the duties which she must learn are how to write a check, . . . how to **reconcile** a bank statement. . . .

p. 513   . . . you must take care that all transactions are completed accurately . . . and that all information about them is kept strictly **confidential**.

p. 528   . . . so the remittance (which means the money sent to pay the bill) was not **deducted** from the new bill.

p. 531   He will then write a check for the specific amount, payable to the person whom you **designate**.

p. 533   The dash is used . . . in place of a comma to show emphasis or to guard against **obscurity**.

p. 533   The dash is used . . . to give special emphasis to an **appositive**.

p. 536   Some firms make **periodic** payments throughout the year on their income taxes.

PART 1 PETTY CASH—HANDWRITTEN

Elaine Ryan, secretary to Mr. David Black, just completed a secretarial course in which she learned that when a package is sent *COD* it means that the person who receives the package must pay cash for it when it is delivered. She remembered that the initials COD meant *Collect on Delivery*. She knew what to do, therefore, when the delivery man delivered a package to her desk and said, "Here is a COD, Miss Ryan." Since this was a small expense, Elaine knew that she must pay cash for the package out of the petty cash fund. As one of her office duties she makes a cash payment for her firm. What records must Elaine keep for this petty cash payment?

Many firms have a special fund called a *petty cash fund* from which they pay small expenses. The petty cash fund can be used to buy stamps, to pay COD charges, to pay for inexpensive office supplies, or any other small expense items. Since most of the records on petty cash are handwritten, it is important that they be written so that you, as well as your employer, can read them easily.

THE PETTY CASH FUND

The petty cash fund is for small expenses and should be handled by one person, usually the secretary or the receptionist.

You should understand how the fund is started, how payments are made from it, and how the fund is replenished. About $25 is usually placed in the petty cash fund; however, the amount may range from $10 to $100, depending upon how much money is spent from the fund. The money in the fund is usually kept locked in a metal cashbox in the desk of the person handling it, and is placed in the office safe at night.

Starting the Fund

To establish a petty cash fund:

1. Write a check payable to Petty Cash for the amount to be placed in the fund, $25 for example. The check may be written by your supervisor or boss if you are not responsible for writing checks.

2. Have the check signed by an authorized person and cashed at the firm's bank.
3. Place the money in the petty cash box.

Making Payments from the Fund

Should a small order of store supplies arrive for which you must make payment, you should immediately make out a receipt which the deliveryman signs. Each time that you make a payment from the petty cash fund, you should make out a receipt for the amount and have it signed by the person receiving the money. The receipts should be numbered consecutively. Each should show the date, to whom the payment is to be made, and the purpose of the payment. The signed receipts should be kept in the petty cash box. At all times the cash on hand plus the total amount of the receipts should equal the original amount placed in the fund. Be sure to get a receipt each time you make a payment because *you* are responsible for the money, and the receipts are proof of your proper use of the fund.

Illus. 14-1
Petty cash receipt

Replenishing the Fund

Additional cash should be placed in the fund whenever the amount of cash gets low. To replenish the fund, follow these steps:

1. Add all receipts and count the cash in the petty cash box.
2. "Prove" the petty cash fund by adding the amount of cash on hand to the total of all petty cash receipts. The sum should equal the amount originally set aside for the fund. An illustration of a proof follows:

Total of petty cash receipts.................	$22.04
Petty cash on hand.......................	2.96
Total....................................	$25.00

3. Prepare a summary report of petty cash expenditures and attach the receipts for them.

SUMMARY REPORT OF PETTY CASH

July 1 to 31, 197–

```
Balance on hand July 1..............  $25.00

Expenditures:
  Office Supplies............  $6.29
  Store Supplies.............   1.25
  Advertising................   4.75
  Messenger Service..........   1.35
  Miscellaneous..............   8.40

Total expenditures.................   22.04

Balance on hand July 31............  $ 2.96
```

4. Write a check payable to "Petty Cash" for the total amount of the receipts shown in the summary report ($22.04 in the illustration).
5. Submit the summary report and the attached receipts to your employer with the check payable to the petty cash fund.
6. After your employer has signed the check, cash it and place the money in the petty cash box, thus replenishing the fund.

Sometimes a more permanent record is made of the petty cash fund in a petty cash book as illustrated below. The columnar petty cash

PETTY CASH BOOK

DATE		EXPLANATION	RECEIVED	PAID
19 Nov.	1	Balance	25 —	
	3	Telegram		75
	30	Postage stamps		3 —
	30	Totals	25 —	23 65
	30	Balance		1 35
			25 —	25 —
	30	Balance	1 35	
	30	Check No. 315	23 65	

Illus. 14-2   Simple petty cash book

book makes it easy to determine how the petty cash was spent when each of the columns is totaled.

PETTY CASH BOOK

Date	Explanation	Receipts	Payments	Office Supplies	Store Supplies	Advertising	Messenger	Miscellaneous
July 1	Balance	25 00						
2	Ad in school program		4 75			4 75		
10	Registered letter		90					90
15	Cleaning office		7 50					7 50
19	Delivery of a contract		1 00				1 00	
20	Twine for store		1 25		1 25			
22	Ink		75	75				
25	Immediate delivery of a sale		35				35	
27	Postage Stamps		4 85	4 85				
29	Miscellaneous office supplies		69	69				
31	Totals	25 00	22 04	6 29	1 25	4 75	1 35	8 40
31	Balance		2 96					
		25 00	25 00					
31	Balance	2 96						
31	Check No. 475	22 04						

Illus. 14-3 Columnar petty cash book

OTHER RECORDS KEPT BY THE SECRETARY

Thus far, we have been discussing jobs that you would handle as a secretary not only in the small firm but also in the large firm. There is one job, however, that is usually handled by the secretary in a small firm — the payroll. In a large firm a special department handles this responsibility, but in a small firm the secretary may keep all the records and even make the payments. How much time you will spend on the payroll will depend on where you work. Some small firms are now having their payrolls prepared by their banks or by companies which specialize in preparing payrolls.

What other types of records would you keep? Well, there are your employer's travel expense reports; there's the record of premium payments on his various insurance policies; there's a record to remind you to pay the rent not only on the office space but also on the various machines your executive may lease, such as computing machines, dictating and transcribing machines, and possibly the automobiles which are used by members of the firm. These are some types of records that you may be expected to keep when you become a secretary. The more accurate the records you keep the more valuable you will be as a secretary.

IMPORTANCE OF HANDWRITING

Illegible penmanship costs United States businessmen enormous sums in scrambled orders, lost time, missent shipments, clerical mistakes, and other forms of inefficiency. The Handwriting Foundation estimates that poor penmanship costs business about $100 million a year.[1]

In keeping records, the secretary fills in forms, posts information to visible card files, and uses her handwriting in many other ways. Neat and legible handwriting is very important.

Did you ever receive a note you could not read? Have you ever had difficulty reading your own handwriting? Then you can imagine how aggravating poor handwriting is to an employer, especially when a mistake in a figure or date, or the illegibility of a name or number, can mean a loss of time, money, and goodwill.

In many cases your writing speed has an influence upon the quality of your writing. If you write at too fast a rate, your letters and numbers will be carelessly formed; and, if you write too slowly, the lines will waver. If you write with excessive speed, it will affect the exactness, alignment, and evenness of your strokes. Remember, if you are writing longhand, write it to be read. Keep your writing speed at the rate at which you can write effortlessly letters and numbers that are readable.

Like all other skills, good handwriting cannot be retained long without conscientious practice. At one time you probably had training in penmanship, but you may have become careless and lost some of this valuable business skill. If you are to keep readable records, you must have clear, legible handwriting.

QUESTIONS

1. What is a petty cash fund?
2. How is a petty cash fund established?
3. Why should a receipt for each payment from the petty cash fund be kept?
4. What steps are necessary to have the petty cash fund replenished?
5. What records may you have to keep in your secretarial position?
6. Why is it important for a secretary to be able to write legibly?

JUDGMENT

1. Why should you exercise care in maintaining a petty cash fund?

---

[1]Costello, John, "Executive Trends," *Nation's Business*, Washington: Chamber of Commerce of the United States (July, 1970), p. 11.

2. It is often said that a person who types well does not need to write well in longhand. What is your opinion of this point of view?
3. What measures can you take to improve your handwriting?
4. In what types of secretarial duties is handwriting important?

PERSONAL QUALITIES

Lou Ann Smith is secretary to Mr. Paterson, who is away on a business trip. He has left written instructions about a report which must be submitted to the directors of the company before he returns. His handwriting is so illegible that the only word Lou Ann can decipher in one section is the word *urgent*. She becomes quite concerned about which course of action she should take. Should she

(a) Ask Mr. Paterson's former secretary to help her?
(b) Look at other specimens of his handwriting which may be of help to her?
(c) Attempt to reach him by telephone to get him to repeat his instructions verbally?
(d) Let the whole thing wait until he returns?
What would you do if you were in Lou Ann's position?

LANGUAGE USAGE

On a separate sheet of paper write the plurals of the following words.

analysis	genius
good-for-nothing	teaspoonful
tomato	shelf
hoax	dwarf
parenthesis	two-year-old
sister-in-law	child
attitude	ox
library	life
passer-by	half
belief	appendix
self	leaf
gentleman	crisis
cargo	lawyer
photocopy	memorandum
money	proof

SECRETARIAL WORK

1. How does your handwriting rate when compared with penmanship which observes the basic rules of good handwriting? On page 511 are examples of letters and figures which are correctly written.

Compare your handwriting with these examples. Do you need to improve your handwriting? Try to make your letters uniform and the spacing between letters and words even. If there are any letters or figures which you or your teacher cannot read, practice writing them until they are similar to the examples below.

a b c d e f g h i
j k l m n o p q r
s t u v w x y z

A B C D E F G H I
J K L M N O P Q R
S T U V W X Y Z

1 2 3 4 5 6 7 8 9 0

2. Some business organizations make a practice of having their monthly statements handwritten. In your best handwriting, with pen, make the two statements below to be mailed by a dry cleaner. If you do not have blank statement paper, draw up your own in the style of the one shown on page 215. (The abbreviation *pr* means *pressed*, and *dc* means *dry cleaned*.)

April 30, 197–. Mr. Frank L. Porton, 32 Washington Place, Freehold, NY 12431.

Mar 31	4 suits, pr............................	4.00
Apr 5	suit, pr...............................	1.00
7	suit, pr...............................	1.00
8	2 suits, dc...........................	4.00
	3 suits, pr...........................	3.00
	quilted robe, dc.....................	2.00
	suit, pr...............................	1.00
12	suit, dc..............................	2.00
21	tux, dc...............................	2.00
	suit, dc..............................	2.00
	jacket, pr............................	1.00
	2 pants, pr..........................	1.00
	suit, pr...............................	1.00
28	2 jackets, dc........................	2.00
	2 suits, pr...........................	2.00

Part 1 / Petty Cash — Handwritten

December 31, 197–. Mr. Frank L. Porton, 32 Washington Place, Freehold, NY 12431.

Dec.	1	4 suits, pr	4.00
	5	1 topper, dc	1.50
	10	2 suits, pr	2.00
		2 chair, 3 cushion covers, dc	6.00
	11	2 suits, altered	19.00
	12	2 suits, pr	2.00
	15	1 dress, dc	3.00
		2 black velvet dresses, dc	6.00
		1 red velvet dress, dc	3.00
	17	2 suits, pr	2.00
	21	2 suits, pr	2.00
	24	1 suit, pr	1.00

3. The following transactions pertain to the petty cash fund kept by the Jones Drug Company during the months of September and October.

Sept. 1 Check No. 175 for $25 was cashed to establish a petty cash fund.
    3 Paid Bill Smith $6 for cleaning the store and office.
   13 Paid the Lake Supply Company 95 cents for miscellaneous store supplies.
   17 Paid Johnny Stone 75 cents for delivering merchandise.
   24 Paid $3 for postage stamps.
   29 Paid the Stevens Hardware Company 50 cents for a duplicate key for the office.
   30 Check No. 221 for $11.20 was cashed to replenish the petty cash fund.

Oct. 4 Paid the Howsam Stationery Company $1.15 for miscellaneous office supplies.
   10 Paid Bill Smith $6 for cleaning the store and office.
   17 Paid Central High School $5 for advertisement in school paper.
   22 Paid the Jackson Paper Company 85 cents for miscellaneous store supplies.
   29 Paid REA $6.75 for collect charges on merchandise purchased.
   31 Check No. 256 for $19.75 was cashed to replenish the petty cash fund.

Prepare a summary report of petty cash expenditures similar to the one illustrated on page 507. If receipt forms are available, write a receipt for each of the payments made during the month of September.

PART 2 THE CHECKBOOK AND THE BANK

Jessica Hughes is a secretary to Mr. Robert L. Blanch, owner of the Taho Automobile Company. She has worked for Mr. Blanch for several years and knows the business very well. Mr. Blanch has come to depend on Jessica in many ways and has decided that she is now experienced enough to write the checks for the company. Jessica knows this will include several new duties which she must learn to do efficiently. Among the duties which she must learn are how to write a check, how to deposit money in the bank, how to reconcile a bank statement, and how to properly endorse checks for the company.

Have you ever thought that you might be handling bank accounts of hundreds, thousands, or hundreds of thousands of dollars? As with most of your other duties, the size and type of firm for which you work will determine the extent of your contact with banks. For example, if you are employed by a large firm with a separate accounting department, your dealings with banks may be limited to handling the personal financial affairs of your immediate employer. On the other hand, if you are employed by a firm engaged primarily in financial transactions, whether it is a large brokerage house or a small collection agency, dealing with banks may be one of your most important daily tasks.

When you deal with a bank or handle money in any other capacity for your firm, you must take care that all transactions are completed accurately and promptly and that all information about them is kept strictly confidential.

BANK ACCOUNTS

You know that business firms use the services of commercial banks rather than risk loss of large sums of money left in the office. Money is deposited in bank accounts, and checks are drawn against these accounts to make payments. Generally cash is used to pay only small business expenses.

Payment is made by check because the canceled check is ultimately returned to the one who wrote it and is a receipt for payment. Furthermore, a person receiving a check can easily transfer it to someone else or deposit it in his own bank account. When a check is deposited in an account, the bank in which it is deposited will collect the amount from the bank on which the check was drawn.

If you are handling bank accounts, it will be your responsibility to make deposits, write checks, keep the checkbook stubs up to date, endorse checks, and reconcile bank statements. You may even have to take the first step of opening the bank account. Let's look at these various duties to see how you can handle them.

Opening a Bank Account

When you open a personal bank account the bank may want to have you identified and/or introduced by one of its depositors. If you are not known by a depositor, the bank may ask for one or more references — preferably a reference from another bank where you may have had an account or a reference from your present employer. This request is made so that the bank may check the references to be reasonably sure that it is dealing with a responsible person who will use the account properly.

Before your account is opened you will be asked to fill out a *signature card*, which will be kept on file at the bank. The signature which you use to sign your checks should always agree with your signature on the card. If you have used a given name and a middle name on the signature card, *Mary Alice Downs*, for example, you should not use initials, such as *M. A. Downs*, when you sign your checks.

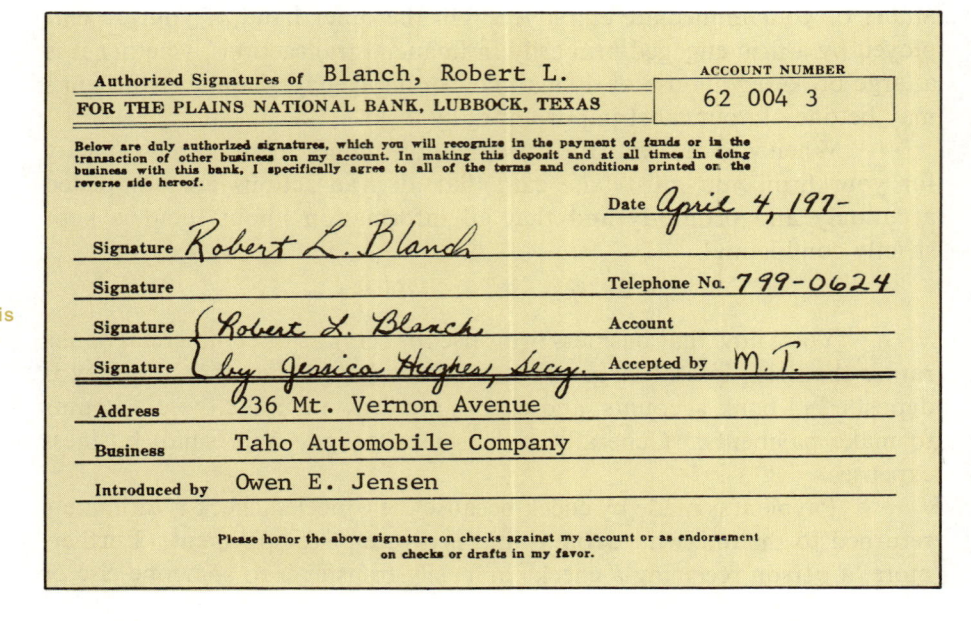

Illus. 14-4

Signature card

This card shows that the secretary is authorized to sign checks for her employer.

When more than one person is to sign checks for a firm — the president, vice-president, and the treasurer, for example — all must fill out signature cards. When you, as the secretary, are asked to handle a checking account for a businessman, a letter must be sent to the bank authorizing your signature; and you will have to fill out a signature card before you will be permitted to sign checks.

Making Deposits

Before making a bank deposit you must list all the amounts in detail on a deposit slip. This form is supplied at the bank's writing counters, and you should have a supply of them at the office, so that you may complete and double-check all entries before you go to the bank with your deposits. Two copies of the deposit slip are prepared.

The information you must fill in on a deposit slip includes the number of the checking account, the name of the depositor, the date, and the items to be deposited. Many banks now supply customers with deposit slips on which the customer's name and account number are already printed. The deposit may consist of currency (paper money), silver (coins), endorsed checks, and/or money orders. In listing checks you may identify them in one of three ways:

1. By transit number which appears in fraction form in the upper right-hand corner of the check and is assigned to

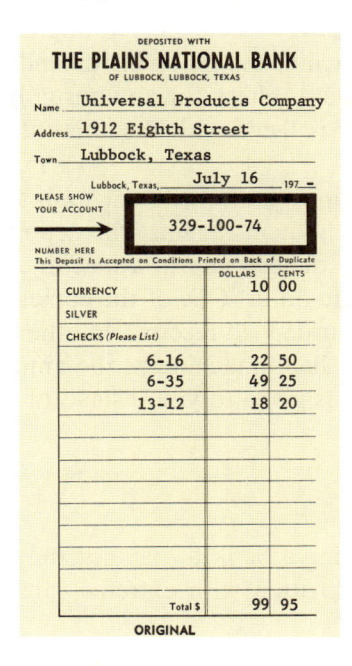

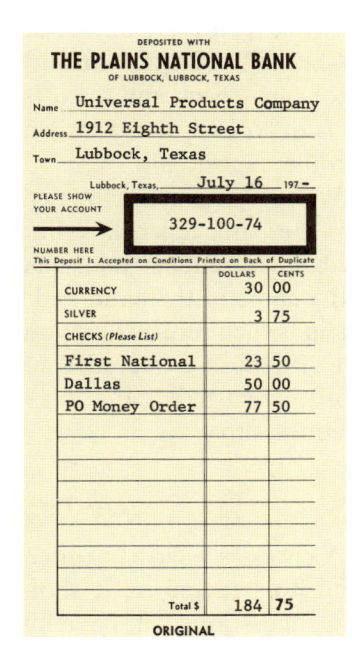

Illus. 14-5

Deposit slips

Part 2 / The Checkbook and the Bank

each bank by the American Bankers Association. An illustration of a check is on page 517.
2. By name, if the bank is a local one.
3. By the city and state of out-of-town banks.

When the deposit you are making consists of large quantities of coins and bills, the bank prefers to have you put the money in wrappers which it provides for its depositors. Pack coins in paper rolls in the following quantities:

Denomination	Number of Coins to a Roll	Total Value of Coins in Roll
Pennies	50	$ .50
Nickels	40	2.00
Dimes	50	5.00
Quarters	40	10.00
Halves	20	10.00

If you have many bills of different denominations, you should package each denomination in amounts of $50, $100, and so on. Be sure that all bills face the same way. Put a bill wrapper — a narrow paper strip with the amount printed on it — tightly around the bills and glue it securely. You should write or stamp the name of the depositing firm on each roll of coins and each package of bills to insure that it is deposited to the right account should it become separated from the rest of the money.

If you have a large number of checks, instead of listing the amount of each check separately on the deposit slip, you may show only the total under "Checks" and attach an adding machine tape showing the individual amount of each check and the total. When a check for an unusually large amount is deposited, the transit number is listed with the amount of the check on the deposit slip.

When you present the deposit slip together with the cash and the checks to the bank teller, he will check the items against the deposit slip. In some banks the teller then places the deposit slip in a machine which stamps the name of the bank and the date on it. One of the copies of the deposit slip is then returned to you as your deposit receipt. In other banks a receipt of deposit is recorded on the teller's machine as the amount of the deposit is registered, and this receipt is given to you instead of a copy of the deposit slip.

WRITING CHECKS

A check is a written order directing a bank to pay out the money of a depositor; therefore, it should be written with extreme care. The following suggestions will be helpful.

1. *Type checks or write them in ink* — never in pencil.
2. *Number* each check, if numbers are not printed on them. Be sure that the number of the check corresponds with that of the check stub.
3. *Date* the check on the exact date that it is written. Do not postdate a check, that is, date it ahead with the hope that there will be sufficient funds in the account by that time to cover the check.

Illus. 14-6
Check with stub

4. Write the name of the payee, the person who is to receive the money, in full. If you are not sure of the correct spelling, try to verify it in the telephone directory or from previous correspondence. Omit titles such as Mr., Mrs., Miss, Dr., or Prof.
5. *Write the amount* of the check in large, bold figures next to the printed dollar sign and close enough to prevent the insertion of other figures. In spelling out the amount, start at the extreme left, capitalize the first letter only, and express cents as fractions of one hundred:
Three hundred thirty-four no/100- - - - - - - - - -*Dollars*
One thousand five hundred fifty 75/100- - - - - -*Dollars*
If you should write a check for less than a dollar, precede the spelled-out amount with the word *Only* and cross out the printed word *Dollars* as:
Only eighty-nine cents- - - - - - - - - - - - - - - - - -*Dollars*
6. *Fill in all blank spaces* before and after the names of the payee and after the written amount with hyphens, periods, or a line.
7. *You may wish to write the purpose of the check*, such as *In Payment of Invoice 3960*, at the bottom of the check. Some checks have a special blank line for this purpose.
8. *Do not erase* on a check. If you should make an error in writing a check, write the word *Void* across the face

of both the check and the check stub. Save the voided check and file it in numerical order with the canceled checks when they are returned by the bank.
9. *Do not sign blank checks.* Anyone can fill them out and cash them.
10. *Do not make a check payable to "Cash"* unless you plan to cash it at once.
11. *Write legibly.* An illegible signature creates difficulties at the bank and is no protection against forgery.

A firm issuing a large number of checks usually will print the amount of each check with a checkwriter, a machine that perforates and inks the amount into the check paper to prevent any alteration.

The Check Stub

Don't run the risk of writing checks when you do not have enough money in your account to insure their payment. To prevent this, fill out the check stub *before* you write a check. Otherwise you may forget to fill it out and to deduct the amount from the account balance. You will then have no record of the check except a blank stub until the bank returns your canceled checks or notifies you that your account has been overdrawn.

The check stub is often bound into the checkbook to the left of the blank checks. The stubs provide space for recording the original balance, deposits, new balances, and information about each check that you write. This information includes the check number, the date, the name of the payee, the amount, and the purpose. The amount of the check should be deducted from the previous account balance and the new balance entered on the stub.

Duplicate Checks

Your firm may prefer to prepare checks in duplicate with a ball-point pen, a typewriter, or some other writing machine instead of taking the time to fill out regular check stubs. The check is sent out, but the duplicate copy is kept for reference purposes and for entering the transaction in the company records.

Endorsing Checks

When your firm gives a check to a person for his services, he cannot cash, deposit, or transfer that check until he endorses it. The endorsement is made by signing the check across the back at the top of the left end. There are different types of endorsements which you will see and use. The most common types of business endorsements are *restrictive*, *full* or *special*, and *blank* endorsements. A knowledge of endorsements will help you safeguard checks.

A *restrictive endorsement* allows you to send an endorsed check safely through the mail. It transfers the ownership for a specific, stated purpose. For example, the following words may be written above the signature of the endorser: *For Deposit Only*. If you endorse a check in this way it can only be deposited in your account. Since the check cannot be cashed by anyone else, there is little danger if the check is misplaced, lost, or stolen.

Endorsements are usually written in ink, but restrictive endorsements made with rubber stamps are often used for depositing checks. This type of endorsement is satisfactory because it makes the checks payable only to the account of the depositor and would not benefit anyone who might obtain a rubber stamp and attempt to use it improperly.

An *endorsement in full*, or a *special* endorsement as it is sometimes called, shows the name of the person to whom the check is being transferred. For example, the words *Pay to the order of Lawrence Trent* may be written before the endorser's signature. A check endorsed in this way cannot be cashed by anyone without Lawrence Trent's signature. Therefore, you may send a check endorsed in this manner through the mail without danger in case of loss.

A *blank endorsement* consists only of a signature across the back of the check. It makes the check payable to anyone who may possess it.

Illus. 14-7

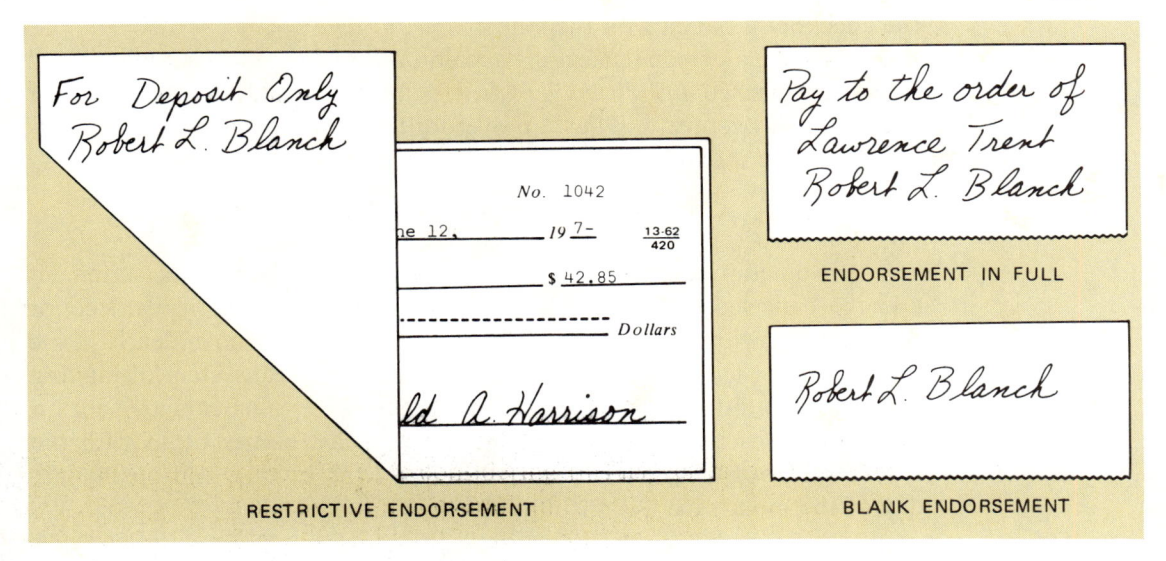

RESTRICTIVE ENDORSEMENT

ENDORSEMENT IN FULL

BLANK ENDORSEMENT

You should use this type of endorsement only when you plan to cash or deposit a check immediately. It is not the correct endorsement for a check that is being sent through the mail or for a check that could be lost or misplaced because the check can be cashed by anyone who holds it — even if he has no right to it.

STOPPING PAYMENT ON CHECKS

One of the firm's employees calls to say that he has lost his paycheck. You must call the bank immediately to stop payment on the check. If the check has not already been cashed or deposited, the bank will refuse payment when it is presented. Payment may be stopped for a number of reasons — if a check is lost or stolen, if it is made out incorrectly, or if it represents payment for goods or services which have been canceled.

You must give the following information to stop payment on a check: the name of the drawer (the one who signed the check), the date of the check, the amount of the check, and the name of the payee. You should also send a confirming letter to the bank immediately or fill out a stop-payment form supplied by the bank. This form gives the bank written instructions not to cash the check described.

OVERDRAFT

An overdraft occurs when a depositor writes a check on an account in which he does not have sufficient funds to cover the full payment. This happens when checks that have not been entered and deducted on the check stubs are cashed or when an error is made in computing or recording the checkbook balance on the stubs.

When a personal checking account is overdrawn, a bank may return the check marked *Insufficient Funds*. A charge is made by the bank for handling the overdraft. Thus, an overdraft is expensive as well as embarrassing to the individual.

RECONCILIATION OF THE BANK STATEMENT

Sometime during each month you will receive a bank statement and the canceled checks that the bank paid out of your firm's account during the previous month. Some banks send such a statement early in the month to all their customers. Other banks use a cycle system of mailing statements at different times of the month; that is, statements are sent on the tenth of each month to customers whose last names begin with the letters *A* through *H*, on the twentieth from *I* through *Q*, and on the last day of the month from *R* through *Z*.

As shown below, the Statement of Account will list the Statement Period — *A*; the Beginning Balance — *B*; Total Deposits — *C*; Total Checks — *D*; the Service Charge — *E*, deducted by the bank for handling the account; and the Ending Balance — *F* — of the period.

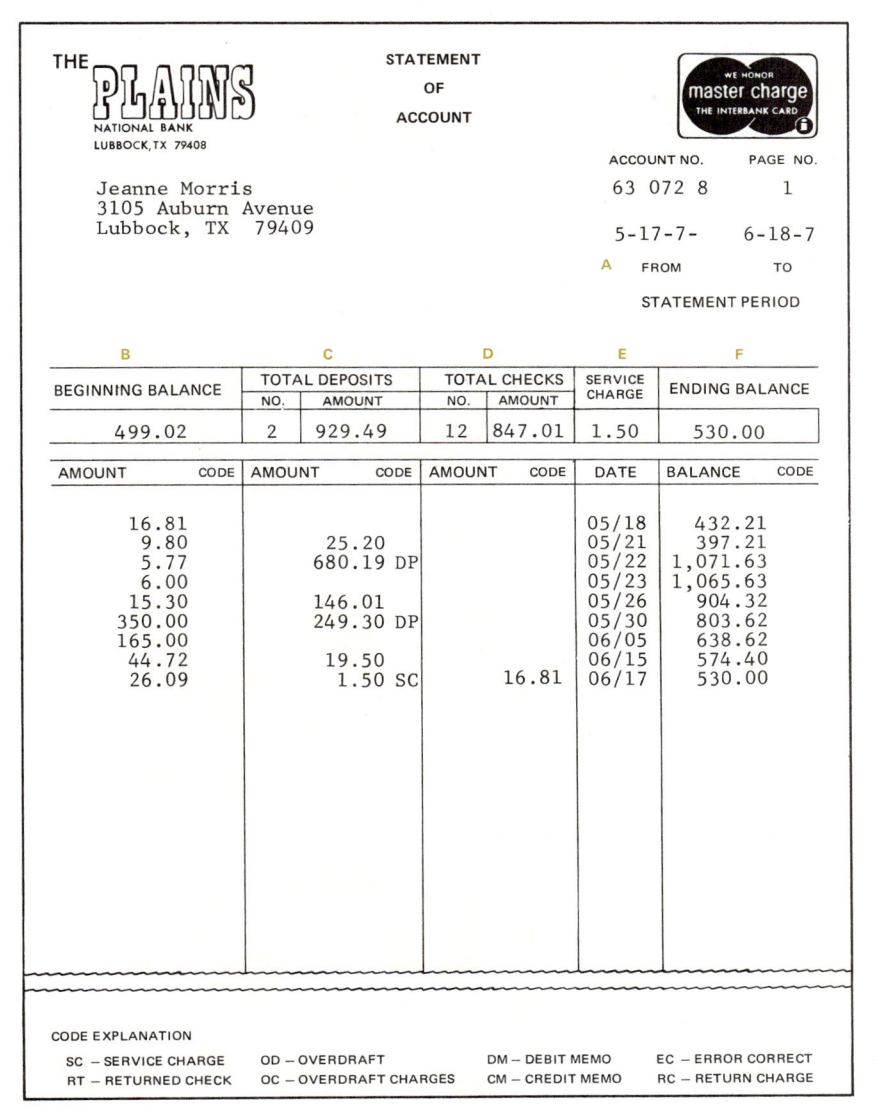

THE PLAINS NATIONAL BANK
LUBBOCK, TX 79408

STATEMENT OF ACCOUNT

WE HONOR master charge THE INTERBANK CARD

Jeanne Morris
3105 Auburn Avenue
Lubbock, TX 79409

ACCOUNT NO. 63 072 8   PAGE NO. 1

5-17-7-   6-18-7
A FROM   TO
STATEMENT PERIOD

B	C		D		E	F
BEGINNING BALANCE	TOTAL DEPOSITS		TOTAL CHECKS		SERVICE CHARGE	ENDING BALANCE
	NO.	AMOUNT	NO.	AMOUNT		
499.02	2	929.49	12	847.01	1.50	530.00

AMOUNT CODE	AMOUNT CODE	AMOUNT CODE	DATE	BALANCE CODE
16.81			05/18	432.21
9.80	25.20		05/21	397.21
5.77	680.19 DP		05/22	1,071.63
6.00			05/23	1,065.63
15.30	146.01		05/26	904.32
350.00	249.30 DP		05/30	803.62
165.00			06/05	638.62
44.72	19.50		06/15	574.40
26.09	1.50 SC	16.81	06/17	530.00

CODE EXPLANATION
SC — SERVICE CHARGE   OD — OVERDRAFT   DM — DEBIT MEMO   EC — ERROR CORRECT
RT — RETURNED CHECK   OC — OVERDRAFT CHARGES CM — CREDIT MEMO   RC — RETURN CHARGE

Illus. 14-8

Statement of account

This banking service permits you to check the accuracy of your checkbook with the bank records and to file the canceled checks as proof of the firm's payments.

Part 2 / The Checkbook and the Bank   521

After you have received the canceled checks and the bank statement, you should compare the final balance on the bank statement with the checkbook balance and account for the difference. This process of accounting for the difference is called *reconciling the bank statement*. For the convenience of their depositors, many banks print a reconciliation form on the back of the monthly statement. The following steps should be taken to reconcile an account:

1. Compare the amount of each canceled check with the amount listed on the bank statement. This step will show any error made by the bank or the depositor in recording a check. Place a check mark beside each verified amount.
2. Arrange the canceled checks in numerical order.
3. Compare the returned checks with the stubs in the checkbook. Place a check mark on the stub of each check that has been returned.
4. Make a list of the outstanding checks — those that have not been paid and returned. Include on the list the number of each outstanding check and the amount.
5. Add the amounts of outstanding checks and deduct the total from the balance shown on the bank statement.
6. Subtract the amount of the service charges listed on the bank statement from the checkbook balance.
7. After the service charge has been deducted from the checkbook balance, the remaining amount should agree with the balance shown on the bank statement after the total of the outstanding checks has been deducted.

Here is an example of a reconciliation:

RECONCILIATION OF BANK ACCOUNT
June 18, 197–

Balance as shown on bank statement...	$530.00	Balance as shown by checkbook........	$375.50
Less checks outstanding:		Less June service charge..........	1.50
143....... $50.00			
144....... 16.00			
147....... 90.00	156.00		
Adjusted bank balance..........	$374.00	Adjusted checkbook balance..........	$374.00

Unit 14 / Secretarial Accounting

CHECKS OUTSTANDING NOT CHARGED TO ACCOUNT		THIS FORM IS PROVIDED TO HELP YOU BALANCE YOUR BANK STATEMENT	
NO.	$		
143	50 00	1. Check Book Balance	$ 375.50
144	16 00		
147	90 00	2. Less Service Charges (if any) shown on this statement (This amount) should be deducted from your book balance.)	$ 1.50
		ADJUSTED CHECK BOOK BALANCE (Item 1 Less Item 2)	$ 374.00
		Bank Balance Shown on This Statement	$ 530.00
		ADD +	
		Deposits not shown in this statement (if any) $_____ $_____ TOTAL	$
		Subtract- Checks Outstanding	$ 156.00
		BALANCE (should agree with adjusted check book balance above)	$ 374.00
TOTAL	156 00		

Illus. 14-9
Bank reconciliation prepared on the printed form shown on the back of the bank statement.

These are the duties that you may perform for your employer or for your firm. They are not difficult, but they demand accuracy, neatness, dependability, and efficiency on your part.

Illus. 14-10
Accuracy, neatness, dependability, and efficiency are necessary for the secretary who handles banking transactions for her employer.

Vincent Nanfra

THE PATH OF A CHECK

A check is passed from person to person and finally returns to the person who wrote it. When a check is written on a bank and deposited in another bank, the check follows the path illustrated on page 524.

The Path of a Check

Illus. 14-11

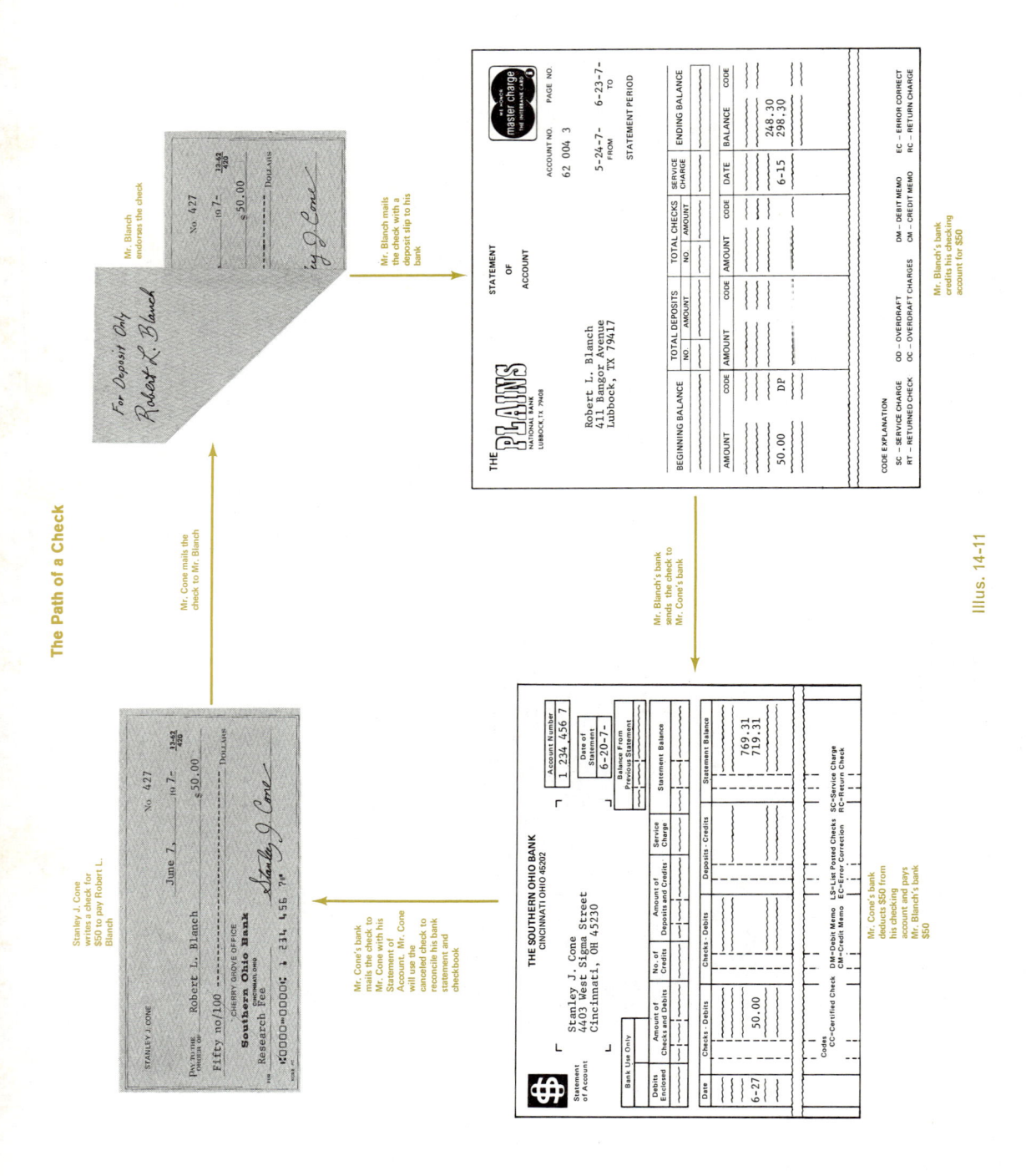

524　　　　Unit 14 / Secretarial Accounting

QUESTIONS

1. As a secretary why should you understand banking procedures?
2. Why is actual cash seldom used in business transactions?
3. List the duties of a secretary who handles a bank account.
4. How is a bank account opened?
5. What is the purpose of a signature card?
6. A deposit slip contains what information?
7. Give ten suggestions that will enable you to write checks correctly.
8. What is a checkwriter?
9. When should the check stub be filled in, and what information should be on it?
10. For what purposes are duplicate checks used?
11. Name three types of endorsements and explain the use of each.
12. Under what conditions should payment be stopped on a check, and what procedure should be followed?
13. What causes overdrafts and why should they be avoided?
14. What information is included on a bank statement?
15. How is a reconciliation of the bank statement made?

JUDGMENT

1. When would you recommend that endorsement in full be used?
2. If you were going into a bank to cash a check, which form of endorsement would you use?
3. If you were endorsing a check to be sent to someone through the mail, what form of endorsement would you use?
4. If you were unable to go to your bank and were planning to send checks through the mail for deposit, which form of endorsement would you use?
5. Who, if anyone, loses when payment on a check is stopped?
6. Must the records that are kept by a secretary be as accurate as those kept by a bookkeeper who devotes his full time to that type of work?
7. What measures may be taken to make it less likely that a check could be altered?
8. Some persons believe that making a bank reconciliation is too much trouble. What is your reaction to this opinion?

PERSONAL QUALITIES

Nancy Dever is the secretary to Mr. Tuttle, Business Manager for a small dry cleaning business. Mr. Tuttle asked Nancy to deposit a check for him in the bank, and he endorsed it by writing his name on the back of the check. While on her way to the bank, Nancy's purse, which contained Mr. Tuttle's endorsed check, was stolen.

Was this check properly endorsed? Could whoever found the check cash it? What should Nancy do?

LANGUAGE USAGE

Three common usages of parentheses are:

A. Around explanatory, nonessential material used within a sentence.

Example: The number of applications was 35 (or was it 38?).

B. To enclose references, directions, and sources of information.

Example: Additional student training is provided by government agencies (United States Department of Labor).

C. Around numbers or letters indicating listings or divisions within a sentence.

Example: He explained his reasons for leaving his present position: (a) his chance to earn a higher salary, (b) his preference for the type of work he would be doing, (c) his opportunity to travel.

Type the following sentences on a separate sheet of paper and insert parentheses where necessary.

1. Her employer's uncle his father's brother came to the office for a visit.
2. When she balanced the petty cash, she found that she was short $2.50 or maybe it was $3.50.
3. In her class in secretarial accounting she learned how to 1 open a bank account 2 write a check correctly 3 reconcile a bank statement and 4 balance a petty cash fund.
4. Stopping payment on checks see page 520 requires immediate action.
5. The date on the check the day she left on vacation and the day the check was lost June 7, 1972 were the same.

SECRETARIAL WORK

1. The checking account balance of the Art Craft Company on the first of March was $932.15. During the month the Art Craft Company deposited $2,530.15 and issued checks totaling $2,777.81. Checks amounting to $298.60 have not been cashed. What is the checkbook balance at the end of the month? What is the bank balance?

2. You are employed by Johnson & Sears and have been authorized to write and sign the checks and keep the checkbook during the absence of the employee who ordinarily does it. During this period, the following checks were written and deposits made. If forms are available, write the checks, prepare the deposit slips, and complete the check stubs. If forms are not available, find the checkbook balance at the end of each day.

Nov. 10 Balance according to last check stub, $1,073.51.

11 Check 532, Washington Square Service Company, $169.25, for invoice of November 2.

12 Check 533, Howard A. Johnson, $50, for personal use.

13 Deposit: currency, $14; silver, $2.25; checks — First National Bank, $59.70; Syracuse, New York, $212.75; Cincinnati, Ohio, $193.80.

15 Check 534, J. W. Combs Co., $549.62, for invoice of November 5.

15 Check 535, City Electric Co., $13.95, for electric bill.

16 Deposit: currency, $15; checks — Central Trust Company, $221.40; First National Bank, $129.62; Rochester, New York, $279.33.

18 Check 536, Franklin Paper Co., $42.50, for wrapping paper and cartons.

3. During the month of June the following checks were issued by the Fuel Oil Products Company:

No. 146	$ 16.10	No. 166	$ 65.00
" 147	4.31	" 167	191.84
" 148	4.24	" 168	84.56
" 149	10.23	" 169	2.04
" 150	166.81	" 170	254.68
" 151	204.68	" 171	27.13
" 152	15.31	" 172	19.00
" 153	4.06	" 173	118.34
" 154	.52	" 174	125.00
" 155	18.93	" 175	50.00
" 156	16.77	" 176	6.60
" 157	22.54	" 177	8.14
" 158	18.30	" 178	14.67
" 159	281.69	" 179	178.34
" 160	346.06	" 180	101.47
" 161	2.85	" 181	11.12
" 162	46.81	" 182	219.00
" 163	5.00	" 183	1.92
" 164	8.50	" 184	10.13
" 165	105.25		

The check stub balance on June 1 was $932.15. The deposits for the month were as follows: $401.68, $664.00, $593.45, $432.18, $187.67, $251.17.

The bank statement for the month of June showed a balance of $981.59. A service charge of $1.50 had been deducted. All checks written were returned with the bank statement except Checks 173, 179, 183, and 184.

Prepare the reconciliation of the bank statement.

PART 3 — MAKING CASH PAYMENTS

Rozelle has worked as a secretary to the treasurer of a manufacturing company for the last three years. When she first started to work she was awed by the many financial duties of the other secretaries. She is now required to do many of these duties. She writes all the checks for the company to pay the monthly bills, to replenish the petty cash fund, to pay quarterly insurance premiums, and to pay any other item which is due. She also cashes checks for her employer, records cash which comes into the firm, and reconciles the bank statement. Through a secretarial course and observation of the other secretaries, Rozelle learned the correct procedures to follow in performing the many financial duties required in her job.

On your first job, you may not be required to perform a great variety of financial duties; however, as you gain experience and are promoted, you will be required to know how to perform additional financial tasks.

PAYING MONTHLY BILLS

To pay the monthly bills for such services as light, rent, and telephone, you will write many checks. Before writing the checks, you should verify the balances of all bills to be sure that you are not being charged for services for which you have already paid. Your last check may have been received after the bill was prepared; so the remittance (which means the money sent to pay the bill) was not deducted from the new bill. Your records will tell you what has been paid and when.

VOUCHER CHECKS

Your company may use voucher checks as illustrated on page 529 instead of regular checks. By using this type of check, you can indicate on the face of the check, or on a detachable stub, the specific invoice, bill, or service for which payment is made. When the invoices are paid, the invoice number, the amount of the invoice, the amount of the discount, and the net amount of the check are recorded in a special block at the left end of the voucher check or on the stub.

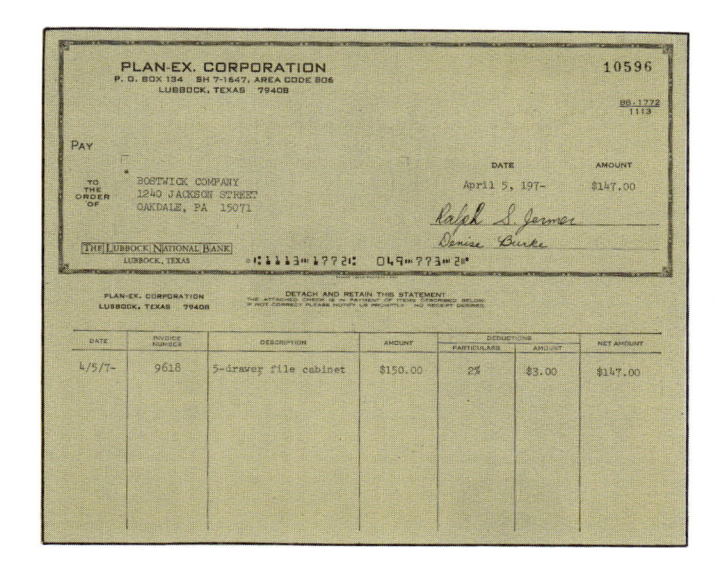

Illus. 14-12
Voucher check

Plan-Ex. Corporation

You should check the accuracy of all figures on an invoice — the extensions, additional charges, discounts, and the net amount — before preparing a check in payment. When you receive a voucher check with a detachable stub, the stub should be detached and filed before the check is deposited.

OTHER FORMS FOR CASH PAYMENTS

In addition to ordinary checks and voucher checks, other forms that are used in making cash payments include

1. Certified check
2. Bank draft
3. Cashier's check
4. Postal and express money orders

Certified Check

Sometimes a check must be *certified* before it will be accepted by a firm. If your employer does not know the credit standing of a new customer, he may ask that a certified check accompany the purchase order.

If your employer asked you to get a check certified, you would take it to a bank official and ask to have it certified. After investigating to see that there are enough funds in your employer's account to cover the check, the bank official would stamp CERTIFIED on the face of the check and then add his official bank signature. Your employer's account would be immediately charged with the amount of the check. This amount is

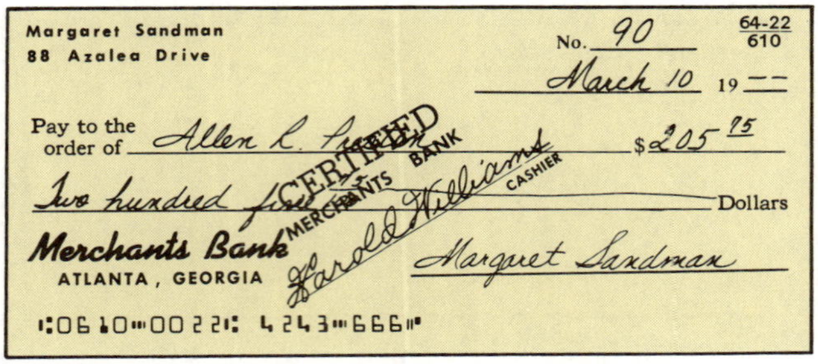

Illus. 14-13
Certified check

transferred by the bank to a special account to be used in paying the check when it is returned. The bank, and not the drawer of the check (in this instance, your employer), becomes responsible for the payment of the certified check. Because the bank guarantees payment of a certified check, any payee will gladly accept it. Like an ordinary check, however, it should be cashed or deposited promptly.

Bank Draft

Another type of cash payment is the bank draft. If you are ordering materials from a distant city, you may send a bank draft to bind the contract. A bank draft is an order drawn by one bank on its deposits in another bank to pay a third party. Since this type of draft, like a certified check, has the bank's assurance of payment, it is accepted more freely than an ordinary check. In the illustration the Bank of Middleton is the drawer; The First National Bank of San Francisco, California, the drawee, is the bank that must pay the draft; and the payee is K and S Construction Co. The cashier of the Bank of Middleton, Anna Jarvis, merely signs for the drawer.

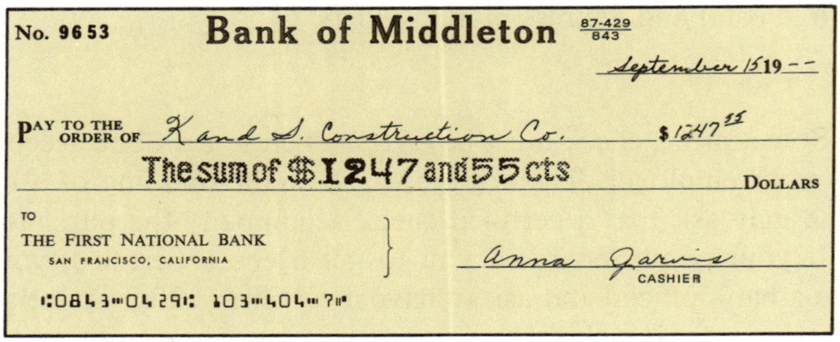

Illus. 14-14
Bank draft

You may purchase a bank draft by presenting cash or your employer's check to a bank. The cashier will make out the draft, which is merely a bank's check drawn on its deposits in another bank. Ordinarily banks make a small charge for bank drafts.

A bank draft is usually used to remit to an individual or firm in a distant city who might not care to accept an ordinary check from a person or firm unknown to them. Although bank drafts and certified checks should be passed with equal confidence, business firms prefer bank drafts.

Cashier's Check

Another type of cash payment you or your employer might use is the cashier's check. A cashier's check is written by a bank on its own funds. It serves somewhat the same purpose as a bank draft. It differs in that it is drawn by the cashier on funds in his own bank, whereas a bank draft is drawn upon deposits in another bank. When you wish to pay a person who may be unaware of your credit standing or to cash a check in a distant city, where you are not known and your personal check might be questioned, you could use a cashier's check.

You need not be a depositor in a bank to purchase a cashier's check. You may give the cashier your employer's check or cash to cover the amount of the cashier's check. He will then write a check for the specific amount, payable to the person whom you designate. A small charge is usually made by the bank for issuing a cashier's check.

Postal and Express Money Orders

Finally, you may make payment by sending domestic and international postal money orders or express money orders. You may send a money order to your salesman in Seattle or Honolulu. Domestic postal money orders may be purchased at all post offices, branches, and stations in the United States and its possessions; international postal money orders at many of them. Express money orders may be purchased at any American Express Company or REA office.

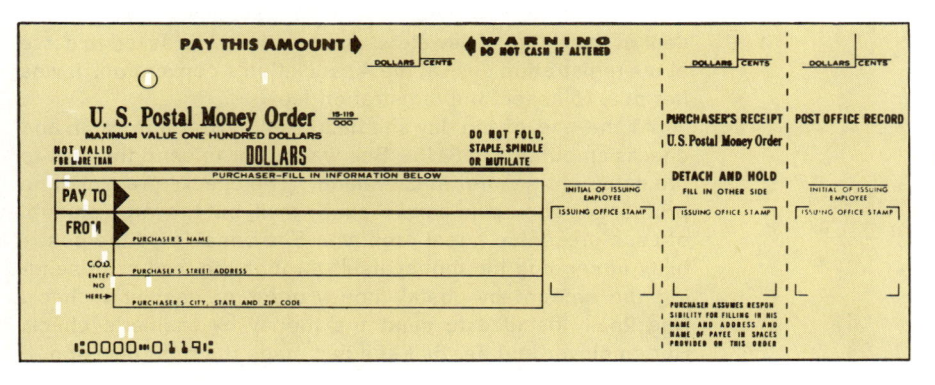

Illus. 14-15

Domestic postal money order

If you are sending an international money order, you must fill out a printed application form. None is required for a domestic money order or an express money order. When you purchase a domestic money order, you are required to enter on the appropriate lines the name of the payee, your own name, and your address. The fees for domestic postal money orders and American Express money orders are the same; the fees for international money orders are double the domestic fees. Postal money orders are limited to $100, but two or more may be purchased to make up any desired amount. For example, to send $450, four for $100 and one for $50 are required; to send $500.02, six money orders are necessary. If equally convenient, it normally would be better to send one cashier's check for the full amount.

To cash a postal money order, take it to any money order office within thirty days after issue; after that time, the orders will be paid only at the office designated on the order.

You may cash express money orders either at express offices or at banks.

QUESTIONS

1. Describe a voucher check.
2. How would your employer have a check certified?
3. Name the three parties to a bank draft.
4. What is a cashier's check and under what circumstances might you use one?
5. Where and in what amounts may postal money orders be procured?
6. Where may express money orders be purchased?

JUDGMENT

Describe circumstances in which a businessman might use (a) a bank draft, (b) a cashier's check, (c) a postal money order, and (d) an express money order.

PERSONAL QUALITIES

Rosanne Morrow, secretary to Mr. Stanley Walker, President of the National Jewelers' Association, was asked to serve at the registration desk at the Association's convention. It was her duty to collect the registration fees.

At the end of the day she had taken in $1,395 in cash, and checks amounting to $415. She was eager to send the fees to the national treasurer in Cleveland. The checks presented no problem as she could send them by mail, but the large amount of cash presented a real problem. She considered the possibility of sending the money itself through the mail or of sending the amount by postal money order or cashier's check. She finally decided to send the money by cashier's check. Her employer told her that she had made the right decision.

What problems would be created by sending the money through the mail? by sending the money by postal money order?

Why do you think that Mr. Walker approved of the cashier's check?

LANGUAGE USAGE

The dash is used

A. To show a sudden break in the thought.

Example: She could deal with both banks — but why should she work with more than one?

B. In place of a comma to show emphasis or to guard against obscurity.

Example: If — and only if — great care is taken, the records will be accurate.

C. Before a statement, or even a single word, which summarizes a series.

Example: Employees, relatives, friends, neighbors — all attended the company's open house in its new building.

D. To give special emphasis to an appositive.

Example: One of the applicants for the job — a girl named Eleanor Nelson — impressed Mr. Mills the most.

Type the following sentences on a separate sheet of paper and insert dashes where required.

1. When will the report be finished if it ever is?
2. The checkbook the heart of the cash payments system must always be kept up to date.
3. A secretary is worth her weight in gold if her work is good.
4. Mr. Adams, of our company, and Mr. Jones, our customer both checked the figures on the statement.
5. Certified checks, bank drafts, money orders I cannot recall the other form are used in making cash payments.
6. The Petty Cash Fund, The Checkbook and the Bank, Making Cash Payments, Income Tax Records these are the subjects covered under "Secretarial Accounting."
7. Truth is stranger than fiction at least that is what they say.
8. Use your office procedures courses typing, shorthand, secretarial office procedures to learn basic business procedures, to help you find a position when you graduate, and to enable you to earn a good salary.
9. When if ever will we receive the annual report?
10. We have learned how to take care of mail, how to answer the telephone, how to file and maintain records all important secretarial skills but the most important is getting along with our co-workers.

SECRETARIAL WORK

1. Here are six different ways of making payment:

    Bank draft
    Cash
    Certified check
    Check
    Express money order
    Postal money order

    In the following situations, give the type of remittance you would use and the reason for your choice.

    (a) We desire to pay in full an account with a firm in Denver with whom we have done business for seven years. The amount is $156.86.
    (b) It is necessary to send a salesman his salary while he is on the road.
    (c) We order a few items from The Chicago Implement Company. They desire payment with the order, for we have never done business with them before.

2. Your employer, Mr. Lewis J. Stockdale, has received a letter from Mr. Phillip B. Olinger, the purchasing agent for Broadwell Manufacturing Company, 1214 Bonway Drive, Decatur, Georgia 30032. Mr. Olinger desires to submit an order for $750 worth of merchandise and wishes to know which method of payment your company requires. Since this is a routine letter, Mr. Stockdale has asked you to reply to Mr. Olinger.

    Your company follows the policy of requesting that a certified check accompany all orders from new customers. The first order makes it possible for a new customer to be integrated into your company's electronic data processing system. After the initial order, a credit check is made of the standing of the new customer. If the credit check proves satisfactory, all additional orders are billed at terms of 2/10, n/30.

    Draft the letter to Mr. Olinger. Prepare one carbon copy.

PART 4 — INCOME TAX PROCEDURES

> Mr. Benson, a tax consultant, is helping Eva Garza prepare records for her employer's tax return. Mr. Benson says that it will be necessary to have carefully kept records of income and expenditures so the tax return will be accurate. Mr. Benson also tells Miss Garza that she should be well informed about federal income tax regulations.

Keeping tax records accurately and carefully is very important to businesses as well as to individuals. Making an error in recording your employer's income or forgetting to keep a record of a deductible expense can make a considerable difference in the amount your employer must pay the United States Government. Do you know what tax duties a secretary is normally required to perform?

SECRETARIAL TAX DUTIES

Your tax duties as a secretary will vary depending upon the firm for which you work. Some firms have the Accounting Department keep all tax records and you, as a secretary, will have very few tax duties. Other firms, however, may require you to perform a variety of duties involving your employer's tax records. Some of these duties may be:

1. *Keep records of deductible items.* The federal and state tax laws are constantly changing the guidelines on which items are deductible and which are not. The checklist on page 537 gives you a general idea of the types of items which are deductible. If you are required to keep a list of deductible items for your employer, this checklist will be of help to you.
2. *Keep records of taxable income.* Many kinds of incomes are taxable. For example, such things as rents from property and interest must be reported as income on your employer's tax report. You should have a general knowledge of what should be reported so that you can keep adequate records.

3. *Organize records.* The records that you keep for your employer on deductible items and taxable incomes should be well organized so that they can be referred to easily and quickly. A file folder should be established each year for income tax materials. All records and supporting documents needed should be put in this folder, so that all data will be in one convenient place.

4. *Make sure your employer does not miss a deadline.* Some firms make periodic payments throughout the year on their income taxes. If this is the case, you should make sure these payments are made on time and that records are kept for each payment.

5. *Provide information to tax consultant if needed.* Some records may not be entirely clear to the tax consultant. You should be informed enough about your employer's tax records so that you can answer the questions for the tax consultant. If you cannot answer a question, you should contact your employer immediately.

TAX INFORMATION NEEDED BY A SECRETARY

Among the tax information you will need will be a knowledge of taxable incomes and deductible expenses. You must make sure that you know the current regulations on taxable income. Generally the following types of income are considered taxable:

1. *Wages and salaries.* The total amount received from wages, salaries, fees, tips, commissions, *honoraria* (which means money paid a person for giving a speech), and similar items are considered taxable income. The records should show the gross amount, that is, the amount before any deductions are made. Bonuses, awards, or prizes are also considered taxable income.

2. *Dividends.* Generally dividends on stock when paid in cash are taxable. However, some dividends may be partially or wholly exempt from taxation. It is best to keep a complete record of all dividends.

3. *Interest.* Most interest payments are taxable. Interest on state and municipal bonds and some United States Government bonds is not taxable.

4. *Rents from properties.* Rent from all properties owned is taxable. The owner, however, is allowed to deduct expenses for maintaining the property, including services and repairs.

INCOME TAX CHECKLIST

When keeping income tax records for your employer, check the following list of common deductible and nondeductible items.

	DEDUCTIBLE	NON-DEDUCTIBLE
Automobile expenses (car used only for pleasure) —		
Gasoline taxes	x	
Interest on automobile loans	x	
License fees		x
Ordinary upkeep and operating expenses		x
Burglary losses over $100, if not covered by insurance	x	
Casualty losses over $100, if not covered by insurance (fire, flood, windstorm, lightning, earthquake, etc.)	x	
Charitable contributions to approved institutions	x	
Dues, social clubs for personal use		x
Fees paid to employment agencies	x	
FICA taxes withheld by employer		x
Fines for violation of laws and regulations		x
Funeral expenses		x
Gifts to relatives and other individuals		x
Income taxes imposed by city or state	x	
Interest paid on personal loans	x	
Life insurance premiums		x
Medical expenses over 3% of adjusted gross income, if not covered by insurance (including the cost of artificial limbs, artificial teeth, eye glasses, hearing aids, dental fees, hospital expenses, premiums on hospital or medical insurance)	x	
Property taxes, real and personal	x	
Residence for personal use —		
Improvements		x
Insurance		x
Interest on mortgage loan	x	
Rent paid		x
Repairs		x
Taxes	x	
Sales taxes, state and local	x	
Traveling expenses attending professional meetings	x	
Traveling expenses to and from place of business or employment		x
Uniforms for personal use including cost and upkeep, if not adaptable for general use (nurses, police, athletes, firemen)	x	
Union dues	x	

Illus. 14-16   Income tax checklist

5. *Profits from sale or exchange of real estate.* Profits from the sale of real estate are usually taxable, however, this, too, will vary depending on the circumstances. It is best to keep detailed records of all transactions involving property in the tax folder.
6. *Royalties.* Royalties usually include income from books, patents, and inventions. This income is taxable; however deductions are allowed for any expenses in producing the item that provides the royalty.

In addition to a knowledge of taxable incomes, you will also need to know the most common types of deductible expenses so that, as the deductible expenses occur throughout the year, you may keep a record of these items. The checklist on page 537 gives you a general idea of the types of expenses that your employer can deduct for income tax purposes. The Income Tax Record on page 539 provides a convenient way of keeping and organizing taxable income and deductible expenses. If you have any questions about whether or not an income is taxable or an expense deductible, you may call your tax consultant or the local Internal Revenue Service office.

A convenient way of keeping track of deductible expenses is to have a form which is filled out whenever the expense occurs and to place it in the file folder at that time. An example of a deductible expense form follows:

DEDUCTIBLE EXPENSE

DATE: January 13, 197–

ITEM: Luncheon

EXPLANATION: Lunch at the Townhouse with Joe Morrow and Ted Rowe from Jackson & Jackson Company. Possible new customer.

TOTAL COST: $15.35

You should attach a receipt to the Deductible Expense form if one is available, especially for the larger amounts. You should explain the expense clearly enough so that there is no question about how the money was spent.

Income Tax Record

Date	Explanation	Income				Deductible Expenses				
		Salary	Dividends	Interest	Rents & Royalties	Misc.	Contributions	Interest	Taxes	Medical & Dental	Misc.
Jan. 3	Acme Mfg. Co. - dividend		35 00								
5	A. C. Larson - rent				75 00						
8	Merchants Bank - interest on mortgage							52 50			
10	Dr. Thomas Weber - dental work									36 00	
11	Profit on sale of Bentex Corp. stock					600 00					
14	Salem County - real estate taxes								52 50		
15	Salary	300 00									
16	Sam's Auto Repairs - repairs from accident										139 75
18	F. M. West - interest on loan			10 00							
22	Red Cross - donation						25 00				
23	Salem County - personal property tax								15 00		
24	George & Co. - dividend		11 25								
25	Queen Optical Co. - eyeglasses									30 00	
28	Southern Publishing Co. - professional books										7 50
31	Salary	300 00									
31	Christ Church - donations for month						20 00				
31	Totals	600 00	46 25	10 00	75 00	600 00	45 00	52 50	67 50	66 00	147 25

Illus. 14-17 Income tax record

Part 4 / Income Tax Procedures 539

You may be responsible for typing and mailing your employer's income tax report. The information on the tax report is considered confidential, and you should be very careful about giving others any information. The report must be typed neatly, and all figures should be checked twice to make sure they are accurate. It is best to mail the tax return personally to be sure that it is mailed on time.

QUESTIONS

1. Why does a secretary need to be well informed about federal and state income taxes?
2. Name five types of taxable income.
3. Name four medical expenses that may be deducted.
4. What kinds of personal expenses are deductible?
5. What personal qualities are essential to the secretary who works on tax records and returns?

JUDGMENT

1. In what ways can a secretary be most helpful in connection with the income tax returns of her employer?
2. What precautions should the secretary take to keep her employer's income confidential?
3. Mary, a secretary to Mr. Albers, is helping her employer with his income tax return. She is in doubt about the deductibility of several items. What should Mary do?

PERSONAL QUALITIES

Judy Ames, secretary to Mr. Howard Downing, has recently had several of her office friends ask her about Mr. Downing's income. Judy has kept Mr. Downing's tax records for several years and, therefore, has the information that her friends are seeking. Judy knows this information is confidential. What should Judy say to her friends when they question her about her employer's income?

LANGUAGE USAGE

Type the following paragraph and insert the necessary capitalization.

on wednesday i met with a committee that was planning a picnic. it will be held on july fourth at the glenwood city park located on the banks of the ohio river. mr. james j. kay will act as chairman of the committee. he is vice-president of the peoples savings bank of watertown. he is a westerner by birth but has made his home in the state of kentucky for many years. mr. kay has invited charles de forest, of brookfield township, to take charge of the sporting event of the day. de forest is a vice-president of the howard hardware company and is treasurer-elect of the watertown rotary club. a group of policemen from division g will control traffic at the picnic grounds, and a reporter from the watertown herald will be on hand to give the affair good news coverage.

SECRETARIAL WORK

1. Mr. Jack Loomey, your employer, has just returned from a business luncheon with two representatives, James Jordan and Neal King, of the National Sash & Door Company. Mr. Loomey is trying to make a sale to the National Sash & Door Company. As he passes your desk, he drops a charge slip for $10.62, the amount of the business luncheon. You know a record should be kept of every deductible expense so you fill out a form similar to the one on page 538 for each deductible expense. Be sure to give an adequate explanation of the expense.

2. You have been asked by Dr. Arthur J. Boles, a professor at Central State University, to keep a record for him of (a) all income other than salary that he receives during the year and (b) all expenditures made by him that are deductible for income tax purposes.

    Dr. Boles reports income and expenditures for October, November, and December as listed below. Not all the expenditures reported are deductible expenses for income tax purposes. Using the checklist on deductible expenses and information in your text about taxable income, record on an income tax record similar to the one on page 539 all income that is taxable and all expenditures that are deductible.

    Oct. 2 Received royalties of $1,063.40 from Sutton Publishing Co.
    5 Paid $18 to Dr. Ernest Sewall for medical services.
    6 Gave $5 to a needy family.
    9 Paid $3 for a dog license.
    10 Received an honorarium of $15 from the Women's Club for making a speech.
    13 Received a dividend of $75 from the Ford Motor Company.
    15 Paid $157.50 to First National Bank for interest on mortgage.
    19 Paid $35 to Thomas Opticians for eyeglasses.
    23 Paid $24 to Photographers, Inc., for professional pictures.
    25 Paid $178.67 for a professional trip to Chicago for which he was not reimbursed.
    27 Paid $45 to Harry's Garage for repairs to his automobile caused by a collision with another automobile. This loss was not covered by insurance.
    28 Gave $10 to Trinity Church.
    30 Received notice from the First National Bank that interest of $19.78 had been credited to his savings account.
    Nov. 7 Received $90 royalties from Century Film Company.
    11 Received an honorarium of $25 from the Rotary Club for making a speech.

Nov. 15 Paid $238.06 to the state tax commissioner for state income tax.
 19 Paid $137.50 to Southern Life Insurance Company for a premium on a life insurance policy.
 22 Paid $20 dues to the Association of University Professors.
 26 Paid $15 interest on a note to the First National Bank.
 28 Contributed $25 to the American Foundation for Scholarships.
 30 Gave $10 to Trinity Church.
Dec. 1 Received a dividend of $12.50 from Radio Corporation of America.
 4 Paid $114.40 to the Town of Westport, Connecticut, for taxes on real estate.
 7 Paid $10 to Dr. Leonard Smith for dental services.
 18 Received $300 from Jack Callan for three months' rent of the Westport property.
 22 Paid $30 to the Hartford Insurance Company for a premium on a hospitalization insurance policy.
 28 Gave $20 to Trinity Church.
 31 Received notice from the First National Bank that interest of $19.78 had been credited to his savings account.

Unit 15

YOU AS A SECRETARY

Part 1. Job Opportunities
    2. The Personal Data Sheet and the Application Form
    3. The Interview
    4. Specialized Secretarial Positions
    5. Up the Secretarial Ladder and Beyond

The secretary who is thoroughly trained need not worry about finding a position. There are positions available in business or in one of the specialized fields, such as education, medicine, or law. Secretaries with administrative knowledge and ability are often promoted to higher level positions.

VOCABULARY BUILDER

*Silence is a book
Before you read it.*

   Mark Mayhall

initial..............................
    adjective: beginning; first

range..............................
    verb: set in a row or in proper order; place among others in a position or situation

objectively..............................
    adverb: expressing the nature of reality as it is apart from personal reflections or feelings

evaluating..............................
    verb: determining or fixing the value of; examining; judging

concise..............................
    adjective: marked by brevity of expression or statement

aspect..............................
    noun: a particular status or phase in which something appears or may be regarded; manner; air

comprehension..............................
    noun: the act or action of grasping with the intellect; the capacity for understanding

isolated..............................
    adjective: set apart from others; alone

assessing..............................
    verb: making an official evaluation of; determining the importance, size, or value of

litigation..............................
    noun: a legal contest carried on by judicial process; a legal dispute; a contest in law

p. 546   Her **initial** position was in the production department. . . .

p. 547   Organizations **range** all the way from small ones where an individual works alone with an office assistant to giant ones. . . .

p. 547   She knew that her performance would be reviewed **objectively** and that promotions would be based on her achievement.

p. 554   In **evaluating** candidates, prospective employers review references carefully.

p. 555   A letter of application is a direct, **concise** letter in which you state clearly the position in which you are interested.

p. 567   When the interviewer is considering this **aspect** of his evaluation he is thinking primarily of the overall impression of the prospective. . . .

p. 567   Does the applicant have a good **comprehension** of business as well as the world in general?

p. 568   As you have learned through your studies, business is not an **isolated** activity.

p. 568   The interviewer will be particularly interested in **assessing** how well you are likely to get along with co-workers. . . .

p. 573   You must have acquired a knowledge and understanding of legal procedures, . . . and **litigation** procedures.

PART 1   JOB OPPORTUNITIES

Karen soon will complete a secretarial program in her high school and plans to work in an office after her graduation in June. She is ready to work and to put into practice what she has learned in her courses. She has had many opportunities to judge her qualifications and her personal interests. She looks forward to being part of a working team in a busy office. She doesn't want to make a mistake in her efforts to seek and select a position.

THE JOB MARKET

What jobs are available in the modern business community? Is there a need for office workers? While automation has transferred many tasks from the desk of an office worker to a machine, there continues to be great demand for office workers of all types. Beginners with limited or no experience find many jobs available to them. Beginners do not become executive secretaries immediately upon graduation from high school. However, there are many instances where high school graduates who do superb work in their beginning jobs are quickly moved into positions of greater responsibility. Businesses are eager to use all the talents and skills of their workers, and their efforts to reward new employees who show special interest in their work result in many promotional opportunities for good workers.

The types of positions that beginners generally fill are typist, clerk-typist, transcribing machine operator, junior stenographer, receptionist, and office machine operator.

ORGANIZATIONAL TYPES

Organizations are classified in a number of ways. A classification based on the nature of activity carried on in the organization is given on page 546.

You will want to consider the type of organization in which you would find it especially interesting to work.

ORGANIZATIONS CLASSIFIED BY ACTIVITIES

Organization	Activity
Manufacturing	Producers of household appliances, glass products, pianos, carpeting, textiles, and the whole range of manufactured products
Mining	Coal, copper, silver
Construction	Housing construction, mobile house construction, office construction, hospital and other institutional construction
Transportation and Public Utilities	Trucking, airlines, railroads, bus lines, electricity, gas, telephone
Trade	Wholesale, central retailing chain, department store, grocery store, specialty store
Finance, Insurance, and Real Estate	Commercial banks, savings banks, security dealers and brokers, insurance companies, real estate brokers
Health Services	Hospitals, clinics, doctor's office, dentist's office
Community Agencies	YMCA, YWCA, Red Cross, 4-H, Boy Scouts, Girl Scouts
Religious	Church, mission services of coordinated groups of churches
Communications	Periodicals, newspaper, book publishing, radio, television
Government	City government, state government, federal government
Education	Preschool centers, elementary school, secondary school, community college, college, university, research center
Professional	Law office, counseling service, consultant services, architect's office

Illus. 15-1

Ellen was a very active Girl Scout from her Brownie days to the present. When she completed her high school program of secretarial studies, she applied for an office job at the local Girl Scout Council office. She was hired. The personnel interviewer was impressed not only with her secretarial skills but also with her excellent background in Girl Scouting that would be very valuable in the work she would do.

Doris, on the other hand, had thoroughly enjoyed the home economics courses that she took in high school and was particularly interested in textiles. When she graduated, she sought and secured a position in a large textile manufacturing company in New York City, to which she could commute daily from her home in northern New Jersey. Her initial position was in the production department; and she soon realized that she would learn much about textiles, which pleased her very much. One of the fringe benefits in her company was the privilege of purchasing fabric at cost price — a valuable benefit for a young woman who sewed her own wardrobe!

Office workers are needed everywhere. Don't fail to give thought to the environment in which your interests will have an opportunity to develop fully.

SIZE OF ORGANIZATION

Organizations range all the way from small ones where an individual works alone with an office assistant to giant ones where there are thousands of employees located in a large office complex. What size do you prefer? You will want to give attention to this question. Some office workers like to be a part of a large company that is fully organized with specific rules and policies about job tasks, promotional possibilities, and salary scales. Others, however, choose to work in very small, informal surroundings where everyone is fully acquainted with everyone else in the organization and promotional opportunities are limited.

When Lenore was considering her first job, she knew that she wanted to work in a large corporation in a large city. She believed that such an organization would have the promotional opportunities she sought. She knew that her performance would be reviewed objectively and that promotions would be based on her achievement. She didn't believe that she had to know every person in the company. She thought it was exciting to be in a corporation that was the largest in its field and considered a leader in international business affairs.

Illus. 15-2

Promotional opportunities are many and varied in large organizations.

Ohio National Life Insurance Company

Part 1 / Job Opportunities   547

> Josette, however, was a quiet young woman who felt more comfortable if her work environment was fully familiar to her and if she knew everyone. She chose to be the second office worker in a small suburban elementary school where there were a principal, an assistant principal, and twelve teachers. She liked the attractive new school built near a wooded area and she thoroughly enjoyed the children and the teachers with whom she associated each day.

LOCATION

Where do you want to work? Your choice is wide! There are jobs in downtown centers of large metropolitan areas, in suburban communities, in small villages. Jobs are available in places as different as Portland, Maine, and Miami Beach, Florida, or London, England, and Lima, Peru. Some beginning office workers expect to commute from their homes when they are working; others plan to relocate so that they may live near the place of their work.

> Denise commutes daily from her suburban home into the financial district of Chicago, where she is working as a stenographer. She drives to work with two friends who also work in the financial district. She says that she enjoys the trip in and back and finds the financial district an exciting, alive place in which to spend her working days.
>
> Beth, who lives in a small village near the eastern tip of Long Island in New York, chose to work in a lawyer's office, which is within walking distance of her home. She rode a school bus to high school, and she says she loves walking to where she must be each day.

BECOMING ACQUAINTED WITH JOB OPPORTUNITIES

There are many ways for you to become acquainted with job opportunities in the community where you seek employment. Use as many as necessary to aid you in securing a position that is best for you.

Placement Office in Your School

Many secondary schools have placement offices as a part of the counseling services provided students. Possibly you used such a service for securing a part-time position or a summer position. Plan to talk with a placement counselor about job opportunities that match your interests and skills. Once a placement counselor knows of your interests, you will undoubtedly receive notices of positions that are available. You should follow through immediately on each job lead and report as requested to the placement office. Many companies seek employees through school placement offices, and you may find that this source is the only one you need in order to secure a position.

Employment Agencies

In many communities there are both private and public employment agencies that will provide aid to you in your efforts to find a position. Private employment agencies are sometimes specialized; so you will want to be sure that you are inquiring at one that does place office personnel. Private employment agencies earn their income from fees which are paid either by the individual who secures a position through services provided by the agency or by the company that hires the new employee. The fee is a percentage of salary, generally based on a week's or a month's salary.

Public employment agencies provide a service without fee. Such agencies are supported through public funds. You may register at a public employment agency for aid in seeking a position. In large cities public agencies are specialized; so you will want to be sure that you visit the department that handles office vacancies.

Classified Advertisements

Many companies as well as employment agencies use the classified section of newspapers to announce vacancies. While many of the advertisements identify the company or agency seeking personnel for positions, some are listed as blind advertisements. A *blind advertisement* is one that lists only a box number so that the identity of the company seeking an employee is not revealed. Blind advertisements are used so that some preliminary screening can be done on the basis of a written letter and data sheet that are submitted by interested applicants.

SECRETARY, JR.
—Free Airline Travel—
Interesting position working with executives of growing national company. Good office skills required (some IBM typing, steno speed 80-100 wpm). Starting salary $100; $110 after 6 months. Outstanding benefits program.
CALL FOR INTERVIEW APPOINTMENT
697-2131, EXT 45
SKY CHEFS, INC.
(subsidiary of American Airlines)

An identified advertisement
for a junior secretary

EXECUTIVE SECRETARY
to the
KEY EXECUTIVE
Leading national sales organization offers a lifetime career for a highly talented top-level secretary. She must have excellent typing and stenographic skills, strong administrative capabilities, a basic understanding of bookkeeping or figure work and all the charm and poise necessary for this top-level position. Relocate to large East Coast city (expense paid). Salary commensurate with previous experience. Reply in confidence.

Y8423 TIMES

A blind advertisement for
an executive secretary

Illus. 15-3

Direct Inquiry to Organization

Some people learn about office positions through relatives and friends who are employed in companies that are seeking new employees. If you are informed of an opening through such a source, your relative or friend may make the initial inquiry to the personnel department and arrange an interview for you. You will be expected to visit the company and indicate to the personnel officer who made the suggestion to you.

Illus. 15-4

A company will form its first impression of you in the personnel office.

Ohio National Life Insurance Company

If there is a company in which you have special interest, it is fully proper to write a letter of inquiry and to indicate your skills and the type of position you are seeking. If you are writing to a company that often hires beginning workers, your chances of being granted an interview are very good.

Civil Service Announcements

Many positions in government require that candidates take examinations and, therefore, there are general public announcements about the dates of such examinations. If you are interested in employment in government, you will want to note the announcements that are posted in public buildings and that appear in newspapers. Announcements for federal positions are often displayed in post offices and in regional civil service offices throughout the country. You can also write directly to the United States Civil Service Commission, Washington, D.C. 20415, asking for information on forthcoming examinations. Announcements of city civil service examinations are usually posted in the City Hall; announcements of county and state examinations, in the County Courthouse or principal county building. Also, you can check your local telephone directory to find the Civil Service Commission office in your city and request information directly from that office.

QUESTIONS

1. What kinds of jobs are generally available to beginning office workers?
2. If you were interested in communications, in what type of organization would you plan to work?
3. In what ways would working for a large company differ from working for a small company?
4. What considerations would influence you in selecting the location for your first job?
5. What kinds of services are provided by school placement offices?
6. Why do private employment agencies charge a fee?
7. How do public employment agencies differ from private employment agencies?
8. In what section of the newspaper can you find notices of job openings?
9. What information is missing in a *blind* advertisement?
10. How can you learn about examinations for civil service positions in the federal government?

JUDGMENT

1. A friend of yours has always been interested in travel. She thinks all aspects of travel are exciting. She is now considering the types of positions for which she should apply since she will be graduating from high school and has taken secretarial skills and secretarial procedures courses. She asks you, "Where should I look for a job?"

   What would you say to your friend?

2. You are interviewed for a position in a small law office in your own home town. There are two office workers in the office now, and you will be the only new person to be employed. There are two lawyers who share the practice. As you walk home following the interview, which ended with the lawyers offering you a position at a fully acceptable salary, what kinds of questions will you ask yourself to determine if this is the job you wish to accept?

PERSONAL QUALITIES

A friend is interested in moving to a large city and working in an office in the center of the city. She talks to you about going to the city with her. She says, "I know we can get a job. We can wait until we get there to find a job. Why worry ahead of time? We can find a place to live, and then we can begin to look for jobs."

What is your reaction to your friend's suggestion?

LANGUAGE USAGE

Several words below are misspelled. Type the entire list correctly.

1. civill
2. classified
3. advertisment
4. recomendations
5. muncipal
6. federel
7. diversified
8. undoubtedily
9. placement
10. specilized
11. comumications
12. utilites
13. principal
14. suburrban
15. initial
16. personnel
17. receptionst
18. comission
19. especiaily
20. comute

SECRETARIAL WORK

1. Make a list of the sources of placement information that are available to you and your classmates who are seeking employment as office workers.
2. From the newspapers read in your community, clip the advertisements for secretarial and related office positions that have appeared in the past week which you are qualified to fill. Be ready to discuss these job opportunities in class indicating why you believe you are able to meet the job requirements.
3. Write an advertisement for an office position that you would find fully satisfactory. In your advertisement indicate the factors that you believe are important in the position which you would like to have.

PART 2: THE PERSONAL DATA SHEET AND THE APPLICATION FORM

Maria Edwards knows that it is important that she describe her qualifications for an office position carefully and accurately, because interviewers not only read personal data sheets thoroughly but they are also impressed with the attractiveness of the format used. Maria also plans to fill in all application forms with care. In order to have all her information absolutely accurate, she has written out the names and full addresses of all the organizations where she has worked part-time and during the summers. She has also received permission from three persons whom she plans to list as references.

THE PERSONAL DATA SHEET

When you are applying for a job, you will want to prepare a personal data sheet. The personal data sheet tells a potential employer who you are and what you are trained to do.

Its Purpose

A prospective employer needs to become acquainted with you in very little time. A personal data sheet is helpful in achieving this purpose. A personal data sheet outlines in clear form the important facts about your background that will be of value in determining whether you are a good candidate for a position.

Its Content

Generally personal data sheets are divided into the following parts:

Personal information   Experience
Education   References
Extracurricular activities

Personal Information. The personal information includes your name, home address, telephone number, your age (date of birth), your height, your weight, your marital status, and your physical condition (a general statement is sufficient).

Education. Under education you will give the complete name of your high school, plus the curriculum that you studied or the major courses taken, and the secretarial skills that you have developed. You will want to add any scholastic awards that you received while in high school.

Extracurricular Activities. Extracurricular activities are of interest to prospective employers; so you will want to list all your organizational activities while you were a student and those activities in the community in which you continue to be active. Any offices that you held in a class or club should also be listed. This section of your personal data sheet reflects your special interests, your ability to work with others, and your leadership qualities.

Experience. Experience at work, even though limited, should be listed. Begin with your most recent experience and list all jobs you have held. Give the job title first, then the name of the firm or organization, and the dates of your employment. If you have had little or no work experience for which you were paid, you will want to list all volunteer jobs that you have held in the community.

References. In evaluating candidates, prospective employers review references carefully. You will want to list as references persons who know you sufficiently to judge you on the traits and attitudes that employers are concerned about. Generally it is a good idea to give at least one name for each of the following:

1. Experience — the recommendation of your present employer or a former employer or supervisor to indicate the quality of your work and your ability to get along with people with whom you work.

2. Scholarship — the recommendation of a former teacher is valuable to indicate your scholastic accomplishments and your potential ability to perform on a job.

3. Character — the recommendation of a person who has known you for several years and can comment on your integrity, loyalty, and reliability is useful. Clergymen, businessmen, and other professional people are appropriate references. You should not list relatives or neighbors. You should telephone or write notes to persons you wish to list as references. It is courteous to request approval before listing a person's name.

Its Appearance

Your personal data sheet should be organized logically and typewritten carefully. You will want to send an original copy to a prospective employer, and you will want to b sure to proofread your copy so that no uncorrected errors are on the copy. Be sure your data sheet reflects the type of person you will be on the job.

LETTER OF APPLICATION

A short letter indicating your interest in a position accompanies your personal data sheet. A letter of application is a direct, concise letter in which you state clearly the position in which you are interested. If you are not certain if the company to which you are applying has a vacancy for the type of job in which you are interested, then your letter of application is also a letter of inquiry.

Below are guides to follow in writing your letter of application:

1. Be sure to include your full address above the date of your letter.

2. Address the letter appropriately: If you are responding to a classified advertisement that provides a return box only, you should use the address given and the salutation should be *Gentlemen*.

    If you have learned about a position through your high school placement office or through a friend, you will be given the name of the firm and perhaps the name of the person in charge of employment. If a person's name is given, address your letter in this manner:

    ```
    Mr. T. G. Gaines, Personnel Manager
    The Abraham Jones Corporation
    3689 Jefferson Street
    Charleston, WV 25309
    ```

    The salutation should be *Dear Mr. Gaines:*

3. State your interest in the first paragraph:

    ```
    May I present my qualifications for the
    stenographic position which you advertised
    in The Charleston Times on Monday, June 3?
    ```

    or

    ```
    Miss _____ _____, the Placement Counselor
    at _____ High School, has suggested that I
    apply for the stenographic position which
    is available in your firm. May I present
    my qualifications for this position?
    ```

2309 Vernon Avenue
Joliet, IL 60431
June 16, 197-

Mr. Frederick C. Moore
Personnel Director
Constitution Life Insurance Company
209 West Fourth Street
Joliet, IL 60432

Dear Mr. Moore

Miss Dorothy Fowler, one of your employees who attended Central High School with me, told me that there will be an opening in your stenographic pool on July 1. I should like to apply for the position. As I have indicated on the enclosed personal data sheet, my secretarial qualifications meet the high standards of your company.

I graduated in the upper fourth of my high school class. During the fall term I plan to take courses in business and finance in the evening division of Joliet Community College. My application for admission has already been approved.

During the past two summers I have had experience as a clerk-typist with the Metropolitan Life Insurance Company, as listed on the data sheet. The office manager, Mr. Arthur T. Sweeney, has given me permission to list his name as one of my business references.

I enjoyed my work with the Metropolitan Life Insurance Company, and I should like to continue in the life insurance field. May I expect to be called for an interview? My telephone number is 555-2368.

Sincerely yours

Margaret Jean Collins

(Miss) Margaret Jean Collins

Enclosure

Illus. 15-5
Letter of application

P E R S O N A L   D A T A   S H E E T

NAME: Margaret Jean Collins HEIGHT: 5'6"
ADDRESS: 2309 Vernon Avenue WEIGHT: 116 pounds
         Joliet, IL 60431
TELEPHONE: Area Code 815 555-2368 MARITAL STATUS: Single
AGE: 18 years   PHYSICAL CONDITION: Excellent

EDUCATION

Graduated from Central High School, Joliet, Illinois, on June 13, 197-, after completing the Secretarial Studies program. Admitted to the Evening Division of Joliet Community College for the fall semester of 197-.

Secretarial Skills:
  Typewriting rate--60 words a minute
  Shorthand dictation rate--120 words a minute
  Transcription rate--35 words a minute
Awards and Certificates:
  Central High School Student Service Award
  Alphabetic Filing Certificate
  Dictaphone Transcription Proficiency Certificate
Office Machines Operated:
  Dictaphone, Mimeograph, Multigraph, Olivetti printing calculator, Call Director

EXTRACURRICULAR ACTIVITIES

Treasurer of the Secretarial Service Club
Secretary of the Central High School Chapter of the Future Business Leaders of America
Reporter for Spot Light, school newspaper

EXPERIENCE

Clerk-typist in the office of the Metropolitan Life Insurance Company in Joliet, Illinois, for the last two summers
Part-time secretary for the Placement Director during senior year at Central High School

REFERENCES

Mr. Arthur T. Sweeney, Office Manager, Metropolitan Life Insurance Company, 236 Main Street, Joliet, IL 60634, Telephone 555-2200
Miss Helen C. Harris, Chairman, Secretarial Studies Department, Central High School, Joliet, IL 60433, Telephone 555-1715
Dr. August W. Brustat, Pastor, Trinity Church, 23 Crane Road, Joliet, IL 60432, Telephone 555-8230

Illus. 15-6
Personal data sheet

556 Unit 15 / You As a Secretary

4. In the second paragraph, you will want to refer to your personal data sheet which is enclosed. This paragraph should highlight the main points of your education and experience. You might write:

```
As you will note from the enclosed data
sheet, I will graduate from Forest Hills
High School in June.  While in high school
I successfully completed several business
courses, including typewriting, shorthand,
secretarial procedures, and bookkeeping.
I have also held two summer jobs where I
have had opportunities to use my business
skills and abilities.  During the last two
years I have been a volunteer secretary in
the high school and have worked for a num-
ber of school administrators and teachers.
```

5. In the final paragraph of your application letter, you will want to indicate your interest in a personal interview as well as the times when you are available:

```
May I have an interview for the steno-
graphic position which you have available?
I complete my school day at three each
afternoon and would be free to come to
your office any afternoon after that time.
```

6. The complimentary close may be a simple *Sincerely yours* or *Yours very truly*, depending upon your salutation (see page 78). Be sure to sign your name and indicate the enclosure.

If you apply for a job through an agency, you will generally go to the firm for an interview. No letter of application will be necessary. In such a case, be sure to take a copy of your personal data sheet with you, for the details on it will be useful in filling in an application form.

THE APPLICATION BLANK

Most companies request that job applicants complete an application blank. Some companies will send you the application blank, and you are to have the form completed when you appear for the employment interview. Other firms will wait until you appear for the interview before requesting that you complete the form.

APPLICATION FOR EMPLOYMENT
WITH
ACME MANUFACTURING COMPANY

(0124)

GENERAL INFORMATION

Name	Wright, Valerie Rose
Date	July 1, 1972
Street Address	3466 Border Lane
Phone Number	621-1046
City	Shreveport	Zone 77109	State LA
Social Security Number	368-05-6133
In Case of an Emergency Notify	Mrs. John A. Wright
Address	3466 Border Lane
Phone Number	621-1046
Date of Birth	May 12, 1951
Sex	F
Age	21
Height	5'5"
Weight	115
Type work desired	Steno-Secretarial
Any defects in sight, hearing, or speech?	No
How much time have you lost through illness in the past two years?	Two days
Nature of Illness	Cold

Give names of any members in our organization with whom you are acquainted: Betty Morris

Are you related to any of these people? No
If so, to whom?

Marital status	Single
No. of minor Children	
Other dependents	
Who referred you to us for employment?	Campbell Business School
If married, is your spouse working?	
If so, where?	
Do you have any other source of income?	No
Do you live with parents? (X)	Board? ( )	Rent? ( )	Own home? ( )
Father's occupation	Accountant
Make and model of car owned	None
Insurance carried Life (amt.)	$5,000
Car Liability (amt.)	
Health & Accident (Type)	
Have you ever served in the United States Armed Forces?	No
Rank and branch of service	
Date of induction	
Date of discharge	
Type of discharge	
Primary service duties	
Are you now employed?	Yes
If so, where?	William Paulson Advertising Company

EDUCATION

High School attended	South High School	City & State Shreveport, LA	Year Graduated 1969
Business School attended	Campbell Business School	City & State Shreveport, LA	Number of months attended One year
College or University attended		City & State	Year graduated	Degree

Business subjects studied while in school:
- HIGH SCHOOL: Typing, Shorthand, Office Practice
- BUSINESS COLLEGE: Typing, Shorthand, Accounting, Office Machines, Letter Writing, Secretarial Procedure
- COLLEGE: Economics

Are you studying now? Yes   If so, what? Economics   Where? LSU Shreveport Branch

Other special training: Successfully completed one-year secretarial training program at Campbell School

System of shorthand studied: Gregg

In the space to the right indicate your present speed in shorthand and typing, if you have these skills. Place an (X) after the office machines you can operate.

Shorthand	100 words a min.	Typing	60 words a min.	Dictaphone	X
Billing Machine		Bookkeeping Machine	X	Mimeograph	X
Addressograph		Calculator		PBX Board	X
Comptometer		Key Punch		Adding Machine	X
Verifier		IBM Tabulator		Other	X

Illus. 15-7

Page 1 — Application blank

EXPERIENCE AND REFERENCES

Business Experience & References (Show last position first)

	From	To	Period Yrs.	Period Mos.	Name of Company	City & State	Person to whom you reported
1	7/70	Now	2		Wm. Paulson Advertising Co.	Shreveport, LA	Thomas Adams
2							
3							
4							

Business Experience and References (Continued)

	GIVE TITLE AND NATURE OF YOUR WORK	Monthly Earnings	Why did you leave?
1	Stenographic and General Clerical Duties	$325	Am seeking work with more responsibility and higher potential earnings.
2			
3			
4			

Character References: Do not refer to previous employers or relatives.

NAME	ADDRESS	OCCUPATION
Mrs. C. C. Clark	3470 Poplar St., Shreveport	Purchasing Agent
Mr. Donald Calhoun	South High School, Shreveport	Teacher, business subjects
Miss Mary Wagner	1312 Pearl St., Shreveport	Owner of clothing store

By signing this application I affirm that all statements made herein are true to the best of my knowledge. If employed by the company, I agree to consider my salary a confidential matter and to refrain from discussing it with other employees.

Valerie Rose Wright
Signature of Applicant

APPLICANTS SHOULD NOT WRITE BELOW THIS LINE

Interviewed by: | Date of interview | Date applicant available for work | E G F P

Remarks:

Date Employed	Clock Number	Department	Classification

Enrolled in Group Insurance | Enrolled in Pension Plan | Blue Cross — Blue Shield Coverage ☐ Ind. ☐ Fam. ☐ Surg.

Date Employment Terminated | Reason | Consider for Re-employment

Illus. 15-8

Page 2 — Application blank

Purpose

Companies have developed standard forms for obtaining from applicants the information they need so that the processing of a new employee can be taken care of easily and quickly.

Interviewers read an applicant's information carefully. In fact, the applicant is evaluated on the basis of her application blank in many instances. Interviewers note the completeness of the form, the neatness of the handwriting (or typewriting), and the extent to which the answers are related to the questions asked.

Cautions in Filling in the Application Blank

When you are asked to fill in an application blank, you should read the instructions carefully before you write anything on it. Also, you should sit at a table or desk so that you will be able to write easily. If you are asked to type the form, insert a scrap sheet of paper in the typewriter and practice a few lines of typewriting so that you become familiar with the machine before you begin to fill in your form. Start at the beginning of the form, filling in each item that applies to you. Note if you are to write your last name first or your first name first, *before* you begin to write your name. For each item that does not apply, draw a short line in the space provided for the answer or write in *NA* (not applicable).

After you have completed filling in all the spaces for which you can supply answers, go back to the beginning and read what you have written to be sure it is accurate and complete before returning it.

Illus. 15-9

Be sure the application blank is complete and accurate before returning it to the personnel office.

Ohio National Life Insurance Company

TESTING

In many companies applicants for positions are asked to take tests along with filling in application blanks. The tests provide additional evidence for the interviewer to use in determining the skill and ability of potential employees as well as their level of general education and their health status.

You should be prepared to take tests when you apply in person for a position. Many applicants find it helpful to carry with them a shorthand pad, pen, pencil, and eraser.

While the specific tests that companies use vary considerably, there are some commonly used tests for office workers. Performance tests in typewriting and stenography are frequently given. The typewriting tests may be simply copying tests that are timed, or they may be job-like tests that require the applicant to set up material appropriately and to make carbon copies and corrections. Companies are interested not only in the rate of typewriting but in the skill of applicants in handling jobs such as the typing of letters and tabulated material. The stenographic test is used to determine the skill of an applicant in preparing a mailable transcript in a reasonable period of time.

In addition to performance tests, some companies administer general aptitude tests, clerical aptitude tests, and general information tests. Most of these tests are relatively short and are similar to the types of tests you have taken as a student in school.

Illus. 15-10

A typewriting performance test is usually required of all stenographic and secretarial applicants.

Vincent Nanfra

PHYSICAL EXAMINATION

A physical examination is also required by many companies. Good health is important if workers are to be fully productive on their jobs. Companies, therefore, have established health standards which applicants must meet if they are to be employed. Furthermore, many companies provide health insurance for workers, and such coverage requires evidence of good health of the worker at the time of employment.

QUESTIONS

1. What is the purpose of a personal data sheet?
2. What information is included in a personal data sheet?
3. What kinds of references should be included in the personal data sheet?
4. Why should you ask the persons whom you are thinking of listing as references if you may list their names?
5. How should you address a letter of application if you are responding to a blind advertisement? Indicate the salutation you should use.
6. What information should you include in a letter of application?
7. Why should an application blank be filled in neatly?
8. How should you indicate on an application blank that a question does not apply to you?
9. What are some types of tests that office workers may be expected to take when applying for jobs?
10. What does the interviewer evaluate when she reviews the transcript of an applicant who took a stenographic test?

JUDGMENT

1. How will your personal data sheet aid a prospective employer in evaluating your qualifications?
2. Why is a personal data sheet not a substitute for an application blank?
3. Why do many companies require a physical examination of new employees?

PERSONAL QUALITIES

When applying for a position in a local insurance company, Marilyn Conway was asked to take a series of tests, including a typewriting test and a reading comprehension test. When she looked at the spelling test, she said to the young woman administering the test, "This is a silly test; I haven't had words to spell since I was in the ninth grade." Later, when she began the typewriting test, she commented, "How do you expect me to do a good job on this test since this is an old typewriter and I have never used one like this in school? Can't you see from my grade in typewriting that I am a good typist. Why is this test necessary?"

How would you evaluate Marilyn's behavior? What would you do if you found that the typewriter was not functioning properly when you began a typewriting test in a company where you were being considered for a position?

LANGUAGE USAGE

Three important uses of the colon are:

A. To introduce a long or formal *direct* quotation

   Example: The President began his talk with these words: "It is on an occasion such as this that we must all remember that we are bound by ties of brotherhood, tradition, and learning."

B. To introduce a number of examples or a formal list of any sort which contains a *summarizing* word

   Example: I have been trained in five skills: typing, shorthand, bookkeeping, filing, and secretarial office procedures.

C. To introduce an independent sentence or clause when the second gives an illustration of a general statement in the first

   Example: The purpose of a newspaper should be twofold: It should be the friend of all that is good and the foe of all that is evil.

Type the following sentences on a separate sheet of paper and apply the above colon uses correctly.

1. The company introduced five new products in one year Filcron, Vinylplas, Polycrest, Nycrin, and Depron.

2. The Chairman of the Board began his address by saying it is with deep emotion that I must submit my resignation to the officers of this company effective June 30, since the United States Government has requested that I assume the presidency of an organization in South America dedicated to relieving the poverty and suffering of our neighbors in Peru and bordering countries.

3. Bring with you your shorthand pad, a pencil, an eraser, and some blank sheets of plain white paper for typing.

4. Her original contention was justified that in time those who study, prepare their assignments, and apply themselves to their classes will receive good grades and be ready to accept positions in business offices.

5. Every detail indicated that Mary was interrupted at her work and intended to return to it the open stamp pad on her desk, the unfinished letter in her typewriter, the shorthand notebook lying open and ready for use, the fountain pen with the point uncapped.

SECRETARIAL WORK

1. Type a letter of application in response to a local newspaper advertisement. Give only the facts related to your experience, education, and other qualifications. Include all your

qualifications in the body of the letter of application; that is, do not use a separate data sheet. Attach the advertisement to your letter. Submit your letter to your instructor for suggestions for improvement.

2. Using an assumed name of a business that has not advertised for help but which is the type of business in which you would like to seek office employment, type a letter of application with the details of your qualifications listed on an enclosed personal data sheet.

3. Assume that you have been asked to complete an application form for a position as a stenographer. If an application form is available, complete it carefully with pen and ink. If a form is not available, type a copy of the illustration on pages 558 and 559 and fill in the required information with pen and ink.

PART 3 THE INTERVIEW

Beth's letter to a local manufacturing company, to which her placement counselor had referred her, resulted in a request that she come in for an interview. Beth looked forward to her 9:30 a.m. appointment. She knew that the interview was an important part of the employment procedure. She planned carefully for this occasion so that she would be dressed appropriately and would be sure to be at the employment office on time. As she thought ahead to the appointment, which was just a day away, she considered the kinds of questions she would likely be asked and the kind of information she would hope to get from the personnel interviewer.

THE PURPOSE OF AN INTERVIEW

Companies differ in many ways. Each has its own manner of conducting business, its own policies that direct the relationships among employees and between employees and the outside world. Companies also have various benefits for their workers. Because of these differences, each company is careful in choosing its employees; for it wants them to be able to fill the job qualifications specified for individual positions. Companies, therefore, talk with prospective employees as a way of determining who will be best suited for their environment. As a prospective employee, you also want to be sure the company meets your desires as the place in which you will want to work. The interview provides a means for this two-way exchange of understanding.

TOPICS DISCUSSED IN AN INTERVIEW

You can expect the interviewer to give you the following types of information:

1. A description of the position (or positions) for which you have applied or for which the interviewer believes your education and experience fit you

2. Information regarding the number of hours that you will work each day, the number of days that you will work each week, and other responsibilities that you will assume
3. The salary and other benefits that are provided employees including such items as coffee breaks, vacation, holidays, hospitalization, pension plans, tuition payment plans
4. The future opportunities in the company for those who are successful in their work

As a candidate for a position, you should not hesitate to ask questions about any of these topics if the interviewer should fail to discuss them adequately. Your primary attention, of course, is on the basic job requirements and the degree to which you are qualified to meet them. Interviewers are not favorably impressed with beginning workers who are primarily interested in salary, fringe benefits, and promotional opportunities. Such an attitude leaves the impression that the beginner is more concerned with what she can get from a position than with what she can give to a position.

Other questions that come to mind while you are talking with the interviewer can be asked. For example, you may be planning to drive to work and will wish to know if a parking lot is provided.

Try to behave as naturally as possible during the interview giving attention to *learning about the job*. Any question that is related to that subject is appropriate for you to ask. Don't think of the interview as an *oral test* of your ability to assume a job. The interview provides mutual information. Remember that *you were asked* to come for an interview. This realization should give you sufficient confidence to handle the situation comfortably.

THE INTERVIEWER'S EVALUATION

While the interviewer talks with you, he is developing an impression of you as a member of his organization. When you come to the end of the interview, the interviewer may be prepared to offer you a position or to indicate to you when you will hear from the company. Policies differ in regard to hiring procedures. In some companies, for instance, all invitations to join the organization are mailed to prospective workers. Decisions are not made in the presence of a prospective employee. In such companies, the interviewer will write a report or fill in a form that gives a full evaluation of each candidate who has applied for a position. Among the considerations of interviewers are these:

Appearance

As soon as a prospective candidate steps into the office of the interviewer the first impression is formed. Is she dressed appropriately and neatly? Is her posture good? Does she walk with assurance? Does her facial expression reveal a pleasant, relaxed, congenial personality?

Voice and Language Usage

Some interviewers have a special interest in the voice of a prospective employee. Is her voice pleasant? Does it indicate an interest in what is being discussed? Does she use the English language with skill? Does she speak clearly and with attention to the precise meanings of words? Does she talk smoothly but not glibly?

Personality

When the interviewer is considering this aspect of his evaluation he is thinking primarily of the overall impression of the prospective employee's behavior. Is she likable? Is she courteous, gracious, considerate of others? Is she likely to be tactful? Is she alert? Does she have energy and a zest for living? Does she have a sense of humor?

Temperament

While the interviewer understands that the interview is not a fully natural situation and that the applicant may not be fully at ease, he attempts to determine the underlying temperament of each candidate. If the applicant is very ill at ease in the situation, is she *likely* to handle emergencies on the job with calmness and confidence? Can she talk about herself without appearing unduly self-centered or too shy?

Knowledge and Skills

While the personal data sheet and the application blank indicate educational background and skills developed, the interviewer will try to learn how thorough the preparation is. Does the applicant have a good comprehension of business as well as the world is general? Does she show ability to work through problems, or does she quickly dismiss something she doesn't understand or hasn't encountered previously? Does she possess the technical skills needed for the job?

Mental Attitude

Interviewers like to hire young workers who have a positive, optimistic view of life, for they then tend to be cooperative and enthusiastic about what they do. Some of the questions the interviewer wants answers to while he talks with you are: Is this applicant open-minded and tolerant? Is she likely to be willing to make changes in her work? Is she likely to become fully involved?

Objectivity

An ability to view a situation clearly and without undue influence because of your personal feelings is considered valuable in an office. An interviewer will seek to answer the questions: Is the applicant objective? Can she make use of facts in a logical way and view them impartially without regard to her own personal interests?

Self-Confidence

What does the applicant think of herself? This is a key question to an interviewer. He hopes to find an applicant with sufficient self-confidence and self-reliance so that she will be willing to take initiative and responsibility on the job. However, he is not favorably impressed with an applicant who *thinks she knows everything and is right at all times*, for such an individual is not likely to realize when she is going beyond the bounds of initiative and responsibility set for her position.

Effectiveness with People

As you have learned through your studies, business is not an isolated activity. It requires the cooperative efforts of many who can work well together. The interviewer will be particularly interested in assessing how well you are *likely* to get along with co-workers as well as with customers and other visitors to the office.

Illus. 15-11

An interview provides the setting for a mutual evaluation of a future business relationship between a company and an employee.

Job Interest

Interviewers are looking for workers who will be keenly interested in doing the job for which they have applied and are willing to remain with the company for a reasonable period of time. The interviewer will ask questions that will give him clues as to how you view your future.

Adaptability

Interviewers, as they think about an applicant in a particular position, also look to the future and try to determine how she will fit into the organization over a period of time. Is this applicant one who is willing to learn new skills and accept new assignments? Has she approached her studies and her extracurricular activities eager to increase her knowledge? Is she able to determine what is needed in a given situation? Companies find workers who can *measure up to new demands* extremely valuable in carrying out the many tasks that must be completed each day.

THE CONCLUSION OF THE INTERVIEW

At the end of the interview, the interviewer will generally thank you for having come in and will indicate to you what the next step is. He may offer you a position and suggest that you let him know in writing or by telephone whether you will accept it. He may indicate a date by which he will expect to hear from you. If he fails to give you details as to how you are to follow up or when you are to do so, it is proper to question him. For example, you may say, "Mr. Stout, do you want me to write you a letter and when would you like to have it?"

The interviewer may say to you that you will receive a letter within a week informing you of the outcome of the interview.

Before you leave the office be sure that you clearly understand whether the company will inform you only if you are successful, or whether the company will write to each applicant letting her know the exact status of her application.

When you have a clear idea of what is to occur next, thank the interviewer in a very brief, sincere manner and leave his office. A slow, reluctant departure will not leave a favorable impression.

THE FOLLOW-UP

It is always appropriate to write a brief letter thanking an interviewer for a pleasant, informative interview. Such a letter should be written as soon as possible following the interview.

Any correspondence or telephone call from a company that has interviewed you should be acknowledged. If you take a position with one company but receive invitations from other companies that have interviewed you, you must write to each company expressing your appreciation and stating that you have accepted another position.

You must also write to the company that offers you a position to inform them that you accept the position. Letters following up job interviews may be brief, but they should be courteous and complete.

QUESTIONS

1. Describe appropriate dress for a job interview.
2. What information can an applicant expect an interviewer to provide about the job?
3. What information can an applicant expect the interviewer to provide about the company and working conditions?
4. What are some questions you might ask an interviewer about a job for which you are applying?
5. Why does an interviewer seek to determine an applicant's mental attitude?
6. How does an interviewer determine the job interest of an applicant?
7. Why do companies consider adaptability an important trait of workers?
8. Why would an interviewer be interested in an applicant's clubs and other organizational activities while in school?
9. How does an interviewer generally conclude an interview?
10. Why should an applicant write a letter following a job interview?

JUDGMENT

1. What factors would you keep in mind when answering each of the following questions:
    (a) Did you enjoy your business courses in high school?
    (b) Why do you want to work for this company?
    (c) What do you expect to be doing in two years?
2. At the conclusion of an interview, the interviewer says, "Thank you for coming in for an interview, Miss Lanz." He says nothing further. What should Miss Lanz say?

PERSONAL QUALITIES

Alice Pickett was asked to appear for an interview at 10:15 a.m. at the office of the Jones Realty Company. She arrived on time, but the interviewer was in a meeting. Alice was required to wait 15 minutes before the interviewer could see her. When she did finally get in, she complained about being required to wait. She remained rather sullen during the entire interview.

What is your evaluation of Alice's behavior?

LANGUAGE USAGE

Colloquialisms are words or phrases acceptable in informal speech, but not generally acceptable in formal writing. (They are also generally acceptable local or regional expressions.)

On a separate sheet of paper, type each sentence below using an acceptable substitution for each italicized word, phrase, or expression.

1. The young man promised that he would be here *around* three.
2. She will plan a *date* with the executive if you will call the office.
3. Will he ever *get hold of* his new tasks in this office?
4. *Most* everyone in the conference room felt that it was too cold.
5. At what hour did he finally *show up*?
6. Her employer will not *stand for* any personal telephone calls at the office.
7. Will Sally *take a try* at the dictating machine?
8. He will want to order *lots* of boxes of duplicating paper.
9. What do you *calculate* will be the topic for the meeting next month?
10. He has *got to* complete that job before he goes out to lunch today.

SECRETARIAL WORK

1. Write a list of questions that you believe an interviewer should ask you if he is to become acquainted with your ability to fill the position of stenographer that is currently available.
2. In the particular business where you have applied for a position, the following qualities and characteristics are carefully checked on an appraisal sheet by the interviewer:

    Appearance: neat, well-groomed, slovenly, average build, thin, stout, tall, short

    Dress: good taste, worn, careless, flashy, untidy

    Posture: well-balanced, very erect, slightly relaxed, slightly stooped, round-shouldered

    Facial Expression: radiant, happy, thoughtful, solemn, sullen

    Hands and Face: healthy looking, well cared for, physical impairment, heavy makeup, blemished, dirty

    Approach: poised, alert, forward, timid, awkward

    Volume of Voice: too loud, easily heard, too low, pleasant, shrill, monotone

    Enunciation: very clear, clear, passable, indistinct, omits syllables

    Pronunciation: faultless, occasional mistakes, frequent mistakes

Grammar: faultless, occasional mistakes, frequent mistakes, poor, extremely poor

Personality: magnetic, animated, pleasant, tactless, conceited, disagreeable

Temperament: calm, confident, shy, excitable, sullen

Knowledge: clear perception, good comprehension, understanding, uninformed, ignorant

Attitude: cooperative, enthusiastic, attentive, indifferent, arbitrary, argumentative

Self-opinion: modest, confident, timid, self-assured, conceited

Interest in Position: exceptional, normal, below average

Standing in Class: first quarter, second quarter, third quarter, fourth quarter

Summary: superior, above average, average, below average

Recommend Employment: yes, no

Comments:

Prepare an appraisal sheet listing all these items. Interview a fellow student for a stenographic position and fill in the appraisal sheet.

PART 4 SPECIALIZED SECRETARIAL POSITIONS

When Laura was considering the kind of secretarial position for which she could train, she realized that there were many opportunities available. In addition to business positions, opportunities exist in the medical profession, in the legal profession, in research, and in all levels of government. Laura realized that each of these fields presents a different kind of challenge and working environment. She also realized that some of these specialized areas require technical training.

SPECIALIZED FIELDS

Today's complex operations require the skills of many specialists who have training far beyond that possessed by informed laymen. Those who assist such specialists require an understanding of the work of the office beyond that which can be acquired through ordinary study and observation. While secretarial workers continue to master technical vocabulary on the job and learn the technical duties required, there is more and more training provided prospective workers. Technical institutes, community colleges, and business schools often offer specialized education. You may want to consider additional training on either a part-time or full-time basis if you decide that becoming a specialized secretary is your goal.

THE LEGAL SECRETARY

To qualify as a legal secretary, you must have a high degree of skill in shorthand and transcription, in which accuracy is of prime importance. You must have acquired a knowledge and understanding of legal procedures, legal instruments, court functions, and litigation procedures. You must possess the administrative and organizational ability to keep the attorney's office functioning smoothly. You must have the judgment and integrity to maintain the professional relationships of the law office in working with the lawyer's clients, the courts, and the public.

A posthigh school program of one or two years, offered in a junior college, community college, or private business school, will provide you with the necessary background and skills for this specialized field.

Job Opportunities

Your beginning position, however, is not usually that of a legal secretary. It is usually necessary to have general office experience before entering law office work. With a large firm, your initial job would be that of a stenographer in a pool of hopeful secretaries. As you grow in your knowledge of the firm's practices and procedures, you will prepare yourself for a legal secretarial position.

Your starting salary as a stenographer with a law firm is usually not higher than that of a general secretary with a business firm; but once you have added a year's office experience to your record, your professional worth will be enhanced. Beginning salaries in large cities for legal secretarial graduates of community colleges range from $100 to $140 a week, with the greater number at the lower point. After you have had anywhere from three to five years' legal secretarial experience, your salary range should then extend from $125 to $170 a week.

Illus. 15-12

Accuracy is of prime importance when the legal secretary transcribes dictation.

Administrative Management Society

Specific Duties

Unlike the general secretary, who deals with a limited number of customers and callers, as a legal secretary you will constantly deal with all your employer's clients and potential clients. Your attitude in working with them will have a direct bearing upon your employer's effectiveness in counseling them. You must remember that you should always follow the legal code of ethics — everything you know about a client, a case, or a written document is confidential information. You will be required to maintain a reminder system: diaries, card tickler files, and follow-up files so that legal action can be taken at the required time. You will be expected to have the ability to code and file legal papers and related correspondence in clients' folders and to find them when they are called for without delays.

You should understand legal terminology thoroughly; otherwise, the dictation will become complex and meaningless and the transcription extremely difficult. You will be asked to set up and type legal instruments such as bills of sale, deeds, leases, and wills. You may be expected to type affidavits, bills of particulars, and other court papers, and to keep a progress record of court matters.

The legal field has become so broad that you may find employment in one of its many subdivisions, and your work in the office may be completely involved in the legal procedures and legal documents of a special phase of law, such as corporation law, tax law, insurance law, patent law, international law, or criminal law.

For a more extensive study of the specific duties of a legal secretary, review the *Legal Secretary's Complete Handbook*.[1] It offers guidance for most law office tasks, from preparing a brief to taking question-and-answer testimony. Examine the *Handbook for the Legal Secretary*[2] if you are interested in legal dictation. The handbook contains material written in shorthand for reading practice with a word-counted key for dictation practice. It was written to serve three groups: (1) the legal secretarial student, (2) the general secretary whose goal is a legal secretarial position, and (3) the legal secretary who would like a better background in law and law office procedure.

THE MEDICAL SECRETARY

The basic qualification for a medical secretary is the ability to take and transcribe medical dictation efficiently combined with a complete

---

[1] Besse Mae Miller, *Legal Secretary's Complete Handbook* (2nd ed.; Englewood Cliffs, N.J.: Prentice-Hall, Inc., 1970).
[2] Louis Leslie and Kenneth Coffin, *Handbook for the Legal Secretary* (Diamond Jubilee edition; New York City: McGraw-Hill Book Company, 1968).

mastery of the medical secretarial practices and procedures followed in a doctor's office or in a hospital. A dedication to the profession of medicine is the greatest single qualification you must possess if you are to become an efficient medical secretary. The demands and adjustments of the position are unusual. The medical assistance required of you would depend entirely upon the office in which you work. One doctor may expect quite a bit of assistance from you in dealing with his office patients; another, none at all. You may be required to work at odd hours because doctors and hospitals have schedules that differ from those in business offices. You would not disclose any information about a patient.

A two-year medical secretarial program, usually offered at the community college level, will provide you with the necessary background and skills. The technical courses offered in the program include medical dictation and transcription; medical terminology; anatomy; the operation of medical equipment, such as the cardiograph and the audiometer; medical office procedures; accounting for the doctor's office; and a work-study course which would give you some actual working experience in a doctor's office and/or a hospital.

Job Opportunities

There is an increasing demand for trained medical secretaries. Most of them find employment in the offices of physicians or in large hospitals and clinics. However, sanitariums, nursing homes, insurance companies, public health departments, firms that manufacture and distribute medical supplies, and medical research and medical publishing companies all offer opportunities to the secretary who has specialized in the medical field. The enactment of Medicare legislation which provides medical assistance for people 65 years of age and older has increased the demand for the services of physicians and medical secretaries who will process the Medicare records in their offices.

Unlike other areas of secretarial work, the medical secretary is a beginning position. The salary you would receive without experience is about equal to that of a beginning secretary in the average business office. If you are employed in a doctor's office, your salary will probably remain constant after a few years. In hospitals, laboratories, medical associations, and other large medical institutions, however, you would have opportunities for advancement to managerial and administrative posts with commensurate increases in salary.

Specific Duties

In addition to your secretarial work, you will perform most of the following duties if you are employed as a medical secretary:

Illus. 15-13

Numerous job opportunities are available in health services for the medical secretary.

Eastman Kodak Company

1. Receive patients, salesmen, and all other callers
2. Receive and place telephone calls
3. Make and schedule patients' appointments
4. Keep files — patients' files, general files, personal files, card tickler files, and follow-up files
5. Maintain case histories
6. Keep financial records — the doctor's checkbook, daily record of collections, patients' accounts, cashbook, and general ledger
7. Send out statements to patients
8. Collect fees
9. Write collection letters and letters about appointments and referrals, insurance, fees, supplies, and equipment for the medical office
10. Fill out forms for insurance companies

If you are to act as the doctor's medical assistant as well as his secretary, you may have to perform the following additional tasks:

1. Prepare patients for medical examinations
2. Care for medical and surgical instruments
3. Set up laboratory equipment
4. Make laboratory tests and operate medical equipment

For a detailed presentation of the specific duties of a medical secretary, read the *Medical Secretary's Guide*.[3] Medical dictation and transcription are covered in the *Medical Secretary*.[4]

THE ENGINEERING SECRETARY

To qualify as an engineering secretary you must possess the intelligence, ambition, and integrity required of all other competent and conscientious secretaries, in addition to having an above average aptitude for mathematics. If you are to become of increasing assistance to your employer, you must acquire a thorough knowledge and understanding of the technical language used in his office. This you will gain gradually with advanced training and on-the-job experience; however, you can accelerate your progress by reading articles published in engineering magazines.

Job Opportunities

Secretarial courses specifically designed to prepare you for employment in engineering offices and in related technical offices are now offered in regions of the country where the demand for them is greatest — in concentrated areas of electronics industries, in aerospace industries, and in communications centers. They are usually offered in two-year programs at the community college level. The salary you would receive upon completion of the program would be approximately the same as you would receive with comparable training as a legal secretary.

Specific Duties

Your ability to take engineering dictation easily and to transcribe it accurately will depend to a large extent upon your engineering vocabulary. To increase your vocabulary, prepare a list of the technical words that occur frequently in your employer's dictation. Look up or devise a shorthand outline for each of them so that you can write them without hesitation during the dictation. Consult a technical dictionary every time you add to the list so that you will know the exact technical meaning and the correct syllabication and spelling of each word.

Numbers and fractions are typed more often in engineering correspondence than in general business correspondence. You will also be required to type equations and mathematical formulas as you prepare

---

[3]Elaine F. Kabbes, *Medical Secretary's Guide* (Englewood Cliffs, N.J.: Prentice-Hall, Inc., 1967).

[4]Kathleen Root and E. E. Byers, *Medical Secretary* (New York City: McGraw-Hill Book Company, 1967).

tables, graphs, and engineering reports. To make the typing of this technical material easier, your typewriter probably will be equipped with four additional keys at the right of the standard keyboard. These special keys will permit you to type eight engineering symbols.

You probably will use a numeric system in filing and cataloging engineering materials. When numbers are assigned to drawings and prints, they are usually filed in a terminal-digit system. Original drawings may be filed flat, rolled, or vertically. Prints are usually folded and filed in vertical files or in open shelf files.

For a more extensive review of the duties of an engineering secretary, examine *The Engineering Secretary's Complete Handbook*[5] by Laird. It covers secretarial duties in an engineering office from assisting with drafting to acting as administrative assistant to a chief engineer.

Illus. 15-14

This engineering secretary prepares a computations analysis chart.

Administrative Management Society

THE EDUCATIONAL SECRETARY

Increased enrollments on all educational levels have created more job opportunities for still another type of specialized secretary, the educational secretary. To qualify as an educational secretary you must possess the secretarial skills and knowledges required of all other competent secretaries, and, most important of all, a genuine liking for students. You

---

[5]Eleanor S. Laird, *The Engineering Secretary's Complete Handbook* (2nd ed.; Englewood Cliffs, N. J.: Prentice-Hall, Inc., 1967).

must have, or work diligently to acquire, the ability to work with the students and all the other people whom you will meet daily — parents, co-workers on the administrative staff, teachers, and the administrators of the educational institution or system.

It is possible to qualify as an educational secretary in a small school system with a high school diploma; this, however, is the exception rather than the general rule. Many large public school systems require a minimum of 30 college credits with additional in-service courses to be completed during your probationary period of employment. Included in the 30 college credits are specific course requirements covering the general principles of educational psychology, the role of the school in the community, and the proper processing of school records and accounts.

Job Opportunities

Openings for educational secretaries are not limited to schools and colleges. You may find a position with your local board of education, with a state or federal department of education, or with one of the many educational associations. While beginning salaries are not on the average as high as those offered to other specialized secretaries, the fringe benefits often are greater. They include more paid holidays and longer vacation periods at Christmas, Easter, and during the summer months.

Illus. 15-15

This educational secretary is checking student schedules prepared by a computer.

Ohio National Life Insurance Company

Specific Duties

Your duties as an educational secretary would vary with the size and type of educational organization in which you find employment. In an elementary or a secondary school, you might be called upon to register new and transfer pupils, to meet parents and other callers, to keep teachers' attendance records, to order supplies, and to handle the correspondence of the school administrators. Your secretarial duties in a college would be limited to a specific department or to an administrative office, such as the office of the president, the registrar's office, the business office, or the office of the dean of students. With an educational association, you would probably be required to deal extensively with communications — membership campaigns, the preparation and distribution of the organization's publications, and the correspondence of the officers of the association. For a more complete description of the duties of an educational secretary, review the *School Secretary's Handbook*.[6]

As an educational secretary you may qualify for membership in the National Association of Educational Secretaries, a department of the National Education Association. The Association conducts workshops and publishes manuals, handbooks, and a magazine, *The National Educational Secretary*, all designed to improve the professional status and efficiency of educational secretaries.

OPPORTUNITIES FOR FEDERAL EMPLOYMENT

Since government is one of the largest fields of employment in the United States, employing approximately three million men and women, you may be interested in knowing about the secretarial opportunities it offers. Almost half the employees of the federal government are office workers, the majority of whom are women.

After you have successfully completed a four-year high school course, you may qualify for a secretarial civil service position without any previous business experience. Equal opportunities are given to all candidates regardless of race, creed, color, or sex.

Civil Service Tests

Performance tests are given for all branches of civil service for office positions requiring such measurable skills as typewriting, shorthand, transcription, and office machine operation. A minimum typing rate of from 40 to 50 net words a minute on copy material is usually required for

---

[6]John Allan Smith, *School Secretary's Handbook* (Englewood Cliffs, N.J.: Prentice-Hall, Inc., 1962).

Illus. 15-16

All branches of government present employment opportunities for qualified young women.

Vincent Nanfra

initial employment as a typist. Shorthand dictation is generally given at rates ranging from 80 to 100 words a minute. The notes must be transcribed on a typewriter within a reasonable time at a transcription standard set by the examining board.

Under certain circumstances arrangements may be made with some schools for teachers to issue a certificate (on a Civil Service Commission form) attesting to the required degree of proficiency in typing or stenography. The certificate must show that the applicant, not more than six months previous to the filing of the certificate, demonstrated the required proficiency to a teacher of typing or stenography in a public, parochial, or private four-year high school, or an accredited institution such as a business school, community college, or college. The typing or stenographic portion of the written tests will not be required of applicants who present a certificate.

Written tests designed to measure intelligence, aptitudes, and general information possessed by the candidates are administered by the Civil Service Commission. Short answer questions, which can be scored by machine, are used in preference to essay questions. They are presented in a number of forms — multiple choice questions, true-false statements, and the matching of related facts.

All candidates must pass the verbal and clerical aptitude tests (including arithmetic computation) given as part of the examination.

Qualifications Requirements

In addition to passing the written tests, one must meet the following requirements to be eligible for the positions and grade levels included under the examination:

For Position of	The Requirement Is
TYPIST GS-2 STENOGRAPHER GS-3	Successful completion of a four-year high school course OR Six months of appropriate experience
TYPIST GS-3	Successful completion of one academic year of substantially full-time study in a resident school above the high school level OR One year of appropriate experience

General Requirements

In addition to educational and experience requirements, there are some general requirements you will have to meet.

Age. There is no maximum age limit for federal civil service employment. The usual minimum age limit is 18, but for most jobs high school graduates may apply at 16. When an examination has a different minimum, the announcement will say so.

Citizenship. Examinations are open only to citizens or to people who owe permanent allegiance to the United States.

Physical Condition. You must be physically able to perform the duties of the position, and you must be emotionally and mentally stable. This does not mean that a physical handicap will disqualify an applicant so long as she can do the work efficiently without being a hazard.

Selection

When an agency wants to hire a new employee, the appointment officer of the agency asks the Civil Service Commission for the names of the persons who are eligible. The Commission then sends the agency the names of the top three persons on the eligibility list. The officer makes a selection from the three. In deciding which candidate to appoint, the officer may ask all three to come in for personal interviews. The names of those who are not selected are retained for future consideration.

Veteran's Preference

Candidates who establish veteran's preference and make passing grades on civil service examinations have five or ten points added to the scores they make in open competition examinations for appointment to jobs in the federal government. Extra points contribute to a higher ranking on eligibility lists.

Salary

A modern position classification plan is used to determine the salary for each job according to the level of difficulty and responsibility of the work involved. Congress sets nationwide scales for 18 pay grades of classified positions. Employees receive periodic within-grade increases for satisfactory service.

The following table of salary rates for the first 15 grades of positions with the federal government was issued in January, 1971, by the United States Civil Service Commission, Washington, D.C. 20415:

STARTING SALARY RATES FOR FEDERAL EMPLOYEES

Grade	Salary
GS-1	$ 4,326
GS-2	5,223
GS-3	5,708
GS-4	6,202
GS-5	6,938
GS-6	7,727
GS-7	8,582
GS-8	9,493
GS-9	10,470
GS-10	11,517
GS-11	12,615
GS-12	15,040
GS-13	17,761
GS-14	20,815
GS-15	24,251

Depending upon their qualifications, typists are classified GS-2 or GS-3, stenographers GS-3 or GS-4. Most secretaries are classified GS-5.

Foreign Service Secretaries. The United States Department of State needs secretaries to work in its embassies and consulates overseas. The nine basic requirements for these positions are listed on the following page.

1. *Age* — You must be at least 21 years of age.
2. *Marital Status* — You must be single and without dependents.
3. *Citizenship* — You must have been an American citizen for at least five years.
4. *Worldwide* — You must be available for assignment to any one of the more than 300 American embassies, legations, or consulates maintained in more than 100 countries throughout the world.
5. *Duration of Employment* — You must remain at your post abroad for at least two years before becoming eligible for transportation back to the United States at government expense.
6. *Physical Condition* — You must pass a physical examination comparable to United States military standards.
7. *Education* — You must be a high school graduate, or you must pass the General Educational Development Examination.
8. *Tests* — You must qualify on aptitude, spelling, typing, and shorthand tests. Stenotyping and Speedwriting are acceptable.
9. *Background Investigation* — You are subject to a background investigation which may require from four to six months to complete.

The specific qualifications in shorthand, typewriting, and office experience for foreign service secretaries in Grades FSS-9 and FSS-10 are as follows:

1. *GRADE FSS-9, SECRETARY*
    (a) *Dictation.* You must be able to take dictation at a speed of at least 80 words a minute.
    (b) *Typewriting.* You must be able to type at a speed of at least 40 words a minute by the touch system.
    (c) *General Work Experience.* One year of general business experience, or the equivalent, is required. Generally you may substitute one year of training at a business school or one year of college work which included pertinent business experience for general work experience.
    (d) *Office Experience.* You are required to have at least one year of specialized office experience which includes stenography, typing, filing, or record keeping, in addition to your general work experience.

2. *GRADE FSS-10, SECRETARY*
   (a) *Dictation.* You must be able to take dictation at a speed of at least 80 words a minute.
   (b) *Typewriting.* You must be able to type at a speed of at least 40 words a minute by the touch system.
   (c) *General Office Experience.* At least two years of general office experience, or the equivalent, are required.
   (d) *Specialized Secretarial Experience.* You are required to have at least two years of specialized, continuous experience in secretarial duties involving shorthand dictation in addition to your two years of general office experience. The two years of secretarial experience must be gained within the three years immediately preceding the date of your application for employment.

OPPORTUNITIES FOR STATE AND MUNICIPAL EMPLOYMENT

There are secretarial positions available in all state government offices for qualified high school and college graduates. There are many opportunities in state government for high school graduates who have had no work experience. In New York State, for example, there is such great need for stenographers and typists that applications are accepted continuously. A portion of a bulletin seeking applicants is shown on page 587.

Ohio also provides continuous, open competitive civil service examinations for office typists and stenographers. A portion of a recent bulletin included the information shown on page 588.

State Civil Service

While working conditions in state civil service vary slightly from state to state, the following prevail in most states:

1. State employees work a five-day week ranging from 35 to 40 hours in state office buildings that are noted for their modern, air-conditioned facilities.
2. The states maintain a salary schedule for the different job classifications that is in keeping with the prevailing rates of pay for comparable jobs in private industry and in federal and municipal civil service systems.
3. Promotions to higher positions in state governments are generally filled from within the state civil service. As a

Stenographer – Typist

OPPORTUNITIES

There is a position for you as a Stenographer or Typist in New York State Government. You can start a rewarding career right now in one of our offices or installations located throughout the State.

JOB DESCRIPTION

This will vary according to your assignment. It may be in any one of the many State departments and agencies. You might work in a group of Stenographers and Typists that serves several people, or you might be assigned to a small office. You'll do typing, including mimeograph stencils. Stenographers take and transcribe dictation, of course. Very likely, you will have other secretarial duties, such as answering the phone and generally keeping things running smoothly.

SALARY

The starting salary for Stenographers in most State offices is $4,615 a year (about $89 a week), and for Typists, $4,200 yearly (about $80 a week). Annual raises, over a five-year period, will increase salaries to $5,760 for Stenograpers and $5,235 for Typists.

Starting salaries in Nassau, Suffolk, Westchester and Rockland Counties will be $4,815 for Stenographers and $4,400 for Typists.

Starting salaries in the five counties of New York City will be $5,044 for Stenographer and $4,607 for Typist.

HOW DO YOU QUALIFY?

You take an examination which includes a qualifying spelling test; a typing test (you have to type 35 words a minute to qualify for a Stenographer or Typist position); a test in dictation for Stenographers only, requiring 80 words a minute.

These examinations are not limited to residents of New York State. However, the tests will be given only in New York State.

TRAINING OPPORTUNITIES

In Albany and New York City there may be training opportunities for candidates whose abilities in typing and dictation are close to, but not as high as, the above standards.

HOW DO YOU APPLY FOR THE TEST?

These examinations are given regularly at local offices of the New York State Employment Service and at the Department of Civil Service. To make an appointment to take this examination

in New York City, call or visit: in Albany:

New York State Employment Service   New York State Employment Service
575 Lexington Avenue   194 Washington Avenue
Telephone: 759-1020   Telephone: 474-4980

OR   OR

New York State Department of Civil Service   New York State Department of Civil Service
1350 Avenue of the Americas   The State Office Building Campus
Telephone: 765-9790   Telephone: 457-2326

In other locations, call or visit the New York State Employment Service nearest your home. Consult your telephone book for the address and telephone number of offices in the locations listed on the next page.

Albion	Geneva	Massena	Port Jervis
Amsterdam	Glen Cove	Middletown	Poughkeepsie
Auburn	Glens Falls	Monticello	Riverhead
Batavia	Gloversville	Mount Morris	Rochester
Bath	Great Neck	Mount Vernon	Rome
Bayshore	Hempstead	Newark	Saranac Lake
Beacon	Herkimer	Newburgh	Saratoga Springs
Binghamton	Hicksville	New Rochelle	Schenectady
Buffalo	Hornell	Niagara Falls	Sodus
Canandaigua	Hudson	Norwich	Spring Valley
Catskill	Huntington Sta.	Ogdensburg	Staten Island
Cedarhurst	Ithaca	Olean	Syracuse
Corning	Jamestown	Oneida	Tarrytown
Cortland	Kingston	Oneonta	Tonawanda
Dansville	Lackawanna	Oswego	Troy
Dunkirk	Lancaster-Depew	Patchogue	Utica
Elmira	Little Falls	Peekskill	Warsaw
Freeport	Lockport	Plattsburgh	Watertown
Fulton	Malone	Port Chester	White Plains
			Yonkers

WHEN YOU PASS THE TEST

In many areas, such as New York City or Albany, you will be offered a job right away. In other places, it may be soon afterward, depending upon how many positions are open at the time and how high you score. If you are not appointed right away, your name will be on a list to be used as jobs become available.

OTHER OPPORTUNITIES

The eligible list for Typist may also be used to fill positions of Dictating Machine Transcriber and for other positions for which it is considered appropriate.

PROMOTIONS

After a year's service as a Stenographer, you will be eligible for promotion to a Senior Stenographer position. This job will pay from $5,775 to $7,135*. Higher level jobs are also filled by promotion.

As a Typist, you will be eligible for promotion to positions such as Senior Typist and Senior Clerk, with a salary range of $5,160 to $6,410*, and Senior Account Clerk $5,775 to $7,135*.

BENEFITS

State employees have a paid vacation each year of 13 days to start and increasing up to 20 days. They also have fully paid sick leave of 13 days a year. Working conditions are good. You may also take advantage of the comprehensive health insurance plan which is entirely paid by the State. The liberal retirement plan and Social Security coverage help you provide for security in later years.

Plus $200 annual salary differential for appointees in Bronx, Kings, Nassau, New York, Queens, Richmond, Rockland, Suffolk, and Westchester Counties.

Illus. 15-17

Portion of a bulletin seeking applicants for New York State government employment rule, only the highest posts (policy-making and administrative positions or positions requiring highly specialized technical training and experience) are filled from outside the state civil service system. Most states maintain a wide variety of training programs designed to increase employee efficiency and to prepare employees for advancement within the system.

4. State employees usually receive a four-week paid vacation and pay for ten or eleven legal holidays each year, which is more than the average number granted to employees in private industry and in federal civil service.

5. Most state employees are members of a retirement system and are permitted to retire at half pay after 35 years of service. The tendency is to reduce the retirement age — at least one state has an optional plan of retirement at age 55.

Illus. 15-18

Portion of a bulletin seeking applicants for Ohio state government employment.

SCOPE OF EXAMINATIONS: The examinations for Clerk Typists will consist of two parts: a written test and a typing test. The examinations for Clerk Stenographers will consist of three parts -- a written test, a test of dictation and transcription, and a typing test. Applicants must obtain a score of at least 65 percent on each part of the examination and make a final average grade of 70 percent or more to place on the eligible list.

All Clerk Typists and Clerk Stenographers must be able to type at a rate of 40 net words per minute. The Clerk Stenographers must be able to take dictation at the following rates: Grade I, 80 words per minute; Grade II, 85 words per minute; and Grade III, 90 words per minute.

The written examination will consist of items dealing with Spelling, English Usage, Filing, Office Procedure, Arithmetic, Word Definition, and Syllabication.

Special Note: Applicants for the Clerk Typist I or Clerk Stenographer I examination who attain a final average grade of 80 percent or more will be placed on the Grade II eligible list, unless they indicate a preference to be placed on the Grade I list only.

NATURE OF WORK AND QUALIFICATIONS

24-1011 Clerk Typist I -- This is simple and routine clerical work involving full-time or substantial part-time typing.
Qualifications: No experience required.

24-1012 Clerk Typist II -- This is advanced clerical work involving varied and occasionally complex work methods and related typing duties.
Qualifications: One year of clerical experience which included some typing.

24-1013 Clerk Typist III -- This is supervisory clerical work or independent clerical work of comparable difficulty requiring highly skilled typing ability.
Qualifications: Two years of clerical experience which included some typing.

24-1021 Clerk Stenographer I -- This is routine stenographic and clerical work in taking and transcribing dictation and in performing related general office duties.
Qualifications: No experience required.

24-1022 Clerk Stenographer II -- This is advanced stenographic and clerical work which includes taking and transcribing dictation and involves occasionally complex work methods and problems.
Qualifications: One year of clerical experience which included some stenographic work.

24-1023 Clerk Stenographer III -- This is responsible secretarial work or stenographic work of a supervisory or technical nature.
Qualifications: Two years of clerical experience which included some stenographic work.

NOTE: Business school training or college training with course work in secretarial practices or business education may be substituted for an equal amount of experience for any of these examinations, to a maximum of one year. College training in other fields may be substituted on the basis of one year of college for six months of the required experience.

Municipal Civil Service

The number of municipal civil service employees in a city or town varies with the size of the municipality, ranging from fewer than one hundred employees in small communities to over a quarter of a million in some large cities. Employment policies vary with the size of the municipalities. Large municipalities tend to follow closely the civil service policies and practices of their respective states. Municipal salaries and working conditions for office workers compare favorably with those offered by private industry in the same regions of the United States and Canada.

QUESTIONS

1. Why does there continue to be a need for more and more secretaries with specialized training?
2. What type of posthigh school training is available for high school graduates who desire to be specialized secretaries?
3. In what ways does the legal secretary's job differ from a medical secretary's job?
4. What are some duties of engineering secretaries?
5. In what kinds of offices do educational secretaries work?
6. What types of tests are included in the federal civil service examinations?
7. Where do foreign service secretaries work?
8. List five requirements of a foreign service secretary.
9. What are some of the working conditions in state civil service positions?
10. What are two advantages of municipal civil service employment?

JUDGMENT

1. What specialized secretarial position do you think you would prefer and why?
2. What do you consider to be the advantages and disadvantages of taking an overseas secretarial position with the Department of State?

PERSONAL QUALITIES

Arlene Martin has had secretarial training in high school and part-time experience in industry. She has decided that she would like to work for the federal government because she believes that the salaries are higher than those paid in private industry and that the fringe benefits are greater. The Civil Service Commission has announced a performance test for a *Data Typist*, a new position in the electronic computing field, described as follows:

"Operates electric typewriter equipped with special keyboard to transcribe coded program instructions or data on magnetic tape."

Part 4 / Specialized Secretarial Positions

Arlene prefers typing to stenography because she has the ability to type accurately at the rate of 60 words a minute, but she cannot take dictation at speeds higher than 100 words a minute. If she passes the performance test, she will be called for an interview. She will also be asked to furnish references as to her education and experience.

Should Arlene take the performance test for the position of data typist? Should she take the job even though it may mean never using her shorthand?

LANGUAGE USAGE

The following ten terms have been taken from the Vocabulary Builder at the beginning of each unit. You will use each word frequently when you begin your working career. On a separate sheet of paper write a sentence relating to something that you have learned in this course and use the word correctly. If you do not recall the meaning, you may check it in the dictionary before composing the sentence.

1. analysis (noun)
2. capacity (noun)
3. conference (noun)
4. initial (verb)
5. maintain (verb)
6. maximum (adjective)
7. participate (verb)
8. procedure(s) (noun)
9. range (noun or verb)
10. specific (adjective)

SECRETARIAL WORK

1. Assume that you are planning to interview a medical secretary in your community or a nearby community. Write out the list of questions you would plan to ask her in order to learn about her duties and her evaluation of her job.

2. Assume that you have decided to prepare for a specialized secretarial position (choose one of the specialties described in this section). Develop an outline of the courses that you believe you should complete in order to be fully prepared for the type of position you seek. Then compose a letter that could be sent to a community college in your area. In the letter explain what your goal is and inquire as to whether the school offers the specific courses you need.

PART 5 UP THE SECRETARIAL LADDER AND BEYOND

Marilyn Sharkey had served as secretary to Mr. Dennis Paige for three years when he was promoted to vice-president of the food processing company for which he had worked for ten years. In his new position his office became an extremely busy place; and Marilyn was given an assistant, Jill, who was hired as a clerk-typist. Marilyn assumed a number of new responsibilities that required much of her time, so that Jill was able to handle the more routine activities, such as typing reports, filing correspondence, answering the telephone, and transcribing machine dictation. Marilyn introduced Jill to the procedures and policies followed in their office. She was also responsible for planning and supervising Jill's work.

THE SECRETARIAL LADDER

The ranking of secretarial positions is based on the rank of executive positions. For example, a secretary to the president of a company has a higher rank than a secretary to the director of the advertising department. Secretarial positions are not subdivided into the same number of levels from company to company. In some companies there may be only two to three levels of secretarial positions, while in other companies there may be as many as a dozen levels. Regardless of the number of levels, in general, the positions range from junior secretary to executive secretary or administrative assistant. Secretaries may move up the secretarial ladder in two ways. When executives are promoted, their secretaries may receive promotions, too. In such situations the secretaries have the qualifications to handle the more responsible tasks of the executives. Secretaries are also promoted independently of their employers if positions should become available, and the personnel officer feels that a particular secretary is ready for a more responsible position.

PREPARATION FOR HIGHER LEVEL RESPONSIBILITY

While on-the-job experience is one of the key ways of learning about a company and how the tasks are handled in the company, secretaries who move ahead in their companies often combine this on-the-job

Illus. 15-19

With on-the-job experience and specialized training, many secretaries move up to positions of greater responsibility.

Qantel Corporation

experience with further educational studies and professional activities. Personnel officers are favorably impressed with efforts of their staff to increase their knowledge and improve their skills. Secretaries who wish to move ahead often attend local community or four-year colleges during the evening hours to take courses in business administration and secretarial studies. Some secretaries work toward college degrees and thus increase their general educational background as well as their professional knowledge. The general education courses which provide a broad understanding of society and the behavior of man are of value in one's work life, too. Many companies encourage further education by providing a tuition-payment plan to any employee who attends evening classes. As a beginning worker, you will want to inquire about the educational benefits provided in the company where you accept a position.

SECRETARIAL ASSOCIATIONS

Secretaries are organized into a variety of associations in the United States. The largest organization of secretaries is the National

Secretaries Association, International. This organization invites secretaries with a specific amount of experience to join local chapters and to participate in a wide range of professional activities. This organization through its Institute for Certifying Secretaries sponsors a professional examination for all secretaries who meet work experience and educational requirements. This examination leads to the title of Certified Professional Secretary. The examination is a two-day 12-hour examination given once each spring in many centers throughout the United States and Canada. The content is based upon an analysis of secretarial work and includes personal adjustment and human relations, business law, business administration, secretarial accounting, secretarial skills and procedures.

You may want to consider joining an organization of secretaries when you meet the requirements for membership. Such an organization provides a means of becoming acquainted with people who are engaged in the same type of work that you are, and association with them broadens your understanding and awareness of your field of work. Personal friendships also develop. Furthermore, organizations of professional workers generally engage in projects and activities that provide services to the community and to the membership. Many, for example, plan workshops and conferences that help the members to keep up to date about secretarial work and the business world.

BEYOND A SECRETARIAL ASSIGNMENT

Secretarial activities provide background experience from which to move into other types of positions in many organizations. There are former secretaries in all types of executive positions. Here are just a few instances:

1. A former secretary is a vice-president in charge of personnel for a large cosmetic manufacturing company.
2. A former secretary is an assistant treasurer of a large metropolitan bank.
3. A former secretary is vice-president in charge of personnel for a large international firm of consulting engineers.
4. A former secretary is a partner in a small interior decorating company.
5. A former secretary is vice-president for industrial sales for a large manufacturing company.

Companies frequently review their personnel talent and attempt to assign people to positions where they will be most productive for the organization. Many skills that competent secretaries possess are also valuable in other situations. However, secretarial skills are not sufficient for promotion to management positions. In fact, secretaries who wish to be considered for management positions will have to develop a far more comprehensive understanding of business than is required for a secretarial assignment.

ADMINISTRATIVE MANAGEMENT

One field into which secretaries are sometimes promoted is the field of administrative management. Administrative management refers to a wide range of positions and includes the woman who supervises a small typing pool to a vice-president responsible for administrative services. In general, the responsibilities of administrative management include the following:

1. Maintaining sufficient office services
2. Maintaining communication facilities
3. Assessing facilities and equipment
4. Organizing the flow of paper work
5. Supervising and evaluating office personnel
6. Managing the office

Maintaining Sufficient Office Services

Considerations in this area include determining how much clerical and secretarial assistance is required in each of the offices of the company and making recommendations to the personnel department about in-company training programs.

Maintaining Communication Facilities

Managers of mail services and of telephone services are performing in the field of administrative management. The supervisor will be responsible for overseeing the functions of these departments to assure smooth, effective communications within the organization as well as with outside individuals.

Assessing Facilities and Equipment

With the increasing numbers of innovations in the ways in which office work is handled, administrative managers spend a great deal of time in looking at new equipment and facilities and determining what changes should be made in their own organizations.

As companies expand, their need for office services generally increases; and administrative managers must determine what facilities are needed and make appropriate selections. They ultimately organize and furnish such new facilities.

Organizing the Flow of Paper Work

Modern companies process a great deal of paper during each working day, and this processing can become unduly complex if there is no one person overseeing the total function. To administrative management falls the responsibility of the total function. Generally periodic studies are made to check on the adequacy of the procedures followed and to make recommendations for change. The need for the paper work to be coordinated among many departments makes the centralization of such function wise in modern businesses. Preparation of manuals that outline procedures in handling office tasks and correspondence is the responsibility of administrative managers.

Supervising and Evaluating Office Personnel

How productive are our typists? What is the extent of the tasks that one stenographer can handle? How well is each file clerk meeting the standards set for the tasks completed? These are some of the questions that are of concern to administrative managers. Further, administrative managers, ranging from supervisors of small staffs of clerical workers to a vice-president who oversees all aspects of administrative functions, are concerned with maintaining high morale among the staff and motivating personnel to greater levels of productivity. Administrative managers participate in determining salaries for various positions and in assessing fringe benefits.

Managing the Office

In many offices secretaries serve as managers. A secretary generally supervises much of her own time through planning, organizing, and completing the tasks to be done. Furthermore, she may, to some extent, organize the work of her employer by providing him with information that he will need and directing his attention to matters that require his supervision. In some offices secretaries have supervision of typists, stenographers, and other office personnel. Through such activities secretaries are, to some degree, administrative managers. Those who are especially skillful in planning and executing tasks — in other words, those who get the job done — are likely candidates for promotion to management positions. Along with their first-hand experience, secretaries should become acquainted with the professional aspects of management and with its technical aspects, such as data processing procedures, office space planning, evaluative techniques for office tasks — all of which must be based on a thorough knowledge of the company's operations and its competitive place in industry. Studying on one's own, through special workshops and seminars in the company or in the local community, and through a college or university are ways of developing the background needed for promotional opportunities. Keeping informed of industry trends by reading trade journals and financial newspapers and magazines is also a valuable trait.

YOUR FUTURE

The pattern of one's career is extremely difficult to predict in a society where an individual has both freedom of choice and many opportunities. With basic education in secretarial skills and procedures, you are prepared to enter many types of organizations where you may pursue your livelihood in whatever you aspire to do. As you become acquainted with the nature of tasks from experience inside an organization, you will want to reassess your career objectives and make plans for further study that will prepare you to meet newly formulated goals.

Opportunities abound. If you combine your wishes with realistic effort and sincere commitment, your achievements will bring you personal satisfaction and at the same time contribute to the organization with which you are associated.

Illus. 15-20

Newspaper Enterprise Association

"Remember, Miss Blatherskite, it's a poor workman who blames his tools!"

QUESTIONS

1. On what basis are secretarial jobs ranked?
2. Are all secretaries promoted when their employers are promoted? Explain.
3. Why would a secretary go to college in the evenings?
4. What is the name of a large organization for secretaries?
5. What is the content of the examination administered by the Institute for Certifying Secretaries?
6. For what reason would a secretary be promoted to a management position?
7. List some responsibilities of administrative managers.
8. What kinds of tasks are related to organizing the flow of paper work through an organization?
9. In what ways is a secretary a manager?
10. In what ways may a secretary prepare for a position in management?

JUDGMENT

1. Assume that you are employed in a large company as a stenographer. After you have been on your job for about a week, you learn that a secretary is leaving. You think you would like the job and you feel confident that you can handle it. You have been observing the secretary for a week. Should you talk with your employer about your interest?
2. A friend of yours is working in the same company in which you are working. It is a large company and, during the orientation, the personnel officer makes clear that there are promotional opportunities in the company and that there is a full tuition-refund plan for any employee who continues to go to school. Your friend has decided to enter a local community college to work toward an Associate Degree. She asks you to join her. What would you decide? Explain your decision.

PERSONAL QUALITIES

Margaret Simpson has recently been promoted to a secretarial position where she is responsible for supervising two clerk-typists. One of the clerk-typists, Sharon, is about three years older than Margaret and has been with the company longer. Sharon is a good worker but it seems she always objects to the assignments Margaret gives her or makes some unnecessary comment. For example, recently when Margaret gave Sharon a statistical table to type, Sharon said, "I'm not supposed to do statistical tables. They are done in the typing pool. After you have been here longer you will know that."

What do you think of Sharon's attitude? How would you handle Sharon if you were Margaret?

LANGUAGE USAGE

The following sentences are based on the important rules of punctuation which have been presented in the Language Usage sections of this book. On a separate sheet of paper type each sentence and punctuate it correctly.

1. Your basic skills your educational training your personal and professional qualities all will be given consideration when you present yourself for an interview.
2. You may be tested on your general knowledge as well as how you take dictation prepare transcripts and how you use a transcribing machine.
3. The personnel director said to her Mr. Baker will expect you to take dictation compose some letters yourself type reports answer the telephone and in general be his Girl Friday do you think you can handle such a job.
4. He asked me if I knew all the parts of a letter and how to type a letter attractively on a letterhead.
5. In preparation for the meeting her employer told her to bring the following pencils a notebook the necessary files the report for the stockholders and would you believe it a bottle of aspirin.
6. She had only a slight knowledge of data processing but her new employer said that with on-the-job training and outside class study she would become efficient.
7. She was greeting an applicant for the position when the telephone call came in however the applicant waited while she located the file for the personnel manager.
8. He asked her to bring the numeric the geographic and the subject files.
9. What would a telegram cost as compared with a long-distance call he asked.
10. A secretary will prepare an itinerary make hotel and transportation reservations balance a petty cash fund and make a bank deposit attend a meeting take the notes and type a report and then say this was a quiet day maybe tomorrow will be more exciting.

SECRETARIAL WORK

1. Assume that you are inquiring about studying on a part-time basis in a local college. What are the courses that you believe would be most helpful in becoming better acquainted with the technical aspects of administrative management. Make a list of the courses that you think would be helpful. Describe briefly what you would want each course to include.
2. Assume that you have accepted a position as a clerk-typist in a local company with many promotional opportunities. In this company all beginning office workers start as clerk-typists. Many move out of such positions within twelve to eighteen months. Write a brief report in which you describe the type of position you would like to have within three years. Also, indicate in your report how you will prepare for the position you hope to have in three years.

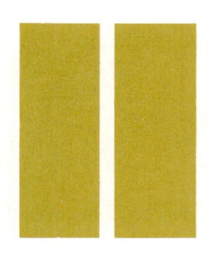

APPENDIX A

GRAMMAR

Grammar is important in speaking and writing. Knowing the rules of grammar is necessary if you are to carry out your responsibilities confidently.

Grammar is a study of the words of a language, but particularly a study of the relationship of those words to one another. Words are divided into nine classifications that are known as parts of speech.

   I. Nouns
   II. Pronouns
   III. Adjectives
   IV. Articles
   V. Verbs
   VI. Adverbs
   VII. Prepositions
   VIII. Conjunctions
   IX. Interjections

I. Nouns

A noun is a word that is used as

   A. A name of a person (Thomas Jefferson)
   B. A place (Washington, D.C.)
   C. A thing (desk)
   D. A quality (goodness)
   E. An action (fishing)
   F. An idea (immortality)

Proper Noun. A proper noun names a particular being or thing. It is always capitalized.

   Alexander Graham Bell, New York, Empire State Building

Common Noun. A common noun names any of a class of beings or things.

   man (men), tree (trees), table (tables)

Collective Noun. A collective noun is a common noun that names a group.

   company, committee, crowd, jury, group

II. Pronouns

A pronoun is a word that is used instead of a noun. Most of the problems with pronouns involve personal and relative pronouns. Use of the correct pronoun after the verb *be* may also present a problem.

Grammar

Personal Pronouns and Their Antecedents. A personal pronoun is a pronoun that shows by its form whether it represents the

A. Speaker (first person)
B. Person spoken to (second person)
C. Person spoken of (third person)

The antecedent of a pronoun is the noun for which it stands. The pronoun must be in agreement with its antecedent in person, number, and gender. There are several uses of antecedents that require particular attention.

1. When two or more singular antecedents of a pronoun are connected by *and*, the pronoun must be plural.
   The clerk and the mail boy received *their* checks.
   If, however, the antecedents are merely different names for the same person or thing, the pronoun must be singular.
   The well-known businessman and public servant has received *his* award.

2. When two or more singular antecedents of a pronoun are connected by *or* or *nor*, the pronoun must be singular.
   Either Joyce or Linda must bring *her* notebook.
   If one of the antecedents is plural, it should be placed last, and the pronoun should be plural.
   Neither the general manager nor his assistants realized that *they* had so little time.

3. If the antecedent of a pronoun is a collective noun that expresses unity, the pronoun must be singular.
   The committee quickly reached *its* decision.
   If the collective noun refers to the individuals or parts that make up a group, however, the pronoun of which it is the antecedent must be plural.
   The class brought *their* own lunches.

4. The number of an antecedent is not changed when it is followed by such connectives as *in addition to* and *as well as*.
   The boy, as well as his brothers, did *his* duty.

5. Since there is no third person, singular number, common gender pronoun, the masculine *he*, *his*, or *him* is generally used when the antecedent requires such a pronoun.
   Each office worker must do *his* best.
   When it is especially important to be accurate, both masculine and feminine pronouns may be used.
   Every employee should be careful about *his* or *her* personal appearance.

Relative Pronouns. A relative pronoun is one that joins a subordinate clause to its antecedent. *Who*, *which*, *what*, and *that* are the relative pronouns.

Secretaries *who* know grammar are valuable.

Some compound relative pronouns are *whoever, whosoever, whichever, whichsoever, whatever,* and *whatsoever.* Relative pronouns present two problems:

1. Using the correct relative with reference to persons and things.

2. Using the correct case form — for example, *who* refers to persons and, sometimes, to highly trained animals; *which* refers to animals or things; *that* refers to persons, animals, or things.

Who, whoever, and *whosoever* are in the nominative case and are the correct forms when a relative pronoun is the subject of a subordinate clause.

Mr. Johnson is a man *who* can do the job.

Whose is in the possessive case and is used as is any possessive.

Whose hat is this?

Whom, whomever, and *whomsoever* are in the objective case and must be used when a relative pronoun is the object of a verb or preposition.

Grace is the girl *whom* we are addressing.

The Pronoun after *Be*. The same case must be used after the verb *be* in any of its forms (*am, are, is, was, were, be, being, have been*) as appears before it. This is usually the nominative case. When the object of a transitive verb, however, precedes the infinitive *to be,* the objective case must follow it.

It was *she* (not *her*).
If I were *he* (not *him*).
Did you expect those children to be *them* (not *they*)?

III. Adjectives

An adjective is a word that is used to modify a noun or a pronoun. There are two types of adjectives:

A. A *descriptive* adjective names some quality of or describes the person or object expressed by the noun or pronoun that it modifies.

pretty girl, *handsome* child, *white* frock

B. A *definitive* adjective points out or expresses the number or quantity of the object named by the noun or referred to by the pronoun.

eight people, *this* book, *that* desk, *ten* pages

Proper Adjectives. Proper adjectives are those derived from proper nouns, and they are always capitalized.

French language or *American* interests

Comparison of Adjectives. Comparison is the expression of an adjective to indicate an increasing or decreasing degree of quality, quantity, or manner. There are three degrees of comparison:

1. The *positive degree* is expressed by the simple form of the adjective.

    light, pretty

2. The *comparative degree* is used to compare two objects. The comparative degree of almost all adjectives of *one* syllable, and of a few of two syllables, is formed by the addition of *r* or *er* to the simple form.

    lighter, prettier

    The comparative degree of most adjectives of *two* or more syllables is formed by the placing of *more* or *less* before the simple form of the adjective.

    more beautiful or *less* useful

3. The *superlative degree* is used to compare *three* or more objects. The superlative degree of most adjectives of one syllable, and some of two syllables, is formed by the addition of *est* to the simple form.

    lightest, darkest

    The superlative degree of most adjectives of two or more syllables is formed by the placing of *most* or *least* before the simple form of the adjective.

    most satisfactory or *least* attractive

Some adjectives are compared irregularly. The following are a few:

Positive	*Comparative*	*Superlative*
good	better	best
much	more	most
little	less	least
far	farther	farthest

IV. Articles

A, *an*, and *the* are articles.

A. *A* and *an* are *indefinite* articles since they merely limit a noun to any one in a class.

   a person, *an* application

B. *The* is a *definite* article because it singles out a particular person or thing in a class.

   The manager read *the* application.

V. Verbs

A verb is a word that shows action or state of being of the subject. There are two classifications of verbs:

A. A *transitive verb* is one that requires an object to complete its meaning. The object may be a noun or a pronoun and it *must be* in the objective case. The object is used to complete the meaning of the verb.

Appendix A

To determine the object of a transitive verb, ask *What?* or *Whom?*

He *reported* the accident.

B. An *intransitive verb* does *not* require an object to complete its meaning.

The light *shines*. The boy *ran*.

Many verbs may be used both as transitive and intransitive verbs. For example, in the sentence, *The boy* ran, *ran* is an intransitive verb requiring no object.

The verb *ran* may, however, be used as a transitive verb: for example, *The boy* ran *a* race. Here *race* is the object of the verb *ran*, and the verb becomes transitive.

Some verbs, however, may be used correctly only as intransitive verbs. *Sit*, *lie*, and *rise* are examples of verbs that are always intransitive verbs since they permit no object; while *set*, *lay*, and *raise* are examples of verbs that are always transitive because they require an object to complete their meaning.

Voice of Verbs. Voice indicates whether the subject of the verb is (1) the doer of the action or (2) the receiver of the action that is expressed by the verb.

A verb in the *active voice* identifies the subject as the doer of the action.

The new stenographer *typed* the letter.

A verb in the *passive voice* identifies the subject as the receiver of the action.

The letter *was typed* by the new stenographer.

Any transitive verb may be used in either the active or the passive voice.

In the independent clauses of a compound sentence or in a series of related statements, verbs of the same voice should be used. This is known as *parallel construction*.

(Wrong) The letter *was dictated* by the executive and the secretary *transcribed* it.

(Right) The executive *dictated* the letter and the secretary *transcribed* it.

Tense. Tense expresses the time of the action. There are three primary tenses:

1. The *present tense* of a verb is used to denote the present time. It is used in expressing a general truth or that which is generally customary. The present tense is also used to describe more vividly what took place in past time. This is known as *historical present*.

Washington *crosses* the Delaware and immediately *attacks* Trenton.

2. The *past tense* indicates past time.

We *shipped* your order yesterday.

3. The *future tense* indicates that which will take place in the future. The future tense is expressed by the use of *shall* or *will* with the present form of the verb.

I *shall go* early. You *will arrive* on time.
She *will come* in at eight o'clock.

Frequent errors are made in the use of *will* and *shall*. The future tense may be used to express simple futurity or to express determination or promise. Simple futurity is denoted by the use of *shall* with the first person, and *will* with the second and the third persons.

I *shall be* happy to see you when you arrive.
He *will be* home early.

If determination or promise is to be expressed, the rule for futurity is reversed. Use *will* with a first person subject, *shall* with a second or third person subject.

I *will be* there without fail.
You *shall* certainly *go*.
They *shall return* tomorrow.

In asking questions, use *shall* when the subject is in the first person (I, we).

Shall we go?

When the subject is in the second or third person, either *shall* or *will* may be used, depending upon which form is expected in the answer.

Will you write the letter? (Answer expected: I *will* write the letter.)
Shall you miss your friends when you move? (Answer expected: I *shall* miss my friends.)

In addition to the primary tenses, there are three verb phrases, known as the perfect tenses, that represent completed action or being.

1. The *present perfect* tense denotes an action or an event completed at the present time. It is formed by the placing of *have* or *has* before the perfect participle.

I *have read* several chapters.
He *has studied* his French.

2. The *past perfect* tense indicates an action or an event completed at or before a stated past time. It is formed by the placing of *had* before the perfect participle.

They *had completed* the picture by the time dinner was served.
I *had assumed* you would come by plane before we received your letter.

3. The *future perfect* tense indicates that an action or an event will be completed at or before a stated future time. It is formed by the placing of *shall have* or *will have* before the perfect participle.

I *shall have gone* before you arrive.
He *will have arrived* home before you can get there.

Whether *shall have* or *will have* is used depends upon the basic rule for the use of *shall* or *will*.

Mood. Mood is that property of a verb that indicates the manner in which the action or state of being is expressed.

1. The *indicative mood* is used in asserting something as a fact or in asking a question.
2. The *imperative mood* is used in expressing a command, a request, or an entreaty.
3. The *subjunctive mood* is used in expressing a doubt, a wish, or a condition contrary to reality.
   (a) A condition contrary to *present* reality is expressed with *were*, not *was*.
      (Wrong) If I *was* tall, I could reach the book.
         If Ann *was* going, you could go along.
      (Right) If I *were* tall, I could reach the book.
         If Ann *were* going, you could go along.
   (b) A condition contrary to *past* reality is expressed by *had been*.
      If the plane *had been* on time, this might not have happened.

Agreement of Verb and Subject. The agreement of verb and subject sometimes causes trouble. A verb must agree with its subject in person and number. The verb *to be* has person and number forms: *I am, you are, he is, we are, you are,* and *they are*; *I was, you were, he was, we were, you were,* and *they were*. Other verbs have only one expression for number and person. When the subject is in the third person, singular number, a verb or an auxiliary in the present or the present perfect tense must end in *s*.

Mr. White *dictates* very slowly.
Miss Stewart *has* been his secretary for a long time.

A very common error is the use of a singular verb with a plural subject.

1. When the verb and the subject are separate in the sentence, the verb must agree with its subject. A common error is to make the verb agree with the word near it rather than with the real subject.
   (Wrong) The *activity* of the board at its meetings *are* always interesting.
   (Right) The *activity* of the board at its meetings *is* always interesting.

2. If the subject is plural in form but singular in meaning, a singular verb is required.

   The news *has* been good.

3. Two or more singular subjects connected by *or* or *nor* require a singular verb.

   Neither Kurt nor Bill *is* at the office.

4. When two or more subjects connected by *or* or *nor* differ in number, the plural subject is placed nearest the verb and the verb made plural.

   Neither the office staff nor the executives *are* to have that bulletin.

   When two or more subjects connected by *or* or *nor* differ in person, the verb must agree with the subject that is nearest to it.

   Either you or I *am* at fault.

   It is frequently better to rephrase the sentence so as to use a verb with each subject.

   Either you *are* at fault or I *am*.

5. Two or more singular subjects connected by *and* require a plural verb.

   The typewriter and the adding machine *are* both in need of repair.

6. When the subjects connected by *and* refer to the same person, a singular verb must be used.

   The great novelist and playwright *is* on his way home.

7. When the subjects connected by *and* represent one idea or are closely connected in thought, a singular verb should be used.

   Ice cream and cake *is* a popular dessert.

8. When either or both subjects connected by *and* are preceded by *each*, *every*, *many a*, etc., a singular verb is required.

   Each stock boy and foreman *is* expected to work late on inventory.

9. When one of two subjects is in the positive and the other in the negative, the verb agrees with the one in the positive.

   The teacher, and not the students, *is* planning to attend.

10. The number of a subject is not affected by words connected to it by *as well as*, *and also*, *in addition to*, etc.

    Mother, as well as the rest of the family, *is* expecting to go.

11. When a collective noun expresses unity, a singular verb is used.

    The jury *is* asking that a point be clarified.

Contractions. Contractions may be used in informal communications.

In writing contractions, remember that *don't*, the contraction of *do not*, is plural and is used with plural nouns and the pronouns *I, we, you,* and *they. Doesn't*, the contraction of *does not*, is singular and is used with singular nouns and the pronouns *he, she,* and *it*.

It *doesn't* bother me much, but I *don't* like it.

Infinitives. An infinitive is a form of the verb that asserts nothing, but merely names in a general way the action or the state of being. It is expressed by the word *to* placed before the verb: *to be, to walk, to talk, to cry*. The infinitive may be used as a noun, the subject of a sentence, a predicate noun, or the object of a verb. It may also be used as an adjective or an adverb.

The sign of the infinitive is omitted after such verbs as *bid, dare, feel, see, need, help, hear, let,* and *make*.

She saw him *open* the door.

Participles. A participle is a verb form used as an adjective having the double function of verb and adjective. There are three forms of the participle:

1. The *present participle* is formed by the addition of *ing* to the simple form of the verb. It expresses action as being in progress, usually at the same time as some other action. It is used as an adjective and at the same time retains some of the properties of a verb.

    The clerk *counting* the money is new here.

    In this sentence *counting* is an adjective modifying the noun *clerk*; it also has the property of a verb in that it takes the object *money*.

2. The *past participle* expresses action prior to that of the governing verb. It is used as an adjective and is usually formed by the addition of *d* or *ed* to the present tense of the verb.

    The machine *used* by the secretary was defective.

    The teacher, *interrupted* by the students, did not complete her grading.

3. The *perfect participle* is formed by the combination of *being, having,* or *having been* with some other participle.

    Having written the letters, she was free to go.

    In the preceding sentence the perfect participle *having written* modifies the subject of the sentence *she*.

    A common error is that of putting at the beginning of a sentence a participial phrase that does not modify the subject. This is referred to as a *dangling* participle.

    (Wrong) Having completed the statement, it was time to file the letters.

    (Right) Having completed the statement, she found it was time to file the letters.

VI. Adverbs

An adverb is a word used to modify a verb, an adjective, or another adverb.

A. An adverb modifies a verb by answering the questions *how? when? where?*

She walked *lightly*.
He arrived *early*.
The report is *here*.

B. An adverb modifies adjectives and other adverbs by expressing degree (*how much? how little?*) and by answering the questions *in what manner?* and *to what degree?*

The clerk will file *more*.
She spoke *less*.
He worked *very* hard.
Julia writes *rather* well.

Comparison of Adverbs. Like adjectives, adverbs are compared to show degree.

1. A few adverbs are compared by the addition of *er* or *est* to the positive form of the adverb.

    soon, sooner; often, oftener, oftenest

2. Some adverbs are compared irregularly:

    well, better, best; far, farther, farthest

3. Most adverbs, however, are compared by the use of *more* or *most* or *less* or *least* with the simple (positive) form of the adverb.

    more brightly, *most* often, *less* lightly, *least* likely

Placing the Adverb. Ordinarily an adverb follows the verb it modifies, but it may precede it. It should be placed where its meaning is most clearly shown. *Only, merely,* and *also*, which are sometimes adverbs and sometimes adjectives, give the most trouble in placing, since they may convey very different meanings in different positions in a sentence.

Only I saw him.   I saw *only* him.
I *only* saw him.   I saw him *only*.

Other Problems with Adverbs. There are a few errors in the use of adverbs that frequently are made.

1. *Very* or *too* should not be used to modify participles.

    (Wrong) She was *very* pleased.
    (Right) She was *very* much pleased.

2. *Too*, which is an adverb that means *also* or *more than enough*, should be spelled correctly and not confused with *to* or *two*.

    By *two* o'clock she had *too* much work *to* do.

3. *Well* is usually an adverb. In speaking of health, however, *well* is used as an adjective. Be careful not to use *good* as an adverb in place of *well*.

   (Wrong) He does his work *good*.
               I don't feel very *good*.

   (Right) He does his work *well*.
               I don't feel very *well*.

4. *Very* is an adverb of degree, while *real* is an adjective of quality. Do not use *real* in place of *very*.

   (Wrong) He had a *real* beautiful office.

   (Right) He had a *very* beautiful office.

5. Adverbs of manner, those ending in *ly*, are frequently confused with adjectives derived from the same root. Adverbs of manner modify verbs that express action.

   She sings *sweetly*. (Adverb)
   Her singing is *sweet*. (Adjective)

6. Two negatives should not be used to express negation.

   (Wrong) The clerk will *not* wait for *nobody*.

   (Right) The clerk will *not* wait for *anybody*.

   (Right) The clerk will wait for *nobody*.

VII. Prepositions

A preposition connects a noun or a pronoun with some other element of the sentence and shows the relationship between them. The noun or pronoun that follows the preposition is its object.

There are two kinds of prepositions:

A. Simple — *to, for, at, through, of*

B. Compound — *into, in spite of, instead of, in regard to, on account of, because of, according to, out of, as to.*

Prepositional Phrases. A group of words made up of a preposition and its object, together with any words used to modify the object, is called a *prepositional phrase*. The object of a preposition may be determined by asking *whom* or *what* after the preposition; what the phrase modifies may be determined by asking *what* or *who* before the preposition.

Prepositional phrases, like adjectives and adverbs, should be placed as close as possible to the words they modify to make the sentence as clear as possible.

Choice of Prepositions. Many errors are made in the use of prepositions because some words demand certain prepositions: *angry with* is used in reference to persons, and *angry at* is used in reference to things, animals, or situations. There are many situations in which prepositions are misused. Some of the most common follow.

1. *Into* should be used after a verb that indicates the motion of a person or a thing from one place to another. *In* is used after a verb expressing the idea of rest or, in some cases, motion within a certain place

   The girl went *into* the classroom.
   The clerk is *in* the filing department.

2. *Between* should be used only in reference to two persons or objects. *Among* should be used when referring to three or more persons or objects.

   The two boys divided the work *between* them.
   Gifts were distributed *among* the natives.

3. Prepositions that are not needed should not be used.

   (Wrong) The wastebasket is *in under* the desk. Where is it *at*?
   (Right) The wastebasket is *under* the desk. Where is it?

4. Do not omit prepositions that are needed to make sentences grammatically correct. Avoid telegraphic style in letters.

   (Wrong) Mr. Finley will arrive North Station 11:00 Sunday.
   (Right) Mr. Finley will arrive at the North Station at 11:00 a.m. Sunday.

VIII. Conjunctions

A conjunction is a word used to connect words, phrases, or clauses. There are three kinds of conjunctions:

A. A *coordinate conjunction* connects words or clauses of the same grammatical relation or construction, neither dependent upon the other for its meaning.

   You *and* I are elected.
   Their father is out of town, *and* their sister is on a vacation.

B. A *subordinate conjunction* connects a subordinate clause with some word in the principal clause upon which it is dependent for its meaning.

   The man left hurriedly *lest* he be seen.

C. *Correlative conjunctions* are conjunctions that are used in pairs; the first introducing, the second connecting the elements. They must be placed just before the elements that they introduce or connect.

   (Wrong) I will *either* meet you in Boston *or* Washington.
       I will meet you *either* in Boston *or* Washington.
   (Right) I will meet you in *either* Boston *or* Washington.
       I will meet you *either* in Boston *or* in Washington.

Or should always be used with *either; nor* with *neither*. They are used in reference to two things only.

(Wrong) *Either* Bob, Jack, *or* Don will pitch today's game.
Neither the superintendent, the principal, *nor* the teachers agreed with him.
Neither Jack *or* Don will pitch today's game.

(Right) Bob, Jack, *or* Don will pitch today's game.
The superintendent, the principal, *and* the teachers disagreed with him.
None of them — the superintendent, the principal, the teachers — agreed with him.
Neither Jack *nor* Don will pitch today's game.

As . . . as is used when equality is expressed, while *so . . . as* is used for a negative comparison.

I earn *as* much *as* you do but not *so* much *as* your brother does.

Some things to watch in the use of conjunctions follow.

1. Conjunctions should not be used in place of some other part of speech.

    (Wrong) Seldom *or* ever should such an example be used.
    You should try *and* improve your speech.

    (Right) Seldom *if* ever should such an example be used.
    You should try *to* improve your speech.

2. A clause, which is a part of a sentence containing a subject and a predicate, having meaning in itself, is connected to the other parts of the sentence by either a conjunction or a relative pronoun. A phrase, which contains no verb and has no meaning in itself, is introduced by a preposition, participle, or infinitive, but not by a conjunction.

    The project cannot be completed *without* your help.
    (*Without* is a preposition.)
    The project cannot be completed *unless* you help us.
    (*Unless* is a conjunction.)

3. *Except* and *without* are prepositions and should not be used in place of *unless*, which is a conjunction.

    (Wrong) You will not master shorthand *except* you concentrate.

    (Right) You will not master shorthand *unless* you concentrate.

4. *Like* is not a conjunction and should never be used in place of the conjunction *as*.

    (Wrong) She walks *like* you do.

    (Right) She walks *as* you do.

IX. Interjections

Interjections are exclamatory words or phrases used in a sentence for emphasis or to indicate feeling. They have no grammatical connection with the rest of the sentence. Interjections are set off by commas or by exclamation marks.

Oh, so you saw it?
Ouch! that hurt.

Grammar Reference Books

Although many questions concerning grammar can be answered by using a good dictionary, you should have available a standard reference book on English grammar.

In Appendix G you will find a list of recommended books. A ready reference on grammar will help you produce better letters and reports for your employer.

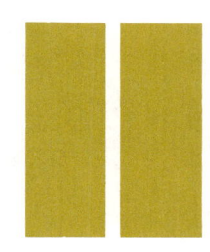

APPENDIX B

PUNCTUATION

Punctuation is used to make more forceful and to indicate more clearly the relationships of written thoughts. Punctuation is the written substitute for the change in voice, the pause, and the gestures that are used in oral expression.

The excessive use of punctuation marks is not considered good form. However, the importance of an accurate usage of punctuation marks is illustrated daily by the serious errors that may be found in office correspondence.

You will be responsible for the correct punctuation of business letters and reports. Although you are not expected to be an authority on punctuation, you should be familiar with the most important rules. The following rules are accepted and generally used wherever English is written.

Period (.)

The period is used

1. After complete declarative or imperative sentences.
   Today we shall study the use of the period.
2. After initials in a name.
   H. L. Andrews
3. After most abbreviations. The following are some exceptions approved by several authorities.
   (a) Mme (Madame), Mlle (Mademoiselle)
   (b) IOU, c/o, OK, SOS, A1
   (c) Chemical symbols: H_2O, Zn, Pb
   (d) Offices and agencies of the federal government: SEC, FBI, FCC
4. Before decimal fractions, and between dollars and cents when expressed in figures, and after the abbreviations *s.* and *d.* for shilling and pence.
   3.45, $16.13, 13s., 7d.
5. For ellipses. Usually three periods or dots are used to indicate the omission from quoted matter of one or more words when the omitted portion does *not* end with a period. Four periods are used when the omitted portion does end with a period.
   The path was long and narrow . . . the weary boys walked slowly . . . .

Punctuation 613

Comma (,)

The comma is the most frequently used form of punctuation; therefore, errors in its use are frequent. The comma is used

1. To set off a subordinate clause preceding a main clause.
   When the bell rings, you may leave.
2. To set off a nonrestrictive phrase or subordinate clause. (A phrase or a clause is nonrestrictive if the main clause in the sentence expresses a complete thought when the nonrestrictive phrase or clause is omitted.)
   My doctor, who is now on his vacation, will prepare the report next week.
3. To separate long coordinate clauses that are joined by the conjunctions *and*, *but*, *for*, *neither*, *nor*, and *or*. The comma precedes the conjunction.
   He worked far into the night, for the deadline was noon the next day.
4. To set off phrases or expressions at the beginning of a sentence when they are loosely connected with the rest of the sentence.
   Nevertheless, we feel the way you do about it.
5. To separate words, phrases, or clauses in a series. Note that a comma precedes the last item in the series.
   The group now has no meeting place, no supplies, and no money.
   They told us when they heard it, where they heard it, and from whom they heard it.
6. To separate two or more adjectives if they both precede or follow the noun they modify, provided each adjective modifies the noun alone. If an adjective modifies a combination of a noun and another adjective, however, no comma is used between the two adjectives.
   An old, shaggy, forlorn-looking dog came limping out to greet us.
   Happy young people come here frequently.
7. To set off words and phrases used in apposition.
   My cousin, whose name is Jean, will arrive soon.
8. To set off parenthetical words, clauses, or phrases.
   Tomorrow, on the other hand, business will be much better.
9. To set off words in direct address.
   Finally, children, we must all be ready when the time comes.
10. To set off *yes* or *no* when used in sentences.
    Yes, you may go now.
    Frankly, no, I don't care.

Appendix B

11. To set off the name of a state when it is used with a city.
    They lived in Denver, Colorado, for many years.
12. To separate the day of the month from the year and to set off the year when used with the month.
    The project must be completed by August 20, 1973, at the latest.
13. To set off a mild interjection.
    Ah, he surely enjoyed that story.
14. To set off a participial expression used as an adjective.
    Smiling pleasantly, she entered the office.
15. To separate unrelated numbers.
    In 1960, 25 new students enrolled.
16. To divide a number of four or more digits into groups of three, counting from right to left.
    1,567,039
17. To set off phrases that denote residence or position.
    Professor William Smith, of Harvard, will speak.
18. To indicate the omission of a word or words readily understood from the context.
    In June the book sales amounted to $523; in July, to $781.
19. Before a short, informal, direct quotation.
    The employer asked, "Have you transcribed those letters?"

Semicolon (;)

The semicolon is used

1. In a compound sentence between clauses that are not joined by a conjunction.
   That is good taste; it suggests discretion.
2. In a compound sentence if either clause contains one or more commas. The semicolon is placed before the conjunction.
   The rainy, windy weather made her cold; but she continued on her journey.
3. Before such words and abbreviations as *e.g.*, *i.e.*, *viz.*, *for example*, *namely*, and *to wit* when they introduce a long list of items. A comma precedes the list.
   Some pairs of words are bothersome to students; for example, affect and effect, loose and lose, sit and set.
4. Between elements in a listing when there are commas within the elements.
   James Craig, Newport High; William Parker, Forest Hills High; and Ken Caldwell, Jefferson High were the winners.

5. Before connectives when such words introduce sentences, principal clauses, or an abrupt change in thought. (The comma follows the connective when used in this manner only if the connective is to be emphasized.) Some of these connectives are *accordingly, consequently, hence, however, in fact, moreover, nevertheless, therefore, thus, whereas, yet.*
It is February; therefore, we have many holidays.

Colon (:)

The colon is used

1. To introduce formally a word, a list, a statement, or a question; a series of statements or questions; or a long quotation.
The book had many good points: it contained an interesting story; it contained humor; it was well illustrated.

2. Between hours and minutes when they are expressed in figures.
   8:30 a.m.   1:45 p.m.

3. After salutations in some styles of business letters:
Dear Sir: Gentlemen:

Question Mark (?)

1. The question mark is used after a direct question, but not after an indirect question.
Are you ready?
He asked what caused the fire.
    It is not necessary to use a question mark after a polite request.
Will you please let us know your decision at once.

2. The question mark is used to indicate uncertainty.
The applicant was born in 1952(?).

3. In a series, a question mark may follow each question if special emphasis is desired. When it is used in this way, it takes the place of the comma; and each element begins with a small letter.
Where is my pen? my notebook? my file?

Exclamation Point (!)

    Like the period, the exclamation point represents a full stop. It is used at the end of a thought expressing strong emotion or command. The thought may be represented by a complete sentence, a phrase, or a word.
    Ha! We caught you this time!

Apostrophe (')

1. To form possessives. There are several rules that govern the formation of the possessive case of words, depending on the final letter or syllable of the word and whether the word is singular or plural. A few important rules follow:

   (a) The possessive of singular and plural common and proper nouns not ending with the *s* or *z* sound (excepting *ce*) is usually formed by the addition of an apostrophe and *s* to the singular form.

   secretary's letter   women's hats
   Shaw's plays   Lawrence's mail

   (b) The possessive of singular and plural common nouns ending in *s* is formed by the addition of only the apostrophe.

   boys' hats   ladies' manners
   committees' reports

   (c) The possessive of a monosyllabic proper noun ending in an *s* or *z* sound is generally formed by the addition of an apostrophe and *s*, although in newspapers addition of only the apostrophe is frequently seen.

   Burns's poems   Marx's ideas
   Liz's book

   (d) The possessive of proper nouns of more than one syllable ending in an *s* or *z* sound (excepting *ce*) is formed by the addition of an apostrophe only.

   Essex' papers   Adams' chronicle
   Burroughs' house

   (e) The possessive of a compound word is formed by the addition of the apostrophe or the apostrophe and *s* [according to Rules (a), (b), and (c)] to its final syllable.

   mother-in-law's visit
   City of Detroit's council
   letter carrier's route
   passers-by's expressions

   (f) The possessive of a series of names connected by a conjunction showing joint ownership is indicated by the apostrophe or apostrophe and *s* to the last name.

   Simon and Walter's garage
   Adams and Anderson's firm

   (g) If joint ownership does not exist in a series of names, the possessive case is formed by the addition of an apostrophe or apostrophe and *s* to each proper name in the series.

   Macy's and Haynes's stores
   Jack's, Joe's, and Bill's gloves

(h) The possessive of abbreviated words is formed by the addition of an apostrophe and *s* to the last letter of the abbreviation.

YMCA's membership
the X's function
the Mr.'s position in the heading
the OK's presence

(i) The apostrophe is *not* used to form the possessive of pronouns.

2. To show contraction or the omission of figures.

don't (for *do not*)   Class of '67 (for *1967*)
it's (for *it is*)

3. To form the plurals of figures, letters, signs, and words.

If you have no *6's*, use *9's* turned upside down.
Her *v's* and *u's* and *T's* and *F's* are too much alike.
The +'s and —'s denoted whether the sentences were correct or not.
There were too many *and's* and *the's* in the essay.

4. Followed by a *d* to form the past tense of arbitrarily coined verbs.

She OK'd the copy.
He X'd out three lines.

Dash (—)

The dash is formed in typewriting by the striking of two hyphens without a space preceding or following them. The dash is used

1. To indicate a change in the sense or the construction of a sentence.
Hemingway, Wolfe, Greene — these are my favorites.

2. Instead of a comma to emphasize or to guard against confusing the reader.
The laborer is worthy of his hire — if his labor is.
If — and only if — we go, the day will be complete.

3. To indicate an omission of letters.
Mr. K—, of P—Street

4. To precede a reference.
No, the heart that has truly loved never forgets.—Moore.

Parentheses ( )

Parentheses are used

1. To enclose figures or letters that mark a series of enumerated elements.

She wanted three things: (1) a promotion, (2) a salary increase, and (3) more responsibility.

2. To enclose figures verifying a number which is written in words.

   twenty (20) dollars
   twenty dollars ($20)

3. To enclose material that is indirectly related to the main thought of a sentence.

   We shall postpone (at least for the present) a decision.

4. To enclose matter introduced as an explanation.

   The answer (see page 200) is puzzling.

The rules covering the use of other marks of punctuation with parentheses are:

1. If needed in the sentence, a comma or dash that normally precedes a parenthetic element is transferred to follow the closing parenthesis.

   He sent a belated, though clever (and somewhat personal), greeting.

2. Punctuation at the end of a parenthetic expression *precedes* the parenthesis if it applies to the parenthetic material only; it *follows* the parenthesis if it applies to the sentence as a whole.

   When I heard him (he shouted, "Who goes there?"), I was surprised.
   (See the discussion on page 78.)
   This experiment had interesting results (see Table I).

Brackets [ ]

Brackets are used

1. To enclose a correction, an addition, or a comment which a writer inserts in matter he is quoting.

   "In 1942 [a typographical error for 1492] Columbus discovered America."

2. To enclose the term *sic*, Latin for *thus*, to show that a misspelling or some other error appeared in the original and is not an error by the one quoting.

   In applying for the job he wrote, "I am very good in atheletics [*sic*], and I can teach mathmatics [*sic*]."

3. When it is necessary to place a parenthesis within a parenthesis; but, in general, such complicated usages should be avoided.

   At 3:30 p.m. (the time agreed upon at the conference [see John Coleman's letter of April 9]) the announcement of the new salary agreement was made to the news media.

Quotation Marks (" ")

Quotation marks are used

1. To enclose direct quotations. Single quotation marks are used to enclose a quotation within a quotation.

    The director said, "I hope you are familar with this play."
    She said, "Unkind as it may be, I can't help saying 'I told you so' to her."

2. To enclose the titles of articles, lectures, reports, etc., and the titles of subdivisions of publications (that is, the titles of parts, chapters, etc.). The titles of books and magazines are not enclosed in quotation marks, but underscored or typed in all capital letters.

    She thought the chapter "Producing Mailable Transcripts" was helpful.

3. To enclose unusual, peculiar, or slang terms.

    Her "five o'clocks" were famous.
    When they saw us, they "flipped."

4. To enclose words used in some special sense, or words to which attention is directed in order to make a meaning clear.

    He said "yes," not "guess."
    The term "title by possession" is often used.

5. To enclose the titles of short poems, songs, and televison and radio shows.

    "Trees" (poem)
    "Fire and Rain" (song)
    "Bonanza" (TV show)
    "Arthur Godfrey Time" (radio show)
    "Lowell Thomas and the News" (radio show)

6. When consecutive paragraphs of the same work are quoted, at the beginning of each paragraph but at the end of only the last paragraph.

Quoted Matter. When quoted matter appears within a letter, an article, or a report, it is advisable that it be indicated as a quotation. This may be done in three ways:

1. The material may be indented from the regular margins on the left and right.

2. It may be underscored throughout.

3. It may be enclosed in quotation marks.

Sometimes the quoted matter is both indented and enclosed in quotation marks. The practice of using quotation marks is the most widely used.

A long quotation is single-spaced, even though the rest of the copy is double-spaced.

Quotation Marks with Other Marks of Punctuation. At the end of quoted material, a quotation mark and another mark of punctuation are often used together. The rules governing the order of these marks are not entirely logical; but since they are well established and generally accepted, you should follow them.

1. A period or a comma should precede the quotation mark even though it may not be a part of the quotation.
   "I saw you," he said, "when you left."

2. A semicolon or colon should follow the closing quotation mark, even though it may be a part of the quotation.
   Mary, Ruth, and John visited that "house of antiques"; and the "antiques" were really unusual.
   There is this to say about his "mission": it is fictitious.

3. Other marks of punctuation should precede the closing quotation mark if they apply to the quotation only, and should follow the mark if they apply to the sentence as a whole and not just to the quotation.
   She asked, "Will you go?"
   Did you read the article "Better Sales Letters"?

Spacing after Punctuation Marks. *One* space is left after punctuation marks within a sentence, with the exception of the colon. *Two* spaces are left after colons and all punctuation marks at the ends of sentences.

Exceptions to the basic rules above are that you do *not* space after:

1. A period used within an abbreviation written in small letters.
   a.m., etc., e.g., i.e.

2. A period used as a decimal point within a series of figures.
   3.111, 10.5

3. A comma used to separate a number into groups of three.
   1,268,749

4. An apostrophe written within a word.
   don't

5. The first punctuation mark when two marks are used together.
   "Why not?"

Italics (The Underscore). A typist can emphasize an important word, phrase, or sentence in typewritten material in several ways. The kind of copy and the purpose for which it is being typed determine to some extent the relative emphasis that should be indicated.

In typewriting, underscoring takes the place of printed italics and is the method most often used to give prominence to a word or group of words.

Emphasis is also achieved by typing in red in the midst of copy typed in black or blue, and by making characters darker by typing over them several times.

In addition to emphasizing a word or words, the underscore (italics) should be used

1. To refer to a word or letter taken out of its context.
    Always dot your <u>i's</u>, and cross your <u>t's</u>.
    Do not write <u>and</u> and <u>the</u> slantwise across the line.
2. To designate a foreign word not yet anglicized.
    Her <u>faux pas</u> was noticeable.
3. To indicate titles of plays, motion pictures, musical compositions, paintings, art objects, books, pamphlets, newspapers, and magazines. (Parts of these, such as chapters in a book or articles in a magazine or newspaper, are designated by quotation marks.)
    Have you seen <u>My Fair Lady</u>?
    El Greco's <u>View of Toledo</u> was on display at the museum.
    We also saw Rodin's <u>The Thinker</u>.
    She found Unit 8, "The Secretary and the Public," in <u>Secretarial Office Procedures</u> very helpful.
    The <u>Wall Street Journal</u> contains a regular feature entitled "Washington Wire."
4. To designate the names of ships, airplanes, and spacecraft.
    U.S.N.S. <u>Nautilus</u>
    Lindbergh's <u>Spirit of St. Louis</u>
    <u>Apollo 15</u>

APPENDIX C
WORD CHOICE AND SPELLING

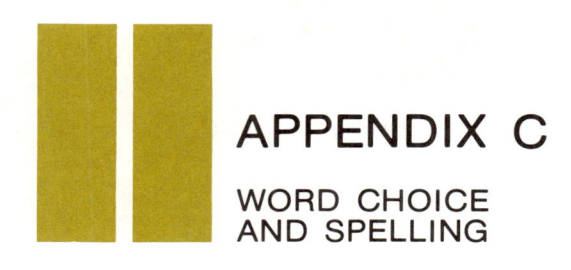

Words are constantly of concern to the secretary. She must know their spelling, their meaning, their appropriateness. Therefore, a secretary must maintain a continuous vigilance over the words she chooses. The competent secretary never becomes indifferent to words. For, if she does, she will soon be letting misspelled words slip by as she proofreads her copy; she will allow words that are not precise for the meaning intended to remain in the copy; and she will soon be guilty of inadequate communication skills.

A dictionary is a regularly used reference by the alert secretary. Become acquainted with your dictionary. Learn to understand all abbreviations that are used. Your dictionary will dispel uncertainties about proper spelling and meanings of words.

Good Usage

To convey messages precisely, it is important that you use words that conform to current good usage. *Colloquialisms*, which are words and phrases that are acceptable in informal conversations and sometimes in letters, are not considered good usage in formal business correspondence. *Provincialisms*, which are terms that are used informally in particular areas of the country, are also to be avoided in formal communications. *Archaic* and *obsolete* words, which are words that were once standard, are no longer in fashion and should be avoided.

Below is a list of *colloquialisms* that should be avoided in business communications.

Incorrect in Formal Writing	*Correct in Formal Writing*
all-round (adj.)	generally serviceable
around	about, nearly
back of, in back of	behind, at the back of
bit	a short time, a little while
calculate	think, plan, expect
cute	clever, amusing
enthuse	enthusiastic
get hold of	to learn, to master
have got to	must, have to

Incorrect in Formal Writing	Correct in Formal Writing
lots of	many, much
most	almost, nearly
not a one	not one
off of	off
over with	finished, done
quite some time	a long time
show up	arrive
stand for	allow, stand

Some *provincialisms* which may fail to convey meaning when used outside a local area, and which should be avoided, are shown below.

Use	Rather than
declare, maintain	allow
raise	rear
short distance	piece
think, suppose, guess	reckon
want to come in	want in
you	you all

Archaic and *obsolete words* that require translation before the meaning is clear should not be used in modern communications — for example:

assoil	(which means absolve)
bespeak	(to address)
damsel	(a young maid of gentle birth)
eke	(to increase, to enlarge)
perchance	(by chance, perhaps)
quoth	(said)
withal	(together with this, besides)

Words That Are Pronounced Alike.

Words that are pronounced alike but differ in meaning are called *homonyms*. These words are often confusing and require close attention to the meaning of the sentence so that the correct word is used.

Some typical homonyms are:

aid, aide	hoard, horde
aisle, isle	incite, insight
allowed, aloud	knew, new
altar, alter	lead, led
bare, bear	lean, lien
bases, basis	loose, lose
berth, birth	right, rite, wright, write
brake, break	role, roll
creak, creek	through, threw
elusive, illusive	ware, wear, where

Words That Are Not Pronounced Alike

There are many words that should not be pronounced alike but often sound alike. Frequently used words of this type include those listed below. Are you able to distinguish the meaning of each?

accept, except	assent, ascent
adapt, adept, adopt	formerly, formally
allusion, illusion	council, counsel
addition, edition	instance, instants
affect, effect	local, locale
carton, cartoon	patience, patients
contend, contest	test, text
costume, custom	personal, personnel
all ways, always	stationery, stationary

Compound Words

In the regular routine of daily business, one class of words that gives considerable trouble is made up of compound words. Compound words fall into three groups: hyphenated compounds, single-word compounds, and two-word compounds.

There are a few rules that will assist you in becoming familiar with certain groups of compound words that use the hyphen.

1. A hyphen is always used in a compound number.

    twenty-one, fifty-eight

2. A hyphen is used between the numerator and the denominator of a fraction written in words, except (a) when one of of the elements contains a hyphen and (b) when the fraction is used as a noun.

    four-fifths share   forty-one hundredths
    two-thirds interest   forty one-hundredths
         one half of the total
         two fifths of the class

3. A hyphen is used between two or more words when the words serve as a single adjective *before* a noun. In applying this rule you must be careful that the words are not a series of independent adjectives. The exception to the rule is that proper nouns made up of two or more words are not hyphenated when used as adjectives.

    a well-liked boy, *but* a boy well liked
    a fresh-water fish, *but* a fish from fresh water
    a New England dinner, a New Jersey product
    a large black horse; a deep, clear pool

4. Groups of three or more words used as a single word are usually hyphenated.

    four-in-hand, well-to-do, sister-in-law, up-to-date

Word Choice and Spelling

5. A hyphen is used after a prefix
   (a) when the prefix is joined to a proper noun
   (b) to prevent confusion between some verbs and a few compounds
   (c) to prevent an awkward piling up of consonants

   Ordinarily, however, a prefix is written as a part of the main word.

   pro-English, re-form (meaning to form again), re-sign (meaning to sign again), bell-like

When *any*, *every*, *no*, and *some* are combined with other words, the compound is a single word: *anything, everyone, nowhere, somehow*. Sometimes, however, the parts of the compound expression are written as separate words: *no one, every one*.

A great many compounds are not covered by these rules. When in doubt, consult a good dictionary. The following compounds are used frequently and therefore deserve attention:

Hyphenated Compounds

by-line　　　　　　　　man-hours
by-product　　　　　　self-confidence
cross-reference　　　　vice-president

Single-Word Compounds

billboard　　　　　　　network
bondholder　　　　　　nevertheless
bookkeeper　　　　　　northeast
bylaws　　　　　　　　notwithstanding
checkbook　　　　　　outgoing
guesswork　　　　　　overdue
handwriting　　　　　overhead
headline　　　　　　　payday
headquarters　　　　　payroll
henceforth　　　　　　policyholder
hereafter　　　　　　　postcard
laborsaving　　　　　　postmarked
letterhead　　　　　　takeoff
meantime　　　　　　　trademark
middlemen　　　　　　viewpoint

Two-Word Compounds

account book　　　　　income tax
bank note　　　　　　　parcel post
card index　　　　　　price list
cash account　　　　　trade union
civil service　　　　　vice versa

Appendix C

The Plural Forms of Words

Some words exist in only the plural form (*annals, news, thanks*), and other words are the same in both the singular and the plural forms (*deer, corps, chassis*). Still other words are irregular in form (*man, men; child, children; foot, feet*). Generally speaking, however, the plural of a word is formed by adding *s* if the plural has the same number of syllables as the singular; or *es* if the plural has an extra syllable. An exception to this rule is found in some words ending in *o* (*motto, mottoes; potato, potatoes*), although other words ending in *o* follow the rule (*piano, pianos; folio, folios; cameo, cameos*).

You will find the following rules for the forming of plural words helpful.

1. Form the plurals of nouns ending with *y* preceded by a consonant by dropping the *y* and adding *ies*. When the *y* is preceded by a vowel, add *s* only.

   lady, ladies   alley, alleys
   salary, salaries   lawyer, lawyers
   story, stories   turkey, turkeys

2. Form the plural of a hyphenated compound noun by changing the principal word of the compound from singular to plural. The principal word of a compound is not always the last word.

   sisters-in-law, cross-purposes, passers-by

3. Form the plural of a single-word compound by adding *s* to the end of the word.

   cupfuls, viewpoints, headquarters

4. The plurals of some words of foreign origin are formed in accordance with the rules of the language from which they are derived.

   axis, axes   datum, data
   alumnus, alumni   alumna, alumnae

5. A few words of foreign origin have both foreign and English plural forms. In some cases, one form is preferred over the other (*strata* instead of *stratums*); while in other cases both forms are considered equally acceptable (*indexes* and *indices, memorandums* and *memoranda*). Consult a dictionary for the preferred usage of plural words of foreign origin.

6. Two persons bearing the same name and title may be referred to in the following manner: *The Messrs. Haviland, The Misses McKenzie, The Doctors Butler,* or *The Mr. Havilands, The Miss McKenzies, The Doctor Butlers.* In formal and business language, the plural form of the title is preferred.

7. The plurals of letters, noun-coinages, proper nouns of more than one syllable ending in a sibilant, and words used as

words only are formed by the addition of an apostrophe and *s*.

p's and *q*'s   Her I-don't-care's were . . .
the and's   The Curtises' house . . .

Word Division

Frequently a word must be divided at the end of a line in order to keep the right margin even. Words should be divided only between syllables. In case of doubt, consult a dictionary. The following rules apply to typewritten copy.

1. When a final consonant preceded by a single vowel is doubled before addition of a suffix, divide the word between the two consonants (prefer-*r*ing, program-*m*ing).
2. A single-letter syllable at the beginning or the end of a word should not be separated from the remainder of the word (*above* not *a-bove*).
3. A two-letter syllable at the end of a word should not be separated from the rest of the word (*calmly* not *calm-ly*).
4. A syllable that does not contain a vowel should not be separated from the rest of the word (*couldn't* not *could-n't*).
5. Hyphenated words should be divided only at the hyphens (*follow-up* not *fol-low-up*).
6. A four-letter word should not be divided; it is seldom permissible to divide five- or six-letter words (*into* not *in-to*), (*camel* not *cam-el*), (*never* not *nev-er*).
7. When a word containing three or more syllables is to be divided at a one-letter syllable, the one-letter syllable should be written on the first line rather than on the second line (*maga-zine* not *mag-azine*).
8. When a word is to be divided at a point where two vowels that are pronounced separately come together, these vowels should be divided into separate syllables (*continu-ation* not *continua-tion*).
9. Compound words are preferably divided between the elements of the compound (*turn-over* not *turno-ver*).
10. Proper names should not be divided; and titles, initials, or degrees should not be separated from names (*President* not *Pres-ident*).

Spelling

Learning to spell correctly requires becoming so familiar with words that you use again and again that you are able to spell them without giving special thought to them. It also means that you should continue to question how you have spelled a word until you are *absolutely* sure of its accuracy. A dictionary will be an important aid in determining whether what you guessed as the right spelling is indeed right. If you find that certain words cause you difficulty frequently, you should make a list of them and take some time to study them so that in the future you will have no uncertainty about them.

There are some spelling rules that will guide you in determining the correct spelling of many words.

1. To spell words containing *ei* or *ie* pronounced like *ee*, use *ie* after any letter except *c*.

belief	grievance
chief	lien
expedient	relieve
field	reprieve
frieze	siege

   Use *ei* after *c*.

ceiling	perceive
conceive	receipt
deceive	

   Exceptions:

either	seize
neither	leisure

2. A final *e* is usually dropped before a suffix beginning with a vowel, unless doing so would change the pronounciation or meaning of the word.

bride, bridal	hope, hoping
force, forcible	manage, managing
college, collegiate	subdue, subduing

   Exceptions:
   dye, dyeing
   change, changeable
   courage, courageous

3. The final *e* is usually retained before a suffix beginning with a consonant.

lone, lonely	hate, hateful
move, movement	pale, paleness

   Exceptions:

judge, judgment	argue, argument

4. Before the suffix *ing*, *ie* is changed to *y*.

die, dying	lie, lying

5. A final double consonant is retained before a suffix.

will, willful	odd, oddly
ebb, ebbing	

6. Usually the final consonant is doubled in words of one syllable, or words ending in a single consonant preceded by

a single vowel with the accent on the last syllable, before a suffix beginning with a vowel.

occur, occurred refer, referring
begin, beginning plan, planned

Exceptions:
fix, fixed refer, reference

7. The final *y* preceded by a consonant is usually changed to *i* before a suffix not beginning with *i*.

    worry, worried happy, happiness

    Exceptions:
    shy, shyness beauty, beauteous

8. The final *y* preceded by a vowel is usually retained before any suffix or the letter *s*.

    annoy, annoyance buy, buyer
    delay, delayed pay, payable
    journey, journeys attorney, attorneys

9. The final *l* is always single in words ending in *ful*.

    careful hopeful
    doubtful regretful

10. Only one word ends in *sede* — *supersede*; only three words end in *ceed* — *exceed, proceed,* and *succeed*; all other words having this sound end in *cede* — *concede, intercede, precede, secede.*

11. When *i* and *e* come together in the same syllable, generally *i* is used before *e*.

12. Avoid dividing words at the end of more than two successive lines, at the end of a page, or at the end of the last complete line of a paragraph.

13. Avoid awkward or misleading divisions that may cause difficulty in reading (*carry-ing* not *car-rying*).

14. When the single-letter syllable *a, i,* or *u* is followed by *ble, bly, cle,* or *cal*, do not separate the single-letter syllable and the suffix.

15. Avoid the division of figures and abbreviations, the parts of an address or date. If it is necessary to separate an address, keep together the number and street name, the city and ZIP Code.

    2143 Market   *not*   2143
    Street   Market Street

    In separating a date, leave the day with the month.

    March 3,   *not*   March
    197–   3, 197–

Appendix C

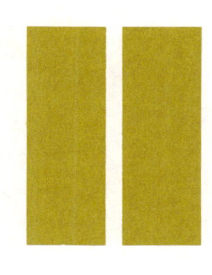

APPENDIX D

ABBREVIATIONS

Abbreviations are abridged contractions. They provide a means of conserving the space required for words and phrases. With the extensive use of computers and related equipment, there has developed the need for the use of more abbreviations than was true at an earlier time. The use of abbreviations is guided by custom and equipment restrictions. A general rule that continues to be followed is that abbreviations are used sparingly in correspondence. Abbreviations, on the other hand, are common in the typing of forms, such as invoices and statements, where there are space limitations.

Abbreviations of Proper Names

For proper names there are generally accepted rules to be followed.

1. A person's family name should never be abbreviated. Given names may be represented by initials, but it is desirable for others to conform to a person's own style or signature. For example, if a person signs his name *Henry R. Grimm*, it is good form for others to write his name that way, rather than *H. R. Grimm*. As a general rule, given names such as *Charles* or *William* should not be abbreviated to *Chas.* or *Wm.*, unless the person himself uses the abbreviation so consistently that it is obvious that it is the spelling he prefers.

2. Names of cities, with the exception of those containing the word *Saint* (*St.*), should not be abbreviated.

3. As a general rule, names of states and territories should be spelled out. For general correspondence, the United States Postal Service has no approved abbreviations for Alaska, Idaho, Iowa, Hawaii, Maine, Ohio, and Utah. Other states and territories *may* be abbreviated as follows:

Ala.	Alabama
Ariz.	Arizona
Ark.	Arkansas
Calif.	California
C. Z.	Canal Zone
Colo.	Colorado
Conn.	Connecticut
D. C.	District of Columbia
Del.	Delaware

Fla.	Florida
Ga.	Georgia
Ill.	Illinois
Ind.	Indiana
Kans.	Kansas
Ky.	Kentucky
La.	Louisiana
Md.	Maryland
Mass.	Massachusetts
Mich.	Michigan
Minn.	Minnesota
Miss.	Mississippi
Mo.	Missouri
Mont.	Montana
N. H.	New Hampshire
N. J.	New Jersey
N. Mex. (or N. M.)	New Mexico
N. Y.	New York
N. C.	North Carolina
N. Dak. (or N. D.)	North Dakota
Nebr. (or Neb.)	Nebraska
Nev.	Nevada
Okla.	Oklahoma
Oreg. (or Ore.)	Oregon
P. R.	Puerto Rico
Pa. (or Penna. or Penn.)	Pennsylvania
R. I.	Rhode Island
S. C.	South Carolina
S. Dak. (or S. D.)	South Dakota
Tenn.	Tennessee
Tex.	Texas
Vt.	Vermont
Va.	Virginia
V. I.	Virgin Islands
Wash.	Washington
W. Va.	West Virginia
Wis. (or Wisc.)	Wisconsin
Wyo.	Wyoming

4. The United States Postal Service has issued an approved list of two-letter all-capital state abbreviations to be used with ZIP Codes. These abbreviations should not be used without the ZIP Codes.

Alabama	AL
Alaska	AK
Arizona	AZ
Arkansas	AR
California	CA
Canal Zone	CZ

Colorado	CO
Connecticut	CT
Delaware	DE
District of Columbia	DC
Florida	FL
Georgia	GA
Guam	GU
Hawaii	HI
Idaho	ID
Illinois	IL
Indiana	IN
Iowa	IA
Kansas	KS
Kentucky	KY
Louisiana	LA
Maine	ME
Maryland	MD
Massachusetts	MA
Michigan	MI
Minnesota	MN
Mississippi	MS
Missouri	MO
Montana	MT
Nebraska	NE
Nevada	NV
New Hampshire	NH
New Jersey	NJ
New Mexico	NM
New York	NY
North Carolina	NC
North Dakota	ND
Ohio	OH
Oklahoma	OK
Oregon	OR
Pennsylvania	PA
Puerto Rico	PR
Rhode Island	RI
South Carolina	SC
South Dakota	SD
Tennessee	TN
Texas	TX
Utah	UT
Vermont	VT
Virginia	VA
Virgin Islands	VI
Washington	WA
West Virginia	WV
Wisconsin	WI
Wyoming	WY

Abbreviations in the Body of a Letter

The shortening of words in the body of a letter can convey a lack of care and time in presenting an attractive, thoughtful message. One should not write: The advt. can be supplied for your dept. @ 50¢ per p. It would be better to say: The advertisement can be supplied for your department at the rate of 50 cents per page.

Abbreviations may be used in the body of a letter when they have become commonly recognized symbols, such as SEC, FTC, CIO, and YMCA. A letter should be understood rather than made to follow a single practice. If, therefore, a letter is written to someone who may not understand an abbreviation it is better to spell it out in the first sentence of its use so that the reader understands the term when it later appears in abbreviated form. For example, the complete term *Securities and Exchange Commission* may be used first; then, in subsequent references, the abbreviation SEC may be used if the document is not a formal one.

Frequently used abbreviations are listed in the dictionary. Each field of work has developed specialized abbreviations, and secretaries learn these when they begin work in a new office.

Periods in Abbreviations

The tendency seems to be to drop the periods from an abbreviation when it is commonly recognized and does not require the periods for clarity. For example, NBC, SEC, and FTC are written without periods and without spaces between the letters. The omission of a period in some abbreviations, however, might be confusing. For example, without the periods, *in.* for *inch* might be mistaken for the preposition; *a.m.* for *morning* might be confused with the verb form. If, in order to avoid confusion, periods are used with an abbreviation, such as *a.m.*, they should also be used in *p.m.* in order to maintain a consistent style.

Abbreviations with Numbers

The abbreviations *st*, *d*, and *th* should not follow the day of the month when it is preceded by the name of the month. Correct usage is

He was planning to leave on the 21st of August.
He leaves for London on August 21.
Mr. Smith went to Los Angeles on the 3d of July.

In enumerations, it is better to write first, second, third rather than 1st, 2d, 3d. The abbreviations *st*, *d*, and *th* do not require the use of a period.

Diagonal Lines in Abbreviations

The use of the diagonal signifies the omission of such words as *per*, *of*, *to*, *upon*. In abbreviated forms, including the diagonal, the period is not usually

Appendix D

used, as in *B/L*. The period is sometimes retained, however, in three- or four-word combinations, as *lb./sq. ft.*

Plurals of Abbreviations

Most plural forms of abbreviations are formed by adding *s* to the singular form. The singular and the plural forms of some abbreviations, however, are the same.

(plural) chgs., lbs.
(singular and plural) cwt., deg., ft., in., oz.

Several plural forms of abbreviations are double single letters.

pp. for pages, ll. for lines.

Plurals of capitalized abbreviations may be formed simply by adding a small *s*. Apostrophe *s* may be added to form the plurals of abbreviations composed of letters (capital and small), signs, and symbols. There is no definite rule, however, that completely governs all cases that may arise.

YMCAs, a.m.s, IOU's, P's, Q's, 6's, FOB's, OK's, #'s.

Coined Verbs

Often an abbreviation is used as a verb in informal correspondence. To make the necessary change, an apostrophe may be added with *s*, *d*, or *ing* to the abbreviation.

OK'd

Possessives of Abbreviations

Generally the singular possessive is formed by adding the apostrophe and *s*, as *Jr.'s, RR's, Sr.'s, SOS's*.

The plural possessive is formed by adding an apostrophe to abbreviations whose plural forms end in *s*, as *Jrs.', Drs.'*.

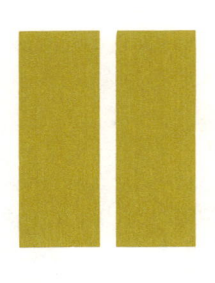

APPENDIX E
TITLES, CAPITALIZATION, AND NUMBERS

Titles

The use of titles is governed by customs that are accepted by the people of a given society. A secretary should learn the correct titles of the persons with whom she associates. There is one principle for the use of titles in oral communication that should always be remembered: *Never use a title alone.* For example, a person who holds a Ph.D. should never be addressed as *Doctor.* The proper address is *Doctor Jones.* Current practice governing the use of titles in writing follows.

Birthright Titles. The title of *Mr., Miss,* or *Mrs.* is customary for adults who have no other title.

Mr. is used before the name of a man who has no other title. *Messrs.,* the abbreviation of *Messieurs* (French for *gentlemen*), is the plural of *Mr.*

Mrs. is the title given to married women and usually to widows. A married woman is usually addressed by her husband's name, as *Mrs. John Brown.* A widowed woman may be addressed by her Christian name, such as *Mrs. Helen Brown,* or by her deceased husband's name, such as *Mrs. John Brown,* whichever she prefers. With the names of two or more married women, the title *Mesdames,* or its abbreviation, *Mmes,* is used, as *Mmes Clark, Wright,* and *Grant.*

Miss is the correct title for an unmarried girl or woman. If there is doubt as to whether the person is married, it is a good policy to use *Miss* or the abbreviation *Ms.,* until her marital status is ascertained. *Misses* is the plural of *Miss,* as the *Misses Alice Henderson* and *Dorothy Jones.*

Doctor. *Dr.* is the title of one who holds any one of the various doctors' degrees. It is usually abbreviated. When two doctors are being addressed, the word *Doctors* or the abbreviation *Drs.* may be used. Since there are so many different types of doctors, doctors of medicine and dentistry frequently use the degree letters after their names and no title preceding, as *Frank B. Dana, M.D.* This practice, of course, could be used by anyone possessing a doctor's degree.

Reverend. This title is properly carried by a minister, priest, or rector. The abbreviation *Rev.* is commonly used, although it is considered better usage to write the word in full. Ordinarily when a person with this title is *spoken* of, the word *the* precedes his title and given name or initials. More than one *Reverend* may be addressed as *Reverend Messrs.* or the repetition of the word *Reverend* before each name.

Abbreviated Titles Following Personal Names. *Senior* and *Junior*, the distinction between a father and son of exactly the same name, are written after the name as the abbreviations *Sr.* and *Jr.* The abbreviation is capitalized, followed by a period, and usually separated from the name by a comma. *Second* and *Third*, the distinction between members of the same family or close relatives whose names are the same, are indicated by the abbreviations *2d* and *3d*, or by the Roman numerals, *II* or *III*. The former style is now more common. Note that these abbreviations are not followed by a period, but they may be separated from the name by a comma.

The abbreviation *Esq.* is used after a gentleman's name in England. In this country it is rarely used. When it is used, the title *Mr.* is omitted.

Double Titles. A title may be used both before and after a person's name if the two titles have different meanings, but two titles that indicate the same honor or degree should not be used. For example, it is correct to say *Dr. H. C. Samuel, Moderator*, but not *Dr. H. C. Samuel, M.D.*

Titles in Addresses and Salutations. Except for *Mr.*, *Mrs.*, and *Dr.*, all titles used in the addresses and salutations of letters are better written in full. Abbreviations, however, are not uncommon. Whenever you are in doubt, type the title in full. No one will be offended by seeing his title in full.

The correct titles and salutations to be used for federal and state officials, educators, and churchmen are given in Appendix F. Whenever you are unsure of a title or salutation, refer to an authoritative source.

Capitalization

A good dictionary is an excellent source for determining practices in capitalization that are most acceptable. A person who must refer to the dictionary for the most elementary information of this type, however, consumes much time. An understanding of the purpose for and a knowledge of the principles of capitalization should be a part of the training of a secretary.

One of the purposes of capitalization is to designate the names or titles of specific things, positions, or persons. Overuse of capitalization, however, tends to detract from the effectiveness of the written matter.

The following are the most common rules of capitalization:

1. Every sentence begins with a capital letter.
2. The pronoun *I* and the interjection *O* are always capitalized.
3. The salutation and the complimentary close of a letter begin with capitals.
4. The days of the week, holidays, and the months of the year are capitalized.
5. All important words in the titles of the main agencies of a government begin with capital letters.
6. Direct quotations begin with a capital letter.

Business Titles and Positions. Titles are capitalized when they immediately precede or follow individual names and are directly related to them, or when they refer to specific persons.

>President W. L. Matthews will speak.
>Mr. R. Hubert McGraw, Jr., Vice-President, Investors Corporation
>Mr. Samuel Jones is Executive Secretary and Treasurer of Hammett Co.

Business titles are not capitalized when they do not refer to specific persons.

>Three men have been president of this company.
>A treasurer will be elected at the meeting tomorrow.

Geographic Names. Names of countries, cities, rivers, bays, mountains, islands, commonly recognized names given to regions of countries, and sections of cities are capitalized.

>Ohio River, Pacific Ocean, Union County, Harlem, the Great Plains, the Mississippi Valley

A geographic term such as *river*, *ocean*, *county*, *city*, and *street* that is not a part of the name but is used before the name, or a geographic term that is used in the plural, should not be capitalized.

>the river Danube
>county of Hamilton
>the city of San Diego
>the Atlantic and Pacific Oceans
>at the corner of Grant and Lee streets

Points of the compass designating specific geographic sections of the country are capitalized.

>the South, the Midwest, the Northwest

The points of the compass that merely indicate direction are not capitalized.

>South Dakota is south of North Dakota.
>The wind is coming from the west.

A noun that refers to the inhabitants of a particular part of the country is capitalized.

>Westerners, a Southerner, a New Englander

Proper names denoting political divisions are always capitalized.

>British Empire, Ward 13, Platt Township, the Papal States

Words before Figures. With the exception of *page*, *line*, and *verse*, words used in connection with figures in typewritten references are usually capitalized. It is important that one rule be followed consistently. If the word *figure* is capitalized when followed by a number in one place, it should be capitalized in all other places in the text.

Chapter XV   Division 3
Figure 8   page iii

Individual Names. Capitalize all names of individuals, except some surname prefixes. *Von, du, van,* or *de,* as a part of a surname, might not be capitalized, depending upon how the person uses it himself, unless it begins a sentence or stands alone within a sentence (that is, is not preceded by a given name or title).

Charles de Gaulle *but* De Gaulle
George Louis du Maurier *but* Du Maurier

Hyphenated Words. In general, there are three rules that govern the capitalization of the parts of a hyphenated word.

1. If both parts of a hyphenated word would ordinarily be capitalized when written alone, then both parts should be capitalized in the hyphenated word.
   Senate-House debate
   Spanish-American War

2. In a heading or title, it is permissible to capitalize the parts of a compound word to conform to a general style.
   Forty-Second Street   Mid-January Sales

3. In straight text material, the manner in which a word is used determines the part of a compound word that should be capitalized.
   Thirty-first Street   anti-Nazi
   mid-January   pro-British
   Treasurer-elect   French-speaking
   ex-President   pre-Pueblo

Headings and Titles of Articles and Reports. Only the first word and important words in headings or titles — nouns, pronouns, verbs, adverbs, and adjectives — are capitalized. Short, unimportant words are not capitalized. Examples of such words are the conjunctions *and*, *but*, and *or*; the articles *a*, *an*, and *the*; and the prepositions *of*, *in*, *to*, and *but*. If the word needs to be stressed, however, it may be capitalized. Frequently long prepositions such as *between*, *after*, *before*, and *among* are capitalized.

Numbers

Numbers can be written as figures or as words. Although figures are used almost exclusively in business forms, both figures and words are used in letters and other types of transcripts that are written in sentence and paragraph form. If there are two or more ways in which an amount can be expressed, it is usually written in the way that requires the fewest words. A number such as 1,300 is written as *thirteen hundred* rather than *one thousand three hundred*. The following rules specify the proper usage in writing numbers.

Numbers at the Beginning of a Sentence. A number that begins a sentence should be spelled out, even though other numbers are expressed in figures in the same sentence. It is wise, therefore, to avoid beginning a sentence with a large number that is cumbersome in words.

Amounts of Money. Amounts of money, except in legal documents, should be written in figures. Amounts less than one dollar are written in figures with the word *cents* following. In writing even sums of money, the decimal and ciphers are omitted.

> We enclose our check for $21.75.
> He paid 22 cents for the paper.
> He will pay $125 for the painting.

Round Numbers. Round numbers are spelled out, unless such numbers are used with others that cannot be expressed conveniently in words.

> We have fifty employees.
> We have 50 salesmen in our group of 295 employees.

Dates. Except in formal or legal writing, the day of the month and the year are usually written in figures. When a date appears in the body of a letter, the year is customarily omitted if it is the same as that which appears in the date line. It is unnecessary to use *st*, *d*, or *th* in dates, unless the day is written before or is separated from the month.

> the 3d of June
> in July, either the 3d or 4th

Streets. It is considered good form to use words for the names of streets that are numbers that are ten or less; figures should be used for numbers above ten. When the name of the street is a number that is written in figures, it is separated from the number of the building by a dash. If the street name is preceded by one of the words *South*, *North*, *East*, or *West*, that word should not be abbreviated.

Tenth Street	Fifth Avenue
72 — 125th Street	72 Fifth Avenue
19 West 115th Street	173rd Street
22 West 110th Street	1 West 12th Street

Time of Day. The abbreviations *p.m.* and *a.m.* may be written in capital or small letters but should be used only with figures. The hour is spelled in full when *o'clock* is used.

> School starts at 8:30 a.m.
> He will leave the office at four o'clock.
> 12 midnight is written 12 p.m. or 12 P.M.
> 12 noon is written 12N. (12M, while correct for 12 noon, can be mistaken for 12 midnight.)

Measurements. Practically all measurements are written in figures.

> Size 7½ AA shoe   12-gal. bottle

Fractions and Decimals. Common fractions appearing alone are spelled out in ordinary reading matter. Mixed numbers are written as figures. Decimals are always expressed in figures.

Miscellaneous Usage. Sessions of Congress and the identifying numbers of various military bodies, political divisions, and dynasties are always written in words.

   the Thirty-sixth Congress Sixteenth Infantry
   Thirteenth Ward

The result of a ballot is written in figures.

   The count was 34 in favor of the motion, 36 against it.

Page, chapter, section, and footnote numbers are always written in figures.

   pp. 45–67   Section 7
   [2]Hawley, J.   Chapter 9

When two numbers immediately follow each other, it is better that the smaller one be spelled out and the larger one be expressed in figures.

   125 two-cent stamps Five 100-dollar bills

Unrelated groups of figures that come together should be separated by commas. Hundreds should be divided from thousands by a comma except in dates, policy numbers, street numbers, and telephone numbers.

   In 1970, 417,296 gallons were sold.

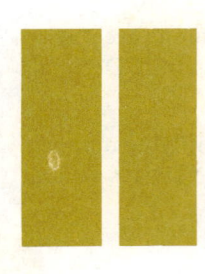

APPENDIX F
SPECIAL FORMS OF ADDRESS, SALUTATIONS, AND COMPLIMENTARY CLOSINGS

Appendix F lists the correct forms of address with appropriate salutations and complimentary closings for the following special groups:

    United States Government officials
    Diplomatic representatives
    State and local government officials
    Members of religious organizations
    School officials
    Individuals

The correct forms of address for envelopes and letters are shown at the left. Open punctuation is used in addresses. The appropriate salutations and complimentary closings are given in the order of decreasing formality.

United States Government Officials

Address	Salutation	Complimentary Closing

The President of the United States

The President The Executive Mansion Washington, DC 20500	Sir Mr. President Dear Mr. President	Respectfully yours Very truly yours

The Vice-President of the United States

The Vice-President United States Senate Washington, DC 20510	Sir Dear Sir Mr. Vice-President Dear Mr. Vice-President	Respectfully yours Very truly yours Sincerely yours

The Chief Justice of the United States

The Chief Justice The Supreme Court of the United States Washington, DC 20543	Sir Mr. Chief Justice Dear Mr. Chief Justice	Respectfully yours Very truly yours Sincerely yours

Associate Justice of the Supreme Court

Mr. Justice (Name) The Supreme Court of the United States Washington, DC 20543	Sir Mr. Justice Dear Mr. Justice	Very truly yours Sincerely yours

The Speaker of the House

The Honorable (Name) Speaker of the House of Representatives Washington, DC 20515	Sir Dear Sir Dear Mr. Speaker Dear Mr. (Name)	Very truly yours Sincerely yours

Member of the Cabinet

The Honorable (Name) Secretary of (Office) Washington, DC 20520	Sir Dear Sir Dear Mr. Secretary	Very truly yours Sincerely yours

Senator (male)

The Honorable (Name) The United States Senate Washington, DC 20510	Sir Dear Sir Dear Senator Dear Senator (Name)	Very truly yours Sincerely yours

Senator (female)

The Honorable (Name) The United States Senate Washington, DC 20510	Madam Dear Madam Dear Senator Dear Senator (Name)	Very truly yours Sincerely yours

Representative (male)

The Honorable (Name) The House of Representatives Washington, DC 20515	Sir Dear Sir Dear Representative (Name) Dear Congressman (Name)	Very truly yours Sincerely yours

Representative (female)

The Honorable (Name) The House of Representatives Washington, DC 20515	Madam Dear Madam Dear Representative (Name) Dear Congresswoman (Name)	Very truly yours Sincerely yours

Head of a Government Bureau

The Honorable (Name), Chairman Commission of Fine Arts Interior Building 18th and C Streets, N. W. Washington, DC 20240	Sir Dear Sir Dear Commissioner Dear Mr. Chairman Dear Mr. (Name)	Very truly yours Sincerely yours

Diplomatic Representatives

American Ambassador

The Honorable (Name) American Ambassador (Foreign City, Country)	Sir Dear Mr. Ambassador Dear Ambassador (Name)	Very truly yours Sincerely yours

American Minister

The Honorable (Name) American Minister (Foreign City, Country)	Sir Dear Mr. Minister Dear Mr. (Name)	Very truly yours Sincerely yours

Special Forms of Address, Salutations, and Complimentary Closings

American Consul General, Chargé d'Affaires, Consul or Vice Consul

(Name), Esq.   Sir   Very truly yours
American Consul General   Dear Mr. (Name)   Sincerely yours
United States Embassy
(Foreign City, Country)

Secretary-General of the United Nations

His Excellency (Name)   Your Excellency   Very truly yours
Secretary-General of the United Nations Sir   Sincerely yours
New York, NY 10017   Mr. Secretary-General

United States Representative to the United Nations

His Excellency (Name)   Your Excellency   Very truly yours
Ambassador Extraordinary and   Sir   Sincerely yours
  Plenipotentiary Permanent Representative Dear Mr. Ambassador
  to the United Nations
New York, NY 10017

Canadian Ambassador to the United States

His Excellency (Name)   Your Excellency   Very truly yours
Canadian Ambassador to the United States Sir   Sincerely yours
1746 Massachusetts Avenue, N. W.   Dear Mr. Ambassador
Washington, DC 20036

State and Local Government Officials

Governor

His Excellency, the Governor of New York Sir   Respectfully yours
The Executive Chamber, Capitol   Dear Governor   Very truly yours
Albany, NY 12224   Dear Governor (Name)   Sincerely yours

Attorney General

The Honorable (Name)   Sir   Very truly yours
Attorney General of Connecticut   Dear Mr. Attorney General   Sincerely yours
State Capitol   Dear Mr. (Name)
Hartford, CT 06115

State Senator

The Honorable (Name)   Sir   Very truly yours
State Capitol Building   Dear Sir   Sincerely yours
Trenton, NJ 08625   Dear Senator (Name)

State Representative

The Honorable (Name)   Sir   Very truly yours
The State Assembly   Dear Sir   Sincerely yours
Albany, NY 12224   Dear Representative (Name)
                                        Dear Mr. (Name)

Mayor

The Honorable (Name)   Sir   Very truly yours
Mayor of the City of Chicago   Dear Sir   Sincerely yours
City Hall   Dear Mr. Mayor
Chicago, IL 60602   Dear Mayor (Name)

Members of Religious Organizations

Bishop (Protestant Episcopal)

The Right Reverend (Name) Bishop of New York The Bishop's House Cathedral Heights New York, NY 10025	Right Reverend and Dear Sir Dear Bishop Dear Bishop (Name)	Respectfully yours Sincerely yours Yours faithfully

Bishop (United Methodist)

The Reverend (Name) Secretary of the General Conference 1540 Westbrook Circle Gastonia, NC 28052	Reverend Sir Dear Sir Dear Bishop Dear Bishop (Name)	Respectfully yours Sincerely yours Yours faithfully

Clergyman (Protestant)

The Reverend (Name) 1841 Euclid Avenue Cleveland, OH 44115	Reverend Sir Dear Sir	Respectfully yours Sincerely yours Yours faithfully

Pope (Roman Catholic)

His Holiness Pope (Name) The Vatican Rome	Your Holiness Most Holy Father	Respectfully yours Sincerely yours Yours faithfully

Cardinal (Roman Catholic)

His Eminence (Name) Archbishop of New York 452 Madison Avenue New York, NY 10022	Your Eminence Dear Cardinal (Name)	Respectfully yours Sincerely yours Yours faithfully

Archbishop and Bishop (Roman Catholic)

The Most Reverend (Name) Auxiliary Bishop of Natchez-Jackson 123 North West Street Jackson, MS 39201	Your Excellency Dear Bishop (Name)	Respectfully yours Sincerely yours Yours faithfully

Monsignor (Roman Catholic)

The Right Reverend Monsignor (Name) Immaculate Heart of Mary Church 8 Carman Road Scarsdale, NY 10583	Right Reverend Monsignor Dear Monsignor (Name)	Respectfully yours Sincerely yours Yours faithfully

Priest (Roman Catholic)

Reverend (Name) St. John's Church 1899 Shepard Road St. Paul, MN 55116	Dear Father (Name)	Respectfully yours Sincerely yours Yours faithfully

Brother (Roman Catholic)

Brother (Name) (Order designation) St. Francis Seminary Louisville, KY 40204	Dear Brother Dear Brother (Name)	Respectfully yours Sincerely yours Yours faithfully

Mother Superior of an Order
(Roman Catholic)

Reverend Mother (Name) Maryknoll Sisters Maryknoll, NY 10545	Reverend Mother Dear Reverend Mother	Respectfully yours Sincerely yours Yours faithfully

Sister (Roman Catholic)

Sister (Name) (Order designation) Catholic Central High School 2701 South Tenth Street Fort Lauderdale, FL 33312	Dear Sister Dear Sister (Name)	Respectfully yours Sincerely yours Yours faithfully

Rabbi (Jewish Faith)

The Rabbi of Congregation Shaaray Tefila 160 West 82nd Street New York, NY 10024	Sir Dear Dr. (Name) Dear Rabbi Dear Rabbi (Name)	Respectfully yours Sincerely yours Yours faithfully

School Officials

President of a University or College

(Name), President Teachers College Columbia University 525 West 120th Street New York, NY 10027	Dear Sir Dear President (Name) Dear Dr. (Name)	Very truly yours Sincerely yours

Dean of a College (male)

(Name), Dean School of Education New York University Washington Square East New York, NY 10003	Dear Sir Dear Dean Dear Dr. (Name)	Very truly yours Sincerely yours

Dean of a College (female)

(Name) Dean of Students Hunter College of the City University of New York 695 Park Avenue New York, NY 10021	Dear Madam Dear Dean (Name) Dear Dr. (Name)	Very truly yours Sincerely yours

Professor of a College or University

(Name) Professor of Business Administration Indiana University Bloomington, IN 47401	Dear Sir Dear Professor (Name) Dear Dr. (Name)	Very truly yours Sincerely yours

Superintendent of Schools

Superintendent (Name) Tupper Lake Central Schools Tupper Lake, NY 12986	Dear Sir Dear Superintendent (Name) Dear Mr. (Name)	Very truly yours Sincerely yours

Principal of a School

(Name), Principal Alexander Hamilton High School Elizabeth, NJ 07202	Dear Sir Dear Mr. (Name)	Very truly yours Sincerely yours

Individuals

One (Male)

(Use *Mr.* when the given name may be that of either a man or a woman.)

Mr. (Name) 65 South Water Street Chicago, IL 60601	Dear Mr. (Name)	Sincerely yours

One (Female)

(Use *Miss* rather than *Mrs.* if there is uncertainty about a woman's marital status. *Ms.* may also be used if a woman's marital status is unknown; but this title should be used with discretion, since it is neither widely nor popularly accepted.)

Miss (Name) 2606 Kanuga Road Hendersonville, NC 28739	Dear Miss (Name)	Sincerely yours

Two (Female)

(*Ladies* is used in preference to *Mesdames* in the salutation for two or more women.)

Misses (Name) and (Name) 3409 Ponce de Leon Boulevard Coral Gables, FL 33134	Ladies	Very truly yours

Three (Male)

(*Gentlemen* is used in the salutation for two or more men — never *Dear Sirs*.)

Messrs. (Name), (Name), and (Name) One Wall Street New York, NY 10005	Gentlemen	Very truly yours

Physician

(Name), M. D. 274 Main Street Springfield, MA 01105	Dear Dr. (Name)	Very truly yours Sincerely yours

or

Dr. (Name)
274 Main Street
Springfield, MA 01105

Attorney

Mr. (Name) Attorney at Law One Pondfield Road Bronxville, NY 10708	Dear Mr. (Name)	Very truly yours Sincerely yours

APPENDIX G

REFERENCE BOOKS

Every secretary should have at least three reference books available for immediate use: a desk-size dictionary, a secretarial handbook, and a telephone directory.

Dictionaries

If you are to carry out your secretarial assignments efficiently and accurately, you should have a modern American desk-size dictionary at your desk. You will find it indispensable in verifying the spelling, syllabification, and proper usage of words as you transcribe your employer's dictation. It contains not only the realistic pronunciation and derivation of words but also the meanings of foreign expressions and standard abbreviations, the names of places and notable people, and other essential information.

Four of the acceptable desk dictionaries with recent additions to the vocabulary of the language are:

The American College Dictionary. New York City: Random House, Inc., 1968.

Funk & Wagnall's Standard College Dictionary, 3d ed. New York City: Harcourt Brace Jovanovich, Inc., 1965.

Webster's New World Dictionary of the American Language, 2d college ed. Cleveland, Ohio: World Publishing Company, 1965

Webster's Seventh New Collegiate Dictionary. Springfield, Mass.: G. &. C. Merriam Company, 1965.

If a desk-size dictionary is not readily available, you should invest in a paperback pocket-size one. The *Merriam-Webster Pocket Dictionary* is recommended as a transcription tool because it contains definitions for 25,000 words. In addition, it includes guides to correct spelling and pronunciation; lists of synonyms and antonyms; commonly used abbreviations, foreign words and phrases; and population figures for the United States and Canada.

Secretarial Handbooks

The secretary's handbook is a compact, thoroughly indexed reference book encompassing a wide range of secretarial practices and procedures. It is an authoritative souce of information on such topics as proper grammatical construction, plural and possessive forms, pronunciation and punctuation, and the correct writing of numbers in letters and reports. It can be of great help in deciding, for example, where to place the *subject line* in a business letter, whether to place the apostrophe before or after the letter *s* in *women's salaries*, and when to capitalize direction in geographic areas such as on the *East Coast* or in *western Montana*.

Some of the outstanding secretarial handbooks are:

Doris, Lillian, and Bessie May Miller. *Complete Secretary's Handbook*, 3d ed. Englewood Cliffs, N.J.: Prentice-Hall, Inc., 1970.

Hanna, J Marshall, Estelle L. Popham, and Rita Sloan. *Secretarial Procedures and Administration*, 6th. ed. Cincinnati: South-Western Publishing Co., 1973.

House, Clifford R., and Apollonia M. Koebele. *Reference Manual for Office Personnel*, 5th ed. Cincinnati: South-Western Publishing Co., 1970.

Hutchinson, Lois Irene. *Standard Handbook for Secretaries*, 8th ed. New York City: McGraw-Hill, Inc., 1969.

Telephone Directories

The most frequently consulted reference book in any office is the telephone directory. It is used not only to find the telephone number of listed subscribers but also to verify the spelling of their names and the correctness of their addresses. The Yellow Pages, or classified section of a telephone directory, may also serve as a buyer's guide because the names, addresses, and telephone numbers of business subscribers are listed under their product or service.

A small booklet supplied by the telephone company, designed for use as a personal telephone directory, can save considerable telephoning time. On alphabetically arranged pages it provides spaces for writing the names, addresses, area codes, and telephone numbers of frequently called local and out-of-town telephones.

Writing References

The content and format of all types of business communications can be improved if appropriate reference books are consulted.

Business Communications. A recommended reference book for the writing of business letters and other communications of a business nature is:

Aurner, Robert R., and Morris P. Wolf. *Effective Communication in Business*. Cincinnati: South-Western Publishing Co., 1967.

Business Reports. Manuals and style books are available to serve as references on how to present papers and reports. Two widely used manuals and a style book are listed at the top of page 650.

A Manual of Style. The University of Chicago. 12th ed., rev. Chicago: University of Chicago Press, 1969.

United States Government Printing Office Style Manual, rev. ed. Washington: U. S. Government Printing Office, 1967.

Perrin, Porter G. *Writer's Guide and Index to English*, 4th ed., Glenview, Illinois: Scott, Foresman and Company, 1968.

Business Speeches. A wide variety of reference books may be consulted to provide the prospective speaker or master of ceremonies at a business function with words, phrases, ideas, and quotations that will enhance and enliven his presentation. Some of these are:

Bartlett, John. *Familiar Quotations*, 14th ed. Boston: Little, Brown and Company, 1968.

Fernald, James C. *Funk & Wagnalls Standard Handbook of Synonyms, Antonyms, and Prepositions*, rev. ed. New York City: Wilfred Funk, Inc., 1947.

Stevenson, Burton E. *Home Book of Quotations*, rev. ed. New York City: Dodd, Mead & Company, 1967.

The Original Roget's Thesaurus of English Words and Phrases. New York City: St. Martins Press, Inc., 1969.

Webster's New Dictionary of Synonyms. Springfield, Mass.: G. & C. Merriam Company, 1942.

Specific References

Reference books in all fields from many different sources, ranging from the *American Library Association Catalog* to the *Zweng Aviation Dictionary*, are listed and annotated in a single volume, the *Guide to Reference Books*. To determine what, if any, reference books are available on a specific subject, the secretary should first consult this guide:

Winchell, Constance M. *Guide to Reference Books*, 8th ed. Chicago: American Library Association, 1967.

Specific information on business and related subjects may be obtained from many reference books. The information includes statistics on all major industries, directories of all large corporations, biographies of notable people, and factual information on a wide variety of business topics. The examples that follow are arranged alphabetically by subjects.

Accounting. The standard handbook in which leading authorities cover the major divisions of accounting is:

Wixon, Rufus, *et. al. Accountants' Handbook*, rev. ed. New York City: The Ronald Press Company, 1956.

Almanacs. Published annually, there are four widely used and comprehensive American almanacs of miscellaneous information.

Information Please Almanac. New York City: Simon & Schuster, Inc.

New York Times Encyclopedic Almanac. New York City: Book and Educational Division, The New York Times Company.

Reader's Digest Almanac and Yearbook. Pleasantville, New York: The Reader's Digest Association, Inc.

World Almanac and Book of Facts. New York City: Doubleday & Company, Inc.

Banks. The Bankers Blue Book, one of the leading bank directories published semiannually with monthly supplements, is:

Rand-McNally Bankers Directory. Chicago: Rand-McNally & Company.

Biographical Information. Revised and reissued every two years, the best known and generally the most useful biographical dictionary, with full biographical sketches of approximately 66,000 notable living American men and women, is:

Who's Who in America. Chicago: Marquis-Who's Who, Inc.

Books. A complete list of all available books, new and old, including hardcovers, paperbacks, trade books, textbooks, and juvenile books is published annually with full ordering information in the following volumes:

Books in Print. Authors, Vol. I, New York City: R. R. Bowker Company.

Books in Print. Titles and Publishers, Vol. II, New York City: R. R. Bowker Company.

Subject Guide to Books in Print. A to J, Vol. I, New York City: R. R. Bowker Company.

Subject Guide to Books in Print. K to Z, Vol. II, New York City: R. R. Bowker Company.

A world list of books in the English language is published annually with monthly supplements in the following:

Cumulative Book Index. New York City: The H. W. Wilson Company.

Business Libraries. A reference book that should be consulted to be sure that the business library is used efficiently and that no available source of business information has been overlooked is:

Johnson, H. Webster. *How to Use the Business Library with Sources of Business Information*, 3d ed. Cincinnati: South-Western Publishing Co., 1964.

City Directories. City directories are compiled, published, and sold commercially for most of the cities of the United States and Canada. Each directory contains the names, the addresses, and the occupations of all individuals residing in a community. It usually contains a street directory and a map of the city.

City Officials. A directory of city officials is usually published annually for each large city. The *City of New York Official Directory*, for example, lists all branches of the city government, the courts, and the state and federal government agencies with offices in New York City. It contains an index of the names of all executives listed in the directory.

> *The City of New York Official Directory.* Room 2213 Municipal Building, New York City 10007.

Colleges. A widely used college guide gives the entrance requirements, accreditation, and other factual information about more than 2,800 American colleges and universities. It also contains related information about junior colleges, community colleges, and technical institutes.

> Lovejoy, Clarence I. *Lovejoy's College Guide*, 11th rev. and enl. ed. New York City: Simon and Schuster, Inc., 1970.

A comparative guide to American colleges analyzes every accredited four-year college in the United States. It provides a sound basis for college selection with data on admission requirements, academic opportunities offered by the institution, special programs, faculty qualifications, and enrollment figures.

> Cass, James, and Max Birnbaum. *Comparative Guide to American Colleges*, rev. ed. New York City: Harper and Row, Publishers, 1970–1971.

Junior Colleges. Information about the 751 recognized, nonprofit junior colleges in the United States, the Canal Zone, and Puerto Rico is published by the American Council on Education. Each exhibit for each college includes full information on admission and graduate requirements, enrollment, curricula offered, calendar, staff, student aid, graduates, foreign students, library, publications, finances, buildings and grounds, history, control, and administrative officers.

> Gleazer, Edmund J. Jr. (ed.). *American Junior Colleges*, 7th ed. Washington: American Council on Education, 1967.

Congress. A directory containing the names, addresses, and brief biographies of all congressmen and chief executives of the federal government is issued annually. In it are also listed the members of all congressional committees, the executives of all departments and agencies of the federal government, and all diplomatic representatives. It may be obtained by writing to the United States Government Printing Office.

> *Congressional Directory.* Superintendent of Documents, U.S. Government Printing Office. Washington 20402.

Corporations. A complete national directory of executive personnel in approximately 28,000 companies engaged in all branches of business and industry is published in *Poor's Register of Corporations, Directors, and Executives.* Each company listing includes the names and addresses of all officers, directors, and other executive personnel; the number of employees and the approximate annual sales; and all products and services of the company in the order of their importance.

The register is sold commercially and is not available in most public and school libraries. It may be obtained from Standard & Poor's Corporation.

Poor's Register of Corporations, Directors, and Executives. Standard & Poor's Corporation. New York City 10014.

Credit Ratings. Credit ratings and credit reports are distributed for retail, wholesale, and manufacturing companies. The reports are not available to the general public, but may be obtained by annual subscription.

Dun & Bradstreet Ratings and Reports. Dun & Bradstreet, Inc. New York City 10007.

Encyclopedias. The value of an encyclopedia is that it provides authoritative information on a great number of subjects in concise and convenient form. Because no other single reference book can offer so extensive a survey of universal knowledge, it is often wise to start an inquiry with an encyclopedia. Two outstanding encyclopedias are:

Encyclopaedia Britannica (24 volumes). Chicago: Encyclopaedia Britannica, Inc., 1971.

Encyclopedia Americana (30 volumes). New York City: Grolier Incorporated, 1971.

A compact single-volume general encyclopedia available for instant reference with concise articles on places, persons, and subjects is published in hardcover and paper editions.

Columbia Viking Desk Encyclopedia, 3d ed. New York City: The Viking Press, Inc., 1968.

Etiquette. Business and social etiquette is covered in a number of books on etiquette but the two most prominent authors are:

Post, Elizabeth L. *Emily Post's Etiquette,* 12th ed. New York City: Funk & Wagnalls, Inc., 1968.

Vanderbilt, Amy. *Amy Vanderbilt's New Complete Book of Etiquette*, rev. ed. Garden City, New York: Doubleday & Company, Inc., 1967.

Geographic Information. Atlases and gazetteers are reference sources for all kinds of geographical information. An atlas is a book of maps with supporting geographical statistics and populations figures for each area. Such a book may be an atlas of the world, of a country, of a state, of a county, or of a city. Two of the atlases frequently used in business offices are:

Rand McNally New Cosmopolitan World Atlas, rev. ed. Chicago: Rand McNally & Company, 1968.

Hammond's Contemporary World Atlas. Garden City, New York: Doubleday & Company, Inc., 1967.

A gazetteer, on the other hand, is a geographical dictionary giving, in alphabetic order, the names and descriptions of towns, villages, cities, rivers, mountains, and countries with pronunciations and related historical and geographical information. One of the most comprehensive gazetteers with information about all important places in the world and all incorporated cities, towns, and villages in the United States and Canada with populations of 1,500 or more is:

Webster's Geographical Dictionary, rev. ed. Springfield, Mass.: G. & C. Merriam Company, 1967.

Law. A three-volume law directory, published annually, with a complete list of the lawyers in the United States and Canada given in Volumes I and II and digests of the laws of the states in the United States and the provinces of Canada in Volume III is available.

Martindale-Hubbell Law Directory. Summit, N.J.: Martindale-Hubbell, Inc.

Magazine Articles. Articles in a selected number of periodicals are indexed according to author, title, and subject and listed in an annual publication with monthly supplements which is available in all public libraries.

Readers' Guide to Periodical Literature. New York City: The H. W. Wilson Company.

Manufacturers. A list of almost all American manufacturers with a classification of their products, trade names, and brands is published annually by the Thomas Publishing Company.

Thomas Register. New York City: Thomas Publishing Company.

Medicine. A register of legally qualified physicians of the United States and Canada with related medical biographies and a list of approved medical schools and hospitals is published every two years.

American Medical Directory. Chicago: American Medical Association.

Newspaper Articles. All items and reports printed in the *New York Times* are briefly summarized, indexed, and cross-referenced by subject and name. They are listed alphabetically with the date, page, and column of publication.

New York Times Index. New York City: The New York Times Company.

Postal Information. A complete listing of the postal services in the United States with detailed regulations and procedures covering these services, together with up-to-date postal rates, is given in the following publication:

Postal Service Manual. Superintendent of Documents, U.S. Government Printing Office. Washington 20402.

Shipping Information. Shipments are frequently made by means other than parcel post — by rail, truck, bus, ship, and, more frequently, by air express. A complete shipper's guide containing rates and routings for parcel post, express, and freight shipments is published in separate editions for different parts of the country. This guide also includes information concerning Canadian and foreign parcel post.

Leonard's Guide. New York City: G. R. Leonard & Company, Inc.

A complete list of all post offices, railroad stations, shipping lines, and freight receiving stations is published.

Bullinger's Postal Shipper's Guide for the United States, Canada, and Newfoundland. Bullinger's Guides, Inc., Westwood, New Jersey.

Information about air express, the newest and swiftest method of door-to-door transportation service, may be obtained by referring to the following publication:

Official Air Express Guide. Air Express Division of REA Express, New York City.

Travel Information. Travel information is available in many forms of guide books, bulletins, and directories.

Guides. Ratings for approximately 20,000 accommodations and restaurants in the United States are published in the paperback editions of the *Mobil Travel Guides* by Simon & Schuster, Inc., New York City. The guides also list the outstanding historical, educational, and scenic points of interest throughout the country. Regional guide books are revised and reprinted annually for California and the West, the Great Lakes Area, the Middle Atlantic States, the Northwest and Great Plains States, the Northeastern States, the Southeastern States, and the Southwest and South Central Area.

Bulletins. Travel bulletins may be obtained from all travel agencies. Two of the better known agencies with offices in all the principal cities of the world are *Thomas Cook & Son* and the *American Express Company*.

Directories. Travelers are almost as interested in their accommodations as they are in their means of transportation. The most frequently consulted directory which annually lists hotels and motels approved by the American Hotel Association with their respective rates, accommodations, and plans of operation is the following:

Hotel & Motel Red Book. New York City: American Hotel Association Directory Corporation.

Overseas Guides. A recent innovation is *The Businessman's Guide to Europe*, available at most overseas airlines offices.

A world guide, containing travel facts about 138 countries, has become a worldwide best seller. It is published by Pan American Airways.

Whitted, Gerald W. (ed.). *New Horizons World Guide.* Distributors, New York City: Simon & Schuster, Inc.

Eugene Fodor edits a complete guide to Europe which is revised annually.

Fodor's Guide to Europe. New York City: David McKay Co., Inc.

Separate editions of Fodor's guides are published for all the major countries and principal cities of Europe. Separate editions are also published for Hawaii, India, Israel, Japan and East Asia, South America, the Caribbean, the Bahamas and Bermuda, and many other areas of the world.

INDEX

A

Abbreviations, 631; in body of a letter, 634; coined verbs, 635; diagonal lines in, 634; with numbers, 634; periods in, 634; plurals of, 635; possessive of, 635; of proper names, 631; state ZIP Code, 632; of states, 632
Accounting machine, 185,197
Accounting, secretarial, *see* Secretarial accounting
Acknowledgment, letters of, 107
Adding machines, *see* Calculating machines
Address, cable code, 335; envelope, 82–83; inside, in a letter, 74; special forms of, Appendix F, 642–647
Addressing machines, 245
Addressing services, 245
Addressograph, 245
Adjectives, 42, 257, 601; comparison of, 601; definitive, 601; descriptive, 601; proper, 601
Administrative management, 594; communication facilities, maintaining, 594; facilities and equipment, assessing, 594; office, managing the, 595; office services, maintaining, 594; paper work, organizing flow of, 595; personnel, supervising and evaluating, 595
Adverbs, 72, 316, 608; comparison of, 608; placing the, 608; problems with, 608
Affidavit, defined, 168
Agenda, defined, 170
Air express, 252
Airmail service, 240
Air parcel post, 252
Airport limousines, 480
Air shuttle flights, 480
Air travel, 476; flight information, 477; helicopter service, 480; limousines to airport, 480; reservations, cancellations of, 480; reservations for, 478; schedules, illustrated, 478; service, classes of, 477; shuttle flights, 480; tickets, pickup of, 479; transportation to airport, 480
Almanacs, *see* Reference books
Alphabetic card files, 461, 462
Alphabetic files, advantages of, 453; disadvantages of, 453
Alphabetic indexing for business firms and other organizations, *see* Indexing, alphabetic for business firms and other organizations
Alphabetic indexing for individuals, *see* Indexing, alphabetic for names of individuals
Alphabetic name files, 370
Alphabetic subject files, 371
Alpha-numeric filing, 446
American Automobile Association (AAA), 483
Annotating and underlining mail, 224
Annual reports of corporations, 155; circle graph, illustrated, 156; highlights of the year, 155; line graph, illustrated, 156; tabular report, illustrated, 156
Answering service, telephone, 294
Antecedents of pronouns, 600
AO mail (articles, other), 241
Apostrophe, 105, 617
Appearance, for interview, 567
Appendix A, Grammar, 599; B, Punctuation, 613; C, Word Choice and Spelling, 623; D, Abbreviations, 631; E, Titles, Capitalization, and Numbers, 636; F, Special Forms of Address, Salutations, and Complimentary Closings, 642; G, Reference Books, 648
Appendix to a report, 141
Applicant, 567; adaptability of, 569; appearance, for interview, 567; effectiveness with people, 568; job interest of, 569; knowledge and skills of, 567; language usage and voice during interview, 567; mental attitude of, 567; objectivity of, 568; personality of, 567; self-confidence of, 568; temperament of, 567; voice and language usage during interview, 567
Application blank, 557; cautions in filling in, 560; purpose of, 560
Application, letter of, 555
Appointment, canceling, 265; letters of, 108
Appointments, scheduling, 262
Archaic words, 623, 624
Articles, 602
Assets, defined, 148
Attention line in a letter, 75
Audit tape, illustrated, 117
Automatic dialing telephones, 313; Call-A-Matic, 314; Card Dialer, 313; Magicall, 314
Automatic typewriter, 345
Automobile clubs, 483
Automobile travel, 483; automobile routing, 483; rental services, 483

B

Balance sheet, 148; illustrated, 150; similarities in, 152
Bank account, 513; deposits, making, 515; opening a, 514; overdraft on, 520; signature card, illustrated, 514; statement of reconciliation of a, 520
Bank draft, 530
Bank statement, reconciliation of a, 520
Banking transactions, 513; endorsing checks, 518; making deposits, 515; opening an account, 514; reconciling bank statement, 520; stopping check payment, 520; writing checks, 516
Bellboy, 315
Bibliography, illustrated, 141
Billing, 214; cycle, 214; invoices, calculating and checking, 214; invoices, preparing, 214; punched card, 200; statements, 215
Billing machines, 197
Blind carbon copies, 49
Block style of letter, 66, 67
Body of a letter, 76
Bookkeeping machine, 197
Brackets, 619
Bus express shipments, 253
Bus travel, 482
Business, learning about employer's, 35
Business correspondence, vocabulary of, 98
Business data processing, *see* Data processing
Business forms, 206–216; continuous, illustrated, 215; credit memorandum, 213; design of, 207; installment order, 212; invoice, 207; invoice, calculating and checking, 214; invoice, preparing the, 214; layaway, 212; purpose of, 206; purchase invoice, 211, 212; purchase order, 210; purchase requisition, 209; for purchasing, 209; sales book, 212; sales invoice, 211; sales order, 212; statement, 207, 215
Business reply card, 92
Business reply envelope, 92

Index 657

Business reports, preparing, 123; *see* Financial statements; *see also* Reports
Button telephone, arrangement of buttons, 311; operating a, 312

C

Cable code addresses, 335
Cablegrams or radiograms, *see* International telegraph service
Cable letters (LT), 335
Calculating machines, 193; electronic, 194; full-keyboard listing, 195; operating, 9; printing, 195; rotary, 196; ten-key listing machine, 194
Calendar, maintaining a, by secretary, 263
Call-A-Matic telephone, 314
Call Director, 310
Callers, assisting, 267; greeting, 261; handling difficult, 269; recording, 268
Capitalization, 381, 637; business titles, 638; geographic names, 638; headings of articles and reports, 639; hyphenated words, 639; individual names, 639; position, 638; surname prefixes, 639; titles of articles and reports, 639; words before figures, 638
Carbon copies, of financial statements, 155; of interoffice memorandums, 71; paper for, 90; preparing blind, 49; separation from letters after transcription, 50
Carbon copy notations on a letter, 81
Carbon pack, assembling, 46
Card, business reply, 92; requisition, 433; signature, illustrated, 514; substitution, 435; tickler files, 436
Card Dialer, 313
Card files, for cross-referencing, 460; vertical, 461; visible, 462
Card index, for geographic filing, 452
Card punch, 185, 200
Card sorter, illustrated, 201
Card verifier, illustrated, 201
Cards, index control, 443
Cards, mailing lists on, 243
Carrier folder, 434
Cash payments, by bank draft, 530; by cashier's check, 531; by certified check, 529; by money order, international, 532; by money order, postal and express, 531; forms of, 529; making, 528
Cash register, 197
Cashier's check, 531
Central files, 369
Central processing unit, 203; control section, 203; process section, 203; storage section, 203
Certified check, 529
Certified mail, 242
Chain feeding of envelopes, 244

Charge out, *see* Records management
Checkbook and the bank, *see* Bank account, Checks
Checks, *see* Endorsement; cashier's, 531; certified, 529; duplicate, 518; overdraft, 520; endorsing, 518; path of, illustrated, 529; stopping payment on, 520; stub, 518; suggestions for writing, 516; transit number on, 515; voucher, 528; writing, 516
Chronological files, 371
Circle graph, illustrated, 156
Civil service, *see* Federal employment; announcements, 550; municipal, 589; state, 586; tests for, 581
Claim for loss of shipment, 256
Classified advertisements, 549
Clothes, selection by secretary, 19
COD mail service, 242
Code messages by international telegraph, 335
Code-a-phone, 294
Coded letter, illustrated, 396
Coding, 420; for subject filing, 449
Collator, 185, 346
Collect long-distance calls, 38
Collective nouns, 599
Colloquialisms, 280, 571, 623, 624
Colon, 563, 616
Comma, 158, 175, 614
Commercial filing systems, 454
Common nouns, 599
Communication facilities, maintaining, 594
Communications, *see* International telegraph service, Letters, Letter writing, Reports, Telegrams, Telephone; secretarial skills in handling, 8, 9; maintaining facilities for, 594
Company travel policy, 498; *see* Travel policy
Complimentary close in a letter, 78
Complimentary closings, special forms of, 642–647
Compound words, 625
Computer addressing, 246
Computer tapes and disks, 468
Computers, 202; accuracy of, 187; central processing unit, 203; electronic system, illustrated, 203; input unit, 188, 202; output unit, 189, 203; program in, 187; speed of, 186; storage in, 187
Computing machines, 193–204; *see* Calculating machines; bookkeeping machines, 197; cash registers, 197
Computyper, 199
Conference, interrupting and terminating a, 270
Conference calls, 319
Conference room, arranging for, 266
Conjunctions, 93, 337, 610; correla-

tive, 610; coordinate, 610; subordinate, 610; things to watch in use of, 611
Contract, essential information in a, 165; illustrated, 168; simple, defined, 165
Contractions of verbs, 607
Copying, by microfilm, 467
Copying and duplicating, by secretary, 10
Copying and reproducing machines, 341; automatic typewriters, used as, 345; collators, used with, 346; correspondence, answering by use of, 343; electrostatic, 342; features of, 341; infrared, 343; Thermofax, 343; types of, 342; Xerox, 343
Cord switchboard, 309
Cordless switchboard, 310
Corrections, making, in copy, 48
Correspondence, *see* Letters; copying and reproducing machines used for answering, 343; organizing, 226; sorter, illustrated, 423
Courtesy, when using telephone, 290
Credit, letters of, 495
Credit approval, 214
Credit card long-distance calls, 318
Credit cards, 495; company, 498
Credit memorandum, 213
Cross-reference sheet, illustrated, 396, 422
Cross-referencing, 395, 421; coded letter, illustrated, 396, 422; company known by more than one name, for a, 397; for geographic filing, 451; married woman, for name of, 397; to a subject file, 449
Customs declaration form, 241
Cycle billing, 214; *see* Billing

D

Dash, 533, 618
Data communication, 331
Data-phone service, 322
Data processing, 181–189; *see* Electronic data processing, Integrated data processing machines, Punched card data processing machines; accounting machines used in, 185; card punch, used in, 185, 200, 468; collator, used in, 185; by a computer system, 186, 202, 468; cycle, 188; defined, 182; electronic, used in filing, 468; flow chart, used in, 189; interpreter, used in, 185; manual, 184; mechanical, 185; methods of, 184; need for, 183; program, used in, 178; by a punched card system, 185, 202, 468; reproducer, used in, 185; retrieval of information, 468; by a tabulating system, 185, 202; sorter, used in, 185, 201; verifier, used in, 185, 201
Data processing cycle, 188; flow chart used in, 189; input of data, 188, 202; origin of data, 188; out-

put of data, 189, 203; source documents, 188
Data sheet, personal, 553
Date line, in letters, 73
Dating the mail, 223
Deductible expense form, 538
Deed, defined, 165
Deposit, in bank account, making, 515
Desk, leaving the, 271
Desk-Fax, 330
Dictating machines, 55; combination units, 56; portable units, 55; remote control systems, 57; secretary's need for using, 57; standard units, 56; suggestions for using, 59
Dictating suggestions, 59
Dictation, 33–41; basic skills for taking, 33; changes in, making, 39, 51; equipment for, 55; indicator slip, illustrated, 58; instructions for, 58; kinds of, 39; learning your employer's work, an aid in taking, 35; position for taking, 37; procedures for taking, 38; readiness for taking, 36; taking and transcribing, 8; tools, 37
Diction, 280
Dictionaries, *see* Reference books
Direct distance dialing (DDD), 302
Directories, 648, 649; alphabetical, 300; personal, 300; using telephone correctly, 299; Yellow Pages, 301
Direct quotations, in a report, 138
Domestic mail service, airmail, 240; certified, 242; classes of, 238; COD, 242; first-class, 239; fourth-class (parcel post), 240; insured, 242; mixed classes of, 240; postal services, special, 241; recalling mail, 243; registered, 242; second-class, 239; special delivery, 241; special handling, 241; special postal services, 241; third-class, 239; tracing, 243
Drawer labels, 413
Dress of a secretary, 19
Duplicating and copying by secretary, 10
Duplicating machines, 349; fluid, 356 (*see also* Fluid duplicating); offset, 359 (*see also* Offset duplicating); stencil, 350 (*see also* Stencil duplicating)
Duplicating by microfilm, 467

E

Educational secretary, 579; job opportunities for, 580; specific duties of, 581
Electronic calculators, illustrated, 194
Electronic computer system, illustrated, 203
Electronic data processing, 468; computer tapes and disks, 468; retrieval of information, 468; tabulating (punched) cards, 468
Electronic stencil maker, 362
Electrostatic copiers, 342
Elevator files, 466
Elliot addressing machine, 245
Ellipses, use of, 613
Employment, opportunities for secretarial, 13
Employment agencies, 549
Enclosure notations on a letter, 80
Endorsement, blank, 519; check, 518; full, 519; restrictive, 519; special, 519
Engineering secretary, 578; job opportunities for, 578; specific duties of, 578
Engineering Secretary's Complete Handbook, The, 579
Enunciation, 279
Envelopes, addressed, illustrated, 82; addressing, 83; business reply, 92; chain feeding of, for a mailing list, 244; Nos. 6 and 10, 234; precanceled, 235; sealing, 234; sizes of business, 91; special notations on, 83; stamped, 235; window, 91, 234
Environment, a factor in success, 26
Equipment and facilities, assessing, 594
Erasing procedure, 48
Erasures, in legal papers, 162
Etiquette, *see* Reference books
Exclamation point, 616
Expense reports, 496; company credit cards, 498; company travel policy, 498; illustrated, 497; living expenses, 498; travel advances, 498; travel insurance, 498
Express and Parcel Post Comparative Rate Guide, 251
Express money order, 531

F

Facilities and equipment, assessing, 594
Facsimile telegraph service, 330
Federal employment, age requirement for, 583; citizenship requirement for, 583; civil service tests for, 581; for foreign service, 584; general requirements for, 583; opportunities for, 581; physical condition for, 583; qualifications requirements for, 583; salaries for, 584; selection for, 583; veteran's preference for, 584
Files, *see* Records management; arranging materials in folders for, 425; basic procedure for, illustrated, 424; card, 460; card tickler, 436; central, 369; chargeout of, 433; coding, 420, 449; collecting papers for, 419; cross-referencing, 421, 449; elevator, 466; file copy, 420; indexing, 420, 449; inspecting, 419, 449; job, 444; key name, used in, 420; legal, 444; letter, coded for, 422; letter released for, 422; management, 368; numeric correspondence, 444; placing records in the, 425; project, 444; random, 465; records center for, 438; release mark on, 419; rotary wheel, 465; special, and information systems, 460; transfer of, 437, 438; secretary, kept by a, 369; sorting for, defined, 423; vertical card, 461; visible card, 462
Filing, *see* Filing systems, Records management; alpha-numeric, 446; basic procedure, illustrated, 424; business, 368; business intelligence, a role in, 368; central, 369; consecutive number, 443; defined, 369; geographic, 450; information retrieval, 368; important records, 372; nonessential records, 372; numeric, 441; records, care of, 372; records control, 368; records disposition, 369; records protection, 368; records retention, 369; subject, 447; systems of, 370; terminal-digit, 445; twenty hints for, 425; useful records, 372; vital records, 368, 372
Filing equipment, 405; lateral files, 407; shelf files, 407; vertical files, 406
Filing methods, summary of, 452
Filing procedures, basic, 419–428; illustrated, 424
Filing rules, alphabetic, for business firms and other organizations, *see* Indexing, alphabetic for business firms and other organizations; alphabetic, for names of individuals, *see* Indexing, alphabetic for names of individuals
Filing supplies, 408; accessories, 415; auxiliary guides, 409; carrier folder, 434; drawer labels, 413; folder labels, 413; folders, 411, 412, 434, 447, 448; guides, 409, 434, 447, 448; guides and folders used in numeric filing, 447; guides and folders used in subject filing, 448; labels, 412; number of, 410; out folders, 434; out guides, 434; primary guides, 409; requisition card, 433; secondary guides, 409; special name guides, 409; substitution card, 435
Filing systems, 370; alphabetic name, 370, 375, 384; alphabetic subject, 371, 441; card, 460; chronological, 371; commercial, 454; electronic data processing, 468; geographic, 371, 450; information, and special, 460; microfilming, 466; numeric, 371, 441; tickler, 371; which to use?, 469
Financial statements, 147; balance

Index 659

sheet, 148, 150; calculations, check accuracy of, 149; carbon copy of final draft, 155; consistency in, test for, 153; income statement, 148, 150; previous statements, study of, 149; proofreading the, 154; responsibilities in producing, 149–155; similarities in, 152; typewritten, 149; understanding, 147
First-class mail, 239
Fiscal period, defined, 148
Flexowriter, 198
Flow chart symbols, illustrated, 189
Fluid duplicating, 356; electronic master maker, 362; errors, correcting, 358; features of, 356; illustrated, 357; master, preparing a, for, 357; principles of, 357
Folder, trip, 488
Folders, 411; arranging material in, 425; capacity of, 412; carrier, 434; dated follow-up, 437; hanging, 411; individual, 412, 425; legal size, 411; letter size, 411; miscellaneous, 411, 425; numeric filing, used in, 447; one-fifth cut, 411; one-third cut, 411; out, 434; placing material in for subject filing, 449; position of, 414; special, 412, 425
Follow-up, 436; card tickler files used for, 436; dated follow-up folders, 437; interview, after an, 569
Follow-up letters, 113
Footnote, illustrated, 126
Footnotes, in a report, 138–140
Foreign service secretaries, 584
Foreign travel, 483; passports, 484; vaccinations, 484; visas, 484
Form, Civil Service Commission, 582
Form letters, 117
Forms, see Business forms; charge-out, 434; continuous, illustrated, 215; customs declarations, 241; deductible expense, 538; income tax record, 539; legal, printed, 163; selling, 212
Fourth-class mail (parcel-post), 240, 251
Full-keyboard listing machine, illustrated, 196
Full-rate international message, 334
Full-rate telegram, 326
Future of the secretary, 596

G

Geographic files, 371
Geographic filing, 450; advantages of, 453; arrangement, 450; card index used in, 452; cross-reference for, 451; disadvantages of, 453; procedure for, 452
Grammar, Appendix A, 599
Grammar reference books, 612
Graphs, 156
Greeting callers, 261

Guide sheet for reports, illustrated, 129
Guides, filing, see Filing supplies; numeric filing, used in, 447; out, 434; position of, 414

H

Handbook for the Legal Secretary, 575
Handbooks, secretarial, Appendix G, 648
Handwriting, importance of, in keeping records, 509
Hard copies, definition, 467
Helicopter service, 480
Homonyms, 283, 624
Hotel and Motel Red Book, 493, 655
Hotels, 493; directories of, 493; reservations, making, 493

I

Ibid, use of, 140
Important records, 372
Income statement, 148; illustrated, 151; similarities in, 152
Income tax procedures, 535
Income tax record, illustrated, 539
Incoming mail, 221
Incoming telephone calls, 290; answer promptly, 290; automatic answering set, 294; automatic recording set, 294; Code-a-phone, 294; identify yourself, 290; information, getting, 292; information, giving, 292; messages, taking accurately, 292; mouthpiece, location of, 290; personal, at office, 295; screening calls, 291; telephone answering service, 294; terminating, 295; tips, 295; transferring, 294
Indexing, alphabetic, for business firms and other organizations, 384, 385; abbreviations, 387; articles, how to index, 386; churches, 391; compound geographic names, 389; compound names and words, 387; conjunctions, how to index, 386; cross-reference for a company known by more than one name, 397; cross-referencing in, 395; federal government offices, 393; foreign names, 390; geographic names, 389; government offices, 393; hyphenated names and words, 387; identical business names, 391; magazines, 393; newspapers, 393; numbers, 389; political subdivisions, 394; possessives, 390; prepositions, 386; schools, 392; single letters, 387; synagogues, 381; titles in business names, 388; two words considered as one, 388
Indexing, alphabetic, for names of individuals, 375; abbreviated first

or middle names, 378; compound last names, 377; given names (first names), 377; identical personal names, 379; initials, 378; last names containing prefixes, 376; married woman, cross-reference for, 397; married women, names of, 380; personal names, 376; seniority in identical names, 379; surnames (last name), 376; titles, 380; unusual names, 378
Indexing, defined, 375, 420; for subject filing, 449
Indicator slip, defined, 58; illustrated, 58; purpose of, 59
Infinitives of verbs, 607
Information, retrieval, 368
Information systems, see Special files; electronic data processing, 468; microfilming, 466
Infrared copies, 343
Initiative, definition of, 25
Input unit of a computer, 188, 202
Inquiry, letters of, 115
Inspecting, for filing, 419; for subject filing, 449
Institute for Certifying Secretaries, 593
Insured mail, 242
Integrated data processing machines, 198; computyper, 199; Flexowriter, 198; punched tape, 198
Interjections, 612
International mail, 241
International telegraph service, 334; cable code addresses, 335; cable letters (LT), 335; code messages, 335; differences in time, a factor in, 336; full-rate messages (FR), 334; kinds of, 334; ship radiograms, 335
International travel, 483
Interoffice memorandums, 69, 71; illustrated, 70
Interpreter, 185
Interview, conclusion of, 569; evaluation of applicant during the, 566; follow-up after an, 569; purpose of, 565; topics discussed in an, 565
Interviewer's evaluation of an applicant, 566; adaptability, 569; appearance, 567; effectiveness with people, 568; job interest, 569; knowledge, 567; language usage, 567; mental attitude, 567; objectivity, 568; personality, 567; self-confidence, 568; skills, 567; temperament, 567; voice, 567
Invoice, 207; calculating and checking the, 214; preparing the, 214
Invoicing, see Billing
Italics (underscore), 621
Itinerary, definition of, 11, 489; distribution of the, 492; domestic, illustrated, 490; overseas, illustrated, 491; planning on, 489; preparation of an, 489

J

Job, test for, 561
Job files, 444
Job market, the, 545; locations of the, 548
Job opportunities, *see* Secretarial job opportunities

K

Key name, used in filing, 420

L

Labels, *see* Filing supplies
Language usage, 22, 275; colloquialisms, 280; courtesy, 281; diction, 280; enunciation, 279; ideas, expressing, 277; mannerisms, 280; pronunciation, 278; slang, 280; speech habits, 276; voice, 277
Lateral files, 407
Layaway forms, 212
LC mail (letters and cards), 241
Lease, defined, 165
Lease, illustrated, 166
Legal document, 161; affidavit, defined, 168; contract, simple, 165; deed, 165; lease, 165; lease, illustrated, 166; power of attorney, 169; typical, 164; will, 165; will, format of, 167
Legal files, 444
Legal forms, printed, 163
Legal papers, 161; *see* Legal documents; dates on, 162; erasures on, 162; notarized, 163; numbers on, 162, 163; spacing on, 162; specifications for, 161; titles on, 162
Legal secretary, 573; job opportunities for the, 574; specific duties of the, 575
Legal Secretary's Complete Handbook, 575
Leonard's Guide, 251, 655
Letter, abbreviations in body of, 634; of application, 555; appropriate opening in, 102; attention line in a, 75; body of a, 76; carbon copy notations on a, 81; city, state, and ZIP Code line in a, 74; coded, illustrated, 396; company line in a, 74; complimentary close in a, 78; cross-reference for, illustrated, 396, 422; cross-referencing a, in subject filing, 449; date on a, 73; block style, 66, 67; enclosure notations on a, 80; first impression, 65; information, importance of accurate in a, 99; inside address on a, 74; language, importance of appropriate and clear in a, 100; logical presentation of, 103; mailing notation on a, 81; margins, 66; message, importance of complete in a, 101; message, importance of courtesy in a, 101; message, structure of, in a, 102; model, illustrated, 77; modified block style, 66, 67; name of a person in a, 74; paragraph division in a, 102; parts of a, 73; placement and styles, 65–71; placement table, 68; postscript to a, 83; punctuation, 66; reference initials in a, 80; released and coded for filing, illustrated, 422; salutations in a, 75; second page of a, 76; separate cover notations on a, 81; signature in a, 78; simplified style, 66, 67; spacing, 66, 67; street address line in a, 74; steps in organizing, 103; styles, 66, 67; subject line in a, 76; title, official, in a, 74; title, use of, in a, 78; transmittal for a report, 135, 136; typed name on a, 78; understanding the, 99; *you* approach in a, 101
Letter placement table, 68
Letter telegram, 335
Letter writing, *see* Letter; English grammar, knowledge of, necessary in, 97; message, planning your, in, 99; message, structure of, in, 102; secretarial, 97–120; steps in organizing, 103; *you* approach in, 101; vocabulary of business correspondence used in, 98
Letterhead, 73, 90
Letterheads, typical, illustrated, 90
Letters of credit, 495
Letters, acknowledgment, 107; appointment, 108; composed by secretaries, 107–118; folding, 233; follow-up, 113; form, 117; of inquiry, 115; inserting in envelope, 233; items to check before mailing, 238; meetings, regarding, 110; ordering goods, 116; ordering services, 116; prospective customer, 118; remittance, 114; requesting reference, 118; reservations, making, 109; simplifying typing of, 69; thank you, 114; of transmittal, 111; typing, 45; *you* approach in, 101
Liabilities, defined, 148
Line graph, illustrated, 157
Loc. cit., use of, 140
Long-distance calls, collect calls, 318; conference call, 319; cost for, 305; credit card calls, 318; direct distance dialing (DDD), 302; overseas calls, 319; person-to-person calls, 302; person-to-person DDD, 303; person-to-person without DDD, 304; placing, 302; station-to-station calls, 302; station-to-station DDD, 302; time factor in, 304; wide area telephone service (WATS), 319
Loyalty, definition of, 26

M

Magicall magnetic tape dialing telephone, 314
Mail, *see* Domestic mail service; annotating the, 224; arrangement of, on executive's desk, 226; dating the, 223; envelopes, precanceled, 235; envelopes, stamped for, 235; folding letters, 233; handling the, 232; incoming, 221; inserting letters for, 233; international, 241; items to check before mailing letters, 238; memorandums, special, 228; metered, 235; *National Zip Code Directory*, 237; opening the, 221; optical character reader (OCR), 237; organizing correspondence, 226; outgoing, 232; photocopying, 226; postage meter, 232; postal cards, stamped, 235; referral slip, illustrated, 227; referring the, 226; register of expected, 228; register of insured, special delivery, and registered mail, 228; related materials, attaching, 225; routing slip, illustrated, 227; routing the, 226; sealing envelopes for, 234; stamps, applying, 234; stamps, precanceled, 235; time stamp for dating, 223; underlining the, 224; ZIP Code, defined, 236
Mail service, domestic, *see* Domestic mail service; mixed classes of, 240
Mailing lists, 243; on file cards, 243; chain feeding of envelopes for, 244; up-to-date, 244
Mailing notations on a letter, 81
Mailing volume, *see* Volume mailing
Margins, letter, 66
Master maker, electronic, 362
Medical Secretary, 578
Medical secretary, 575; job opportunities for, 576; specific duties of the, 576
Medical Secretary's Guide, 578
Meeting facilities, arranging for, 266
Meetings, letters regarding, 110
Memorandums, interoffice, 69–71; register of mail, 228; special, 228
Message, *see* Letter
Messages, taking telephone, 292
Metroliner, 481
Microfilming, 466; copying, 467; duplication, 467; hard copies, 467; retrieval, 467; what to microfilm, 468
Mimeograph, *see* Stencil duplicating
Minutes, 169; agenda, 170; correcting the, 172; defined, 170; information, gathering for, 170; illustrated, 171; parliamentary procedure, 169; points to be covered in typing the, 172; *Robert's Rules of Order*, 169; *Standard Code for Parliamentary Procedure*, Sturgis, 169
Misused words, 323, 501

Index **661**

Mobil Travel Guides, 493, 655
Mobile telephone, 315
Model letter, illustrated, 77
Money orders, international, 532; postal and express, 531; telegraphic, 332
Monthly bills, paying, 528
Motels, *see* Hotels
Municipal civil service, 589
Municipal employment, opportunities for, 586

N

Nanosecond, defined, 186
National Records Management Council, 438
National Secretaries Association, International, 592
National Zip Code Directory, 237
Net loss defined, 148
Net profit, defined, 148
New York Times Index, The, 142
Nonessential records, 372
Notarized legal papers, 163
Notary public, statement of, illustrated, 164
Nouns, 15, 599
Numbers, abbreviations used with, 634; amounts of money, 640; at beginning of sentence, 640; dates, 640; fractions and decimals, 641; measurements, 640; miscellaneous use of, 641; round numbers, 640; streets, 640; time of day, 640; use of, 639
Numeric correspondence files, 444
Numeric files, 371
Numeric filing, 442; advantages of, 453; alpha-numeric, 446; arrangements for, 443; consecutive number filing, 443; correspondence, 444; disadvantages of, 453; guides and folders used in, 447; job, 444; legal, 444; project, 444; terminal-digit, 445

O

Obsolete words, 623, 624
Office, managing the, 595
Office positions, table of, 6
Office services, maintaining, 594
Official Airline Guide, 478
Offset duplicating, 359; electronic master maker, 362; errors, correcting, 361; features of, 360; illustrated, 360; master, preparing an offset, 361; photo-offset master, 361
Offset masters, 361
Op. cit., use of, 140
Optical Character Reader, 237
Order letter for goods or services, 116
Organizations, direct inquiry to, for employment, 550; size of, 547; types of, 545
Out folders, 434
Outgoing calls, 299; *see* Long-distance calls, Telephone directories
Outgoing mail, *see* Mail
Outline, 124
Output unit of a computer, 189, 203
Overdraft on a bank account, 520
Overnight telegram, 326
Overseas telephone calls, 319

P

Packaging, 255; recent developments in, 251
Paper, letter, *see* Stationery
Paper work, organizing flow of, 595
Parallel construction of verbs, 603
Parcel post, air, 252; fourth-class mail, 240, 251
Parentheses, 526, 618
Parliamentary procedure, 169
Participles of verbs, 607
Passports, 484
Path of a check, illustrated, 524
Payments, cash, *see* Cash payments, Petty cash fund
PBX switchboard, 309
Per diem living expense while traveling, 498
Period, 613; in abbreviations, 634
Person-to-person telephone calls, 302
Personal data sheet, 553; appearance of, 554; content of, 553; education in, 553; experience in, 554; extra-curricular activities, 554; personal information in, 553; purpose of, 553; references in, 554
Personal pronouns, 600
Personal qualities of a secretary, 17–26
Personnel, supervising and evaluating office, 595
Petty cash fund, 505; payments, making from, 506; replenishing the, 506; starting the, 505; summary of, illustrated, 507
Photocopies, used in filing, 435
Photo-offset masters, 361
Physical examination for a secretarial position, 562
Picturephone, 314
Poise, definition of, 21
Possessive abbreviations, 635
Postage meter, 232, 235, 236
Postal cards, stamped, 235
Postal money order, 531
Postal Service Manual, 251, 654
Postscript to a letter, 83
Power of attorney, defined, 169
Prepositions, 84, 609; choice of, 609
Printing calculator, illustrated, 195
Priorities, establishing, by secretary, 12
Private branch exchange (PBX) system, 309
Private wire telegraph service, 331
Professional qualities of a secretary, 17–26
Professional secretary, definition of, 12
Program, in data processing, defined, 187
Project files, 444
Pronouns, 29, 457, 599; after *be*, 601; antecedents of, 600; personal, 600; relative, 600
Pronunciation, 278
Proofreaders' marks, illustrated, 127
Proofreading suggestions, 142; for financial statements, 154
Proper noun, 599
Proprietorship, defined, 148
Prospective customer letters, 118
Provincialisms, 623, 624
Punch card, 200
Punched card data processing machines, 200; card punch machine, 200; sorter, 201; tabulator, 202; verifier, 201
Punched tape, illustrated, 198
Punctuation, Appendix B, 613; letter, 66; quotation marks with other marks of, 621; spacing after, 621
Purchase invoice, 211, 212
Purchase order, 207, 210, 211, 212
Purchase requisition, 209, 210
Purchasing, forms for, 209

Q

Qualities, personal and professional, of a secretary, 17–26; secretarial, developing, 41
Question mark, 143, 616
Quotation marks, 191, 620; with other marks of punctuation, 621
Quotations, how to arrange, 138
Quoted matter, 620

R

Railway freight service, 254
Random files, 465
REA Express, 252
Reader's Guide to Periodical Literature, 142
Reconciliation of a bank statement, 520
Record retention schedules, 438; factors affecting, 439
Recording machines, 193–204; *see* Calculating machines; bookkeeping machines, 197; cash registers, 197
Records, *see* Filing; care of, 372; handwriting, importance of, in keeping, 509; important, 372; maintained by secretary, 10; nonessential, 372; placing in file, 425; useful, 372; vital, 368, 372
Records center, 438
Records control, 367, 368; *see* Filing; disposition, 369; files management, 368; information retrieval, 368; protection, 368; retention, 369; and the secretary, 373

Records management, 419–470; see Files, Geographic filing, Numeric filing, Subject filing; charge-out, 433; charge-out forms, 434; charge time, length of, 435; electronic data processing, 468; follow-up, 436; microfilming, 466; photocopies, used for, 435; records center for, 438; requisition card, used for charge out, 433; retention schedules, 438; special files and information systems, 460; system to use?, 469; transfer of files, 437, 438
Reference, letters of, 118
Reference books, 648–656; accounting, 650; almanacs, 650; banks, 651; biographical information, 651; book lists, 651; business communications, 649; business libraries, 651; business reports, 649; business speeches, 650; city directories, 651; city officials, 652; colleges, 652; Congress, 652; corporations, 652; credit ratings, 653; dictionaries, 658; encyclopedias, 653; etiquette, 653; geographic information, 653; grammar, 612; junior colleges, 652; law, 654; magazine articles, 654; manufacturers, 654; medicine, 654; newspaper information, 654; postal information, 654; secretarial handbooks, 648; shipping information, 655; specific, 650; telephone directories, 649; travel information, 655; writing references, 649
Reference initials on a letter, 80
Reference visible systems, 464
Referral slip, illustrated, 227
Refreshments, handling, 270
Register of expected mail, 228
Register of insured, special delivery, and registered mail, 228
Registered mail, 242; insuring, 242; return receipt of, 242
Relative pronouns, 600
Release mark, used in filing, 419
Remittance letters, 114
Report, appendix to a, 141; bibliography, with a, 141; body of a, 132, 137; conclusions of a, 140; cover of a, 133; final draft of a, 127; footnotes in a, 126, 138–140; guide sheet for, 129; headings in a, 134; importance of a, 123; information, gathering for a, 142; introductory parts of a, 132; letter of transmittal for a, 135; margins for a, 128; numbering pages in a, 134; outline of a, 124; page of a, illustrated, 139; parts of a, 132; preface of a, 135; preparing a business, 123; proofreaders' marks in a, 127; proofreading the, 142; quoted material in a, 138; recommendations in a, 140; rough draft of a, 125; specifications for a, 127; summary of a, 137; supplementary parts of a, 132; table of contents for a, 136, 137; tables, listed in a, 137; tabular, illustrated, 156; title page of a, 133; typing the, 127; writing, steps in, 124
Report writing, steps in, 124
Reports, typing, 45; see Annual reports of corporations, Financial statements, Report
Reproducer, 185
Reproduction machines, see Duplicating machines
Requisition card, 433
Reservations, hotel and motel, 493; letters making, 109
Resolutions, 173
Retention schedules, 438; factors affecting, 439
Retrieval of microfilmed information, 467; of information in a computer, 468
Return receipt for registered mail, 242
Road Atlas, 483
Robert's Rules of Order, 169
Rotary calculator, illustrated, 196
Rotary wheel files, 465
Rough draft, suggestions for preparing a, 125; with proofreaders' marks, illustrated, 128
Routing slip, illustrated, 227
Rules of Order, Robert's, 169

S

Safeguard filing system, illustrated, 456
Salaries, civil service, 584; engineering secretary, 578; legal secretary, 574; medical secretary, 576; secretarial, 14
Sales order form, 212
Salutation, formal and informal, 76; in a letter, 75
Salutations, special forms of, Appendix F, 642–647
Schedule, kept by secretary, 12; maintaining a, 270
School placement office, 548
School Secretary's Handbook, 581
Second-class mail, 239
Second page of a letter, 76, 78
Secretarial accounting, see Bank account; Cash payments, making; Checks; Income tax procedure; Petty cash fund; Secretarial tax duties
Secretarial associations, 581, 592, 593
Secretarial job market, 545
Secretarial job opportunities, 548; civil service announcements, 550; classified advertisements, 549; direct inquiry to organization, 550; employment agencies, 549; placement office in school, 548
Secretarial ladder, up and beyond, 591–596
Secretarial letter writing, 97–120; see Letter, Letters, Letter writing
Secretarial positions, rewards for, 13; training for, 12
Secretarial responsibility, preparation for high level, 591
Secretarial tax duties, 535; checklist, income tax, 537; deductible expense form, 538; income tax record, illustrated, 539; tax information needed 536
Secretary, see Educational secretary, Engineering secretary, Legal secretary, Medical secretary, Secretary and the public; administrative management by a, 594; appearance, 276; assignment beyond a, 593; associations for the, 581, 592, 593; basic skills of a, 8; civil service tests for a, 581; clothes, selection by, 19; cooperation of, 23; copying and duplicating done by, 10; courtesy, 281; deductible expense form for a, 538; definition of (National Secretaries Association), 5; communications, handling, 8; data processing and the, 181; day's work, planned by, 12; dictating skill, need for, 57; dictating suggestions for, 59; dictation, taking, 8, 33–41; employment opportunities for, 13; environmental influence on the, 26; federal employment, opportunities for, 581; files kept by, 369; forms, business, used by, 206–216; fulfillment in serving society, 13; future of, 596; hair styles of, 19; health needs of, 20; income tax checklist for a, 537; income tax record form for a, 539; initiative of a, 25; Institute for Certifying Secretaries, 593; involvement, 23; job market for the, 545; language, usage of a, 22, 275; letter writing responsibilities, 97–120; loyalty of, 26; makeup worn by, 20; manners, 276; office workers, among, 5; operating calculating machines, 9; orderliness of, 24; personal and professional qualities of, 17, 18; personal care, 18; personality of, 275; posture and poise necessary for the, 21; priorities, establishing, 12; professional, definition of, 12; public responsibilities to the, 261; records control and the, 373; records maintained by, 10, 508; responsibility, preparation for high level, 591; responsibilities of, 7–12, 57; responsibility while employer travels, 499; salaries for, 14; schedule, kept by, 12; specialized fields for the, 573; speech habits, 276; tax duties of a, 535; tax information needed

Index 663

by a, 536; transcribing, 8; travel arrangements, handled by, 10, 476; trustworthiness of a, 24; typewriting, 8; voice of, 22; working conditions of, 13
Secretary and the public, 261–282; *see* Language usage, Secretary; appearance, 276; appointments, canceling, 265; assisting callers, 266; calendar, maintaining a, 263; delays, handling, 269; desk, leaving the, 271; difficult callers, handling, 269; greeting callers, 261; manners, 276; meeting facilities, arranging for, 262; personality, 275; person-to-person meetings, 261; recording callers, 268; handling refreshments, 270; reminding employer of appointments, 264; responsibilities to the public, 261; schedule, maintaining the, 270; scheduling appointments, 262; speech habits, 276
Selling forms, 212; credit memorandum, 213; installment order, 212; layaway, 212; sales book, 212; sales order, 212
Semicolon, 230, 615
Sender's Application for Withdrawal of Mail, Form 1509, 243
Separate cover notations on a letter, 81
Shelf files, 407
Ship radiograms, 335
Shipment, claim for loss, 256; marking goods for, 254; tracing, 256
Shipping, air, 250; air express, 252; air parcel post, 252; claim for loss, 256; developments, recent, in, 250; guide books, 251, 655; methods of, 251; packages, marking for, 255; tracing, 256
Shipping, surface, 250; bus express, 253; claim for loss, 256; developments, recent in, 250; guide books, 251, 655; methods of, 251; packages, marking for, 255; parcel post, 251; railway freight service, 254; REA Express, 252; tracing shipments, 256; truck transportation, 254; United Parcel Service, 253
Shipping information, 655
Shorthand notebook page, illustrated, 40
Signals on visible records, 463
Signature card, illustrated, 514
Simple contract, 165
Simplified letter, 66, 67
Slang, 280
Sorter, 185, 201
Sorting, for filing, defined, 423; for subject filing, 449
Source documents, defined, 188
Spacing, in legal papers, 162; letter, 66
Speakerphone, 313
Special delivery mail, 241

Special files, 460; card, 460; elevator, 466; random, 465; reference visible systems, 464; rotary wheel, 465; signals on visible records, 463; vertical card, 461; visible card, 462
Special handling mail, 241
Speech, when using telephone, 289
Spelling, 628; exceptions, 629, 630
Spreading, in correcting errors, 49
Squeezing, in correcting errors, 49
Stamps, precanceled, 235; postage, 234
Standard Code for Parliamentary Procedure, Sturgis, 169
State civil service employment, 586
Statement, Income, 148, 151, 152
Statement of notary public, illustrated, 164
Statements, financial, and reports, 147–156
Station-to-station telephone calls, 302
Stationery, office, paper used for, 89; size of paper used for, 89; types of, 88
Stencil duplicating, electronic stencil maker, 362; errors, correcting on stencils, 354; features of, 350–356; illustrated, 351; principles of, 350; stencil sheet markings, illustrated, 352; typing a stencil, 351
Sturgis' *Standard Code for Parliamentary Procedure*, 169
Subject filing, 447; advantages of, 453; coding, 449; cross-reference to, 449; disadvantages of, 453; folders, placing material in, for, 449; guides and folders used in, 448; indexing, 449; inspecting, 449; procedures, 449; sorting for, 449
Subject line in a letter, 76
Substitution cards, 435
Suffixes, 204
Super-Ideal filing system, illustrated, 455
Switchboard, Call Director, 310; cord, 309; cordless, 310

T

Table of contents for a report, illustrated, 136
Tables, listed in a report, 137
Tabular report, illustrated, 156
Tabulating (punched) cards, 468
Tabulator, 202
Telegram, cash for, 332; charge account, use of, for, 332; chargeable words, 326; collect service for, 332; delivery of, 333; Desk-Fax, 330; domestic, 325; facsimile service, 330; filing a, 330; full-rate telegram, 326; money, sent by, 332; overnight telegram, 326; over-the-counter service, 330; over-the-telephone service, 330; preparing a, 328; private wire systems,

331; repeat back service, 333; report delivery of, 334; teleprinter service, 331; Telex, 331; tie line service, 330; time zone difference, a factor in sending, 334
Telegraph service, domestic, 325; *see* Telegram; international, 334; *see* International telegraph service
Telegraphic money orders, 332
Telephone, *see* Incoming telephone calls, Long-distance calls, Outgoing calls; calls, placing, 299; cost of service, 305; courtesy on the, 290; local calls, cost for, 305; personal calls, 295; personality, 287; speech, suggestions for improving, 289; terminating calls, 295; tips, 295; vocabulary on the, 290; voice, suggestions for improving, 287, 288
Telephone directories, alphabetical, 300; personal, 300; using correctly, 299; Yellow Pages, 301
Telephone equipment, automatic dialing, 313; Bellboy, 315; button telephone, 311; button telephone, operating a, 312; Call Director, 310; Call-A-Matic, 314; cord switchboard, 309; cordless switchboard, 310; Magicall, 314; mobile telephone, 315; Picturephone, 314; speakerphone, 313; special, 309; switchboard (PBX), 309; touchtone, 311
Telephone service, cost of, 305; local calls, 305; long-distance calls, 305
Teleprinter telegraph service, 331
Teletype, definition of, 320
Teletypewriter service, 320; Dataphone service, 322; exchange service (TWX), 321; private line service (TWPL), 322
Telex telegraph service, 331
Ten-key listing machine, illustrated, 194
Terminal-digit filing, 445
Testing for a secretarial position, 561
Thank you letters, 114
Third-class mail, 239
Tickler file, defined, 12, 371
Tie line telegraph service, 330
Time, differences in, a factor in international telegraph service, 336
Time, factor in long-distance telephone calls, 304
Time factors in travel, 484
Time stamp, illustrated, 223
Title page of a report, illustrated, 133
Titles, abbreviated, following personal names, 637; in addresses, 637; birthright, 636; business, 638; doctor, 636; double, 637; position, 638; reverend, 636; in salutations, 637
Titles, official, in a letter, 74, 78
Topical form of a business report, defined, 124

Topical outline of a report, illustrated, 125
Touch-tone telephone, 311
Tracing shipments, 256
Train travel, 481; coach accommodations, 481; first-class accommodations, 481; railroad timetables, 482; service, classes of, 481
Transcribing, improving your skill, 51; process of, 45; taking dictation and, 8
Transcribing machines, 55; combination units, 56; remote control systems, 57; standard units, 55; suggestions for using, 59, 60
Transcription, completing the, 50; desk organized for, 44; equipment for, 55; organization of, 44
Transfer file, 438
Transit number, 515
Transmittal, letters of, 111
Transportation, air, 476; airport limousines, 480; automobile, 483; bus, 482; helicopter service, 480; train, 481; truck, 254
Transportation departments, 475
Travel agencies, 476
Travel arrangements, handling by secretary, 10
Travel funds, 494; checks, personal used for, 496; credit cards, 495; letters of credit, 495; travelers' checks, 494
Travel information, 655; bulletins, 655; directories, 655; guides, 655; overseas guides, 655; reference books on, 655
Travel policy, advances, 498; company, 498; company credit cards, 498; insurance, 498; living expenses, 498
Travel services and arrangements, 475–500; air travel, 476; automobile travel, 483; bus travel, 482; credit cards used in making, 495; expense reports, 496; foreign travel, 483; funds for traveling, 494; hotels, selection of, 493; itinerary, the, 489; letters of credit used in making, 495; motels, selection of, 493; secretary's responsibilities for, 476; time factors in arranging, 484; train travel, 481; transportation departments, 475; travel agencies, 476; trip, checklist for, preparing a, 498; trip, planning a, 475; trip folder, 488
Travelers' checks, 494
Trip, checklist for preparing, 498; planning a, 475
Trip folder, 488
Truck transportation, 254
Typewriting, 8; see Legal papers, Minutes, Report; financial statements, 149; letters, suggestions for simplifying, 69; secretarial, 123–178

U

Underlining and annotating mail, 224
Underscore (italics), 621
United Parcel Service, 253
Universal Air Travel Card, 479
Useful records, 372

V

Vaccinations for foreign travel, 484
Variadex filing system, illustrated, 454
Verbs, 54, 62, 602; active voice of, 603; adding *ing*, 297; agreement of subject and, 605; coined, 635; contractions of, 607; infinitives of, 607; intransitive, 603; parallel construction of, 603; participles of, 607; passive voice of, 603; tense of, 603; transitive, 602; voice of, 603
Verifier, 185, 201
Vertical card files, 462
Vertical files, 406
Visas, 484
Visible card files, 462; reference systems, 464; signals on, 463
Vital records, 372; defined, 368
Vocabulary, archaic words, 623, 624; of business correspondence, 98; of misused words, 323, 501; obsolete words, 623, 624; when using telephone, 290
Voice, 277; secretary's, 22; on telephone, 287
Volume mailing, addressing machines for, 245; addressing services for, 245; aids for, 243; chain feeding of envelopes in, 244; file cards of mailing lists for, 243; mailing lists for, 243; up-to-date mailing lists for, 244
Voucher checks, 528

W

Wide area telephone service (WATS), 319
Will, defined, 165; format of, 167
Window envelope, 91, 234; illustrated, 92
Word choice, *see* Appendix C, 623; division of, 628
Word Division Manual: The Fifteen Thousand Most Used Words in Business Correspondence, 98
Words, archaic, 623, 624; compound, 625; counting chargeable, in a telegram, 326; misused, 323, 501; obsolete, 623; plural forms of, 627
Working conditions, secretarial, 13; in state government jobs, 586
World Almanac, The, 142
Writing, steps in organizing, 103

Y

Yellow Pages, 301; use of, in filing, 371
You approach in letters, 101

Z

ZIP Code, 74, 236; abbreviations of states used with, 632; defined, 74, 236